CONTEMPORARY Black Biography

ISSN 1058-1316

CONTEMPORARY

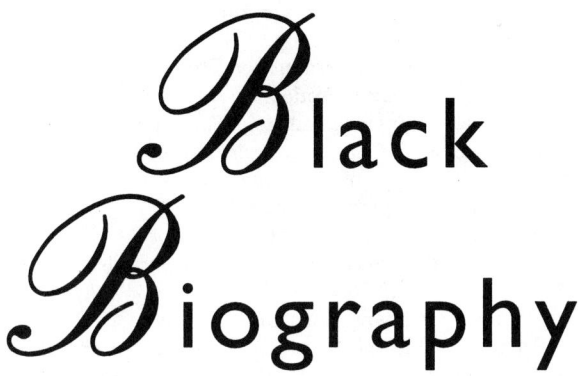
Black
Biography

Profiles from the International Black Community

Volume 19

Shirelle Phelps, Editor

DETROIT • LONDON

STAFF

Shirelle Phelps, *Editor*

Carol Brennan, John Cohassey, Eileen Daily, Ed Decker, Mike Eggert, Brian Escamilla, Ellen French, Carrie Golus, Ashyia N. Henderson, Robert R. Jacobson, Mary Kalfatovic, Jeanne Lesinski, James Manheim, David G. Oblender, Rebecca Parks, Paula P. Scott, Sandy Stiefer, Alison Carb Sussman, Michael Watkins, Lisa Weitzman, *Contributing Editors*

Linda S. Hubbard, *Managing Editor, Multicultural Department*

Susan Trosky, *Permissions Manager*
Margaret Chamberlain, *Permissions Specialist*

Mary Beth Trimper, *Production Director*
Deborah L. Milliken, *Production Assistant*
Cynthia Baldwin, *Product Design Manager*
Barbara J. Yarrow, *Graphic Services Manager*
Christine O'Bryan, *Desktop Publisher*
Randy Bassett, *Image Database Supervisor*
Pamela A. Reed, *Imaging Coordinator*
Robert Duncan, Michael Logusz, *Imaging Specialists*

Victoria B. Cariappa, *Research Manager*
Barbara McNeil, Andrew Guy Malonis, Gary Oudersluys, *Research Specialists*
Jeffrey D. Daniels, Tamara C. Nott, Cheryl L. Warnock, *Research Associates*
Corrine A. Stocker, *Research Assistant*

While every effort has been made to ensure the reliability of the information presented in this publication, Gale Research does not guarantee the accuracy of the data contained herein. Gale accepts no payment for listing; and inclusion in the publication of any organization, agency, institution, publication, service, or individual does not imply endorsement of the editors or publisher. Errors brought to the attention of the publisher and verified to the satisfaction of the publisher will be corrected in future editions.

This publication is a creative work fully protected by all applicable copyright laws, as well as by misappropriation, trade secret, unfair competition, and other applicable laws. The authors and editors of this work have added value to the underlying factual material herein through one or more of the following: unique and original selection, coordination, expression, arrangement, and classification of the information.

All rights to this publication will be vigorously defended.

Copyright © 1999 by Gale Research
27500 Drake Rd.
Farmington Hills, MI 48331-3535

All rights reserved including the right of reproduction in whole or in part in any form.

Printed in the United States of America

No part of this book may be reproduced in any form without permission in writing from the publisher, except by a reviewer who wishes to quote brief passages or entries in connection with a review written for inclusion in a magazine or newspaper.

ISBN 0-7876-1275-8
ISSN 1058-1316

10 9 8 7 6 5 4 3 2 1

Contemporary Black Biography Advisory Board

Emily M. Belcher
General and Humanities Reference Librarian
Firestone Library, Princeton University

Dr. Alton Hornsby, Jr.
Professor of History
Morehouse College

Ernest Kaiser
Editor, Contributor
Retired Librarian, Schomburg Center for Research in Black Culture

Jeanette Smith
Librarian
Julia Davis Branch, St. Louis Public Library

Dr. Ronald Woods
Director, Afro-American Studies Program
Eastern Michigan University

Wendell Wray
Retired Librarian, Schomburg Center for Research in Black Culture
Retired Professor of Library Science, University of Pittsburgh

Contents

Introduction ix

Photo Credits xi

Cumulative Nationality Index 225

Cumulative Occupation Index 233

Cumulative Subject Index 247

Cumulative Name Index 283

Arinze, Francis Cardinal............................. 1
Potential Roman Catholic pontiff

Avant, Clarence..4
Highly respected record company executive

Bailey, Radcliffe... 7
Multi-talented versatile artist

Berry, Halle...10
Beautiful actress

Bizimungu, Pasteur....................................14
Rwandan leader

Brown, Donald..18
Sculptor of genius

Byrd, Michelle..21
Innovative film industry executive

Caesar, Shirley...25
The queen of gospel music

Camp, Kimberly...29
Dynamic museum administrator

Carter, Betty...32
Matriarch of Jazz

Cheadle, Don..35
Versatile actor

Cleveland, James..39
Legendary king of gospel music

Coltrane, John..42
Great jazz innovator

Crawford, Randy..47
Versatile jazz vocalist

Crothers, Scatman......................................50
Lovable character actor

Davis, Piper...53
Negro League's pioneer player

Delaney, Beauford......................................56
Impressionist painter

Donegan, Dorothy......................................60
Flamboyant "Queen of the Keys"

Downing, Will...64
Mellow jazz crooner

Edelin, Ramona Hoage...............................67
National Urban Coalition leader

Flack, Roberta..70
Grammy award-winning pop vocalist

Frazier, Joe...74
"Smokin" former heavyweight boxing champion

Freeman, Charles.......................................79
Chief justice of the Illinois Supreme Court

Goines, Donald...83
Author of gritty crime novels

Golden, Marita...86
Critically acclaimed author and educator

Graves, Denyce..90
Vibrant operatic vocalist

Harkless, Necia Desiree.............................94
Multi-talented scholar

Harris, Jay..97
Newsworthy newspaper publisher

Hemsley, Sherman...................................100
Television's George Jefferson

Henry, Aaron..103
Tireless civil rights advocate

Hill, Calvin..................................107
Rising star of corporate consulting

Hill, Janet...................................107
Rising star of corporate consulting

Hounsou, Djimon.......................111
Up-and-coming African movie star

Hyman, Phyllis...........................115
Tragically talented vocalist

Ingraham, Hubert A. 118
Reformist prime minister of the Bahamas

Jackson, George........................121
Motown's president and CEO

Jackson, Michael.......................124
The King of Pop

Jackson, Samuel L....................129
Dynamic actor of stage and film

Joyner, Tom...............................134
Nationally syndicated radio host

King, Gayle................................137
Journalistic jewel

Lampkin, Daisy.........................140
NAACP's first field secretary

Langhart, Janet.........................143
Highly-visible media personality

Lee, Spike..................................146
Prominent filmmaker

Lewis, Thomas..........................151
Dedicated "fisherman" for disadvantaged children

Maynor, Dorothy 155
Harlem School of the Arts esteemed founder

Mogae, Festus Gontebanye....................159
Botswana's capable leader

Moorer, Michael........................162
Talented former boxing champion

O'Neil, Buck...............................165
Baseball's goodwill ambassador

Parker, Pat.................................168
Outspoken feminist poet and activist

Patterson, Floyd.......................171
Boxing's heavyweight hero

Perry, Lee "Scratch"..................175
The father of reggae music

Petry, Ann..................................179
Novelist who captured Harlem's soul

Razaf, Andy...............................182
Heralded blues lyricist

Reason, J. Paul..........................185
Navy's four-star admiral

Richmond, Mitch.......................188
Washington's new basketball wizard

Roberts, Marcus........................191
Innovative proponent of neoclassical jazz

Robinson, Patrick.....................194
Fashion designer extraordinaire

Scott, Wendell Oliver, Sr. 197
Pioneering race car driver

Stewart, Maria W. Miller...........201
Pioneering female lecturer

Sweat, Keith..............................205
New Jack Swing vocalist

Taulbert, Clifton Lemoure........208
Prolific author

Towns, Edolphus......................212
Influential New York Congressman

Walker, Cedric ``Ricky"............215
Colorful UniverSoul Circus founder

Wesley, Dorothy 219
Howard University's librarian extraordinaire

Introduction

Contemporary Black Biography provides informative biographical profiles of the important and influential persons of African heritage who form the international black community: men and women who have changed today's world and are shaping tomorrow's.

Contemporary Black Biography covers persons of various nationalities in a wide variety of fields, including architecture, art, business, dance, education, fashion, film, industry, journalism, law, literature, medicine, music, politics and government, publishing, religion, science and technology, social issues, sports, television, theater, and others.

In addition to in-depth coverage of names found in today's headlines, *Contemporary Black Biography* provides coverage of selected individuals from earlier in this century whose influence continues to impact on contemporary life. *Contemporary Black Biography* also provides coverage of important and influential persons who are not yet household names and are therefore likely to be ignored by other biographical reference series. Each volume also includes listee updates on names previously appearing in CBB.

Designed for Quick Research *and* Interesting Reading

- **Attractive page design** incorporates textual subheads, making it easy to find the information you're looking for.

- **Easy-to-locate data sections** provide quick access to vital personal statistics, career information, major awards, and mailing addresses, when available.

- **Informative biographical essays** trace the subject's personal and professional life with the kind of in-depth analysis you need.

- **To further enhance your appreciation** of the subject, most entries include photographic portraits.

- **Sources for additional information** direct the user to selected books, magazines, and newspapers where more information on the individuals can be obtained.

Helpful Indexes Make It Easy to Find the Information You Need

Contemporary Black Biography includes cumulative Nationality, Occupation, Subject, and Name indexes that make it easy to locate entries in a variety of useful ways.

Available in Electronic Formats

Diskette/Magnetic Tape. *Contemporary Black Biography* is available for licensing on magnetic tape or diskette in a fielded format. Either the complete database or a custom selection of entries may be ordered.

The database is available for internal data processing and nonpublishing purposes only. For more information, call (800) 877-GALE.

Online. *Contemporary Black Biography* is available online through Mead Data Central's NEXIS Service in the NEXIS, PEOPLE and SPORTS Libraries in the GALBIO file.

We Welcome Your Suggestions

The editors welcome your comments and suggestions for enhancing and improving *Contemporary Black Biography*. If you would like to suggest persons for inclusion in the series, please submit these names to the editors. Mail comments or suggestions to:

The Editor
Contemporary Black Biography
Gale Research
27500 Drake Rd.
Farmington Hills, MI 48331-3535
Phone: (800) 347-4253

Photo Credits

PHOTOGRAPHS AND ILLUSTRATIONS APPEARING IN *CONTEMPORARY BLACK BIOGRAPHY*, VOLUME 19, WERE RECEIVED FROM THE FOLLOWING SOURCES:

All Reproduced by Permission: **Arinze, Francis Cardinal,** photograph. Reuters/Archive Photos. **Berry, Halle,** photograph. AP/Wide World Photos. **Bizimungu, Pasteur,** Reuters/Patrick de Noirmont/Archive Photos. **Brown, Donald,** photograph. Donald Brown Enterprises. **Caesar, Shirley,** photograph by Kathleen Barry. **Camp, Kimberly,** photograph courtesy of Kimberly Camp. **Carter, Betty,** photograph by Jack Vartoogian. **Cheadle, Don,** photograph by Susan Sterner. AP/Wide World Photos. **Cleveland, James,** photograph. Fisk University Library. **Coltrane, John,** photograph. AP/Wide World Photos. **Crawford, Randy,** photograph by Daniel Ray. Atlantic Records. **Crothers, Scatman,** photograph. Corbis-Bettmann. **Donegan, Dorothy,** photograph by Ron Sachs. Archive Photos. **Downing, Will,** photograph by Jack Vartoogian. **Flack, Roberta,** photograph by Jack Vartoogian. **Frazier, Joe,** photograph. Archive Photos. **Freeman, Charles,** photograph by Seth Perlman. **Goines, Donald,** photograph. Holloway House Publishing Company. **Graves, Denyce,** photograph by J. Henry Fair. Suzanne Stephens Arts Services. **Harkless, Necia Desiree,** photograph. Courtesy of Entertainment 2000. **Harris, Jay,** photograph. *San Jose Mercury News*. **Hemsley, Sherman,** photograph by Nick Ut. AP/Wide World Photos. **Henry, Aaron,** photograph. AP/Wide World Photos. **Hounsou, Djimon,** photograph. AP/Wide World Photos. **Hyman, Phyllis,** photograph by Tom Gates. Archive Photos. **Ingraham, Hubert A.,** drawing by Bill Bourne. Gale Research. **Jackson, George,** photograph. Motown Record Company. **Jackson, Michael,** photograph. France Presse/Corbis-Bettmann. **Jackson, Samuel L.** photograph (c) 1993 Deidre Davidson. Archive Photos. **Kenya Black Wizards,** photograph by Mike Derer. AP/Wide World Photos. **Langhart, Janet,** photograph. Reuters/Cameron/Archive Photos. **Lee, Spike,** photograph. AP/Wide World Photos. **Lewis, Thomas,** photograph. Courtesy of Thomas Lewis. **Maynor, Dorothy,** photograph. UPI/Corbis-Bettmann. **Mogae, Festus Gontebanye,** drawing by William Bourne. Gale Research. **Moorer, Michael,** photograph by Jim Palmer. APd/Wide World Photos. **O'Neil, Buck,** photograph by Ed Zurga. AP/Wide World Photos. **Patterson, Floyd,** photograph. Popperfoto/Archive Photos. **Petry, Ann,** photograph. AP/Wide World Photos. **Razaf, Andy,** photograph. Frank Driggs Collection/Archive Photos. **Reason, J. Paul,** photograph. U.S. Navy. **Richmond, Mitch,** photograph. AP/Wide World Photos. **Roberts, Marcus,** photograph by Nana Watanabe. Marcus Roberts Enterprises, Inc. **Robinson, Patrick,** photograph by Adam Nadel. AP/Wide World Photos. **Scott, Wendell Oliver, Sr.,** photograph. AP/Wide World Photos. **Sweat, Keith,** photograph by Kevin Westerburg. Elektra Entertainment. **Towns, Edolphus,** photograph. UPI/Corbis-Bettmann.

Francis Cardinal Arinze

1932—

Roman Catholic cardinal

Francis Cardinal Arinze is part of an inner realm of leading authority figures inside the Roman Catholic Church. His prominence in Vatican administrative circles reflects the Church's newfound focus on the numerical strength of a large number of relatively recent converts in developing regions of the world. Arinze, the Archbishop of Nigeria, rose to prominence in the 1970s in Africa and was called to serve within the offices of the Vatican in 1984 by Pope John Paul II. He is widely rumored to be one of the most promising cardinals in line to succeed the pope.

Arinze was born in 1932 in Eziowelle, in the Onitsha state of Nigeria. His family of seven, headed by parents Joseph Nwankwu and Bernadette M. Arinze, followed the traditional religious practices of the Onitsha region, but Arinze was baptized into the Roman Catholic religion at the age of 9. "I was very impressed by that parish priest who baptized me, and after watching him for a long time, I felt the desire of becoming myself a priest," Arinze told *Our Sunday Visitor* in a 1996 interview. He entered the seminary at the age of 13, and took his priest's vows in 1958. Seven years later, in 1965, he was consecrated a bishop in the Titular Church of Fissiana, and two years later was named archbishop of Onitsha. At the age of only 34, he became the youngest metropolitan archbishop in the world.

Career Moved to Vatican

While still working in Africa Arinze served as president of the Nigerian Council of Bishops. After the end of the three-year civil war in Nigeria in 1970, Arinze became one of the key players in a serious effort to bring Roman Catholicism to more Nigerians. His efforts were very successful. Only a few years later, the number of Catholics in the Onitsha area had risen over 65 percent, in comparison to 11 percent in the rest of Nigeria. His efforts were noticed by Pope John Paul II, and Arinze was called to the Vatican—the small state inside the city of Rome that serves as world headquarters for the Roman Catholic Church—in 1984. A year later he was elevated to cardinal and became part of the College of Cardinals, which traditionally elects the popes.

"Nowhere in the world is Catholicism flourishing as it is in Africa," wrote Paul Wilkes in the *New York Times Magazine,* who interviewed Arinze and several other

At a Glance...

Born November 1, 1932, in Eziowelle, Onitsha, Nigeria; son of Joseph Nwankwu and Bernadette M. Arinze. *Religion:* Roman Catholic.

Career: Ordained Roman Catholic priest, 1958; consecrated Bishop in the Titular Church of Fissiana, 1965; made archbishop of Onitsha, 1967; Nigerian Council of Bishops, president; called to Vatican, April, 1984; elevated to Cardinal, 1985; Pontifical Council for Inter-Religious Dialogue, The Vatican, president.

Addresses: *Home*—Vatican City, Italy. *Office*—Pontifical Council for Inter-Religious Dialogue, 00120 Vatican City, Italy.

leading cardinals in 1994. Arinze told him that a large part of traditional "African belief is animism, and animism is very, very close to Catholicism, so there is a natural attraction, an affinity. In animism, there is one God, spirits good and evil, worship of ancestors, rituals." Like many of the other cardinals appointed during John Paul II's tenure, his views are in line with his superior's conservative views. For instance, Arinze has spoken publicly on the subject of clerical celibacy, although some Catholics believe priests should be allowed to marry and have children.

At the Vatican, Arinze was named by Pope John Paul II to head the Pontifical Council for Inter-Religious Dialogue. In this capacity, Arinze served as spokesperson for the world's 968 million Catholics on issues concerning cooperation and relations—especially of a political nature—with those of other faiths. This is an especially crucial concern in the Middle East, where wars of religion continue in the modern era. It is also a pressing concern in Africa, where Islam is attracting a growing number of converts. Arinze heads a Joint Liaison Committee with his Muslim counterparts, and has made numerous statements regarding the need for increased concord and tolerance between the Muslim and Christian world. Christians in some Muslim-dominated countries, for example, are forbidden to gather in public for worship.

A Candidate for the Pontificate

With the declining health of Pope John Paul II, Arinze is widely rumored by Vatican insiders to be one of the most likely candidates among the 166 cardinals to succeed as pontiff. Should that occur, he would become the first African pope in the Roman Catholic Church's history. For the past five hundred years popes have usually been Italian, but the election of Karol Wojtyla, a Pole who was formerly Archbishop of Krakow, as Pope John Paul II in 1978 marked the beginning of a new, groundbreaking era for the church. When Wojtyla was elected, authorities feared massive unrest in then-Communist Poland. John Paul II's leadership of the Church, and his outspoken political views, had numerous ramifications in the Eastern European politics, and he has been credited with lighting the fire that became the Solidarity labor movement. That, in turn, sparked other important political events that helped lead to the end of Soviet-style Communism in that region of the world.

> "I was very impressed by that priest who baptized me, and after watching him for a long time, I felt the desire of becoming myself a priest."

Arinze knew Pope John Paul II when he was still Karol Cardinal Wojtyla, Archbishop of Krakow. Arinze was in Ireland on a lecture tour when he heard the news of the College of Cardinals' selection in 1978. "We are going to have order in the Church," Arinze reportedly told listeners that day in Belfast, according to Jonathan Kwitny's *Man of the Century: The Life and Times of Pope John Paul II*. Kwitny termed it an "accurate insight. Of course, Arinze had no idea that he would soon be whisked from Nigeria to Rome to help create that order, or that the African Church was about to be rendered independent, a marked change from its status as a colony to European missionary societies."

The election of Arinze to succeed Pope John Paul II "would capture the world's imagination," speculated Peter Hebblethwaite in the *National Catholic Reporter*. "If the future of the world depends on cooperation between the world's largest religious groups, Christians and Muslims," wrote Hebblethwaite, "then Arinze would be the man for the post-communist world just as John Paul was the right man to bring the communist world down." Arinze frequently appears on Catholic television programs in North America, such as the Eternal World Television Network. "To be Catholic by definition is universal—a religious family for all nations," he said in a speech in Sydney, Australia reported in the *Sydney*

Morning-Herald. "If everybody followed what the Catholic Church preached we would have a paradise on Earth."

Selected writings

Partnership in Education, 1965.
Sacrifice in Ibo Religion, 1970.
Answering God's Call, 1983.
Alone with God, 1986.
Church in Dialogue, 1990.

Sources

Books

Kwitny, Jonathan, *Man of the Century: The Life and Times of Pope John Paul II,* Henry Holt, 1997.

Periodicals

Christian Century, July 13-20, 1994.
National Catholic Reporter, September 11, 1992, pp. 5-7; June 18, 1993.
New York Times, February 28, 1998.
New York Times Book Review, October 19, 1997.
New York Times Magazine, December 11, 1994.
Our Sunday Visitor, August 4, 1996.
Sydney Morning-Herald, July 26, 1997.

—Carol Brennan

Clarence Avant

19(?)(?)—

Recording industry executive

Clarence Avant has long been known for his shrewd business acumen and deal-making skills. During his 30-year career, he has been actively involved in promoting opportunities for African Americans in the recording industry, and campaigning for Democratic political candidates. "He's been there for everybody, and if he'd helped himself as much as he's helped everyone else along the way, he'd be a billionaire by now," remarked Quincy Jones, a record producer and good friend of Avant's, in a 1991 *Black Enterprise* article.

Avant has helped foster the reputations of numerous performers and producers, and advised prominent Americans in both government and business. His success has been achieved mostly through individual effort, rather than collaboration with others in the recording industry. As was noted in *Black Enterprise,* "Often dressed in sweatsuits and sneakers discussing deals in the rough-and tumble language of the street, this power broker has developed the strategies, chutzpah, and contacts to become the most influential black in the music business and some say in the entire entertainment industry."

Avant's road to success began in the early 1960s, when he managed the careers of a variety of people in the music industry. Among those he represented were the blues artist Little Willie John, jazz organist Jimmy Smith, composer Lalo Schifrin, jazz producer Creed Taylor, and rock-and-roll recording pioneer Tom Wilson. Later in the decade, Avant exhibited his talent for making successful deals when he engineered the first joint venture between an African American artist and MGM, a major record company.

In 1971, Avant strengthened his presence within the music industry by forming his own record company, Sussex Records. He quickly signed recording artists Bill Withers, Dennis Coffey, Gallery, The Presidents, and Wadsworth Mansion to his new label. Avant also purchased KAGB-FM, which became one of the first African American-owned FM radio stations in metropolitan Los Angeles. In 1975, he formed Tabu Records. Tabu became a very successful venture and notable artists such as the S.O.S. Band, Alexander O'Neal, Cherrelle, and Kool & the Gang were signed to the label. Avant's skills as a producer and deal maker played a key role in the successful rise of African American producers Jimmy Jam and Terry Lewis. He also helped "L.A." Reid and Kenny "Babyface" Edmonds create LaFace Records in the 1980s.

Despite his own personal success, Avant lamented on the continued lack of African American representation within the upper echelons of the recording industry. "Black music is responsible for [about] 20% of the revenues in the record industry ... but we sure as hell aren't pulling 20% of the dollar or enjoying 20% of the power," he told *Black Enterprise* in 1991. In the same interview, Avant placed some of the blame at the feet of

> At a Glance...
>
> Born in Greensboro, NC; married to Jacqueline Avant; children: Nicole, Alex.
>
> **Career:** Managed Willie John, Jimmy Smith, Lalo Schifrin, Creed Taylor, and Tom Wilson, early 1960s; engineered first joint venture deal for an African American with a major record company (MGM), late 1960s; formed Sussex Records, 1971; became owner of KAGB-FM, 1970s; founded Tabu Records, 1975; served as delegate to the Dominican Republic, late 1970s; was member of the Trade Mission to the African Nations for United Nations Ambassador Andrew Young; helped guide the careers of producers Jimmy Jam and Terry Lewis; helped Antonio "L.A." Reid and Kenny "Babyface" Edmonds launch of LaFace Records, late 1980s; became chairman of Motown Records, 1993; became part of investment group for New Age Beverages, a partnership with PepsiCo in South Africa, 1994; co-investor of Royal Palm Crowne Plaza Hotel, Miami, FL, 1997; became first African American to serve on International Management Board of Polygram, 1997; serves as Resident Jamaican Trade Counsel.
>
> **Memberships:** board member, NAACP Legal Defense Fund; board member, Recording Industry Association of America (RIAA); board member, PolyGram International Management; board member, Motown Cafe; Apollo Theater Foundation; Los Angeles World Affairs Council; Inner City Broadcasting Corporation; Qwest Broadcasting.
>
> **Awards and honors:** The Brotherhood Crusade's Tribute Award; The Operation P.U.S.H. Award; Neil Bogart Children's Choice Award; Thurgood Marshall Lifetime Achievement Award; American Achievement Award.
>
> **Addresses:** *Business*—Motown Records, 825 Eighth Avenue, New York, NY 10019.

African Americans. "There will never be an African American running an entire majority-owned record company, business affairs, or legal department unless black record executives look beyond black music, learn about financing, and aspire to own something," he remarked.

In 1993 Avant was named chairman of Motown Records, the label that propelled legendary artists such as Stevie Wonder, the Temptations, Diana Ross, and Lionel Richie to stardom. He also became involved in other lucrative business ventures. In 1994, Avant and a group of other notable African American investors created a $20 million investment partnership in South Africa called New Age Beverages. New Age soon teamed with PepsiCo to build a bottling plant in South Africa. This plant was PepsiCo's first venture in the country since 1985, when it left South Africa to protest the policies of apartheid. The plant was to be completely managed by South Africans and financing was provided to truck drivers at the plant so that they could eventually purchase their own trucks.

In 1997, Avant and a group of other African American investors purchased the Royal Palm Crowne Plaza Hotel in Miami. This purchase marked the establishment of Miami's first African American-owned luxury hotel. That same year, Avant became the first African American to be appointed to the international management board of PolyGram Records.

In 1996, Avant and Quincy Jones were presented with the Thurgood Marshall Lifetime Achievement Award. At the award ceremony in Washington, D.C. Elaine Jones, director-counsel of the NAACP Legal Defense and Educational Fund, praised Avant and Jones for their contributions, "Clarence Avant and Quincy Jones have earned our highest respect and esteem for the work they've done over the span of a lifetime."

Avant has been an active member of the Democratic party, both at the local and national levels. During the Carter administration, he was a delegate to the Dominican Republic and served as a member of the Trade Mission to the African Nations for United Nations Ambassador Andrew Young. During the 1990s, Avant played key roles in President Clinton's presidential campaigns and currently serves as Resident Jamaican Trade Counsel.

Avant continues to be a major figure in the recording industry, where his reputation as a trailblazer and mentor to generations of African American artists is legendary.

Sources

Periodicals

Black Enterprise, December 1991, p. 50; March

1997, p. 17.

Jet, June 3, 1996, p. 4; December 1, 1997, p. 54.
Music Week, August 14, 1993, p. 5.
San Francisco Chronicle, October 4, 1994, p. B1.

Other

Additional information for this profile was obtained from the Motown Records Publicity & Media Relations Division.

—Ed Decker

Radcliffe Bailey

1968—

Artist

The works of Atlanta-based artist Radcliffe Bailey have earned the young painter comparisons with other African-American artists, including Romare Bearden and Jean-Michel Basquiat. Bailey's "uneven carpentry, smeared paint, and weathered objects function as window dressing for an examination of the environmental moorings that shape black culture," wrote Anastasia Aukeman in *ARTnews*. Thousands see one of Bailey's most arresting works when they pass through Atlanta's Hartsfield International Airport, the second-busiest terminal in the world; it was hung in time for the 1996 Olympic Summer Games.

Few artists achieve such recognition and acclaim so early in their career, but critics have often remarked upon Bailey's solid training in and incorporation of many European-based artistic traditions, such as the geometric forms of Russian constructivism, along with his ability to bring in subtle, but provoking ideas reflecting the African American experience to his art. "His stance makes it possible for many different kinds of people to relate to his work," wrote Joe Lewis in *Art in America*.

Bailey was born in New Jersey in 1968. As a child, he spent time with his grandfather, a blacksmith. The birdhouses the two made together helped spark in Bailey both a love of creative work and an appreciation for everyday objects. Choosing to pursue art as a career, he attended the Atlanta College of Art, from which he received a B.F.A. in 1991. His first brush with celebrity, however, came as a result of his appearances in two 1992 video clips from the musical group Arrested Development; Bailey made cameos in songs for both "Mr. Wendal" and "Tennessee." He also remained in the Atlanta area and began pursuing a career as serious painter.

"Uncanny Silence"

Much of Bailey's work begins with vintage sepia-tone photographs of African Americans from decades past; many of them were given to him by his grandmother. Bailey works them into mixed-media collages on wood or canvas that incorporate other found objects and thick bands of bright color—but the photos give a decidedly human dimension to his work. In the New Orleans publication *Gambit Weekly*, D. Eric Bookhardt wrote of their impact: "Formally posed and attired, they return our gaze with the impassive eyes of those who have seen much but are in no great rush to talk about it. Instead, it is their uncanny silence that speaks to us."

Doors are also another symbolic object that appear frequently in Bailey's works; sometimes he constructs a canvas to resemble an entire dwelling. His use of weatherbeaten wood reminds the viewer of sharecropper lean-tos in the Deep South and other ramshackle buildings. Critics have often commented upon Bailey's adept evocation of the Old South in his art, his ability to effortlessly summon up the intergenerational character

> **At a Glance...**
>
> Born in 1968, in NJ. *Education:* Atlanta College of Art, B.F.A., 1991.
>
> **Career:** Artist, 1991–.
>
> **Addresses:** *Home*—Atlanta, GA. *Gallery*—David Beitzel Gallery, 102 Prince St., New York, NY 10012.

and mood of this region of the United States—"an ethos that includes superstition, racial turmoil, deterioration, and regeneration," as Aukeman pointed out in *ARTnews*. Upon his canvases Bailey has also sometimes laid tar (once a hate-crime ingredient) and cotton, the crop which depended on legalized slavery for its ability to turn a profit.

A Transatlantic Canvas

Bailey's range of artistic materials echoes his African American heritage. The colors he uses are often bright and almost tropical in intensity. He also uses them in thick strokes, which in some cases appear as "ritualistic curved lines that recall the old wrought-iron grillwork found in Haiti and New Orleans," wrote Bookhardt in *Gambit Weekly*. Often he brings *nkisi,* African votive figurines, onto his canvases.

Within a few years Bailey's growing body of work had found admirers. In 1994, he was invited to participate in a group exhibition titled "Equal Rights & Justice" at the High Museum in Atlanta. He also signed on with a prominent Atlanta dealer, the Fay Gold Gallery. *ARTnews* reviewer Amy Jinkner-Lloyd found his first show at Fay Gold praiseworthy, especially for his exploration of African-American themes with a "restraint ... which is remarkable for such a young artist." She found fault only with one work, *For Four Little Girls, Birmingham, Alabama,* which, like most of Bailey's art, serves to commemorate a specific moment in history—in this case, the church firebombing deaths of four girls during the worst days of the civil-rights struggle in the 1960s.

Bailey has also expanded into more three-dimensional confines with the occasional piece of sculpture. In the 1994 show, one of these was an anvil covered with shards of mirror—a piece, Jinkner-Lloyd asserted, that "entices visually. It also suggests savagery decorated with civility," which she considered a fitting symbol for the history of race relations throughout the course of American history.

"Art That Bridges Class and Race"

Bailey's 1995 solo show at Fay Gold was critiqued by *Art in America*'s Lewis. He termed Bailey's works "culturally literate and introspective without being sentimental," and singled out *The Magic City* in particular as evidence of Bailey's talents. This mixed-media work, 8 by 12 feet in dimension, recalls a dilapidated shack; onto it Bailey has worked in branding marks from an iron, a reference to one of the slave era's more barbaric practices. Yet the work also incorporates other, less gruesome, symbols from African-American culture, such as a team emblem from one of the Negro League baseball teams that thrived in the first half of the twentieth century. Lewis found effusive praise for Bailey's work in his *Art in America* review, especially in light of the relatively youthful artist's sensitive handling of cultural themes. Bailey's paintings and sculptures, wrote Lewis, "are what I hoped the '90s would bring—an art that bridges class and race." Pop singer Elton John also found favor with Bailey's art, buying a work from the Gold Gallery as a result of attending one of the artist's first shows. In a dramatic honor, one of Bailey's works—a large 40 by 12 foot mural—was selected to welcome visitors at in a hall at Atlanta main airport just in time for the 1996 Summer Olympics in that city.

Not surprisingly, Bailey's career has taken him to the center of the art world. New York City's David Beitzel Gallery has represented him since 1995. At a spring 1997 show there, Bailey showed several large mixed-media pieces. *Mound Magician* was fan-shaped, a baseball diamond with baseballs embedded in it, slashed by yellow, black and red stripes of paint. Other works, smaller in dimension, took the shape of musical instruments—*Mingus,* for instance, looked like a bass fiddle. Another, *Black and Tan,* resembled a grand piano suspended from a wall with orange, yellow and black color chords predominating. In place of a keyboard at the top, however, Bailey had instead put in flickering electric candles, an effect which pleased critic David Ebony; in his review, published on the web site *artnet.com,* Ebony declared, "this work, and the show as a whole, is exhilarating music for the eye."

Music as Metaphor

Art in America's Calvin Reid also reviewed the Bailey show at David Beitzel, and found it impressive in both execution and scope. "Splattered by energetic brush patterns, portentous inscriptions and a spooky evocation of historical triumph, these works record a potent convergence of Pan African romanticism, downhome black mythology and the antic hipsterism of black

American urban life," Reid declared. In 1997, Bailey was also invited to contribute to "As Time Goes By: History, Memory, and Sentimentality" at the Stamford, Connecticut branch of New York's famed Whitney Museum. Bailey sent *Shango* and *Soular Taps,* both of which continued the theme of incorporating vintage photographs; in this case, he used images of infants.

> "I'm like free jazz. I'm not concerned about where I'm going, just as long as I'm moving forward and documenting life."

Bailey lives in a loft in Atlanta's warehouse district, which is stacked with found objects that will someday find their way into his work. In his *Art in America* review, Lewis pointed to Bailey's appropriation of found objects into his works as evidence of the artist's solid grounding in the modernist traditions of twentieth-century art, but with a new twist; Lewis likened Bailey's ultimate visual patterns to the use of samples in modern hip-hop music—"Bailey creates 'real time' within old space," Lewis declared. The artist himself has used also the rhythms of African American culture as a metaphor on more than one occasion. "I like to think of my artworks as similar to the music of Thelonius Monk," Bailey told Aukeman in *ARTnews*. "They're like rituals that just happen." In an interview with *Vibe*'s Kevin Powell a year later, Bailey stated, "I'm like free jazz. I'm not concerned about where I'm going, just as long as I'm moving forward and documenting life."

Selected exhibitions

"As Time Goes By" (solo), Whitney Museum, Stamford, CT 1997.

Sources

Periodicals

Art in America, March 1995, p. 110; February 1998, p. 103
ARTnews, April 1994, p. 180; November 1995, p. 112.
Gambit Weekly (New Orleans), October 27, 1997.
New York Times, July 27, 1997; December 24, 1997.
Vibe, August 1996.

Other

"David Bailey's New York Top Ten," published at http://www.artnet.com/mag/magazine/reviews

—Carol Brennan

Halle Berry

1968—

Actress, model

"I don't want to be just a sex goddess," film and television actress Halle Berry divulged to Lawrence Chua in *Elle,* "but then I don't want to play just crackheads either." Notable whether playing ingenues or junkies, she has performed roles in films as diverse as *Boomerang,* which starred Eddie Murphy, and filmmaker Spike Lee's controversial *Jungle Fever.* A former model and first runner-up in the Miss USA pageant, Berry, who also appeared on television as Debbie Porter on *Knots Landing,* postulates that planning helped her leap to leading lady status in the film industry. The actress told Chua, "Preparation, luck and opportunity seemed to come together at the same time."

Born to a white mother and black father, Berry grew up in Cleveland, Ohio. Her parents separated when she was four years old. Halle and her sister Heidi were raised by their mother, Judith, a registered nurse. Throughout her childhood, Berry recalled, she was so shy her mother had to coax her to leave home to go downtown. Being the offspring of a biracial couple, Berry had her initial encounter with prejudice as a youngster, when her family moved from an inner-city neighborhood to suburban Cleveland. "People would call me `zebra' and leave Oreo cookies in our mailbox," she recounted to Chua. When she questioned her mother about these incidents, Berry related in *Ebony,* her mother explained, "I'm white, and you are Black.... What do you see when you look in the mirror? You see what everyone else sees. They don't know that you're biracial. They don't know who your mother is, and they aren't going to care."

Entered Beauty Contest

From the time she was in grade school, Berry wanted to be an actress. She related to Laurie Werner in *USA Weekend,* "I would imitate scenes from *The Wizard of Oz.* I even had the right dog." A cheerleader, Berry also became prom queen and class president during her high school years. When she was 17 years old, Berry was surprised to learn one of her high school boyfriends had entered her name in the Miss Teen Ohio beauty pageant. Winning the title, she then entered a succession of other pageants, including Miss World, in which she won the dress competition. Berry was also named first runner-up in the Miss USA competition after her selec-

At a Glance...

Born August 14, 1968; daughter of Judith (a registered nurse) Berry; married David Justice (a professional baseball player), 1993, divorced, 1997. *Education:* Attended Cuyahoga Community Coll., Cleveland.

Career: Actress and model; appeared on Bob Hope's USO Tour; television appearances include "Living Dolls," ABC, "Knots Landing," CBS, and "Queen," "Solomon and Sheba," made for cable television movie, "Oprah Winfrey Presents: The Wedding," 1998; motion picture appearances include *Jungle Fever, Strictly Business,* and *The Last Boy Scout,* all 1991, and *Boomerang,* 1992, *Father Hood,* 1993, *The Progam, The Flintstones* in 1994, *Losing Isaiah,* 1995, *Executive Decision, Rich Man's Wife* in 1996, *B.A.P.S.,* 1997, *Bulworth, Why Do Fools Fall In Love?* 1998; has competed in beauty pageants. Volunteer, Juvenile Diabetes Association.

Selected awards: Named Miss Teen Ohio and Miss Ohio, 1985; first runner-up, Miss USA Pageant, 1985; winner of dress competition, Miss World Pageant, 1986; NAACP Image Award; voted one of the "50 Most Beautiful People" by *People* Magazine.

Addresses: *Home*—Los Angeles, CA. *Other*—Halle Berry's Fan Club, 250 West 57th Street, Suite 2517, New York, NY 10019.

tion as Miss Ohio in 1985.

In 1986 Berry enrolled at Cuyahoga Community College in Cleveland to study broadcast journalism. When she took an internship at a local radio station, Berry discovered she disliked reporting. She left college before completing her degree to pursue modeling and study acting in Chicago. Her mother encouraged the career transition, Berry divulged to Chua: "When I left home to start acting, [my mother's] attitude was, 'Keep your chin up, go do it; but if you fail, home is always here.'"

While in Chicago, Berry auditioned for a role in producer Aaron Spelling's television pilot *Charlie's Angels '88.* Although the show did not materialize, Spelling was impressed with Berry's screen test. He encouraged her not to give up acting. Two big breaks in the young actress' career came with a three-week USO tour with Bob Hope and a starring role as a teenage fashion model in the short-lived television series *Living Dolls.* Berry remarked in *Ebony,* "Here I was an ex-model, a former beauty queen and when *Living Dolls* was canceled, I was playing a model. People weren't taking me seriously."

Became A Success

Hoping audiences would view her differently, Berry prepared for her next role as a crack addict named Vivien in *Jungle Fever* by interviewing several crack addicts and going ten days without a bath. Although her role brought her acclaim, Berry took a recurring part in the television series *Knots Landing* for financial purposes. "I'm a real miser," the actress told Werner. "I want a cushion," she added.

After Berry's 1991 appearance as a femme fatale in the motion picture *Strictly Business,* Peter Biskind wrote in *Premiere,* "Berry may still be playing somebody's girlfriend, but clearly her star is ascending." The actress almost lost the leading role of Natalie in the comedy. She recalled to Chua, "I found out that they hired me, thought I was too light-skinned, hired someone darker, realized that was a mistake, and then hired me again. And I understood that I had gone through all of this agony for two weeks just because of my skin color."

Although critics were divided in their reviews of the film, Berry's portrayal marked a turning point in her career. Her appearance in leading roles was assured with her selection as Damon Wayans' exotic dancer girlfriend in the movie *The Last Boy Scout.* Vincent Canby of the *New York Times* wrote, "The best thing in the film is Halle Berry. She is an actress who is going places." Berry researched her role in the movie by paying the owner of a Hollywood strip joint to let her dance. After the film's success, Berry commented to Biskind, "I don't want to rise to superstardom overnight, like Julia Roberts. There's no place to go but down."

"Though she is an imposing beauty ... Berry's radiant looks belie the strengths that have made her a young actress worth watching," wrote Chua in 1992, after the release of the comedy *Boomerang.* Judy Gerstel of the *Detroit Free Press* lauded Berry in the film as "versatile," noting that her role as Angela was "played to doe-eyed perfection." The year *Boomerang* was released, *Ebony* profiled the young actress as an image breaker: "A down-to-earth, drop-dead gorgeous woman, Berry exudes confidence, having already shattered the Hollywood adage that models can't act."

Married, Then Divorced

As her film career picked up steam, Berry began a relationship with Atlanta Braves baseball player, David Justice. Their whirlwind courtship began in 1992 and ended when Berry proposed to him, and the couple were married on New Year's Day in 1993. She told *Ebony* in 1994 that Justice was her "soulmate, my rock, my prince on a white horse." Compared to the other men Berry had been involved with, Justice was Prince Charming. One of her ex-boyfriends sued her and sold his story to a national tabloid newspaper. Another ex hit her in the ear so hard she lost 80 percent of her hearing in that ear.

The couple were likened to another famous couple, Marilyn Monroe and Joe Dimaggio. And like them, the marriage ended in divorce. Just a couple of months after celebrating their third anniversary, Justice asked for a divorce. It devastated Berry. She told *Ebony* in 1997: "I was numb for probably two months. I was walking around in a daze. I didn't know how to function. I would wake up in the middle of the night and think this is just a bad dream. I kept saying, 'No, this isn't really real. David's just on a road trip.'"

Her friends rallied to support Berry—her mother even flew to Los Angeles to be with her. But she still had self-doubts and thoughts of suicide. Berry even made an attempt by getting in her car to inhale toxic fumes, but she recalled to *Ebony*, "somewhere in my heart, I think I knew I didn't really want to end my life. I just wanted to end the pain."

Berry entered therapy and threw herself into her work. Her next film, *B.A.P.S.*, was a comedy directed by Robert Townsend. She described to *Ebony* how working on this film helped her heal, "It's a comedy, and I wasn't feeling very funny, so I wasn't confident that I would be able to be in that space. But it turned out to be therapeutic. I could laugh and be silly and let go of all that negative energy."

Sought-After Actress and Model

Throughout her acting career, Berry has sought roles that were diverse. She went from a hip-hop dancer in *Strictly Business* to a college co-ed in *The Program* to playing a recovering drug addict fighting for her son in *Losing Isaiah*—she won raves for this portrayal. She is also known to play characters of the past. She portrayed Alex Haley's paternal grandmother in "Queen," a television miniseries. She took a turn as a pre-historic secretary in the live-action film, *The Flintstones*, and she played Sheba in "Solomon and Sheba," a made for cable television movie. This also marked the first time an African American has portrayed Sheba, who was an Ethiopian. In one year alone, Berry portrayed the love interest of Warren Beatty in *Bulworth,* then a young woman trying to choose between two men while dealing with her past in "The Wedding," produced by Oprah Winfrey, and *Why Do Fools Fall In Love?,* a movie based on singer Frankie Lymon's life, where she played Zola Taylor, a member of the singing group The Platters and one of Lymon's wives.

> "I don't want to be just a sex goddess, but then I don't want to play just crackheads either."

In addition to becoming one of Hollywood's best known African American actresses, Berry returned to modeling when she signed with Revlon Cosmetics. She will begin filming "The Dorothy Dandridge Story," sometime in 1998. Berry and a handful of other African American actresses are in a race to get Dandridge's story told. Unlike Dandridge, who fought racism in Hollywood, only to succumb to the pressure in the end, Berry has risen above her circumstances and proven to herself—and others—that she is a fighter and will continue to do so.

Selected works

(Films)

Jungle Fever, 1991.
The Last Boy Scout, 1991.
Strictly Business, 1991.
Boomerang, 1992.
The Program, 1994.
The Flintstones, 1994.
Losing Isaiah, 1995.
B.A.P.S., 1997.
Bulworth, 1998.
Why Do Fools Fall In Love?, 1998.

(Television and cable)

"Living Dolls," ABC.
"Knots Landing," CBS.
"Queen," 1994.
"Solomon and Sheba."
"The Wedding," ABC, 1998.

Sources

Detroit Free Press, July 1, 1992.
Ebony, February 1992; October 1992; December 1994; March 1997.
Elle, April 1992.
Essence, October 1996.
Jet, November 11, 1991.
People, November 25, 1991; December 23, 1991; July 20, 1992; May 11, 1998.
Premiere, December 1991.
Upscale, June/July 1992; October/November 1992.
USA Weekend, November 8-10, 1991.

Other

Information obtained from the Internet at www.cleveland.com and http//:e1.eonline.com.

—Marjorie Burgess and Ashyia N. Henderson

Pasteur Bizimungu

1951—

President of Rwanda

Pasteur Bizimungu became president of Rwanda in July of 1994 after a political crisis that attracted international notice for its scenes of horrific bloodshed as one of Rwanda's two main ethnic groups attempted to annihilate the other. A onetime civil servant, Bizimungu is of Hutu heritage, but has been allied with a political rebel group of the Tutsi minority since the early 1990s. Working from abroad, the Rwandan Patriotic Front, or RPF, attempted to overthrow a corrupt Hutu regime, and Bizimungu was a key player during this era; after a 1994 crisis that resulted in civil war and the RPF's victory, he was named president of the troubled country.

Bizimungu was born in 1951 and hails from the northwest region of Rwanda. His career has been closely tied to the political fortunes of his land for much of his adult life. The small, impoverished Central African nation shares many similarities with Burundi, a neighboring country which, along with Rwanda, was once administered under the Belgian colonial regime. Rwanda's other neighbors are Uganda to the north, Tanzania on the east, and the Republic of Congo (formerly Zaire) at its western border. About the size of Vermont, it is a hilly but fertile country and its population of about 8.2 million (pre-civil war estimates) supports itself mainly through farming. About 80 percent of Rwandans are Christian, with two-thirds of that number Roman Catholic; the rest are Muslim or maintain traditional African tribal beliefs. The country's per-capita income in 1997 was $234 a year, and the life expectancy for an average Rwandan is 49 years. It has an extremely high rate of AIDS cases and HIV infection, and many also die of malaria, tuberculosis, and malnutrition.

Hutu and Tutsi

Rwanda is divided along two main ethnic lines, Hutu and Tutsi. As Bizimungu explained in a welcome speech to American president Bill Clinton in March of 1998, the genocidal bloodshed of the 1994 civil war "was not a product of centuries old ethnic hatred as it is often assumed. The ideology that led to genocide was planted in our society in the early part of the 20th century when the seven-century old Rwanda was conquered by Europeans. It was based on the contemporary European racist theories. Discriminatory policies were applied to

At a Glance...

Born 1951. *Education:* Attended the National University of Rwanda, early 1970s. *Politics:* Rwandan Patriotic Front.

Career: Electro-Gas (state-owned public utility), Kigali, Rwanda, manager until 1990; political activist and member of Rwandan Patriotic Front (RPF); appointed president by RPF in July, 1994, for five-year term.

Addresses: *Office*—Residence de la Republique, Kigali, Rwanda. *Embassy*—The Embassy of the Republic of Rwanda, 1714 New Hampshire Ave. NW, Washington, DC 20009.

all walks of life."

Though the two ethnic groups were similar, far different social customs arose over generations. The Tutsi gained an advantage over the Hutu by means of the "cattle-contract," which first gave them economic power, then social and political hegemony. Belgian colonial authorities helped maintain this inequality, but a peasant uprising in 1959 led to the overthrow of the Tutsi monarchy and power passed to the Hutus. Rwanda gained independence from Belgium on July 1, 1962, and the political changeover led to the exile of a great number of Tutsi. The Republic of Rwanda was structured around a president, prime minister, and National Assembly, with the president controlling a great deal of power. France trained and supplied the Rwandan Army for many years after independence and maintained close ties with the Hutu regime. A military coup in 1973 installed Major General Juvenal Habyarimana, a Hutu, as president. There was one political party, the Mouvement Revolutionnaire National pour le Developpement (MRND).

A Corrupt Dictatorship

At the time of this event, Bizimungu was a student at Rwanda's only university, the National University of Rwanda. Over the years he rose through the civil service ranks and, until 1990, served as manager of Electro-Gas, the state-run utility. The utility was in dire financial straits, so Bizimungu campaigned Habyarimana to allow Electro-Gas to raise its rates, lay off some of its bloated payroll, and shut off service to those who were in severe arrears, which included many government agencies. He resigned in protest in 1990 when Habyarimana refused. He also accused the president and his government of rampant nepotism and other corrupt practices that fomented a political instability for the benefit of the Hutu regime.

Inside Rwanda there was a push for a multi-party, multi-ethnic democracy, and the Rwandan Political Front (RPF) formed in exile around this idea. It was primarily Tutsi, but there were also many disillusioned Hutu like Bizimungu who allied with it. When he went to Uganda to meet with RPF leaders in the summer of 1990, he informed rebels there, according to Gerard Prunier in *The Rwanda Crisis: History of a Genocide,* that the country's political system was very weak and could be easily brought down. That same year RPF launched an invasion, and guerrilla fighting continued for the next three years.

Mysterious Plane Crash

Bizimungu eventually went to the Belgian capital of Brussels, where the RPF maintained offices. There he served as the RPF's primary spokesperson and was a key player in the delegation that negotiated a peace settlement in Arusha, Tanzania in August of 1993. According to the terms of the settlement, President Habyarimana pledged to move Rwanda toward a more democratic era that included sharing power with Tutsi. But, as BBC correspondent Fergal Keane wrote in *Season of Blood: A Rwandan Journey,* "for several years prior to the [1994] genocide Hutus were exposed to an ongoing and virulent campaign of anti-Tutsi brainwashing." This propaganda centered around "ten commandments" to guide Hutu-Tutsi relations, which condemned miscegenation and "urged Hutus to 'stop having mercy on the Batusi,'" wrote Keane. "This last injunction was to be obeyed by thousands of Hutu peasants when the genocide began."

In April of 1994, both Habyarimana and the president of Burundi died in a plane crash after their aircraft was fired upon and brought down near his palace's landing strip. The event launched massive bloodshed in Rwanda as the RPF moved to take control and Hutus responded. A radio station owned by Hutu extremists and supported by the late Habyarimana himself broadcast the words "Tutsis need to be killed." News footage of the carnage and reports of the systematic murder of children made international news. Machete-wielding gangs of militia roamed; women were beheaded in front of their children. Hutus who were in support of the RPF were also slaughtered in large numbers.

Bizimungu and other RPF leaders, after gaining control of the major cities, declared a cease-fire on June 15; pressure from other African states also helped halt some of the carnage. The political crisis was far from over, however. When Zaire (now the Republic of Congo) opened its border in mid-July, Rwandans crossed it in huge numbers. Overall, about 2.1 million (of a population of just over 8 million) fled to refugee camps there and elsewhere. The United Nations estimated those refugees at about half Hutu, half Tutsi in makeup. Conditions were desperate and dangerous in the camps, to say the least. Many died of cholera, and as late as 1997 opposing sides fired on the segregated camps.

Named President

"Because there were only a handful of Hutu in the rebel leadership ranks, human rights officials believe Mr. Bizimungu was important as a symbol of their multi-ethnicity," noted a *New York Times* report. Indeed, the new Tutsi government (installed in place of Habyarimana's Hutu-dominated one) had several key leaders of Hutu ethnicity. Bizimungu was one of them, as was his prime minister, Faustin Twagiramungu. Yet Twagiramungu had not been a member of the RPF, but rather of the provisional government in Rwanda since the assassination of Habyarimana. Only the RPF military chief, General Paul Kagame, was a Tutsi. Bizimungu was thought to be close to Kagame, but was at odds with Faustin Twagiramungu from the start. On one occasion Twagiramungu hinted that there was a potential for a dictatorship if Bizimungu did not call elections soon. Bizimungu ousted him in August of 1995, along with three other cabinet members.

The new president of Rwanda faced far more serious threats than the ones in his administration, however. "One of the new Government's biggest challenges will be to persuade Hutu to return," wrote the *New York Times*'s Raymond Bonner not long after Bizimungu and the RPF took over. A large, exiled Hutu population was more dangerous abroad than if they were confined in Rwanda under the eye of the RPF—as the exiled Tutsi had proven to the Habyarimana/Hutu regime. Many Hutu soldiers fled during the summer of 1994—some with their weapons—and vowed to return as an army to overthrow the RPF and Tutsi.

War crimes and Rwanda's international standing were also pressing concerns for Bizimungu. In late 1994 he spoke before the United Nations General Assembly and requested the swift formation of an international tribunal to investigate the genocide. He said further delay could portend more bloodshed; his government detained nearly six thousand suspects in the atrocities.

Bizimungu and France

Bizimungu also chastised France and its role in the 1994 civil war. The French military had set up a "safe zone" in a southern section of Rwanda, and were accused of sheltering ousted Hutu leaders there. A year later, Bizimungu accused France of withholding assistance until some Hutu were allowed back into power. In late 1995, according to a Reuters report, Bizimungu declared that "France has had a hand in the genocide in this country, because it wanted to protect its agents who were in power here and to make of this country what it would have liked it to become ... What the French are after now is to restore these people to power. France is interested in the French language and the protection of its policies here."

In late 1996 Bizimungu also encountered problems with neighboring Zaire: Tutsi were accused of firing on Hutu refugee camps in eastern Zaire, but Bizimungu said his government forces did not have the weaponry to do so. The new Rwandan government was also accused of giving military help to Banyamulenge Tutsi in Zaire; in the summer of 1997 rebel forces, led by Laurent Kabila, overthrew the dictatorship of Mobutu Sese Seko and restored the country to its previous name, Congo. Bizimungu attended Kabila's inauguration ceremony, which was heralded as a sign of hope and stability in this region of the world. But a year later, in August of 1998, tensions had increased between the two countries, and forces hostile toward Kabila were gaining ground. Kabila accused Bizimungu and other African leaders of fomenting the conflict; many Rwandans helped to train the Congolese army inside the country, while dissatisfaction over Kabila's authoritarian rule spread. Conversely, Bizimungu accused the Congolese military of training exiled Rwandans (primarily Hutu militia responsible for the genocide) hostile to his RPF government.

Most nations would be devastated after a civil war that resulted in the death of about ten percent of its population and the exodus of one-quarter of that number, but Rwanda had so little in the first place. Bizimungu struggled to put a National Assembly together, restore some semblance of normality, and put the economy back into operation; he also campaigned the international community for relief aid. In December of 1997 he hosted U.S. Secretary of State Madeleine Albright, with whom he visited refugee camps. There were still attacks on camps—during her stay, a Tutsi camp housing refugees from the Congo was shelled by Hutu forces—

but Albright pledged a nearly $4 million aid package. The Secretary of State also said publicly that Western nations like the United States need to accept some of the blame for not intervening in Rwanda when the genocide began in April of 1994. Bizimungu also hosted President Bill Clinton on his tour of Africa in March of 1998.

Sources

Books

Keane, Fergal. *Season of Blood: A Rwandan Journey.* Viking, 1995.
Prunier, Gerard. *The Rwanda Crisis: History of a Genocide.* New York: Columbia University Press, 1995.

Periodicals

Chicago Tribune, December 11, 1997.
New York Times, June 15, 1994, p. A11; July 20, 1994, p. A6; July 25, 1994, p. A7; October 9, 1994, sec. 1, p. 19.

Other

BBC World News, http://bbc.co.uk
Reuters Information Service, http://www.reuters.com, December 2, 1995.
Rwanda Information Exchange, http://www.rwanda.net

—Carol Brennan

Donald Brown

1963—

Artist

Donald Brown has emerged to become one of the premier sculptors of recent years, noted especially for his ability to capture the likenesses of real people in portrait busts. While successfully incorporating the European influences of his youth with an understanding of his African ancestry, Brown's style enjoys an international reputation for excellence. On his resume Brown writes that his aspirations are "to celebrate heroes and heroines of African descent, upholding their legacies for future generations to remember through the art of sculpture and creating an awareness and acknowledgment of our ongoing contributions to this planet."

Brown is most well known for his evocative sculpture, *A Genius With Four Masters MA,* which portrays Mahatma Gandhi, Marcus Garvey, the Reverend Dr. Martin Luther King, Jr., Malcolm X, and Nelson Mandela. The sculptor's works include portrait busts of South African president Nelson Mandela, writer Maya Angelou, and New Jersey Governor Christine Todd Whitman, and a series of figurines commissioned by the actor John Amos. Among the owners of his works are Whitney Houston, Gladys Knight, General Colin Powell, John Amos, Wynton Marsalis, the parents of Tiger Woods, and Michael Jordan's mother. Brown's pieces also are in the Baltimore NAACP headquarters, the National Black Theatre Festival offices, and the National Black Arts Festival offices in Atlanta. His portrait busts start at $50,000, while his limited edition sculptures start at $5,000.

Recognized His Talent Early

Donald Brown was born September 21, 1963, in a town called Dudley in the West Midlands of England, close to Birmingham. He spent the first twenty-six years of his life in Wolverhampton, about six miles from Dudley. There were only two children in his family, him and an older brother. His father, Abram Brown, was a foundry worker who made enamel baths. His mother, Mildred Maud (Kelly) Brown, was an auxiliary nurse for the local hospital.

Brown went to a variety of schools, including one for asthmatics because he has asthma. When he was eleven, he discovered his talent for sculpting in a woodworking class. After the teacher told the class to take a piece of wood and do whatever they wanted to it, Brown got very excited. "I snuck it in my pocket and took it home," he

At a Glance...

Born Donald Brown, September 21, 1963, in Dudley, West Midlands, England; son of Abram Brown (a retired foundry worker) and Mildred Maud (Kelly) Brown (a retired auxiliary nurse); children: Michael James Brown. *Education:* Wolverhampton University, England, BA (honors), 1989.

Career: Foremost a sculptor. Comic actor with an independent duo, 1980-96; art teacher, 1990-96; photographic and runway model, Manchester Model Agency and Dreams Model Agency, 1991-96; sales manager, Northern Pressure Washers, 1991-92.

Awards: 7th Day Adventist Gospel Songwriter of the Year, 1991; BBC Gospel Awards original music/rap composition, 1993; numerous medals in track-and-field events.

Addresses: Residence—51 Dimmock Street, Parkfield, Wolverhampton WV46HF, England; *Office*—The Moss Side and Hulme Business Federation, Unit 1-3, Greenheys Business Center, 10 Pencroft Way, Hulme, Manchester M156JJ, England.

recalled in a *CBB* interview. "And I polished it and shaped it and it was round and smooth [and] began to shine. I was a bit nervous because I thought I was going to get in trouble for taking it home. But instead I got the attention that I never expected from the tutor who then brought in other tutors to see what I'd done.... [A]t that young age, getting approval from authority as well as my peer group was an indication that I was good at something."

Another discovery came at 13 when Brown accidentally split the head of a figure of a man he was carving. After initial disappointment, he saw the sculpture in a whole new way, as an abstract realistic piece, with all the veins and striations laid bare. He left it the way it was, using the accident as a means to further the significance of his work. "That really put me on the map in terms of being recognized as a quality sculptor within the school," he said.

By the time Brown was 14 a portrait of himself cast in resin had appeared on national television as part of the Children's Cadbury Arts exhibition and many proclaimed him to be a prodigy. He studied for his Bachelor of Fine Arts degree at Wolverhampton University and received the degree with honors when he was in his early twenties in 1989. From 1990 to 1996 he taught art at schools in Birmingham, Wolverhampton, Manchester, and Bristol.

In spite of his personal enthusiasm for his art, Brown did not initially receive support from his family. His mother became concerned about his choice of profession because it did not seem like an economically stable endeavor. According to Brown, his mother wanted him to go into the ministry and be a preacher or a teacher or a doctor. "I actually went to the ministry college to check it out and spend a weekend," Brown reminisced to *CBB*. "And I was shocked that there wasn't an art studio, and immediately I thought well this is not for me. I felt that I had an ability to create the kind of work that would in itself be [a] ministry to people in a different way. And now that I'm meeting with success [my mother] accepts fully what I'm doing."

Learned to Sell Himself

While still in school Brown created a bust of a man in clay in a shopping mall in Oldham as part of a residency, and learned to work and talk to passersby at the same time. After graduation he decided he did not want to be a struggling artist or one who was successful only after he died so he gave himself a crash course in business, first by working in the finance department of Wolverhampton University and then by working for several sales companies, selling everything from televisions to garage materials.

Brown's ultimate aim was to learn how to promote himself and his work as a product, without having to go through an agent. "In as much as other agents and galleries might be successful," he explained. "Very often you have to comply with certain rules and regulations or a certain kind of style. And at the moment I want to make sure I maintain my freshness, my ability to create as and when I want to, without having certain restrictions."

Created "Narrative" Sculpture

Initially Brown only aimed to create a sculpture that looked like somebody, but now he tries to instill his work with meaning, symbolism, and depth as well. A case in point is his affecting personal bonded bronze sculpture *A Genius With Four Masters MA*. In it, Marcus Garvey and Mahatma Gandhi are depicted high in the background while in the foreground on either side Malcolm X and the Reverend Dr. Martin Luther King, Jr. pull apart prison bars so Nelson Mandela can climb out to freedom.

"It's almost like trying to create sculpture which is like a narrative, like a story, whereby it's educational and informative," Brown said. "There's a reason why Martin Luther King and Malcolm X are breaking these prison bars open, there's a reason why there's locks but no keys, because they themselves are the keys, there's a reason why all the five heads are linked in a certain way which is symbolic of the five Olympic circles, which is a sign of global unity." Brown also told *The News and Observer* of Raleigh, North Carolina, "These men were all masters in their own right." As Brown explains it, their names all have the letters MA, and a master's degree is considered a sign of excellence.

In the beginning Brown's influence came from studying the sculptures of European masters like Michelangelo, Rodin, and Bernini. But after visiting America he became cognizant of his African history, something he had not been made aware of in Britain, and it made an impact on his work. However, he does not want to limit himself to one style or the other. "I can create a European style," he commented to *CBB*. "I can create an African American style. A lot of people say, 'Is your work European? Or is your work African American or Africanized?' I would like to be able to produce commissions from any particular nationality."

Critics have praised Brown for the detail and likeness in his portrait busts. In addition, "Critics are very quick to say that I'm the artist of the moment or an artist [who's] going to explode or an artist [who] is art's best kept secret," he said. "They admire the fact that an artist can work in public and switch at regularity from sculpting to talking." The exposure has resulted in an increasing demand for more of his original works.

Currently, the artist is working on "an action-packed sculpture with a deep rooted message for a lot of African Americans" about the Middle Passage, the journey taken by the slave ships from Africa across the Atlantic to America and England. "I'm focusing on the atrocities that occurred during that passage, being cramped in small spaces, many sick and dying flung overboard, literally millions," he said. "[I'm] creating a piece which brings attention to that time lest we forget." The sculpture is scheduled to be cast from clay into bonded bronze. Brown also is starting a new work that is the female equivalent to *A Genius With Four Masters*. "It will be celebrating female heroines [who] contributed immensely to our history."

In addition to sculpting, Brown has managed to excel in track-and-field as a hurdler and long-jumper, and he also has another career as a gospel songwriter. Exhibiting boundless talent, he also works as an actor, model, and stand-up comedian.

Selected major works

A selection of figurines, commissioned by actor John Amos, 1998.
Portrait bust of New Jersey Governor Christine Todd Whitman, commissioned by John Amos, 1998.
A Genius With Four Masters MA, 1997.
Portrait bust of author and performing artist Maya Angelou, commissioned by the Atlanta National Black Arts Festival, 1996.
The official celebrity figurine for the 1996 National Black Arts Festival.
Portrait bust of Larry Leon Hamlin, the founder and artistic director of The National Black Theatre Festival in North Carolina, commissioned by John Amos, 1995.
A miniature face of British comedian Rowan Atkinson, known as "Mr. Bean," commissioned by Barrow Models, 1991.

Sources

Periodicals

Essence, May 1988, p. 78.
Manchester Evening News (U.K.), May 10, 1994, pp. 26-27; May 25, 1996, p. 47; January 30, 1998, p. 29.
Monthly Magazine (U.K.), November 1995, pp. 28, 30.
National Black Theatre Festival program (NC), August 4-9, 1997, p. 14.
National Voice, (NC) April 1998, pp. 9, 15.
News & Observer (NC), August 8, 1997.
Winston-Salem Chronicle, August 1997, vol. 1, no. 2, p. 16.

Other

Interview with Donald Brown and assistance from Perri Gaffney at Donald Brown Enterprises, NYC.

—Alison Carb Sussman

Michelle Byrd

1965—

Film industry association executive

Michelle Byrd is not an actress or a screenwriter. In fact, neither she nor anyone else in her family has previously been involved in the world of film. And yet, in an artistic world so often controlled by big money, big names, and big movie production companies, Michelle Byrd plays a big role: she is the executive director of the Independent Feature Project, the largest non-profit association of independent directors, producers, screenwriters, distributors, and other film industry professionals dedicated to promoting independent films and encouraging creativity and diversity in film.

Byrd was born in 1965 in Brooklyn and later moved with her family to Westchester, New York. For a variety of personal reasons, she did not want to attend college far from home and thus decided to enroll at Fairfield University, a Jesuit university in Connecticut. While she had grown up in predominantly white neighborhoods, she nonetheless felt out of place at this heavily Italian and Irish Catholic school. In her mind, her interests, already focused on the arts, diverged too greatly from those of her peers.

Despite the progressive, arts-focused curriculum of her high school, Byrd had never heard of independent films nor seen a foreign-language film before she entered college. While at Fairfield she took a class entitled "New German Cinema." As she claimed, "This class opened my eyes to the fact that the world is larger than the old movies I watched on television as a kid or whatever was current in the movie theater." Through her exposure in this class, Byrd developed a real interest in foreign-language films. The art house cinema in nearby South Norwalk showed foreign films along with such independent films as *Stop Making Sense, Married to the Mob*, and *She's Got to Have It*. Even though unhappy at school, these films touched and inspired Byrd.

Discovered Independent Feature Project

When she graduated from Fairfield in 1987 with a degree in English and began to plan her future, Byrd did not forget her class on German cinema or the evenings she spent in the theater in South Norwalk. Immediately after graduation, she found a job in publishing as an editorial assistant in the children's book division of Scholastic, Inc. While working on trade paperbacks, writing copy, and covering unsolicited materials, she began to explore job possibilities in the film industry.

After several years at Scholastic and still struggling to determine her professional focus, Byrd considered moving from children's to adult magazine publishing. While exploring options with various magazines and doing free-lance copyediting, she stumbled across *Off Hollywood Report,* a publication of the Independent Feature Project (IFP). She quickly made the connection with her time at the South Norwalk movie house and began volunteering as a proofreader and copyeditor for the

> **At a Glance...**
>
> Born 1965 in Brooklyn. *Education:* BA, Fairfield University.
>
> **Career:** Editorial assistant, Scholastic, Inc., 1987-90; grant writer, Natural Resources Defense Council, 1990-91; deputy drector, Independent Feature Project, 1994-97, eecutive director, 1997-.
>
> **Member:** New York Women in Film and Television; Film Society of Lincoln Center; Association of Independent Video and Filmmakers; National Society of Fundraising.
>
> **Addresses:** Independent Feature Project, 104 West 29th Street, 12th Floor, New York, NY 10001-5310.

magazine while still employed by Scholastic.

When Byrd first joined the IFP, it was still a relatively small organization. It was born in 1979 as a result of a national organizing conference of filmmakers in conjunction with the New York Film Festival. The organization was originally founded to "produce a small sidebar program of American independent films during the New York Film Festival (then focused mainly on European films." Since its inception, the IFP has grown in the size and breadth of its programming. It now acts as a liaison between the business and artistic communities, promoting the best in independent films and enabling the films to reach the audiences they deserve both domestically and internationally. As stated in its promotional materials, the IFP rests "on the belief that a truly vital American cinema must include the personal, idiosyncratic, sometimes controversial voices of filmmakers working outside the established system."

As she continued to volunteer for *Off Hollywood Report*, Byrd realized that finding a paying job in the film industry would not be easy; most jobs required an initial two to three months of non-paid work. On her own financially after college, she could not afford this situation. Thus, she continued to volunteer for IFP, taking vacation time to participate in its Independent Feature Film Market (IFFM). Concurrently, she further broadened her exposure to the film industry by working as a production assistant for an independent film. Through this experience, she determined that she did not have the personality for the production side of the business and all of its emotional and physical demands but continued to remain active with IFP.

Eager to leave the low-paying market of children's publishing and still unable to find a financially-viable position in the world of film, Byrd made a complete break and in 1990 joined the Natural Resources Defense Council, a national environmental organization, as a foundation grant writer. While on the surface this move may seem to be a divergent path, it did provide Byrd with valuable work experience in a non-profit environment. While still at the Natural Resources Defense Council, Byrd was offered a position as Ernest Dickerson's camera assistant for *Jungle Fever*. Much to her disappointment, Byrd had to refuse the position, for it was nonpaying. This opportunity, though, compelled her to recommit herself to finding a way into film.

Launched IFP Career

In 1991, during the course of her job hunt, Byrd found an advertisement in *Variety Magazine* for an entry-level position at IFP. Michelle arrived for the interview—and has been there ever since. Initially, she envisioned staying with IFP for one year, for she did not perceive it to be a career move but instead simply a paying job in film. At the time, IFP had only two other year-round full-time employees: the executive director and the program director. The marketing director worked full-time for only eight months each year. All other employees were independent contractors.

IFP proved ideal for Byrd. At the onset, the organization provided her with a superb vantage point for understanding the inner workings of the film industry. The job enabled her to meet filmmakers, writers, and those involved in production, distribution, sales, and festival programming. Still not knowing exactly what she wanted to do, Byrd came to realize that she had landed in the perfect place.

Byrd's entry into IFP coincided with the organization's gaining increased financial stability and with the development of more extensive programming. At first, the IFFM, which emerged from IFP's first presentation of 15 American independent films at the 1979 New York Film Festival, stood as IFP's primary program. The IFFM remains to date to be the largest project in which IFP is involved. Through the Film Market, IFP initially sought to attract the attention of the film industry, for at that time there was no formal distribution and exhibition mechanism for independent film producers. As Byrd described it, "What our market does is level the playing field."

As detailed in IFP's own materials, the IFFM has emerged as the premier Market for emerging American independent talent, now annually previewing over four hundred new works. The IFFM also educates 800 filmmakers and screenwriters in all aspects of the film industry and publishes a development guide of projects in progress for the industry. It attracts buyers from around the world to view feature and short films, works-in-progress, and scripts seeking financing. It further gives filmmakers an opportunity to have festival directors examine their work and to make important business connections.

In essence, the IFFM ensures that, after hours of work, films are actually seen. Says Byrd, "The Market has become for numerous filmmakers that stamp which helps legitimize filmmaking as a viable career option." In the end, in Byrd's mind, the Marketplace "lets people discover things for themselves ... It's a convergence of all these different people with all their different needs that creates a kind of magic." *The Brothers McMullen, El Norte, Metropolitan, Reservoir Dogs, Roger & Me,* and *Stand and Deliver* are just some of the films which have been showcased at IFFM.

The growing consumer interest in independent films certainly catalyzed the broadening of the IFP's mission to include year-round programming in addition to the annual IFFM. Films like *The Brothers McMullen* proved that movies could be made successfully by filmmakers without film school degrees. In Byrd's words, "You could just be a guy doing films in New Jersey." Moreover, as the tools of the trade have become increasingly accessible to the general public and as the industry maintains its aura of glamour, so has the number of films produced risen—and thus the need for an expanded IFP. Having viewed IFP as an initial stepping stone, Byrd suddenly found herself in the middle of its growth. By 1994 she was the deputy director, and in 1997 she assumed the position of executive director.

Articulated Vision for IFP

Byrd's objectives with the project have evolved as her role with the organization has grown. As deputy director, she oversaw year-round programming, managed daily operations, and developed and implemented new programs and services. She was also instrumental in launching No Borders, an international co-production mini-market. An outgrowth of IFP's involvement in international festivals, No Borders selects films primarily at script stage which have obtained at least 30% of the required financing. Explained Byrd in a film festival news release, "The filmmaker or producer needs to have a track-record and an ability to attract international co-financing." Through No Borders, IFP then helps to find contacts for international partners. Sundance Film Institute, Filmstiftung Nordrhein-Westfalen, and the CineMart of International Film Festival Rotterdam are No Borders' partners who track and suggest projects for this Market.

Under Byrd's guidance, the IFP's reach is extensive. Not only does it promote independent films through numerous screenings, but it also seeks to assist filmmakers through programs focused on consultations with media and entertainment experts, a professional skills database, newsletters, and the coordination of panels, seminars, and receptions at film festivals worldwide. It also helps to promote relationships between American filmmakers and potential partners both domestically and overseas. Byrd has also overseen a tremendous growth in membership. Together with IFP/West in Los Angeles, IFP/North in Minneapolis, IFP/Midwest in Chicago, and IFP/South in Miami, the organization in 1998 includes nearly ten thousand members.

While obviously pleased with the continued growth in popularity of independent films, Byrd cautioned that the IFP cannot become static. In her mind, while there are increasingly more people making movies, the local theaters are not necessarily showing a wider range of films. Increasingly, what were once considered art house films are now perceived as more mainstream. At the same time, those films which, she explained, "require slower release, do not have overt marketing handles, or do not speak to a niche audience" have few viable screening venues. Byrd's goal with IFP, then, is to position the organization so that it ensures a place for as wide a range of voices as possible. One must remember, Byrd pointed out, that "independent film is not unique in that it is independent. It is the independent voices which are unique, and the IFP must ensure that these films are picked up for distribution" before they slip through the cracks.

Towards this end, Byrd has focused on expanding the scope of IFP beyond the artistic community to include the general public as well. Under her guidance, IFP will promote an audience development campaign for independent films. She has also established gatherings such as Director's Take and the monthly series, Independents Night, which enable film enthusiasts to attend a variety of screening events. During the Independents Night series, filmmakers interact directly with the public in order to gain an understanding of how an audience responds to a particular work. Without the onus of a large advertising and marketing budget which demands revenues from large turnouts on opening weekends, IFP has the flexibility to preview arty, obscure films as well as larger, more mainstream ones. IFP itself thus embodies Byrd's mission.

Having initially committed herself to one year at IFP and declaring that IFP was not a career move, Byrd now finds herself in her seventh year there. "I guess I should say this is a career now," Byrd laughed. She has signed a contract to remain with IFP through 1999. Life in the non-profit world, she has learned, is draining, and she cannot predict where she will be beyond her contract date. But for now she remains committed to IFP and to ensuring that ever more people hear the voices on the fringe.

Sources

Periodicals

Variety, March 31–April 6, 1997, pp. 9, 12; February 9, 1998, p. 28.

Others

Film Festivals Server, Berlin News.
Independent Feature Project Promotional Brochure.
Independent Feature Project Web Site.
Independent Film Channel Online Interview.

—Lisa S. Weitzman

Shirley Caesar

1938—

Gospel vocalist, evangelist

Often called the first lady of gospel music, award-winning Shirley Caesar has inspired many people for forty years. She and her singing group perform all over the country to packed audiences. Not only have many of her recordings been reissued, but they have been nominated for seventeen Grammy Awards, more than any gospel artist in history. Praising God through music, however, was not enough. Caesar went on to preach, eventually becoming the co-pastor of the Mt. Calvary Holy Church with her husband, Bishop Harold Ivory Williams.

Shirley began to sing in church at an early age, with her family, which was headed by gospel singer Big Jim Caesar. In 1950, tragedy struck the family when her father died of a fatal seizure. For years Caesar thought her father had died because he whipped her that day for breaking some street lights. She was twelve years old. That same year, Caesar began to take her singing seriously, especially since her mother, a semi-invalid, was left with 13 children to raise. Caesar started touring as a gospel soloist with evangelist Reverend Leroy Johnson. A year later, Caesar had made her first recording, the single, "I'd Rather Have Jesus."

While attending a concert of Albertina Walker's Caravans, the top female gospel singing group of its day, Caesar wrote a request on a slip of paper: "Please call Shirley Caesar to sing a solo." Walker called her up on stage and when she finished, Caesar told Howard Reich in the *Chicago Tribune,* that Walker had remarked, "I want that woman in my group." In 1958, after Walker's invitation, Caesar interrupted her business education studies at North Carolina State College, sold her biology book for ten dollars, took a bus to Washington D.C., and joined the Caravans. Besides Walker, the group included Inez Andrews, a three-octave range contralto known as the "High Priestess of Gospel," and ballad singer Sarah McKissick, and gospel great, Rev. James Cleveland.

Satisfied with Her Life Choice

The early years on the road with the Caravans were difficult for Caesar. Many restaurants in the sixties posted "Whites Only" signs. Eateries that would serve her singing group often put little care into the preparation of the food. Caesar will always remember a bout

> **At a Glance...**
>
> Born on October 13, 1938, in Durham, NC; daughter of "Big Jim" (tobacco factory worker, gospel singer) and Hallie Martin (homemaker) Caesar; married Bishop Harold Ivory Williams (a pastor), 1983. *Education:* North Carolina State College (now North Carolina Central University), 1956-58; Shaw University (Raleigh, NC), B.A., 1984, business administration.
>
> **Career:** Began singing as "Baby Shirley;" joined Albertina Walker's Caravans, 1958-66; evangelist, 1961-; formed Shirley Caesar Singers, 1966-; Durham City Council, 1987-1991; co-pastor, Mt. Calvary Holy Church in Winston-Salem, NC and Raleigh, NC; Shirley Caesar Outreach Ministries, Inc.
>
> **Selected awards:** Nine Grammy Awards, including an award for "Put Your Hand in the Hand of the Man from Galilee", 1972, best soul gospel performance, contemporary for *Rejoice,* 1981, and best single for "Martin", 1985; *Ebony Magazine* Award for best female gospel singer, 1975; nine Dove Awards for Gospel; named annual spokeswoman for McDonald's Salute to Gospel Music, 1987; Dr. Martin Luther King Jr. Drum Major Award, 1987; ten Stellar Gospel Awards; two NAACP Image Awards; Pride of SESAC Award for lifetime achievement, 1997; 3 gold albums; inducted into the Gospel Music Hall of Fame.
>
> **Addresses:** *Office*—Shirley Caesar Outreach Ministries, Inc., P.O. Box 3336, Durham, NC 27702.

with food poisoning that left her "Sick, sick, sick!" she told Mike Nappa of *CCM Magazine.*

Throughout her life's work, Caesar has focused on gospel music, considered the fastest growing genre in the music industry in the 1990s. Gospel music enthusiasts often compare her to singer Mahalia Jackson, the "Grand Dame of Gospel." Caesar herself has earned the moniker "Queen of Gospel." Caesar, happy with that role, told *Ebony,* "America will never outgrow its need for gospel [music] because it will never outgrow its need for God."

When Caesar was twelve, she heard the Lord's voice calling her name and calling her to preach. Until 1961 Caesar just used her voice to sing, but with the recording of the single, "Hallelujah, It's Done," Caesar found that incorporating scripture and sermon into her songs was a natural style for her. Although this "song and sermonette" technique was created by Mother Willie Mae Ford Smith and Edna Gallmon Cooke, Caesar developed it with enthusiasm. In 1966, after eight years with the Caravans, Caesar left to organize her own group, the Caesar Singers. Recording executives often approached Caesar to "crossover" into rhythm and blues, but she adamantly refused throughout her career.

A 1997 *CCM Magazine* writer, Jamie Lee Rake, noted that Caesar's voice is "an inventive, passionate, nimble instrument." In 1998, *Atlanta Journal and Constitution* reporter Sonia Murray referred to Caesar's voice as "a gale force instrument." That voice has praised the Lord and blessed His people around the world with a traditional style of gospel music. Besides the comparison to Mahalia Jackson, Caesar has been likened to gospel singer Clara Ward and makes no apologies for sticking with gospel music throughout her career. Her style may be traditional but she keeps her music's message up-to-date, passionate, and heartfelt. Her concerts attract listeners who rarely darken a church step.

A Life Devoted to Ministry

Not surprisingly, Caesar's singing style also led her to work as an evangelist. In 1983, Caesar married Bishop Harold Ivory Williams and became co-pastor of Mt. Calvary Holy Church in Winston-Salem, North Carolina and later in Raleigh-Durham. After her elaborate wedding—there were 140 people in the wedding party—Caesar would pursue the education that was interrupted 25 years earlier. In 1985, Caesar obtained a degree in business management from Shaw University. The degree prompted her to immediately pursue a master of divinity degree at Duke University.

Caesar lives what she preaches. In 1990 she told *Jet* magazine, "Fifty percent of everything I earn on the road I put back into the community." Shirley Caesar Outreach Ministries, Inc., which is in her hometown of Durham, North Carolina, serves those in need by providing food, clothing, and emergency funds. During its first year alone, more than 500 families received help. The ministry relies entirely on contributions and income donated by Caesar and Bishop Williams since they are unwilling to rely on public funding as other charities do.

The outreach ministry has greatly affected Caesar's music. She tackles contemporary issues like drugs, cocaine babies, homeless people, AIDS, teenage mothers, broken marriages, and even cancer in the songs she has written. Many of her songs, for example, "Don't Drive Your Mother Away," focus on families. Caesar was close to her mother and family and wanted others to understand the value and need for that kind of bond. Caesar is grateful that her mother was an inspiration, an encourager, and a conscience. By using her gifted voice, Caesar never let her mother down.

Ministry Led to Public Office

In 1988, while Caesar was a member of the Durham City Council, she commented to *Ebony* magazine, "My main objective is to make sure we focus on the needy and not the greedy." Many wondered how she managed to fit the twice-monthly council meetings into her busy life, but Caesar saw the council as an opportunity to continue what she had started with the Outreach Ministries. Fair housing, along with programs for the poor and the elderly were issues that concerned her and many on the council, especially since the 150,000 population of Durham had grown consistently in the eighties.

> "America will never outgrow its need for Gospel [music] because it will never outgrow its need for God."

After her four year term, Caesar felt a stronger pull to serve as a pastor than as a council member, especially since Mt. Calvary Holy Church had grown from 15 to 600 members by the end of her term. In 1990, while on the council, Caesar was ordained as a pastor. Wanting only to serve with her husband, Pastor Caesar takes no money for her position. Serving the Lord takes precedence over her concerts even. The Caesar Singers often drive all night so Pastor Caesar can be in the pulpit on Sunday. Noted Howard Reich in the *Chicago Tribune,* Caesar wants to be a "real pastor who also happens to sing gospel."

Never Pursued Fame and Fortune

Caesar has recorded more than 30 albums and gives more than 150 concerts a year. For many years she has also hosted an annual Crusade Convention. Judges in the music industry have recognized Caesar's musical talent with numerous awards. As of 1998, she had earned nine Grammys, 15 Dove Awards, and ten Stellar Gospel Awards. Caesar has also received two NAACP Image Awards. Though Caesar has been inducted into the Gospel Music Hall of Fame, sung for President Jimmy Carter, and performed at the 1996 Olympics in Atlanta, fame and fortune were never important to her. What continues to be important to her is reaching needy people and bringing the hope offered by Christ into their lives.

Whatever means Caesar could use to reach people, she used. Caesar has done four Broadway shows, contributed to *The Preacher's Wife* and *Rosewood* movie soundtracks, guest-starred on United Paramount Network's television show, "Good News"(where she now has a recurring role), performed on *The Arsenio Hall Show* and *Live With Regis and Kathie Lee,* and even on a large home-shopping network. Singer Bob Dylan, when chosen as a Kennedy Center honoree, asked her to perform his song, "Gotta Serve Somebody." In 1997 Caesar performed in the theatrical production, *This Is My Song,* which traces the history of gospel music. The play was set in the fictitious Mt. Zion Church of Faith with Caesar as the pastor, Cissy Houston as its music director, and Tramaine Hawkins as a special guest. *USA Today* reviewer Steve Jones called the performance of the three famous gospel singers more a "soul-stirring church service" than theater. As the story unfolded through song, the audience often joined with foot-stomping, singing, and working its way to the stage to shake Pastor Caesar's hand. By whatever means, Caesar is determined to reach people.

In a 1987 interview with *USA Today* Caesar commented, "Gospel music teaches us to love, respect, to uphold. It may speak of hell, damnation, and fire, but it also speaks of the bright side, that the Lord is faithful, and he is loving, kind, and forgiving. You won't find that in other songs, that no matter where you have fallen, the grace of God will pick you up. Gospel music will tell you that when you pray, God listens." Many would say that Shirley Caesar's powerful and message-filled singing points the way to God's grace.

Selected discography

Albums

Rejoice, Myrrh Records, 1982.
Christmasing, 1992.
He's Working It Out for You, Sony Music, 1992.
I Remember Mama, Sony Music, 1992.
Jesus, I Love Calling Your Name, Sony Music, 1992.
First Lady, 1993.
Her Very Best, Sony Music, 1993.
Live in Chicago, Sony Music, 1993.
Stand Still, Word Records, 1993.

Why Me Lord, 1993.
Gold, 1994.
He Will Come: Shirley Caesar Live, Sony Music, 1995.
Best of Shirley Caesar & The Caravans, Malaco/Savoy Gospel, 1995.
Just a Word, Sony Music, 1996.
Sailin', Sony Music, 1996.
Treasures, 1996.
Shirley Caesar Convention Choir, Word Records, 1996.
Miracle in Harlem, Sony/Word Records, 1997.
Shirley Caesar & The Caravans, Malaco/Savoy Gospel, 1997.
The Very Best of Shirley Caesar, Collectibles Records, 1998.
Shirley Caesar: The Lady, the Melody, and the Word, 1998.

Videos

Oh Happy Day, University of Missouri Agricultural Press, 1989.
Caesar: Live in Memphis, Cmvca Press, 1992.
Caesar: He Will Come, Cmvca Press, 1995.
Caesar: I Remember Mama, Cmvca Press, 1995.
Shirley Caesar in Concert, University of Missouri Agricultural Press, 1998.
Also author of *The Lady, the Melody, and the Word: The Inspirational Story of the First Lady of Gospel Music,* Thomas Nelson Publishing, 1998.

Sources

Books

Black Women in America: An Historical Encyclopedia, edited by Darlene Clark Hine, Elsa Barkley Brown, and Rosalyn Terborg-Penn, Indiana University Press, 1993.
In Black and White, Gale Research, 1980.
Notable Black American Women, Gale Research, 1992, pp. 151-152.

Periodicals

Atlanta Constitution, April 25, 1993, p. N; July 22, 1996, p. SS39; January 29, 1998, p. 4E.
Billboard, October 2, 1993, p. 57; August 3, 1996, pp. 48-50; March 29, 1997, p. 17; November 29, 1997, p. 10; January 10, 1998, pp. 14-15.
CCM Magazine, July 1997.
Chicago Tribune, January 17, 1992, p. 3.
Christian Herald, June 1981, p. 60; June 1983, p. 36.
Ebony, December 1988, pp. 66-70; March 1994, p. 20; April 1994, pp. 76-79; February 1996, p. 44; December 1996, pp. 36-37.
Entertainment Weekly, November 29, 1996, p. 88.
Essence, April 1985, p. 42.
Jet, March 19, 1981, p. 64; July 18, 1983, p. 13; March 25, 1985, p. 21; January 8, 1990, p. 53.
Los Angeles Times, October 13, 1997, p. F.
News, July 9, 1997.
People Weekly, November 9, 1987, pp. 85-86; January 13, 1997, p. 22.
USA Today, October 1, 1987, p. 11; March 21, 1997, p. D; January 12, 1998, p. D3.
Washington Post, February 22, 1998, p. G1.

Other

Additional information found on the *Southern Folklife Collection* Website, http://www.lib.unc.edu/mss/sfc/ncfolk.html.

—Eileen Daily

Kimberly Camp

1956—

Museum administrator, artist

The director of Detroit's Charles H. Wright Museum of African American History, Kimberly Camp presides over the largest black-oriented museum in the United States. As a museum administrator with a widely noticed record of accomplishment in both the exhibition and management arenas, Camp is one of the country's brightest young stars in museum work, a field in which African Americans have historically been underrepresented. In addition to her ambitious and consuming career as an administrator, Camp is an important artist in her own right—another rarity among museum administrators.

Kimberly Camp was born on September 11, 1956 in Camden, New Jersey. The only child of Hubert Camp, an oral surgeon and jazz trumpeter, and Marie Dimery Camp, an office worker and artist, she grew up in an artistic environment. "I always went to museums, all different kinds of museums," she told Constance Prater of the *Detroit Free Press*. Another childhood memory involved trips to visit relatives in a steel town in Pennsylvania. She told Prater that the trips gave her "a sense of perspective on how people live, on family values, on how you're supposed to treat the elderly." The visits would influence both Kimberly Camp the artist, who often painted family scenes, and Kimberly Camp the administrator, whose career would involve her deeply in the effort to preserve and interpret black history.

Made African Dolls

Camp finished high school at the age of sixteen, and went on to earn a degree in fine arts and art history at the University of Pittsburgh, graduating in 1978. For several years after that she engaged in various activities that deepened her creativity and honed her skills in museum work. She worked on exhibitions at various museums in a freelance capacity, began making and selling African dolls called Kimkins, and headed an anti-graffiti mural project in her hometown of Camden. Camp reamins chairman of the board of the company she founded, Kimkins, Inc. Realizing that she combined a creative streak with strong business acumen and an aptitude for building community support for artistic institutions and activities, Camp returned to school and earned a Master's degree in arts administration from Drexel University in Philadelphia in 1986.

Hired by the Pennsylvania Council for the Arts as program director for its artists-in-education and minor-

At a Glance...

Born September 11, 1956, in Camden, New Jersey, daughter of Hubert Camp (an oral surgeon) and Marie Dimery Camp (an office worker and artist). *Education:* University of Pittsburgh, B.A., 1978; Drexel University, M.S. in Arts Adminstration, 1986.

Career: Arts administrator, city of Camden, early 1980s; program director, Pennsylvania Council for the Arts, 1986–89; director, Experimental Gallery, Smithsonian Institution, 1989–94; director, Charles H. Wright Museum of African American History, Detroit, 1994–98; The Barnes Foundation, executive dir, 1998–; creator and chief executive, Kimkins, Inc. (maker of African dolls), 1982–; numerous exhibitions of painting and "soft sculpture" (dolls); public art commissions in Pittsburgh and in Cape Coast, Ghana, 1998.

Awards: Named fellow, Kellogg National Leadership Program, 1997; Spirit of Detroit award, 1994; Award of Distinction, Kentucky Art and Craft Foundation, 1994; Purchase Award, J. B. Speed Art Museum, 1988.

Addresses: *Office*—Executive Director, The Barnes Foundation, 300 N. Latch's Lane, Merion, PA 19066.

ity-arts divisions, Camp quadrupled annual awards funding during her three-year tenure. In 1989, a friend suggested she apply for the directorship of the newly formed Experimental Gallery in Washington, D.C., a new unit of the Smithsonian Institution. Chosen as founding director, Camp took bold steps. "We pushed the envelope," Camp recalled in an interview with *Black Enterprise;* with Camp at the helm, the museum offered such controversial exhibitions as *Etiquette of the Undercaste,* an exploration of homelessness that viewers entered by lying down on a model of a morgue drawer slab and being pushed in. "My point is that you spend so much on exhibitions, they ought to change you," Camp later told the *Detroit Free Press.* "They ought to inform. They ought to stick."

Chosen Director of New Museum

In 1994, Camp was persuaded by a recruiter to apply for the directorship of Detroit's new Museum of African American History (since renamed the Charles H. Wright Museum of African American History after its founder).

She was selected for the job and presided over the construction of a new 119,000-square-foot building that is the country's largest facility devoted to African American culture; it was four times as large as the space the museum had formerly occupied. After the new building opened in April of 1997, the museum experienced a 300 percent increase in attendance and an increase in its annual budget from $1.2 million to $6.7 million.

Once again, Camp masterminded a dramatic entrance to the exhibition space. Designed by Ralph Appelbaum, famous for his design work on the exhibits at the U.S. Holocaust Memorial Museum in Washington, the new museum's exhibits are accessible by way of a steel bridge flanked by a model of a ship's hold, to which are shackled human beings, mostly children—a slave ship and its cargo. Local black teenagers volunteered to pose for the models of the slaves, re-enacting the tragedy that had befallen their ancestors.

The museum drew large crowds in its first months of operation, attracting generally favorable notices from museum critics. On several occasions it provided space for significant community events, the most important of which occurred when the body of former Detroit Mayor Coleman A. Young lay in state in the building's spectacular rotunda. Camp has experienced her share of criticism, however. Local artists and vendors protested the participation of white personnel in the museum's design and construction. Sellers at the museum-sponsored African World Festival took to the street in front of the museum to protest increased fees for display space. Journalists raised questions about the proportion of the museum's budget devoted to administrative costs, salaries, and travel. Also, museum founder Charles H. Wright led a group of former personnel who took issue with Camp's emphasis on prestigious traveling exhibitions at the expense of locally generated material. Attendance and fundraising figures, while impressive, failed to meet ambitious goals.

Responded Forcefully to Critics

Camp, whom acquaintances have credited with considerable stubbornness and strength of will, met her critics head-on. She took particular issue with those who deplored white participation in the construction of the museum, telling the *Detroit News,* "Excluding people puts it on a bigotry theme. I want everybody to come to this museum, to experience the best of our culture." In 1998, the museum unveiled a major exhibition of photographs and other memorabilia from the old eastside Detroit Black Bottom neighborhood that was designed to appeal to the local community. There were also signs that year of a rapprochement with former director Wright, whose name was added to the museum's official designation. Camp also contended that general budget classifications gave a misleading impression of how the museum allocated its resources. She pointed out, for example, that the institution's large travel budget served mainly to bring speakers and other presenters to the museum itself, not to facilitate staff junkets to other destinations.

> "I want everybody to come to this museum, to experience the best of our culture."

Despite all of the controversy surrounding her new position in Detroit, Camp remained active as an artist. The Kimkins dolls continued to rack up commercial sales, and Camp's dolls were featured in a number of local and national art museum and gallery exhibitions of "soft sculpture." Camp has also exhibited her paintings widely. *Detroit News* critic Joy Hakanson Colby remarked, "Camp's paintings celebrate her family and ancestors by lifting black and white images from old snapshots and giving them a new life on canvas. She uses hot, singing colors, indulging her imagination and sense of fun when she dresses her father in a brilliant turquoise suit and her stern great-great-grandmother in a scarlet dress." Her works are included in the permanent collections of such prestigious organizations as the J. B. Speed Museum in Louisville and *Reader's Digest*.

Appointed a fellow of the Kellogg National Leadership Program in 1997, Camp has received numerous awards, including a National Endowment for the Arts fellowship, a New Jersey State Senate citation, the Spirit of Detroit award, and selection as one of the Outstanding Young Women of America. In late 1998, Camp's talents received even more recognition: it was announced that she would be leaving Detroit to assume the position of executive director of the Barnes Foundation, a prestigious private art museum in Philadelphia. Known for its collection of French post-impressionist masterpieces, the Barnes Foundation museum is also home to a large collection of African art.

Sources

Periodicals

Black Enterprise, May 1998, p. 58.
Detroit Free Press, February 17, 1994, p. C1; April 6, 1997, p. E1; September 25, 1998, p. B1.
Detroit News, March 31, 1995, p. C11; January 12, 1996, p. B2; May 1, 1996, p. C1; April 30, 1998, p. E6; May 18, 1998, p. A1; May 27, 1998, p. S4.
Emerge, February 1997, p. 72.
Essence, September 1997, p. 78.
National Geographic World, December 1986, p. 22.
New Orleans Times-Picayune, April 19, 1998, p. A40.
U.S. News and World Report, May 26, 1997, p. 54.
Washington Post, January 30, 1991, p. B1.

—James M. Manheim

Betty Carter

1930–1998

Jazz vocalist

Betty Carter is acclaimed as a giant of modern jazz, a role model who passes along the ideal of artistic integrity to younger jazz artists, and a female trailblazer in a musical genre long dominated by men. Accompanied by a pure small-jazz combo—piano, drums, and bass—Carter evolved a complex but personal vocal style rooted in the classic bebop music of Charlie Parker, Dizzy Gillespie, and Miles Davis. She is a vocal virtuoso and an utter original.

Betty Carter was born Lillie Mae Jones in the auto-manufacturing city of Flint, Michigan, on May 16, 1930 (some sources give the year as 1929, but the 1930 date seems preferable in view of the fact that Carter as a teenager often lied about her age in order to gain admittance to jazz clubs). Carter's family endured the devastation that the Great Depression wreaked upon Flint, and moved to Detroit in search of work in munitions factories.

Fascinated by Jazz in High School

While her father became a choir director at the Chapel Hill Baptist Church, Carter studied piano at the Detroit Conservatory of Music and became fascinated by jazz while a student at the city's Northwestern High School. She frequented a soda counter with a jukebox full of 45 RPM records that introduced her to the musicians who created the daring new improvisatory music called bebop. Using the stage name Lorene Carter, she entered talent contests and toured small clubs in Michigan and Ohio, sometimes performing with nationally known bebop ensembles as they toured the area.

These performances attracted the notice of swing bandleader Lionel Hampton, who hired her for regular engagements with his band beginning in 1948. Carter herself preferred the more modern music of bandleader Dizzy Gillespie, and the annoyed Hampton reacted by giving Carter the nickname Betty Bebop, which evolved into Betty Carter. Carter toured with Hampton's band through 1951, making a well-received appearance at Harlem's Apollo Theater. However, she was fired as a result of disagreements with the bandleader.

After leaving Hampton's ensemble, Carter spent most

At a Glance...

Born Lillie Mae Jones, May 16, 1930, in Flint, MI; Married James Redding, later divorced; children: two sons—Myles and Kagle Redding. *Religion:* raised Baptist. Died September 26, 1998 in Brooklyn, NY.

Career: Jazz vocalist. Toured with Lionel Hampton's band, 1948–51; toured and recorded album with Ray Charles, 1960–61; formed own record company, Bet-Car Productions, 1969; appeared in stage show *Don't Call Me Man,* 1975; continued performing and recording through 1990s; released critically acclaimed album *I'm Yours, You're Mine,* 1997, at age of 66.

Awards: Three Grammy nominations for Best Jazz Album; numerous jazz industry awards.

Addresses: *Production company*—Bet-Car Productions, 117 St. Felix St., Brooklyn, NY 11217.

of the 1950s building a name for herself, appearing at small jazz clubs up and down the East Coast and carving out an original style as she interacted with such prominent jazz figures of the time as Sarah Vaughan, Thelonious Monk, and Miles Davis. She recorded an album, *Betty Carter,* for the Epic label in 1953, and continued to record sporadically over the next few years. By the end of the decade her efforts had paid off to such an extent that she was tabbed to tour with R & B singer and pianist Ray Charles, then in the midst of his jazz phase.

Recorded Duets with Ray Charles

Charles at the time was one of the most popular musicians in the country, and the duet album the two singers recorded, 1961's *Ray Charles and Betty Carter,* remains a jazz classic. Carter had no trouble keeping up with her more famous partner. She told *Pulse* magazine: [W]e didn't go over anything more than one time, because I was capable of understanding everything he said to me about what to do and how to do it."

Like those of many other jazz musicians, Carter's career suffered during the ascendancy of rock music in the 1960s. Pressured to release a commercially oriented album, Carter stuck to her guns and defended the sometimes inaccessible bebop style that she cultivated and loved. She married, but even her husband pressured her to commercialize her style, and the marriage ended in divorce, leaving Carter with two young sons. At the decade's end, finding herself without recording opportunities, Carter formed her own label, Bet-Car, and began to chart a wholly independent creative course. Her music deepened, and she began to cultivate an uncanny capacity for rhythmic surprises within a tightly controlled framework. She found a ready audience for her musical experimentation on the nation's college campuses, where young female fans especially admired her.

> "[W]e didn't go over anything more than one time, because I was capable of understanding everything he said to me about what to do and how to do it."

During the 1970s and 1980s, Betty Carter's audience continued to grow. Major milestones were a New York stage show, *Don't Call Me Man,* in 1975 and appearances at the prestigious Newport Jazz Festival in 1977 and 1978. Maintaining control over not only her recording career but her production and booking schedules, Carter became a fixture of jazz nightclub scenes nationwide. In 1988 she was signed to the Verve label, perhaps the premier purveyor of top-quality recorded jazz; her deal with the label included reissues of her earlier Bet-Car releases.

Focused on Jazz Education

Carter has relished her role as a senior figure and standard-bearer of jazz and black culture generally. In recent years her efforts have been geared more and more toward jazz education. Her band has been a proving ground for a long succession of young players; her concerts gain piquancy from the interplay between energetic youth and artistic mastery. Carter has conducted school workshops and crusaded for the inclusion of jazz in college coursework, especially at black institutions. Her influence on jazz of the 1990s has been enormous, with the phenomenally successful vocalist Cassandra Wilson citing her as a major influence. In 1995 *Down Beat* writer John Ephland pointed to Carter's "playful and ingenious approaches to lyrics and overall sound" as a basis for Wilson's style.

Carter's own recording activities continued to generate critical acclaim in the 1990s. In 1997 *Down Beat* critic Thomas Conrad, calling Carter "the most instrumentally conceived of jazz vocalists, capable of melodic improvisations as unpredictable as any saxophonist this side of Ornette [Coleman]," wrote of Carter's new album, *I'm*

Yours, You're Mine, that "[t]he cumulative effect is narcotic.... How many singers can you name who have made one of their strongest recordings in their 66th year?" Conrad likewise pointed to the way Carter could find young players "who always sound exceptional when they play with her." At century's end, she was nothing less than the matriarch of jazz. Carter died of pancreatic cancer at home in the Fort Greene section of Brooklyn, New York on September 26, 1998. She will be surely missed by her fans.

Selected discography

The Carmen McRae–Betty Carter Album, Hall/Fantasy, 1988.
Look What I Got, Verve, 1988.
Ray Charles and Betty Carter, Dunhill, 1988 (reissue).
Whatever Happened to Love?, Verve, 1989.
Droppin' Things, Verve, 1990.
Finally, EMI, 1991 (reissue).
It's Not About the Melody, Verve, 1992.
Feel the Fire, Verve, 1994.
Inside Betty Carter, Capitol, 1994 (reissue).
Meet Betty Carter and Ray Bryant, Columbia, 1996 (reissue).
I'm Yours, You're Mine, Verve, 1997.

Sources

Books

Contemporary Musicians, volume 6, Gale, 1992.
The New Grove Dictionary of Jazz, Macmillan, 1988.
Smith, Jessie Carney, ed.; *Notable Black American Women,* Gale, 1992.

Periodicals

Down Beat, January 1995, p. 22; January 1997, p. 49; January 1998, p. 66.
Pulse, August 1988.
Vogue, October 1983, p. 538.
Washington Post, March 21, 1997, p. WW13; March 24, 1997, p. B7.

Other

Additional information found online at http://www.nytimes.com/yr/mo/day/news/national/obit-carter.html.

—James M. Manheim

Don Cheadle

1964(?)—

Actor

Don Cheadle has been working steadily in films, television and theater since 1985, when he was still in drama school. Typical struggling actor jobs such as waiting on tables or parking cars are not part of Cheadle's story. "I've been blessed beyond belief. I've only been an actor to support myself. To complain would be sinful," Cheadle told Justine Elias of *Interview*. Among Cheadle's credits are a stint as a district attorney on television's *Picket Fences* and a much praised supporting performance in the movie mystery *Devil in a Blue Dress*. "Don Cheadle does a frighteningly funny turn as a completely amoral little man who finds it easier to kill someone than to talk to him," wrote David Denby in *New York*. Many critics felt Cheadle's not earning an Academy Award nomination for *Devil in a Blue Dress* was an outrage. Cheadle tried to take a more practical view of the situation. "My folks sent me a slew of magazine and newspaper articles that asked why I wasn't nominated, so in the end I got more buzz for being overlooked," Cheadle told Elias.

Cheadle was born in Kansas City, Missouri in about 1964, the second of three children of a psychologist father and a schoolteacher mother. His father's pursuit of educational and job opportunities took the family to Lincoln, Nebraska, and Denver, Colorado. The role of Templeton the Rat in a fifth grade production of *Charlotte's Web* got him interested in acting. "I remember carrying my script around and studying it like I do now—I don't know why, but I was serious about acting even then," Cheadle told Kristine McKenna of the *Los Angeles Times*. After performing in numerous high school plays and musicals, Cheadle moved on to the California Institute for the Arts in Valencia, California, near Los Angeles. "I loved Cal Arts. I knew I would be acting all the time there. You might not get the part you want, but you know you're going to be in twenty-four plays no matter what," Cheadle told *Interview*.

Upon graduation in 1986, Cheadle was given five hundred dollars by his parents to help him start off his professional career. Fortunately, after about a month, just as the money was running out, Cheadle landed a role in the film *Hamburger Hill,* a drama about a group of soldiers battling to secure a strategic hill during the Vietnam War. Shot on location in the Philippines, the film was directed by John Irvin and featured a roster of

At a Glance...

Born in Kansas City, MO, c. 1964, the son of a psychologist and a teacher. Father of two. *Education:* Califronia Institute of the Arts, Valencia, CA, B.F.A., 1986.

Career: Appeared in feature films *Hamburger Hill,* 1987; *Colors,* 1988; *Roadside Prophets,* 1992; *Meteor Man,,* 1993; *Things to Do in Denver When You're Dead,* 1995; *Devil in a Blue Dress,* 1995; *Rosewood,* 1997; *Volcano,* 1997; *Boogie Nights,* 1997; *Bulworth,* 1998; *Out of Sight,* 1998. Television films include *Rebound: The Legend of Earl "The Goat" Manigault,* 1996; *The Rat Pack,* 1998. Also appeared in regular roles on the television series *The Golden Palace,* 1992-1993, and *Picket Fences,* 1993-1995; had recurring roles on *Fame,* c. 1985, and *The Fresh Prince of Bel Air,* c. 1990. Stage appearances include *The Screens* and *Leon, Lena and Lenz,* Guthrie Theatre, Minneapolis, MN; *The Grapes of Wrath* and *Liquid Skin,* Mixed Blood Theatre, Minneapolis, MN; *Cymbeline,* Public Theater, New York City, 1989; *'Tis a Pity She's a Whore,* Goodman Theatre, Chicago, IL; *The Blood Knot,* Complex Theatre, Hollywood, CA. Author of the play *Groomed,* New Works Festival, the Mark Taper Forum, Los Angeles, CA, 1997.

Awards: Named Best Supporting Actor by the National Society of Film Critics and the Los Angeles Film Critics Association for *Devil in a Blue Dress,* 1995; National Association for the Advancement of Colored People Image Award nomination for Best Supporting Actor in a Motion Picture for *Rosewood,* 1997.

Addresses: *Home*—Venice, CA. *Publicist*—Steven Huvane, Huvane, Baum, Halls Public Relations, 8383 Wilshire Boulevard, Suite 444, Beverly Hills, CA 90211.

new young performers including Dylan McDermott, Courtney B. Vance, and Steven Weber, along with Cheadle.

Returning from the Philippines, Cheadle quickly found work at the Guthrie Theater in Minneapolis in a production of Jean Genet's *The Screens* staged by renown experimental director JoAnne Akalaitis. From there Cheadle moved on to the film *Colors,* a gritty tale of Los Angeles gang warfare between the Bloods and the Crips. Directed by Dennis Hopper, the film starred Robert Duvall and Sean Penn as police officers investigating a "drive-by" shooting of a gang member. Cheadle played Rocket, the leader of the Crips who dies in a shoot out at the film's end. A happier film project was 1993's *The Meteor Man,* a socially conscious fantasy about a man who finds himself with superhuman power after being struck by a meteor and uses the new power to clean up his troubled neighborhood. Robert Townsend wrote, directed, and starred in the film. Again, Cheadle played a gang member, only this time for satirical humor.

Cheadle's breakthrough film was *Devil in a Blue Dress,* a moody "film noir" based on a Walter Mosley mystery novel. Released in 1995, the film starred Denzel Washington as Easy Rawlins, an unemployed aircraft worker turned private detective investigating a murder in Los Angeles' vibrant black community in the 1940s. Cheadle played Mouse, Rawlins' violent and vicious friend who became his partner in the investigation. "Cheadle almost steals the show from Washington with his matter-of-fact humor," wrote Sibylla Nash in the *Los Angeles Sentinel.* Cheadle told Stephen Farber of the *New York Times:* "At first I was surprised that audiences laughed at Mouse. I wasn't attempting to get laughs. But in any farce, the energy a character spends pursuing a single goal is funny. And it's scary, too. I think one reason people laugh is that they're feeling 'I'm glad I'm not in that room with Mouse.'"

Devil in a Blue Dress was directed by Carl Franklin, in whose American Film Institute student film *Punk,* Cheadle had appeared several years before. Initially Franklin did not want Cheadle for the role of Mouse, thinking him too young to play a contemporary of fortyish Washington. Cheadle was refused an audition. Fortunately, an accidental encounter between Cheadle and Franklin at a doctor's office lead to Cheadle being asked to read for the part. After a second reading with Washington, during which the two actors clicked, secured the part for Cheadle. "I had six weeks to prepare so I did lots of research that included spending a week in Houston, which is where Mouse is from. I met a few people from the '40s who were of the world Mouse lived in, and having talked with some of them I can tell you that gangsters of that era were different from gangsters today. There was more honor among thieves then, and they had a strong sense of community and all kept each other in check. Crack, of course, has put an end to all that," Cheadle told the *Los Angeles Times.*

Though well-received by critics, *Devil in a Blue Dress* failed at the box office. "That was very disappointing because it was a wonderful film, with wonderful performances," critic Orlando Peters explained to the *Jacksonville Free Press*. "I would have bet a bundle that film would have done well. It had a proven star, and it was based on a popular book. It wasn't even a matter of it failing to cross over, because black people alone could have made that film a success, and the final numbers say black audiences were not interested in the film." For his work as Mouse, Cheadle was named best supporting actor by the Los Angeles Film Critics Association and by the National Society of Film Critics. Cheadle's name, however, was not on the list of Academy Award nominees. "Now that I know how [Oscar nominees] get picked, and how the selection process works, I could give a (expletive) if I ever get one. I mean it would be nice because your money goes up, and it shows appreciation on a wide level, but what does my performance have to do with the political lobbying and machinations that go on inside the Academy that I am not privy to? Nothing. If I never get an Oscar, it doesn't mean anything about my work," Cheadle told Mark Ebner of *Premiere*.

Though Cheadle has so far specialized in supporting roles, a film where he played the lead was *Rebound: The Legend of Earl "The Goat" Manigault*. Made for the Home Box Office (HBO) cable channel in 1996, *Rebound* told the near-autobiographical story of a Harlem basketball wizard of the 1960s whose chance for a career in professional basketball was ruined by his descent into drug addiction and crime. Manigault's eventual recovery from addiction and his work with New York City youth were also depicted. "Cheadle's performance in portraying the once promising basketball star who traded his skills for the foolish pleasures of snorting and injecting his way to a temporary high is superb," wrote Jaime C. Harris in the *Amsterdam News*. *Rebound* was directed by actor Eriq LaSalle, of television's *ER*, and featured James Earl Jones, Forrest Whitaker, and Clarence Williams III.

Another story based on past events in which Cheadle appeared was *Rosewood*, a look at the burning down by angry, bigoted whites of Rosewood, an African American community in central Florida. Believing a white woman's false accusation that she had been attacked by a Rosewood man, and jealous of Rosewood's prosperity, white residents of the neighboring mill town of Sumner torched the nearly all-black town in 1923. Cheadle played Sylvester Carrier, a piano teacher who risked his life by deciding to stand his ground and not run away from the racist mob. The film was directed by John Singleton. "I had seen Don Cheadle's portrayal of Mouse in *Devil in a Blue Dress* and was impressed with his performance. I called him up afterward and told him we had to work together. I didn't know what it would be at the time, but when we were casting *Rosewood*, I realized he would be a great Sylvester," Singleton told the *Indianapolis Recorder*. Released in 1997, *Rosewood* garnered some excellent reviews. Joan H. Allen of the *Amsterdam News* called the film "powerful and compelling." Despite critical praise, *Rosewood* barely registered at the box office. "It was a hard sell," Cheadle explained to Elias. "Very few movies take on the risk of trying to teach you something, or illuminate something so that people who just want escapism will digest it too ... The Rosewood tragedy wasn't that long ago: It took place in our grandparents' day, and the xenophobic attitude it shows is prevalent today. And when the mirror is held up to that attitude, well, I think people feel pretty resentful when they've just paid $7.50," he continued.

> "I remember carrying my script around and studying it like I do now—I don't know why, but I was serious about acting even then."

Cheadle admitted that money was the primary impetus for his appearance in the disaster film *Volcano*, in which an unprepared Los Angeles is threatened with an overwhelming flow of lava. His role in the 1997 film as assistant chief of the city's emergency management squad was not written specifically for a black actor. Cheadle said non-race specific roles are relatively rare and not necessarily desirable. "Color blindness is ridiculous ... You don't need to ignore your race ... There are issues you can't *not* confront. I'm glad people try to write roles that anyone can do, but I also don't ever want to end up in movies where the fact that I'm a black man is a nonissue. In America, it's always an issue," Cheadle told *Interview*.

In *Boogie Nights*, an unsparingly frank examination of the pornographic film industry of the 1970s, Cheadle played Buck Swope, an X-rated movie star. "My backstory on him would be that he's from a broken home, and he's fallen into this family of misfits that have welcomed him," Cheadle said of his character in the film to Ebner. At first, Cheadle was reluctant to accept the part, worried that the film might be tawdry. He requested that he not have to take off his clothes for the camera. "I didn't want to be naked and exploited. I wanted the film to take a deep look at these people and it does," Cheadle recalled in *Interview*.

On series television, Cheadle's most notable work was

his two years as a straight-arrow district attorney on the quirky small town life drama *Picket Fences.* He also had a regular role on the situation comedy *The Golden Palace,* an unsuccessful sequel to *The Golden Girls,* and recurring roles on *Fame,* and *The Fresh Prince of Bel Air.* More television is not something Cheadle sees in his future. "I plan to focus on films and theater because with television you're forced to deal with major script changes every day. There's no time to refine things, and they so often cut things that are key to where you're trying to take your character. I find it very frustrating," Cheadle said in the *Los Angeles Times.*

Cheadle is the founder of an artists company called Elemental Prose, which has as its goal the passing down of oral history through words and music. He has directed plays, including his own work *Groomed,* about four black men attending a wedding in Nebraska, which has been produced in Los Angeles and Hartford, Connecticut. As a screenwriter, he has written the script for a remake of the 1973 "blaxploitation" film *Cleopatra Jones,* and hopes to direct the film, envisioning Jada Pinkett Smith or Viveca A. Fox as the title character. In an HBO film about Hollywood's legendary "Rat Pack," Cheadle will play Sammy Davis, Jr., with Ray Liotta as Frank Sinatra, and Joe Mantegna as Dean Martin. Cheadle, who lives in Venice, California, with his girlfriend, actress Bridget Coulter and their two young children, is pleased with how his life and career have evolved. He told *Premiere*—"When I sit back and think about it, relaxed on my front porch, feeling a breeze and listening to the wind chimes, I go, 'Damn, this came out right. This is really nice.'"

Sources

Periodicals

Amsterdam News (New York), November 23, 1996, p. 56
Bay State Banner (Boston), March 20, 1997.
Entertainment Weekly, October 10, 1997, p. 66.
Indianapolis Recorder, February 22, 1997, p. B2.
Interview, August 1997, p. 80-85.
Jacksonville Free Press, March 5, 1997, p. 13; June 4, 1997, p. 11.
Los Angeles Sentinel, October 4, 1995, p. A3.
Los Angeles Times, September 30, 1995, p. F1.
New York, October 2, 1995, p. 82.
New York Beacon, May 14, 1997, p. 26.
New York Times, October 22, 1995, sect. 2, p. 18.
Philadelphia Tribune, January 31, 1997, magazine section, p. 4.
Pittsburgh Courier, February 12, 1997, p. B3.
Sun Reporter, February 20, 1997, p. 9; April 24, 1997, p. 9.

Other

Information also provided by Huvane, Baum, Halls Public Relations

—Mary Kalfatovic

James Cleveland

1932(?)–1991

Gospel vocalist, minister, composer

A prolific composer of pieces that remain gospel standards, a distinctive vocal performer, and a tireless teacher and organizer of huge gospel conventions, James Cleveland spent a lifetime "at the forefront of America's gospel music experience," in the words of his *Billboard* magazine obituary in 1991. Cleveland paved the way for modern gospel music by incorporating blues and jazz influences, and directly shaping the careers of soul superstars Aretha Franklin and Billy Preston. He was a towering figure, a man considered by many as the "King of Gospel Music" and the "Crown Prince of Gospel."

James Cleveland was born in Chicago, perhaps on December 5, 1932 (his birthday has also been given as December 23, and his birth year as 1931, but the date proposed here accords with that given by gospel music authority Horace Boyer in the *New Grove Dictionary of American Music*). His earliest musical experiences occurred when his grandmother took him to Chicago's Pilgrim Baptist Church, where the renowned choir director and composer Thomas B. Dorsey was responsible for the music. Dorsey was greatly impressed with the young man's vocal talent and asked him to sing a solo. Cleveland rapidly broadened his musical abilities. He told *Gospel Sound* author Tony Heilbut that although his parents could not afford a piano, "I used to practice each night right there on the windowsill. I took those wedges and crevices and made me black and white keys."

Wrote Three Songs A Week

Influenced by gospel songstresses Mahalia Jackson (whose home was located on Cleveland's paper route) and Roberta Martin, Cleveland began performing and composing regularly while still in his teens. As his voice changed, he strained to hit high notes and caused some damage to his vocal cords. As a result, his singing voice took on a rough and raspy quality that became his trademark in later years. Martin, who was active in the gospel music publishing field, began paying Cleveland to write songs for her and he developed into an extremely prolific songwriter. Between 1956 and 1960, he wrote approximately three songs per week.

In 1953 Cleveland joined a gospel group called the Caravans as pianist, arranger, and occasional singer.

At a Glance...

Born December 5, 1932 (some sources give the birthday December 23 and the year 1931) in Chicago; son of Ben Cleveland (a WPA worker); children: LaShone; died of heart failure, February 9, 1991. *Religion:* Baptist.

Career: Minister and gospel singer, songwriter, and pianist; sang with the Thorn Gospel Crusaders and many other groups, 1940s and 1950s; formed own group, the Gospel Chimes, 1959; co-director of music, New Bethel Baptist Church, Detroit, 1960; signed to Savoy label, c. 1961; released over 100 albums; founded James Cleveland Singers, 1963; organized Gospel Music Workshop of America, 1968; founded Southern California Community Choir, 1969; founder and pastor, Cornerstone Institutional Baptist Church, Los Angeles, 1970.

Awards: Sixteen gold records; Grammy award for *Amazing Grace*, 1972; Image Award from National Association for the Advancement of Colored People, 1976.

With Cleveland on vocals, the group had some success with two recordings, "The Solid Rock" and "Old Time Religion." Seeking to put into action his own creative vision, Cleveland left the Caravans in 1959 and formed his own group, the Gospel Chimes. Over the next several years, Cleveland achieved a series of creative breakthroughs. He moved to Detroit in 1960 to take a position as music director at the famed New Bethel Baptist Church where the Reverend C. L. Franklin, father of soul vocalist Aretha Franklin, was pastor. In 1972, he collaborated with Aretha on the Grammy-winning multimillion-selling LP *Amazing Grace*.

Signed to Savoy Records

While recording with various Detroit choirs, Cleveland attracted the attention of New York–based Savoy Records and was signed to the label early in the 1960s. He went on to record more than 100 albums for Savoy, sixteen of which were gold albums. One breakthrough recording was Savoy's 1963 release *Peace Be Still*. On the title track of the record, which paired Cleveland with the Angelic Choir of Nutley, New Jersey, Cleveland crystallized his choral work and hit on a powerful formula that he would follow many times throughout the rest of his career. In the words of Horace Boyer, writing in the *New Grove Dictionary of American Music*, "Cleveland half croons, half preaches the verse, shifting to a musical sermon at the refrain; towards the end of the songs the choir repeats a motif over which Cleveland extemporizes a number of variations." *Peace Be Still* remained on the gospel music charts for fifteen years.

> "Anyone who heard him, you were touched by him. He was a motivator, and innovator. He leaves the greatest legacy."
> —Aretha Franklin

Cleveland moved to Los Angeles in 1963, serving as pastor of the New Greater Harvest Baptist Church. In 1970 he opened his own church, the Cornerstone Institutional Baptist Church. Cornerstone would eventually grow into one of the city's largest congregations. Cleveland always insisted that his work as a preacher was integral to his career, remarking to a *Billboard* interviewer that gospel was "an art form, true enough; but it represents an idea, a thought, a trend."

After a brief hiatus, Cleveland soon redoubled his musical efforts. He formed several successful new groups, including the James Cleveland Singers and the Southern California Community Choir. In 1968, Cleveland founded the Gospel Music Workshop of America. The purpose of the workshop was to bring together singers from all over the country in order to perpetuate the art of gospel music. The workshops eventually attracted thousands of adherents and laid the groundwork for the popularity of gospel music.

Maintained Unswerving Allegiance to Gospel

By the 1970s and 1980s, Cleveland had become a gospel music legend. Disc jockeys, impressed by the sheer power of Cleveland's voice, played his music and several of his records became minor pop hits. However, unlike talented gospel artists like Sam Cooke and Aretha Franklin who crossed over to pop careers, Cleveland maintained an unswerving allegiance to gospel. His imaginative arrangements are credited with introducing jazz and pop rhythms to gospel and paved the way for gospel-pop fusion artists such as Edwin Hawkins and Andrae Crouch.

Cleveland suffered severe respiratory problems in his later years and died of heart failure on February 9, 1991, in Los Angeles. Aretha Franklin memorialized Cleveland in the *New York Times* with these words: "Anyone who heard him, you were touched by him. He was a motivator, and innovator. He leaves the greatest legacy."

Selected discography

(All albums recorded on Savoy label).

This Sunday in Person, 1961.
Rev. James Cleveland with the Angelic Choir, Vol. 2, 1962.
Peace Be Still, 1963.
Songs of Dedication, 1968.
I Stood on the Banks of Jordan, 1970.
Amazing Grace (with Aretha Franklin), 1972.
In the Ghetto, 1973.
Tomorrow, 1978.
Lord Let Me Be an Instrument, 1979.
James Cleveland Sings with the World's Greatest Choirs, 1980.
It's a New Day, 1982.
This Too Will Pass, 1983.
Jesus Is the Best Thing That Ever Happened to Me, 1990.

Sources

Books

Anderson, Robert, and Gail North, *Gospel Music Encyclopedia,* Sterling, 1979.
Contemporary Musicians, volume 1, Gale, 1989.
New Grove Dictionary of American Music, Macmillan, 1986.
Romanowski, Patricia, and Holly George-Warren, *The New Rolling Stone Encyclopedia of Rock & Roll,* Fireside, 1995.

Periodicals

Billboard, February 23, 1991, p. 4.
Library Journal, February 15, 1998, p. 181.
New York Times, February 11, 1991.

—James M. Manheim

John Coltrane

1926–1967

Jazz saxophonist, composer

Jazz saxophonist and composer John Coltrane led, between 1960 and 1966, one of most influential groups in the history of jazz. Since his first jobs with nationally known band leaders in the late 1940s, Coltrane's career—which included stints with Miles Davis and Thelonious Monk—went through several phases and stylistic changes before culminating in the playing of "free jazz" based upon the omission of a harmonic center. Like saxophonist Charlie Parker, he opened up new improvisatory variations by expanding the musical vocabulary of jazz. Apart from bringing into vogue the playing of chords on the saxophone, Coltrane often led groups which employed either two basses or two drummers. His solemn manner, spiritual outlook, and chronic drug use made him an avant garde cultural hero among countless jazz artists and 1960s rock musicians. Inspired by the music of Africa, India, and the Far East, Coltrane brought together disparate musical and cultural elements (including modern symphonic music by such composers as Igor Stravinsky), which made him one of the founders of a world music consciousness, and a creative force whose profound impact has yet to be fully recognized.

John Coltrane was born on September 23, 1926, in Hamlet, North Carolina, to John Robert Coltrane—a tailor—and Alice Gertrude Blair, members of the African Methodist Episcopal Church who displayed talent as amateur musical instrumentalists. A few months after the birth of their son, the Coltranes moved one hundred miles north to High Point, North Carolina. Not long after, Coltrane's father separated from the family, leaving Alice and her sister to raise John Jr. A bright student in grammar school, Coltrane's subsequent musical interests shifted his attention away from his school studies which earned him average grades. Around the time of his father's death from stomach cancer in 1939, Coltrane took up alto saxophone and then clarinet. Shortly afterward he played in a local community band, and in the fall of 1940, became a member of William Penn High School's newly formed music ensemble. During this time, he spent countless hours in private musical practice which became an obsessive endeavor.

After graduating from high school in May of 1943, Coltrane joined his mother in Philadelphia, and enrolled in the Ornstein School of Music, where he received private saxophone lessons from Mike Guerra. "[Col-

At a Glance...

Born John William Coltrane, September 23, 1926, in Hamlet, North Carolina; died of liver cancer July 17, 1967; son of John Robert Coltrane (a tailor) and Gertrude Blair; married Naima Grubbs October 3, 1955, and divorced in 1966; married Alice McCleod (pianist/harpist) in 1966; children: John W. Jr., Ravi John Coltrane; *Education:* Ornstein School of Music circa 1943; Granoff Studio.

Career: Played alto saxophone in a Navy Band, 1945-46; free-lanced with various musicians in Philadelphia, 1946-49; with Eddie "Cleanhead" Vinson, 1948-49; with Dizzy Gillespie, 1949-51; performed with saxophonist Earl Bostic, 1952; toured with saxophonist Johnny Hodges, 1954; performed with organist Jimmy Smith before joining Miles Davis' quintet, 1955; performed and recorded with Thelonious Monk, 1957; returned to Miles Davis' group and recorded with Kenny Burrell, 1958; quit Miles Davis' group and recorded album *Giant Steps,* 1959; led own group, 1960-65; added Eric Dolphy to group, 1961; played jobs with Wes Montgomery and recorded with Duke Ellington, 1962; recorded with singer Johnny Hartman, 1963; performed with two drummers and recruited saxophonist Farrell "Pharoah" Sanders, 1965; led with new ensemble, 1966; *Military service:* U.S. Navy 1945-46.

Awards: *Down Beat* Jazz Musician of the Year, International Critic's Poll, Reader's Poll, Best Saxophone, and Best Miscellaneous (soprano saxophone), New Star Combo, 1961; *Down Beat* Jazzman of the Year, 1965; album *Love Supreme* voted Album of the Year by *Down Beat* and *Jazz,* 1965.

Naval Tour Of Duty

Inducted into the Navy in 1945, Coltrane was first stationed in California and then spent a tour of duty on the Hawaiian island of Oahu. Between regular military duties Coltrane, called "Trane" by other naval personnel, performed on clarinet and alto saxophone in a dance band, The Melody Masters. Shortly before his discharge in August of 1946, and while still in Oahu, Coltrane took part in his first recording session with a small group of Navy musicians, playing bebop-style numbers on alto saxophone. Back in Philadelphia, Coltrane, funded by Veteran's Administration benefits, continued his musical education at the Granoff Studios. Like many young jazzmen of the post war period, Coltrane balanced his study of music between formal and informal training. "Philadelphia's jazz scene had high technical standards in comparison with many local scenes outside New York," noted Lewis Porter in *John Coltrane: His Life and Music.* "This clearly had an impact on Coltrane, who was fascinated with technical and theoretical matters. He both contributed to and benefitted from this aspect of the Philadelphia jazz life," he continued.

In 1947 Coltrane spent three months in the band of trumpeter King Kolax, and then continued to study music and free-lance around Philadelphia, until joining Jimmy Heath's big band. After disbanding his group in Philadelphia, in November of 1948, alto saxophonist Eddie "Cleanhead" Vinson hired Coltrane as a tenor saxophonist as part of his new unit. Coltrane toured with Vinson until leaving the band in the summer of 1949, and by September was hired as lead alto saxophonist for Dizzy Gillespie's big band. Though honored to be a member of Gillespie's ensemble, Coltrane's position on alto offered him little room for improvisation. In between playing Gillespie's new bebop novelty material, Coltrane did manage to perform complex modern compositions such as Gillespie's "Night in Tunisia" and Thelonious Monk's "Round Midnight."

When financial troubles caused Gillespie to break up his big band in 1950, the trumpeter formed a small unit which included Coltrane on tenor saxophone. As a member of the Dizzy Gillespie Sextet, Coltrane was joined by vibraphonist Milt Jackson, bassist Percy Heath, and drummer Specs Wright. In March of 1951 Coltrane recorded on Gillespie's Detroit-based Dee Gee label with Milt Jackson, Kenny Burrell, both of whom he would later collaborate on solo recording projects. In New York that same year, Coltrane, as a result of his increasing drug use, was fired by Gillespie.

trane] was easily the best student in my class," accounted Guerra in *Chasin' the Trane.* "I wrote out complex chord progressions and special exercises in chromatic scales, and he was one of the few who brought his homework back practically the next day and played it on sight," he continued. At this time, Coltrane befriended such Philadelphia jazzmen as Jimmy Heath, Benny Golson, and Ray Bryant—musicians with whom he often performed with in small groups around the city.

Free-lanced In Philadelphia

Back in Philadelphia, Coltrane continued his study of music through relentless practice and free-lance jobs. In April of 1952 he toured with alto saxophonist Earl Bostic. Coltrane free-lanced around Philadelphia, until joining Johnny Hodges in March of 1954. In a *Down Beat* interview with Don Demichael, Coltrane described the musical value of his stint with Hodges: "I was getting first hand information about things that happened way before my time." Despite an enthusiasm for Hodge's music, Coltrane's drug habit forced the bandleader to fire him.

In September of 1955 Coltrane worked in Philadelphia with organist Jimmy Smith. In *John Coltrane: His Life and Music,* Lewis Porter noted that during this period, "Coltrane utilized a very slow vibrato, lending to poignant delicacy to his sound. At faster tempos, Coltrane's tone became more raspy and intense." When tenor saxophonist Sonny Rollins left Miles Davis' band, the trumpeter invited Coltrane to fill the job. At first, Coltrane found playing with Davis uneasy and frustrating. After a very brief return with Jimmy Smith, he rejoined Davis' band later that month. Two months later, Coltrane appeared on the Prestige album *The New Miles Davis Quintet,* soon to be followed by sessions that yielded Davis' classic works, *Cookin', Relaxin', Workin' With Miles Davis,* and *Steamin'*. He then appeared on Davis' first solo Columbia release, *'Round About Midnight.* By 1957 Coltrane's increasing drug use began to take its toll. In his memoir *Miles,* Davis recalled his waning tolerance for Coltrane's addiction: "Trane was a beautiful person, a real sweet kind of guy, spiritual, all of that. So you really couldn't help loving him and caring about him, too. I figured he was making more money than he ever made in his life, and so when I talked to him I thought he would stop, but he didn't." Without heeding his bandleader's advice, Coltrane was fired by Davis in April of 1957.

Apprenticeship With Thelonious Monk

In the summer of 1957 Coltrane, bassist Wilbur Ware, and drummer Shadow Wilson, backed pianist Thelonious Monk at New York's Five Spot on the city's lower east side. Though it lasted only several months, Coltrane's stint with Monk proved an invaluable musical experience. Monk's habit of leaving space behind the soloist (termed "laying out") allowed Coltrane freedom to explore various harmonic possibilities. Ted Goia wrote, in *The History of Jazz,* "Rather than emulating Monk's use of space or compositional style of improvisation, as so many others did when playing with the pianist, Coltrane stayed true to his own emphatic style." As Goia added, "In an amazing turnaround, Monk came to adapt to Coltrane, even going so far as not playing behind some of the horn solos, allowing the tenorist to stretch out with just bass and drum backing (as the saxophonist would do a few years later with his own band)." Shortly before joining Monk, Coltrane cut the number, "Monk's Mood," which later appeared on the Prestige album *Thelonious Himself.* As a regular of Monk's group, he attended an April 1957 session which yielded material featured on the album *Thelonious Monk With John Coltrane,* a work containing such Monk classics as "Ruby My Dear," "Trinkle Tinkle" and "Nutty." Several years later, in *Down Beat,* Coltrane recalled, "Working with Monk brought me close to a musical architect of the highest order. I felt I learned from him in every way—through the senses, theoretically, technically."

Solo Trane

In May of 1957 Coltrane recorded his debut album, entitled *Coltrane,* for Prestige Records (over the next months he would record material which make up the albums *Dakar,* and *Traneing In).* That same year, Prestige arranged a deal with Blue Note Records allowing Coltrane to record one album, which brought forth, *Blue Train,* a modern jazz classic, yielding such Coltrane numbers as the twelve bar-structured "Blue Train" and "Moment's Notice"—a sixteen-bar original which Lewis Porter noted, in *John Coltrane: His Life and Music,* that displayed Coltrane's "preoccupation with placing changing harmonies under a repeated note in the melody."

At this time, Coltrane's musical explorations coincided with an increasing interest in world religions and spiritual consciousness. In the liner notes to *A Love Supreme,* Coltrane wrote, "During the year 1957, I experienced by the grace of God, a spiritual awakening which led me to a richer, fuller more productive life ... All Praise to God." As Valerie Wilmer noted, in *As Serious as Your Life,* "[Coltrane] was not the first musician to speak of spiritual matters, but his example was one of the most compelling and persuasive"—one that exemplified the "hip" element by becoming "a musician of value or worth to the community," and African American culture.

Rejoined Davis

In 1958, after periodically kicking his drug habit, Coltrane rejoined Davis' expanded-unit which included alto saxophonist Cannonball Adderly. In February and March of 1958 the sextet recorded *Milestones*. During this two-month period, he also recorded two solo efforts *Soultrane* and *Trane's Reign,* and co-led a date with guitarist Kenny Burrell. In the spring of 1958, Coltrane recorded on Davis' album the classic numbers "On Green Dolphin Street" and Richard Roger's "My Funny Valentine"—material which comprised the album *'58 Sessions*. In March and April of 1959 Coltrane took part in sessions which produced Davis' classic album *Kind of Blue*. Despite his invaluable experience with Davis' sextet, Coltrane had, by 1959, desired to expand his own musical horizons, and spent many hours at the piano working out harmonic variations [Coltrane composed most of his work on the keyboard]. As he told Ralph Gleason, in the liner notes to *Ol'e Coltrane*, "All the time I was with Miles I didn't have anything to think about but myself so I stayed at the piano and chords, chords, chords! I ended up playing them on my horn."

Continued Solo Career

A work with an immense impact on the jazz world, Coltrane's Atlantic album, *Giant Steps,* was cut in three sessions held between April and December of 1959. His original numbers, "Giant Steps" and "Countdown," became test pieces not only for saxophonists but for other instrumentalists as well. In the album's liner notes, Coltrane explained that he titled "Giant Steps" for the intervals of the composition's bass line which moved from "minor thirds to fourths ... in contrast fourths or in half-steps."

After a European tour with Davis, Coltrane left the trumpeter's group in April of 1960, and five months later, (after several personnel changes) assembled a quartet with pianist McCoy Tyner, bassist Steve Davis, and drummer Elvin Jones. In Jones' inventive musicianship Coltrane found the ideal drummer whose revolutionary circular-style of playing and furious sense of swing seemed to anticipate his musical ideas. In October the quartet recorded the Atlantic album, *My Favorite Things,* featuring Rodgers' and Hammerstein's title selection, on which Coltrane's eastern-sounding soprano saxophone inspired numerous jazz interpretations of the original stage number. In May and June of 1961, he gained the Impulse labels' permission to record an eighteen-piece orchestral work, *Africa/Brass*. In November of the same year, the quartet cut [with Reggie Workman on bass and a guest appearance by Eric Dolphy] *Live at the Village Vanguard* which included the feral blues "Chasin' the Trane." Coltrane's extended soloing, noted Nat Hentoff in the album's liner notes, "... is particularly fascinating for the astonishing variety of textures Coltrane draws from the full range of his horn and the unflagging intensity of his inventions."

During the early 1960s, Coltrane's agonized saxophone cries and atonal intervals led critics to label him "the angry tenor," (a title he despised). Despite criticism, Coltrane's fierce attack and astonishing display of unique musical ideas were balanced by his tasteful playing of ballads and blues. In describing the man behind the media image, Elvin Jones commented, in *Thinking in Jazz:* "[Coltrane] was so calm and had such a peaceful attitude, it was soothing to be around him....To me, he was like an angel on earth. He struck me deeply. This is not just an ordinary person, and I'm not a believer to think very seriously about that. I've been touched some way by something greater than life." Coltrane's deepening religious consciousness inspired him, in December of 1964, to record the album *Love Supreme*. A four section suite, *Love Supreme* became *Down Beat* magazine's album of the year, and emerged as Coltrane's best-selling recording.

New Musical Explorations

In 1965 the Impulse label released *Ascension,* Coltrane's first tonally free effort. "This forty-minute performance," observed Ted Gioia in *The History of Jazz,* "found Coltrane and his rhythm section supplemented by a half-dozen horn players in a wild free-for-all—a superheated encounter that, for many listeners, served as the fitting logical and anarchistic end point to this quest of freedom." In September of 1965 tenor saxophonist Ferrell "Pharoah" Sanders joined Coltrane's ensemble. Frustrated that his piano had taken a background role, Tyner left the band at the end of 1965, and was replaced by pianist and harpist Alice McCleod, a former Detroiter who became Coltrane's second wife in 1966. After Coltrane's addition of drummer, Rashied Ali, the group's two-drum line-up found disfavor with Elvin Jones, who soon left the group (Jimmy Garrison stayed with Coltrane's group until the summer of 1966).

The Art Of Free Jazz

By 1967 Coltrane's music no longer employed the use of a steady beat (most notably in the absence of a walking bass), and abandoned the use of a tonal center in his compositions. As saxophonist Dave Leibman noted in *Down Beat,* "In '66 and '67, Trane employed no harmonic basis at all, but worked on the base level of harmonic minimalism, which he could paint any picture over, moving in and out of the stated key, playing in many keys at once." In February and March of 1967 Coltrane recorded the album *Expressions*. He also recorded, in February, a number of duets with drummer Rashied Ali, posthumously released as the Impulse! album *Interstellar Space*. At this time, Coltrane's chronic use of LSD attributed to his worsening health. After complaints of pains in his stomach in May of the same year, he was hospitalized. Two months later, Coltrane was admitted to Huntington Hospital, in New York City, where he died of liver cancer on July 17, 1967.

Despite his untimely death, Coltrane left behind a musical legacy of profound human message. In an interview quoted in the book *John Coltrane: His Life and Music*, Coltrane expressed his ultimate creative purpose: "I think music can make the world better and, if I'm qualified, I want to do it. I'd like to point out to people the divine in a musical language that transcends words. I want to speak to their souls."

Selected discography

(with Dizzy Gillespie)

The Champ, Savoy, 1992.

(with Miles Davis)

The New Miles Davis Quintet, Prestige 1955.
Cookin', Prestige, 1956.
Relaxin', Prestige 1956.
Workin' With Miles Davis, Prestige, 1956.
Steamin', Prestige, 1956.
Miles Davis and the Modern Jazz Giants, Prestige, 1956.
Round About Midnight, Columbia, 1956.
Milestones, Columbia, 1958.
Miles Davis '58 Sessions, Columbia, reissued material, 1991.
Kind of Blue, Columbia, 1959.

(with Thelonious Monk)

Thelonious Monk With John Coltrane, Jazzland, reissued on Original Jazz Classics, 1987.
The Thelonious Monk Quartet Featuring John Coltrane, Live at the Five Spot/Discovery! Blue Note.

(solo)

Dakar, Prestige, 1957.
Blue Train, Blue Note, 1957.
Traneing In, Prestige, 1958.
Kenny Burrell and John Coltrane, New Jazz, 1958, reissued on Original Jazz Classics, 1987.
Giant Steps, Atlantic, 1960.
My Favorite Things, Atlantic, 1961.
Ol'e Coltrane, Atlantic, 1961.
The Complete Africa Brass Sessions, Impulse!, 1961.
Live at the Village Vanguard, Impulse!, 1962.
Coltrane, Impulse!, 1962.
Ballads, Impulse!, 1962.
John Coltrane in Stockholm 1963, Charly Records, 1986.
A Love Supreme, Impulse!, 1964.
Cresent, Impulse!, 1964.
Ascension, Impulse!, 1965.
Sun Ship, Impulse!, 1965.
Meditations, Impulse!, 1965.
Coltrane Plays the Blues, Atlantic, 1966.
Expression, Impulse!, 1967.
Interstellar Space, Impulse!, 1967.

Boxed Sets

John Coltrane: The Prestige Recordings.
The Last Giant, Rhino Records.

Sources

Books

Berliner, Paul F., *Thinking in Jazz: The Infinite Art of Improvisation,* University of Chicago Press, 1994.
Davis, Miles with Quincy Troupe, *Miles the Autobiography,* Simon & Schuster, 1989, p. 209-210.
Gioia, Ted, *The History of Jazz,* Oxford University Press, 1997, pp.245-246. Thomas, J.C., *Chasin' The Trane: The Music and Mystique of John Coltrane.* Da Capo, 1976.
Porter, Lewis, *John Coltrane: His Life and Music,* University of Michigan, 1998.
Wilmer, Valerie, *As Serious as Your Life: The Story of Jazz,* Pluto Press, 1977, p. 25-44.

Periodicals

Down Beat, October 16, 1958; September, 29, 1960; June 1988, pp. 20-27.

Other

Additional information for this profile was obtained from the liner notes to: *Giant Steps,* Atlantic, 1960; *Live at the Village Vanguard,* by Nat Hentoff, 1962; *John Coltrane, A Love Supreme,* 1964; *Ol'e Coltrane,* by Ralph Gleason, Atlantic, 1961.

—John Cohassey

Randy Crawford

1952—

Vocalist

Proving herself to be a versatile interpreter of jazz, soul, rhythm and blues, and pop, singer Randy Crawford has been an active presence on the music scene since she began performing in local night clubs as a teenager. Her recordings have run the gamut from smooth ballads such as "One Day I'll Fly Away," which became her trademark song, to covers of songs made famous by Bob Dylan ("Knockin' on Heaven's Door"), Brook Benton ("Rainy Night in Georgia"), and the artist formerly known as Prince ("Purple Rain").

Whether recording new songs or established favorites, Randy Crawford has long been known for her signature sound that makes every song seem new. "Before you know it, regardless of whatever category the tune was at its inception, it is a Randy Crawford song," noted the *Atlanta Constitution* in its review of her 1997 release *Every Kind of Mood*. The singer has also been lauded by critics for her ability to create a personal link with listeners that brings them right into the sentiment of the song. As Jeremy Helligar noted in *People*, "Crawford's great assets are her intimate singing style and vocal restraint—the way she lightly tugs her vowels when she's caught up in the heat of passion and unleashes gentle tremolos when she's suffering the agony of heartache."

Despite being frequently praised for her mastery of many different musical styles, Crawford's versatility has in some ways hampered her career. As Ron Wynn remarked in *The All-Music Guide to Rock,* "Crawford's quivering delivery and eclectic nature has made it difficult for record companies to target and market her materials." Although she has not attracted a wide audience within the United States, she has been a popular star in Europe for nearly two decades. From 1979 to 1984, eleven of her singles reached the top 75 in Britain.

As a child in Cincinnati, Ohio, Crawford's vocal talent was developed by singing in church and social choirs. By the time she was 15, she was performing in local night clubs. In 1967, she made her international debut in St. Tropez, France during a summer vacation trip to Europe. Crawford has cited singers such as Dinah Washington and Aretha Franklin as important early career influences. As a young girl, she discovered gospel music by listening to recordings of Aretha Franklin. "I used to listen to all of those records for many, many hours,"

> *At a Glance...*

Born Veronica Crawford on February 18, 1952, in Macon, GA; one of five children.

Career: Sang in church and school choirs and local night clubs as a teenager, Cincinnati, OH; performed in St. Tropez, France, 1967; began performing with George Benson, 1972; released first single, "If You Say the Word," 1972; sang at World Jazz Association tribute concert to Cannonball Adderley, Los Angeles, CA, 1975; released first album, *Everything Must Change*, on Warner Brothers, 1976; sang lead on "Street Life" for The Crusaders, 1979; completed tour of Europe, 1984; performed with London Symphony Orchestra, 1988; collaborated with Italian performer Zucchero at a performance in the Soviet Union, 1990; performed at Christmas concert at he Vatican for Pope John Paul II, 1991; released *Every Kind of Mood* on Mesa/Blue Moon Label, 1997.

Awards and honors: Most Outstanding Performer, Tokyo Music Festival, 1980; Best Female Artist, BRIT Awards, U.K., 1982.

Addresses: *Management*—Barry Gross, 930 Third Street, Suite 102, Santa Monica, CA 90403; *Record company*—WEA Records Germany; licensed by Mesa/Bluemoon Recordings, Inc.; manufactured and distributed by Atlantic Recording Corporation, 1290 Avenue of the America, New York, NY 10104.

Crawford remarked in *Ebony Man*.

Opened for George Benson

As a teenager, Crawford was lead vocalist in a group that included bassist William "Bootsy" Collins, who taught her how to play piano. A television appearance attracted the attention of a Los Angeles booking agent, who helped land her a gig as an opening act for noted jazz guitarist/singer George Benson. In 1972 she began opening for Benson at Nico's, a popular jazz/soul club in New York City. "I got discovered while I was singing with George Benson," Crawford later told *Ebony Man*. During her first year with Benson, she released her first single "If You Say the Word."

Crawford's career received another boost in 1975, when Warner Brothers signed her to a contract after she appeared with Benson and Quincy Jones at the World Jazz Association tribute concert for the late Cannonball Adderley. Her debut album, *Everything Must Change*, "displayed her ability to interpret songs in a variety of styles with a voice that was rich in inflection and capable of a wide range of expression," according to *The New Grove Dictionary of American Music*. Although reviews of the album were largely positive, sales were only mediocre. In 1977, Crawford appeared as a backup vocalist on *Please Don't Touch*, the second solo album of former Genesis member Steve Hackett.

In 1979 Crawford recorded *Raw Silk*, which featured songs written by Allen Toussaint, Ashford & Simpson, and Oscar Brown. That same year she sang lead vocals on the title track of *Street Life*, an album by the popular jazz group The Crusaders. The song topped jazz charts in the United States for 20 weeks and made Crawford a star on the international music scene. The Crusaders co-wrote, produced, and provided instrumental support on Crawford's 1980 release *Now We May Begin*. The title track from this album was "a beautiful ballad that established her independent career," claimed *The Guinness Encyclopedia of Popular Music*. Although *Now We May Begin* failed to climb music charts in the United States, it reached number ten in Britain. In 1981, Crawford recorded the love theme for the soundtrack of *The Competition*, a film starring Richard Dreyfuss and Amy Irving.

Had Chart Success in England

Crawford continued to experience tremendous success in Europe. Her song "You Might Need Somebody" rose to number 11 on the British charts. Her next album *Secret Combination* climbed to number two in Britain and number 71 in the United States. This album featured a mix of smooth ballads, as well as funkier music, and utilized a wide range of musical styles. *Secret Combination* also marked the first time that a Crawford album charted in the top 100 on the American music charts.

In 1984, Crawford launched a successful tour of Europe. She returned to the United States that same year and recorded a duet with pop star Rick Springfield entitled "Taxi Dancing." In 1986 Crawford released *Abstract Emotions*, which reached number 14 on the British charts. In 1988, she appeared in two sold-out concerts with the London Symphony Orchestra. She also performed at jazz festivals throughout the world with such notable jazz musicians as Al Jarreau, Joe Sample, and

Ray Charles. She traveled to the Soviet Union in 1990 and performed in the Kremlin with the Italian superstar Zucchero.

During the early 1990s, Crawford experienced a slow period in her career. In 1995, she released a new album on the WEA Germany label entitled *Naked and True* and began another tour of Europe. The album was soon released in the United States by the Mesa/Bluemoon label. *Naked and True* became Crawford's third most successful album, selling 250,000 copies in the United States and over 500,000 copies worldwide. The album featured songs in a wide range of styles, including "Give Me the Night," which hit number one on the Smooth Jazz/NAC radio charts.

Crawford remains active as a performer and recording artist after some 30 years of professional singing, and her music continues to attract critical acclaim. "Crawford's unique vocal styling gives life to the fifteen tracks that emote love, heartbreak, sympathy, and passion," raved John Norment in his review of Crawford's 1997 release *Every Kind of Mood*. In the liner notes of *Every Kind of Mood,* Ahmet Ertegün offered even higher praise. "I listen to Randy Crawford and hear something so familiar," wrote Ertegün. "It's a sound that's timeless, beautiful, and honest. It's the sound of one of the most truly soulful voices of our time."

Selected discography

Everything Must Change, Warner, 1976.
Now We May Begin, Warner, 1980.
Abstract Emotions, Warner, 1986.
Naked and True, Mesa/Bluemoon, 1995.
Every Kind of Mood, Mesa/Bluemoon, 1997.

Sources

Books

Clarke, Donald, ed., *The Penguin Encyclopedia of Popular Music,* Viking, 1989, pp. 295–296.
Erlewine, Michael, Vladimir Bogdanov, and Chris Woodstra, eds., *All Music Guide to Rock,* Miller Freeman, 1995, pp. 211–212.
Hitchcock, H. Wiley, and Stanley Sadie, eds., *The New Grove Dictionary of American Music, Volume 1,* Macmillan, 1986, p. 531.
Larkin, Colin, ed., *The Guinness Encyclopedia of Popular Music, Volume 3,* Guinness Publishing, 1992, p. 976.
Rees, Dafydd, and Luke Crampton, eds., *Rock Movers & Shakers,* ABC-CLIO, 1991, pp. 126–127.

Periodicals

Atlanta Constitution, January 29, 1998, p. E-4.
Billboard, October 28, 1995, p. 29; March 7, 1998, p. 60; March 21, 1998, p. 98.
Ebony, June 1998, p. 22.
Ebony Man, July 1996, p. 8.
People, March 9, 1998, p. 29.

Other

Additional information for this profile was obtained from Atlantic Recording Corporation publicity materials.

—Ed Decker

Scatman Crothers

1910–1986

Actor, musician

To anybody who watched much television in the 1970s and early 1980s, very few faces or voices were more familiar than those of Scatman Crothers. Crothers is best remembered for his portrayal of Louie the Garbage Man on the NBC series *Chico and the Man,* but through his constant appearances on television talk shows, dramas and sitcoms, and in such movies as *One Flew Over the Cuckoo's Nest* and *The Shining,* Crothers became one of the period's most visible cultural icons. He achieved this fame after toiling in near-anonymity for more than 50 years. During that time, he performed as a drummer, guitar-banjo-ukeleleist, singer, songwriter, and actor in entertainment settings ranging from prohibition-era speakeasies to high-tech 1980s movie studios.

Scatman was born Benjamin Sherman Crothers on May 23, 1910, in Terre Haute, Indiana. His father was a cobbler and the proprietor of a second-hand clothing store. At the age of 14, Crothers began teaching himself to play both drums and guitar, and to sing in the scat style later made popular by Louis Armstrong and others. Still in his teens, Crothers landed a job entertaining customers at one of the local speakeasies, a place frequented by Chicago mobsters trying to lie low. He received no salary at the roadhouse, but the lavish tips made him "the richest kid in high school," Crothers recalled in a 1981 *Jet* article.

Serenaded the South

When Crothers was 19, he and his brother Louis set out for Indianapolis, where Scatman hoped to find work as an entertainer. Unable to find employment as a ukulele-plucking minstrel, Crothers ended up taking a job cleaning and blocking hats. He became close friends with the owner of the business, a Greek immigrant, and the owner's son. He even learned to speak some Greek. Crothers never gave up his musical aspirations, however, and he eventually landed a job with a traveling band called Montague's Kentucky Serenaders. With the Serenaders, Crothers toured the South, and experienced for the first time the harsh racism of the region.

Crothers left the Serenaders in 1931, and the following year he moved to Dayton, Ohio, where friends had suggested work could be found. It was in Dayton that he acquired his distinctive nickname. Upon arriving in town, Crothers immediately went to local radio station

> **At a Glance . . .**
>
> Born Benjamin Sherman Crothers on May 23, 1910, in Terre Haute, IN; died November 22, 1986, in Los Angeles, CA; father was a cobbler and used clothing store proprietor; married Helen Sullivan, 1937; children: Donna. *Religion:* Christian.
>
> **Career:** Performed at local speakeasies in Terre Haute, 1924; traveled across US as leader of own band, 1930s; made television debut in *Dixie Showboat*, 1948; made film debut in *Meet Me at the Fair*, 1952; frequent appearances in character roles and guest spots on film and television, 1950-86; cast member of NBC series *Chico and the Man*, 1974-78; film roles include *Hello Dolly*, 1969; *Lady Sings the Blues*, 1972; *One Few Over the Cuckoo's Nest*, 1975; *Bronco Billy*, 1980; *The Shining*, 1980; and *Twilight Zone, the Move*, 1983.

KSMK to audition for a spot on the air. The program director was impressed with Crothers's talent, but felt that his name was too bland. Off the top of his head, Crothers immediately came up with the moniker "Scatman." It quickly became his de facto first name.

Crothers spent the next few years performing primarily as a solo act, with a few exceptions that included a stint in 1933 and 1934 with Eddie Brown and His Tennesseans. In the mid-1930s he formed his own band, with which he traveled throughout the Midwest. In many of the venues the group played, they were the first black entertainers ever to perform. The audiences were almost always entirely white. While performing in Canton, Ohio in 1936, Crothers met Helen Sullivan, a white woman from nearby Steubenville. He married her the following year. Their marriage remained intact for the rest of Crothers' life.

Brought Bebop to Tinseltown

By the early 1940s, Crothers was a regular at the popular jazz clubs in Chicago, both in the Loop and on the South Side. Crothers was playing drums and singing at this point. His band, which included Oliver Michaux on piano, Jimmy Harris on alto sax, and Leroy Nabors on trumpet, was dabbling in bebop, the new jazz style being pioneered by the likes of Dizzy Gillespie and Charlie Parker, by this time. In about 1945, Crothers decided to ditch his Midwestern band and head westward. Settling with Helen in Hollywood, he found scattered bookings in Los Angeles and San Francisco, sometimes as a solo act, other times as leader of his own small combo. He also worked occasionally as a sideman in other people's bands. During a very slow period in 1946, Crothers signed on as drummer with the Slim Gaillard Trio. Working with Gaillard, best known for writing the novelty hits "Flat Foot Floosie" and "Cement Mixer," Crothers was able to earn a stable income and establish connections in the West Coast music scene.

Within a year, Crothers had left the Gaillard group and was back on his own. In 1948 Crothers was introduced to Phil Harris, a radio star and regular on Jack Benny's program. He and Harris—like Crothers a native of Indiana—immediately hit it off. Together Crothers and Harris recorded a song called "Chattanooga Shoeshine Boy," which they introduced on Harris's NBC radio show *The Phil Harris—Alice Faye Show*. Crothers recorded two more hits later that year: "On the Sunny Side of the Street" and "Dead Man's Blues." He became a regular guest on Harris's show, and the pair continued to collaborate on records and in films for years to come.

Crothers was in the right place at the right time as the television age began to dawn. His new show-biz connections led to a spot on the TV show *Dixie Showboat*, making him the first African American on television in Los Angeles. Crothers spent four years on that show, then moved on to the *Colgate Comedy* with Donald O'Connor. Meanwhile, he continued to perform live in area clubs, in particular a steady gig at an L.A. nightspot called The Oasis. Crothers's television work led naturally to a career in film. While working at The Oasis, Crothers met actor Dan Dailey, who offered him a part in a movie he was making. The resulting film, *Meet Me at the Fair* (1952), became a semi-classic. Crothers received sixth billing in the credits, and the movie effectively launched his Hollywood motion picture career.

Became Popular Variety Show Guest

Over the next two decades, Crothers appeared in a huge assortment of character roles and guest spots on television and film. In the early 1950s, he was a regular on the "Beulah" comedy series. He guested on *The Jack Benny Show* and *The Steve Allen Show*. Crothers' television and movie exposure led to bigger and better club bookings as well, and when he was not acting he was performing his musical comedy act at various live venues in Los Angeles, Las Vegas, New York, and elsewhere. He also continued to make records, including the 1950s hit "Walkin' My Baby Back Home." In addition, Crothers began his cartoon voice career during this period in *Beany and Cecil*.

In spite of these accomplishments, however, genuine stardom continued to elude Crothers. As the 1950s continued, quality work became scarce. He landed bit parts in a couple of 20th Century Fox movies: *Between Heaven and Hell,* starring Robert Wagner, in 1956, and *The Gift of Love* in 1958. He performed with a trio at military installations as part of the USO. He continued to work at nightclubs throughout the decade, and remained in demand for television variety shows. As the 1960s began, film roles remained few and far between. He had a small part in the 1960 Warner Brothers feature *The Sins of Rachel Cade,* and another in the Olivia de Havilland vehicle *Lady in a Cage* in 1964. The same year, he was cast as a shoeshine boy in *The Patsy,* which starred Jerry Lewis. While working on that picture, Crothers and Lewis became close friends, leading to parts for Crothers in two other mid-1960s Lewis films, *The Family Jewels* and *Three on a Couch.*

It was in the 1970s that Crothers finally broke through as a fixture in the big leagues of the entertainment industry. In 1970 Crothers played the voice of Scat Cat in the animated Walt Disney feature *The Aristocats.* That work led to further cartoon voice work, beginning with a job as the voice of Meadowlark Lemon on the television cartoon series *The Harlem Globetrotters.* He appeared in the flesh in two more 1970 films, *The Great White Hope* and *Bloody Mama.* Several more bit parts followed in quick succession, prompting Crothers to finally hire a Hollywood agent. A veritable flood of character roles on both film and television followed in the early 1970s, including spots in the movies *Lady Sings the Blues* starring Diana Ross, and *The King of Marvin Gardens.* In 1972 he appeared in such television mainstays as *Adam 12, Love American Style, Kojack,* and *Ironside.*

Rode Trashy Role to Stardom

As the 1970s continued, Scatman's television résumé was bursting with entries. He appeared on, among other series, *Sanford and Son, Mannix, McMillan and Wife,* and *The Odd Couple.* Returning to cartoons, he provided the voice of Saturday morning canine superhero *Hong Kong Phooey.* Crothers's "big break" finally came in 1974, when he was cast as Louie, the lovable garbage man in the NBC sitcom *Chico and the Man.* Crothers played Louie until 1978, when star Freddie Prinze's suicide brought the show to an abrupt end. By that time, however, Crothers had made a permanent mark in the television industry. He was also finally making a more than comfortable living after half a century in showbiz.

His success on the small screen helped breathe some life into his previously lackluster big screen career. Jack Nicholson, with whom Crothers had worked in *The King of Marvin Gardens,* got him a role in his hit 1975 movie *One Flew Over the Cuckoo's Nest,* based on the novel by Ken Kesey. Crothers teamed up with Nicholson again five years later in *The Shining,* in which both actors gave perhaps the most memorable performances of their very different careers.

From the mid-1970s on, Crothers was a constant presence on television, making scores of appearances on talk shows, sitcoms, and dramas. He had starring roles in three shortlived 1980s television series: *One of the Boys* (1982), *Casablanca* (1983), and *Morningstar/ Eveningstar* (1986). His film credits included roles in *Bronco Billy* (1980), *Zapped* (1982), and *Twilight Zone: The Movie* (1983). In 1985 Crothers developed a malignant tumor behind his left lung. He continued to work through his illness, but in 1986 the inoperable tumor spread to his esophagus. He died on November 22, 1986.

Throughout his career, Crothers's most conspicuous characteristic—in addition, of course, to his unmistakable talent as an entertainer—was his omnipresent smile. He was by all accounts a genuinely happy individual. In Hollywood, notorious for backbiting and superficiality, Scatman stood out for his authentic charm and nearly universal popularity. It was simply impossible not to like him, so positive and unaffected was the energy and love that he projected. As Jim Haskins wrote in *Scatman,* his biography of Crothers, "There was no dark side to Scatman Crothers.... No one endured more happily, or had a better time living."

Sources

Books

Haskins, Jim, *Scatman: An Authorized Biography of Scatman Crothers,* William Morrow, 1991.

Periodicals

Ebony, July 1978, p. 62.
Jet, June 11, 1981, p. 28; December 15, 1986, p. 62.
New York Times, November 23, 1986, p. 45.
TV Guide, March 13, 1976, p. 21.

—Robert R. Jacobson

Piper Davis

1917–1997

Professional baseball player

Lorenzo "Piper" Davis was born on July 3, 1917 in Piper, Alabama. The company-owned town is no longer on the map, but Davis's legacy lives on as one of the most talented and versatile athletes of his generation. Davis's father John worked at Piper Coal Company as a miner and lived with his wife Georgia and their nine children. Davis attended high school in nearby Fairfield playing baseball and basketball. He was so good in basketball that he earned a scholarship to attend Alabama State University in nearby Montgomery. After one year of college Davis was forced to quit school and get a job to help support his family.

In the late thirties with the country in the depths of the Depression a man could make one dollar a day in the mines, so Davis signed up with Piper. Life as a miner being lowered into a black hole by a rope did not agree with the young athletic star and he quit after only three months. He got a job at a Birmingham steel mill and soon joined the black squad of American Cast Iron Pipe Company (ACIPCO) in the city's Industrial League. The company had two teams—one for whites and one for blacks. The 19-year-old played well enough to be signed by the Omaha Tigers in 1936. The Nebraska-based Negro team traveled throughout the Midwest playing local clubs and performing exhibitions. After the 1936 season the Tigers had financial problems which forced Davis to return to Birmingham and the ACIPCO team. That squad included Artie Wilson, Ed Steele, Bill Powell, and Herman Bell—the nucleus of what would become one of the legendary Negro League teams—the Birmingham Black Barons.

Davis as a Baron

The Black Barons manager Winfield Welch signed Davis in 1942 for five dollars a game and seven dollars and fifty cents a double-header. In 1943 Davis's salary doubled and he joined the team as a full-time player. He chose baseball over his job at ACIPCO for which he earned three dollars and 36 cents a day. Davis became a fixture at second base for the most impressive Negro American League (NAL) team of the 1940s. The Black Barons won the NAL Pennant in the 1943, 1944, and the 1948 seasons, but each time the team lost the Negro World Series to the Homestead Greys.

Two-Sport Star

In Davis's career with the Black Barons he appeared in eight All-Star games beginning in 1945. Four times Davis represented the West in the East-West All-Star Classic. His All-Star totals included eight runs in 26 at-bats with four runs batted in (RBI) and a .308 batting average. But Davis did not excel in baseball alone. His Black Barons manager was also the coach of the Harlem Globetrotters. Welch found out about Davis's basketball skills and signed him to play for the Globetrotters when

At a Glance...

Born Lorenzo Davis, July 3, 1917 in Piper, Alabama; died May 22, 1997 in Birmingham, Alabama; son of John (a coal miner) and Georgia. *Education:* Attended Alabama State University for one year.

Career: Signed by the Birmingham Black Barons in 1942; Player-Manager for the team in 1948 and 1949; Played basketball for the Harlem Globetrotters, 1943-46; First African American player in the Boston Red Sox organization, 1950; Played for the Oakland Oaks, 1951-55; Played for the Los Angeles Angels, 1955-57; Player-Manager of the Ft. Worth Cats, 1958; Scouted for the Detroit Tigers, St. Louis Cardinals, and Montreal Expos.

Awards: Made eight Negro League All-Star Game appearances; Elected to the Alabama Sports Hall of Fame in 1993.

---

the Black Barons' season was over. Davis made $350 a month plus two dollars a day for meal money and another dollar if a player rode the bus all night instead of staying in a hotel. Davis played for the Globetrotters for three years through the 1946 season.

At the end of the 1947 season after Jackie Robinson had integrated the Major Leagues, the American League St. Louis Browns offered to sign Davis to a minor league contract, but he turned it down. Davis recognized the offer for what it was; a cynical attempt to put more people in the stands by a hapless and failing franchise. He returned to the Black Barons and became the team's player-manager in 1948. Although he led his team to the 1948 Negro World Series, his stint as manager will be remembered for the discovery of a 16-year-old outfielder named Willie Mays. Davis told Dave Kindred of *The Sporting News* about the first time he put Mays in the lineup: "I had a fella pick up ballplayers and bring 'em to the game. So I see this li'l ol' boy out of high school and I say to him, 'Don't you know if they catch you out here playing ball for money, they won't let you play high school ball no more?' And Willie says, 'I don't care.' So I called Kat (Mays's father) and Kat says if Willie wants to play, let him play. I let him play the second game of a doubleheader out in left field. My center fielder could out-run Willie, but he couldn't out-throw him." Mays, still a student at Fairfield High School, ended up driving in the winning run of the only game the Black Barons won in the 1948 Negro World Series. By 1949 Mays was gone and then in 1950 Davis also left.

Red Sox Rebuff

In 1950 the Boston Red Sox minor league affiliate in Scranton, Pennsylvania purchased Davis's contract for $7,500. Tom Hayes, the Black Barons owner, was promised another $7,500 if Davis was still with the team on May 15. Far from being well received, Davis was forced to stay and eat in the servants quarters on the road apart from the rest of the team and even dress in the visitors' locker room all by himself. When May fifteenth came around Davis was called into the general manager's office believing that he was on his way to Boston's Triple A affiliate. At that time he led the team in batting average (.333), home runs (3), and RBI (10). But the first black player in the Red Sox organization was not promoted. Davis was paid $500 and released. The organization claimed that it could not afford him. Davis finished the 1950 season in Guadalajara, Mexico and tried again to make the Red Sox in 1951, but he was cut.

After the disappointment with the Red Sox the 34-year-old ballplayer got a call from his old Black Barons and ACIPCO teammate Artie Shaw. Shaw was in California playing for the Oakland Oaks. Davis joined Shaw and played minor-league ball there for the next five seasons. Midway through the 1955 season Davis joined the Los Angeles Angels and played three years in southern California. From Los Angeles Davis secured a job as player-manager for the Fort Worth Cats in the Texas League. He stayed only one season with the Cats. At the age of 41 he had had enough of life on the road for a black ballplayer in the deep South of 1958. He was rarely able to eat in a restaurant or stay in a hotel, or even play in some ballparks. Davis went back to Birmingham in 1959 to manage the Black Barons, but by this time the team was a side show—a shadow of the squad's formidable past tradition. In the early sixties Davis coached and drove the team bus for the Harlem Globetrotters but then returned to baseball full-time. He served as a scout for the Detroit Tigers, St. Louis Cardinals (1968-76), and the Montreal Expos (1984-85). Davis was elected to the Alabama Sports Hall of Fame in 1993. According to the state shrine Davis was inducted as "One of the state's all-time best athletes—major league caliber in baseball and basketball. One of the most versatile players in baseball history, he could play any position expertly, as well as run, and hit with power and average." Lorenzo "Piper" Davis died on May 22, 1997 at the age of 79. Davis will be remembered as a proud representative of the Negro Leagues and one of the Black Barons' brightest stars. He told Kindred of *The Sporting News*: "Wasn't no crusading ... We looked to play ball is all ... Wasn't nothing the white Barons did, we couldn't do. We outdrew 'em playing in the same ballpark. We'd have a few whites come to see us, couple hundred a night. They appreciated good ball."

Sources

Books

Ribowsky, Mark. *A Complete History of the Negro Leagues: 1884 to 1955,* Birch Lane Press: New York, 1995.

Periodicals

The Sporting News, June 30 1997, p. 6.

Other

Alabama Archives website: http//www.asc.edu/archives/famous/sports/piper.htm. Major League Baseball website: http://www.majorleaguebaseball.com/nbl/nl35.sm.

Negro Leagues website: http://www.the-coop.com/nlb/players/davis.htm.

—Michael J. Watkins

Beauford Delaney

1901–1979

Painter

Beauford Delaney, one of the foremost American expatriate painters of the twentieth century and friend to such prominent artistic figures as James Baldwin, Georgia O'Keefe, and Henry Miller, was born in Knoxville, Tennessee on December 30, 1901. He was the eighth of ten children in the family, though only four survived into adulthood. Delaney's mother Delia Johnson Delaney was born a slave in Richmond, Virginia in 1865. She was a talented quilt maker and took in laundry and cleaned houses for a living. Delaney's father John Samuel Delaney came from a sharecropping family and served as a Methodist preacher and barber. The family enjoyed life in Knoxville, but soon moved to Jefferson City where Delaney's father served as pastor to a poor and rural black community. Since the position came with no salary the whole family was involved in working to support themselves and the fledgling church. Despite the lack of free time Delaney's mother encouraged Beauford and his brother Joe to draw scenes from the family Bible. In 1915 the family moved back to Knoxville so that Delaney's father could take on the pastor's position at the church where he had earlier been assistant pastor. By this time only Beauford and his brother Joe were at home and soon after Joe was sent to a private school because he had behavioral problems and needed discipline.

If Joe was somewhat wild as a boy, Beauford was just the opposite. He was an excellent student and at the age of 14 got a job cleaning tables after school at the Vine Street Cafe and also worked shining shoes. His first commissioned painting was for his boss at the shoe shine place. Delaney was supposed to paint a seascape in oil though he had never seen the sea nor worked in oil before. The painting so impressed his first patron that he introduced Delaney to a local impressionist painter named Lloyd Branson. Branson, a white man who admired the Confederacy, recognized the talent of the 14-year-old artist and agreed to give him art lessons in exchange for Delaney serving as his assistant. Delaney learned to work in pastels, oils, and watercolors and also received encouragement and financial help from Branson.

The Delaneys' life was fairly tranquil at this time in Knoxville until April 30, 1919 when John suffered a heart attack and died. In addition to this personal tragedy for Beauford there was a race riot in the city that same year which spoiled a relatively progressive atmosphere between the races in Knoxville. Delaney had been increasingly curious about the outside world and these two events seemed to give him the impetuous to explore. In September of 1923, with the encouragement and financial help of Branson, Delaney departed for Boston to pursue his dream of becoming an artist.

Life in Boston

Delaney arrived in Boston with a few letters of introduc-

At a Glance...

Born Beauford Delaney, December 30, 1901 in Knoxville, Tennessee; died on March 29, 1979 in Paris, France; son of John Samuel Delaney (a Methodist minister) and Delia Johnson Delaney; *Education:* Informally enrolled at several art schools in Boston including the Copely Society, the South Boston School of Art, and the Lowell Institute.

Career: Painted his first commissioned work at the age of 14; received first prize in his first New York show at the Whitney Studio Gallery, 1929; first one-man show at the New York Public Library, 1930; first fully expressionistic show at New York's Artist's Gallery, 1948; moved to Paris, France, 1953; first Paris exhibitions, 1954; first Parisian solo show at the Galerie Paul Facchetti, 1961; major retrospective show at the American Cultural Center, 1969; last major show while living at the Studio Museum in Harlem, 1978.

Awards: Received a $5,000 grant from the National Council of the Arts, 1968.

tion and a small amount of money Branson had given him. One of the first families he called on was the white, liberal, quasi-aristocratic Bryants. Through the Bryants Delaney was introduced in salons all over the city to the most influential people of liberal Boston society. This group was known in the 1920s as the Boston Radicals and included Edna St. Vincent Millay and a young Countee Cullen.

Despite the rich intellectual life Delaney was absorbing, he found that he still needed money. He found a job at Western Union working the midnight shift as a janitor. He seemed to live several different lives—a faceless janitor, a quiet and polite observer of elite Boston society, and a third self which he had yet to come to terms with—his homosexuality. It was also as a young man in Boston that Delaney began to hear voices in his head, a condition which would plague him for the rest of his life. As a respite from his own inner turmoil he turned to art. He was enrolled informally in several art schools because he was not allowed to register as a regular student because of his race. He took classes at the Copely Society, the South Boston School of Art, and the Lowell Institute. He also copied works at the Massachusetts Normal Art School and at different Boston museums. By the spring of 1929 when he left Boston he was no longer a "self-taught" artist. He had a solid classical background with influences from impressionists such as Claude Monet and John Springer Sargent. In addition he was introduced to activist politics which were some of the most radical racial ideas of his time.

Delaney and the Harlem Renaissance

Delaney arrived in Harlem in November of 1929 at the end of its famed "Renaissance" period. Some of the greatest African American minds of the time were active in Harlem—Cullen, Langston Hughes, W.E.B. Du Bois, and Marcus Garvey. Though the academic world of New York soared, the reality of arriving there knowing no one was somewhat more down to earth. On his first day in New York, Delaney was robbed of all his possessions and that night, while sleeping on a park bench, he had his shoes stolen. Through an artist contact he was able to get a job as a bellhop at the Grand Hotel and rent a small room. During his time off, he painted. He again gained entry into the elite class by painting portraits, though he also painted the people on the streets of Harlem. It was in these portraits for which he would receive no money that he began to experiment distorting faces and drawing more blurred images. It was this experimentation that led to paintings such as "Can Fire in the Park," which now hangs in the National Museum of American Art (NMAA). The NMAA Research Bulletin described the painting: "In its integration of brilliant color, bold patterning, rhythmic lines, and tactile surfaces, the work hovers between representation and abstraction."

Through his work in portraits, Delaney was invited to enter a show at the Whitney Studio Gallery, which he won. His work so impressed the owners, they hired him at the gallery. He then moved from Harlem to Greenwich Village. He followed his success at the Whitney with a one-man show at the New York Public Library and joined the Art Students' League, which included such influential artists as Don Freeman, Jackson Pollock, Charles Alston, and in November of 1930, his brother Joe. He and his brother differed in their approaches to art and life and rarely spoke about art though Joe did follow his brother to Greenwich Village in 1931. After his early success Delaney quit his job at the Whitney to devote himself to his art.

In the mid-thirties Delaney seemed to live separate lives. One life he lived with his African American artists and friends, and he lived the other with his white, bohemian, and largely homosexual friends. With his fellow black artists he was serious and committed as he shared the tribulations of being an artist of color in the midst of the

Depression. With his white friends he could be openly gay and enjoyed their care-free outlook on life as this circle of friends often included young men from wealthy families who helped support him. His two worlds never interacted. Dante Pavone was one of Delaney's white Bohemian friends with whom he would have a relationship from 1936 to 1953. Pavone was one of the painter's main subjects of this time period. Though Delaney was in love with Pavone, the two never had a physical relationship.

After a financially difficult summer of 1938 Delaney had a major breakthrough in the fall. He had two one-man shows and was featured in *Life Magazine*. In 1941 Delaney made another artistic stride in a one-man show at the Vendome Gallery. These new paintings were more modern, designed not to depict the likeness of the subject but to produce a particular compositional effect. His work was favorably reviewed by *The New York Times* and *Art Digest*. The Vendome show also presented a painting of nude white women and another called "Dark Rapture" which featured a 16-year-old James Baldwin with whom Delaney would remain friends for the rest of his life. Delaney saw much of himself in the young Baldwin who was also the son of a preacher struggling to find his own sexual identity. Delaney introduced him to jazz and classical music, the arts, and the New York intellectual scene.

Throughout the 1940s Delaney continued to battle psychological problems, suffered through grinding poverty, and in 1942 was the victim of a racist and homophobic gang and was badly beaten. Despite his physical and emotional difficulties, he continued to progress in his art moving fully into the modernist tradition. His 1945 "Portrait of James Baldwin," which the Philadelphia Museum of Art acquired in February of 1998, showed him moving more and more towards abstract expressionism. In 1945 Henry Miller published his essay "The Amazing and Invariable Beauford De Laney" and he became a Greenwich Village institution, albeit an eccentric one. In 1948 he had a solo exhibit at the Artists Gallery which was fully expressionist for which he was hailed by *The New York Times* and *Art News*. In the late forties and early fifties he had several one-man shows at the Roko Gallery, but in 1953 he had his final show in New York. His thoughts were turning to Paris, where all the great modernist painters worked. He made up his mind to visit the city and after a quick stay with his family in Knoxville, he embarked for Paris on August 28, 1953. He left his apartment and his studio with all his paintings intact believing he was only going to be gone for a short time, but he would never see New York again.

Life in Paris

Delaney found that he enjoyed Paris, though he spoke almost no French. There was little obvious racism and he was able to meet like-minded Americans in the cafes to discuss art and society. He even met Baldwin again by chance and though he intended to return to New York, he settled in France more solidly. In many ways Baldwin mentored Delaney in Paris as he had mentored the young writer in New York introducing Delaney to friends and taking him to night clubs and gay bars. Delaney stayed in Paris through the winter of 1953 painting almost continuously (and almost totally in the abstract) to keep the voices in his head at bay. He survived on small donations from his friends back in the United States. He had his first exhibitions in the summer of 1954 at the Salon des Réalités Nouvelles Musée d'Art Moderne and the Ninth Salon at the Musée des Beaux Arts. He continued to appear in exhibitions throughout the late fifties and though he would receive critical acclaim, he sold few paintings.

In the spring of 1955 Delaney showed his paintings in Madrid, Spain. In 1956 he appeared in a show of "Abstract American" artists which was exhibited in Paris and Iserholn, Germany. In May he had his first solo show in Europe. In 1961 Delaney had a major exhibition at the Galerie Paul Facchetti in Paris, though only two paintings sold. Personally this period of Delaney's life was full of turmoil. Though he appeared calm on the outside, his inner voices were tormenting him. After moving in with Baldwin in 1955 the two argued and Delaney moved out. The two quickly repaired the rift, and Delaney was sad and lonely whenever Baldwin was gone—which was quite often.

Delaney's mental and emotional problems became apparent during a trip to Greece in 1961. He began to hallucinate that people were trying to rob and murder him. On the boat from Italy to Greece he threw his overcoat which contained his wallet and passport over the side of the boat. He then jumped over the other side into the sea. He was soon discovered by a local fisherman cold and half-drowned. After attempting suicide in a hotel, he was put in a sanitarium. A friend brought him to a clinic where it was found that he had kidney and liver problems probably brought on by excessive drinking. Friends finally insisted that he see a psychiatrist who diagnosed acute paranoid delusions which were aggravated by his alcoholism. He checked into a clinic at Nogent where he spent his sixtieth birthday alone.

Delaney appeared to improve as he slowed his drinking and was put on medication to aid in quieting the voices. He moved to Rue Vercingétorix and began a fruitful part of his career. He was helped by his friend and patron Madame du Closel who also paid his rent from 1962 to 1975 with the occasional painting as compensation. Delaney was moved by Baldwin's descriptions of the civil rights battles in the United States and began a series of Rosa Parks paintings. In 1964 he held an exhibition in Copenhagen and in the fall at Farleigh Dickinson University. Delaney also had a one-man show of portraits and abstractions at the Galerie Lambert in Paris.

In the late sixties he balanced a growing notoriety and success with the struggle to keep his sanity. He had several shows in 1966 and 1967 including one at the American Embassy. The Embassy bought some of his paintings and hung them there. He also traveled to northern France, Venice, and Istanbul to be with Baldwin. In 1968 Delaney was awarded $5,000 by the National Council of the Arts in December. In March of 1969 he had a retrospective show at the American Cultural Center.

Through all of these professional high points and honors, Delaney suffered emotionally, especially when he drank. The murder of Martin Luther King Jr., sent him into a depression. During the Paris riots of 1968 he was wandering the streets dazed and disoriented. He was also having trouble with his memory. He gave much of his $5,000 grant to people who would come around him when he had money because he thought nothing of giving it all away. He made a short Christmas visit to Knoxville in 1969. His family was so distressed about his health that they urged him to stay, but he returned to France in January of 1970.

In the 1970s Delaney's mental condition became more unstable. He would forget or refuse to take his medication or start to drink again. He was unable to participate in a University of Tennessee exhibit that was created for him and his brother Joe. Ironically, as his health started to falter, his renown as a painter was growing. He had a painting at the Smithsonian Institute and was featured in several exhibitions as well as in *Jet* and *Playboy* magazines. In February of 1972 Delaney had a major show at the Speyer Gallery in Paris with tributes written by Henry Miller, James Jones, and Georgia O'Keefe. After undergoing a hernia operation and a short time of improvement, his health took a turn for the worse. Many of his friends thought he was suffering from the onset of Alzheimer's disease. He was becoming more forgetful, careless, and sloppy in appearance and inviting homeless people into his apartment where they would eventually stay and abuse his real friends who would stop by.

In the spring of 1975 Delaney was found sick and passed out in the street. Baldwin had himself declared responsible for his old friend's welfare and soon thereafter Delaney was committed to the St. Anne's Hospital for the Insane. Baldwin tried to get Delaney's affairs in order, but when he went to the painter's apartment he found it cleaned out with two angry homeless men residing there with whom he got into a fist fight. While he lay in the hospital in Paris, Delaney had the most important exhibition of his career back in New York in April of 1978. The Exxon Corporation and the National Endowment for the Arts sponsored a show of his at the Studio Museum in Harlem. The show, which highlighted his Paris work, was well received. But seemingly as ever, professional success was overshadowed by personal tragedy as his health was becoming more and more fragile. By the time of the exhibition he was not able to recognize anyone and slipped in and out of consciousness. Beauford Delaney died on March 29, 1979.

Death did not stop the rising acknowledgment of Delaney's mastery. His work was still being exhibited in places such as the Studio Museum in Harlem and the Michael Rosenfeld Gallery in the late 1990s. In Jabari Asim's article on Delaney's biography in the *Washington Post,* the reviewer offers some viewpoints on the twentieth century master: "To James Baldwin he was 'a cross between Br'er Rabbit and Saint Francis of Assisi.' To Henry Miller he was 'the summum and optimum of all the solar energies and radiances combined.' To most scholars and followers of African American art, Beauford Delaney was one of the most gifted men ever to wield a brush."

Sources

Books

Leeming, David. *Amazing Grace: A Life of Beauford Delaney.* Oxford University Press: NY, 1998.

Other

Information also found at the following websites: http://www.artincontext.com/listings/pages/artist/g/3en39z9g/exhib.htm.

http://nmaa-ryder.si.edu/deptdir/cursub/rb1-1-21.htm.

http://www.libertynet.org/pma/pressrel/delaney.htm.

http://www.washingtonpost.com/wp-srv/style/books/reviews/amazinggrace.htm.

—Michael J. Watkins

Dorothy Donegan

1922–1998

Pianist

Dorothy Donegan rose to prominence in the male-dominated world of jazz music with unique flamboyancy and musical style. Mixing swing, boogie-woogie, vaudeville, pop, ragtime, and classical music styles with a heavy dose of "visual antics" and an outrageous sense of humor, she was best known as a performer rather than as a recording artist. While her recordings remain strikingly absent from most jazz anthologies, she made a lasting impression on her art form.

Donegan was born in Chicago on April 6, 1922. Her father, Donazell Donegan, was a cook on the Chicago, Burlington, and Quincy Railroad, and her mother, Ella Donegan, contributed to the family income by renting out rooms in the family's large apartment. Donegan's mother used this rent money to support her daughter's music studies. Donegan readily admitted that it was her mother who truly appreciated her talent, who listened to her, and encouraged her to put feeling into her music. Her mother even served as her first business manager.

With her mother's encouragement, Donegan began taking piano lessons when she was five years old and obtained her musical education in Chicago's public schools. For the first five years, she studied with Alfred N. Simms. Later, the legendary Walter Henri Dyett, who tutored many celebrated jazz musicians, worked with her while she was a student at DuSable High School. She may have claimed, as Sally Placksin noted in *American Women in Jazz,* that she practiced to avoid housework, but clearly her dedication exploited her natural talent. By the age of ten, she was already performing as a church organist, and began playing jazz professionally in local nightclubs during her high-school years. As a 14-year-old, she played in southside Chicago nightclubs for $1 a night and even crossed the color barrier by performing at Costello's Grill in downtown Chicago. At the age of 17, she was hired to play jazz piano with The Bob Tinsley Band.

In 1942, Donegan recorded her first album of blues and boogie-woogie on the Bluebird label. However, despite her early jazz success, she still aspired to be a classical pianist. Consequently, she continued her classical music education, studying piano with Rudolph Ganz at the Chicago Musical College and later attending the University of Southern California. One year after releasing her first jazz album, Donegan became the first African

At a Glance...

Born Dorothy Donegan, April 6, 1922 in Chicago; died May 19, 1998, in Los Angeles; daughter of Donazell Donegan, a railroad chef, and Ella (Day) Donegan; married and divorced to John McClain, Walter Eady, and William Miles; children: John, Donovan. *Education:* Studied at the Chicago Conservatory of Music; Chicago Music College, 1942-44; University of Southern California, 1953-54.

Career: Classical and jazz pianist who performed in the United States, Canada, and Europe; selected festivals included Newport Jazz Festival, 1978; Kool Jazz Festival, 1981; Festival De Frauen, 1988; Floating Jazz Festival, 1991; White House Jazz Festival, 1993; Playboy Jazz Festival, 1994.

Selected awards: American Jazz Masters Hall of Fame, National Endowment for the Arts, 1992.

American performer and first jazz pianist to perform in concert at Chicago's Orchestra Hall. In the first half of her program, she performed Grieg and Rachmaninoff, then switched to a jazz format in the second half of her performance. The concert earned Donegan a front-page review in the *Chicago Tribune* and caught the attention of legendary jazz pianist Art Tatum.

Intrigued by Donegan's "wide repertory and blizzard-fast fingers," Tatum paid a visit to her home. She played for him, and he shared some of his techniques with her. He quickly became her mentor, and she particularly liked to watch how he "fingered all the runs." While Donegan's style reflected the art of other such jazz greats as Earl Hine and Errol Garner, she was most strongly influenced by Tatum.

Defined Her Own Style

In defining her own style, Donegan remarkably blended her varied musical talents, often putting together spontaneous melodies from unrelated songs. She moved easily between the worlds of jazz and classical music, often blending them within a single composition. As Don Heckman of the *Los Angeles Times* pointed out, Donegan was best known "for her versatility, for her ability to move, without a moment's hesitation, from boogie-woogie, to stride, to a classical piece to straight-ahead contemporary jazz." "[Y]ou never know where she's going to go, she's so creative she builds the song as she goes along," commented fellow musician Illinois Jacquet in the notes accompanying the 1991 recording of *Live at the Floating Jazz Festival.* "She can do that because she knows so many songs and has such a great ear.... She doesn't play in bands because she's a band all by herself." Donegan was blessed, as Heckman remarked in the *Los Angeles Times,* with "a musical imagination that saw no limits, that found fascinating, unexpected linkages between seemingly unrelated music."

In addition to blending different musical styles, Donegan would add humor to her performances. As Ben Ratliff related in the *New York Times,* "She often would act out songs, mocking their words; do devastating parodies of pianists and singers, especially if they were in the audience, or get up and shake her hips while keeping up a left-handed riff." Donegan perceived herself as an entertainer and justified her antics by coupling them with her supreme musical talent. In a 1991 interview with Whitney Balliet of the *New Yorker,* she recounted a story regarding her performance style. In the 1950s, the government taxed clubs an additional 20 percent if they had dancers or singers in addition to musicians. As Donegan described it, "I was doing a lot of wiggling then, moving my derriere around and snapping my fingers and carrying on, and the I.R.S. decided that I was entertainment and put the tax on. That hurt business, so I went to the musicians' union, and the union asked, can she wiggle as long as she's playing? And they said yes, and took the tax off. A wiggle never hurt anybody."

Donegan's flamboyant, highly energetic performances complemented her incredible musical talent. Not only was she in constant motion, but she was also known for her repertoire of off-color jokes. As Antoinette Handy pointed out in *Black Women in American Bands and Orchestras,* Donegan was often referred to as "the wild one," "the triumphantly unfettered, "the shoulder-shaking, finger-popping, hip-slapping lioness of piano rooms." At the same time, however, critics also were quick to add that Donegan was, "wild but polished," "possessor of enormous technical skill," and "brilliant, ridiculously talented."

Performed Nationally in Intimate Clubs

Bedecked in opulent gowns and turbans, Donegan had a natural rapport with her audiences. Her playing style and showmanship were well-suited for intimate clubs, and it was in this venue where she most often performed. Following a stint in Hollywood, where she turned down a five-year contract with MGM Studios to appear in the United Artists film *Sensation of 1945,* and on Broadway in the show *Star Time,* Donegan played in jazz clubs in Los Angeles and New York. She also performed in a traveling show with the legendary African American comedienne, Moms Mabley. In 1949, Donegan headlined the cast of the first all-black show at Hollywood's famous Tom Breneman Café.

During the 1950s, word of Donegan's skill and showmanship spread. She began a series of engagements at the London House in Chicago, and was recruited by other top clubs in New York, Chicago, and Los Angeles. Donegan's managers, Music Corporation of America, also signed her to a ten-year, $3,000 a week contract with the Embers, a posh supper club on East 54th Street in New York City. Her husband, John McClain, confidently promised to reimburse the club's owner if he ever lost money on Donegan's performances. It was a debt he never had to pay.

McClain owned several clubs in Los Angeles and Donegan played in many of them. He admired her virtuosity on the piano and believed, according to Leslie Grouse in *Madame Jazz,* that "she should have received more recognition for being one of the best from Bach and Beethoven to dirty blues and boogie-woogie." During their marriage, McClain helped Donegan manage her career. They had a son, John, who is also a musician.

Donegan and McClain eventually divorced in 1959, although they remained good friends. She then married Walter Eady, with whom she had another son, Donovan. Donegan and Eady also divorced and she was married for a third time to William Miles. That marriage also ended in divorce. With characteristic humor, Donegan told Balliet, "I think I've been married three times too many. Every time there were dry periods in the sixties and seventies, I'd marry again. Then, when I got work, I'd drift away." She also told the *Los Angeles Times* in 1992, "I think artists should be by themselves."

Troubled by Recording Difficulties

There is much debate surrounding the existence of Donegan's early recordings. McClane confirmed, for instance, that she had recorded a number of albums for the Decca, Continental, and Capitol labels during the 1950s. However, neither he nor Donegan knew what happened to them. As Placksin recounted in *American Women in Jazz,* Donegan believed Decca sold her recordings to a company which combined them with other recordings by women pianists. "They put us all together like a supermarket of goods," Donegan claimed.

By the 1970s, Donegan was an established jazz performer and supported herself by playing in festivals in the United States, Canada, and Europe. Although she appeared most often as a soloist, she also performed occasionally as part of The Dorothy Donegan Trio. In addition, she maintained her reputation as an accomplished classical pianist. In 1976, she performed a Grieg concerto with the New Orleans Philharmonic at Tulane University and with the Southeast Symphony in Los Angeles.

"A wiggle never hurt anybody."

Although Donegan performed frequently throughout the world, she never achieved true stardom. She attributed her lack of fame, in part, to racism within classical music. Donegan performed in an era when African Americans received few opportunities to play with symphony orchestras. Although racism was less prevalent within the world of jazz, Donegan often had to battle sexism. Throughout her long career, she was always quick to point out the discrepancies she perceived between male and female jazz performers. While female jazz musicians often asked their male counterparts to perform with them onstage, the men rarely reciprocated. While Donegan had, according to Grouse, "the musical mastery, charisma, and prestige to impress any man [she] calls to play for [her] group," she rarely received return invitations. She bluntly told reporters that sexism caused her obscurity, along with "her insistence on being paid at the same scale as her male colleagues," as Ratliff pointed out. In a 1958 article in *Ebony,* Donegan remarked, "I've snowed them [male jazz pianists] all under except one (the late Art Tatum). Most of them play like women."

Donegan continued to perform until the fall of 1997 when health problems, including diabetes and cancer, forced her to end her career. On May 19, 1998, Donegan died of colon cancer at her home in Los Angeles. While this "queen of the keys" may not have achieved the fame she desired or deserved, she certainly left a distinctive mark on the development of contemporary jazz. Donegan was imbued with a talent and spirit which burst forth not only through her fingertips, but also through her feet, which danced on the pedals. Often caught up in the intensity and energy of her music, Jacquet remarked that Donegan appeared as though "[s]he'd probably still be playing if someone hadn't told her it was time to clear the theater." She was what Grouse termed a "witty, wily, and warm performer," and for this she will always be remembered.

Selected discography

Piano Boogie, Bluebird, 1942.
Dorothy Donegan's Musical Compositions, 1942-1954, 1954.
Dorothy Donegan, 1959.
Makin' Whoopee, Black and Blue, 1979.
Brown Gal, Krazy Kat, 1987.
Dorothy Donegan Live!, Capitol, 1990.
Incredible Dorothy Donegan Trio, Chiaroscuro Records, 1991.
Live at the 1990 Floating Jazz Festival, Chiaroscuro Records, 1991.
Dorothy Donegan Trio, Chiaroscuro Records, 1994.
Dorothy Romps—A Piano Retrospective (1953-1979), Rosetta Records, 1994.
Explosive Dorothy Donegan, Audiophile, 1995.

Sources

Books

Dahl, Linda, *Stormy Weather: The Music and Lives of a Century of Jazz Women,* Pantheon Books, 1984, pp. 72-73.
Grouse, Leslie, *Madame Jazz,* Oxford University Press, 1995, pp. 8, 10, 15-17, 21, 183-89.
Handy, D. Antoinette, *Black Women in American Bands and Orchestras,* The Scarecrow Press, 1981, pp. 184-85.
Hine, Darlene, Brown, Elsa, Terborg-Penn, Rosalyn, eds., *Black Women in America,* Indiana University Press, 1993, pp. 345-46.
Placksin, Sally, *American Women in Jazz,* Seaview Books, 1982, pp. 193-95, 197.
Smith, Jessie, ed., *Notable Black American Women*, Gale Research, 1992, pp. 283-85.
Southern, Eileen. *Biographical Dictionary of Afro-American and African Musicians.*
Walker-Hill, Helen, *Piano Music by Black Women Composers,* Greenwood Press, 1992, pp. 32-33.

Articles

Ebony, July 1958, pp. 15-19.
Los Angeles Times, May 21, 1998, p. B10; May 22, 1998, p. F23.
New Yorker, February 18, 1991, pp. 37-38, 40-41.
New York Times, May 22, 1998, p. A23.
Northeast Ohio Jazz Society Jazz Central, July 1998, pp. 7-8.
Record Notes from Live at the Floating Jazz Festival, 1991.
Time, November 3, 1958, p. 78.

—Lisa S. Weitzman

Will Downing

19(?)(?)—

Vocalist

Rising from anonymity as a journeyman session singer in the 1970s to become a popular solo crooner in the 1990s, Will Downing has been a popular fixture on the mellow jazz music scene since releasing his debut album in 1988. Serving as "a reliable source for potent R&B music that nourishes the mind," according to *Billboard* magazine, he successfully bridged the gap between contemporary jazz and rhythm and blues with hits such as "In My Dreams" and "A Love Supreme." Downing has been especially popular in the United Kingdom where, for over a decade, he has been a big draw in major concert venues and his albums have frequently gone gold or platinum.

Built Crossover Appeal

Downing's crossover appeal helped him build audiences in both the jazz/adult and uptempo rhythm and blues genres. The singer frequently covers R&B classics and jazz standards on his albums, and has had hits with remakes of songs such as Deniece Williams' "Free," Rose Royce's "Wishing on a Star," Nat King Cole's "When Sunny Gets Blue," and Phyllis Hyman's "I Don't Want to Lose You." In a 1993 article in *Billboard,* Downing referred to his singing as "warm, sensitive, and sensual at the same time. Very inviting and trusting. There are a lot of singers who sing at you and not to you. That's the kind of vocalist I try not to be." Because he likes to create an intimate mood with listeners, Downing prefers performing in small settings rather than large arenas.

"I grew up listening to jazz and I was born when soul music was at its height," said Downing, according to the Mercury Records home page on the Internet. While attending Erasmus Hall High School in Brooklyn, he listened fervently to singers such as Donny Hathaway, Aretha Franklin, Ray Charles, and Nat "King" Cole, all of whom influenced his style. In *Billboard,* Downing said that he is also a long-time fan of D.J. Rogers, Stevie Wonder, and Phil Perry.

Became Active Session Singer

Downing kept busy in the recording studio in the 1970s as a background singer for Rose Royce, Billy Ocean, Jennifer Holliday, Stephanie Mills, Kool and the Gang,

> **At a Glance...**
>
> Born in Brooklyn, NY.
>
> **Career:** Was background session singer for Jennifer Holliday, Kool & the Gang, Billy Ocean, Stephanie Mills, and others, 1970s; began working with producer/performer Arthur Baker, mid-1980s; contributed vocals to recordings by Wally Jump Jr. & Criminal Element, mid-1980s; solo albums: *Will Downing*, 1988; *Come Together as One*, 1989; *A Dream Fulfilled*, 1991; *Love's the Place to Be*, 1993; *Moods*, 1995; *Invitation Only*, 1997.
>
> **Awards and honors:** Best Album of the Year (*A Dream Fulfilled*), Vocalist of the Year, and Best Live Performer of the Year, all from *Blues & Soul* magazine, 1992.
>
> **Addresses:** *Record company*—c/o Mercury, 825 Fifth Avenue, New York, NY 10019.

Nona Hendryx, and others. His career got a major boost after he met the producer/performer Arthur Baker in the mid-1980s. At that time Downing teamed up with Baker's group, Wally Jump Jr. and the Criminal Element, whose members included Wally Jump, Craig Derry, Sonny Calvin, Dwight Hawkes, Jeff Smith, and Michigan and Smiley. Downing's voice contributed to a number of dance hits by the group, including "Don't Push Your Luck."

After recording songs for Baker's label as part of Wally Jump Jr. and the Criminal Element, Downing signed a deal with Island Records. Success came quickly with his first album as a solo artist—a self-titled LP released in 1988. The album generated two hits in England that launched the LP into the Top 20 overseas, including the chart-topping "A Love Supreme." Downing assumed more control over his next album, *Come Together as One*, serving as producer, as well as co-writer on many of the songs with Brian Jackson. While skimming the edges of popularity in the United States, this 1989 release was very popular abroad and increased the singer's following across the Atlantic. Each of Downing's first two albums sold over 100,000 copies in the United Kingdom, and built up legions of fans for the new solo star. Their popularity resulted in Downing playing numerous sold-out shows at the Hammersmith Ballroom, a renowned concert hall in London.

Downing's career soared with his acclaimed *A Dream Fulfilled*, which hit the stores in 1991. This album made him an even bigger concert draw, and he toured on a steady basis for nearly three years after its release. His popularity even drew the attention of England's royal family, resulting in an invitation for him to perform for Prince Charles and Princess Diana in the renowned Prince's Trust Concert in England. In 1992 *Blues & Soul* magazine bestowed three major awards on him: Best Album of the Year, Vocalist of the Year, and Best Live Performer of the Year.

The singer continued riding the crest of fame in 1993 with his first release on the Mercury label, *Love's the Place to Be*, which remained a fixture on *Billboard* magazine's Black Album Chart for an entire year. In her review of the album in *Billboard*, Danyel Smith wrote that "the soulful croonings of Will Downing are bluesy, romantic, and most of all, formidable." Joan Anderman's review in the *Boston Globe* added that the singer is "blessed with a warm voice and sensible enough to avoid excess ornamentation." Downing's first single release from the album, "Have I Told You," was referred to as "a pulsating strong song" by Talise D. Moorer in the *Amsterdam News*. Once again, Downing struck a major chord with British listeners, with buyers bringing home 300,000 copies of *Love's the Place to Be* to make it a certified platinum release.

In 1995, Downing created the album *Moods*, which reflected his own experiences and observations on everyday life and relationships. The album was a highly personal one for the singer, not only because its subject matter was a compilation of his thoughts on life, but also because it featured many of Downing's long-time friends and creative collaborators, including Rex Rideout, Ronnie Foster, and Art Porter. He tapped into the talents of his musician friends again for the 1997 release, *Invitation Only*, an album that continued the evolution of his observations on love and relationships.

Ignored Popular Trends

In recent years Downing has often appeared in concert with his long-time friend, the gifted saxophonist Najee. During the 1990s he lamented changes on the music scene that have reduced his listening audience on the radio. "Within the last six years, the music has changed so much," he told *Ebony Man* in 1998. "What I used to do was considered the norm and rap was the specialty. Now it's just flipped. Radio stations look at what I do as quiet storm-type of music. They only play it at night, and then I don't get the radio and listener play that could be possible." Despite the trends working against him, Downing continues to stay the musical course he originally charted for himself. As he told *Billboard* in 1993, "There's a definite place for my type of music. The public has to make a concerted effort to let the radio stations know that they really want to hear it. This music was once the mainstream. Now it's becoming alternative."

Selected discography

Will Downing, Island, 1988.
Come Together as One, Island, 1989.
A Dream Fulfilled, Mercury, 1991.
Love's the Place to Be, Mercury, 1993.
Moods, Mercury, 1995.
Invitation Only, Mercury, 1997.

Sources

Books

Larkin, Colin, ed., *The Guinness Encyclopedia of Popular Music, Volume 3,* Guinness Publishing, 1992, p. 976.

Periodicals

Amsterdam News, October 30, 1997, p. 49.
Atlanta Constitution, November 19, 1997, p. B2.
Billboard, August 14, 1993, p. 18; September 27, 1997, p. 26; April 4, 1997, p. 65.
Boston Globe, November 26, 1997, p. E6.
Ebony Man, January 1998, p. 6.

Other

Additional information for this profile was obtained from the Web site of Mercury Records on the Internet, as well as from the Motown Records Publicity & Media Relations Division.

—Ed Decker

Ramona Hoage Edelin

1945—

Organization executive

Ramona Hoage Edelin is an intellectual in action. Since 1988 she has been the chief executive of the National Urban Coalition. She works to bring educational opportunities to schoolchildren in urban environments and to shape a range of government urban policies from her Washington D.C. office. Edelin came to her activist career from a background in higher education. The holder of Ph.D. degree in philosophy, she made a conscious decision to put her ideals to work in the everyday world. Yet she is still widely known for an idea: Edelin introduced the term "African American" into general circulation, and may in fact have coined it.

Edelin's educational background began with the environment of her youth. Both her grandfather and her mother were university professors. Born Ramona Hoage in Los Angeles on September 4, 1945, she moved with her parents to college campus areas in Atlanta, Georgia, Orangeburg, South Carolina, and Carbondale, Illinois. Her early childhood education took place at the Oglethorpe Elementary School in Atlanta, a "laboratory school" run by Atlanta University. Laboratory schools, often established in inner-city areas by institutions of higher learning, strive to implement progressive educational ideas and to develop the talents of exceptional urban youngsters. This one launched Ramona Hoage on a stellar educational career.

Standout Student at Fisk University

Graduating from the Stockbridge School in Stockbridge, Massachusetts in 1963, she entered Fisk University in Nashville. In the top rank of the nation's historically African American institutions, Fisk offered a competitive environment. But she compiled an impressive record that included a B.A. (magna cum laude) in philosophy, election to Phi Beta Kappa, and numerous university honors. She graduated in 1967, and soon afterward married Kenneth Edelin, a recent graduate of Nashville's prestigious Meharry Medical College; they divorced some years later.

Kenneth Edelin's tour of military service sent the young couple to England, where Ramona cared for their son, Kenneth, Jr., and somehow found time to complete an M.A. degree in philosophy at the University of East Anglia in Norwich, England. Returning to the United States, she enrolled in the doctoral program in philosophy at Boston University and settled on the writings of the pioneering black intellectual W. E. B. Du Bois as a dissertation topic. In a 1996 interview with *Emerge* she recalled that "what I needed to do was prove to a department of philosophy that, in fact, Dr. Du Bois was a philosopher." "I don't think anybody has said as well [as Du Bois], let alone better, what our reality is," she added.

Popularized Term "African American"

Edelin's academic career was off to an impressive start

At a Glance...

Born September 4, 1945 in Los Angeles; only child of George and Annette Hoage. Married Kenneth Edelin, a physician, ca. 1967 (later divorced); children Kenneth, Jr., Kimberley. *Education:* B.A., Fisk University, 1967; M.A., University of East Anglia (Norwich, England), 1969; Ph.D., Boston University, 1981.

Career: Chief executive officer of action and advocacy organization. Joined faculty of Northeastern University, 1972; contributed to founding and naming of program in African American Studies, early 1970s, possibly originating term "African American" at that time; became program chairperson, 1974; moved to Washington, D.C., 1977, as executive assistant to president, National Urban Coalition; named director of operations, 1979; named vice president of operations, 1981; named vice president of programs and policy, 1982; became chief executive officer, 1988; promoted usage of term "African American" in meeting with Rev. Jesse Jackson, its key popularizer, 1988; headed commission promoting appointment of African American women at beginning of Clinton administration, 1992; spearheaded *Say YES to a Youngster's Future* educational program, late 1980s–.

Awards: Phi Beta Kappa, Fisk University, 1967; "Women to Watch," *Ebony* magazine, 1982.

Addresses: National Urban Coalition, 727 15th St. NW, 9th floor, Washington, DC 20005.

---

even before she completed her dissertation and received the Ph.D. degree in 1981. She taught at various institutions in the Boston area: Emerson College, Brandeis University, and Northeastern University, where she founded and chaired the school's program in "African American Studies," a new description that diverged from the usual "Afro-American Studies" and "Black Studies" usages of the time. "I had also used it in my scholarship for years before that," she told *Emerge*.

While the precise moment of the new term's coinage is unknown, Edelin several times took crucial steps toward gaining for it the attention of the general public. The most important of these steps was raising the issue at a December 1988 meeting of black leaders chaired by the Rev. Jesse Jackson. Jackson adopted the "African American" usage, paving the way for its general acceptance. As a result, Jackson has sometimes been credited as the originator of the term, but Edelin recalled in the *Emerge* interview that initial press reports of the meeting correctly attributed the idea to her. She continued to argue in favor of the adoption of "African American," telling *Ebony* in 1989 that "[c]alling ourselves African Americans is the first step in the cultural offensive. Our cultural renaissance can change our lot in the nation and around the world."

As might be gathered from that statement, the focus of Edelin's efforts in life had changed fundamentally since the days of her academic career in the 1970s. To put it simply, she had begun to hunger for concrete applications of her ideas. As she put it in the *Emerge* interview, "I ... saw the opportunity to apply much of what I had developed intellectually to help, because I am just despairing of the condition of our people. When I say despairing, I simply mean that I decided that I had to do what I could do about it." In 1977 she took what must have been a drastic step: she relinquished her position at Northeastern and joined the National Urban Coalition as an executive assistant to then president Carl Holman.

Became National Urban Coalition (NUC) CEO

The NUC had been founded in 1967 in response to the riots that paralyzed many large American cities in the summer of that year, and it proved a perfect fit with Ramona Hoage Edelin's new ambitions. She rose steadily through the ranks, becoming director of operations in 1979, vice president of operations in 1982, and chief executive officer in 1988. The organization aimed to make policy recommendations that benefited inner cities, and under Edelin's tenure has particularly emphasized the implementation of innovative educational programs that work to open up opportunities for inner-city young people. As of 1996, Edelin oversaw educational, economic, and leadership development programs in 32 cities in 19 states.

The NUC's largest program is *Say YES to a Youngster's Future,* which works in 100 schools nationwide to bring up-to-date math, science, and technology instruction not only to young students, but to their families and teachers as well. Other programs include the M. Carl Holman Leadership Development Institute (a think tank that brings together leaders of diverse organizations to explore ways in which they might affect the course of public policy) and the Executive Leadership Program, which attempts to instill leadership qualities into selected students.

Edelin's profile grew higher through the 1990s. A familiar face in official Washington, she chaired a National Political Congress of Black Women commission established in 1992 in an effort to place black women in prominent positions within the administration of President Bill Clinton. Journalists often sought her out for opinions, especially on issues facing African American young people, and in 1998 she participated in a Black Entertainment Television roundtable discussion entitled "Empowering Our Communities: A Talk with Vice President Al Gore." Through the late 1990s, Ramona Hoage Edelin continued to work on the front lines of change, as a committed thinker and doer.

Sources

Books

Smith, Jessie Carney, ed. *Notable Black American Women,* Gale, 1992.

Periodicals

Ebony, July 1989, p. 76.
Emerge, September 1996, pp. 34–37.
Jet, January 16, 1989, p. 53; December 21, 1992, p. 5.
Omaha World Herald, April 8, 1990, p. 14A.
Washington Post, April 2, 1998.

—James M. Manheim

Roberta Flack

1940—

Singer, songwriter

So timeless is the appeal of Roberta Flack's soulful singing that some of her hits of the 1970s are now being embraced by a generation of listeners far too young to remember when those hits were current. Her style, which has remained fairly consistent over the decades, contains hints of jazz, gospel, and blues. Flack's music has a broad appeal that makes a mockery of the demographic borders of race, age, and gender.

Flack was born on February 10, 1940, in Black Mountain, a small town in the mountains of North Carolina. Both of her parents, Laron and Irene Flack, were skilled musicians. Laron was a self-taught jazz piano stylist, while Irene, with the benefit of a few formal lessons, played piano for the local Methodist church. At an early age Roberta picked out melodies while sitting in her parents' laps. When she was about five years old, the family moved to Virginia and settled in Arlington, a suburb of Washington, D.C. Laron found work as a draftsman and Irene got a job cleaning and cooking at a high school, so Flack grew up in a comfortable working-class setting.

Interested Mainly in Music and Food

Flack began taking formal piano lessons at the age of nine. At 13, her rendition of "Carry Me Back to Old Virginny" earned her second prize in a state-wide piano competition among black students. Her only other interests were church, food, and school. As a result, she became a very religious, obese scholar. "I weighed over 200 pounds. All I did was play the piano and eat all day ... and study and go to church," she was quoted as saying in a 1971 *Ebony* article.

Flack graduated from high school at 15 and earned a piano scholarship to Howard University. After a short time, however, she switched her major from piano to music education, which required her to study voice in addition to instrumental music. Flack graduated from Howard in 1958 with a B.A. in music education and began working on a master's degree, but when her father died in 1959, she quit school in order to go to work to help the family out financially. Still only a teenager, Flack took a job teaching English at an all-black rural school in Farmville, North Carolina. The following year, she found a position teaching junior high

At a Glance...

Born February 10, 1940, in Black Mountain, NC; daughter of Laron (a draftsman) and Irene (a cook and cleaning person) Flack; married Stephen Novosel (a jazz bassist), 1966 (divorced 1972); children: Bernard Wright. *Education:* Howard University, BA, 1958; University of Massachusetts, postgraduate work in music education.

Career: English teacher, Farmville, NC, 1959; English and music teacher, Washington, D.C. public schools, 1960-67; began performing in local clubs, mid-1960s; became full-time performer, 1967; Atlantic Records recording artist, 1968--; released first album, *First Take*, 1969; starred in ABC television special, "The First Time Ever," 1973; Has toured extensively worldwide since 1969. Has also scored for motion pictures and television, performed as a concert pianist, and conducted opera; formed own music publishing and record production company.

Awards: *Down Beat* Female Vocalist of the year, 1971-73; Roberta Flack Human Kindness Day, Washington, D.C., 1972; Grammy Awards for: Record of the Year, 1972, for "The First Time Ever I Saw Your Face," and 1973, for "Killing Me Softly With His Song;" Best Pop Vocal Performance by a Duo (with Donny Hathaway), 1972, for "Where Is the Love?;" Best Pop Vocal Performance by a Female Solo Artist, 1973, for "Killing Me Softly."

Addresses: *Record company*—Atlantic Records, 75 Rockefeller Plaza, New York, NY 10019; *Booking agency*—Associated Booking Corp., 1995 Broadway, Suite 501, New York, NY 10023.

grades in the Washington D.C. school system, where she spent the next seven years.

Meanwhile, music remained a central part of Flack's life outside of the workplace. She directed church choirs and began taking voice lessons, concentrating primarily on opera, with Frederick "Wilkie" Wilkerson. She also began taking on voice students of her own. Eventually, Wilkerson convinced Flack to give pop music a try. At first she considered the suggestion an insult, but over time she began making appearances at local clubs, both as a pop singer and as a piano accompanist for others. By 1967 Flack had gained a healthy local following, and was singing five nights a week at a nightclub on K Street in Washington. She was discovered there by Henry Yaffe, who brought her to his trendy new Georgetown club Mr. Henry's. By 1968 she was drawing such a crowd to the club that Yaffe opened a special room at his other location near Capitol Hill to showcase her talent. She also found time for a social life during this period, culminating in her 1966 marriage to Stephen Novosel, a jazz bassist.

Demo Led to Atlantic Contract

As Flack's style continued to mature, she began to draw the attention of many show-biz types, who swarmed to hear her perform when they were in town. Among those celebrity admirers was jazz pianist Les McCann. McCann was so impressed with Flack's singing that he made a demo tape and took it to Atlantic Records, which immediately signed Flack to a recording contract. Flack's debut album, *First Take*, was released in late 1969. It sold well over 100,000 copies, but that was only a warmup for what was to take place over the next few years.

Flack emerged as a superstar of major proportions in 1970. Her follow-up album, *Chapter Two*, sold over a million copies within a few months of its release. Flack was suddenly in demand for live performances everywhere. She played at the Montreux Pop Festival in Switzerland, the Newport Jazz Festival, and at other important festivals and top nightclubs across the United States. She also created a sensation with her guest performance on a 1970 Bill Cosby television special. She followed that with many other TV appearances. Flack ended the year with a triumphant concert in front of a capacity crowd at New York's Philharmonic Hall in December. *Downbeat* magazine named Flack Female Vocalist of the Year for 1970, breaking a string of 18 straight years in which Ella Fitzgerald received that honor.

Flack's third album, *Quiet Fire*, was released in 1971, and it quickly won both great critical acclaim and strong sales. Later that year, Flack's single "The First Time Ever I Saw Your Face" was used in the soundtrack of the Clint Eastwood film *Play Misty for Me*. Its exposure in that movie helped catapult the song to the top of the pop charts. The song earned Flack her first Grammy award in 1972, and also sparked a new wave of sales for her first album, on which it had originally appeared. Although 1972 was a tumultuous year in Flack's personal life, with her marriage to Novosel ending in divorce, it was another banner year in her professional life. She initiated an ongoing collaboration with singer Donny Hathaway with the release of their joint album *Roberta Flack and Donny Hathaway.* That album spawned the hit single "You've Got a Friend." The pair also earned a Grammy for the single "Where is the Love?" as Best Vocal Performance by a Duet, Group, or Chorus.

Slew Audiences Softly

Flack shone as one of the music industry's brightest stars through the middle part of the 1970s. By this time, her sound was beginning to veer away from her gospel and jazz roots toward more of a middle-of-the-road pop sensibility. Her 1973 album *Killing Me Softly,* which featured the number one hit "Killing Me Softly With His Song," went gold within two weeks of its release. She earned Grammies for both the single and the album. Flack topped the charts again the following year with the single "Feel Like Makin' Love," and her 1975 album of the same title quickly went gold, like its predecessors. Following this string of successes, Flack decided to slow down the pace of her recording career in order to both assume more creative control over her projects, and to spend more time pursuing other interests. She began doctorate studies at the University of Massachusetts in Amherst. She also launched her own music production and publishing company, and became involved in composing and producing musical scores for television and motion pictures.

Even with her energies distributed more widely, Flack was able to put out another successful album, *Blue Lights in the Basement,* in 1977. Although critics were generally more reserved in their praise than they had been in the past, *Blue Lights* was among the top selling albums of the year. It included a duet with Hathaway, "The Closer I Get to You," which reached number two on the pop charts. Flack joined forces again with Hathaway a few years later to record the album *Roberta Flack Featuring Donny Hathaway,* which included the hits "You Are My Heaven" and "Back Together Again." Before the album's 1980 release, however, this fruitful collaboration came to an abrupt end when Hathaway jumped to his death from the 15th floor of a New York hotel.

Celebrated Love With Bryson

Flack wasted little time in finding another male singing partner. She recorded two albums in the early 1980s with vocalist Peabo Bryson, *Live and More* (1980) and *Born to Love* (1983). The latter album contained the major hit "Tonight I Celebrate My Love." Meanwhile,

Flack kept busy composing and producing the soundtrack for the 1981 movie *Bustin' Loose,* starring Richard Pryor and Cicely Tyson. She also released two Atlantic albums in 1982: *I'm The One,* and a collection of greatest hits called *The Best of Roberta Flack.* During the mid-1980s, Flack was absent from the recording studio. She returned after a five-year hiatus to make the album *Oasis* in 1988. *Oasis,* whose title track rose to number one on the R&B charts, represented a bit of a shift in musical strategy. It was a much more heavily-produced album than her previous efforts, although the intimacy and depth of her vocals was as clear as ever. The album featured support from a host of celebrity collaborators that included Quincy Jones, Maya Angelou, Ashford & Simpson, Marvin Hamlisch, and Brenda Russell.

> "I weighed over 200 pounds. All I did was play the piano and eat all day ... and study and go to church."

1991 found Flack in the studio once again. The resulting album, *Set the Night to Music,* produced yet another top ten hit in the title track, a duet with Maxi Priest. In 1994 Flack co-produced *Roberta,* a Grammy-nominated collection of jazz, blues, and pop classics celebrating her 25th year as an Atlantic recording artist. Two years later, Flack found herself in the limelight again, though not through her own efforts. When the popular hip-hop act The Fugees scored a huge hit with its cover version of "Killing Me Softly With His Song," Flack was suddenly introduced to new generation of listeners, many of whom had not even been born when she first recorded the song more than twenty years earlier. She even made a cameo appearance in the Fugees' video.

Taking their cue from the Fugees, other younger artists have begun covering classic Flack hits. By now a performer of legendary status, Flack continues to perform concerts for adoring audiences at nightclubs, concert halls, festivals, and in other settings. She has also continued to produce great music through collaborations with other artists. In 1997 she performed a series of concerts in five cities with folksinger Judy Collins to benefit the Nina Hyde Center for Breast Cancer Research at Georgetown University and a handful of other breast cancer organizations. As one of the premier pop vocalists of the last thirty years, Roberta Flack's voice has penetrated deeply into the consciousness of American popular culture, and will likely remain there for years to come.

Selected discography

(albums)

First Take, Atlantic, 1969.
Chapter Two, Atlantic, 1970.
Quiet Fire, Atlantic, 1971.
Killing Me Softly, Atlantic, 1973.
Feel Like Makin' Love, Atlantic, 1975.
Blue Lights in the Basement, Atlantic, 1977.
Roberta Flack, Atlantic, 1978.
Bustin' Loose (soundtrack), MCA, 1981.
Best of Roberta Flack, Atlantic, 1981.
I'm the One, Atlantic, 1982.
Oasis, Atlantic, 1988.
Set the Night to Music, Atlantic, 1991.
Roberta, Atlantic, 1994.

(with Donny Hathaway)

Roberta Flack and Donny Hathaway, Atlantic, 1972.
Roberta Flack Featuring Donny Hathaway, Atlantic, 1980.

(with Peabo Bryson)

Live and More, Atlantic, 1981.
Born to Love, Capitol, 1983.

Sources

Billboard, August 27, 1994, p. 12.
Ebony, January 1971, p. 54.
Essence, December 1982, p. 58.
High Fidelity, May 1978, p. 121.
Interview, May 1996, p. 76.
New York Times, March 23, 1997, p. 34.
People Weekly, October 9, 1978, p. 124; June 17, 1996, p. 65.
Saturday Review, June 17, 1972.
Time, June 5, 1972, p. 73; May 12, 1975, p. 62.

—Robert R. Jacobson

Joe Frazier

1944—

Professional boxer, entertainer, businessman

Joe Frazier had many moments in boxing history. It began in 1964 when he won the Olympic gold medal in Japan, and peaked when he became the first American Olympic heavyweight champion to also win the heavyweight title of the world. When he was champion he held the highest knockout percentage in history, and while he had been knocked down a few times, he had never been knocked out. Frazier was involved in "the fight of the century" when he fought Muhammad Ali in 1971 for the world heavyweight title, which Frazier held. The Frazier-Ali fight was the first of three battles, but this fight of the century set an indoor boxing record for attendance and revenue, and along with their third fight, is considered classic boxing and an example of athletic courage and endurance.

Influenced By Televised Boxing

Born in Beaufort, South Carolina, on January 17, 1944, Frazier grew up on the ten-acre family farm with his twelve brothers and sisters. A thirteenth child, David, died of diphtheria as an infant, making Frazier the youngest in the large family. His parents, Rubin and Dolly Frazier, grew vegetables and raised hogs but their main income came from working on the large farms of white landowners. His mother worked in the fields while his father was an overseer. Nicknamed Billy Boy, Frazier was, by his own admission, his father's favorite and was frequently at his side. He said in his autobiography, "... my daddy was my hero, my heartbeat. We were always together." Frazier's mother was a devout Baptist who was strong on love and discipline and Frazier occasionally felt the "switch" made of braided tree vines. His mother's word was law and the kids were expected to listen and obey. Frazier's childhood was a rural Southern existence; he spent much of his time helping his father operate a still and pitching in to do the daily chores. And just as his parents and siblings did, he worked in the fields of one of the large farms.

When television became generally available in the early 1950s, Frazier's family was the first to have one in the Laurel Bay section of Beaufort. In those early days of television, boxing was a large part of the limited programming. Frazier's family would watch the fights and saw boxing greats Sugar Ray Robinson, Rocky Mar-

> **At a Glance...**
>
> Born January 12, 1944 in Beaufort, South Carolina; son of Rubin and Dolly Frazier; wife: Florence; children: Marvis, Weatta, Jo-Netta, Natasha, Jacqui, Hector, Marcus. *Religion:* Baptist.
>
> **Career:** Began pro boxing career 1958; owner, member of the rock-blues group Smokin' Joe and the Knockouts; owner of Smokin Joe's Corner restaurant; owner, president, Joe Frazier & Sons Limousine Service, 1974-; owner, Joe Frazier's Gymnasium, 1974-.
>
> **Selected awards:** Philadelphia Golden Gloves novice heavyweight title, 1962; Middle Atlantic Golden Gloves heavyweight championship, 1962, 1963, 1964; Olympic gold medal in boxing 1964; heavyweight champion, NY, MA, IL, ME, 1968; World Boxing Association, heavyweight champion, 1970-73; inducted Boxing Hall of Fame, 1980.
>
> **Addresses:** *Business*—c/o Lynne & Reilly Agency, 6290 Sunset Blvd Ste 326, Los Angeles, CA 90028.

ciano, Willie Pep, and Rocky Graziano. At the time eight-year-old Frazier was not particularly interested in boxing but he did know who former heavyweight champion Joe Louis was. When an uncle commented on young Frazier with his stocky build being the next Joe Louis, it made quite an impression on the boy. From that time on Frazier worked to fulfill that prophecy. He rigged a heavy bag from a burlap sack and rags, corncobs, brick, and Spanish moss. He hung the bag from the branch of an oak tree in the yard and began hitting it almost daily for the next several years. He was ridiculed by many, including his own family, when he told them he was going to be a champion of the world like Joe Louis. He relates in his autobiography that he replied to them, "You all can laugh but I'm gonna be world champion some day." Segregated Beaufort had no gyms and the playgrounds could not be used by blacks. He says, "All I had to build my dream on was that homemade heavy bag."

Frazier attended a segregated school and did not find much to interest him there. Learning did not come easily for him but he admitted in his autobiography, "Lots of times my work day would begin after school and run past midnight....I'd be too tired to pay much attention the next day in school ... after walking four miles to get there. Not that I was any more eager for learning when I was rested." He frequently skipped school and dropped out when he was 14. Frazier's early teens were spent doing farm work, running around with friends to clubs and parties, street fighting, and "chasing girls." Frazier met Florence Smith, his future wife, when he was almost 14 and she was 16. But Frazier's life took a turn when he ran into trouble with the owners of the farm he worked on. Tensions ran high in those days when whites and blacks argued. Frazier lost his job and became determined to leave the racist South. It was almost a year later before he made enough money for the bus fare to leave. He worked first as a delivery man for Coca-Cola and then as a construction worker at the Marines training depot on Parris Island in South Carolina. He headed for New York to live with relatives and to begin a new life.

Boxing Career Began in Slaughterhouse

After an unsuccessful attempt to find regular work in New York, the young Frazier decided to move on to Philadelphia, where he had relatives. Eventually he got a job with Cross Brothers, a slaughterhouse, where he did a variety of chores. The pay was barely enough to get by, and now he was feeling the responsibility of being a family man—back home in Beaufort his girlfriend Florence had just given birth to their son, Marvis. While working at Cross Brothers, Frazier developed a habit that would later be immortalized by actor Sylvester Stallone in the boxing movie, *Rocky:* Frazier practiced his punches on the hanging sides of beef when he moved them into the refrigerator. But he gradually stopped training and gained weight until he was 220 pounds. It was not until late in 1961 that he decided he was going to change his life and revive his Joe Louis dream.

When the overweight Frazier joined the Police Athletic League gym in Philadelphia, he was determined to trim down and pursue his dream of being a professional boxer. It did not take him long to find out that even though he had been the street fighter to contend with in Beaufort, his skills were not enough to keep him from taking a beating in the gym ring. His first sparring session hurt and he realized he had a long way to go. But Frazier knew from that first session on that he was where he wanted to be, and that with hard work he would find the success he craved.

Won Olympic Gold Medal

With regular boxing instruction and training Frazier gained a reputation in the gym. With the guidance of

Duke Dugent, the gym manager, and trainer Yancey (Yank) Durham, Frazier developed a healthier lifestyle as well. By 1962 Frazier had trimmed down to 190 pounds and was a "lean, mean fighting machine." He saw the first reward for his hard work when he won the Philadelphia Golden Gloves novice heavyweight title that year. He went on to win the Middle Atlantic Golden Gloves heavyweight championship in 1962, 1963, and 1964.

In the fall of 1963 Frazier and Florence were married. Frazier continued to work at Cross Brothers during the day and to train in the gym at night. In the gym his style of fighting was compared to a boxer he admired, Rocky Marciano. Marciano had been known as an aggressive fighter and had retired undefeated as heavyweight champion in 1956. Frazier also developed a reputation for his devastating left hook, and frequently voiced his intention of becoming the heavyweight champion of the world.

Frazier's only loss while an amateur was to Buster Mathis, a big, heavy, yet agile man. When the U.S. Olympic Boxing Team was being decided for the 1964 games in Tokyo, Frazier and Mathis met in the finals of the trials. Frazier was eager to redeem his only amateur loss, but Mathis won again. It was a big disappointment for Frazier, who considered quitting boxing. But he was convinced by Duke Dugent and Yank Durham to not only continue boxing but to get on as a sparring partner for the Olympic team as an alternate to Mathis.

Frazier was concerned about losing his job if he went to the Olympics. He and Florence now had three children and her job at Sears Roebuck was not enough to keep the family afloat. When Cross Brothers agreed to hold his job Frazier went to the Olympic training camp in San Francisco. During this time Frazier worked hard at sparring and roadwork. During an exhibition one evening Mathis broke a knuckle while boxing with Frazier. The injury opened up a spot on the team and suddenly Frazier had a chance to prove himself at the Olympics. In the Olympics Frazier was one bout away from the gold medal when he hurt his left thumb. He was not sure how badly it was damaged and while he sought medical treatment, which consisted of ice and wrapping, he turned down an X-ray, fearing he would be dropped from competition if the finger was broken. Despite using his right hand more than his devastating left hook, which gave him severe pain each time he used it, he beat his opponent, Hans Huber of Germany, to win a gold medal for the United States. Frazier says in his autobiography, "The thrill of representing the U.S. and winning despite a handicap—well, there was no feeling quite like that. I had taken a giant step toward my uncle Israel's casual prediction that Billy Boy would be the next Joe Louis."

With his Olympic victory Frazier thought he would finally begin to see some financial and professional success. But surgery on his thumb left him unable to work in the slaughterhouse. Frazier decided it was time to find a sponsor to help him establish his professional boxing career, but he did not have much luck finding one even after winning the gold medal. The Christmas of 1964 was a dismal one for Frazier, who did not have money for gifts. A timely story in the local paper changed things for the family as gifts and money poured in from a concerned public.

Frazier continued to fight and to scratch for income. His pay for his first professional bout in August of 1965 was from selling tickets to the fight. Also that year, Frazier's father, Rubin, died of lung cancer at age 53. Frazier took it hard, trying to find comfort in the fact that his father had been alive when he won the gold medal. His financial problems ended in late 1965 when a group of financial backers came together and formed Cloverlay, Inc. to run his professional boxing career. Part of the agreement was that Frazier would receive a salary of 100 dollars per week and this would increase as the purses did. During this lean time Frazier went to work as a salesman.

Frazier's nickname, 'Smokin' Joe,' came from Yank Durham when he used to tell Frazier before a fight, "Go out there ... and make smoke come from those gloves. You can make smoke, boy. Just don't let up." Frazier continued to fight and develop, striving to remain undefeated and heading for the championship. He was nearly beaten in a bout with Oscar Bonavena in September of 1966 when Bonavena knocked him down twice in the second round. By New York rules the fight ended if an opponent went down three times in the same round. Frazier managed to stay up and went on to win by a split decision.

The Fight Of The Century

There were suggestions that Frazier should fight Muhammad Ali, the current heavyweight title holder. But Yank Durham wanted Frazier to have the chance to develop properly so that when he eventually did face Ali or another champion, he would win. Frazier began to study Ali. When he went to watch him fight in March of 1967 the two began what would become years of competitive bantering. While Ali had changed his name from Cassius Clay to Muhammad Ali in 1964 when he converted to the Black Muslim faith, Frazier insisted on calling him Cassius Clay. Ali had been known from the start of his own career as being a loud-mouthed self-promoter, yet the public and sports writers seemed to love him rather than despise him for it. Ali constantly put Frazier down and while Frazier took it in stride in the beginning, he soon deeply resented it.

In June of 1967 Muhammad Ali was stripped of his title and lost his boxing license for resisting the Vietnam draft because of his religious beliefs. This action left the heavyweight title vacant so the World Boxing Association (WBA) held a tournament to name a new champion. Frazier did not participate though and instead took a different route, fighting his nemesis Buster Mathis for the heavyweight title in New York, Massachusetts, Illinois, and Maine in March of 1968. He won by knockout. After defending the title through 1969 Frazier fought Jimmy Ellis, who had won the WBA tournament. Frazier beat Ellis to become the heavyweight champion of the world. But Frazier did not win respect from the boxing public—many felt Ali's license and title should not have been taken and they still considered him the champion.

When Ali's boxing license was restored in 1970 by a federal court, he returned to the ring determined to regain the heavyweight title. On March 8, 1971, Frazier and Ali faced each other at Madison Square Garden, with the heavyweight title of the world on the line. By this time Eddie Futch was assisting Yank Durham in Frazier's training. More than 20,000 people attended this fight, among them celebrities like actor Burt Lancaster doing radio commentary and singer Frank Sinatra photographing the fight for *Life* Magazine. Futch told *Sports Illustrated*, "I have never seen any boxing event that had so many celebrities." The attendance (gate) and admission fees collected over a million dollars and set indoor boxing records. Closed-circuit television allowed another half million viewers, and viewers in foreign countries also tuned in for a total audience of about 300 million viewers. The fighters each received 2.5 million dollars for the bout. The 15-round fight has been considered among the best in history both for its gate and revenue as well as the action in the ring. It was a hard-fought battle that left the crowd breathless and wondering how long either fighter could continue giving and taking such brutal battering. In the fifteenth round Frazier's left hook put Ali on his back. Ali quickly got up, but Frazier won the fight by unanimous decision and retained the title. Both fighters went to the hospital. The thrill of rightfully winning the title consoled Frazier during the next 10 months when he suffered from "athlete's kidney" and could not box.

After his match with Muhammad Ali Frazier earned, in addition to financial rewards, a certain amount of celebrity. He had started the Smokin' Joe Musical Revue and toured the United States and Europe. He appeared on the Dean Martin television show and later bought a plantation in South Carolina. He eventually moved his mother to the plantation. He was also invited by Governor John C. West to speak to the South Carolina legislature.

Frazier only fought twice in 1972 and on January 22, 1973, he fought and lost his title to George Foreman in a second-round TKO. When Ali and Frazier fought again on January 28, 1974, at Madison Square Garden, the fight could not be compared to their first meeting. This time Ali had worked out a strategy of clinching and keeping Frazier from being effective—he won in a 12-round decision. That same year Frazier lost his longtime trainer and friend Yank Durham when the older man suffered a massive stroke and died at the age of 52.

Ali later won the heavyweight title by defeating Foreman. The title was on the line when Ali and Frazier met again on October 1, 1975, in Manila, the Philippines. Ali had predicted an early knockout but the fight went for 15 grueling rounds that left observers breathless. The pugilists hit so hard that each sent the other's mouthpiece flying. Frazier's eyes swelled shut until he could not see Ali's fists coming but he still fought on. As the bell for the fifteenth round start was about to go off, Eddie Futch threw in the towel to Frazier's protests, saying, "Sit down, son. It's all over. No one will ever forget what you did here today." Ali retained the title but they both fought as true champions. Despite the seeming animosity between the two men Ali told the press that the fight with Frazier could be compared with dying. He was reported in *Sports Illustrated* as saying, "I always bring out the best in the men I fight, but Joe Frazier, I'll tell the world right now, brings out the best in me." In November of 1996, after years of reports of Frazier harboring bad feelings about Muhammad Ali and his vilifications, Frazier publicly apologized to Ali in *Jet* magazine, saying, "It's about time to bring it to an end. I'm willing to say I'm sorry if I said anything to hurt [Ali]."

In November of 1975 Frazier underwent surgery to remove a cataract on his left eye. He had developed the problem years earlier but had not wanted to have the surgery for fear it would halt his boxing career. He had been getting by with medication but by this time it was clear that without surgery he would be blind. But while the surgery removed the cataract and kept the eye from further deterioration, it was too late—he was legally blind in his left eye and now wore contacts to fight, which he did with a rematch of George Foreman in June of 1976. When the fight was stopped in the fifth round, Frazier knew his career was over.

After retiring and making the musical group a full-time

venture, Frazier renamed it "Smokin' Joe and the Knockouts" and made it an eleven-piece revue. In 1977 the group began to travel around the United States to give performances, to favorable reviews. Frazier also bought the gym he had trained in, which had been owned by Cloverlay, his management team. With the gym came several aspiring fighters that had been under contract with Cloverlay. Frazier became a manager and trainer, although the majority of training in his gym was done by Eddie Futch, George Benton, Van Colbert and Sam Hickman. It was the late 1970s and Frazier was also busy with his restaurant, "Smokin' Joe's Corner," and a limousine service.

Joe Frazier came out of retirement in December of 1981 to fight Floyd Cummings, but even though the bout was a draw he had to admit it was time to hang up the gloves for good. In 1985 Florence and Joe Frazier filed for divorce. His son, Marvis Frazier, runs the Smokin' Joe Frazier, Inc. businesses and Frazier's daughter Natasha assists him. Frazier is proud of all of his children, who have become successful in their own right. Joe Frazier can be proud of his own accomplishments, including boxing his way into the history books.

Sources

Books

Frazier, Joe, with Berger, Phil, *Smokin' Joe,* Macmillan, 1996.

McCallum, John D., *The Encyclopedia of World Boxing Champions since 1882,* Chilton Book Company, 1975.

Periodicals

Jet, May 20, 1996; November 18, 1996, p. 5.

Sports Illustrated, October 3, 1994, p. 30; September 1996, p. 58.

—Sandy J. Stiefer

Charles Freeman

1933—

State Supreme Court Justice

On May 12, 1997, the justices of the Illinois Supreme Court made a historic decision—but this time, no defendants or plaintiffs were involved. Rather than deciding the outcome of a court case, they were choosing which of their colleagues would become chief justice. In a near-unanimous vote, they elected Charles E. Freeman, making him the first African American to be chief justice of the state's highest court.

It was not Freeman's only "first" in the Illinois judicial system. In 1990, he had become the first African American elected to the state's supreme court. "He's talented, quiet, and unassuming," R. Eugene Pincham, who served with Freeman on the Illinois Appellate Court, was quoted as saying in the *Chicago Tribune*. "Probably only 20 percent of the black population of Chicago even knows he's on the Supreme Court....He's a behind-the-scenes force, not an adamant, dogmatic, outgoing rabble-rouser," he added.

According to Bob Sector and Christi Parsons, writing in the *Chicago Tribune,* "Freeman is hardly a household name in Illinois, yet he has figured in some of the most historic moments in local black political empowerment." These moments included the successes of others as well as himself. In 1983, as a Circuit Court judge, Freeman administered the oath of office to Harold Washington, Chicago's first African American mayor, and Freeman's former law partner.

Charles Eldridge Freeman was born on December 12, 1933 in Richmond, Virginia. He was the son of William Isaac Freeman and Jeanette Rena Winston Freeman. In 1954, Freeman earned a B.A. in liberal arts from Virginia Union University in Richmond, Virginia. From 1956 to 1958, during the Korean War, he served in the US Army as a courts and boards reporter. Freeman married Marylee Voelker on August 12, 1958 (according to one source, August 27, 1960); the couple has one son, Kevin, who was born in 1969.

After the war, Freeman moved to Chicago, where he earned his law degree at John Marshall Law School in 1962. From 1959 to 1964, he worked as a property and insurance consultant for the Cook County Department of Public Aid. Freeman was admitted to practice in Illinois in 1962, and set up a legal office in Chicago, where he specialized in divorce and real estate work. For many years, his law partner was Harold Washington,

At a Glance...

Born Charles Eldridge Freeman, December 12, 1933, Richmond, VA; son of William Isaac Freeman and Jeanette Rena Winston Freeman; married Marylee Voelker, August 27, 1960; one son, Kevin. *Education:* Virginia Union Univ., B.A. in liberal arts, 1954; John Marshall Law School, J.D., 1962. *Politics:* Democrat. *Religion:* Presbyterian.

Career: Property and insurance consultant, Cook County Dept. of Public Aid, 1959-64; Asst. attorney general, 1964; Asst. state's attorney, 1964; Asst. attorney, Bd. of Election Commissioners, 1964-65; Arbitrator, IL Industrial Commission, 1965-73; Commissioner, IL Commerce Commission, 1973-76. Elected to Circuit Court of Cook County, 1976; First District of IL Appellate Court, 1986-90; Justice, IL Supreme Court, 1990-; Chief Justice, IL Supreme Court, 1997-.

Selected awards: Chosen to administer oath of office during swearing-in ceremonies for Harold Washington, Mayor of Chicago, 1983, 1987; honorary LL.D, John Marshall Law School, 1992; Kenneth E. Wilson Award, Certificate of Merit, Ida Platt Award, Presidential Award and Judicial Award from Cook County Bar Assn.; Earl B. Dickerson Award from Chicago Bar Assn.; Cornelius Francis Stradford Award from the State's Attorney of Cook County; Kenneth Wilson Memorial Award and Guardians Award of Appreciation; Certificate of Achievement from Intl. Christian Fellowship Missions.

Member: Bar Associations of Chicago, Cook County, DuPage County and IL; IL Judges Assn.; Judicial Council of IL; American Judges Assn.; American Judicature Soc.; Third Ward Democratic Headquarters; Ralph H. Metcalfe Youth Fund; Garfield Park Community Growth Center (Bd. of Dirs.; Englewood Businessmen and Civic League (Past VP); Conference to Fulfill These Rights (Bd. of Dirs.), Phi Beta Sigma Fraternity.

Addresses: *Home*—Chicago, IL. *Office*—Supreme Court of Illinois, 160 N. LaSalle Street, Room N2104, Chicago, IL 60601.

who would later become the first African American mayor of Chicago.

In addition to his private practice, Freeman held a wide variety of government positions, serving as assistant attorney general, as a prosecutor for Cook County, and as an attorney for the Board of Election Commissioners. In 1965, he became an arbitrator for the Illinois Industrial Commission, which hears worker's compensation disputes.

In 1973, Freeman was appointed to the Illinois Commerce Commission, the state agency that reviews utility rates. In that position, he became the target of a newspaper investigation; it was revealed that he regularly used complimentary passes provided by railroads that were regulated by the commission. The practice was not illegal, and Freeman defended it as "an entitlement," as quoted in the *Chicago Tribune*. The controversy did not prevent Freeman from being elected to the Cook County Circuit Court three years later, in 1976.

That same year, Freeman gave up his private practice. He still maintained close ties with his former law partner, Washington, however. When Washington was elected mayor of Chicago in 1983 and again in 1987, Freeman was chosen to administer the oath of office during the swearing-in ceremonies; he was the first African American to do so. For Freeman, it was one of the highest honors he had received in his career.

Elected to Illinois Supreme Court

In 1984, Freeman joined the race for a seat on the Illinois Appellate Court, which serves as the first check on the legal and factual decisions of trial judges. Although he won the backing of the Democratic Party, he was defeated by former Chicago Mayor Michael Bilandic.

Two years later, Freeman ran for the court a second time, again with the support of the Democratic Party; he also won an endorsement from the *Chicago Tribune,* which praised his "strong reputation." This time, Freeman won the election, and served on the appellate court for four years.

In 1990, the voters of Illinois faced a historic election: three of the justices on the state's supreme court were retiring. Unlike US Supreme Court justices—who are appointed to their positions for life—Illinois Supreme Court justices are elected, and their terms run for just ten years, with mandatory retirement at age 75.

Freeman decided to join the race for one of the two seats from Cook County, an area which includes Chicago. During the campaign, he stressed his experience and his productivity as an appellate judge; but he also said he thought it was important for an African American to run for the court. In the supreme court race, Freeman again had the support of the Democratic Party—though its support was almost a disadvantage in this case. For the last two decades, candidates backed by the party had lost contested primaries in Cook County.

Still, in March of 1990, Freeman defeated three other candidates to become the Democratic candidate for the seat. "I believe voters looked at me without regard to race and thought me a viable candidate," Freeman told the *Chicago Tribune*. "The Democratic Party reached out for qualified candidates this time, which was a break with the tradition of cronyism that, I think, may have caused the party-endorsed candidates to lose in the past," he added.

According to a profile of candidates that appeared six months later in the *Chicago Tribune*, Freeman was a self-described "judicial moderate." During a candidates forum sponsored by the Chicago Bar Association, Freeman said that he would consider overturning the death penalty in Illinois. While he expressed respect for the legal principle that past decisions should serve as precedents in future cases, he said, "I believe that if cases come before the Supreme Court again—and certainly they will—testing the constitutionality of the death penalty, that I would again look at the constitutionality of the current statute," he was quoted as saying in the *Chicago Tribune*.

Among Freeman's many backers was the *Chicago Tribune*, which listed him in its endorsements for the state's supreme court. "He has the confidence to say he wouldn't be a justice for defendants or a justice for victims. He would just be fair-minded," the editorial board wrote. "He has a deep respect for the law and a keen understanding of the need to streamline the state's judicial system. He would be an excellent choice for the seat opened by the retirement of Justice Seymour Simon," they continued.

On November 6, 1990, Freeman—along with Michael Bilandic and former appellate judge James Heiple—was elected to a ten-year term on the Illinois Supreme Court. During the swearing-in ceremony, Freeman acknowledged his unique role as the first African American justice on the state's highest court. "To each decision and policy, I bring a unique background to a diverse and distinguished court," he was quoted as saying in the *Chicago Tribune*. "I hope to implement those changes that were so long in coming as was the election of an African American to this court."

Freeman also promised to push for administrative changes. "I believe as much attention should be focused on administering this court system as is placed on our judicial decisions," he told the *Chicago Tribune*. "The public perception of the judicial branch of government is at an all-time low. We must address that perception," he continued.

Freeman offered a long list of possible changes that the court, with its three new members, should discuss. These proposals included changing the way judges are selected; requiring lawyers to do some free legal work for the poor; allowing cameras in the courtrooms during trials; and hearing oral arguments for some cases in Chicago rather than in Springfield, the state's capital.

Elected Chief Justice

Seven years later, the Illinois Supreme Court was embroiled in controversy. James Heiple, who had recently been chosen by the court to be chief justice, was accused of trying to use his position to avoid traffic tickets; an Illinois House committee was investigating the case, to determine if he should be impeached. Heiple appeared to be protecting himself from such charges by appointing a close friend to chair the Illinois Courts Commission, the body in charge of disciplinary proceedings.

During the investigation, Freeman had been openly critical of Heiple, a former ally on the court. In a letter to his fellow justices, he wrote, "It may very well appear to some that this court is more concerned with the grabbing of power and control that it is with the public's perception and the integrity of this court. In the words of Thurgood Marshall, ... 'we must never forget that the only real source of power that we as judges can tap is the respect of the people'" (quoted in the *Chicago Tribune*).

On May 2, after being censured by the Illinois Courts Commission, and still under threat of impeachment, Heiple resigned his position. Despite the fact that Freeman had testified against him during the investigation, it was Heiple, along with former Chief Justice Michael Bilandic, who nominated Freeman for the top post. Freeman was elected chief justice by six of his seven colleagues on May 12, 1997, with one justice abstaining from the initial vote. That justice registered his vote the following day, making the decision unanimous.

Though symbolically significant, the chief justice position on the Illinois court—which runs for three years—is not as powerful as the top job in many other states or on the

U.S. Supreme Court. The U.S. chief justice, if in the majority, can assign the writing of court opinions, a power that can strongly influence the tone of rulings. The Illinois chief justice does not have that authority; instead, the job mainly entails administrative oversight of judicial assignments and the annual budget.

One of his top priorities as chief justice, Freeman told the *Chicago Tribune*, would be to repair the battered reputation of the Illinois judicial system. "The judiciary kind of thrives on and survives on the respect that the public gives it, and without that respect, our ability to function and administer the court system becomes little more difficult," he was quoted as saying in the *Chicago Tribune*.

"He has a reputation of being a very solid judge, a very competent judge," Jeffrey Shaman, law professor at Chicago's DePaul University, was quoted as saying in a *Chicago Tribune* article about Freeman's appointment. "His opinions are well crafted. He's intelligent. He's respected in the legal community."

Politically, Freeman tends to be on the liberal side, according to Shaman. "I think that he probably more often than any justice dissents in criminal cases on the side of protecting" the rights of the accused, he told the *Chicago Tribune*. As well as his years of experience in the Illinois judicial system, he also brings other strengths to the job, he was quoted as saying in the *Chicago Tribune:* "I'm patient. I'll listen. I'm open to suggestions. I don't bruise easily."

Takes Time to Inspire Others

Freeman has received numerous awards from the Chicago, Cook County, and American Bar Associations, including recognition for his work helping minorities in the profession. He received an honorary LL.D. from his alma mater, John Marshall Law School, in 1992.

In his spare time, Freeman pursues several hobbies, which include photography and collecting cameo glass and soapstone. On weekends during the summer, he enjoys spending time on his motorboat in Lake Michigan. Giving back to the community is also one of his priorities; he sits on the board of directors of several community organizations, and gives inspirational lectures to young people.

In February of 1998, Freeman spoke to a group of African American high school students at Shell Youth Training Academy in southside Chicago. "If you want something and you think it's worth getting, you reach for it," he told the group (quoted in the *Chicago Tribune*). According to one of the students who heard him (also quoted in the *Chicago Tribune*), "His life and career makes you realize, if you're dedicated, you can do anything."

Sources

The American Bench: Judges of the Nation, edited by Mary Reincke and Nancy Lichterman, Reginald Bishop Forster & Associates, 1979.

Chicago Tribune, Feb 28, 1986, sec. 1, p. 14; Nov 27, 1986, sec. 2, p. 18; Mar 21, 1990, sec. 2, p. 1; Mar 22, 1990, sec. 2, p. 7; Oct 14, 1990, sec. 3, p. 11; Oct. 25, 1990, sec. 1, p. 26; Nov 4. 1990, sec. 4, p. 4; Dec 4, 1990, sec. 2, p. 2; June 12, 1991, sec. 2, p. 3; Feb 17, 1997, sec. 5, p. 1; May 13, 1997, sec. 1, p. 1; May 14, 1997, sec. 2, p. 9; Feb 11, 1998, sec. 2, p. 8.

—Carrie Golus

Donald Goines

1937(?)–1974

Novelist

The novels of Donald Goines, described by *Entertainment Weekly* reviewer Suzanne Ruta as "nasty, brutish, and short," are slices of life in the inner-city underworld. They describe, in graphic detail, the short careers of black crime kingpins, hit men, drug pushers and other criminals. Set mostly in Detroit, his hometown, Goines's novels teem with scenes of violence and mayhem and the language of the characters is laced with obscenities. The plots of most of Goines's novels center around the workings of a criminal enterprise and proceed to a grim and tragic conclusion. Goines, a career criminal and heroin addict who was arrested fifteen times and served seven prison terms, drew deeply upon his own life experiences when writing his novels and they have been eagerly devoured by generations of African American readers.

Goines was born in Detroit between 1935 and 1937. His childhood was relatively stable and his parents, who owned a small dry-cleaning store, sent him to a Catholic elementary school. Goines dropped out of school as a teenager and joined the Air Force, using false identification to enlist. While stationed in Japan during the Korean War, he became addicted to heroin. According to Eddie Stone, who wrote Goines's biography *Donald Writes No More*, Goines saw action on the front lines in Korea as an ambulance driver.

After returning home from the Korean War, Goines supported his worsening drug habit by committing crimes, including bootlegging and pimping for a ring of prostitutes. Goines was eventually arrested and convicted for his crimes. In 1965, he was assigned to Jackson State Prison in Michigan. While an inmate at Jackson, Goines began writing short stories with Western themes. Another inmate introduced him to the writings of Robert "Iceberg Slim" Beck in 1969 and, in those writings, Goines found inspiration. Working at a typewriter in his cell, Goines rapidly produced his first novel, *Whoreson: The Story of a Ghetto Pimp*. Within weeks, it was accepted for publication by Holloway House.

Whoreson was actually published after Goines's second novel, *Dopefiend: The Story of a Black Junkie*. *Dopefiend,* which likely drew its creative energy from Goines's own drug addiction, focuses on the destruction that heroin wreaks upon a middle-class African American couple. Literary critic Greg Goode called the set-

At a Glance...

Born c. 1937 in Detroit, Michigan; died October 21, 1974, in Highland Park, Michigan; son of Joseph (a dry cleaner) and Myrtle Goines. married Shirley Sailor; two children. *Education:* Attended Catholic schools in Detroit.

Career: Novelist; served in the United States Air Force, 1952-55; engaged in criminal activity, later described in detail in his writings, 1950s and 1960s; served prison sentences totaling 6 1/2 years; novel *Whoreson: The Story of a Ghetto Pimp*, written in Jackson State Prison, MI, accepted for publication by Holloway House, Los Angeles, 1969; published 16 novels after release from prison in 1970; published five novels as Al C. Clark ("Kenyatta" series); consistent sales of books through 1990s; *Daddy Cool* republished by W. W. Norton, 1996.

tings and characters in *Dopefiend* "repulsively memorable," pointing to the novel's detailed depictions of the horrors of a shooting gallery presided over by a sadistic dealer named Porky. According to his biographer Eddie Stone, Goines described heroin as "the drug of the damned" and tried to warn his younger sister of its dangers by forcing her to watch him inject the drug.

Following the success of *Whoreson* and *Dopefiend*, Goines continued to write novels that featured criminals and their violent pursuits. His 1972 novel, *Black Gangster*, tells the story of a hustler who organizes a criminal gang under the guise of a black revolutionary organization. Another novel, *Eldorado Red*, revolves around the robbery of a cash-collection house in a "numbers" operation, an illegal lottery that flourished in many African American neighborhoods. Many of Goines' novels depict cycles of revenge killings that accomplish nothing and impulsive characters who often meet their death at the hands of brutal white police officers. Although he was not a person given to overt moralizing, Goines may have intended such depictions as a protest against the mindless violence of the ghetto. In the *Village Voice*, Michael Covino described Goines as "a chronicler of the black ghetto during the precipitous decline of the 1970s."

In 1974, Goines began writing a new series of novels that sought to take a broader view of ghetto violence and address its root causes. Using the name of a close friend, Al C. Clark, as a pseudonym, Goines penned what became known as the Kenyatta series. Each novel features Kenyatta, a powerful leader influenced by Muslim and Marxist thought, who organizes an army to rid African American neighborhoods of white police officers on the one hand and violent criminals on the other. The Kenyatta series includes the novels *Crime Partners*, *Cry Revenge!*, *Death List*, *Kenyatta's Escape*, and *Kenyatta's Last Hit*, in which Kenyatta dies in a shootout with the forces of a white financier who profits from the flow of drugs into the ghetto.

Although he became a successful novelist, Goines was never able to overcome his strong addiction to heroin. Much of the income from sales of his novels went toward the purchase of drugs. In an attempt to break the patterns that were feeding his addiction, Goines and his wife moved from Detroit to Los Angeles. While in Los Angeles, Goines entered several drug treatment programs. Eventually, he and his wife returned to the Detroit area and settled in the enclave of Highland Park. On October 21, 1974, Goines and his wife were murdered in their apartment during a robbery.

Goines' writings have remained extremely popular among African American readers. All of his novels remain in print and some adherents of gangster rap have proclaimed themselves fans of his writing. In 1996, Goines's 1974 novel *Daddy Cool* was reissued as part of the "Old School" series published by the W.W. Norton Company. Donald Goines, who regarded his writing as the pinnacle of his life's work, would have been proud.

Selected writings

Dopefiend: The Story of a Black Junkie, Holloway House, 1971.
Whoreson: The Story of a Ghetto Pimp, Holloway House, 1971.
Black Gangster, Holloway House, 1972.
Black Girl Lost, Holloway House, 1972.
Street Players, Holloway House, 1973.
White Man's Justice, Black Man's Grief, Holloway House, 1973.
Daddy Cool, Holloway House, 1974 (reissued by W. W. Norton, 1996).
Eldorado Red, Holloway House, 1974.
Never Die Alone, Holloway House, 1974.
Swamp Man, Holloway House, 1974.
Inner City Hoodlum, Holloway House, 1975.

As Al C. Clark (series: Kenyatta)

Crime Partners, Holloway House, 1974.
Cry Revenge!, Holloway House, 1974.
Death List, Holloway House, 1974.

Kenyatta's Escape, Holloway House, 1974.
Kenyatta's Last Hit, Holloway House, 1975.

Sources

Books

Contemporary Authors, volume 124, Gale, 1988.
Contemporary Literary Criticism, volume 80, Gale, 1994.

Pederson, Jay P. ed., *St. James Guide to Crime & Mystery Writers,* St. James Press, 1996.
Stone, Eddie, *Donald Writes No More,* Holloway House, 1974, repr. with epilogue 1988.

Periodicals

Entertainment Weekly, July 25, 1997, p. 66.
Melus, Fall 1984, p. 41.
Village Voice, August 4, 1987, p. 48.

—James M. Manheim

Marita Golden

1950—

Author

Marita Golden has won renown not only for her African American-centered novels, but she also has attracted critical acclaim for nonfiction works whose focus has been her own immediate family. She has written of her experiences coming of age in the post-civil rights era and of her sojourn in Africa, and she has also penned a well-received treatise on the dangers faced by young black men, such as her own son, in urban America. Golden has incorporated many of these same themes into her fiction as well, and the force and fluency of her prose has earned her comparisons to other African American women writers, such as Toni Morrison and Alice Walker. "Fiercely intelligent, brimming with ethical questions, never overtly political, the novels of Marita Golden have an old-fashioned earnestness about them," declared *Washington Post* writer Donna Rifkind.

Golden grew up in the District of Columbia's black community. Her mother—a woman whose early life provided the basis for a character in one of Golden's later novels—had left a hardscrabble life in the South behind. Beatrice Reid Golden first worked as a maid, but eventually parleyed her meager funds into a more prosperous existence by means of some creative investments. She married three times, and by the time her only child was born in 1950, the senior Golden had become a landlord who owned rooming houses near 14th Street in the northwest quadrant of the city. Yet, as her daughter recalled in a 1993 article for *Essence,* Beatrice Golden's third marriage was a rocky one.

"Both my parents were gamblers," Golden wrote in *Essence.* "They played the numbers and won often.... I remember the black Lincoln Continental [my father] bought once and how it sat sleek and somehow fitting before our three-story rooming house, until it was repossessed three months later."

Moved to Nigeria

Thanks in part to her father's extroverted, ebullient nature, Golden said she learned from him "that I was worth listening and talking to," she told Colman McCarthy in the *Washington Post.* As a teen, Golden attended Western High School (now renamed Duke Ellington High School), and was awarded a scholarship to American University, also in the nation's capital. After receiving her undergraduate degree there in 1972, Golden worked for a time at the *Baltimore Sun* newspaper before heading to graduate school in New York. She earned a master's degree from Columbia University, and took a job in 1974 as an associate producer at a New York City public television station. In New York she met her first husband, Femi Ajayi, a student from Nigeria, and moved with him to his country when they married. After giving birth to a son, Golden left her husband and returned to the United States in the late 1970s. She had found life in Lagos difficult, especially for an American woman, and she wrote of these differences in customs and cultures in her first book, *Migra-*

At a Glance...

Born April 28, 1950, in Washington, DC; daughter of Francis Sherman (a taxi driver) and Beatrice Lee (a property owner; maiden name, Reid) Golden; married Femi Ajayi (an educator), mid-1970s (divorced, late 1970s); married a public school teacher; children: Michael Kayode (first marriage). *Education:* American University, B.A., 1972; Columbia Univ., M.Sc., 1973.

Career: Affiliated with the *Baltimore Sun,* Baltimore, MD, early 1970s; WNET-Channel 13, New York City, associate producer, 1974-75; University of Lagos, Lagos, Nigeria, assistant professor of mass communications, 1975-79; Roxbury Community College, Roxbury, MA, assistant professor of English, 1979-81; Emerson College, Boston, MA, assistant professor of journalism, 1981-83; writer, 1983–; George Mason University, creative writing program, senior writer, c. 1995; Virginia Commonwealth University, Richmond, VA, professor, c. 1996–. Member of nominating committee for the George K. Polk Awards; executive director of the Institute for the Preservation and Study of African American Writing, 1986-87; consultant for the Washington, D.C., Community Humanities Council, 1986-89.

Member: Afro-American Writer's Guild (president, 1986)

Addresses: *Home*—Mitchellsville, MD. *Office*—Virginia Commoenwatlh Unviersity, Richmond, VA 23284. *Agent*—Carol Mann, 168 Pacific St., Brooklyn, NY 11201.

tions of the Heart (1983).

Golden settled in Boston as a single mother, and took a job as an assistant professor of English at Roxbury Community College in 1979. She eventually became an assistant professor of journalism at nearby Emerson College, but decided to return to the Washington area around the time *Migrations of the Heart* was published. Golden followed *Migrations of the Heart* with two novels—*A Woman's Place,* published in 1986, and *Long Distance Life,* published in 1989. *A Woman's Place* revolved around the intertwined lives of three African American women whose friendship dates back to their student years at a prestigious Boston university. All three choose different paths as educated, self-aware African American women, and all three experience their own particular difficulties.

Critical Acclaim for Second Novel

Golden's second novel, *Long Distance Life,* became a bestseller in the DC area. A multi-generation family saga, it begins with Naomi Johnson, a character whose journey from the sharecropper South to urban prosperity was similar to that undertaken by Golden's own mother. Johnson's daughter, Esther, comes of age in the 1960s, as Golden herself did, and becomes active in the civil rights movement. She leaves a young son behind in the partial care of his father, a man who will not leave his wife for Esther. When Esther finally returns—radically transformed, carrying a Bible and a journal—Randolph ends his marriage in order to marry Esther and become a full-time father to their son. Tragically, he dies of a heart attack just before their wedding day, leaving Esther carrying their second child.

The rest of *Long Distance Life* charts the lives of those sons. The elder of the pair, Logan, becomes a doctor. Several years ahead of Nathaniel, who never got to meet his own father, Logan's years away at college unintentionally rob Nathaniel of a much-needed steady male presence in his life. Nathaniel eventually becomes a drug dealer, though as a middle-class youth he is far removed from the violence and poverty of the world in which he operates. "The economic security his mother and brother provide for him produces a curious boredom," wrote reviewer Nagueyalti Warren about Nathaniel's plight in *Black American Literature Forum.* Warren praised Golden for her talent for characterization, especially regarding men like the once-philandering Randolph. "In her fiction, Golden creates men who are strong, yet gentle, perceptive, wise, and kind," reflected Warren.

Female Friendship and the Freedom Rides

In Golden's third novel, *And Do Remember Me* (1992), the civil rights movement of the Sixties and its attendant violence again serves as an important catalyst for her characters. Its protagonist, Jessie, is a young woman who flees an abusive home in the Deep South. She becomes involved in the organized efforts at voter registration and desegregation known as the Mississippi Freedom Summer, and in the process finds romance with a fellow activist and future playwright named Lincoln, and a mentor and friend in Macon, an African American woman of a far different background than her own. Over the course of the novel, Jessie moves with Lincoln to New York and becomes a stage actor. Patricia Smith, reviewing *And Do Remember Me* for the *Boston Globe,* found some fault with its narrative structure, but noted that "Golden has always been her own artist, crafting clean, straightforward prose that never gets in the way of the story it is trying to tell."

Golden's gift for language took a more personal turn in 1995 with the publication of *Saving Our Sons: Raising Black Children in a Turbulent World.* The work's origins dated back to a journal she began keeping for her son Michael in 1993 as he entered his high-school years. They lived in Washington, a city whose reputation for violent crime was unparalleled during those years. Golden knew that in her city the leading cause of death among young African American males was homicide—and she also knew that her middle-class life, her college degree, and her safe and loving home were perhaps not enough to keep Michael from becoming a statistic. Even if he escaped physical assault, she realized that as her son grew into a young adult, he would come to "inhabit that narrow, corrupt crawl space in the minds of whites and some black people too," Golden wrote in *Saving Our Sons*, "a space reserved for criminals, outcasts, misfits, and black men. Soon he would become a permanent suspect."

Saving Our Sons a Commercial Success

In the book, Golden wrote of the problems her son faced and theorized as to their origins. She worked in socioeconomics and African American history, and compared his life in the United States with what might have been had they remained in Nigeria. The denouement of the book comes with his reunion with his birth father, whom he never knew. Golden hopes in *Saving Our Sons* that this connection to his past will set Michael on solid ground. Eventually she also decides to send him to a boarding school near Philadelphia, and concedes that even her best efforts might not portend success: "And although I have paved a straight and narrow path for my son to tread, always there is the fear that he will make a fatal detour, be seduced, or be hijacked by a White or Black cop, or a young Black predator, or a Nazi skinhead, or his own bad judgment, or a weakness that even I as his mother cannot love or punish or will out of him," Golden wrote.

Golden returned to the novel format with her fifth book, *The Edge of Heaven,* published in 1997. Another multigenerational saga, it begins with the third generation, the college student Teresa, as she works as an intern in a prestigious law firm. At home, however, she and her grandmother Adele are preparing for the imminent release of Teresa's mother Lena from prison. Lena, a once-successful accountant, served several years for the murder of Teresa's 11-year-old sister Kenya. The details of the crime, however, are murky, and Golden only slowly reveals what really happened through the course of the story. This was a plot contrivance that *New York Times* writer Janet Kaye found confusing, but Kaye did concede that Golden "tells an often affecting story of dashed hopes and domestic discord without succumbing to either preaching or melodrama." *Washington Post* writer Rifkind reviewed it and called it "a departure from Golden's previous novels ... Lena's troubles can be traced not to oppression by the white world but to her eager participation in that world."

A Catalyst for a Younger Generation

Golden is a contributor to *Sisterfire: Black Womanist Fiction and Poetry,* and edited *Wild Women Don't Wear No Blues,* both collections of works by African American women writers. She is also determined to help pave the way for a new generation to follow hers. While at George Mason University, she noticed how few African American students were enrolled in the Master of Fine Arts program. To help remedy this, she launched the Zora Neale Hurston/Richard Wright Foundation with her own funds, bestowing prizes to African American students at the school who submitted fiction to a call for submissions. Later, her project grew into a nationwide competition, and Toni Morrison and other prominent writers sit on its advisory board.

Out of the Foundation and Golden's activism also came an annual seminar for writers at Virginia Commonwealth University, where she is a professor. Golden has conceded that while many African American novelists have enjoyed unparalleled success in the 1990s, she asserts "there still remains a kind of divide before of that has yet to be crossed. We tend to get pigeonholed with the types of stories we choose to tell, whereas a white story can be about anything," she said in an interview with D'Lena M. Ambrose in the *Journal of Higher Education.*

Selected writings

Migrations of the Heart (autobiography), Doubleday, 1983.
A Woman's Place (novel), Doubleday, 1986.

Long Distance Life (novel), Doubleday, 1989.
And Do Remember Me (novel), Doubleday, 1992.
(Editor) *Wild Women Don't Wear No Blues,* Doubleday, 1993.
(Contributor) *Sisterfire: Black Womanist Fiction and Poetry,* edited by Charlotte Watson Sherman, HarperPerennial, 1994.
Saving Our Sons: Raising Black Children in a Turbulent World, Doubleday, 1995.
The Edge of Heaven, Doubleday, 1997.

Sources

Periodicals

American Visions, October-November 1993, p. 35.
Black American Literature Forum, Winter 1990.
Boston Globe, July 27, 1992, p. 30.
Entertainment Weekly, February 3, 1995, p. 49.
Essence, September 1993, p. 79; February 1995, p. 52.
Harvard Educational Review, Winter 1996, pp. 879-881.
Jet, June 12, 1997, p. 12.
Journal of Higher Education, June 14, 1996, pp. A45-46.
Library Journal, November 1, 1997, p. 115.
New York Times, April 5, 1998.
Publishers Weekly, June 7, 1993, p. 58; July 11, 1994, p. 74; October 27, 1997, p. 52.
Washington Post, December 21, 1989, p. D1; June 21, 1992, p. X3; January 15, 1995, p. X5; March 25, 1995, p. A19; July 16, 1995, p, X1; December 21, 1997, p. X1.

—Carol Brennan

Denyce Graves

1964—

Opera singer

A much-loved native daughter of Washington, D.C., celebrated mezzo-soprano Denyce Graves is international opera's newest star. *USA Today* has predicted that Graves will likely be one of the twenty-first century's operatic superstars. In her signature role as Bizet's sultry, passionate Carmen, she has won glowing reviews worldwide. Jerry Schwartz noted in the *Atlanta Journal-Constitution* that critics have called her Carmen "one of the most stunning performances ever of that storied role." *The Wall Street Journal* called her "the hottest Carmen on the opera circuit today," and Martin Feinstein, former general director of the Washington Opera, stated simply, "she is the definitive Carmen."

Following a three-year apprenticeship with the Houston Grand Opera, where she made her debut as Hansel in *Hansel and Gretel* in 1989, Graves took the operatic world by storm. She has sung with tenor legends Placido Domingo, Luciano Pavarotti, and Jose Carreras. She has appeared on the stages of the world's most famous opera houses, including the Vienna State Opera, La Scala in Milan, and the Royal Opera in London's Covent Garden. Graves made her debut at New York's Metropolitan Opera to critical acclaim in the fall of 1995, in the title role of *Carmen*.

Reviewers have been effusive in their descriptions of Graves's voice. In 1997 Tony Kornheiser wrote in the *Washington Post,* "Denyce Graves's voice is spectacular. It's so clear and clean you feel you can see through it." Herbert Kupferberg described it as "sumptuous but mercifully light and flexible" in *Parade* in 1994 and in a 1994 article for *American Record Guide,* David Reynolds called it "a full and voluptuous instrument indeed." Others were more specific. Reviewer Anthony Tommasini wrote in the *New York Times* in 1995 that Graves has "a classic mezzo-soprano voice with dusky colorings and a wide range, from her chesty low voice to her gleaming top notes." Schwartz described it as "quite distinctive—rich, burnished, deep." He concluded, "Her wonderfully tasteful musicianship allows it to project with a directness that few singers in any age have been able to manage."

Nurtured on Galveston Street

Denyce Antionette Graves was born March 7, 1964 to Charles Graves and Dorothy (Middleton) Graves-Ken-

At a Glance...

Born Denyce Antoinette Graves, March 7, 1964, in Washington, D.C., daughter of Charles Graves (now a minister) and Dorothy (Middleton) Graves (now Graves-Kenner, then a clerk typist at Federal City Coll.). *Education:* B. Mus. New England Conservatory of Music, 1988.

Career: Mezzo-soprano opera singer. Debuted as Hansel in *Hansel and Gretel,* 1989, Suzuki in *Madame Butterfly,* 1990, Houston Grand Opera; as Maddalena in *Rigoletto,* D.C., Opera, 1991; as Carmen in *Carmen,* Minnesota Opera, 1991, Metropolitan Opera, Dallas Opera, Opernhaus Zurich; as Baba the Turk in *The Rake's Progress,* Chatelet, Paris; Charlotte in *Werther,* Genoa, Italy; Cuniza in *Oberto,* Royal Opera, London; Adalgisa in *Norma,* and many others. Performed on numerous PBS progs, 1990-91; TV panel member, BET TV, 1990; many solo recitals and concerts; participant in educ. outreach progs. with Opera, Grand Rapids, MI, 1991, Opera Theatre of St. Louis, 1990, and Houston Grand Opera, 1990; performer, Gala Concert, Tucker Found., 1990, broadcast nationally on PBS *Great Performances,* 1991; performer, with Placido Domingo, *Concert for Planet Earth,* for United Nations Summit on the Environment, Rio de Janeiro, 1992.

Memberships: Amer. Guild of Musical Artists; Panel mem., Washington Opera Open Forum, 1991; active supporter, African Natl. Congress, Boston, 1985.

Selected awards: First place, Northeast MetroOpera Regional Auditions, 1987; recipient, Richard F. Gold Career grant, Houston Grand Opera, 1989; recipient, Grand Prix du Concours Intl. de Chant de Paris, 1990; recipient, Jacobsooon Study Grant, Richard Tucker Music Found., NYC, 1990; recipient, Natl. Endowment for the Arts grant, 1990; recipient, Metro Opera grant, 1990; recipient, Grand Prix Lyrique, Assn. des amis de l'opera de Monte-Carlo, 1991; Marion Anderson Award, 1991; Honorary Doctorate, Oberlin College Conservatory, 1998.

Addresses: *Public Relations*—c/o Suzanne Stephens Arts Services, 1714 N. Bryan St., Arlington, VA 22201; *Mgr*—c/o William G. Guerri, Columbia Artists Mgmt. Inc., 165 West 57th St. New York, NY 10019.

ner. The middle child of th Denyce and her siblings were raised by their mot on Galveston Street in southwest Washington, D.C. Charles Graves walked out on his family when Denyce was not yet two and his youngest daughter not yet born. Dorothy Graves worked hard to support her family, first as a laundress and then as a clerk typist at Federal City College—now the University of the District of Columbia. "Our neighborhood was tough and chaotic ... and very poor," Graves told Marilyn Milloy of *Essence.* "Violence, drugs, hopelessness, despair—it was all there. Yet with all that, my mother held her ground and built a solid foundation for our little family."

Dorothy Graves built that foundation on a bedrock of love, discipline, and faith. She was strict, making sure her children had no spare time in which to find trouble. Regular chores and homework filled much of their after-school time, and Dorothy took care of the rest by scheduling various activities for the evenings, such as sewing, report writing, gospel singing, and church attendance. "Thursday night was always for our singing group. I loved to sing early on," Graves told *Essence.* Popular music was forbidden in the Graves home, as were certain television shows that Dorothy felt portrayed blacks in a demeaning manner. As a result of this sheltered upbringing, Denyce was neither familiar with nor especially interested in whatever was considered "cool" at the time. Consequently, she stood out as different from her peers. Classmates called her "Hollywood" merely because she was aloof. Her mother balanced the discipline with encouragement. She told her children they were special, that their throats and brains had been kissed by God, that they could do anything.

Discovered Opera

Graves's first mentor was her elementary school music teacher, Judith Grove, who, through a series of job changes, followed her to Friendship Junior High and on to high school. Impressed by the girl's commitment to hard work and her serious attitude toward music, in 1977 Grove encouraged her to apply to Duke Ellington School of the Arts, a public performing arts high school in Georgetown. Graves won admittance by passing an audition. Although her mother had serious qualms at the prospect, Graves did not.

She felt immediately at home at Ellington. She no longer stood out; all the students there were committed, working toward similar goals. She recalled in an article in the *Washingtonian,* "I felt that I could finally breathe. There have been few things in my life where I said 'This is it,' but when I walked through that door, there was a rightness in my bones about it."

While a student at Ellington, Graves saw her first opera. She was 14. Attending a dress rehearsal at the Kennedy Center for Beethoven's *Fidelio,* she was captivated. Some time after that, a teacher gave her a recording of Marilyn Horne singing an aria from the opera Cavalleria Rusticana. Playing the aria until she had it memorized, Graves determined to become an opera singer.

Graves finished high school in just two years, graduating in 1981. She was offered scholarships to several colleges, but chose the Oberlin College Conservatory in Ohio. The school had offered only a partial scholarship, so she worked several jobs to make ends meet. At Oberlin she studied under reknowned voice teacher Helen Hodam. Reaching mandatory retirement age in 1984, Hodam left Oberlin to teach at the New England Conservatory of Music in Boston, and Graves followed her there. Working up to three jobs at a time to support herself, it would take her four more years to graduate. She earned her Bachelor of Music in 1988.

Throat Ailment Suspended Career Plan

Before she graduated, Graves entered the Metropolitan Opera Regional Auditions in 1986. She won. "I had to win," she told the *New York Times.* "I was four months behind in my rent. I couldn't pay for the rented dress I was wearing." When she got to New York to sing in the finals, however, she was stricken with a mysterious throat ailment. It got worse as she sang. Forced to withdraw from the competition, she saw 11 specialists before the problem was diagnosed as a treatable thyroid condition. Disheartened, she took a secretarial position and did not sing again for a year.

Then Graves received a series of phone calls that would change her life. The Houston Grand Opera called to invite her to audition for its opera studio, a young artists training program. The disaster of the Metro finals was too fresh an experience, and Graves said thank you, but her singing days were over. Houston called again a couple of months later and renewed the offer. Her answer was still thanks, but no thanks. Six weeks passed and Houston called a third time. This time, friends persuaded her that this was meant to be, so she flew to Texas to audition. She had not sung in more than a year. She took her time warming up, and then sang Carmen's seguidilla. *New York* quoted Graves as saying of the experience, "That day I sang better than when I was well and in good voice. It was a revelation from God."

Graves spent three years in Houston. She told *Essence* that her life changed completely. "My job there was to do supporting roles or cover for other mezzos as well as grunge work—singing in the malls at Christmas time, things like that," she said. "But I also met the great tenor Placido Domingo, and from that point on things began to happen." Impressed with her talent and drive, Domingo became her mentor.

The World's Reigning Carmen

Her debut in a lead role came in 1989 in Houston, as Hansel in *Hansel and Gretel.* Graves was invited to sing in the Tucker Foundation's 1990 Gala Concert, which was broadcast nationally in 1991 on PBS's *Great Performances.* Building on her Houston apprenticeship, she has proven herself a major talent ever since. She has sung leading roles in all the most respected opera houses in the world. Although she had sung other roles early in her career, her characterization of Carmen generated the most excitement. By early 1996 she had sung in more than 30 productions of that opera. Hailed by enthusiastic critics as "the world's reigning Carmen," it has become her signature role. In a 1995 review in the *New York Times,* Tommasini wrote, "She is a compelling stage actress who exude[s] the sensuality that any Carmen must have but few do." Tim Page observed in the *Washington Post,* "We do not merely listen to her Carmen, we experience it; she not only sings the role of the fiery Gypsy girl, she embodies her." She made her much-anticipated debut at New York's Metropolitan Opera in 1995 as Carmen. Linda Killian noted in the *Washingtonian* in 1996, "Whenever an opera house anywhere in the world thinks about doing a production of *Carmen,* Graves is at the top of the list. She has reached the point where she says no to Carmen as often as she says yes." The reason, Killian explained, is that "Domingo and others have warned her that she mustn't become typecast, that she needs to expand her repertoire and her voice by doing other roles."

Graves explained the benefit of other roles to her voice in *New York*. "Mozart and bel canto—I swear to God, they make your voice better. They're difficult, especially for a voice like mine. My voice is broad. It's fat. I need to work to line it up, to make it skinny. With *Carmen* you have to watch out. It's so theatrical. It can take the sheen off the voice and get it out of line, make it hard." Recent seasons have found her in roles as varied as Baba the Turk in Stravinsky's *The Rake's Progress,* Charlotte in Massenet's *Werther,* and Dalila in Saint-Saens's *Samson et Dalila.* In 1997 and 1998 she sang several recitals and concerts around the United States. She has sung at the White House and performed with Placido Domingo on his *Concert for the Planet Earth,* which was broadcast worldwide from the United States summit on the environment in Rio de Janeiro in 1992.

In 1990 Graves married classical guitar importer David Perry. They met the year before while performing with the Wolf Trap Opera Company in Virginia. Perry was a lutenist in the orchestra. He travels with Graves much of the time, handling details for her and calming her nerves before performances by playing classical guitar for her. "My husband is a rock in this whole crazy turbulence of a career," Graves told the *Christian Science Monitor.* They have a home in Leesburg, Virginia.

Graves is conscious of being a role model for black children, just as Leontyne Price was an early inspiration for her. She is also grateful to those who broke the operatic color barrier before her. Her own struggles to reach the top, she told *Ebony,* "are nothing in comparison to the suffering of those people who allowed me to be in the position that I'm in today." In spite of her meteoric rise to stardom, Graves has encountered racism, and believes she has lost out on roles because she is black. And, having pursued a career in what has been traditionally an elitist art form dominated and controlled by whites, she has been criticized by blacks for wanting to be "white." Responding to those who would try to pigeonhole her as one thing or another, Graves had this to say to the *Atlanta Journal-Constitution* in 1996: "Anyone who thinks the world of international opera is any easier for black people than anything else has never been there. But bitterness can eat a hole in your soul." Killian noted in *The Washingtonian* that Graves strives to leave race aside as she hones her craft. She wrote, "Graves does not want to be a black opera singer. She want to be an opera singer who happens to be black."

Having reached the top, Graves's struggle continues. "The key in this business is not only about getting your foot in the door," she told *Essence,* "it's about demanding such a standard of excellence from yourself that you stay in the room. The ultimate goal, in my opinion, is for people to flock to the theatre not only to see *Carmen,* but to see Denyce Graves." If her bookings—which stretch into the next century—are any indication, Denyce Graves will be staying in the room for many years to come.

Selected discography

Angels Watching Over Me, NPR Classics, 1998.
Denyce Graves: A Cathedral Christmas, PBS Productions, 1998.
Recital Denyce Graves: Heroines de l'Opera romantique Francais, FNAC Music, 1993.
Hamlet, EMI, 1993.
Concert For Planet Earth, Sony Classical, 1993.
Otello, Deutsche Grammophon, 1993.

Sources

Periodicals

American Record Guide, September/October 1994.
Atlanta Journal-Constitution, November 16, 1997, November 17, 1997.
Christian Science Monitor, July 24, 1996.
Ebony, February 1996.
Essence, September 1996.
Glamour, December 1997.
Los Angeles Times, January 21, 1996.
New York, September 11, 1995.
New York Times, December 28, 1997, October 14, 1995, October 9, 1995.
Parade, May 29, 1994.
People Weekly, October 23, 1995.
Reader's Digest, February 1997.
Theatre Bio, Suzanne Stephens Arts Services, June 1998.
Wall Street Journal, April 4, 1995.
Washingtonian, December 1996.
Washington Post, January 19, 1997, June 8, 1996, October 9, 1995, March 26, 1995, February 24, 1991, September 28, 1989.

—Ellen Dennis French

Necia Desiree Harkless

1920—

Scholar

Educator, writer, pianist, and painter, Necia Desiree Harkless is a woman of many talents and interests. Over the decades she has worked as a social worker, music teacher, kindergarten teacher, and university professor of education. Her specialties in education were curriculum development, multicultural education, African American history, and the ancient African kingdoms of Egypt, Nubia, and Nigeria. After retiring from Georgetown College in 1985, Harkless became a Donovan Scholar at the University of Kentucky. With a grant for "refueling or retooling," Harkless pursued her longtime passions for cultural ethnography and fine arts.

Harkless grew up in Hamtramck, a section of Detroit largely populated by people of Polish descent, the eldest of three children born to James and Ethel Harkless. Her family attended the Second Baptist church in the community known as Greektown. She found the blending of diverse ethnic communities with their different cultures that make up Detroit stimulating in many ways. Moreover, because Harkless attended the Detroit Settlement schools, which taught art and music as well as the basic curriculum, she became interested in the fine arts. From an early age, she learned to play the piano and also took cello and organ lessons. Later she studied music with Madame Manebaca, a piano soloist with the Detroit Symphony Orchestra, and earned a bachelors degree in piano and organ performance and musical theory from the Detroit Institute of Musical Arts.

Embarked on Career in Education

For fifteen years Harkless taught children to play the piano, but her interest in teaching did not stop there. In 1942 she earned a bachelors degree in education from Prairie View State Agricultural College, in Hempstead, Texas. She worked as a caseworker for the Michigan Department of Social Welfare for a decade, and for several years she taught kindergarten in the Detroit public school system. Focusing on early childhood education, she developed a curriculum guide for early childhood teachers at a time when the federally supported Head Start programs were not yet year-round programs. Later she conducted research in education during her graduate studies at Wayne State University in Detroit, from which she earned a doctorate in education in 1974.

At a Glance...

Born June 25, 1920, in Detroit, MI; daughter of James and Ethel Harkless. *Education:* Prairie View State and Agricultural College, (Hempstead, Texas), B.A. (education and social science), 1942; Detroit Institute of Musical Arts, B.A. (piano, organ, and musical theory), 1960; University of Illinois at Champaign-Urbana, M.A. (education), 1969; Wayne State University, Detroit, MI, Ph.D. (education), 1974.

Career: Michigan Department of Social Welfare, caseworker, 1946-56; Detroit Institute of Musical Arts, music teacher, 1954-65; Detroit Public Schools, teacher, 1965-68; Wayne State University College of Education, researcher, 1968-74; University of Kentucky, associate professor of education, 1974-81; Georgetown College, associate professor of graduate education, 1981-85.

Awards: University of Kentucky Donovan Scholar.

Member: Lexington-Fayette County Historic Commission, Prichard Committee for Academic Excellence, Advisory Board of the Governor's School for the Arts, Lexington Art League.

Addresses: c/o Heart to Heart, P.O. Box 2017, Lexington, KY 40594.

Harkless taught in the College of Education at the University of Kentucky from 1974 through 1981 and at Georgetown College, a private Baptist college in Georgetown, Kentucky, from 1981 until her retirement in 1985. Among her projects while at the University of Kentucky was the development and field testing of curriculum guides to teach American students about Nigeria, a country in west central Africa to which many African Americans can trace their ancestry. As a professor emerita and University of Kentucky Donovan Scholar, Harkless continued to receive financial support to pursue her research interests, among them the Black Madonnas of Europe, ancient African culture and art, the Nubian and Meroitic kingdoms of ancient Egypt and Sudan, and the contributions of black American women in America from 1776 to 1986. She has spoken often on these topics to interested groups of all ages as part of the Kentucky Humanities Council's speakers bureau.

Also a visual artist, Harkless started painting in oils during retirement because she wanted to depict the Nubian experience. She often paints on silk, which is then mounted on linen. Such works as "Nubian Mothers," "Nubian Water Carrier," and "Nubian Art Class" celebrate the beauty and majesty of the Nubian form. In addition, Harkless created a line of silk scarves, which she called "Simply Joy," that are made with shiburi, a Japanese technique similar to batik.

Discovered the Black Madonnas

At an early age, Harkless became enthralled with the Black Madonnas, statues that can be found in more than a thousand churches throughout Europe. "Love of the Black Madonna was planted before I was born," Harkless told *Contemporary Black Biography (CBB)*. As a soldier during World War I, her father had fought for the French because at that time black American soldiers were not allowed to fight alongside white American forces. Although he was stationed near Paris, Harkless, like his fellow black American soldiers, was told that Paris was off-limits, so he visited other areas of the country. At a church in Chambery in the French Alps, James Harkless first discovered a Black Madonna--a statue of Mary the Mother of Jesus holding the infant Jesus--and sent a postcard of it home to his wife, Ethel. "Dear Love, This is the Black Madonna. Her gown is pure gold.—Jim," the card read. In 1994, Necia Harkless traced the path her father had traveled in France, visiting the famous Notre-Dame de Myans in Chambery, as well as other churches housing Black Madonnas. "People didn't know about the Black Madonnas. I felt I should educate them," Harkless told *CBB*. "When you go into churches, they'll say because of smoke from candles, the Madonnas have turned black, but from what we now understand, the prototype came from Isis (an ancient Egyptian fertility goddess)," she explained. In her chapbook of poems, *Heart to Heart,* Harkless reproduced photographs and briefly told the stories of three Black Madonnas.

Investigated Ancient Civilizations

As an ethnographer—a person who studies a civilization in terms of its culture at a particular place and during a certain time—Harkless spent over a decade researching and recovering the true history of the dark-skinned peoples of the Middle East, especially in ancient Egypt between the Red Sea and the Nile River. Her efforts centered on the kingdoms of Kush that are mentioned in the Bible and in ancient classical writings. Artifacts from these kingdoms have been preserved in museums worldwide and are only in the 1990s being recognized as

Nubian, that is, originating from the ancient black-skinned inhabitants of Nubia, and recategorized to reflect this new information. Harkless has traveled widely and seen many of the artifacts and archaeological sites firsthand. "I feel like a Sherlock Holmes ... or an Alice in Wonderland," Harkless told *CBB* of her research efforts. Harkless has shared her research with colleagues at professional meetings of archaeologists and ethnographers. In 1998 she was completing a lengthy work on the subject, tentatively entitled *Nubian Pharaohs and Meroitic Kings: Rulers of the Kingdom of Kush*. In this work, she described the oral, classical, and biblical traditions that shed light on the kingdom of Kush. She also detailed the archaeological efforts of nineteenth- and twentieth-century scholars to preserve artifacts from the kingdoms, described the Nubian temples and tombs, and provided information on the ancient geography, climate, vegetation, and animal life. Because the classic work on this subject has long been out of print and further research has revealed new insights, Harkless felt some urgency to complete this scholarly work. Furthermore, Harkless has often stressed the need for African Americans to remember that they are the descendants of kings and queens, not only slaves.

Sources

Books

Harkless, Necia Desiree, *Heart To Heart: Poems and Images by Necia Desiree Harkless,* Heart To Heart and Associates (Lexington, KY), 1995.

Other

Interview with Necia Harkless, July 7, 1998.

Further information was provided by Entertainment 2000, P.O. Box 2017, Lexington, KY 40594.

—Jeanne M. Lesinski

Jay T. Harris

1948—

Newspaper publisher

Jay T. Harris, publisher of the *San Jose Mercury News,* is considered one of the most influential minority newspaper executives in the United States. Head of the influential West Coast daily since 1994, he has enhanced the reputation of the already well-regarded *Mercury News* and continued to expand its role as an important media source in California, especially in its coverage of Silicon Valley. The paper itself made headlines in late 1996 when it published a controversial story that linked the crack cocaine epidemic and drug traffickers to a right-wing Central American political group that received erstwhile covert support from the Central Intelligence Agency. Harris was praised for allowing the story to run, and for sticking by the paper and the reporter after the story generated intense scrutiny.

Harris began his career in journalism not long after earning a degree in English from Pennsylvania's Lincoln University in 1970. His first job was as a reporter with the *Wilmington News-Journal,* a Delaware paper, where he made a name for himself relatively early in his professional career for an expose on heroin trafficking in the city. The series won Harris an Associated Press award, and he was soon promoted to an editor's desk. Within a few years he had been singled out for a fellowship by the Frank E. Gannett Urban Journalism Center at the Medill School of Journalism. Medill, at Northwestern University in suburban Chicago, is considered one of the foremost training grounds for journalism in the United States. Harris was made a Gannett Fellow, the first ever, when the Urban Journalism Center was created. In 1975, Harris left the day-to-day world of newspapers when he was offered a job at Medill. There he taught classes as an assistant professor of journalism and urban affairs; he also served as associate director of the Urban Journalism Center and associate dean at Medill before leaving in 1982.

Top Job in Philadelphia

Harris returned to newspaper work that year when he arrived in Washington, D.C., to take a job with Gannett News Services, one of the largest print media companies in North America and publisher of *USA Today.* There, he served as a national correspondent and wrote a weekly column. In 1985, he left Gannett when he was

At a Glance...

Born 1948. Married; three children. *Education:* Lincoln University, B.A., 1970.

Career: Began as reporter for *Wilmington News-Journal,* Wilmington, DE, 1970, editor, until 1975; Northwestern University/Medill School of Journalism, assistant professor of journalism and urban affairs, 1975-82; also served as associate director of the Frank E. Gannett Urban Journalism Center and associate dean of Medill School of Journalism; Gannett News Services, Washington, D.C., national correspondent, 1982-85; *Philadelphia Daily News,* executive editor, 1985-88, and vice-president of Philadelphia Newspapers, 1987-88; Knight-Ridder Newspapers, Miami, FL, assistant to the president, 1988-89, vice-president of operations, 1989-93; *San Jose Mercury News,* San Jose, CA, chair and publisher, 1994-.

Awards: Par Excellence Award, Operation PUSH, 1984, for distinguished service; special citation from the Institute for Journalism Education for contributions to the cause of racial diversity in American newspaper journalism, 1991; Ida B. Wells Award, National Association of Black Journalists, 1992.

Member: American Leadership Forum-Silicon Valley.

Addresses: *Office*—San Jose Mercury News, 750 Ridder Park Dr., San Jose, CA 95190.

---

wooed away by its top competitor, the Knight-Ridder News Corporation. He was hired by the family-owned media company to helm its *Philadelphia Daily News.* Not yet forty years old, he became one of the youngest executive editors of a major metropolitan daily in the country. He also became one of a few minority newspaper executives in such a post as well. A 1988 article on his achievement by George Garneau in *Editor & Publisher* called Harris's rise, especially at such a young age, "exceptional ... in a field dominated but middle-aged, white men." Harris remained optimistic that that particular demographic would change: "I think more people will do what I do over time," he told Garneau, and remained philosophical about his own situation. "My color is a factor in everything in my life," he told *Editor & Publisher.* "Race is a factor in American society.

Obviously, some people think I'm pretty good."

In 1987, Harris was made a vice-president of Philadelphia Newspapers, and remained in the number-two spot at the *Daily News* until he was summoned to Knight-Ridder headquarters in Miami for a post there. From 1988 to 1989 he served as assistant to the president, and was named vice-president for operations in 1989. In this post he oversaw Knight-Ridder's newspaper holdings in the Midwest and Plains states, including its dailies in Akron, St. Paul, Gary, Duluth, and Grand Forks. In 1993 Harris was offered the plum position of chairman and publisher of the *San Jose Mercury News* upon the retirement of its top executive. The newspaper, based in the northern California city of San Jose, was a widely-read, respected newspaper with a circulation of 300,000 and considered the "Wall Street Journal" of Silicon Valley. In Santa Clara County, located at the south end of the San Francisco Bay, it was estimated that 57 percent of the population read the *Mercury News*'s daily edition.

A Vital News Source

Harris stepped into the publisher's job in San Jose in 1994. Some notable accomplishments of his tenure include the launch of a foreign bureau in Hanoi, Vietnam—the first permanent news bureau there since the Vietnam War ended—and the paper's on-line edition, the Mercury Center, with its special focus on high-technology business news and a customizable personal news service called NewsHound. About two million visitors "hit" the paper's Internet site at peak hours. Harris also oversaw the launch of *Nuevo Mundo,* a Spanish-language weekly paper and the only such news source in Northern California.

But it was the newspaper's publication of "Dark Alliance: The Story Behind the Crack Explosion," that made headlines around the country and made the *San Jose Mercury News* known to a far more extensive number of people than just residents of Santa Clara County. Written by an investigative reporter on its staff, Gary Webb, the three-part series detailed possible links between some California-based supporters of "contras"—the anti-Communist guerrillas in Nicaragua—the crack cocaine problem in Los Angeles in the 1980s, and the Central Intelligence Agency. Webb obtained information from informants who were involved with the first two. There arose a massive controversy about the reports, and the story was in some cases misconstrued as an allegation that the CIA had flooded South Central L.A. and other pockets of urban misery with crack. As Harris clarified in an interview with Victoria Valentine in

Emerge magazine, "the heart of the story is ... that close associates of the Nicaraguan Contras, in the early 1980s, were selling very significant amounts of pure cocaine in the United States; that much of that was going into South Central L.A.; that others, persons in L.A., including people associated with the gangs there, were turning it into crack; and that, finally, these same persons associated with the Contras were sending money back to support that effort."

Story Unleashed Furor

Some in the African American community had long suspected a tie between the government and the rise of crack, a drug that was cheap, addictive, and deadly. Unusual methods of financing the Nicaraguan contras, a pet cause of the Reagan Administration, were not unknown: during the 1980s, it was discovered that agents for the U.S. government were secretly selling arms to Iran, a sworn foe of the United States, and using the money to finance the contras, who were struggling to overthrow a leftist Sandinista government in Nicaragua. Though the story Harris had okayed initially caused little stir, its publication on the Mercury Center site and subsequent rapid dissemination throughout cyberspace— as well as the interest given it on talk-radio programs hosted by such prominent pundits such as Joe Madison— helped the "Dark Alliance" story gain notoriety. Several prominent political figures, including U.S. Attorney General Janet Reno, Los Angeles Mayor Richard Riordan, and U.S. congresswoman Maxine Waters, called for an official government investigation into Webb's allegations.

Other newspapers and media outlets found fault with the "Dark Alliance" story, and Harris had to weather criticism that the reporter's tactics and conclusions were flawed. Peter Kornbluh, writing in the *Columbia Journalism Review,* remarked that "their editorial decision to assault, rather than advance, the *Mercury News* story has, in turn, sparked critical commentary on the priorities of those pillars of the mainstream press."

Harris is married and has three children. He is involved in numerous professional and philanthropic organizations, and is a trustee of the John S. and James L. Knight Foundation. He is also the recipient of numerous professional accolades, including a 1991 citation from the Institute for Journalism Education for his contributions to racial diversity in American newspaper journalism, and the Ida B. Wells Award from the National Association of Black Journalists in 1992. His prediction in the *Editor & Publisher* interview proved prophetic: a decade later, even the first newspaper that had hired Harris, the *News-Journal* in Wilmington, had an African American executive editor.

Sources

Columbia Journalism Review, January/February 1997; May/June 1998, p. 26.
Editor & Publisher, May 7, 1988, pp. 11, 38.
Emerge, December/January 1997, pp. 34-37.

Additional information for this profile was provided by press materials from the *San Jose Mercury News* and Knight-Ridder Newspapers.

—Carol Brennan

Sherman Hemsley

1938—

Actor

Comedic actor Sherman Hemsley so embodied his role on television's long-running series *The Jeffersons* that many fans still think of him only as George Jefferson. Donald Bogle described Hemsley in *Blacks in American Films and Television* as "one of America's best-known [by character, not name] but least publicized performers." Hemsley was a stage actor at the beginning of his career. He broke into television in 1973 when producer Norman Lear cast him as George Jefferson, Archie Bunker's neighbor in the popular series *All in the Family*. His character proved so strong that Hemsley was cast in a starring role with Isabel Sanford in the spinoff series, *The Jeffersons*. *The Jeffersons* became wildly popular in its own right with audiences both black and white, and enjoyed a ten-year run on CBS, from 1975 to 1985. In the years that followed, Hemsley's career has continued to thrive. He has had several film roles and has made numerous guest appearances on television shows including *Family Matters, Me and the Boys,* and *Fresh Prince of Bel Air*.

Although a popular and very successful actor who has worked steadily since he began in New York theatre in the sixties, Hemsley has managed to keep the spotlight of publicity focused on his professional career only. As a result, most of the details of his personal life have remained private.

Sherman Hemsley was born February 1, 1938 in Philadelphia. He attended school there through the tenth grade. He served in the U.S. Air Force sometime after the Korean War, stationed in both Japan and Korea. In the mid-fifties Hemsley enrolled in the Bok Vocational-Technical School in South Philadelphia to learn tailoring. As the *Philadelphia Daily News* noted in 1996, "If Sherman Hemsley had been able to sew a fine seam, TV might never have been the same." Luckily for George Jefferson fans, tailoring proved intimidating for Hemsley, who told the paper he opted out when he saw "how hard it was to do those little stitches." He traded vocational school for a retail sales position. This he did not care for either, and moved on to restaurant training, lured by the prospect of being able to eat what he cooked. "But," Hemsley told the *Daily News*, "I always knew I wanted to be an actor." He finally landed a position with the U.S. Postal Service, where he would work for eight years. During those early years Hemsley also attended Philadelphia's Academy of Dramatic Arts

At a Glance...

Born February 1, 1938, in Philadelphia, PA. *Education:* Attended Philadelphia Academy of Dramatic Arts, also studied with Lloyd Richards in New York; served in U.S. Air Force in Japan and Korea.

Career: Worked for U.S. Postal Service for eight years; performed with Negro Ensemble Company, New York City. Television: *Black Book* (Philadelphia local series); George Jefferson, *All in the Family*, 1973-75; George Jefferson, *The Jeffersons*, 1975-85; Deacon Frye, *Amen*, 1986-91; voice, B.P. Richfield, *The Dinosaurs*, 1991-94; Willie Goode, *Goode Behavior*, 1996-97; numerous guest appearances on series and specials. Made-for-television movies: *Purlie*, 1981; *Alice in Wonderland*, 1985. Films: *Love at First Bite*, 1979; *Stewardess School*, 1986; *Ghost Fever*, 1987; *Club Fed*, 1991; *Home of Angels*, 1993; *Mr. Nanny*, 1993; *Sprung*, 1997. Theatre: debuted with Negro Ensemble Company, New York City; appeared in *The People vs. Ranchman*, 1968; *But Never Jam Today*, 1969; *Old Judge Mose is Dead*, 1969; *Moon on a Rainbow Shawl*, 1969; *Purlie*, 1970; *Purlie Victorious* and others with the Theatre XIV Company; *The Blacks; The Odd Couple; Norman, Is That You?* 1986; *Under the Yum-Yum Tree; Death of a Salesman; Don't Bother Me, I Can't Cope*, 1973; *I'm Not Rappaport*, 1987. Owner, Love Is, Inc., a production company.

Memberships and awards: Member, AFTRA, Vinette Carroll's Urban Arts Corps, Actors' Equity Association, Screen Actors Guild, American Federation of Television and Radio Artists; recipient, NAACP Image Award, 1976, 1987, Hollywood Foreign Press Association Award, Golden Globe Award.

Addresses: c/o Kenny Johnston, 6290 Sunset Boulevard, Suite 403, Los Angeles, CA 90028.

and pursued roles in small theaters. Notably, he starred in a local Philadelphia TV comedy series called *Black Book*. Although he has admitted he sometimes had his doubts about whether he would make it as an actor, he explained the dream to *Parade's* James Brady in 1996: "You have this burning desire. You're sure this is the path to take. Yeah, I had doubts. But a buddy at the post office said, 'Hey, you're the only one of us who's going to get out of here.'"

Began Theatre Career

Hemsley obtained a transfer to New York City in the late sixties. Once there, he joined the Negro Ensemble Company. He also studied acting with Lloyd Richards and performed with Vinette Carroll's Urban Arts Corps. 1968 found him cast in the off-Broadway production *The People vs. Ranchman* as the assistant executioner. In 1969 he appeared with the Urban Arts Corps on a double bill combining the one-act *Old Judge Mose is Dead* and the three-act tragicomedy *Moon on a Rainbow Shawl*. *New York Times* reviewer McCandlish Phillips singled out Hemsley's performances for praise, noting, "In both ends of the evening, Sherman Hemsley shows himself to be an actor whose instinct for the comic line and the comic gesture ... is wholly natural and just about perfect." Phillips credited Hemsley with "sustain[ing] ... the one-act comedy throughout." He also observed that as Charlie Adams in *Moon on a Rainbow Shawl*, "he stirs laughter at every turn until, in a moment of overwhelming grief, he weeps."

In 1970 Hemsley was cast as Gitlow in the Broadway musical *Purlie*. Although *New York Times* theatre reviewer Clive Barnes noted that "Novella Nelson and Sherman Hemsley were smooth as silk as Purlie's family," he also suggested that the play would make stars of performers Cleavon Little and Melba Moore. As it turned out, *Purlie* was instrumental in making a star of Sherman Hemsley as well. Producer Norman Lear saw Hemsley's performance in that production and was impressed. Three years later, Lear was trying unsuccessfully to cast the role of Archie Bunker's neighbor in the CBS series *All in the Family*. Remembering Hemsley's performance in *Purlie*, Lear tracked him to San Francisco, where he was performing in *Don't Bother Me, I Can't Cope*.

Cast as George Jefferson

Hemsley was perfect as George Jefferson. Pamala S. Deane described the part in the *Encyclopedia of Television*. "The George Jefferson character was conceptualized as a black equivalent of Archie Bunker. George was intolerant, rude, and stubborn," she wrote. In two years' time George was so well-liked by audiences it was decided *The Jeffersons* would become a spinoff series.

Premiering January 17, 1975, the show became, after a somewhat rocky start, an enduring success. In this series, the Jeffersons' dry cleaning business has expanded to seven stores and has made them very wealthy. They have moved from Queens to a luxury high-rise apartment on Manhattan's East Side. Focusing on their lives, the series co-starred Isabel Sanford as Louise Jefferson—or "Weezy," as George called her. It was the first television show since *Amos 'n Andy* to feature blacks in starring roles with a mostly black cast, noted the *Encyclopedia of Television*. Featuring Roxie Roker and Franklin Cover, the show also broke ground as the first to portray an interracial married couple. Roker and Cover, played the Willises, the Jeffersons' neighbors. *Jet* noted in 1983 that despite strong initial ratings, the show suffered through some poor time slots and several times faced the specter of cancellation. Ratings stabilized when the show was moved to Sunday nights in a plum lineup led by the venerable *60 Minutes*. Although an excellent writing team and inimitable cast chemistry are also credited for the series' success, *Jet* concluded that "for a generation that has grown up with George and Weezy, the most attractive aspect of the show is the relationship between these two. Their ups and downs, likes and dislikes transcend race and have universal appeal."

The Jeffersons ended its ten-year run in 1985. Hemsley was soon cast in another series, this time opposite actor-turned-real-life-minister Clifton Davis in the CBS church board hit, *Amen*. Board member Deacon Frye, Hemsley's new character, bore some similarities to George Jefferson. Frye was also feisty, overbearing, witty, and sometimes unscrupulous. Hemsley pointed out to *Jet* in 1986 that although "this character has the same energy level as George ... they are basically different people." Again, good cast chemistry and writing helped sustain the show beyond the excellent acting of its principals, and the series ran for a respectable five years, ending in 1991.

Hemsley was the voice of B.P. Richfield on the series *The Dinosaurs* from 1991 to 1994, and was cast in 1996 as ex-con Willie Goode in the short-lived UPN series *Goode Behavior*. Hemsley has made numerous guest appearances on various television series and specials from 1975 to the present. He has had film roles in *Love at First Bite* (1979), *Stewardess School* (1987), and *Ghost Fever* (1987). In 1996 he won a $2.8 million lawsuit against Wolf Schmidt, a film distributor who, according to *Jet*, "denied him his share of profits from the 1987 movie *Ghost Fever.*" Hemsley also appeared in the made-for-TV movies *Purlie* in 1981 and *Alice in Wonderland* in 1985.

Deane noted in the *Encyclopedia of Television* that "Hemsley as a person is quite unlike the high-strung character he has popularized on television." Rumors that Hemsley is difficult to work with were settled by Clifton Davis. "I'm here to tell you that's a lie," he told *Jet* in 1986. "He's very shy. He's giving, and is not on an ego trip. He's terrific." Other *Amen* cast members had similar praise for Hemsley. *Jet* reported in 1987 that "Roz Ryan, who plays Amelia Heterbrink, gives Hemsley much of the credit for keeping the show laid back." "He's a peach," Ryan told *Jet,* and added, "Sherman is like a Black Charlie Chaplin. He's wonderful."

Sources

Books

Bogle, Donald. *Blacks in American Films and Television: An Encyclopedia*. New York: Garland Publishing, Inc., 1988.

Brown, Les. *Les Brown's Encyclopedia of Television*, 3rd Edition. Detroit: Gale, 1992.

Contemporary Theatre, Film, and Television, Vol. 3. Edited by Monica M. O'Donnell. Detroit: Gale, 1986.

Encyclopedia of Television, Vol. 2. Edited by Horace Newcomb. Chicago: Fitzroy Dearborn Publishers, 1997.

Terrace, Vincent. *Encyclopedia of Television Series, Pilots and Specials, 1974-1984*. New York: Zoetrope, 1985.

McNeil, Alex. *Total Television: The Comprehensive Guide to Programming from 1948 to the Present*, 4th Edition. New York: Penguin Books, 1996.

Facts on File, 1992.

Periodicals

Jet, October 3, 1983, October 27, 1986, November 23, 1987, March 25, 1996, April 7, 1997.

New York Times Theatre Reviews, Vol. 8.

Philadelphia Daily News, August 22, 1996.

—Ellen Dennis French

Aaron Henry

1922–1997

NAACP leader, civil rights leader, politician

A fiery, outspoken civil rights leader, Aaron Henry was also a moderate who sought to heal the wounds that divided blacks and whites in the 1960s. For more than thirty years, Henry was a leader of the National Association for the Advancement of Colored People (NAACP) in Mississippi and was on the front lines of virtually every civil rights event of the era. By his own account, he was arrested 38 times in the effort to secure equal rights for African Americans. Most of these arrests occurred in Henry's home state of Mississippi, which zealously supported segregation. Overwhelmingly elected governor of Mississippi in a "mock" election in 1964, Henry would eventually serve his state as a legislator. His death in 1997 marked the end of a prestigious life shaped by the fight for racial equality.

Aaron Edd Henry was born in Dublin, Mississippi on July 2, 1922, the son of Edd, a sharecropper, and his wife Mattie Logan. After attending high school in nearby Clarksdale, Henry enlisted in the Army and was stationed in Hawaii. While there, he took part in his first protest by initiating a demand for integrated military housing. Henry later recalled that his grandmother had instilled in him the notion that he was as worthy of justice as any white man. "They put on their pants the same way you do," she told him according to his *New York Times* obituary, "one leg at a time."

Joined NAACP

Following his discharge from the Army, Henry attended Xavier University in New Orleans on the G.I. Bill. He quickly demonstrated his leadership abilities at Xavier, serving as student body president and president of his junior and senior classes. In 1950, with a pharmaceutical degree in hand, Henry and an Xavier classmate returned to Clarksdale and opened a pharmacy. Henry's new role as a successful businessman soon propelled him to a leadership position within the local black community.

In 1954, Henry joined the Mississippi chapter of the NAACP. By 1960, his fierce determination to fight segregation led to his election as president of the state chapter, an office he would hold until stepping down in 1993. A year after joining the NAACP, Henry organized the Council of Federated Organizations (COFO). Designed to unify and coordinate the activities of the NAACP, the Student Nonviolent Coordinating Commit-

At a Glance...

Born Aaron Edd Henry July 2, 1922 in Dublin, Mississippi to Edd, a sharecropper, and Mattie Logan Henry. Married Noelle Michael, 1950 (died 1994); children: Rebecca. *Education:* Xavier University, B.A.

Career: Civil rights leader; opened pharmacy in Clarksdale, Mississippi with Xavier classmate, 1950; joined National Association for the Advancement of Colored People (NAACP), 1954; founded Council of Federated Organization (COFO), 1955; elected president of the Mississippi chapter of NAACP, 1960; arrested in Freedom Rider protest, 1961; organized boycott of stores in Clarksdale, Mississippi, 1961; won "mock" election as governor of Mississippi, 1963; helped found Mississippi Freedom Democratic Party (MFDP), 1964; selected as "at-large" delegate at Democratic National Convention, 1964; helped to organize Loyalist Democratic party in Mississippi, 1965; chaired the Loyalist delegation at the Democratic National Convention, 1968 and 1972; co-chaired the Mississippi delegation at Democratic National Convention, 1976; elected to Mississippi House of Representatives, 1982-96.

tee (SNCC), the Southern Christian Leadership Conference (SCLC), and the Congress of Racial Equality (CORE), the Council lay dormant for years until the early 1960s, when they initiated large-scale voter registration and adult education.

COFO also became involved in the defense of the Freedom Riders. The Freedom Riders were a group of black and white activists who were organized by CORE to protest the existence of segregated interstate bus facilities. Although the Supreme Court ordered the integration of all bus stations and terminals serving interstate travelers in December of 1960, blacks in the Deep South who tried to use bus terminal facilities designated for whites or use the front seats of buses were often beaten, thrown off the bus, or jailed. In May of 1961, the Freedom Riders began their protest in Washington, DC and rode the Trailways and Greyhound bus systems to New Orleans, with the white protesters sitting in the back seats and the black protestors sitting up front. If challenged, the black protestors would refuse to give up their front seats. Additionally, at each station or terminal, blacks would attempt to use whites-only facilities. Along the route, the protest was marked by violence as segregationists confronted the Riders at nearly every stop. When the Riders arrived in Jackson, Mississippi, Henry was among those arrested.

Won Mock Election

In late 1961, Henry initiated a boycott against stores in Clarksdale that refused to hire black workers or discriminated against black customers. City officials responded by arresting Henry and six other protestors on the grounds of "conspiring to withhold trade." Although Henry and the others were convicted in local courts, the convictions were reversed on appeal and the boycott continued. Henry was then arrested on what he called a "trumped-up" charge of sexually harassing a white hitchhiker, for which he was convicted in March of 1962. An appeals court eventually reversed the conviction. When Henry claimed that the local prosecutor and police chief falsified the sexual harassment charge on the basis of his civil rights activities, the two men sued him and were awarded $80,000. The appeals court again reversed the decision. By the time the boycott ended, Henry's pharmacy had been firebombed and his wife Noelle was fired from her job as a public school teacher.

In June of 1963, the civil rights community in Mississippi was dealt a serious blow when leader Medgar Evers was murdered in the driveway of his home after taking Henry to the airport. The two close friends had met in the early 1950s and Henry vigorously supported Evers in his quest to become field secretary of the Mississippi NAACP. Henry was later told that a flip of a coin had determined that it would be Evers who was assassinated and not him. "Ever since Medgar died," Henry is quoted as saying in his *New York Times* obituary, "I have been making sure he didn't die in vain."

In the fall of 1963, under the auspices of COFO, a mock election was held for the office of governor of Mississippi. Voter registration tests that were biased against blacks and violent attacks against voter registration workers had severely hampered the ability of blacks to participate in elections. In response, the Freedom Vote was staged. Henry ran as a candidate for governor with Edwin King, a white chaplain at the all-black Tougaloo College, as lieutenant governor. Unofficial freedom ballots were printed and distributed in churches and meeting places. The Henry-King duo won the election handily. Roughly 80,000 blacks had participated in the mock election, nearly three times the number of officially registered black voters.

The success of the mock election encouraged the SNCC and COFO to increase their voter registration efforts.

They designated the summer of 1964 as Freedom Summer and began a massive voter registration campaign with the help of 800 volunteers, many of whom were white college students from the North. Also that summer, Henry co-founded the Mississippi Freedom Democratic Party (MFDP), a biracial coalition which challenged the exclusion of black members by the Democratic Party in Mississippi. Henry was elected chairperson of the MFDP, whose principal goal was to have a delegation seated at the 1964 Democratic National Convention in Atlantic City, New Jersey.

Participated in 1964 Democratic Convention

Although the MFDP had chosen 68 delegates to attend the convention, the administration of President Lyndon Johnson declared that they would not be allowed to participate. In addition, the attorney general of Mississippi issued an injunction against the MFDP delegates and threatened to jail any who tried to attend the convention. The MFDP delegates, including Henry, ignored the injunction and traveled to the convention. They received support from delegates from other states, who insisted that the MFDP delegates be seated on the convention floor. After a three-day standoff, a compromise was reached. The MFDP delegates were offered "at-large" status which would not allow them to vote for a candidate or represent any state. The delegates refused this compromise.

> "I think that every time a man stands for an idea or speaks out against injustice, he sends out a tiny ripple of hope."

A second compromise was offered which gave "at-large" delegate status only to Henry and Edwin King. This development angered and insulted the other MFDP delegates. "It's a token of rights on the back row that we get in Mississippi," outspoken leader Fannie Lou Hamer is quoted as saying in *Mississippi Challenge*. "We didn't come all this way for that mess again." The compromise, however, was accepted without the knowledge of the MFDP delegates. On the first night of the convention, the MFDP delegates arrived and took the seats of the regular Mississippi delegates, which created a stir. The next morning, Henry, Martin Luther King, Jr., and Senator Wayne Morris tried to convince the rest of the MFDP delegates to accept the compromise. They still refused and at the convention that night, they arrived to find all of the seats in the Mississippi section removed except for three, where the white delegates sat surrounded by security guards. The 68 MFDP delegates remained and stood throughout the evening.

Later in 1964, Henry attempted to run for Congress as an independent, as did Fannie Lou Hamer and Annie Devine. However, election officials claimed that the candidates had failed to obtain the required number of signatures to put their names on the ballot. The next year, Henry won another Freedom Vote mock election for the U.S. Senate and was elected to the national board of directors of the NAACP. In addition, Henry sensed that the MFDP was becoming too radical and did not represent his more moderate views. He left the MFDP and helped to form the Loyalist Democrats, a group of blacks, white liberals, and organized labor activists who sought to distinguish themselves from the conservative "regular" democrats. Henry became a chief architect for the new party and chaired the Loyalist delegation to the 1968 and 1972 Democratic National Conventions.

Henry eventually initiated a unification program with the regular democrats in which the two sides would split convention delegates and positions on the party executive committee. Complete unification was accomplished in time for the 1976 Democratic National Convention which was co-chaired by Henry and a regular democrat. This unification paved the way for more blacks to be elected to the state legislature. In 1980, Henry filed a lawsuit which led to the reapportionment of districts and allowed for the election of more representatives. Henry was elected to the Mississippi House of Representatives in 1982 and held the seat until 1996.

Although Aaron Henry's name is largely unknown outside his home state of Mississippi, his impact on civil rights in that state and around the country is undeniable. For Henry, there was no such thing as a small victory and each victory usually led to an even greater success. "I think," Henry told *Historic World Leaders*, "that every time a man stands for an ideal or speaks out against injustice, he sends out a tiny ripple of hope."

Sources

Books

Carrow, David J., *Bearing the Cross,* Vintage Books, 1996.

Lowery Charles D. and John F. Marszalek, eds., *Encyclopedia of African-American Civil Rights,* Greenwood Press, 1992.

Maisel, Sandy L, ed., *Political Parties and Elections in the United States,* Garland Publishing, 1991.

Nossiter, Adam, *Of Long Memory: Mississippi and the Murder of Medgar Evers,* Addison-Wesley Publishing Co., 1994.

Parker, Frank R., *Black Votes Count: Political Empowerment in Mississippi after 1965,* University of North Carolina Press, 1990.

Salter, John R., Jr., *Jackson Mississippi,* Robert E. Krieger Publishing Co., 1987.

Sitkoff, Harvard, *The Struggle for Black Equality, 1954-1980,* Hill and Wang, 1981.

Stern, Mark, *Calculating Visions: Kennedy, Johnson, and Civil Rights,* Rutgers University Press, 1992.

Walter, Mildred Pitts, *Mississippi Challenge,* Aladdin Paperbacks, 1992.

Williams, Juan, *Eyes on the Prize: America's Civil Rights Years, 1954-1965,* Penguin Books, 1987.

Periodicals

Jet, June 9, 1997, p. 55.
New York Times, May 21, 1997, p. D-23.
Time, June 2, 1997, p. 27.

—Brian Escamilla

Calvin and Janet Hill

Corporate consultants

The husband-and-wife team of Calvin and Janet Hill has become a respected resource on "how to"—how to raise a family, how to create diversity in the workplace, and how to survive the pressures of being a professional athlete. Perhaps best known as the parents of NBA All-Star Grant Hill, the Hills are prominent corporate consultants whose overlapping interests and skills have sometimes led to their working together. In April of 1997, the Hills were both hired by the Dallas Cowboys to help rescue a football team embarrassed by criminal charges and drug suspensions. Independently, they serve as consultants to other leading corporations; Janet acts as vice president of a Washington D.C. consulting firm, while Calvin has become an independent consultant after working for many years as a vice president for the Baltimore Orioles.

Calvin Hill's first career, however, was as a professional football player. With a degree from Yale University, he became the Dallas Cowboys' number one draft pick in 1969. As a running back, he went on to win Rookie of the Year honors and played in four Pro Bowls and two Super Bowls. During his early career with Dallas, Calvin also considered becoming a minister and for three years he attended Southern Methodist University's Perkins School of Theology while he played football. After six years as a Cowboy, Calvin played for one season in Hawaii in the short-lived World Football League. Next, he became a Washington Redskin in 1976 and, although he announced his retirement in 1977, returned to play three seasons for the Cleveland Browns.

Left Field for Front Office

Calvin's 13-year stint as a professional athlete was followed by a job in the Browns' front office. From 1987 to 1994, he was a vice president for the Baltimore Orioles. Calvin left the Orioles in order to pursue the possibility of bringing professional baseball back to Washington, D.C. with a group of like-minded investors. The group had made an unsuccessful bid to purchase the Washington Bullets and Capitols in 1994. In 1996 another effort was focused on purchasing the Astros, a deal that also fell through. Ultimately, Calvin wants to run and own part of a sports franchise. After having left the Orioles, he commented in the *Washington Post,* "I didn't want to turn into somebody who'd just be there collecting his paycheck....You're out front, you're visible, but you reach this glass ceiling....Ownership has been on my mind for a long time. It's a way to effect change and build something. You just have a lot more power to create as an owner."

These achievements and aspirations were born of a can-do attitude that was passed from father to son. Calvin's father was a sharecropper who moved north from South Carolina to become a construction worker. He wanted his son, who was born in Baltimore, to graduate from college. Calvin described the close relationship he had

At a Glance...

Born Calvin Hill, January 2, 1947, in Baltimore; son of Henry and Elizabeth Hill. Born Janet McDonald in 1947; married 1970; children: Grant Henry Hill. *Education:* Calvin graduated from Yale University, B.A., 1969; attended Southern Methodist Univ., Perkins School of Theology, 1969-71. Janet graduated from Wellesley College, B.A. (mathematics), 1969; M.A. (math education), Univ. of Chicago, 1972.

Career: Calvin played professional football as a running back for the Dallas Cowboys, 1969-74; Hawaiians (World Football League), 1975; Washington Redskins, 1976-78; Cleveland Browns, 1978-81; worked in Browns front office until 1987; vp for Baltimore Orioles, 1987-94; independent consultant, 1994-; . Janet worked as a teacher and scientist before serving as special asst. to the Secretary of the Army, 1978-81; founded corp. consulting firm Alexander and Assoc., 1981.

Awards: Calvin's honors include the Pro Bowl NFL All-Star Game, 1969, 1972, 1973-74; NFL Rookie of the Year, 1969; *Sporting News* NFL Eastern Conf. All-Star Team, 1969; All NFL Team (Pro Football Writers of America), 1969, 1973; 1000 Yard Club, 1972; *Sporting News* NFC All-Star, 1973; Maryland Hall of Fame.

Memberships: Calvin's include: Yale Club of Washington, DC; exec. board, Yale Devt. Bd; Yale Univ. Council, 1982-86; bd mem, NCAA Found.; President's Council on Physical Fitness; adv. bd, Rand Corp. Drug Policy Research Ctr. Janet's include: bd mem, Wellesley Coll. Center for Research on Women; Wellesley Business Leadership Council; former pres, Wellesley Coll. Alumnae Assn.; bd mem, Wendy's Intl.; bd mem, NY Cotton Exchange; board mem, McDonald Dental Lab.; bd mem, Fuqua School of Business at Duke Univ.

Addresses: *Home*—Great Falls, VA. *Office*—Alexander and Associates, 400 C Street N.E., Washington, D.C. 20002.

---

with his father in the *Washingtonian:* "I was very fortunate to have a father who was like clockwork. He came home every day and wanted to hear about my day. He was there for me when I didn't do well in Little League, taking me out in the back yard to practice. He was there when I went to prep school, to college, even to the Cowboys. When he died—I was 34—I felt like I'd lost my biggest supporter."

Teacher Turned Entrepreneur

Janet Hill is a vice president at Alexander & Associates, a Washington D.C.-based consulting firm that she co-founded in 1981. Her partner is Clifford Alexander, who she worked for as special assistant and White House liaison when he was secretary of the Army from 1978 to 1981. Among its clients, the firm numbers Major League Baseball, IBM, ABC News, the Ford Foundation, and the U.S. General Accounting Office. In addition to other services, Janet helped her clients establish an "inclusive" work force, that is, one including women and minorities. She sought to teach corporations how to hire qualified women and minority employees without relying on quotas, affirmative action, or sensitivity training. Importantly, Janet talked about inclusiveness because she considers the concept of "diversity" to be divisive. Moreover, her goal is to show businesses that a white male work force is not in their best interest financially. She explained in the *Detroit News,* "I don't have a moral message with this; I'm only talking with a business, pragmatic message....there [is] no reason one would want to recruit only white males, for example....You're not going to get the very best people. To get them, you have to canvass the universe. All the employers I know are in competitive businesses. They want the very best people."

Corporate consulting is also a career change for Janet, who first worked as a teacher after college. A graduate of Wellesley College, where she was a suite-mate of first lady Hillary Rodham Clinton, she earned a B.A. in mathematics in 1969. She also received a masters degree in math education from the University of Chicago. She has worked as a teacher at the high school, junior college, and college levels, and was a scientist at a private consulting firm.

Both of the Hills have extended their influence as members of corporate and university boards. Janet's appointments include the boards of Wendy's International, The New York Cotton Exchange, and McDonald Dental Laboratory; she also sits on the board of the Fuqua School of Business at Duke University. Calvin serves on the boards of the NCAA Foundation, the President's Council on Physical Fitness, and the Rand Corporation Drug Policy Institute. Both of the Hills are actively involved with several boards and organizations serving the institutions from which they graduated.

Joined Forces to Help Cowboys

Having worked together previously, the Hills were hired by the Dallas Cowboys in 1997 to improve the team's player-development programs. Several players had recently been involved in ugly incidents off the field that resulted in drug suspensions and a rape allegation. It was the Hills' job to create a support system that would try to teach players how to keep their personal lives safer and saner. They created a number of programs including family assistance, drug and alcohol abuse treatment, and career counseling. Calvin was enthusiastic about the Cowboys' future a year later, when he spoke to *The Hartford Courant:* "When I went to Dallas, I was expecting a team full of characters....what I found was a team of character. People tend to let a couple of incidents color the perception....Fame is a microscope, and with the Cowboys, it's an electron microscope."

> "We think our educations have served us every day for the last 26 years since we've been out of college, and that's part of the drumbeat we have given Grant."

The Cowboys clearly are not alone in their need to assist players who are dealing poorly with fame and fortune. The Hills' work with the NFL team is part of a larger trend towards support programs in college and professional sports. When Calvin met with a group of All-American college football players in 1998, he hoped to give them some warning of the overwhelming pressures they would face as professional athletes. "I wish I could tell each guy here to put all the money away for a couple of years until they figure out what to do with it," he said in the *Hartford Courant:* "The problem is, these young men are socialized a certain way ... and then they are given more money than they ever could have envisioned. They get all that money and fame too quickly, before they know how to handle it," he continued. The personal problems professional athletes face are well known to the Hills, not only because of Calvin's experiences in the NFL, but because of their son Grant's career in the NBA. Speaking of Grant's entry into professional basketball in the *Dallas Morning News,* Calvin remembered, "We were scared to death ... because we know what's out there."

Raised a Scholar-Athlete

Many sports fans think the Hills' defining role is being the parents of NBA All-Star Grant Hill. The Hills would probably agree with this notion, given their ideas on child-rearing. The Hills, particularly Janet, often speak publicly about their relationship with Grant—their only child—and about how proud they are of him. During such discussions, Janet and Calvin Hill's distinctly different personalities become apparent. Sitting with the Hills at one of Grant's first games as Detroit Piston, *Sporting News* reporter Michael P. Geffner saw a fascinating side-by-side comparison of an almost grimly intense Calvin and a smiling and hollering Janet. Geffner described the father's ritualistic approach to watching his son play: "His eyes will never leave the court, and he'll talk to no one, breaking that silence only rarely to lean sideways and mutter one-line critiques to no one in particular." Meanwhile, Janet commented, "It's like he's out there playing along with Grant....and it's a long draining season. I have faith in Grant making it through OK, but Calvin I wonder about."

In subsequent years in the NBA, Grant Hill has become known as the league's "Mr. Nice Guy." Fans have been curious to know about the family background of this star player and Janet has often detailed their approaches to parenting. Because of her commitment to spending as much time as possible with Grant as he grew up, she came home from work to make dinner every night; "...[F]or 18 years his father and I never went anywhere," she remembered in *Jet.* She also believes in spanking, and because of her strict system of rules and punishments earned the nickname "The General" from Grant. And in a family where sports was very important, school was always the first priority. She is very proud that Grant earned a B.A. in history from Duke University and reflected in the *Detroit News,* "We think our educations have served us every day for the last 26 years since we've been out of college, and that's part of the drumbeat we have given Grant."

The Hills have encouraged Grant to take an active role in his business relationships with the Pistons and the companies for which he does product endorsements. Not surprisingly, Janet and Calvin are full of opinions and ideas when it comes to Grant and his career, and in their professional capacities have a wealth of experience to share. In 1997 all three of the Hills were named by *Fortune* as among the most influential black business people. But as Janet commented in *The New York Times,* "We're trying very hard to stay in our roles as parents. Not coach, not agent, not general manager. Parents." Similarly, Calvin put aside the importance of wealth and accomplishment when he commented in the *Washingtonian,* "Simple things are the most important. I've achieved some success in school, my profession. But I'm proudest of raising my son to be a good person."

Sources

Dallas Morning News, July 20, 1997, p. 1A.
Detroit News, December 3, 1995.
Fortune, August 4, 1997, p. 72.
Hartford Courant, February 14, 1998, p. C1.
Jet, May 12, 1997, p. 50; March 9, 1998, p. 51.
New York Times, December 23, 1994, p. B9.
PR Newswire, May 16, 1994.
Sporting News, January 16, 1995, p. 24.
Washingtonian, April 1997, p. 33.
Washington Post, March 30, 1994, p. F5.

—Paula Pyzik Scott

Djimon Hounsou

1964—

Actor

Djimon Hounsou, from the West African nation of Benin, stands on the brink of becoming the first black African international movie star. Hounsou's performance in the historical epic *Amistad* was widely praised and drew much attention to the previously little known actor. Directed by Steven Spielberg and produced by Debbie Allen, *Amistad* told the true story of a bloody uprising on a slave ship bound for Cuba in 1839. The captured Africans demanded that the crew members remaining alive take the ship back to Africa. Instead, the crew sailed north to the United States where the Africans were jailed while their fate was decided in a court battle pitting American abolitionists against pro-slavery forces who viewed the Africans as property belonging to slaveholders. Hounsou played Cinque, the leader of the revolt. The film also starred Morgan Freeman as an African American observing events, Anthony Hopkins as John Quincy Adams, the former president who pleaded the cause of the Africans before the Supreme Court, and Matthew McConaughey as a fervently Abolitionist attorney. "It is a great movie that should be seen because it enables us to get in touch with a history that is only 160 years in our past. Like *Roots*, it forces us to look reality in the face," wrote B.B. Robinson about *Amistad* in the *Chicago Independent Bulletin*. S. Allen Counter in the *Bay State Banner* called Hounsou "the reincarnation of Cinque" adding that "*Amistad* deals in a straightforward and honest manner with the most neglected subject of the American past, namely unrequited chattel slavery. More importantly, it informs the subject and demonstrates better than any other film on American slavery how much good can be achieved when persons of different racial and religious backgrounds work together for what is right."

Djimon Hounsou (pronounced JI-mon HON-sou) was born in Cotenou, Benin, in 1964, the youngest of five children. His father's occupation as a cook made the family relatively prosperous by West African standards. "We were not a rich African family. Everything was very basic. If you knew the way I lived then, and the way I'm living now...it's day and night," Hounsou told Lindsay Bishop of *Venice*. Hounsou grew up speaking French and several dialects of Goun, the Beninois language. The packed movie showings in his television-less home village got him thinking about a career in show business. "Once you were in you couldn't move. Every space was

At a Glance...

Born in Cotenou, Benin, in 1964, the son of Pierre (a cook), and Albertine Hounsou. Attended schools in Lyons, France, c. 1977-84.

Career: Worked as a fashion and photographer's model in France and the U.S., c. 1987-93; moved to U.S. in 1990; film appearances include *Without You I'm Nothing*, 1990; *Unlawful Entry*, 1992; *Stargate*, 1994; *Amistad*, 1997; *Deep Rising*, 1997; *Ill Gotten Gains*, 1998; also appeared in music videos with Steve Winwood, Paula Abdul, Madonna, and Janet Jackson, c. late 1980s-early 1990s.

Awards: National Association for the Advancement of Colored People Image Award for outstanding actor in a motion picture for *Amistad*, 1998.

Addresses: *Home*—Beverly Hills, CA; *Publicist*—Rogers and Cowan, 1888 Century Park East, Los Angeles, CA, 90067.

---

filled with people. That's when I knew I wanted to be an entertainer," Hounsou told Carol Day of *People*.

At the age of thirteen, Hounsou was sent to Lyons, France to live with an older brother and study to become a doctor. To the great disappointment of his family, he proved to be a lackadaisical student with no interest in medicine. "I wanted a different life from the one my family planned," Hounsou told Day. Leaving school at age twenty, Hounsou drifted to Paris after being thrown out of the house by his brother. Without a place to live or working papers that allowed him to get a job, Hounsou found himself sleeping on benches and bathing in fountains. "Going through people's garbage at night to find a piece of bread to eat—that was not a pretty sight. I didn't want any trouble with the police, so I kept a low profile, " Hounsou told Daniel J. Sharfstein of the *New York Times*. After living on the street for over a year, Hounsou's impressive, six feet, two inch physique was noticed by a passerby who handed him the business card of a photographer. Hounsou followed up on the idea. "I never pictured myself that good-looking [but] I had nothing to lose," Hounsou told Day. Hounsou's photograph was circulated to modeling agencies and he soon found himself on fashion show runways and appearing in an advertisement campaign for designer Thierry Mugler. "It's a very surreal world, modeling, but it kept me off the streets, literally," Hounsou said in an interview posted on the Irish Film and Television Net website.

> "I want to work, because that is the only way my acting will improve. But I can't just take a job now to work. I need to be very careful not to screw this up."

Hounsou's work with Mugler led to his being cast in three music videos directed by David Fincher—Steve Winwood's "Roll with It," Madonna's "Express Yourself," and Paula Abdul's "Straight Up." The videos got the attention of noted photographer Herb Ritts and Hounsou soon became one of Ritts' favorite models. For Ritts' book *Men and Women* Hounsou posed with an octopus on the top of his head. "At the time I didn't speak English, so I didn't understand what [Ritts] was talking about, what octopus meant," Hounsou said to Bishop. "And they brought in this big container. I was looking at him and trying to communicate with my face like 'What?!?!'...In less than ten minutes he got the picture. The picture came out. It was a beautiful photo. At the time I didn't think so, but it was nice working with him." Hounsou worked with Ritts again on Janet Jackson's video "Love Will Never Do Without You." Ritts said of Hounsou to Sharfstein—"I just loved his inner soul in combination with his physical stature. He has an incredible sensitivity. The way he make shapes—he really understands his body. That comes from an inner sense."

In 1990, Hounsou moved to Los Angeles, hoping to break into acting. He began taking drama classes and taught himself English by listening to the narration on cable television documentaries. "The first few years when I was learning English I had to think in French before I said the things I wanted to say in English. Now I dream mostly in English. Now it's almost the reverse. I have to think in English now to write in French sometimes," Hounsou told Bishop. In the United States, Hounsou found his race mattered much more, to both whites and other black people, than it had in France. "It never occurred to me that there was a way to behave 'black' in order to be black ... That was one of my first encounters with, I guess, the American lifestyle. It was difficult for me. Growing up in France, I was just a human being. I came here and they tell you, 'Hey, he behaves like a white boy.' I didn't know there was a way to be black. So that was shocking," Hounsou told Bishop.

Hounsou's first film appearance came in comedienne Sandra Bernhard's screen adaptation of her Off-Broadway show *Without You I'm Nothing* in 1990. Hounsou, who could not yet speak English, played the silent role of Bernhard's ex-boyfriend. He then landed small roles in 1992's *Unlawful Entry,* a crime thriller starring Kurt Russell, and in the 1994 science fiction film *Stargate,* also starring Russell.

It was *Amistad,* director Steven Spielberg's highly touted follow up to his Academy Award winning based-on-truth Holocaust story *Schindler's List,* that brought Hounsou to the attention of the public. Making a movie out of the story of the Amistad uprising was the idea of dancer/actress Debbie Allen, who produced the film. While browsing through the bookstore at her alma mater Howard University several years ago, Allen happened upon the book *Black Mutiny: The Revolt of the Schooner Amistad* by William A. Owens. "I was inspired, overwhelmed and upset that I had not heard the story," Allen told Bennie M. Currie of *American Visions.* Allen acquired the film rights to Owens' book but found no movie studio interested in the Amistad tale. Finally, she took the idea to Spielberg. He was willing to help get the project off the ground but was reluctant to direct the film himself, suspecting that a black director might be more appropriate. Allen disagreed. "I think if there was a ever a movie done by a man who understands people in bondage, people suffering, people overcoming, it was *Schindler's List.* And besides, I needed a hot, strong filmmaker—someone who could handle a story that was epic," Allen explained to Currie.

In landing the role of Cinque, Hounsou won out over more than one hundred actors who auditioned for the role. "Djimon just has an enduring quality, a real sense of destiny. He's extremely powerful and charismatic and charming. I saw him, and he was just how I imagined Cinque to look and sound....He was Cinque at first sight," Spielberg told Sharfstein. Cinque speaks just a single line of English in the entire film—"Give us free!" The rest of the role is in Mende, a West African language spoken in Sierra Leone, the area from which Cinque was taken. Though Hounsou's native tongue, Goun, is also West African, it is no closer to Mende than English is to French.

Hounsou was given only ten days to learn the basics of Mende. This linguistic chore added to the pressure of tackling his first major acting assignment. "It was very hard. I would go home every night and work, work, work on the script, and then sometimes I would show up the next day feeling disappointed in myself. Morgan Freeman gave me good advice. He said acting is like life, and that some days you are good at it, and some days you just have to get through by doing the best you can," Hounsou told Terry Lawson of the *Knight-Ridder/Tribune News Service.* Hounsou viewed Cinque as an ordinary man. "He never intended to lead this whole thing in the first place. He only did what he did to free himself. I don't really like that he's called a slave, because there's no such thing in Cinque's mind as being a slave. He's somebody who never chose to be anything but a human being," Hounsou told Scharfstein.

Freeman found that Hounsou completed his task with flying colors. "Djimon's perfect. He'll be on people's minds for a while. What he's personifying is the strength and conviction of a person who's decided: 'This is not my destiny. This is not my fate, My destiny is not in the hull of this ship,'" Freeman told Scharfstein. Matthew McConaughey was similarly impressed by Hounsou. "He's completely unaffected. He was so good and so raw because of what he did not know. He had a range. He could make the transition from fear to weeping in all sincerity. And that was innate for him. I don't know where it comes from. He's also one of the most sensitive and compassionate men I've ever met," McConaughey told Andy Seiler of *USA Today.*

Released in December 1997, *Amistad* garnered mostly favorable reviews. "If you were wondering what Steven Spielberg could possibly do for an encore after *Schindler's List,* the answer is *Amistad*. If the first film finally established his credentials as a serious filmmaker as well as a master fabricator of big pop entertainments, *Amistad* confirms them. It's a big, bold noble juggernaut of a film that literally and figuratively brings to light a pivotal piece of American history," wrote Jay Carr in the *Boston Globe.* The film did only modest business at the box office and was far outdistanced by a more sensational based-on-fact film, *Titanic,* which was released at approximately the same time.

After completing *Amistad,* Hounsou appeared in *Ill Gotten Gains,* another slave story, this one a low-budget feature directed by young newcomer Joel Marsden and co-starring Eartha Kitt. *Deep Rising,* a horror film Hounsou made before *Amistad,* was released in early 1998.

In his private life, Hounsou shares a Beverly Hills apartment with his girlfriend, actress/screenwriter Victoria Mahoney. He enjoys working out at the gym, horseback riding, and polo. The pride he feels towards his association with *Amistad* has made him more choosy about future projects. He explained to Lawson—"Yes, I want to work, because that is the only way my acting will improve. But I can't just take a job now to work. I need to be very careful not to screw this up."

Sources

American Visions, December 1997-January 1998, p. 39.
Amsterdam News (New York), January 7, 1998, p. 20.
Bay State Banner (Boston), August 12, 1998, p. 26.
Boston Globe, December 12, 1997, p. C1.
Chicago Independent Bulletin, February 12, 1998, p. 13.
Detroit News, December 12, 1997.
Knight-Ridder/Tribune News Service, December 8, 1997.
Maclean's, December 15, 1997, p. 62.
New Republic, December 22, 1997, p. 24.
Newsweek, December 8, 1997, p. 64.
New York Times, December 7, 1997.
Oakland Post, December 24, 1997, p. 8.
People, December 15, 1997, p. 19; January 12, 1998, p. 82.
Time, December 15, 1997, p. 108.
USA Today, December 9, 1997, p. D1.
Variety, December 2, 1997, p. 27; December 8, 1997, p. 110.
Venice, December 1997, p. 36-40.

Other

Information also provided by Rogers and Cowan Publicity Agency and the Irish Film and Television Net Website (www.iftn.ie).

—Mary Kalfatovic

Phyllis Hyman

1949(?)–1995

Vocalist

When Phyllis Hyman committed suicide in June of 1995, she closed the book on a career that had long been deeply appreciated by connoisseurs of romantic jazz and rhythm-and-blues singing. A commanding physical presence and riveting stage performer, Hyman was a tragic figure beset by personal troubles. Never quite achieving the popularity that her prodigious talent seemed to justify, she nevertheless left behind a legacy of deeply felt recordings and unforgettable live performances.

Phyllis Hyman was born in Philadelphia, most likely on July 6, 1949, and raised in Pittsburgh. (Some sources give the year as 1950, but numerous press reports of her death mentioned that she had been ready to celebrate her forty-sixth birthday.) She was the oldest of seven brothers and sisters. An elementary school teacher noticed and nurtured her vocal talents, but she grew up poor and aimed at first toward a solid career as a legal secretary, attending the Robert Morris Business College.

Formed Own Band

A six-foot, one-inch beauty, Hyman made her way to New York in her early twenties, dreaming of a career in the entertainment industry. Almost immediately she began to find work at least intermittently as a vocalist, and by 1974 she had formed her own band, Phyllis Hyman and the PH Factor. By the next year she had become a fixture of New York's stylish Upper West Side, making regular appearances at two clubs a few blocks apart, Rust Brown's and Mikell's. Influential figures in the black music industry circulated through these clubs, and Hyman in 1976 attracted the attention of percussionist and producer Norman Connors, who gave her a shot at wider exposure—a featured-performer slot on his album *You Are My Starship*. The album included Hyman's hit remake of the Stylistics' ballad "Betcha By Golly Wow," which dented R & B charts and helped Hyman make the acquaintance of the song's co-composer, Linda Creed.

On the strength of "Betcha By Golly Wow" and other songs on the album, Hyman was signed to the Arista label in 1977 and released the album *Phyllis Hyman*. Arista specialized in sophisticated black vocal music with a hint of jazz—the lifeblood of the emerging "quiet storm" format that had gotten its start at the radio station of the premier black educational institution Howard

> ### At a Glance...
>
> Born in Philadelphia, PA on July 6, 1949 (some sources give year as 1950), oldest of seven brothers and sisters; raised in Pittsburgh. Married Larry Alexander, late 1970s (later divorced). Died by suicide on June 30, 1995. *Education:* Attended Robert Morris Business College.
>
> **Career:** Jazz and R & B vocalist. Moved to New York, early 1970s; formed band Phyllis Hyman and the PH Factor, 1974; featured on Norman Connors album *You Are My Starship*, 1976; signed to Arista label, 1977; worked with producer Barry Manilow, late 1970s, resulting in hit "Somewhere in My Lifetime"; cast member *Sophisticated Ladies* (Duke Ellington tribute), late 1970s–early 1980s; signed with Philadelphia International label, 1986; recorded albums *Living All Alone*, 1986, and *Prime of My Life*, 1991; appeared in Spike Lee film *School Daze*, 1988. Several posthumous album releases.
>
> **Awards:** Tony award nomination, for *Sophisticated Ladies*, 1981.

University. The label offered the young singer a congenial environment, and demonstrated its faith in its new recruit by having high-flying vocal star Barry Manilow produce one of her early releases, resulting in the R & B top-fifteen hit "Somewhere in My Lifetime." Hyman also scored a hit with the disco-inflected "You Know How to Love Me."

Hyman married her manager Larry Alexander in the late 1970s, but both the personal and professional associations ended in divorce. For the rest of the singer's life the search for a romantic partner would cause her emotional trouble. She told *Jet* magazine in 1981 that she hoped for a relationship: "I don't really want to say need because to me—an aggressive, liberated woman—need sounds too pathetic. But maybe I'm wrong. Maybe need and want sometimes go together. Maybe I do need and want a man."

Nominated for *Sophisticated Ladies*

At the time, though, the singer was very much occupied with her still-growing career. She won a spot in Broadway's Duke Ellington revue *Sophisticated Ladies*, and once again flourished in a role where her talent as a live performer could be showcased. Hyman was nominated for a Tony award in 1981, and remained with the cast of the show for three years. (The musical's original cast LP includes Hyman's rendition of "In a Sentimental Mood.") Her recordings made after the run of the musical were only modestly successful; some have attributed the singer's problems at retail to the difficulty fans and music-industry figures encounter when they try to categorize her music: did Hyman sing R & B? jazz? pop? The question was never definitively answered, for Hyman's talent crossed lines.

In 1986 Hyman moved to the Philadelphia International label, where she worked with "Philly Soul" producers Kenneth Gamble and Leon Huff and made what some feel were her best recordings, although the upper reaches of stardom continued to elude her. On 1986's *Living All Alone* (which carried, in the words of *Boston Globe* writer Frederic Biddle, "very dark emotional undertones" with its title-track refrain of "I can't stand this living all alone") and 1991's *Prime of My Life* (which featured a brief venture into rap music), Hyman hit her stride with lush, sad romantic ballads that may fairly be called tragic.

By the late 1980s Hyman's live shows reliably filled large urban theaters—Harlem's Apollo, Oakland's Paramount, the gloriously ornate Fox in St. Louis. Often dressed in African-inspired clothing, a fez atop her head, Hyman as a stage performer had few peers. Never resting on the natural beauty of her contralto voice, she was given to surprises like a perfectly whistled version of the title track of "Living All Alone" at a Blue Note performance in 1993. Hyman's short performance in Spike Lee's film *School Daze* also gives an idea of her capabilities.

Confessed Loneliness and Unhappiness

Living All Alone featured a new Linda Creed composition entitled "Old Friend" which increasingly often became part of Hyman's live show. The two women had long been good friends, and Creed's death in 1993 may have been one of the events that started Hyman on a downward spiral. She gained weight and was rumored to be battling drug and alcohol addictions. During her appearance on television's *Arsenio Hall Show* viewers were touched and saddened by her frank confession of loneliness and unhappiness. On June 30, 1995, just before she was slated to appear at the Apollo with star vocal group The Whispers, Phyllis Hyman committed suicide by taking an overdose of pills. At her memorial service her sister Sakeema said that the singer had suffered from "addiction and depression."

Her death only intensified the admiration that fans felt for her music, and no fewer than four posthumous releases appeared over the next three and a half years: *I Refuse to Be Lonely* and *Forever with You* consisted of unreleased Philadelphia International material, and Arista and Roadshow, Norman Connors' label, released compilations. A different sort of tribute came from The Whispers, who starred and toured in a stage musical about Hyman's career entitled *Thank God! The Beat Goes On*. Jazz vocalist Nancy Wilson, quoted in *Jet* magazine, said, "When I think of all the talents that I've known over the years, I considered Sarah Vaughan and Phyllis Hyman as having the greatest voices, greatest instruments ever, the greatest pipes." It seemed all the more tragic that Hyman's greatness had been so little heralded.

Selected discography

Phyllis Hyman, Arista, 1977.
Somewhere in My Lifetime, Arista, 1978.
Sing a Song, Arista, 1979.
You Know How to Love Me, Arista, 1979.
Can't We Fall in Love Again, Arista, 1981.
Goddess of Love, Arista, 1983.
Living All Alone, Philadelphia International, 1986.
Prime of My Life, Philadelphia International, 1991.

Posthumous releases

I Refuse to Be Lonely, Philadelphia International, 1996.
Forever with You, Philadelphia International, 1998.
Phyllis Hyman Remembered, Roadshow, 1998.
Phyllis Hyman: The Legacy of Phyllis Hyman, Arista, 1998.

Sources

Atlanta Constitution, July 21, 1998, p. F2.
Billboard, August 8, 1998, p. 23.
Fort Lauderdale Sun-Sentinel, July 9, 1995, p. D3 (reprint of article form *Boston Globe*).
Jet, July 24, 1995, p. 52.
St. Louis Post-Dispatch, July 9, 1995, C3.

—James M. Manheim

Hubert A. Ingraham

1947—

Prime Minister of the Bahamas

The rise of Hubert A. Ingraham and his Free National Movement Party has ushered in a new political era for the island nation of the Bahamas. In 1992, Ingraham became only the second prime minister since the country's passage from status as a British colony into independence as a Commonwealth nation. His 1992 win, according to the *New York Times*'s Larry Rohter, "can be seen as the start of the generational change" of politics in this and other Caribbean states. Like several of his colleagues, Ingraham has left behind the party-dominated political campaign, similar to the British system, in favor of a more American-style, candidate-driven contest. More importantly, during his two terms in office Ingraham initiated a series of government reforms that did much to restore the reputation of the Bahamas.

Hubert Alexander Ingraham was born on the island of Grand Bahama on August 4, 1947. Grand Bahama is just one of the archipelago's 700 islands that spread out over 80,000 square miles of Atlantic Ocean territory. With a balmy climate, and a landscape of unequaled beauty, the leading industry in the Bahamas is tourism. Ingraham's father worked as a stevedore, a dockhand who loaded and unloaded ships, and his mother was a maid. He attended schools in Cooper's Town and in the capital of Nassau, and studied for a law degree. Called to the Bar in 1972 while in his mid-twenties, Ingraham eventually became a senior partner in the firm Christie, Ingraham, and Company.

Bahamas Became Self-Governing

Ingraham grew interested in a secondary career in public service during the first years of Bahamian independence. His mentor was the Bahamian political leader Sir Lynden O. Pindling. Pindling had led the fight for self-rule in the 1960s. After the Bahamas were granted independence from Great Britain in 1973, Pindling's Progressive Liberal Party (PLP) won the majority in the first elections and he became prime minister. The country, however, remained part of the Commonwealth, with Queen Elizabeth II serving as Bahamas's official chief of state along with a governor she appointed. Pindling and his PLP continually won re-election until challenged years later by Ingraham.

Ingraham's first foray into government service came

At a Glance...

Born August 4, 1947, in Pine Ridge, Grand Bahama, Bahamas; son of Jerome (a stevedore) and Isabella Laroda (a domestic servant; maiden name, Cornish) Ingraham; married; wife's name, Delores Velma (Miller) Ingraham; six children. *Education:* Studied law. *Politics:* Free National Movement.

Career: Called to the Bahamas Bar, 1972; Christie, Ingraham, and Company, senior partner; Served as member of Air Transport Licensing Authority, and chaired the Real Property Tax Tribunal; elected to the National General Council of the Progressive Liberal Party (PLP), 1975; elected national chair and member of national executive committee of Progressive Liberal Parry (PLP), 1976; elected to Bahamas House of Assembly as PLP candidate, 1977; re-elected, 1982; named Minister of Housing, National Insurance and Social Services, 1982-84; dismissed from cabinet, 1984; expelled from party, October, 1986; elected to National Assembly as independent candidate, 1987; joined Official Opposition, April, 1990; appointed Parliamentary Leader of Official Opposition; became leader of Free National Movement (FNM), May, 1990; became Prime Minister with the FNM's electoral victory in August, 1992. Named to Her Majesty's most honourable Privy Council, July 1993.

Member: Conference of CARICOM Heads of Government (former chair).

Addresses: *Office*—Office of the Prime Minister, Sir Cecil Wallace Whitfield Centre, P.O. Box CB-10980, West Bay St., Nassau, Bahamas.

with a spot on the Air Transport Licensing Authority; he later chaired the Real Property Tax Tribunal. In 1975 he was elected to the PLP's National General Council, and the following year was chosen national chair and member of the national executive committee of the Party. In the elections of 1977, Ingraham won a seat in the Bahamas House of Assembly as a PLP candidate. He was re-elected in 1982, and Pindling named him Minister of Housing, National Insurance and Social Services in the new cabinet that same year.

Though he was considered a protege of Pindling, Ingraham grew increasingly disgruntled by the government corruption he witnessed. He found fault with both official and covert practices and grew critical of Pindling. Ingraham's official biography noted that "in 1984, in the midst of a Commission of Inquiry into illegal drug trafficking and trans-shipment through the Bahamas and the attendant disclosures of corruption inside the government and the civil service, Mr. Ingraham, as a result of his protests against that situation, was dismissed from The Bahamas Cabinet. He continued to speak out on the issue of corruption and other unsavoury practices, and was expelled from the governing party in October, 1986."

The situation in the Bahamas worsened in the late 1980s, when the nation became known as a nexus for drug trafficking. As the *New York Times*'s Rohter explained in a 1992 article, "witnesses in the trials of both Carlos Lehder, a founder of the Medellin drug cartel in Colombia, and Gen. Manuel Antonio Noriega, the deposed Panamanian dictator, testified to payoffs to Sir Lynden, and some United States officials have long recommended that he be indicted on drug-trafficking charges." Ingraham's outspokenness found an audience with the electorate even though he had been expelled from the PLP. He won a seat in the National Assembly in the 1987 elections as an independent candidate, a rather unusual occurrence. He put together the Free National Movement (FNM), a political foe to the PLP, and in the spring of 1990 was named Parliamentary Leader of the Official Opposition. General elections are called in the Bahamas every five years, and in August of 1992 the FNM took a majority of seats in the National Assembly and Ingraham, as its party leader, replaced Pindling as prime minister.

Reforms Began at his Level

Despite the political turmoil of the last few years, Ingraham seemed eager to relegate the less savory aspects of recent politics in the Bahamas to the past. There were calls for an official investigation and perhaps even an attempt at prosecution of Pindling, but Ingraham concentrated on more impacting political and economic matters. He reshuffled the structure of the cabinet in September of 1993, and shortened his own title to Prime Minister and Minister of Finance, transferring some of the duties in his portfolio to other cabinet ministers. In another reorganization taking place in early 1995, Ingraham again cut his title to simply Prime Minister.

Other visible signs of a new era occurred during Ingraham's first term. He launched an infrastructure-improvement program, used a firm hand in eradicating the drug trafficking problem, and reintroduced death by hanging. Ingraham also initiated a plan to boost the island nation's sagging tourism industry by privatizing some of the poorly-run government-owned hotels and resorts. He also began courting foreign investment by rescinding laws that restricted foreigners from holding real estate in the Bahamas, and introduced a new, quick process to officially register a company. Such tactics quickly attracted a growing number of individual and corporate foreign tax exiles, since Bahamas has no personal, sales, corporate or capital-gains taxes.

Under Ingraham, "the Bahamas has started to live down its reputation for corruption and mismanagement," declared the *Economist* in 1997. In that year's election campaign, Ingraham and the FNM reminded Bahamians that not only had they created several thousand new jobs, the new regime had also done much to restore the country's international standing. Ingraham again ran against Pindling and Pindling's PLP, and won another overwhelming victory: the FNM took 34 of the 40 House of Assembly seats. Yet the campaign was marred by a tragic and shocking murder: Ingraham's campaign manager, Charles Virgill, disappeared at a political rally just a week before the election. His body was found, and three suspects were taken into custody. "One of the men accused of shooting Mr. Virgill took part in a bizarre ceremony" at a PLP convention earlier that year, reported the *Economist*. Some young men, associated with Bahamian gangs, took an oath styled after the creed of the Nation of Islam in which they pledged to uphold the family and eschew weapons. The magazine noted that Pindling was unconnected to the crime.

No More Shady Business

It is unlikely that Ingraham will enjoy the long reign of his predecessor, since he is eager to see a term-limit amendment to the Constitution passed before he leaves office. Other goals for his second administration are to further divest the island of large hotel and resort holdings, and sell off some of the government-owned public utilities as well. Ingraham has often spoken of his goal to "conduct the affairs of The Bahamas 'in the sunshine,'" and put in place a system and mindset where the misdeeds of the previous era would not be possible. "What I want to bring about," Ingraham told Peter C. Newman in *Maclean's*, "is to shape a new political culture—to trigger a genuine revolution in ... the way Bahamians see themselves."

Ingraham was named to Her Majesty's most honourable Privy Council in 1993, and has chaired the Conference of CARICOM Heads of Government. He is married to Delores Miller Ingraham, with whom he has six children.

Sources

Periodicals

Detroit News, March 15, 1997.
Economist, March 8, 1997, p. 48.
Jet, April 7, 1997, p. 16.
Maclean's, March 28, 1994, p. 48.
New York Times, August 22, 1992; July 27, 1997.
Travel Weekly, June 17, 1993, p. 47; May 16, 1994, p41; May 11, 1995, p. C21; November 16, 1995, p. C110.

Other

Further information for this profile was obtained at the Government of the Bahamas official World Wide Web site at http:www.bahamas.net.bs/government.

—Carol Brennan

George Jackson

1960(?)—

Record company executive, film producer

After rising through the ranks in Hollywood film studios to become a successful producer, George Jackson has parlayed his media experience into a prominent position in the music industry. Hired as the president and CEO of Motown Records in late 1997, Jackson accepted the challenge of rebuilding the once preeminent pop music label. A Harlem native with a B.A. in Sociology from Harvard, he was chosen for talents that combine creative passion and business acumen. As a film producer, Jackson has made popular films with urban themes, including *New Jack City* and *House Party 2*. His films are notable for their soundtracks and for making nearly double the average gross income for films in their budget range.

The man who is known to his friends and associates as "Poppa George," came to Hollywood in 1982 to work for Paramount Television's sitcom *The New Odd Couple*. The next year, he moved to Universal Pictures to become executive assistant to Thom Mount, the president of Worldwide Production. Jackson's steady climb upwards continued when he spent the next two years as executive vice president of production at Indigo, Richard Pryor's production company at Columbia Pictures. Next, he headed Grio Entertainment Group, a Warner Bros.-based partnership with Quincy Jones and Clarence Avant.

Formed Film Team in Hollywood

In 1985 Jackson set up shop to make his own films when he co-founded Jackson-McHenry Entertainment Company with Doug McHenry. The team produced and sometimes directed youth- and music-oriented films that were more notable for their box office returns than for their artistic impact. Their first film was the 1985 rap-oriented *Krush Groove*. In varying degrees, music would be important in all Jackson-McHenry films, which have generated soundtracks that gained gold and multi-platinum status. Comedies *House Party 2* and *House Party 3* were an opportunity for the pair to mix *Animal House*-style humor with more serious commentary about the experiences of black college students. The first of the two films, which both feature the comedy duo Kid 'N Play, was also Jackson's and McHenry's directorial debut. This endeavor was typical of the hands-on approach favored by the team, who are known for being involved in all aspects of a film's production, including scriptwrit-

> *At a Glance...*
>
> Born in 1960?, in Harlem, NY; married Yuko Sumida, 1998. *Education:* Harvard University, B.A. in sociology.
>
> **Career:** Production assistant, Paramount Television show, *The New Odd Couple,* 1982-83; executive assistant to president of Worldwide Production, Universal Pictures, 1983-84; executive vice president of production, Indigo, Columbia Pictures, 1984-86; head of Grio Entertainment Group, Warner Bros.; co-founder Jackson-McHenry Entertainment, 1985, Elephant Walk Entertainment, 1996; co-produced *Krush Groove,* 1985, *House Party 2,* 1991, *New Jack City,* 1991, *House Party 3,* 1994, *Jason's Lyric,* 1994, *A Thin Line Between Love and Hate,* 1996, TV movie *Body Count,* 1998, and television series *Malcolm & Eddie;* president and CEO, Motown Record Company, 1997-.
>
> **Member:** Producers Guild, American Film Institute Third Decade Council, Independent Film Project West, Black Filmmaker Foundation, Big Brothers Association of America.
>
> **Awards:** NAACP Image Award, Black American Cinema Society Award, Communications Excellence to Black Audiences Award.
>
> **Addresses:** *Office*—Motown Record Co., L.P. 825 8th Avenue, 29th Floor, New York, NY 10019-1736.

ing, music, and marketing.

Perhaps the most successful—and controversial—Jackson-McHenry film is *New Jack City*. The story of a community's battle to bring down a crack-selling drug lord in Harlem, *New Jack City* grossed some $48 million during its first year and was credited by *Los Angeles Times* writer Claudia Puig for being "probably what broke the ice for pictures like 'Boyz N the Hood.'" It also generated considerable criticism, however, when a series of violent events at theaters across the United States were tied to the film. The partnership responded with a *New York Times* editorial that included the comment: "Those who argue, as many have, that our film encourages viewers to imitate the violence they've seen on the screen are wrong. The real cause of violence at the theaters is not cinematic images of drug culture but decades of poverty in our communities." The producers also noted their cinematic intent of condemning drug culture, and their determination to present an accurate picture of it.

> "I wasn't a record man. I was a movie guy, and how dare I try to run a record company, and not just any record company—Motown.... For a lot of people, the jury is still out."

Talking to the *Los Angeles Times* in 1991, reporter Joe Prichirallo noted, "The interesting thing about Doug and George is they want to be more than just creative people. They want to be the black Samuel Goldwyns. They want to be moguls. They want to run studios." This idea was confirmed by the 1996 creation of Elephant Walk Entertainment, in which Jackson became partners with McHenry and Rob Lee. The Elephant Walk company umbrella includes Jackson-McHenry Films, talent agency Elephant Walk Management, Elephant Walk Television—which produces United Paramount Network's *Malcolm & Eddie,* record label JacMac, music publishers Harlem Boys Music and Oaktown Boys Music, and the SLANG music website. Jackson's work as a producer since *New Jack City* includes *Jason's Lyric* (1994), *A Thin Line Between Love and Hate* (1996), and the TV movie *Body Count* (1998). In this last film, Jackson also appeared on screen as a ticket agent.

Accepted Motown Makeover

When Jackson became president and CEO of Motown in 1997, it raised the question of whether his hiring was a sound decision. As Jackson acknowledged in *USA Today* in February of 1998, "I wasn't a record man. I was a movie guy, and how dare I try to run a record company, and not just any record company—Motown....For a lot of people, the jury is still out." Certainly, Jackson had big shoes to fill. Motown Records was a huge hit producer during the 1960s and 1970s under founder Berry Gordy, who signed acts including the Miracles, The Commodores, The Four Tops, The Jackson Five, Diana Ross, The Temptations, and Stevie Wonder. The record label foundered after Gordy sold the company in 1988 to Boston Ventures. Polygram later purchased the company, placing a huge value on the catalog and brand name, but Motown did poorly under the stewardship of

Jackson's predecessor, Andre Harrell.

Describing Jackson's predicament in *Fortune,* Roy S. Johnson said, "he is entering a real quagmire—assuming the leadership of the most recognizable brand in the music business at a time when the company is still reeling from years of disappointing results, poor management, public controversy, and intrigue." Clarence Avant, Motown's chairman emeritus, saw Jackson's role in reviving Motown in a larger context when he commented in *Fortune,* "White people can afford to lose Pan Am, Montgomery Ward, or Woolworth's....There are a million other white-run institutions. Blacks cannot afford to lose even one." And Avant explained why he felt Jackson was up to the task of reviving Motown in *Black Enterprise:* "I've known George for 15 years....He's always been ahead of the marketplace in identifying trends, and music has always been a part of his life and his projects. I think George is uniquely suited to lead the company given his understanding of trends, technologies, music and entertainment in general."

Expanded Roster and Visibility

Jackson began rebuilding Motown's fortunes by making staffing cuts and signing new artists. He presided over Motown's 40th anniversary in 1998, and the many events and promotions related to its celebration. At the time of his hire, Boyz II Men and Queen Latifah were the biggest names on the Motown roster, which had shrunk considerably in size and prominence since the label's heyday. In response to this situation, Motown merged with Polygram's Mercury Records R&B division in February of 1998, and several Mercury acts were transferred to the Motown label including Tony Toni Tone, Brian McKnight, Will Downing, and Raphael Saadiq.

According to *Billboard*'s Anita M. Samuels at the time of the merger, "Although Motown's specialties are R&B and hip-hop, the company's immediate plans include making inroads in rap music." Jackson also hoped to create tour packages resembling the old Motown Revues and supervised the institution of two new television programs, *Motown Mondays* on VH1 and the syndicated *Motown Live.*

In addition to his responsibilities at Motown, Jackson's professional plans include a remake of *The Mack,* a 1973 blaxploitation film about a pimp named Goldie. Working with McHenry and 20th Century Fox, he has tackled the difficult job of reworking a film that some consider politically incorrect. Jackson, however, remarked in the *Los Angeles Times* that he saw the remake as an opportunity to "expose society's hypocrisy, get the roaches out from under the carpet....Gangster films take an uncompromising view of what has come to be known as the 'American way.'" As with *New Jack City,* Jackson seeks to provide his audience with an entertaining film, but one that also expresses the real concerns of the black community.

Sources

Black Enterprise, February 1998, p. 25.
Billboard, November 8, 1997, p. 12.
Fortune, November 24, 1997, p. 133.
Los Angeles Times, October 23, 1991, p. F1; June 30, 1997, p. F1.
New York Times, March 26, 1991, p. A23.
USA Today, February 12, 1998, p. 8B.

—Paula Pyzik Scott

Michael Jackson

1958—

Vocalist, songwriter, businessman

A powerfully creative and disciplined artist, Michael Jackson is a distinctive vocalist, an imaginative and original songwriter with a gift for turning his own experiences into powerful lyrics, and a dancer almost without peer. Keeping control over his own career, he ruled pop and rhythm-and-blues music charts throughout the 1980s. Jackson's private life was just as fascinating as his music and dance moves.

The lead singer of the beloved family group the Jackson 5, Michael Jackson was in his early twenties when *Thriller* catapulted him into the ranks of the rich and famous. He has never matched the success of *Thriller,* and in the 1990s his career suffered serious reversals, the most damaging of which may have been the accusations of child abuse leveled against the singer in 1993. By the late 1990s, the star of the self-proclaimed "King of Pop" seemed to have dimmed. But no one who remembered the explosion of his talent during the previous decade could doubt either his overall impact as a performer or his ability to once again seize the limelight.

Jackson was born on August 29, 1958 in the steel-manufacturing center of Gary, Indiana, outside of Chicago. His father Joseph had played guitar in a local group called the Falcons; his mother Katherine was a country music enthusiast who instilled in her eight children a love of singing. Joseph, a very demanding and rumored—by his children—to be an abusive man, aimed to turn his five male children—Jackie, Tito, Jermaine, Marlon, and Michael—into musical stars, and by 1964, before Michael's sixth birthday, had formed them into the Jackson 5. The group played in local arenas and travelled throughout the Midwest performing before they wre noticed. Attracting the attention of hit singer Gladys Knight and pianist Bobby Taylor—not Diana Ross as some have claimed—the Jackson 5 were signed in 1968 to the Motown label, whose roster of youthful black acts had reliably been generating hits for several years.

Became a Motown Topseller

Michael's exuberant vocals defined such catchy Jackson 5 hits as "I Want You Back," "The Love You Save," "ABC," and "I'll Be There," all of which hit Number One in 1970. He released three albums for Motown as a solo

> **At a Glance...**
>
> Born Michael Joseph Jackson August 29, 1958 in Gary, Indiana; son of Joseph (a heavy equipment operator and part-time musician) and Katherine (a sales clerk, maiden name Scruse) Jackson. Married Lisa Marie Presley, 1994 (divorced 1996); married Debbie Rowe, 1996; two children, Prince Michael Jackson Jr. and Paris Michael Katherine. *Religion:* Raised as a Jehovah's Witness.
>
> **Career:** Performing and recording artist, 1963–. Vocalist with the Jackson 5, 1963–76; group signed with Motown Records, 1969; signed as solo artist with Motown, releasing debut album *Got to Be There*, 1972; appeared in film *The Wiz*, 1978; released Epic Records debut *Off the Wall*, 1979; released *Thriller*, the best-selling album of all time, 1982; released *Bad*, 1987; published autobiography *Moonwalk*, 1988; established Heal the World foundation, 1989; released *Dangerous*, 1991; released *HIStory*, 1995; released *Blood on the Dance Floor*, 1997; invested in and promoted entertainment centers and casinos with cable and casino mogul Don Barden, late 1990s.
>
> **Selected awards:** Numerous Grammy awards for *Thriller*, including album of the year, record of the year, best male rock vocal performance for "Beat It", and best new R&B song for "Billie Jean"; Song of the Year for "We Are the World," 1986; special humanitarian award from President Ronald Reagan, 1984; American Music Awards, Special Award of Achievement, 1989; World Music Awards for Best-Selling American Artist, World's Best-Selling Pop Artist, and World's best-Selling Artist of the Era, 1993; Grammys, Living Legend Award, 1993, Best R & B Single for "Remember The Time," 1993.
>
> **Addresses:** *Record company*—Sony/Epic Records, 550 Madison Ave., New York, BY 10022-3211.

artist, with singles such as "Ben," "Rockin' Robin," and "Got to Be There" reaching top chart levels. With Michael as lead vocalist and choreographer, the group toured extensively, giving audiences electrified shows that made the Jackson 5 more popular with each new show. Joseph Jackson and label founder, Berry Gordy, Jr., never saw eye to eye. Joseph always believed his sons could produce and write, but were limited by Motown's management. The Jacksons left Motown after a dispute over artistic control and signed with CBS's Epic label in 1976.

Motown sued and the Jackson 5 lost its name. The brothers (minus Jermaine, who opted to stay with Motown), now known as The Jacksons—added to the group was youngest brother, Randy—went on to be successful on the Epic label with such hits as "Blame It On The Boogie," "Shake Your Body," and "Heartbreak Hotel," all of which were written by various Jackson brothers.

As the Jackson 5, the brothers appeared in their first TV special, "Goin' Back to Indiana," an ABC network presentation that also starred comedians Bill Cosby and Tom Smothers. ABC also aired a Saturday morning animated series "The Jackson Five" which featured the Jacksons' singing voices. As The Jacksons, they performed in Las Vegas with their sisters Rebbie, La Toya, and Janet. Incidentally, Janet in the 1990s would eclipse Michael in popularity.

New Independence in Career

Michael sought to carve out a career independent of his siblings'. Though he made solo albums as a child on the Motown label, it was on Epic that Michael became a superstar in his own right. He played the Scarecrow in the 1978 film *The Wiz* (opposite longtime friend Diana Ross in the role of Dorothy), and during the making of the film met music executive and producer Quincy Jones.

Jones would become one of the architects of Jackson's grand successes, creating a light, sophisticated production style that effectively showcased Jackson's quiet yet intensely dramatic vocals. A musical eclectic since his jazz days in the early 1960s, Jones also encouraged Jackson to experiment with novel stylistic fusions. The first fruit of their efforts was Jackson's 1979 release *Off the Wall*, which mixed disco and ballad elements and spawned four Top Ten singles.

Jones also produced *Thriller*, the long-awaited followup to *Off the Wall*. After the release of the mild novelty song "The Girl Is Mine" (a duet with ex-Beatle Paul McCartney) as the first single, the album's sales built slowly. But with subsequent single releases Jackson emerged spectacularly as a personality who could appeal to diverse audiences like no one else in American music had been able to for years. "Beat It," featuring rock guitarist Eddie Van Halen, crossed over to attain popularity even among fans of heavy metal music;

"Billie Jean" drew on Jackson's own experience of unjust paternity accusations. Both songs reached number one, and "Billie Jean" made him the first artist to be number one on the pop single, pop album, R & B single, and R & B album charts simultaneously. *Thriller* went on to generate an unprecedented total of seven Top Ten singles. The album roosted atop Billboard magazine's sales charts for thirty-seven weeks, and at its peak was reported to be selling more than 500,000 copies every week.

Strong Sales Throughout the 1980s

In 1985 Jackson co-wrote the international famine-relief single "We Are the World," one of the biggest-selling singles of all time. It seemed that everything Jackson touched turned to gold or platinum. His videos for the *Thriller* album helped to put the Music Television Channel, or MTV for short, on the map. His videos also showcased his dance moves that was still being imitated well into the 1990s. His most famous move, the Moonwalk, became a dance craze. Jackson first displayed the Moonwalk in his video for his song, "Billie Jean." He also began wearing one glove that was covered with rhinestones. He was asked by Barbara Walters on the television show "20/20" why he wore one glove, Jackson replied, "Cooler than two." Glove aside, many were impressed with Jackson's style and moves. Jane Fonda in *Time* magazine, described his music as "A fresh, original sound. The music is energetic, and it's sensual. You can dance to it, work out to it, make love to it, sing to it. It's hard to sit still to."

Jackson could also count as fans of his dancing, such pros as Bob Fosse, Gene Kelly, and Fred Astaire, who was quoted in *Time* as saying, "My Lord, he is a wonderful mover. He makes these moves up himself and it is just great to watch....I don't know much more dancing he will take up, because singing and dancing at the same time is very difficult. But Michael is a dedicated artist."

Jackson reunited with his brothers, including Jermaine, for a "Motown 25" television special. Afterward, the Jacksons released another album, titled *Victory,* and then went on tour. Pepsi, who had signed Michael to a lucrative contract, decided to make a commercial with all the brothers performing. During production, an accident occurred and Michael's hair and scalp was badly burned, but he fully recovered. The tour was his swan song exit. After the end of the tour, Michael left the group and soon afterward, they disbanded.

His next album release, 1987's *Bad,* sold 22 million copies internationally, a disappointment only by the lofty standard *Thriller* had established. *Bad* included five number one singles: "I Just Can't Stop Loving You," "Bad," "The Way You Make Me Feel," Man in the Mirror," and "Dirty Diana." *Dangerous,* released in 1991 with new producer Teddy Riley at the helm, likewise topped 20 million in total sales. *Dangerous* produced "Remember The Time," that won R & B's best single at the Grammys. The album also featured kid rap duo Kriss Kross, rapper Heavy D, and Princess Stephanie of Monaco.

Jackson continued to produce videos. As his popularity grew, he was able to premiere each video during primetime television and MTV. Most videos were short form, that is, lasting the length of the songs, but some were long form which included dialogue, and some were mini-movies.

His song, "Thriller," began the tradition, and the video, "The Making of Michael Jackson's 'Thriller'" garnered sales in the millions. Most notable among the long form videos were "Bad"—which also starred an unknown actor by the name of Wesley Snipes—"Black or White," which featured Macauley Culkin of *Home Alone* fame, and the infamous crotch-grabbing dance routine, and also "Remember The Time," with comedian Eddie Murphy, basketball great Magic Johnson, and super-model Iman. "Remember The Time" also featured Jackson's first on-screen romantic kiss and one of the best choreographed dance routines of the 1990s.

Jackson's songs, "Smooth Criminal" and "Leave Me Alone," were featured in his film, *Moonwalker.* His other film, *Captain Eo,* was shown at Disneyworld and Disneyland theme parks. Although he was not given credit, Michael Jackson's voice appeared on the animated television series, "The Simpsons."

Became a Sought After Recluse

In the years following the release of *Thriller,* Jackson found himself subject to the isolation that artists in the top echelon of fame inevitably experience. A devout Jehovah's Witness, he adopted a disguise and went door to door to promote the religion shortly after the album was released. But the pressures of stardom eventually made it impractical for him to continue his religious activities, and he renounced his membership in the sect in 1987 after his video, "Thriller," was condemned by the group. A public perception of Jackson as a curious recluse began to take shape about this time. He was a constant subject of stories in the nation's tabloid press. Some—such as the story that he slept in a levitating "hyperbaric chamber" for the purpose of extending his life span—were planted by Jackson's own operatives as a way of garnering publicity. Jackson's skin seemed to become progressively lighter, leading to rumors that he was bleaching his skin in order to appear white.

Jackson countered this rumor in a February 1993 interview with television talk show host Oprah Winfrey, claiming that he suffered from vitiligo, a skin disease. But public unease with the star increased markedly as a result of much more serious allegations that surfaced in August of that year. Jackson was accused of sexually molesting a thirteen-year-old boy at his Encino, California compound, called Neverland. The singer had long enjoyed surrounding himself with children; in September, his sister La Toya claimed that he had sometimes spent nights together with them in his bedroom. Jackson strongly denied any wrongdoing, maintaining that he was the victim of an extortion plot on the part of the father of the thirteen-year-old. The case was settled privately for an undisclosed sum in January of 1994, and charges were dropped, but it cost Jackson a lucrative endorsement contract with Pepsi-Cola. He has continued to deny the charges.

Married Lisa Marie Presley

Jackson's musical successes since the time of these allegations have been sporadic, but his personal life has continued to provide surprises. In August of 1994 it was revealed that Jackson had married Lisa Marie Presley, daughter of legendary rock and roll innovator and pop megastar Elvis Presley, ten weeks earlier in a ceremony in the Dominican Republic. The couple was amicably divorced in January of 1996; in November of that year, Jackson married Debbie Rowe, a nurse who had reportedly been artificially inseminated and was pregnant with the singer's child. A son, Prince Michael Jackson Jr., was born in early 1997, and the couple, who often do not reside together, were graced with the birth of a daughter, Paris Michael Katherine, in April of 1998.

Despite a $30 million marketing campaign, Jackson's 1995 release *HIStory: Past, Present, and Future Book I* fell short of expectations with its sales of two million units domestically, twelve million internationally; controversies over the songs "Scream" and "They Don't Care About Us" (the latter contained an allegedly anti-Semitic lyric reference for which Jackson later apologized) and an award for song "You Are Not Alone," did not keep the album from dropping out of the U.S. Top Ten within weeks of its release. A 1997 album, *Blood on the Dance Floor: HIStory in the Mix,* fared even worse, with little marketing and domestic sales in the hundreds of thousands; it consisted largely of remixes by various hit producers of songs from the 1995 HIStory release. Jackson seemed to be attempting to update his style to fit with the technology-driven musical trends of the 1990s.

During the late 1990s the singer was occupied with grandiose schemes to build entertainment complexes in such diverse locales as Poland, South Korea, Paris, and Detroit, where he joined with gambling magnate Don Barden to push for a proposed casino and amusement park. This effort fell through in Detroit, when the people voted no on their proposal to allow the two to bid for a casino license in August of 1998. His charitable foundation Heal the World was reported by *People* magazine to be cutting back on donations as Jackson's total income dropped from an estimated $65 million in 1989 to $20 million in 1997.

That has not stopped Jackson, though. Plans for an upcoming album release and tour are in the works. Michael will reunite with his brothers for another album to be released on his record label, MJJ Music, as well as tour as a group. Michael Jackson himself sums up his 35-year career in his 1993 Grammy Legend Award acceptance speech: "My childhood was completely taken away from me. There was no Christmas, there was no birthdays, it was not a normal childhood, nor the normal pleasures of childhood....But as an awful price, I cannot re-create that part of my life. However, today, when I create my music, I feel like an instrument of nature. I wonder what delight nature must feel when we open our hearts and express our God-given talents." Millions of fans, young and old, black or white, are happy Michael Jackson chose to share those talents with the world.

Selected discography

(as solo performer)

Got to Be There, Motown, 1972.
Ben, Motown, 1972.
Music and Me, Motown, 1973.
Forever, Michael, Motown, 1975.
The Best of Michael Jackson, Motown, 1975.
Off the Wall, Epic, 1979.
Thriller, Epic, 1982.
Bad, Epic, 1987.
Dangerous, Epic, 1991.
HIStory: Past, Present, and Future Book I, Epic, 1995.
Blood on the Dance Floor: HIStory in the Mix, Epic, 1997.

(with the Jackson 5, on Motown)

Diana Ross Presents the Jackson 5, 1969.

ABC, 1970.
Third Album, 1970.
The Jackson 5 Christmas Album, 1970.
Maybe Tomorrow, 1971.
Goin' Back to Indiana, 1971.
The Jackson 5's Greatest Hits, 1971.
Looking Through the Windows, 1972.
Skywriter, 1973.
Get It Together, 1973.
Dancing Machine, 1974.
Moving Violation, 1975.
Joyful Jukebox Music, 1976.
The Jackson 5 Anthology, 1976.
Boogie, 1980.
Farewell My Summer Love, 1984 (recorded 1973, previously unreleased).

(with the Jacksons, on Epic)

The Jacksons, 1976.
Goin' Places, 1977.
Destiny, 1978.
Triumph, 1980.
The Jacksons Live, 1981.
Victory, 1984.

Sources

Books

Jackson, Michael, *Moonwalk,* Doubleday, 1988.

Romanowski, Patricia, and Holly George-Warren, eds., *The New Rolling Stone Encyclopedia of Rock and Roll,* Fireside, 1995.
Taraborrelli, J. Randy, *Michael Jackson: The Magic and the Madness,* Birch Lane Pres, 1991.

Periodicals

Atlanta Journal, November 26, 1996, p. A14.
Billboard, March 30, 1991, p. 5.
Detroit Free Press, August 3, 1998, p. B2.
Los Angeles Times, February 28, 1998, p. D1.
MacLeans, April 20, 1998, p. 11.
New York Times, March 20, 1996, p. D4; June 23, 1997, p. D6.
People, March 1, 1993, p. 46; September 6, 1993, p. 40; May 4, 1998, p. 6.
Time, March 19, 1984, p. 54; September 14, 1987, p. 85.
Washington Post, August 2, 1994, p. F1; January 19, 1996, p. D1.

Other

Barbara Walters' interview with Michael Jackson on "20/20" and Jackson's 1993 Grammy Award acceptance speech was found at the Michael Jackson Internet Fan Club at www.fred.net/mjj/

—James M. Manheim and Ashyia N. Henderson

Samuel L. Jackson

1948—

Actor

"I never get tired of acting because I have a passion for it," Samuel Jackson declared to Paul B. Cohen of the *L.A. Village View*. "Every time I have an opportunity to do it, I will do it." Despite occasional encounters with the implicit racist attitude of Hollywood, he has managed to get cast "color-blind" more often than many of his black colleagues. His versatility and professionalism have been Jackson's keys to survival. As Phillip Noyce, director of *Patriot Games,* told the *New York Times,* "Sam has a remarkable connection with the cinema audience."

Likewise, Jackson is much beloved by those who enjoy live drama. Unlike film work—which tends to offer little immediate reward for the actor—Jackson has acknowledged to Cohen that "theater is such a healthy exchange of energy between the audience and the actors." He added that he can sense audience members "sitting forward, sighing, or getting carried along with the momentum of what we're doing, so it's very invigorating."

Jackson spent years reinvesting that energy in role after role, until finally erupting into widespread public notice in the late 1980s. Before then, his lengthy résumé of film appearances consisted mostly of low-profile character parts until his award-winning performance in Spike Lee's *Jungle Fever* moved him to the top of casting directors' lists. He went on to appear in increasingly varied features with two goals in mind—stretching his range and returning to stage, the arena in which he got his start.

Jackson grew up in Chattanooga, Tennessee, with his mother, grandparents, and his aunt, who was a schoolteacher. His urge to perform emerged while he was still quite young. "As a kid I loved *Treasure Island*," he informed Jean Oppenheimer of the *L.A. Village View*. "My favorite pirate movie was *The Crimson Pirate* with Burt Lancaster. When I was a kid we played pirates in our neighborhood, not sissy stuff like Captain Hook but *serious* pirates." He also participated in rowdy neighborhood recreations of favorite westerns, substituting bicycles for the horses. When he was not pretending to be a high sea rogue, he acted in his aunt's school plays. However, he did not seriously participate in the theater

At a Glance...

Born December 21, 1948 in Chattanooga, TN. Married LaTanya Richardson, an actress, c. 1981; daughter, Zoe. *Education:* Received Dramatic Arts degree from Morehouse College, Atlanta, GA, 1972.

Career: Cofounded Just Us theater company and member of Negro Ensemble Company, Atlanta, c. 1970s; appeared in New York stage productions, including *A Soldier's Play*, 1981; *The Piano Lesson*, 1987; *Sally/Prince*, 1989; *The District Line*, 1990; *Two Trains Running*, 1990; and *Home*. Appeared in Seattle Repertory production of *Fences*; appeared in Coast Playhouse, Los Angeles production of *Distant Fires*, 1993. Made film debut in *Together for Days*; appeared in numerous films, including *Ragtime*, 1981; *Raw*, 1987; *School Daze*, 1988; *Sea of Love*, 1989; *Do the Right Thing*, 1989; *Mo' Better Blues*, 1990; *Def by Temptation*, 1990; *Goodfellas*, 1991; *Jungle Fever*, 1991; *Jumpin' at the Boneyard*, 1992; *White Sands*, 1992; *Patriot Games*, 1992; *True Romance*, 1993; *Menace II Society*, 1993; *National Lampoon's Loaded Weapon I*, 1993; *Amos & Andrew*, 1993; *Jurassic Park*, 1993; *Against the Wall*, 1994; *Assault at West Point: The Court Martial of Johnson Whittaker*, 1994; *Fresh*, 1994; *Pulp Fiction*, 1994; *Kiss of Death*, 1995; *Die Hard: With A Vengeance*, 1995; *Losing Isaiah*, 1995; *A Time To Kill*, 1996; *The Long Kiss Goodnight*, 1997; *Eve's Bayou*, 1997; *187*, 1997; *Jackie Brown*, 1997; *Sphere*, 1998; *The Negotiator*, 1998; *The Red Violin*, 1998.

Awards: Best Supporting Actor award at Cannes Film Festival and New York Film Critics award for *Jungle Fever*, 1991; Academy Award, Best Supporting Actor, nominated for *Pulp Fiction*, 1995.

Addresses: *Home*—San Fernando Valley, CA. *Agency*—International Creative Management, 8942 Wilshire Blvd., Beverly Hills, CA 90211.

---

world until he was in college.

Trustees a Captive Audience

Jackson attended Morehouse College in Atlanta, Georgia, but in order to major in theater he had to take all his theater classes at the college's sister school, Spelman. There he met LaTanya Richardson, an actress whom he would later marry; there too, he made his adult performance debut in the darkly satirical Weill-Brecht classic, *The Three Penny Opera,* making up for his lack of singing acumen with his acting skills. Meanwhile, offstage was becoming radicalized by the burgeoning black liberation movement of the early 1970s. Student anger at the lack of African American studies and the institution's control by a white governing body caused him to participate in an action that involved locking a few Morehouse trustees—including Rev. Martin Luther King, Sr.—in a room until the insurgents' demands were met. For having had a hand in things, Jackson and some of his comrades, were suspended but later reinstated.

Focusing on what would soon become his career, Jackson helped start the Just Us theater company in Atlanta, but he and Richardson ultimately left for New York City in 1976. "All I know is, we pulled into [Greenwich] Village at night, and everyone on the street looked really bizarre," Jackson told Michael Angeli of the *New York Times.* "We were going to live with some friends on Barrow Street. What we didn't realize was that it was Halloween, and we were in the middle of a parade." Though he did not begin his own parade of acting roles until some years later, he did start working in the theater almost immediately.

For the next several years, Jackson appeared in various plays. Film work was sometimes offered, as when he appeared in 1981's *Ragtime,* but it was when he was appearing onstage in *A Soldier's Play* the same year that he began making real connections. He first met fellow African American actor Morgan Freeman, who greatly encouraged him, then a young film student named Spike Lee. Lee came backstage to introduce himself. Jackson recollected to the *New York Times.* "He told me he was a Morehouse alumnus, that he was at NYU [New York University] film school, da-da-da. He was going to, um, be a filmmaker. He said when he started to make films, he would love for me to be in his movies. It was, like, I had my dream, and he had his—a surplus of reality there, you know what I mean?"

Worked With Lee

Lee's dream came true, and Jackson appeared in several of the writer/director's films, including *School Daze* in 1988, and the following year's *Do the Right Thing.* Jackson observed that Lee's tendency to use the same actors in different films lent an *esprit de corps* to the productions. "Bill Nunn, Giancarlo [Esposito]—we knew each other from Morehouse, where we did plays together. There's something to be said for the ensemble feeling, for getting to know other actors and having a feeling for working with them," Jackson explained to Angeli. "And doing Spike's films, that was the one thing we all had to look forward to every year—knowing we were going to get together again. Same crew, same actors," he continued. Jackson also landed character roles in features by other directors; in the late 1980s to early 1990s, Jackson worked in *The Exorcist III, Coming to America, Sea of Love* and Martin Scorsese's *Goodfellas*. But Lee was the creative force behind the film that made Jackson's reputation, *Jungle Fever*.

In that 1991 production, Jackson played Gator, the crack-addicted brother of Flipper Purify, played by Wesley Snipes. This character hit home because Jackson himself was a recovering crack addict. He brought an explosive charisma and unpredictability to the portrayal; Peter Travers of *Rolling Stone* called him "a blistering actor in an unforgettable role." When the film debuted at the Cannes film festival, the judges named Jackson the best supporting actor. The award was a double honor because the Cannes judging had never before extended to that category, but Jackson's performance left an indelible mark on those who would rate him. Besides winning at that prestigious affair, he also received a New York Film Critics award. Jackson even won over the toughest critic of all—himself. Perhaps the greatest satisfaction accorded by the showing was that for once, as he told Lena Williams of the *New York Times,* "I don't want to go back and fix it."

A few months after *Jungle Fever's* release, Jackson was surprised to find that his increased visibility and all the acclaim made some filmmakers think he was unavailable except at high salaries. He emphasized to Williams that he was "not out of anyone's range yet." Nonetheless, he proceeded to take small roles in such offbeat films as *Juice* and *True Romance,* among others. When Jackson was sent the script for the thriller *White Sands,* he assumed he was being considered for the part of the villain—a role eventually bagged by Mickey Rourke.

"Then they call me back and say no, you're Meeker, the FBI agent. What? I had to go back and read it again," Jackson admitted to *Premiere's* Veronica Chambers. "And I like the guy [Meeker] a lot. He's not obviously bad or obviously good. It was a stretch from Gator to that character. And I really would like to display the fact that I have that range." The film's director, Roger Donaldson, praised Jackson to Chambers, saying "He's got enormous resources as an actor. He's extremely talented technically. Sam can do something one take, then go back and build on it. He's spontaneous, but he's well trained.... And he's a nice guy."

"Call Your Agent"

Hollywood did not need to be heavily persuaded about Jackson's willingness to take on different genres. He shared above-the-title billing in two broad comedies, *Amos & Andrew* and *National Lampoon's Loaded Weapon I.* Unfortunately, critics trashed both 1993 films. *Entertainment Weekly's* review of the *Amos & Andrew,* for example, consisted largely of career advice for the actor. Their reviewer wondered, "did Samuel L. Jackson really have to follow up his mesmerizing, out-on-the-edge performance as a homeless crack addict [in *Jungle Fever*] with *National Lampoon's Loaded Weapon I* and the imbecilic mistaken-identity farce *Amos & Andrew?*" The unequivocal pan concluded by urging the actor to "call your agent—and fire him."

Despite such misfires, Jackson continued working regularly in the 1990s, appearing as a technician in the box-office hit *Jurassic Park*—also one of the top-selling movies of all time—as one of Harrison Ford's allies in *Patriot Games,* and in an ensemble role in *Menace II Society. Patriot Games* director Noyce told the *New York Times* that Jackson, despite having his performance severely edited, "made so much out of so little that the audience imagined he had a greater participation than he actually did."

In 1994, Jackson was cast as a killer in writer-director Quentin Tarantino's *Pulp Fiction,* an ultraviolent thriller boasting what Jackson described to Cohen as "one of the best scripts I've read in a couple of years." The plumb role contained "four to five page [long] speeches ... and that's something you don't normally do in a film," though he had done so on stage. Jackson had earlier appeared in such prestigious New York productions as August Wilson's two acclaimed pieces, *The Piano Lesson* and *Two Trains Running*. His appreciation for the dialogues Wilson had written was obvious. Speaking to Cohen, Jackson reflected, "August writes three-hour plays, and when I was doing *Piano Lesson*—I was the original [protagonist] Boy Willie before [actor] Charles Dutton did it—that character talks for about two hours and ten minutes in a three-hour play...."

Back to the Stage

Despite the plethora of motion picture work he obtained in the late 1980s and early 1990s, Jackson pined to appear onstage again. Once he did, he was pleasantly surprised to find a new environment in regards to many playwrights. In a *New York Times* interview, Jackson observed that "the black acting community is relatively small. Especially in New York theater. The funny thing is that when they used to cast black roles, everybody from age 20 to 50 was called because they had no idea what kind of black person they wanted for the role. That kind of let you know that they sort of didn't have a clue as to who these people are."

Though Jackson assumed he would have to maintain himself in New York City for theatrical roles, he was pleasantly surprised at the opportunity to be in the 1993 working-class play *Distant Fires* in Los Angeles. "Everybody's very concerned about the production as a whole and not about their own performances," he enthused to Cohen. He similarly told *Premiere's* Chambers "I always want to get back to theater to make sure that I'm still an actor. You have to convince people who are actually sitting there looking at you that you're doing what you're doing, without all the trappings of reality around you."

Back to Hollywood

Jackson's time on stage was short-lived because Hollywood continued to beckon. Since *Jungle Fever,* he has been in over 30 films. Jackson teamed up with fellow *Pulp Fiction* star Bruce Willis in *Die Hard: With A Vengeance,* the third installment of the *Die Hard* films. He also portrayed Carl Lee Hailey, the father who murdered two white rednecks who brutally raped his daughter in *A Time To Kill,* a film based on the bestseller by John Grisham.

Jackson has also appeared in *Fresh, Losing Isaiah* with Jessica Lange and Halle Berry, *The Long Kiss Goodnight* with Geena Davis, *The Great White Hype,* a satire on the boxing industry—he portrayed a character like boxing promoter Don King—and *U.S. Marshals* with Tommy Lee Jones and Wesley Snipes. He also took part in *Sphere,* a thriller, with Dustin Hoffman and Sharon Stone. He told Bruce Fretts of *Entertainment Weekly,* "The closer together your jobs are, the greater the [producers] think your ability is."

Teamed Up Again With Tarantino

Jackson teamed up again with Quentin Tarantino in *Jackie Brown,* an adaptation of author Elmore Leonard's book, *Rum Punch,* and starring *Foxy Brown* star, Pam Grier—a favorite of Tarantino—Robert DeNiro, Bridget Fonda and Michael Keaton. This film opened to mixed reviews but Jackson shined in them all. Though not as violent as other Tarantino flicks, *Jackie Brown* was still offensive to some, especially concerning the use of the N-word in the film. Director Spike Lee took offense, even accusing Tarantino of wanting to be black. Jackson came to Tarantino's defense, quoted in *Jet* as saying, "Black artists think they are the only ones allowed to use the word. Well, that's bull. This film is a wonderful homage to Black exploitation films (of the 1970s). This is a good film. And Spike hasn't made one of those in a few years."

> "I never get tired of acting because I have a passion for it."

Jackson also starred and co-produced *Eve's Bayou.* Though he hoped the producer title was just ceremonial, it turned out to be real. He told Joe Leydon of MSNBC that once on location, he found that he was "the only producer who's really on the set. So, things start to happen. And you have goals every day." The independent film won raves from critics and Jackson is set to produce another film.

Jackson has completed his part in the first installment of the *Star Wars* prequels. He plays a Jedi Knight. Jackson will also utter that famous line, "May the force be with you." Since this is a prequel to the already released *Star Wars* saga, he is actually the first person to ever say the line. He also appeared in *The Negotiator, The Red Violin,* and a small-barely noticeable part in *Out Of Sight.* To sum up his busy year, Jackson was quoted in MSNBC as saying, "All I can say is, it's been an interesting kind of year for me. I look up one day, and I'm standing across from Dustin Hoffman, and I go 'Wow!' And I look up another day, and I'm next to Robert DeNiro. And last week—I died and went to heaven. I looked up, and there was Yoda."

Trappings notwithstanding, Jackson admitted to *L.A. Village View* writer Jean Oppenheimer that he still wants to play a pirate, as well as a gunslinger, as he had done in his neighborhood as a child. Yet he has never lost sight of the practical necessities of his career. Indeed, Samuel Jackson seems, with each new performance, to guarantee a versatility and commitment that never go out of style.

Sources

Entertainment Weekly, March 5, 1993, p. 42; Febru-

ary 18, 1994, pp. 102-3; November 25, 1994.
Essence, April 1992, p. 48.
Interview, April 1992, p. 50.
Jet, March 9, 1998, p. 36.
L.A. Village View, February 12, 1993, 11; December 3, 1993.
New York Times, June 9, 1991; February 7, 1993, section 2, 13-14.
Premiere, May 1992, p. 57.
Rolling Stone, June 27, 1991, 75-6.

Other

Information also obtained online at www.msnbc.com, The Samuel L. Jackson Home Page at http://member.aol.com/gifhack, and www.canoe.ca/JamMoviesArtistE2K/jackson_samuel.html.

—Simon Glickman and Ashyia N. Henderson

Tom Joyner

1949(?)—

Radio personality

Tom Joyner has always been recognized as a man on the move. He first came to public attention by hosting a morning radio show in Dallas and an afternoon show in Chicago simultaneously for eight years, flying back-and-forth between jobs daily. In the 1990s his popularity soared as the host of a nationally syndicated morning radio program. As nationally syndicated radio programs became a hot trend in the 1990s, Joyner became the biggest star in black radio.

Tom Joyner was born in Tuskegee, Alabama around 1949. As a young man he sang with the Commodores but left before the group became successful. Years later he would tell the *Los Angeles Times* that he would forever kick himself for not staying with the group until it became successful. "This is a bitter subject," he claimed. "I've been friends with Lionel Richie since childhood. We go back to nursery school. And here I am getting up at three in the morning. Do I regret it? Here I am going to the bank every Friday and the bank comes to him. 'Got any checks for us today, Mr. Richie?' Don't get me started," he joked. It was around that same time, however, that Joyner formed a more lasting relationship, marrying his wife Dora.

With his music career over even before it started, Joyner embarked upon a radio career. By the early 1980s he was a fixture in Chicago, working at his third station in that market. In 1983 Joyner got a big break when he was hired by radio station KDKA in Dallas to host its morning program, and within a couple of years his show was the second-rated morning show in that market.

In 1985 Joyner was faced with a difficult career dilemma, and he solved it in a way few people would have considered. He was negotiating a new contract in Dallas, and at the same time, WGCI, a station in his old hometown of Chicago, expressed interest in hiring him as its afternoon host. Negotiations were fruitful, with each station offering him a million dollars over several years. Joyner decided that both jobs were too good to refuse, and took the amazing step of signing contracts with both stations.

"I got to thinking," Joyner told *People Weekly*. "Dallas and Chicago are in the same time zone. There was plenty of time between the morning and afternoon shows," he continued. He looked into travel arrangements, and discovered that between available flights and typical weather patterns, he would likely be able to make both jobs almost 100 percent of the time.

Convincing his bosses and his wife that the dual career was a good idea was the next step. His boss in Dallas was not forthcoming with his opinions about the arrangement. But Marv Dyson, president and general manager of the Chicago station, told *People Weekly*, "It came as sort of a shock to me when I found out that Tom had signed a contract for the morning show in Dallas and the afternoon show with us without really telling either

At a Glance...

Born circa 1949 in Tuskegee, Alabama. Married to Dora; sons: Thomas and Albert.

Career: Worked as disc jockey at three Chicago radio stations. Morning air personality, KDKA in Dallas, Texas, 1983-93. Afternoon host, WGCI in Chicago, 1985-93. Host of nationally syndicated "On The Move," late 1980s; "Tom Joyner Morning Show," 1993—.

Addresses: *Business Address*—13725 Mont fort Drive, Dallas, TX 75240

---

station. But after I talked at length with Tom, with his whole family, with the airlines and with doctors, I knew it would work." Dyson's station took advantage of the situation by staging a promotion in which listeners would guess the date that Joyner would first fail to make it to his afternoon job.

Convincing Dora both jobs were a good idea was another matter. While Joyner had never had a fear of flying, Dora was less confident in airline travel. "Sure, I have an uneasy feeling about him doing so much flying, but he's never worried about it," she explained to *People Weekly*. "So I've tried to accept it. He's worked a long time for this opportunity, so he won me over," she added.

A typical day during the two-market era for Joyner saw him up at 3 a.m., eating breakfast by 4 a.m., on the air in Dallas at 5:30, off the air at 9, on a plane to Chicago by 10, on the air in Chicago from 2-6 p.m., on a plane back to Dallas by 10 p.m., eating dinner with his wife by 11:30 and in bed by midnight. He even found time to play racquetball at the Downtown Sports Club in Chicago between shows. Joyner cut a deal with American Airlines to fly the 8,000 miles a week for a $30,000 annual fee, and was bestowed with the nickname, "The Fly Jock." Fatigue was a factor, but as he told *People Weekly,* "I'm not an air traffic controller, nor am I out digging ditches eight hours a day. I talk and play records. No big deal."

If the arrangement gave pause to executives at the two stations, they need not have worried. Within three years Joyner had both his programs in first place in their respective time slots and markets. His format on both stations was urban contemporary music, but Joyner's easygoing personality was also a key part of his shows' appeal, and raised him above the status of a disc jockey.

During the late 1980s Joyner also first dipped his toes in the syndication pool with a weekly countdown show entitled—what else?—"On the Move."

Although the contracts Joyner originally signed would only have required him to do both shows for five years, he wound up doing both for eight. During that time he logged over seven million frequent-flyer miles. When the run was up, the airline retired two seats in his honor and presented them to him for use in his radio studio.

The opportunity to give up the commute came in 1993, when ABC offered Joyner a syndicated morning show. The arrangement would allow him to be on the air in countless markets while staying in one city. Syndicated radio was having great success, with Howard Stern, Rush Limbaugh, Larry King and many other radio personalities making a strong impact in the ratings in markets large and small.

"The Tom Joyner Morning Show" debuted in January of 1994 on WGCI and 28 other stations from Los Angeles to Washington, D.C. and Miami to Flint, Michigan. The format was not a radical departure from what he had been doing, but there were adjustments to make the show more like television. There was a studio band, like Jay Leno's and David Letterman's, but the band was in a studio in Chicago while the host and his cast were in Dallas. There were also comedy sketches and a steady parade of guests. Joyner's easygoing, agreeable personality was still the factor that made the show work.

Joyner made use of his new national platform to exhibit his political and social consciousness from time to time. He came to Michael Jackson's defense when public and media attention from child molestation accusations was negatively focused upon him. After Jackson agreed to settle a lawsuit out of court, Joyner polled his audience for its reaction and found that 90 percent of his listeners said they supported Jackson. Joyner also stopped an auction of slave posters at Christie's auction house later in the decade, waged a write-in campaign that convinced Fox television to renew "Living Single," rated the most popular TV program among black audiences, and rallied support for the defeat of an anti-affirmative action bill in Houston, a market in which his show was not even heard.

Joyner's morning show was a quick success, expanding to 62 stations within its first two years on the air. While there was some debate within the industry regarding what format Joyner fit into best, it was usually found that his program drew its highest ratings when broadcast on black-oriented stations, and companies that owned two or more stations in a market usually chose to broadcast his show on such stations. The show was considered a hot property in many markets, and when ABC moved it from WGCI to WVAZ in Chicago, it was a major story in that city.

There was also a good deal of debate within black radio circles regarding whether Joyner's program was good or bad for black radio in general. Programmers found it a dream come true. Joyner's program, slickly packaged and highly professional, accrued high ratings, and the only cost stations paid to broadcast it was an agreement to run all ABC network commercials, leaving only station breaks for stations to run their own commercials. But others in the business were concerned that Joyner's show would disrupt the local community aspect which had always been central to black radio's appeal, and would eliminate jobs as prospective morning hosts would find more and more stations opting for Joyner's show and others like it. "I'm not taking jobs," Joyner defended himself to the *Washington Post*. "I'm making sure we have jobs. We have the [ratings] numbers that allow our stations to compete with other stations and we bring those stations a morning show that's difficult for anyone else to compete against."

By early 1998 Joyner's show was heard in 95 markets. His list of guests included Don King, Oprah Winfrey, Sam Donaldson, Tipper Gore, Stevie Wonder, Luther Vandross and President Bill Clinton. His mix of urban contemporary music with talk, comedy, news, politics and sports was making him a force in the highly coveted 25-54 age bracket. His show was highly competitive in many markets, and was the number one morning show in Washington, D.C. No longer a man on the move, Tom Joyner had already arrived, not just as a major player in black radio, but in radio in general.

Sources

Billboard, February 5, 1994, p. 8.
Broadcasting and Cable, September 27, 1993, p. 49; December 18, 1995, p. 66.
Chicago Tribune, October 12, 1988, section 5, p. 6; January 4, 1994, section 1, p. 16.
Inside Media, May 15, 1996, p. 26.
Los Angeles Times, April 21, 1994, p. F1.
Mediaweek, July 22, 1996, p. 33.
Newsweek, February 23, 1998, p. 55.
People Weekly, January 20, 1986, p. 98.
Washington Post, May 14, 1996, p. 1E.

—Mike Eggert

Gayle King

1956(?)—

Television personality, journalist

Gayle King is the well-regarded best friend of one of the most popular and financially successful personalities in television history. The Connecticut newscaster has been close pals with Oprah Winfrey since their humble beginnings at a Baltimore television station, and Winfrey often recounts "Gayle" anecdotes to her viewing audience, which numbers in the millions daily. In contrast to Winfrey, King has led a far more sedate life as a news anchor at a Hartford CBS affiliate since the early 1980s, and is a divorced mother of two. In 1997, she hosted her own half-hour nationally syndicated talk show that enjoyed a year-long run. King, the envy of many, has occasionally found herself on the receiving end of Winfrey's well-publicized generosity. As she told Jim Calio in a 1998 *Redbook* interview, "Who wouldn't want to be her best friend?"

King was the first of four daughters born to Scott and Peggy King. She spent several years as a child in Ankara, Turkey, where her father was stationed; he later became an electrical engineer and King enjoyed a comfortable, middle-class upbringing in Maryland. As a college student at the University of Maryland in the mid-1970s, King obtained her first job in television at WTOP-TV in Washington, DC. Though she was studying psychology at the time, she decided to pursue a career in media instead. In 1976, she was working at Baltimore's WJZ-TV as a $12,000-a-year production assistant. At the station, one of the news anchors was an unknown just a year older than King named Oprah Winfrey. King was still living at home at the time, and during a particularly bad snowstorm one evening, she faced a long and slow drive home. Winfrey invited King to bunk at her place nearby instead.

Friendship Endured

The pair gossiped about co-workers for hours that night, and became fast friends. King recalled being shocked when they went shopping together and Winfrey was able to afford two sweaters at the mall. Even though their career paths soon took them separate ways, they remained close. Each remember spending Friday nights in the late 1970s on the phone, long-distance, watching the popular nighttime soap opera *Dallas* simultaneously. King had been hired in 1978 by WDAF-TV in Kansas City as a news anchor. She eventually began dating a local police officer, Bill Bumpus, and the pair wed in 1982.

King was then hired for the news team at WFSB-TV in Hartford, Connecticut, and has made the city her home since. With her husband—who earned a law degree from nearby Yale University—she had two children in the late 1980s. King and her husband asked Winfrey to become godmother to both. By then an extremely successful talk-show host, Winfrey also helped out by contributing generously to a "nanny fund" she set up for King upon the birth of her second child. King has said

> **At a Glance...**
>
> Born c. 1956, in Chevy Chase, MD; daughter of Scott (an electronics engineer) and Peggy (a homemaker) King; married Bill Bumpus (an attorney), 1982 (divorced, 1993); children: Kirby (daughter), William. *Education:* Received degree from University of Maryland, c. 1977.
>
> **Career:** Worked at WTOP-TV, Washington, DC, c. 1975; WJZ-TV, Baltimore, MD, production assistant, 1976; WDAF-TV, Kansas City, MO, 1978-81; WFSB-TV, Hartford, CT, news anchor, 1982--. Host of NBC daytime program, *Cover to Cover,* 1991; host of own syndicated half-hour show for Eyemark Entertainment, *The Gayle King Show,* 1997-98.
>
> **Awards:** Emmy Award for newscasting.
>
> **Addresses:** *Office*—WFSB-TV/Channel 3, Three Constitution Plaza, Hartford, CT 06103-1892.

that it is only because she has been able to hire a good caretaker for her children that she has successfully balanced both career and motherhood.

Tales of Gayle

Since 1982 King has been co-anchor on the local news of Hartford's CBS affiliate, and has become a popular, Emmy-award winning television personality. Yet she has also achieved a more national celebrity because of Oprah: millions tune into the *Oprah* show daily, and the popular, personable host and the details of her life are well known to viewers. On the air, Winfrey speaks often of King as her best friend, and sometimes recounts the practical jokes she and King play upon one another. "Gayle is the reason I don't need therapy," Winfrey told *People* writer Samantha Miller. "People come up to me, introducing their friends to me all the time, saying 'She's my Gayle.' I wish everybody had a Gayle in their life."

There is also a downside to King's fame. "A lot of people come up to me and I know they have an agenda," King told Calio in *Redbook.* "They have a movie script or they need some bills paid or they need a loan." Yet network executives also saw potential in King: if she was remarkable enough to share a confidential friendship with the divine Oprah, then the viewing public might also love her. King began to be courted by production companies interested in giving her a show of her own. In 1991, she hosted a short-lived NBC newsmagazine called *Cover to Cover,* and in 1997, after much negotiation, found herself with her own half-hour syndicated show bearing her name.

Courted by Syndicater

King had it written into her contract that the show would never appear in the same time slot as Winfrey's show in any of its 200-plus markets around the country. Eyemark Entertainment, connected with the CBS network, also believed so fervently in King's drawing power they built a studio next door to WFSB in Hartford so that maintaining two jobs would be easier for her. Most daytime shows are based out of New York or Los Angeles, but King, divorced in 1993, refused to relocate because of her children, who still spend a great deal of time with their father.

The Gayle King Show debuted in September of 1997. Winfrey, not surprisingly, was a big help to King on a number of matters, advising her about her on-screen wardrobe and even offering critical assessments of the set furniture and theme song. When Winfrey told King that some publicity shots were unacceptable, King heeded her advice and had them redone. But when Winfrey told her to get rid of one particular chair and confessed she hated King's theme music, King had the chair shipped out to Winfrey in Chicago with a computer chip in its seat so that when Winfrey sat on it, the theme music played. Winfrey also helped King and her show in other ways. After a month on the air, Winfrey and Graham, a notoriously reclusive romantic pair, allowed themselves to be jointly interviewed by King on the air. Graham came to the Hartford studio, while Winfrey appeared via a satellite hookup. The satellite linking made television history as the first instance when two daytime talk shows had gone on the air together.

The Perks of Paldom

The Gayle King Show enjoyed a year-long run, but suffered the fate of many personality-driven chat shows that glutted the airwaves in the mid-1990s, and its cancellation was announced in the spring of 1998. Though it was picked up for renewal by 85 percent of the affiliates, ratings had remained too low. King still appears on the 5:30 p.m. newscast on WFSB. Though Winfrey once offered her friend a seven-figure sum to come and work for her thriving production company in

Chicago, King turned it down—again, because of her children.

For fun, King regularly visits Winfrey in Chicago or at the star's digs in Florida, all expenses paid; as the best friend of the richest woman in the entertainment industry (with an estimated wealth of $550 million in 1997, according to the *Forbes 400* list), King is no longer astonished that Winfrey can buy what she wants at the mall. "People always amaze me by asking, 'Aren't you jealous of Oprah?'" King told *Ladies Home Journal* writer Audrey Edwards. "I say, 'Why would I be?' I'm happy with my own life, and I'm so thrilled for her. When I visit Oprah I'm wined and dined and chauffeured around in a limo. And when I come home and can't remember where I parked the car at the airport or trip over the kids' toys, I think the visit was great, but I really like my life, too."

Sources

Broadcasting & Cable, August 18, 1997, p. 26; October 13, 1997, p. 36.
Jet, October 6, 1997, p. 32; October 20, 1997, p. 54.
Ladies' Home Journal, October 1997, p. 136.
MediaWeek, April 20, 1998, p. 8.
People, February 23, 1998, p. 123.
Redbook, February 1998, p. 62.

—Carol Brennan

Daisy Lampkin

1883(?)–1965

Newspaper executive, civil rights advocate

During an era when social biases kept most women out of the political arena, Daisy Lampkin was an invaluable supporter of the adolescent National Association for the Advancement of Colored People (NAACP). Having been active in the fight for women's suffrage in the United States, she turned her energies to the black civil rights movement during the 1920s and assumed an official position with the NAACP in 1930. Lampkin became a key fundraiser for the organization and was highly respected for her tireless enthusiasm and persuasive skills. She was also a prominent figure in Pittsburgh's black community through her involvement in a myriad of organizations and her role as vice president of the *Pittsburgh Courier*.

In Pittsburgh, Lampkin is remembered for her achievements as an advocate for social change and for her remarkable personal attributes. In 1997 Steve Levin wrote in *Pittsburgh Post-Gazette,* "Daisy Lampkin had a way about her that charmed politicians and emboldened the browbeaten....[S]he could fly into a city, give several speeches with her oratorical flair and get even the most parsimonious to donate;" he added, Lampkin is "considered by some to be one of the great American women of the 20th century." A woman with a passion for hats, Lampkin was affectionately known to her friends and colleagues as "Aunt Daisy." At one time, Lampkin rented an apartment to a teacher named K. Leroy Irvis, who later became the Pennsylvania House of Representatives' longest-serving speaker. Irvis recalled in the *Pittsburgh Post-Gazette,* "If she had any vulnerability, I never saw it. She could be soft when it was needed or she could be hard and commanding when she needed to be. She was the one person who could tell me to sit down and shut up and I would sit down and shut up."

Began Activism as Suffragette

Born Daisy Elizabeth Adams on August 9, 1883? in Washington, D.C., Lampkin grew up in Reading, Pennsylvania as the only child of George and Rosa Adams. After graduating from public high school, the young woman came to Pittsburgh in about 1909. She married William Lampkin in 1912 and helped him at his restaurant in a Pittsburgh suburb. Lampkin proceeded to devote her adult life to social causes, beginning with those issues that were important to her as a black housewife. She is believed to have given her first women's rights tea in 1912, and when the couple moved into the city, she became more actively involved in the suffrage movement. The Lampkins had no children, but helped to raise a friend's daughter, Romaine Childs, who became Lampkin's heir.

As a suffragist, Lampkin joined the Negro Women's Equal Franchise Federation, later renamed the Lucy Stone League. In 1915 Lampkin became the organization's president, a position she held for 40 years. After women obtained the right to vote, the group raised

At a Glance...

Born Daisy Elizabeth Adams, in Reading, PA, August 8, 1883?; daughter of George S. (a porter) and Rosa (Proctor) Adams; married William Lampkin (a restaurant owner) in 1912; died on March 10, 1965.

Career: *Pittsburgh Courier,* vice-president, 1925-65; National Association for the Advancement of Colored People (NAACP), regional field secretary, 1930-35; national field secretary, 1935-47; member, board of directors, 1947-65; assisted a great number of organizations, including the Lucy Stone Woman Suffrage League, the National Association of Colored Women, Colored Voters' Division of the Republican National Committee, Allegheny County Negro Women's Republican League, Negro Voters League of Pennsylvania, Pittsburgh Urban League, National Council of Negro Women, Grace Memorial Presbyterian Church.

Awards: NAACP Woman of the Year, 1945; Eleanor Roosevelt-Mary McLeod Bethune World Citizenship Award, 1964; home on Webster Avenue designated a historical landmark, Pennsylvania Historical and Museum Commission; Spirit of King Award, Pittsburgh Port Authority, Kingsley Association, Pittsburgh Pirates, 1997.

money for scholarships. Lampkin's early career as a suffragette included making street-corner speeches and encouraging other black housewives to create a social voice as organized consumer groups.

Once Lampkin had gained the right to vote, she became actively involved in politics. She would become chairman of the Allegheny County Negro Women's Republican League, vice-chairman of the Negro Voters League of Pennsylvania, and vice-chairman of the Colored Voters Division of the Republican National Committee. Lampkin also served twice as an alternate delegate at large to the National Republican Party Convention.

Lampkin involved herself in an amazing number of other organizations and projects. During World War I, she led Allegheny County's black community in raising over $2 million in Liberty Bond sales. Lampkin helped organize the first Red Cross chapter among black women and created local chapters of the Urban League and NAACP. She was a charter member of the National Council of Negro Women, a board chairman for the National Association of Colored Women, and an elder of Grace Memorial Presbyterian Church.

Lampkin became a *Pittsburgh Courier* vice president under editor-publisher Robert L. Vann, who had previously recruited her to help with fundraising. According to one account, Lampkin had won a subscription contest for the black weekly in which a promoter promised a car as first prize; when the promoter disappeared leaving Vann without a car, he rewarded Lampkin out of his own pocket. Another account says that Lampkin was made a stock holder. While a vice president, Lampkin wrote stories and was often named in the newspaper. "The women's pages ... featured an impressive array of clubs which sponsored weekly events in the black community, and Daisy Lampkin was always out in front raising money for orphans and widows, church mortgages and scholarships for youth," Edna B. McKenzie noted in *Pennsylvania Heritage.* By mid-century, she had helped make the *Pittsburgh Courier* the most widely circulated black newspaper in the world.

Became First Field Secretary

In 1930, Lampkin became the first field secretary for the NAACP. She assumed this job under the direction of Walter White, and quickly made her presence felt in the organization. Lampkin is credited with single-handedly arranging for the NAACP's 1931 national convention to be held in Pittsburgh. In 1935 Lampkin was made national field secretary, a role she filled until 1947 when she became a member of the board of directors. This change came about when Lampkin's doctor advised her to slow down in consideration of her poor health. For Lampkin's work for the NAACP was very rigorous, requiring frequent travel and long days. It is believed that she once conducted 40 chapter meetings in a single month. She crossed the country forming new chapters, reviving existing chapters, and raising money. Ultimately, Lampkin could never bring herself to retire and served the organization for some 35 years.

Among the most important episodes of Lampkin's service to the NAACP was when she spearheaded the anti-lynching button campaign of 1937, which was aimed to support the Costigan-Wagner Act that was to be voted on in the U.S. Congress. The act called for federal intervention when local authorities failed to respond to lynchings. To this end, the NAACP was faced with the difficult task of increasing blacks' awareness of lynchings. As Lampkin recalled in a 1962 interview with author Robert L. Zangrando, "We were so ashamed that whites could do that to *us,* that we hardly wanted to talk about it publicly." Some 250,000 buttons were produced that read "Stop lynching! N.A.A.C.P. Defense

Fund." Sold at a time when blacks were still suffering financially from the Great Depression, the buttons grossed $9,378 by April of 1937.

Lampkin was also involved in much behind-the-scenes work, including convincing future Supreme Court Justice Thurgood Marshall to become a member of the association's Legal Defense Committee. She is said to have told the young lawyer in 1938—when he was practicing law in Baltimore—that he should move to New York to be near the NAACP headquarters. By 1954 he had become an attorney for the organization and argued the case of Brown vs. the Board of Education before the U.S. Supreme Court. In particular, Lampkin worked closely with Roy Wilkins, who was head of the NAACP at the time of her death.

Contributions Re-evaluated

Some historians doubt that an accurate measure of Lampkin's contributions as an activist was ever made during her lifetime. Edna B. McKenzie, an emeritus professor at the Community College of Allegheny County, remarked in the *Pittsburgh Post-Gazette,* "the men really depended upon her. I doubt seriously if they could have done it without Daisy Lampkin. She raised the money and she recruited the people. I'm not just talking about Pittsburgh; I'm talking nationally." And Lampkin was described by Paula Giddings in *When and Where I Enter* as an example of "women who performed much of the nuts-and-bolts work of their organizations, yet were hardly expected to gain public recognition or even be in on major policy decisions." However, in some instances her impact was clearly documented: in 1944 she was credited with increasing the NAACP's membership more than any other executive; in 1945 the organization named her its "Woman of the Year;" and during her last year as national field secretary, Lampkin was reported to have raised over $1 million for the NAACP.

During the early 1950s Lampkin renewed her involvement in women's issues when she assisted the black sorority Delta Sigma Theta with a fundraising campaign to create a national headquarters in Washington, D.C. As Paula Giddings noted in *In Search of Sisterhood,* this campaign or "'crusade' would be different from the others. For the first time she would try to raise a significant amount of funds wholly within one organization: an organization whose members, chapters, and regions had varying amounts of resources." The resulting campaign called for chapters to give the prescribed amount of $100 each, for graduate sorors to give at least $10, and for student members to give $5. In this way she helped the sorority to centralize their record keeping and finances and to have a presence in the policy-making center of the nation.

Remained Devoted to NAACP

Hypertension and arthritis were the leading causes that prompted Lampkin to leave her position as NAACP field secretary and the hardship of extensive traveling, but she continued to work as a member of the organization's board. Lampkin died on March 10, 1965 after having a stroke months earlier at a NAACP membership drive event in Camden, New Jersey. As this illustrated, her dedication to the civil rights organization never faltered. Her adopted daughter Romaine Childs remembered in the Pittsburgh Post-Gazette: "They'd call and say, 'Daisy, we need you'....We've got some boys in jail. We need to raise some funds.' She couldn't stay in a hotel (because of segregation) but she'd pack her bags in the middle of the night or day and go raise funds for the NAACP. And that was her life." The Pittsburgh Courier reflected in Lampkin's obituary that the woman was "in herself an institution. There was no line of separation between herself and the National Association for the Advancement of Colored People. She was truly 'Mrs. NAACP.'"

In 1983 Lampkin was recognized in her adopted home town of Pittsburgh by a historical marker on her Webster Avenue apartment building. This was the first time the state of Pennsylvania awarded a plaque to honor an African American in the city. In 1997 she was the recipient of the "Spirit of King" award, which honors civil rights advocates from Pittsburgh who embody the ideals of Dr. Martin Luther King Jr.

Sources

Books

Giddings, Paula, *In Search of Sisterhood,* W. Morrow, 1988.
When and Where I Enter, W. Morrow, 1984.
Salem, Dorothy C., editor, *African American Women,* Garland, 1993.
Zangrando, Robert L., *The NAACP Crusade Against Lynching,* Temple University Press, 1980.

Periodicals

Pittsburgh Courier, March 20, 1965, p. 1.
Pittsburgh Post-Gazette, February 2, 1998, p. A10.
Pennsylvania Heritage, Summer 1983, p. 9-12.

—Paula Pyzik Scott

Janet Langhart

1941—

Media consultant, journalist

As wife of the U.S. Secretary of Defense, Janet Langhart is one of the most prominent spouses in Washington. The former beauty pageant winner, Boston television personality, media consultant—and longtime Democrat—wed a Republican senator in 1996, and their union has been celebrated more as a triumph over multicultural issues in America than political ones. Though there are other high-profile interracial couples in Washington power circles, including Supreme Court Justice Clarence Thomas and his wife, Langhart and her husband William S. Cohen—appointed to his cabinet post in the Clinton Administration in late 1996—are the country's highest-ranking such pair on the official protocol lists. *Washington Post* writer Kevin Merida called them "the best advertisement for the kind of dialogue and interpersonal racial progress President Clinton is now pushing, the kind of progress that can't be legislated."

Langhart was born Janet Floyd in 1941 and grew up in public housing in racially segregated Indianapolis. She was raised by her mother, who worked as a hospital ward secretary. After spending two years at Indianapolis's Butler University, Langhart found success as a model in the 1960s, winning several beauty pageants, including "Miss Sepia" of 1966 and "Miss International Auto Show" two years later. It was a different era, and one that ignited in her a sense of injustice over racial attitudes in America. She recalled that on one occasion, she arrived at an audition for an appliance commercial and caused somewhat of a stir; an African American woman pitching products in a nationwide ad campaign was still a rarity at the time.

Langhart married her first husband, Tony Langhart in 1968, just as her career was taking off. She was working at a Chicago television station (she eventually became a weathercaster there), and the couple married just weeks after the tragic assassination of Martin Luther King Jr. Both were ardent civil-rights supporters, and "it was a kind of sentimental reaction to that loss," Langhart told the *Washington Post*'s Merida in a 1997 interview. They divorced later that year.

Rose to Fame in Boston

As a result of her ratings success in Chicago, Langhart was hired by a Boston television station in 1974 as the co-host of *Good Day,* a local news program. She arrived

At a Glance...

Born Janet Floyd, December 22, 1941, in Indianapolis, IN; daughter of a hospital ward secretary; married Tony Langhart, 1968 (marriage ended, 1968); married Robert Kistner, 1978 (a physician and researcher; marriage ended, 1989); married William Cohen (politician and U.S. cabinet secretary), February 14, 1996. *Education:* Attended Butler University. *Politics:* Democrat.

Career: Began as Ebony Fashion Fair model; affiliated with WISH-TV, Indianapolis, IN; WBBM-TV, Chicago, television weathercaster in Chicago, late 1960s; WCVB-TV (Channel 5), Boston, MA, co-host of "Good Day," 1974-78; affiliated with NBC network, 1978 and the *America Alive* show; served as assistant press secretary in the 1988 presidential campaign of Michael Dukakis; co-host of New England Today, c. 1993; co-anchored *America's Black Forum* with Julian Bond on Black Entertainment Television (BET), c. 1996; founder, Langhart Communications, an image-consulting firm. Former board member, United Negro College Fund, U.. National Arboretum.

Addresses: *Home*—Washington, D.C. *Office*—c/o United States Department of Defense, The Pentagon, Washington, D.C. 20301.

in the city while a vicious battle over school busing was raging, a crisis whose worst moments were captured in news footage of residents of one neighborhood throwing stones at yellow schoolbuses full of children. The racially charged atmosphere lingered in sections of Boston for years afterward. Langhart was overwhelmed. "I felt betrayed because I had a notion of Boston as the cradle of liberty," she told *Boston Globe* writer John Powers. "Boston was our beacon of fairness and justice and in many ways, it is. I didn't get those ideas from romance. So I would go on the air and say: 'Why are you doing this? Why are you stoning black children? How do you reconcile this? Where is the cardinal?'" In response, a local civil rights leader invited Langhart to her home, and gently reminded the newscaster to direct her words not to groups of viewers, but rather "to the good people of Boston. They'll know who they are," Langhart recalled in the *Boston Globe* interview.

Langhart's combination of frankness, affability, and glamour earned her a devoted following. On the streets of Boston, she was a celebrity, a favorite with both black and white viewers. *Boston Globe* reporter Jack Thomas offered praise years later, saying, "Langhart is known for surprises, and for style, passion and ambition." In 1978, NBC hired her to co-host *America Alive,* and that same year she married another prominent Bostonian, gynecologist Dr. Robert Kistner. Several years her senior, the physician had been part of the team of research scientists responsible for the birth control pill. As his wife, Langhart never needed to work again; they lived a lavish lifestyle that included a condominium at the city's posh Ritz Hotel. Yet Langhart was loathe to abandon her career for good. She returned to television in Boston for a time, but was released from her contract in a notorious 1987 incident when she refused to draw lottery numbers, declaring to the press that she had no ambition to become "Vanna Black."

Entered Political Arena

Langhart's skills soon found a more appropriate outlet when she became assistant press secretary for the 1988 presidential campaign of Massachusetts governor Michael Dukakis. The Democratic Party nominee lost the election to George Bush, but her involvement in the high-stakes world of media and politics injected added ambition into Langhart's career plans. By then, Kistner had retired, and was enjoying a more relaxed life in Palm Beach; their marriage failed when the pair realized they had far different goals. They split amicably in 1989, but Kistner tragically committed suicide a year later. In time, Langhart renewed an acquaintance with a politician she had once interviewed in the 1970s, a senator from Maine named William S. Cohen.

Cohen had been raised Jewish but rejected the religion at the age of 12 when he was told he could not have a bar mitzvah unless his Protestant mother converted. A moderate Republican who had served in Congress since 1972, Cohen was often at odds with more conservative elements in the party and was known as one of the few Republicans who still supported affirmative-action programs. He also wrote poetry and novels. When he and Langhart started dating, a well-connected New England family wrote him and asserted that dating an African American woman would ruin his political career. The family had donated large sums of money to his campaigns over the years, and Cohen decisively informed them that their funds and opinions were no longer welcome.

Wed Senator, Surprise in Store

In the early 1990s, Langhart was hired by the cable network Black Entertainment Television (BET) and co-anchored *America's Black Forum,* a talk show, with civil-rights activist Julian Bond. She also founded Langhart Communications, a consulting company that helps corporate executives and government officials improve their on-camera demeanor. After a courtship of several years, Langhart and Cohen married on Valentine's Day in 1996 in a formal room of the U.S. Capitol building. The ceremony was attended by several prominent political figures, including Republican Congressmen Alfonse D'Amato and Trent Lott, as well as journalists such as Andrea Mitchell and Dan Rather.

By this point in his career, Cohen had decided not to run for re-election in the 1996 campaigns. In his farewell speech, he told his colleagues in Congress that bipartisan politics—primarily, the bitter struggle between the Democratic White House and Republican-controlled Congress—was the main reason for his leaving office. He reminded them in his address that "we are all on the same side," the *Washington Post* reported. In a surprise announcement a few months later, Cohen was named Defense Secretary after Clinton won a second Oval Office term. As a member of the Senate Armed Services Committee during his tenure in Congress, Cohen had often locked horns with Clinton's first Defense Secretary, William Perry, but when Perry stepped down, he recommended Cohen to take his place.

Prominent Role Relished

Langhart suddenly became one-half of one of the most prominent interracial couples in the United States. In her new role as the wife of the man who oversees all of the country's armed forces, she travels often with her husband to visit American troops stationed around the globe—including to some of the harsher, troubled regions of the world—and has tried to use her position to call attention to the plight of military families far from home. She is popular with troops and enjoys speaking with them one-on-one. Langhart's marriage to Cohen also provides inspiration to the more than 1.4 million active-duty servicemen and women, many of whom are non-Caucasian. Furthermore, many military personnel marry someone of another background. "It's a military of volunteers and G.I. Janes and whites and blacks and Latinos and Asians who look at [Cohen] and his spouse and see the America of the millennium," wrote the *Boston Globe*'s Powers.

Langhart often queries soldiers and servicepeople about conditions on American bases overseas, conspiratorially telling them, "You can level with me," as she explained in the *Boston Globe* interview with Powers. "Maybe I can't do anything about it, but I can hear you, and I can take it back to my husband." Langhart has also become sensitive to the plight of those who are not sheltered by the benefits of an American passport. In Sofia, Bulgaria, for a NATO summit with Cohen, the wives of American embassy officials told Langhart how abysmal the hospital conditions were in the city for its residents; she returned home, marshalled support from pharmaceutical companies for supplies and had them flown over.

Langhart and Cohen have remarked that as an interracial couple, they have never experienced overt discrimination, although some people feel the need to bring up African American subjects. But she remains nonplused by the attitudes of others. "Look at me," she told the *Globe*'s Powers. "I grew up in the ghetto in a single-parent family. I went to a private college on a scholarship. And here I am on Pennsylvania Avenue with the Secretary of Defense. If that isn't a reflection on how great this country is."

Sources

Boston Globe, March 9, 1989, p. 77; September 16, 1997, p. E1.
Jet, October 10, 1988, p. 33; February 12, 1996, p. 32; March 4, 1996, p. 16.
Washington Post, December 6, 1996, p. A26; December 14, 1997, p. F1.

—Carol Brennan

Spike Lee

1957—

Filmmaker

"Fight the power," the theme song to his 1989 film *Do the Right Thing,* could easily be Spike Lee's personal motto. From his earliest days as a student filmmaker, Lee has shown a willingness to tackle prickly issues of relevance to the African American community—and has savored every ounce of controversy his films invariably produce. "Spike loves to fight," the filmmaker's friend and business associate Nelson George told *Vanity Fair.* "There's a gleeful look he gets, a certain kind of excitement in his eyes when shit is being stirred up, he continued." "I guess you could call me an instigator," Lee admitted in an interview with *Vogue.*

Although the bane of Hollywood executives, Lee's delight in playing the provocateur has not only made his own films profitable, but has also created an industry-wide awareness of an untapped market niche. Following the unforeseen box office success of Lee's earliest films, Hollywood's gates have opened to a new generation of young African American filmmakers. "Spike put this trend in vogue," Warner Bros. executive vice president Mark Canton told *Time.* "His talent opened the door for others." Lee relishes his role as path-paver. "Every time there is a success," he explained to *Ebony,* "it makes it easier for other blacks. The industry is more receptive than it has ever been for black films and black actors. We have so many stories to tell, but we can't do them all. We just need more black filmmakers," he added.

Shelton Jackson Lee was born in Atlanta, Georgia, on March 20, 1957. He grew up in Brooklyn, New York, an area that would become the setting of many of his films. Lee's awareness of his African American heritage was established at an early age. His mother, Jacquelyn, instilled within her children an appreciation for African American art and literature. "I was forced to read Langston Hughes, that kind of stuff," Lee told *Vanity Fair.* "And I'm glad my mother made me do that." His father, Bill, an accomplished jazz musician, introduced him to African American jazz and folk legends such as Miles Davis and Odetta.

By the time he was old enough to attend school, Lee had earned the nickname his mother had given him as an infant, Spike—an allusion to his toughness. When he and his siblings were offered the option of attending the predominantly white private school where his mother

> ### At a Glance...
>
> Born Shelton Jackson Lee, March 20, 1957, in Atlanta, GA; son of William (a musician and composer) and Jacquelyn (a teacher; maiden name, Shelton) Lee. *Education:* Morehouse College, B.A., 1979; New York University, M.F.A., 1982.
>
> **Career:** Screenwriter, director, actor. Directed *Joe's Bed-Stuy Barbershop: We Cut Heads*, 1982; launched Hollywood career with low-budget, black-and-white film *She's Gotta Have It*, 1986; also director of music videos and commercials for Nike, Levi-Strauss, and Diet Coke. Opened film production studio 40 Acres and a Mule, 1987, and first Spike's Joint promotional outlet, 1990.
>
> **Awards:** 1983 Motion Picture Arts and Sciences' Student Academy Award for *Joe's Bed-Stuy Barbershop: We Cut Heads;* Cannes Film Festival's Prix de Jeunesse, 1986, for *She's Gotta Have It;* two Academy Award nominations for *Do the Right Thing.*
>
> **Addresses:** *Office*—40 Acres and a Mule Filmworks, 124 DeKalb Ave., Brooklyn, NY 11217.

taught, Lee decided to enroll in the public schools so that he could experience companionship with African Americans. "Spike used to point out the differences in our friends," recalled his sister Joie, who was a private school student. "By the time I was a senior," she told *Mother Jones,* "I was being channeled into white colleges." Lee decided to major in mass communications at Morehouse College, which is an African American college and his father and grandfather's alma mater.

Pursued Film Career

While at Morehouse College, Lee discovered his true calling. Following his mother's untimely death in 1977, Lee's friends tried to cheer him with frequent trips to the movies. He was greatly impressed with the work of directors such as Bernardo Bertolucci, Martin Scorsese, and Akira Kurosawa. However, it was not until he viewed Michael Cimino's *The Deer Hunter* that Lee realized that he wanted to become a filmmaker. His friend John Wilson recalled their conversation on the ride home from the film in an interview with *Vanity Fair.* "John, I know what I want to do," Lee had said. "I want to make films." Lee was determined to create films that captured the essence of the African American experience and was willing to produce them by any means necessary. "Spike didn't just want to get in the door of the house," Wilson explained. "He wanted to get in, rearrange the furniture—then go back and publicize the password."

Following graduation from Morehouse College, Lee enrolled in New York University's Tisch School of Arts graduate film program. Before long, Lee clashed with his instructors. As his first-year film project, Lee produced a ten-minute short, *The Answer,* in which an African American screenwriter is assigned to remake legendary director D.W. Griffith's classic film *The Birth of a Nation. The Answer* was widely criticized by his instructors. Although the film program's director, Eleanor Hamerow, told the *New York Times,* "it's hard to redo *Birth of a Nation* in ten minutes," Lee suspected that his critics were offended by his digs at Griffith's stereotypical portrayals of black characters. "I was told I was whiskers away from being kicked out," he told *Mother Jones.* "They really didn't like me saying anything bad about D.W. Griffith, for sure."

Lee was unfazed by the criticism *The Answer* received and produced a 45-minute film entitled *Joe's Bed-Stuy Barbershop: We Cut Heads.* The film went on to earn Lee the 1983 Motion Picture Arts and Sciences' Student Academy Award. Although the honor enhanced Lee's credibility as a director, it didn't pay the bills. Faced with the need to survive, Lee worked for a movie distribution house cleaning and shipping film while raising funds for a semi-autobiographical film, *The Messenger.*

A coming-of-age story about a young bicycle messenger, *The Messenger* was aborted prematurely when sufficient funding failed to materialize. "We were in pre-production the entire summer of 1984, waiting on this money to come, and it never did," Lee told *Vanity Fair.* "Then, finally, I pulled the plug. I let a lot of people down, crew members and actors that turned down work. I wasn't the most popular person. We were devastated." But all was not lost; Lee had learned his lesson. "I saw I made the classic mistakes of a young filmmaker, to be overly ambitious, do something beyond my means and capabilities," he said. "Going through the fire just made me more hungry, more determined that I couldn't fail again."

Scored a Surprise Hit

Lee's determination paid off when he filmed *She's Gotta Have It* in 1985. Completed in only 12 days and on a shoestring budget of $175,000, the black-and-white film was shot on one location with a limited cast and edited on a rented machine in Lee's apartment. By the time *She's Gotta Have It* was completed, Lee was so deeply in debt that his processing lab threatened to auction off the film's negative.

After Island Pictures agreed to distribute it, *She's Gotta Have It* finally opened in theaters in 1986. A light comedy centering on sex-loving artist Nola Darling and her relationships with three men, the film pokes fun at gender relations and offers an insightful spin on stereotypical male roles. It was a hit not only with African American audiences, but also with crossover, art-house patrons. Grossing over $7 million dollars, the film was a surprise hit.

A Microcosm of Black Life

With a major hit under his belt and the backing of Island Pictures, Lee released his next film, *School Daze,* in 1988. An exposé of color discrimination within the African American community, *School Daze* draws on Lee's years at Morehouse. "The people with the money," he told the *New York Times,* "most of them have light skin. They have the Porsches, the B.M.W.'s, the quote good hair unquote. The others, the kids from the rural south, have bad, kinky hair. When I was in school, we saw all this going on." This black caste system, Lee explained to *Newsweek,* was not a limited phenomenon. "I used the black college as a microcosm of black life."

School Daze created controversy within the African American community. Although Lee was applauded for exploring a complex social problem, many people were offended by his willingness to "air dirty laundry." When production costs ballooned to $4 million, Island Pictures pulled out of the project. Within two days, Lee had arranged a deal with Columbia Pictures that included an allowance for an additional $2 million in production costs. Although Columbia didn't actively promote *School Daze,* it still grossed $15 million.

Explored Racial Tensions

School Daze established Lee's reputation as a director who was willing to tackle controversial issues. He continued this trend with the release of *Do the Right Thing* in 1989. The story of simmering racial tensions between Italian and African Americans in the Bedford-Stuyvesant section of Brooklyn, *Do the Right Thing* becomes a call to arms when violence erupts in response to the killing of an African American man by white police officers. The meaning of "the right thing," Lee told *People,* is not ambiguous. "Black America is tired of having their brothers and sisters murdered by the police for no reason other than being black." "I'm not advocating violence," he continued. "I'm saying I can understand it. If the people are frustrated and feel oppressed and feel this is the only way they can act, I understand."

Struck a Balance

In 1990, Lee chose a romantic theme for his next film, *Mo' Better Blues.* The film tells the story of a self-centered jazz trumpeter, Bleek Gilliam, whose personal life plays second fiddle to his music. "*Mo' Better Blues* is about relationships," Lee explained to *Ebony.* "It's not only about man-woman relationships, but about relationships in general—Bleek's relationship to his father and his manager, and his relationship with two female friends. Bleek's true love is music, and he is trying to find the right balance."

Although recognized for its technical mastery and snappy score, *Mo' Better Blues* received only tepid reviews. "The movie is all notions and no shape," said the *New Yorker,* "hard, fierce blowing rather than real music." More than one critic took offense at Lee's shallow treatment of female characters and the ethnic stereotyping of Jewish jazz club owners Moe and Josh Flatbush.

Examined Interracial Love

In his 1991 film, *Jungle Fever,* Lee explored the theme of romance from a more provocative slant. Inspired by the 1989 murder of black teenager Yusuf Hawkins by a mob of Italian American youths, *Jungle Fever* revolves around the office affair of a married, African American architect and his Italian American secretary. The film examines the sexual mythology that surrounds interracial romance. "Yusuf was killed because they thought he was the black boyfriend of one of the girls in the neighborhood," Lee told *Newsweek.* "What it comes down to is that white males have problems with black men's sexuality. It's as plain and simple as that. They think we've got a hold on their women." Although it received only mixed reviews, *Jungle Fever* set the stage for Lee's next controversial film, *Malcolm X.*

Created a Masterpiece

The filming of *Malcolm X* became a personal mission for Lee, who had long been an admirer of the legendary

African American leader. He planned a biographical film of epic proportions that required months of research, numerous interviews, and even an unprecedented trip to Saudi Arabia for authentic footage of Malcolm's 1964 pilgrimage to the holy city of Mecca. The film, a three-hour-and-21-minute epic, traces Malcolm X's development from his impoverished, rural roots to his final years as an ever-evolving activist. "I knew this was going to be the toughest thing I ever did," Lee told *Time*. "The film is huge in the canvas we had to cover and in the complexity of Malcolm X."

Although *Malcolm X* received no Oscars, the film was a box office hit and played a significant role in the elevation of Malcolm X to mythic status. It also spawned a cultural phenomenon often referred to as "Malcolmmania." By the time the movie was released in 1992, its logo, a bold "X," was pasted on everything from a ubiquitous baseball cap to posters, postcards, and T-shirts. In addition, a wide variety of spin-off products was born, ranging from serious scholarly studies to a plastic Malcolm X doll, complete with podium and audio cassette. Lee was quick to defend himself against charges of commercialism. He remarked that his merchandising of the film was in line with Malcolm X's own philosophy—that African Americans need to build their own economic base—"I think we've done more to hold ourselves back than anybody," Lee told *Esquire*. "If anybody's seen all my films, I put most of the blame on our shoulders and say, 'Look, we're gonna have to do for ourselves.'... I feel we really have to address our financial base as a people."

Following the success of *Malcolm X,* Lee fell into a moviemaking slump as his next three projects failed at the box office. His 1994 semi-autobiographical film *Crooklyn* grossed only $13.6 million, a poor showing when compared with *Do the Right Thing* and *Jungle Fever,* which made $28 million and $33 million, respectively. *Crooklyn* chronicled the everyday struggles of the Carmichaels, a middle-class African American family living in Brooklyn during the 1970s. Critics criticized the film's structure, which was based more on random incidents in the life of the family than on an actual plot.

Lee's 1995 film, *Clockers,* focused on a murder investigation in a New York City housing project. The plot revolved around a pair of African American brothers—the older one is struggling to get out of poverty through honest means, while the younger works as one of a cadre of drug pushers known as "clockers," because they work around the clock. The brothers become the focus of a murder investigation when the older brother confesses to a killing that the younger brother had been ordered to commit by a local drug lord. The movie did not fare well at the box office.

In 1996, Lee released *Girl 6*. This comedy starred Theresa Randle as an aspiring actress who becomes a phone-sex operator. Relishing the control she exerts over the men who call her, a control which is absent in her own life, Girl 6 becomes obsessed with her work. Critics widely panned the film and criticized its shallow depictions of women. *Girl 6* also fizzled at the box office. That same year, Lee produced the film *Get on the Bus.* The plot revolved around a busload of African American men who are traveling to the historic Million Man March in Washington, D.C. Along the way, the men discuss issues such as manhood, religion, politics, and race. By the time they arrive in Washington, D.C. the men, once strangers, have become brothers and friends. Released one year after the Million Man March, the movie was a critical success although it did not receive widespread distribution.

In 1997, Lee released a documentary film *4 Little Girls*. The film chronicles the events leading up to the September 15, 1963 bombing of an African American church in Birmingham, Alabama by white racists. The bombing claimed the lives of four girls who were in the church at the time. The film, which included archival film footage, photographs, and interviews with people active in the civil rights movement, resurrected a painful chapter in American history and received favorable critical reviews.

Lee married his two great loves—filmmaking and basketball—for the 1998 movie *He Got Game*. The movie depicts the corruption and temptation which are the hallmarks of professional sports recruiting, as experienced by a high school basketball star, Jesus Shuttlesworth. Complicating the decisions surrounding Jesus' career is his convict-father, Jake, who has been temporarily released from jail on orders from the governor to convince Jesus to attend the governor's alma mater. Starring the popular actor Denzel Washington as Jake, and Milwaukee Bucks guard Ray Allen as Jesus, the film received favorable reviews.

In addition to filmmaking, Lee is an astute businessman. He has established Spike's Joint, a chain of apparel boutiques, in several cities and created his own record label, 40 Acres & A Mule Musicworks. He also owns a production company, 40 Acres & A Mule Filmworks. Lee also formed his own advertising agency, Spike/DDB, after partnering with the noted advertising agency, DDB Needham, in early 1997. He also authored *Best Seat in the House: A Basketball Memoir,* which was published in 1997.

In October of 1993, Lee married Tonya Linette Lewis

after a brief courtship. Their daughter, Satchel, was born in 1994. In 1997, Tonya gave birth to their son, Jackson Lewis. The Lee family resides in New York City where Lee, a rabid basketball fan, is a regular spectator at New York Knicks basketball games.

Selected filmography

She's Gotta Have It, Island, 1986.
School Daze, Columbia, 1988.
Do the Right Thing, Universal Pictures, 1989.
Mo' Better Blues, Universal Pictures, 1990.
Jungle Fever, Universal Pictures, 1991.
Malcolm X, Warner Bros., 1992.
Crooklyn, Universal Pictures, 1994.
Clockers, Universal Pictures, 1995.
Girl 6, 20th Century Fox, 1996.
Get on the Bus, Sony Pictures, 1996.
4 Little Girls, 40 Acres and a Mule, 1997.
He Got Game, Buena Vista Pictures, 1998.

Selected writings

By Any Means Necessary: The Trials and Tribulations of Making Malcolm X, Hyperion, 1992.
Best Seat in the House: A Basketball Memoir, Random House, 1997.

Sources

America, August 19, 1989; September 15, 1990; August 10, 1991.
American Film, July/August 1989; September 1989.
Ann Arbor News, October 30, 1992; November 18, 1992.
Chicago Sun-Times, September 13, 1995.
Commonweal, November 8, 1991.
Detroit News, January 26, 1992.
Ebony, November 1991.
Emerge, November 1991, pp. 28-32.
Entertainment Weekly, November 27, 1992.
Esquire, August 1991.
Essence, November 1991, p. 64.
Film Comment, July/August 1989.
Jet, June 10, 1991.
Maclean's, February 17, 1992, p. 60.
Mother Jones, September 1989.
Ms., September/October 1991.
The Nation, June 1, 1998, pp. 35-36.
Newsweek, February 15, 1988; August 6, 1990; June 10, 1991; February 3, 1992, p. 30; November 16, 1992, pp. 67-72; April 22, 1996, p. 75.
New York, June 17, 1991.
New Yorker, August 13, 1990; June 17, 1991; October 12, 1992.
New York Times, August 9, 1987; November 15, 1992; November 29,1992; December 6, 1992.
People, July 10, 1989; March 5, 1990; August 13, 1990; June 22, 1992.
Rolling Stone, November 26, 1992, pp. 36-40, 80-81.
Time, June 17, 1991; March 16, 1992; September 18, 1995.
Upscale, October/November 1992.
Vanity Fair, June 1991, pp. 70, 80-92.
Video, February 1990; February 1991.
Vogue, August 1990.
Washington Post, March 22, 1996; October 18, 1996.

Other

Additional information for this profile was obtained from the IAC Insite World-Wide Web site, http://web4.iac-insite.com/insite, and the CelebSite, last updated January 12, 1998, http://www.celebsite.com/ (accessed September 2, 1998).

—Nina Goldstein and Rebecca Parks

Thomas Lewis

1939—

Fishing school administrator

"If you give a man a fish, you'll feed him for a day. Teach him how to fish, and he will feed himself for a lifetime." This familiar creed stands as the cornerstone of Thomas Lewis's commitment to the youth of Washington, D.C.

Lewis was born in Chadbourn, North Carolina, the sixth of 15 children, and moved to Elizabethtown, North Carolina as a young child. His mother, Martha, picked cotton, and his father, Gaston, worked in a sawmill. Lewis dropped out of school after tenth grade and, like most of his siblings, left home. He found work as a migrant farm laborer picking fruits and vegetables in Virginia, West Virginia, New Jersey, New York, and Florida. In 1959 Lewis moved to New York, was drafted into the U.S. Army, and stationed in France. While in the Army, he earned a high-school-equivalency degree.

After being discharged from the Army, Lewis worked as a postal clerk for one year before joining the Washington, D.C. police force in December of 1965. He remained in contact with his family, often providing them with emotional and financial assistance. As his brother Ed Lewis recalls in an interview with *People Magazine,* "Tom was always, always the guy to make sure the family stood together."

Upon joining the Washington D.C. police force, Lewis served as a beat officer and patrolled the streets of the nation's capital during the riots which occurred following the assassination of Martin Luther King, Jr. in 1968. As a police officer, Lewis was faced with a dilemma. On the one hand, he was sworn to uphold the law and serve as a representative of the police force, a force which routinely discriminated against African Americans. However, Lewis also understood the anger of African Americans and their thirst for justice. Lewis described in a television interview for *Black and Blue* how he was tormented by the idea of arresting the rioters, knowing the depth of their hopelessness and despair. He remarked that he often struggled to control his own outrage and anger.

Defined Personal Direction

After three years on the force, Lewis was transferred to the community relations department. For the next 18 years, Lewis regularly visited classrooms throughout the

At a Glance...

Born Thomas Lewis, in 1939, in Chadbourn, NC; son of Martha Lewis, a cotton picker, and Gaston Lewis, a sawmill worker; married to Lucille; children: Jason, Patrick, Tisha. *Education:* American University, BS, 1975; Sacred Hour Ministerial School of Discipleship, Certificate in Ministry, 1984.

Career: Washington D.C. Police Department, officer, 1965-86; Hope Village Community Treatment Center, vocational counselor, 1986-87; Lutheran Social Services, senior family counselor, 1987-89; For Love of Children, family and child services coordinator, 1989-93; Metropolitan Police Department of Washington, D.C. Boys and Girls Club, early intervention program coordinator, 1992-95; The Fishing School, founder, director, chairman of the board of directors, 1990-.

Selected awards: Washingtonian of the Year, 1997; One and Only Nine Award, 1995; Jefferson Award, Institute for Public Service, 1995; Public Service Award, National Organization of Black Law Enforcement Executives, 1997; Community Service Award, Seventh Day Adventist Church, 1996, 1997.

Memberships: Leadership Washington; Fraternal Order of Police.

Addresses: The Fishing School, 1240 Wylie Street, NE, Washington, D.C. 20002; Mailing address: PO Box 60674, Washington, D.C. 20039.

D.C. public school system to counsel students and to teach good citizenship, drug abstinence, and safety. His dedication and commitment to children embodied the essence of the "Officer Friendly" program, and he was often called by this nickname. Lewis was frequently overwhelmed when he visited classrooms and witnessed the poverty and desperation exhibited by the students. As he related to *People Magazine* in 1996, "I never saw so many filthy, dirty children coming to school in the morning. I stepped out of many classrooms with tears in my eyes." He was also greatly moved by the number of children who asked him to be their "daddy" and who often fought amongst themselves for his attention. Lewis decided to retire from the police force and made a personal vow to God that he would devote the rest of his life to helping children in need.

During his years with the Washington D.C. police department, Lewis's personal life flourished. He married his wife, Lucille, and together they had three children, Jason, Patrick, and Tisha. In 1975, he earned a bachelor of science degree in administration of justice from American University and became a licensed social worker. He organized a gospel music group, the Capitol Community Singers, in 1974 and has written and recorded five albums with the group. A religiously devout man, Lewis completed three years of study at the Sacred Hour School of Discipleship in Glen Arden, Maryland and was ordained a minister in 1984. He served as the assistant to the pastor at Goodwill Baptist Church in Washington until 1997 and since then has served as the staff minister in the interdenominational HIS Church.

On February 14, 1986, Tom Lewis retired from the Washington D.C. police force. From 1986 to 1987 he worked as a vocational counselor at Hope Village Community Treatment Center, the largest halfway house in Washington D.C., helping newly released prisoners to re-enter society. From 1987 to 1993 he worked for two nonprofit agencies, Lutheran Social Services and For Love of Children, first as a family counselor and then as a family and child services coordinator.

In 1989, Lewis had a vision. He decided to convert a rental property that he had purchased in northeast Washington, D.C. into a family service center. Although he was not certain that his vision would come to pass, Lewis relied heavily upon his religious faith. As he stated in *The Washington Informer,* "Success begins with God and if you have everything you want and don't have a relationship with God, I don't think you're going to go far."

Opened The Fishing School

In March of 1990 Lewis opened The Fishing School, a school devoted to providing children with after-school educational, social, and religious training. Lewis's ambitious agenda focuses on teaching children and parents to "fish," to learn how to respect and care for others while also learning to respect and care for themselves. "We are fishing in the rivers of the mind," Lewis often comments. "I want to find out what it is that these children are fishing for and then teach them how they can get it." As the school's mission statement dictates, "The Fishing School endeavors to create and nurture the desire, will, and discipline required for inner-city children to develop into independent, productive members of our society."

Lewis recognizes that children entering The Fishing School bring many "stones" with them: stones of poverty, illiteracy, judgment, hopelessness, sin, pain, and complacency. During an interview on the CBS television show *Window on America,* Lewis poignantly expressed the hope that his children become stone rollers rather than rolling stones. "Our hope," he remarked, "is that once we begin rolling away stones of fear, selfishness, faithlessness, pride, domination, and misunderstanding, those in the neighborhood who are buried in the tomb of hopelessness will come forth. When they do, they'll use their many talents, skills, and ideas to free themselves from their social and economic bonds."

Lewis firmly believes that children are capable of assessing the direction of their life. Given the proper circumstances, moreover, they can be motivated to make all necessary changes. Most importantly, Lewis hopes to help children discover their own inner beauty and develop self-esteem.

Focused on Continuous Improvement

Improving academic performance is one of The Fishing School's primary goals. To accomplish this goal, students are offered Bible study, tutoring, homework assistance, science and rocketry classes, computer classes, gospel choir, dance, drama, and arts and crafts. These disciplines all interact to form a dynamic after-school curriculum. In the rough Washington, D.C. neighborhood that is home to The Fishing School, Lewis has many other aims for his program. As Thomason remarked, "With his free, family-oriented programs, Lewis tries to keep the souls of youngsters from becoming as dilapidated as many of the buildings around them." As Oklahoma Representative J.C. Watts commented in his 1996 address to the Republican Party Convention, "Tom understands that what we build, nourish, and encourage the youth of America to be today is what our country will be 20 years from now."

Involvement by parents and guardians is critical to the success of The Fishing School program. A parent or guardian must accompany each student who applies for admission to the school. Adults are also asked to volunteer five hours each month in the school as compensation for the services which their children receive. Although the school lacks sufficient funding to offer an all-encompassing community program, the school is open to parents before 3:00 p.m. Staff members counsel parents, serve as mentors and tutors, and offer referral services to other community-based organizations. In the fall of 1998, the school will also begin to explore the possibility of providing GED courses. As they do with the children, Lewis and his staff work to motivate parents to succeed.

> "Success begins with God and if you have everything you want and don't have a relationship with God, I don't think you're going to go far."

The Fishing School has been able to celebrate numerous success stories. Several Fishing School students have given poetry readings at Borders Books. One graduate performed at the Washington School of Ballet and another won an $8,000 creative-writing scholarship. Three students have received Free the Children Trust scholarships, one placed first in his school in the Stanford Nine Proficiency Test, and several have been accepted at the Duke Ellington School of Performing Arts in Washington. In 1996, the school boasted its first high school graduate.

Broadened His Mission

In 1998, Lewis expanded The Fishing School concept into other needy areas of Washington, D.C. Plans were announced for the opening of a second Fishing School in September of 1998. Rita Davis, a mother of six grown children, contacted Lewis after viewing a television program about The Fishing School. She donated a two-story home which, after renovation, will become a community child care center. It is expected that this Fishing School will serve an additional 30 children with four paid staff members and several volunteers and consultants.

Despite the success of The Fishing School, Lewis struggles to secure consistent financial assistance. He receives occasional small grants from local foundations and from the United Black Fund, an agency of the United Way. For the first time, the school received some federal money in 1998 from the Department of Housing and Urban Development. As expenses continue to increase, Lewis must rely heavily on private donations. Families are asked to contribute $25.00 each so that children can attend The Fishing School's summer program. However, some families are unable to pay due to financial hardships. Lewis often talks about attending

"Hope Meetings," gatherings where he hopes to meet people who will provide financial help. Since the school's inception, Lewis has never accepted a salary.

Although his job as executive director of The Fishing School presents many challenges, Lewis remains a man of faith who is passionately committed to success. As he remarked on the CBS television show *Window on America,* "The Lord is pleased, and that's my job. This helps me to live out my calling. When I am finished at The Fishing School, I will go home to the Lord to rest."

Sources

Periodicals

Channel 32 Magazine, April 1994, p. 3.
Necessary, Winter 1996, pp. 6-7, 15.
People, September 30, 1996, pp. 59-60.
TwentyFIRST, March 1997, p. 24.
Washingtonian, January 1997, p. 79.
Washington Informer, May 9-15, 1996, pp. 8-9.
Washington Post, May 12, 1994, p. DC2.
World Magazine, 1996.

Other

American Family, NET Television, 1996.
Black and Blue, Washington, D.C. Channel 8.
"The Fleecing Of America," *NBC Television News,* March 6, 1998.
Promotional Materials, The Fishing School.
Washington, D.C. Channel 4, February 1998.
Window on America, CBS Television.

—Lisa S. Weitzman

Dorothy Maynor

1910(?)–1996

Opera singer, educator

Although rarely mentioned in the same breath as divas such as Marian Anderson and Leontyne Price, Dorothy Maynor's influence on classical music is just as impressive. Even more impressive is the influence she's had on thousands of students who've passed through the halls of the Harlem School of the Arts, the school she founded in 1963 in New York's sometimes-troubled uptown neighborhood. Following a singing career that spanned a quarter century in which Maynor delighted audiences in concert halls around the world with her warm, rich soprano, she then spent another twenty-five years as executive director of the school. Though largely forgotten as a singer, Maynor's place in history is assured with her greatest artistic achievement, the Harlem School of the Arts.

Born Dorothy Leigh Mainor in Norfolk, Virginia in 1910 (some sources say 1909) to a Baptist minister and his wife, the Mainor house was constantly filled with music. "My sister played the piano," she reminisced to Noel Straus of the *New York Times.* "It was a rare day when we weren't singing in the house to her accompaniment. But it was just the sort of thing you might find in almost any home anywhere." Maynor also sang in her father's church, but a career in music had never been her intention. At the age of 14, she enrolled in the nearby Hampton Institute where she studied home economics and thought of a career in teaching. Her love for singing prompted Maynor to join the school's choir where for years she was just another voice in the soprano section. On a 1929 tour of Europe, however, she had developed into such an accomplished soloist that Dr. Robert Nathaniel Dett, the choir director and head of Hampton's music department, sought to further her potential.

"While we were on tour Dr. Dett cabled my father from Europe and told him to change my plans from studying home economics and dress design to music," Maynor recalled to Maurice Peterson of *Essence.* I wasn't consulted at all. But it didn't matter. I was happy." Maynor soon won a scholarship to study choral conducting at Westminster Choir College in Princeton, New Jersey, from which she graduated in 1935. The following year, with the financial help of benefactress Harriet Curtis, the dean of women at Hampton during Maynor's years there, Maynor moved to New York to study singing with Wilfred Klamroth and later, John Alan Haughton.

At a Glance...

Born Dorothy Leigh Mainor September 3, c. 1910 in Norfolk, Virginia, to Reverend John J. Mainor and Alice Jeffries Mainor; died February 19, 1996, West Chester, Pennsylvania; married Reverend Shelby Rooks, June 24, 1942. *Education:* Hampton Institute, B.A., 1933; Westminster Choir School, B.A., 1935; studied singing with Wilfred Klamroth and John Alan Haughton, New York City, beginning 1936.

Career: Began singing in her father's church; sang in the Hampton Institute Choir, 1924-33; toured Europe with the Hampton Choir, 1929; moved to New York to study singing, 1936; impromptu performance for Boston Symphony Orchestra conductor Serge Koussevitzky, 1939; made recital debut at New York's Town Hall, November 19, 1939; toured the world as recital singer and made many radio appearances, 1939-63; recorded for RCA, 1953-63; performed at President Harry S. Truman's inauguration, 1949; first black artist to perform at Constitution Hall, Washington, DC, 1952; performed at President Dwight D. Eisenhower's inauguration, 1953; retired from singing and founded the Harlem School of the Arts, 1963; became first black member of the Metropolitan Opera board in New York, 1975; raised $3.5 million to build a new building for the Harlem School of the Arts, 1977; retired as executive director of the Harlem School of the Arts, 1979.

For three years she studied diligently and also at this time, changed the spelling of her name from Mainor to Maynor.

The Debut at Town Hall

In the summer of 1939 Maynor was invited to attend the Berkshire Symphonic Festival—now called Tanglewood—which was the summer home of the Boston Symphony Orchestra. Maynor's patrons arranged a private audition with conductor Serge Koussevitzky who was so impressed with the clarity of her voice and command of material, he arranged for her to perform the next day at a private picnic he was giving for his musicians and some guests. Again, Maynor overwhelmed her audience to such an extent that an article appeared about her performance the next day in the *New York Times,* and an interview with Maynor was published a few days later in which she explained her motivation to sing. "I hope to represent the art of song as well as I can," she told Noel Straus. "That's about all I can say. To accomplish that, to be a worthy representative of the best music, one feels so very small when one thinks of it.... I would like to master all colors of tone and give each type of work what it demands. I am working hard for that."

As word spread of Maynor's success at the festival, expectations ran high for her recital debut, scheduled for November at New York's Town Hall. Once more, Maynor shone in the solo spotlight. "Miss Maynor's voice is phenomenal for its range, character, and varied expressive resources," Olin Downes declared in the *New York Times.* "She proved that she had virtually everything needed by a great artist—the superb voice, one of the finest that the public can hear today; exceptional musicianship and accuracy of intonation; emotional intensity, communicative power.... She should be able to reach almost any height as one of the leading concert singers of her generation." Similar words of praise were echoed in other sources and *Newsweek* reported that following Maynor's final encore, "Depuis le jour" from Charpentier's *Louise,* the house stood and cheered for twenty minutes as tears rolled down the singer's cheeks.

Following her debut, Maynor toured the United States and the rest of the world and performed with the leading orchestras of the day. In 1942 she married the Reverend Shelby Rooks, who became the minister of St. James Presbyterian Church in Harlem. Additionally, Maynor embarked upon a recording career in which she sang arias, spirituals, and operas. Her interpretations of the latter, however, were limited to the recording studio because no opera company of the time would allow a black person to perform in their productions. Although her singing earned Maynor extremely favorable reviews from critics around the world, she wasn't allowed to audition for the Metropolitan Opera. In an ironic twist, she would become the first black member of the Met's board of directors in 1975. "I learned 23 roles and never got to sing them," Maynor lamented to Peterson of *Essence.* In 1952 Maynor became the first black artist to perform at Constitution Hall in Washington, DC, the venue where the Daughters of the American Revolution had barred black contralto Marian Anderson from performing in 1939. In 1955, Anderson broke the Metropolitan Opera's color barrier.

Harlem School of the Arts

The constant touring of the 1940s and 1950s left Maynor little time to spend with her husband, who was devoted to his Harlem parish. In 1963, after Reverend

Rooks suffered a heart attack and required a lengthy convalescence, Maynor decided she would retire from singing and help her husband with his church. Rooks, acknowledging his wife's passion for music and the arts, suggested she start an arts education program in the church's community center. When Maynor found she could not get funding for a school that did not yet exist, she decided to do it on her own. With twenty students and Maynor acting as teacher, fundraiser, secretary, and janitor, the Harlem School of the Arts was born.

> "If you succeed in proving your intelligence and your gifts, then you have helped the next person."

Maynor set out to provide the kind of uplifting environment she received at the Hampton Institute to the children of Harlem. "I had such an exciting childhood," she remarked to Peterson. "Hampton gave us an awareness and an appreciation for discipline and achievement; it was the proper soil for young people and my spirit was nurtured. From my experience at Hampton came the concept for this school."

Maynor was also driven by the fact that she wanted to see African Americans reap the rewards for their work. In the 1940s she recalled watching white bandleaders writing down music played by blacks on the bandstand of the Savoy Ballroom. "It occurred to me then that if we would only take the time and discipline ourselves to be literate in our work, whatever our gifts, then *we* would be reaping the rewards."

After about a year of operation, the school began to get funding from foundations and was able to offer courses in a variety of instruments as well as painting, drama, and dance. One of the early ballet teachers, Arthur Mitchell, whom Maynor had to persuade to teach, went on to found the Dance Theatre of Harlem, itself an important and world renowned cultural institution. As more funds came in so did more teachers and students, most of whom came from low-income families. A sliding tuition scale was established so every child had a chance to learn. Piano lessons for ten cents weren't uncommon. "With our boys and girls in Harlem, life affords them no vista, no ample view of themselves," Maynor explained to Doris Black of *Sepia*. "That is what I want them to have, and I firmly believe the arts are a splendid means of providing this. What I dream of is changing the image held by the children. We have made them believe that everything is beautiful outside this community. I want them to make beauty in this community."

A New Building, Then An Exit

By the late 1970s the school boasted more than 40 instructors and over 1,000 students. Having far outgrown the community center of St. James Church, Maynor took it upon herself to raise about $3.5 million dollars to erect a new 37,000 square foot building on a lot adjacent to the St. James parish. "There is no government money in this building," Maynor enthused to C. Gerald Fraser of the *New York Times*, adding that the school exists because of "foundations, devoted and loyal friends, a hardworking dedicated board and cooperation from the parents and the children." Indeed, with a list of impressive friends and past boardmembers such as Leonard Bernstein, Langston Hughes, Marian Anderson, Agnes de Mille, and Vladimir Horowitz, funding for the new building came easily from private donors as well as the Marion Ascoli Fund and the Ford, Kresge, and Mellon foundations.

With the opening of the new building in 1979, Maynor retired as executive director of the Harlem School of the Arts. Her husband also retired from his parish and the couple moved to Pennsylvania. The couple enjoyed a quiet retirement until Maynor's death in 1996. Although most people are unaware of the gifts she gave while she was alive and the impact she had on so many people, Maynor was never one to seek glory for her efforts. "Anyone is privileged to deal in the arts because it adds a spiritual dimension to life that isn't possible in any other field that I know of," she told Peterson of *Essence* in 1977. "If you succeed in proving your intelligence and your gifts, then you have helped the next person."

Sources

Books

Hitchcock, H. Wiley and Stanley Sadie, eds., *New Grove Dictionary of Music, Vol. 3*, Macmillan Press Ltd., 1986.

Slominsky, Nicolas, ed., *Baker's Biographical Dictionary of Twentieth-Century Classical Musicians*, Schirmer Books, 1997.

Story, Rosalyn M., *And So I Sing*, Amistad Press, 1990.

Rogers, Jr., William F., *Dorothy Maynor and the Harlem School of the Arts: The Diva and the Dream*, Mellen Press, 1993.

Turner, Patricia, *Dictionary of Afro-American Performers,* Garland Publishing, Inc., 1990.

Periodicals

American Record Guide, March-April, 1996, p. 260.
Amsterdam News, March 2, 1996, p. 8; March 16, 1996, p.23.
Ebony, May 1966, p. 80.
Essence, December 1977, p.56.
Jet, March 25, 1996, p. 52
New York Times, August 10, 1939; August 13, 1939, p. D-5; November 20, 1939, p. 15; May 20, 1979, p.55; February 24, 1996, p. A-12.
New Yorker, November 18, 1939, p.18.
Newsweek, August 21, 1939, p. 26; November 27, 1939, p. 25.
Opera News, August 1992, p.45; February 27, 1993, p. 16; June 1996, p. 52.
Sepia, October 1971, p. 21.
Time, August 21, 1939, p. 45; November 27, 1939, p. 58.
Village Voice, February 21, 1977, p. 73.
Washington Post, December 22, 1991, p. G-5; February 26, 1996, p. D-4.

—Brian Escamilla

Festus Gontebanye Mogae

1939—

President of Botswana

Festus Gontebanye Mogae became president of the Republic of Botswana on April 1, 1998, in a peaceful transfer of power that political analysts term exceptional for southern Africa. Mogae was only the third president in Botswana's history since the country gained its independence from the British Empire in 1966. His resume included decades of service in various governmental posts, most of them connected with finance and development. "Unlike his two predecessors who styled themselves as farmers on loan to politics, Mogae is steeped in the world of economics and high finance," noted Darren Schuettlet in *The Namibian*.

Mogae was born on August 21, 1939 and traveled abroad for his higher education. He attended North West London Polytechnic in England, and went on to earn an honours degree at Oxford; he later received a graduate degree in developmental economics from Sussex University. In 1968 he married Barbara Modise and started a family that eventually numbered three daughters. Botswana was granted independence from its status as a British crown colony in 1966, and soon afterward Mogae became a part of its vanguard of young, educated politicians in the new government. Since independence, politics in the Republic of Botswana have been dominated by the Botswana Democratic Party (BDP), of which Mogae is a long-term member. Beginning in 1968 he served first as a planning officer in the Ministry of Development and Planning (restructured into the Ministry of Finance and Development Planning in 1970), then was elevated to senior planning officer in 1971, and became director of economic affairs for the Ministry in 1972. Between 1975 and 1976 he served as Permanent Secretary.

A Prosperous Post-Colonial Legacy

Unlike its neighbors, the Botswana of Mogae's era has enjoyed a long history of political stability. This, many observers note, is partly the result of a largely homogenous population: most of its 1.5 million citizens are of the Tswana ethnic group (the plural of which is "Batswana"). The Tswana native language is Setswana, but English is used in Botswanan government and business, a legacy of its colonial past. About thirty percent of the

At a Glance...

Born August 21, 1939, in Serowe, Botswana; son of Dihabano and Dithunya Mogae; married Barbara Gemma Modise, 1968; children: three daughters. *Education:* Attended North West London Polytechnic; received honours degree from Oxford University; earned degree in development economics from Sussex University. *Politics:* Botswana Democratic Party.

Career: Ministry of Development and Planning for the Republic of Botswana, Gabarone, Botswana, planning officer, 1968-69; Ministry of Finance and Development Planning, Gabarone, planning officer, 1970, senior planning officer, 1971, director of economic affairs, 1972-74, permanent secretary, 1975-76; permanent secretary to President of Botswana, 1982-89; minister of finance and development planning, 1989-98; vice-president, 1992-98. International Monetary Fund (IMF), alternate governor for Botswana, 1971-72, alternate executive director, 1978-80, governor, 1981-82; alternate governor, African Development Bank, 1971-76; representative at the Commonwealth Fund for Technology Co-Operation, 1971—; member of Junior Development Committee of the World Bank and IMF on the transfer of real resources to developing countries, 1992. Mogae has also served as director of Botswana Development Corporation, 1971-74 (chair, 1975-76), DeBeers Botswana Mining Co. Ltd., 1975-76, Bangwato Concessions Ltd., 1975-76, B.C.L. Sales Ltd., 1975-76, and Bank of Botswana, 1975-76 (governor, 1980-81).

Member: Botswana Society, Botswana Society of the Deaf, Kalahari Conservation Society, Commonwealth Parliamentary Association, Parliamentarians for Global Action, Global Coalition for Africa.

Awards: Officier, Ordre National de la Cote d'Ivoire, 1979; Presidential Order of Honour of Botswana, 1989.

Addresses: *Office*—Office of the President, Republic of Botswana, Gabarone, Botswana.

population live in urban areas such as the capital, Gabarone.

Botswana is also considered a leader in Southern African politics, and earns praise for the stable example its sets for its neighbors. In many cases, African leaders have been ousted only with armed intervention. It has been called the continent's "showcase democracy." All three of the nations bordering Botswana—South Africa, Namibia, and Zimbabwe—bear the scars of internal violence and strife. When Mogae became president in April of 1998 as the handpicked successor to outgoing president Ketumile Masire, it contrasted markedly with the reigns of Zimbabwe's Robert Mugabe (in power since 1980) and Sam Nujoma of Namibia; only South African President Nelson Mandela and his announcement of his planned retirement in 1999 compared.

Mogae's stint as Permanent Secretary also gave him a seat on a number of other important official bodies, including the DeBeers Botswana Mining Co. and the Bank of Botswana. He had already served as an alternate representative for Botswana at the International Monetary Fund. Botswana's economic success still rests largely on its mineral wealth, primarily in diamonds. It is the international leader in diamond production, and derives so much income from this—although the powerful DeBeers company co-owns, with the government, the three main diamond mines—that it receives no international aid.

Mogae was well qualified for his new post. From 1982 to 1989 he had served as permanent secretary to President of Botswana under Masire, and was named minister of finance and development planning in 1989. In Botswanian politics, that post is often paired with that of the vice-president, and in March of 1992 Masire elevated Mogae to that office. The vice-presidency is usually considered a stepping stone to the presidency, but there were others within the BDP that were vying for power in the event of Masire's leaving office. Furthermore, as a result of rising unemployment figures in the cities, Mogae's BDP had lost a number of seats in parliament to other parties such as the Botswana National Front in the 1994 elections. Just prior to stepping down in early 1998, Masire enacted a series of reforms that pleased both the BDP and its opposition in parliament, the Botswana National Front, and smoothed the way for Mogae's assumption of power.

Sworn In After Presidential Visit

Mogae was sworn in just two days after a visit to Botswana by U.S. President Bill Clinton. Just prior to the ceremony, *The Namibian* called Mogae "a no-nonsense politician capable of uniting a fractured BDP." His first task was to name a new vice-president and new cabinet. Given the recent internal conflicts within the

BDP, however, his choices could earn him new enemies—or even perhaps create a threatening rival. Vying for the prominent post were Ponatshego Kedikilwe, an American-educated BDP official, and Ian Khama, the son of Botswana's first president and former head of the army. Mogae named Kedikilwe his new minister for finance and development, but not vice-president, and created special post for Khama as minister of presidential affairs and public administration.

In Mogae's first few months in office, he announced a major program to improve Botswana's infrastructure, using the country's revenues to build schools, medical facilities, and offices. The country has enjoyed a budget surplus 16 years in a row—ten of those with Mogae as Finance Minister—and plans to add additional funds to its reserves with the planned privatization of a few major industries. In late 1998, Mogae planned to sell off both the government-run airline, Air Botswana, and the government telecommunications industry. There were no plans, however, to unload the country's water utility, a crucial sector in this draught-plagued area.

Mogae faces elections in 1999 as mandated by the country's constitution. There have been problems with restless—and in some cases riotous—university students, and Mogae has attempted to resolve a longstanding border dispute with Namibia over an uninhabited island situated in the river that serves as border between the two countries. Armed troops on both sides fire the occasional volley, and Botswana claims that its sovereignty over the tiny island, which is under water for much of the year, dates from an 1890 German-British treaty. The dispute has been referred to the International Court of Justice at The Hague for arbitration.

Mogae is considered an outstanding leader in Southern African politics. He is involved with a number of regional coalitions whose aim is to modernize economic conditions in this part of the continent. Mogae's charitable involvements include membership in the Botswana Society of the Deaf and the Kalahari Conservation Society. In his leisure time he enjoys tennis and music.

Sources

Periodicals

African Business, September 1995, p. 12; September 1996, p. 17.
Mail & Guardian (Johannesburg, South Africa), November 17, 1997; March 31, 1998; April 7, 1998.
The Namibian, March 27, 1998; April 2, 1998; May 20, 1998; May 22, 1998.
New York Times, April 1, 1998.

Other

http://www.cnn.com
http://www.theage.com

—Carol Brennan

Michael Moorer

1967—

Professional boxer

In 1993 Michael Moorer was not well known outside of boxing circles, even though he was ranked as the number one heavyweight contender by the International Boxing Federation. However, when he defeated Evander Holyfield in April of 1994, Moorer had become the toast of the boxing world and a celebrity. He has held the International Boxing Federation (IBF) and World Boxing Association (WBA) heavyweight titles and has battled both seasoned veterans and young upstarts.

Moorer was born on November 12, 1967 in Detroit, Michigan and grew up in Boca Raton, Florida. He had a difficult childhood and was often involved in fights. As a high school student, he reportedly started a fight at a football game that resulted in injury to another student. Although police were called to the scene, no charges were filed.

In 1988, Moorer was a young boxer when he was approached by sports agent John Davimos. Davimos recognized Moorer's talent and worked hard to arrange boxing matches for him. By 1992, Moorer had compiled 29 wins and it was becoming increasingly difficult for Davimos to book fights for him. Few boxers wanted to challenge Moorer due to his exceptional talent and devastating left hook. In addition, many boxers demanded a guaranteed part of Moorer's purse before stepping into the ring. As a result, both Moorer and Davimos were losing money with each fight. This situation changed dramatically when Moorer defeated Holyfield and captured both the World Boxing Assocation and International Boxing Federation crowns. That victory completely erased Davimos's financial deficit and earned both men a healthy profit.

Became Heavyweight Champion

In January of 1994, Evander Holyfield announced that he would fight champion Lennox Lewis for the World Boxing Council (WBC) title. Holyfield already held the IBF and WBA championship titles and wanted an opportunity to capture the WBC crown. However, IBF officials declared that Holyfield must fight Moorer, the number one IBF contender, before stepping into the ring with Lewis. Holyfield would be stripped of his IBF title if he fought Lewis first. Faced with few options, Holyfield

At a Glance...

Born November 12, 1967 in Detroit, Michigan; married Bobbie; children: Michael Moorer, Jr.

Career: Defeated Ramzi Hassan to win WBO Light Heavyweight Championship, 1988; defeated Brett Cooper to win WBO Heavyweight Championship, 1992; defeated Evander Holyfield to win the WBA and IBF Heavyweight Titles, 1994; lost IBF Championship to George Foreman, 1994; defeated Axel Schulz to reclaim IBF Championship, 1996; lost IBF Championship to Evander Holyfield, 1997.

Addresses: *Contact*—Main Events, 811 Totowa Road, Suite 100, Totowa, NJ 07512.

---

agreed to fight Moorer.

The two faced off in the ring on August 22, 1994, in Las Vegas. Early in the fight, Holyfield rocked Moorer with a hard punch and sent him to the canvas. Moorer recovered quickly, however, and gradually dominated Holyfield as the fight progressed. After a bruising twelve-round bout, Moorer was declared the winner by a 3-2 majority decision.

Moorer's victory over Holyfield was greeted with sadness by some boxing fans and members of the media. Holyfield, an ordained minister, was viewed by many as a gentleman and worthy champion who had brought an air of decency back to boxing after the scandalous reign of his predecessor, Mike Tyson. He trained hard and worked to improve his boxing skills. Moorer, on the other hand, had a reputation as an undisciplined boxer who took a carefree attitude toward training. Some feared that boxing had entered another period marked by scandal and bad behavior. As Richard Hoffer wrote in *Sports Illustrated* shortly after Moorer's victory, "And so boxing seems—seems—once more to descend to thuggery, its majority heavyweight championship now held by a man who was promoted as "Nasty"; a man whose entourage announced his appearance at a press conference by overturning trays of dishes; a man who once told an interviewer, 'I want to break a cheekbone to see what it looks like pushed in....'"

Lost Title to George Foreman

After defeating Holyfield, Moorer proposed a title defense fight against George Foreman. Foreman had held the heavyweight championship from January 1973 to October 1974, eventually losing the championship to Muhammad Ali. Foreman was in the midst of a comeback and had performed well in fights with lesser opponents. However, many boxing insiders believed that Foreman was too old and overweight to compete with Moorer. When the Moorer-Foreman bout was proposed, the World Boxing Association and International Boxing Federation refused to sanction it and threatened to strip Moorer of his title if he fought Foreman. After Foreman passed a series of medical tests, the WBA and IBF agreed to sanction the fight.

The Moorer-Foreman bout was held on November 14, 1994, in Las Vegas. Many boxing fans felt that Moorer would easily defend his title. For most of the fight, Moorer held the upper hand and seemed to have victory well within his grasp. Two minutes into the tenth round, however, Foreman surprised Moorer with a vicious punch and knocked him out. Moorer announced his retirement from boxing shortly after the fight. Two days later, he announced that he would not retire and had made the previous statement because he was frustrated by the loss to Foreman and difficulties in his personal life. He also declared that he had already agreed to a rematch with Foreman. The second Moorer-Foreman fight was scheduled for February 29, 1996. It was cancelled in January of 1996 after both sides failed to agree on how to promote the fight and distribute the multimillion-dollar purse.

On November 8, 1997, a rematch was held in Las Vegas between Moorer and Holyfield. Holyfield held the WBA title, while Moorer held the IBF belt. Moorer began the fight strongly, employing many of the same tactics that he had used three years earlier to defeat Holyfield. His right jab was very effective during the first three rounds and he landed a strong right hook that buckled Holyfield's legs. Following the third round, Holyfield changed his strategy to counter Moorer's outside boxing style. He quickly took control of the fight and knocked Moorer to the canvas five times—once in the fifth, twice in the seventh, and twice in the eighth. Although Moorer was able to get to his feet after each knockdown, referee Mitch Halpern stopped the fight in the eighth round on the advice of the ringside physician. Holyfield had avenged his earlier loss to Moorer and claimed the IBF title.

In 1998, Moorer was mentioned as a possible opponent for WBC heavyweight champion Lennox Lewis after talks for a fight between Holyfield and Lewis fell through. Moorer was also considered as an ideal first opponent for Mike Tyson when Tyson's suspension from the WBA and IBF are lifted. A hearing was scheduled for the fall of 1998 to determine whether Tyson's boxing license would be reinstated.

Michael Moorer has proven himself to be a competent fighter and a worthy opponent. Although he has often stated that he plans to retire from the ring early in his career, his boxing future continues to look promising.

Sources

Cable World, September 8, 1997.
Forbes, June 20, 1994.
Jet, May 9, 1994; November 21, 1994; December 9, 1996; November 24, 1997.
Multichannel News, January 10, 1994; January 31, 1994; January 1, 1996; October 6, 1997; November 17, 1997.
Plain Dealer (Cleveland), November 7, 1997; December 29, 1997.
Sports Illustrated, May 2, 1994; August 22, 1994; November 14, 1994; November 28, 1994; May 29, 1995; January 29, 1996; November 17, 1997.

—Sandy J. Stiefer

Buck O'Neil

1911—

Professional baseball player

John Jordan (Buck) O'Neil, a former standout Negro League player and manager and one of baseball's greatest spokesmen, was born on November 13, 1911 in Carrabelle, Florida. He was the second of three children born to John Sr., a sawmill worker, and Luella, a restaurant manager. The family moved to Sarasota in 1923. It was there that O'Neil received his first taste of professional baseball.

As a 12-year-old, O'Neil began his semi-professional career as a member of the Sarasota Tigers and traveled throughout Florida. To support himself, he shined shoes and worked as a box boy. O'Neil related a pivotal moment in his life to Steve Wulf of *Sports Illustrated,* "I was considered a good box boy because, while most of the box boys could only carry two crates at a time, I was big and strong enough to carry four. I did that for about three years, at $1.25 a day. One day I was having lunch by myself next to a big stack of boxes, and it was so hot, I said out loud, 'Damn, there has got to be something better than this.'" That "something," O'Neil decided, was baseball.

Following completion of the eighth grade, O'Neil wanted to continue his education. Because of his skin color, however, he was not admitted to the high school in Sarasota. O'Neil was eventually able to obtain his high school diploma and earned a baseball and football scholarship to Edward Waters College in Jacksonville. He completed two years of college before leaving school to play baseball in 1934.

From 1934 to 1938 O'Neil played on various teams, including the Miami Giants, New York Tigers, and the Shreveport Acme Giants. In 1937 he signed with the Memphis Red Sox, earning $100 per month. That same year, he played for one month with the Zulu Cannibal Giants, a barnstorming team. The Giants, owned by Harlem Globetrotters founder Abe Saperstein, wore straw skirts instead of uniforms, but the team paid well and the players did not have to wear war paint as some "African-themed" teams did. In 1938, after four years of moving from team to team, O'Neil earned a spot as the first baseman for the Kansas City Monarchs, one of the elite teams of the Negro Leagues.

Buck and the Monarchs

From 1939 to 1942, Kansas City won four consecutive Negro American League pennants. O'Neil told *Sports Illustrated* about the glory years of the Monarchs: "We

> *At a Glance...*
>
> Born John Jordan O'Neil, November 13, 1911 in Carrabelle, FL; son of John Sr. (a saw mill worker) and Luella (a restaurant owner); married Ora Lee Owen, 1946. *Education:* attended Edward Waters College, Jacksonville, FL.
>
> **Career:** First semi-professional baseball experience with the Sarasota Tigers, 1923; began professional career with the Miami Giants, 1934; New York Tigers, 1935; Shreveport Acme Giants, 1936; Memphis Red Sox, 1937; Kansas City Monarchs 1938-43, 1946-51; managed the Kansas City Monarchs, 1948-55; scout for the Chicago Cubs, 1956-88; first African American coach in Major League baseball, 1962; scout for the Kansas City Royals, 1989-.
> Memberships: Negro Leagues Baseball Museum Board of Directors, chairman; Veterans' Committee of the National Baseball Hall of Fame.
>
> **Awards:** Negro League batting titles, 1940 and 1946; named to the West All Star team of the Negro League East-West Classic, 1942, 1943, and 1949; Missouri Sports Hall of Fame.
>
> **Addresses:** *Residence*—Kansas City, Missouri; *Mailing*—Kansas City Royals Baseball Club, PO Box 419962 Kansas City, Missouri 64141-6969.

were like the New York Yankees. We had that winning tradition, and we were proud. We had a strict dress code—coat and tie, no baseball jackets. We stayed in the best hotels in the world. They just happened to be owned by black people. We ate in the best restaurants in the world. They just happened to be run by blacks. And when we were in Kansas City, well, 18th and Vine was the center of the universe. We'd come to breakfast at Street's Hotel, and there might be Count Basie or Joe Louis or Billie Holiday or Lionel Hampton."

In 1942, O'Neil led the Monarchs to a four-game sweep of the Homestead Grays in the Negro World Series, hitting .353. He won batting titles in 1940 and 1946, hitting .345 and .350 respectively. O'Neil was also named to the West team of the East-West All-Star Classic in 1942, 1943, and 1949 and was a member of Satchel Paige's All Stars. Paige's team, made up of Negro League stars, played a team of white major league players known as Bob Feller's All Stars in a 14-game barnstorming series in 1946. O'Neil remembered that the players who performed in those exhibitions had a mutual respect for the abilities of their opponents. The Negro League All Stars won the majority of the games played.

In 1944, with the United States deeply involved in World War II, O'Neil enlisted for a two-year stint with the U.S. Navy. He was stationed at Subic Bay in the Philippines and worked as a bosun loading and unloading ships. Although he was proud to serve his country, O'Neil regretted the fact that he was not a member of the Monarchs in 1945. That was the year that Jackie Robinson played in Kansas City before signing with the Brooklyn Dodgers.

Following the end of World War II, O'Neil returned to the Monarchs in 1946. He won the batting title that year and also married Memphis schoolteacher Ora Lee Owen. In 1948, O'Neil was named player-manager of the Monarchs. He led Kansas City to league pennants in 1948, 1950, 1951, and 1953 and two Negro World Series titles. Alfred "Slick" Surratt, who played outfield for O'Neil, told Mark Goodman of *People Weekly* about O'Neil's managerial style: "He knew what it took to win a ball game, and he gave you confidence in yourself. After every game, when we got on the bus, he'd go over the game with us, whether we'd won or lost."

Joined the Cubs

O'Neil left the Monarchs in 1956 to become a scout for the Chicago Cubs. He travelled throughout the South searching for talented African American baseball players. He is credited with bringing formidable talents such as Ernie Banks, Lou Brock, Oscar Gamble, Lee Smith, and Joe Carter to the Cubs. In 1962, O'Neil made history by becoming the first African American coach in the major leagues. Although he had broken through an important barrier, O'Neil eventually realized that the Cubs were not interested in making him a big-league manager and returned to scouting. He remained with the Cubs until 1988, capping a 33-year career with the organization. He returned to Kansas City the following year and joined the Kansas City Royals as a scout.

Celebrity Status

In 1990, O'Neil began raising money for a museum to preserve and celebrate the history of the Negro Leagues. His efforts led to the opening of the Negro League Baseball Museum in Kansas City, Missouri. As a co-founder of the museum and one of the most articulate and engaging spokesman for the Negro Leagues, O'Neil began to appear regularly on radio and television programs. In 1994, he was featured prominently on Ken Burns' PBS documentary "Baseball." O'Neil was a key contributor to the segment entitled "Shadow Ball," which chronicled the greatness of the Negro Leagues, but also the pain of discrimination and exclusion from the major leagues. Burns, who won international acclaim for his 1990 documentary about the Civil War, told *People Weekly*'s Goodman about O'Neil's contribution to the nine-part series: "He's the conscience of the program. Because of his dignity, his lack of bitterness and his sense of humor, Buck makes a wonderful ambassador for the game." Although the "Baseball" series was not as well-received as Burns' Civil War documentary, O'Neil's appearance made him a media celebrity.

In 1996, O'Neil published his autobiography *I Was Right on Time: My Journey From the Negro Leagues to the Majors* with *Sports Illustrated* editor Steve Wulf and David Conrads. In the late 1990s O'Neil remained active in the Royals organization, served as the chairman of the Negro Leagues Baseball Museum Board of the Directors, and was a member of the Veterans' Committee of the National Baseball Hall of Fame in Cooperstown, New York. He worked as a spokesman to secure pensions for surviving Negro League players and to preserve the history of the Negro Leagues. He told Dave Kindred of *The Sporting News* that Negro League baseball was not the clowning, barnstorming jumble commonly portrayed in movies such as '*The Bingo Long Traveling All-Stars and Motor Kings*: "Negro League baseball wasn't anything like that. It was like the white major leagues, serious baseball, well organized. There were 16 Negro League ball clubs, each with at least 15 players—the Monarchs had 18 players. There were all those people putting on the games, booking agents, traveling secretaries, trainers. Baseball was black entertainment and was important to black communities."

Buck O'Neil will be remembered as one of the finest players in the Negro Leagues. Through his willingness to share his memories of the Negro Leagues, fans everywhere have a greater understanding and deeper appreciation for a significant period in baseball history.

Selected writings

I Was Right on Time, (with Steve Wulf and David Conrads), Touchstone, 1996.

Sources

Periodicals

People Weekly, September 26, 1994.
Sports Illustrated, September 19, 1994.
The Sporting News, September 5, 1994.

Other

Additional information obtained from the Major League Baseball website at http://www.majorleaguebaseball.com/nbl/nl19.sm; Missouri Sports Hall of Fame website at http://www.mosportshalloffame.com/boneil.htm; and the Negro Leagues website at http://www.nc5.infi.net/~moxie/nlb/players/o'neil.htm.

—Mike Watkins

Pat Parker

1944–1989

Poet, activist

A poet who writes about the world around them is not uncommon. However, when the poet is African American, lesbian and a feminist, their poems follow a decidedly different slant. Pat Parker rose above the stereotypes usually associated with those terms with a gritty honesty that prompted Adrian Oktenberg of *Women's Review of Books* to declare Parker, "the poet laureate of the Black and Lesbian peoples." An anecdotal and autobiographical poet, Parker's poems are the story of her life, a life which ended much too early when she died of breast cancer in 1989.

Born Patricia Cooks in Houston, Texas in 1944, she was the fourth daughter of Ernest, a tire retreader, and Marie Louise, a domestic. Parker was born two months premature and was hospitalized for three months with pneumonia. She reflected upon this event in an early poem entitled "Goat Child." "'You were a mistake'/my mother told me/ever since i've been/trying to make up./couldn't really imagine/her-him in bed &/me coming 4 yrs after/the last sister/& to make things worse/i come blasting in/2 months too soon./maybe the war did it/& to top the whole thing off/i'm the fourth girl/& was my father pissed/caught pneumonia &/ got hung up in incubator/for three months/finally made it out,/but the bed was too big/so my sister lost her doll bed./another enemy quickly made."

The Poet Emerged

Following a poverty-stricken childhood, Parker graduated from high school in 1962 and moved to California to attend Los Angeles City College and later, San Francisco State College. She married Ed Bullins in 1962. They divorced four years later and she married Robert F. Parker. That marriage also ended in divorce and Parker worked a succession of jobs in order to support her two daughters, Cassidy and Anastasia. She settled near Oakland, California and worked as a proofreader, waitress, clerk, and creative writing instructor. In the late 1960s, Parker became immersed in the civil rights, women's rights, and gay rights movements. An impassioned activist, Parker was also beginning to find her voice as a poet.

Parker published her first volume of poetry, *Child of Myself*, in 1972. In the title poem, Parker rebuts the Biblical notion that the woman is the second sex, "To think second/to believe first/a mistake/erased by the motion of years./i, woman, i/can no longer claim/a mother of flesh/a father of marrow/I Woman must be/the child of myself." With the release of *Child of Myself* Parker, who had been known solely among the Lesbian Tide Collective, a group of poets in Northern California, began to reach a wider audience.

Movement in Black

Parker's second volume of poetry, *Pit Stop*, was released in 1973 and focused on a variety of issues. The title poem of the collection dealt with the subject of alcoholism and was told in the vernacular of any corner

> ## At a Glance...
>
> Born Patricia Cooks, January 20, 1944 in Houston, Texas; died June 4, 1989, in Oakland, California; daughter of Ernest Nathaniel and Marie Louise Cooks; married Ed Bullins, June 20, 1962 (divorced, January 17, 1966); married Robert F. Parker, January 20, 1966 (divorced); children: Cassidy Brown, Anastasia Dunham-Parker. *Education:* Attended Los Angeles City College and San Francisco State University.
>
> **Career:** Poet, activist; published *Child of Myself,* 1972; published *Pit Stop: Words,* 1974; released the recording *Where Would I Be Without You: The Poetry of Pat Parker and Judy Grahn,* 1976; appointed director of Feminist Women's Health Center in Oakland, CA, 1978; published *Movement in Black: The Collected Poetry of Pat Parker, 1961-1978* and *Womanslaughter,* 1978; founded Black Women's Revolutionary Council, 1980; published *Jonestown and Other Madness,* 1985.

bar. "Let us drink to your new lover/Let us drink to your lover—gone/Let us drink to my lover/Let us drink to my lover—gone/Hey, let's drink to the good people/Let's drink to the nearest holiday/Let's drink to our ability to drink." In her introduction to Parker's poetry anthology, poet Judy Grahn called "Pit Stop," "the first poem I know of dealing with the subject of alcoholism among women, a serious debilitator of minority communities." Parker later recorded an album with Grahn entitled *Where Would I Be Without You: The Poetry of Pat Parker and Judy Grahn,* which was released in 1976.

The year of 1978 marked the beginning of an active period for Parker. She was appointed director of the Feminist Women's Health Center in Oakland and published her third volume of new poetry, *Womanslaughter.* She also published an anthology of her works entitled *Movement in Black: The Collected Poetry of Pat Parker 1961-1978.* The title poem of *Womanslaughter* revolved around the murder of Parker's sister and Parker's frustration when the murderer was convicted of manslaughter and released after serving only one year in prison. "One day a quiet man/shot his quiet wife/three times in the back./He shot her friend as well/His wife died." Parker admitted in the poem that she was weakened by her sister's death, but made stronger through the passage of time and the support of others. "I have gained many sisters./And if one is beaten,/or raped, or killed,/I will not come in mourning black./I will not pick the right flowers.... I will come with my many sisters/and decorate the streets/with the innards of those/brothers in womanslaughter.... I will come to my sisters,/not dutiful,/I will come strong."

Silenced Too Soon

In 1985 Parker published her fifth volume, *Jonestown and other madness.* Taking its title from the 1978 tragedy in Guyana where a self-proclaimed religious leader, Jim Jones, ordered more than 900 people to commit suicide, Adrian Oktenberg of *Women's Review of Books* proclaimed it Parker's best work. "It is a necessity not only for those who care about poetry," Oktenberg wrote, "but also for those who care about life." In the foreword of *Jonestown,* Parker confesses that the book came about, "because we have become too quiet.... We are a nation in great trouble. It is time for those with vision to speak out loudly before the madness consumes us all."

Rochelle Ratner of *Library Journal* acknowledged Parker's role as a black lesbian mother and a political activist. "At times, the poems become rhetorical," Ratner wrote, "but more often they are saved by Parker's sharp irony and her ability to relate political issues to events in her own life." In her poem "Legacy," which she wrote for her daughter, Anastasia, Parker attempts to dispel the notion that lesbians are ineffective parents who lead their children down the path of depravity. "Take the strength that you may/wage a long battle./Take the pride that you can/never stand small./Take the rage that you can/never settle for less./These be the things I pass/to you my daughter/if this is the result of perversion/let the world stand screaming./You will mute their voices/with your life."

A year after Parker's death Lyndie Brimstone, writing in *Feminist Review,* described Parker as, "this loud and rich-mouthed poet who planted her feet firmly on platforms all over America and demanded that her audiences, whoever they may be, pay attention, was not only working class, she was Black and lesbian: the very first to refuse to compromise and speak openly from her undiluted experience." In an untitled poem, Parker seems to echo Brimstone's sentiments, "I am a child of America/a step child/raised in the back room/yet taught/taught how to act/in her front room." As the poet Audre Lorde wrote in her foreword to *Movement in Black,* "Even when a line falters, Parker's poetry maintains, reaches out and does not let go. It is clean and sharp without ever being neat. Yet her images are precise, and the plain accuracy of her visions encourages an honesty that may be uncomfortable as it is compelling. Her words are womanly and uncompromising."

Sources

Books

Coss, Clare, *The Arc of Love: An Anthology of Lesbian Love Poems,* Scribner, 1996.
Howe, Florence, *No More Masks: An Anthology of Twentieth-Century American Women Poets,* Harper-Perennial, 1993.
McEwen, Christian, ed., *Naming the Waves: Contemporary Lesbian Poetry,* The Crossing Press, 1989.
Moraga, Cherrie and Gloria Anzaldua, eds., *This Bridge Called My Back: Writings by Radical Women of Color,* Kitchen Table: Women of Color Press, 1983.
Morse, Carl and Joan Larkin, eds., *Gay & Lesbian Poetry In Our Time: An Anthology,* St. Martin's Press, 1988.
Whitehead, Kim, *The Feminist Poetry Movement,* University Press of Mississippi, 1996.

Periodicals

Callaloo, Winter 1986, p. 259.
Colby Library Journal, March 1982, p. 9.
Feminist Review, Spring 1990, p. 4.
Library Journal, July 1986, p. 77.
Women's Review of Books, April 1986, p. 18.

—Brian Escamilla

Floyd Patterson

1935—

Professional boxer

Floyd Patterson was born on January 4, 1935 in Waco, North Carolina—the third of 11 children. He grew up in abject poverty and would become the youngest heavyweight champion until Mike Tyson came along. The family moved to Brooklyn, New York in 1936 so that Patterson's father Thomas could look for work. He worked in construction, as a longshoreman, in sanitation, and in a fish market. Thomas Patterson worked every day, but to Floyd's young eyes there never seemed to be enough. The Patterson's constantly moved around Brooklyn trying to accommodate the ever-growing family. As a child, Patterson felt ashame of not having clothes that fit and a sense of helplessness for not being able to help his parents provide for the family.

As a result of his own self-perception, Patterson did not go to school, but avoided the truant officer by staying in the dark all day—in neighborhood cellars, alleys, subway stations, or in the movies. Patterson was not like the other kids; he could not (or would not) read or write, he did not bring friends home, and he would not look people in the eye. Besides skipping school he began to steal to pass the time away. Because his mother could not control him, Patterson was sent to the Wiltwyck School for Boys in 1945, which was an alternative to jail for boys aged eight to 12. It was at this correctional institution that Patterson blossomed. At Wiltwyck he received individual attention and found that white and black kids were treated exactly the same.

It was also at Wiltwyck that Patterson put on boxing gloves for the first time. He was a natural, winning all three bouts in which he participated. At the age of twelve Patterson returned home a new person. He was still shy, but he had overcome the feeling of shame that was so deep-seeded within him as a small child. Patterson went to P.S. 614—a vocational elementary school where he got the idea that he could use boxing to earn money for his family.

A Fighter is Born

In 1949 Patterson entered Gramercy Gym, which was run by Cus D'Amato, who would later train and manage Tyson. D'Amato gave Patterson boxing equipment and taught him the rudiments of the ring, but his first experience at boxing was almost his last. Patterson's

At a Glance...

Born Floyd Patterson, January 4, 1935 in Waco, North Carolina; Son of Thomas Patterson; wife Sandra; children: Seneca, Jennifer.

Career: Won a gold medal in the 1952 Helsinki Olympics; World Heavyweight Champion 1956-59, 1960-62; Last fight in 1972 against Muhammed Ali; Commissioner, New York State Athletic Commission, 1977-84; Commissioner, New York City Sports Commission, 1985; Chairman, New York State Athletic Commission, 1995-98.

Awards: Received "Setting a Good Example Award" from President John F. Kennedy, 1961; Elected to the Boxing Hall of Fame, 1976; Received the "Pioneer of Excellence Award" from the World Institute of Black Communications and CBS Records, 1986.

first fight was against his brother Frank, who was then the 160-pound New York Golden Gloves Champion. He was pummeled by his big brother, but overcame his fear and stuck with the sport. Six months later he had his first amateur fight.

In January of 1950 Patterson entered and won his first AAU tournament bout in the 147-pound weight class. The next year as a 160-pound fighter, Patterson won his weight class and traveled to Chicago to participate in the national AAU Boxing Championships. 1951 was a significant year for Patterson personally because he met his future wife Sandra Hicks. Patterson wanted to turn pro that year as a sixteen-year-old, but D'Amato would not let him. In the back of his mind D'Amato was saving Patterson for the 1952 Olympics in Helsinki, Finland. In 1952 Patterson won the Golden Gloves Championship at Madison Square Garden and the National AAU Championship in Boston. After Patterson won the Eastern Olympic tryouts and was named to the team, he left school for good for a chance at history. Patterson became a member of perhaps the finest United States Olympic boxing team ever assembled as the squad won five gold medals including Patterson's.

On September 12, 1952 Patterson had his first professional bout at the age of 17. He won it with a knockout in the first round to receive the eye-popping sum of three hundred dollars—half of which immediately went to his mother. Soon the family had a telephone, a television, and appliances in the home where Patterson still shared a bed with his little brother Larry. In his first month as a professional he won three fights and $1,000. Patterson was named "Ring Rookie of the Year" in 1953 by the New York Boxing Writers.

There was talk of matching the 19-year-old prodigy up against a ranked opponent, but D'Amato wanted to take it slower. After fighting four light heavyweights, D'Amato signed Patterson for his first big professional fight against veteran Joey Maxim. Patterson returned to Wiltwyck to train for the fight for which he would be paid $5,000. In his debut as a big-time contender, the kid lost to the experience of Maxim. Though Patterson did not believe he had lost in his heart, he was devastated. Later Patterson realized that he had been outsmarted by the ex-champion and developed a respect for Maxim. Patterson soon recovered from his loss and went on a tear of 11 straight knockouts including his first official heavyweight fight against Archie McBride. By the end of 1955 Patterson was fighting in Los Angeles and rubbing elbows with such Hollywood stars as Frank Sinatra and Kim Novack. Despite his new success and notoriety, he was miserable. He missed Sandra who was still in high school back in Brooklyn. When Patterson returned home, he asked Sandra to be is wife and the two were married on February 11, 1956 in a civil ceremony. After Patterson converted to Catholicism later that year the two were married again in a religious ceremony on July 13. Patterson bought a home for his family in Mt. Vernon, New York and he and his new wife moved in with them.

On April 12, 1956 Rocky Marciano retired, leaving the heavyweight division without a champion. On June 8 the 21-year-old Patterson fought Tommy 'Hurricane' Jackson at Madison Square Garden for a purse of $50,000. Despite a broken hand that he had injured two weeks before the fight, Patterson won the bout in a split decision. The path was open to fight for the newly vacated heavyweight championship. In September of 1956, Patterson was signed to fight Archie Moore for the heavyweight championship. As he drove to Chicago Stadium on November 30 he had more than the title belt and its $114,257 purse on his mind. At Queens Memorial Hospital back in New York Sandra was going into labor with their first child. Patterson was able to keep his composure and knocked out Moore in the fifth round. In his dressing room a reporter informed him that he was a father and showed him a picture of his new daughter Seneca. One and a half hours after winning the heavyweight championship Patterson was in a car on his way back to New York.

Patterson ruled the boxing world at the age of 21, but

he learned in reality that his accomplishment meant little to a black man in 1957 America. He was not able to get a meal in a truck stop in Baltimore or eat in a restaurant in Kansas City during a five-city exhibition tour. In Wichita he was greeted by 50 people blocking his path from the station. A Catholic priest intervened and allowed Patterson and his entourage to stay with him at his Parish. After continuing on with his exhibition before a hushed all-white crowd, Patterson vowed that he would never box in front of a segregated crowd again. He insisted that promoters desegregate seating and avoid scheduling him to train in segregated towns. Patterson also became part of an anti-discrimination suit against a beauty parlor which would not take his wife's appointment. Becoming heavyweight champ was a rude awakening in other ways as well. The withdrawn Patterson was constantly stared at, and was criticized by the boxing media both for his youth and for not fighting real challengers to his heavyweight title. Because of D'Amato's dispute with the boxing powers-that-be, the best contenders would not fight Patterson. He fought Jackson again and also two lightly-regarded fighters Roy Harris and Brian London in 1958 before signing to take on the number one contender, Ingemar Johansson from Sweden.

A Champion Dethroned

Johansson was undefeated in 21 fights and had knocked out 13 previous opponents. During his training Johansson played up the fact that he had injured his right hand. He never threw it while sparring. During the championship fight, he also made Patterson a believer. Johansson did not even come close to throwing the right for the first two rounds. After setting up the young fighter to leave his left side open, Johansson delivered a crushing right hand to the side of Patterson's head which punctured his left ear drum and left him dazed for the rest of the bout. Johansson punched Patterson down seven times, but each time the bewildered champ struggled back to his feet. Finally the referee had to stop the fight.

After recovering from the physical beating, Patterson found that the mental anguish was worse to deal with. He had weeks of sleepless nights and even his children began to question if their father was sick. Finally the feelings of self-doubt and self-pity began to evolve into something like a hatred for Johansson. Patterson was also having his troubles with D'Amato after an investigation of the way the first Johansson fight was promoted. D'Amato would eventually have his license revoked on November 24, 1959 and be suspended from boxing. Despite not having his manager, Patterson had developed a burning desire for a rematch and for redemption. He decided not to wait for D'Amato's suspension to end and signed to fight the heavyweight champion again on June 20, 1960 at the Polo Grounds in New York. Patterson overcame another hand injury and his own demons of doubt in the second fight. He started out as the aggressor cutting Johansson's eye in the first round. Patterson worked him over for four more rounds and then at 1:51 of the fifth the ex-champ literally knocked Johansson senseless. Patterson was heavyweight champ again, but in his long climb back to the top of the boxing world he learned something about himself. For Patterson he would rather give up boxing than to develop a hatred for an opponent.

Years after the fight he told *Sports Illustrated*: "I was so filled with hate. I would not ever want to be like that again." He would fight Johansson a third time and though he struggled, Patterson found a way to win. He was knocked down twice in the first round, but then switched his focus to pounding Johansson's body. Patterson won the fight in the sixth round knocking Johansson out with a right. In late 1961 Patterson knocked out Tom McNealey in the fourth round after knocking him down eight times. After the McNealey fight Patterson again heard from the critics claiming that he would not fight any real challengers, but that would change all too soon.

Patterson vs. Liston

The most obvious choice for a title bout was Charles "Sonny" Liston who had been demolishing all the boxers critics claimed Patterson should have been fighting. D'Amato was cautious as ever and did not want Patterson to fight Liston citing the ex-con's ties to organized crime. Even the NAACP did not want Patterson to give Liston a shot at the title because of his unsavory reputation. But Patterson fought Liston anyway on September 25, 1962 in Chicago. Liston outweighed Patterson by 25 pounds and was a nine-to-five favorite. Liston batted Patterson around like an amateur knocking him out in two minutes and six seconds of the first round. In the rematch a year later Liston knocked Patterson down three times before again knocking him out in the first round.

Many thought that Patterson's career was over, but he was only 29 years old and he decided to continue his boxing career. He won two bouts in Stockholm, Sweden and earned another shot at the title against Muhammad Ali. Patterson thought he matched up well with the brash young Ali, but he had no luck in the fight. He injured his back in the first round, but continued even though he was severely hampered. Patterson lasted into the twelfth round when the referee gave the bout to Ali on a technical knock out. Despite the terrible punishment he was receiving in the ring Patterson was not ready to retire. He defeated Henry Cooper in 1966 and fought four times in 1967.

Patterson lost to WBA Champion Jimmy Ellis in a title fight in Sweden despite breaking Ellis's nose and cutting his eye. He then left the ring for two years. He resumed boxing in 1970 mostly fighting washed-up journeymen through 1971. But he would get one last chance at the big-time in 1972. Muhammad Ali was looking to stay sharp while waiting for his rematch with Joe Frazier. He signed to fight the 37-year-old Patterson on September 20 in 1972. Patterson stayed even with Ali for the first four rounds, but Ali cut Patterson badly over his right eye and the ring doctor stopped the fight in the eighth round. Patterson called for a third fight with Ali, but it never happened. The brutal beating by Ali would be his last fight. Patterson's final record was 55-8-1 with 40 knockouts.

Success After Boxing

Though he would never fight again, Patterson remained active in boxing. Patterson opened a gym in New Paltz, New York to bring along young fighters the way D'Amato brought him to boxing prominence. In 1976 Patterson took particular interest in an 11-year-old kid named Tracy Harris, who reminded him of himself as a boy. Patterson took the young boxer under his wing both personally and professionally. He eventually adopted Tracy Juan Harris Patterson as well as becoming his trainer and manager. Patterson guided his new son to two Golden Gloves titles as an amateur and to 97 victories. Patterson seemed to work well with his son as Tracy compiled an excellent professional record and won the World Boxing Council junior featherweight championship. But the newest Patterson wanted a change. In late 1994 he told his adopted father that he wanted a different manager and the bond between father and son was broken. Though Patterson suffered pain in his personal life, his tireless work in the boxing community brought him to the attention of New York Governor George Pataki. He was named the athletic commissioner of the State of New York in June of 1995. Patterson hoped to use casino gambling as a way to bring the marquee fights from Las Vegas back to New York. He also wanted to establish a pension fund for older fighters in the state. In late December of 1995 Patterson presided over the biggest bout in New York in decades pitting Oscar De La Hoya against Jesse James Leiha. What should have been his greatest professional triumph was spoiled by the results of one of the undercard fights. Patterson sat slumped in his chair as he watched his estranged adopted son lose his title.

At 61 years old Patterson appeared to be the picture of health. He still worked out at his gym and remained active running the athletic commission and serving as a Eucharistic minister administering Communion to residents of a nearby nursing home. But all was not well with the former champion. There were rumors that Patterson's memory was slipping. The truth came out after a New York Post report on a deposition that Patterson gave in March of 1998 in regards to "ultimate fighting." During the deposition Patterson could not remember his secretary's name, the name of the man he replaced as athletic commissioner, or the name of Archie Moore, the man he defeated for the heavyweight championship. Patterson's friend and former boxer Jose Torres told *The Sporting News:* "I felt that he was having a little trouble with his memory, and people were talking about it all around boxing ..." The fallout from the revelation led to Patterson's resignation from the athletic commission on April 1, 1998. Since then Patterson has retired to his 17-acre farm in New Paltz having left a legacy as an honest and loyal gentleman in a world of boxing conmen, back-stabbers, and charlatans. He remained as legendary sportswriter Red Smith said, as quoted in *Sports Illustrated:* "A man of peace whose life has been devoted to beating men with his fists."

Sources

Books

Patterson, Floyd and Gross, Milton. *Victory Over Myself.* Bernard Geis Associates; New York, 1962.

Periodicals

Sports Illustrated, March 22, 1993, p. 70; November 18, 1996, p. 4.
The Sporting News, April 1, 1998.

Other

World Boxing Association website: http:www.wbaonline.com/insidewba/history/legends_fpater.htm.

The Cyber Boxing Zone website: http:www.cyberboxingzone.com/boxing/box4_97.htm.

Heavyweight Boxing Championship History website: http://www.nashville.com/wws604/hwbs.htm#Patterson.

—Michael J. Watkins

Lee "Scratch" Perry

1936—

Reggae artist

Lee "Scratch" Perry is a world-music figure of near-mythic status. He has been credited with inventing the form of music that became known as reggae, its stripped-down offshoot called "dub," and the reincarnations of both decades later as drum-and-bass and other dance-club genres. Perry makes records awash in "echoes and distortions, sudden noises and disorienting absences, and they have influenced not only reggae but hip-hop, rock and all sorts of dance music," wrote Jon Pareles of the *New York Times.* Since the 1960s he has enjoyed success as a producer and a recording artist, but is probably better known for his wildly eccentric persona and famously bizarre pronouncements to the press. "I am an alien from the other world, from outer space, I don't have no land, no estate, no property, no house. Not on this earth. I live in space—I'm only a visitor here," Perry once reportedly said, according to a website devoted to him. "Some people are only here to collect property. I am here with my suitcase to collect only the good brains."

Perry was born in Hanover, Jamaica in 1936. Like many rural black Jamaicans of the era, he grew up poor. "I quit school," he recalled, according to the Perry web site. "I learned nothing at all. There was nothing to do except field work, so I started playing dominoes and learned to read the minds of others. This has proved eternally useful to me." As a young man, he moved to the island's capital, Kingston, in the 1950s to find work. He was hired by Clement "Coxsone" Dodd, a well-known figure in the Kingston music scene who ran a label called Studio One. Perry began as an assistant, and worked his way up to a talent scout job. At one point he ran the label's store. Coxsone also made him a "selecter," or disk jockey, at organized ska parties; Perry's style often packed the house. Yet the music scene in Jamaica was a fierce one, and on occasion Perry and his colleagues had to battle thugs employed by Coxsone's rivals who tried to shut down the parties by force.

The Upsetter

Perry made his first records for Studio One in the early 1960s. His backing band was the Skatalites, and he had his first hit with "Chicken Scratch" in 1965. Other tracks were done with the Soulettes, a group fronted by Bob Marley's wife, Rita Marley. These first records, which included "Prince in the Pack" and "Mad Head" among others, noted the author of an essay on Perry in the *Guinness Encyclopedia of Popular Music,* "featured a bluesy, declamatory vocal style" that became Perry's trademark. His lyrics, moreover, addressed certain issues in Jamaican life, such as political violence and social injustice. They also contained occasional sexual innuendos and scathing diatribes against his competitors in the Jamaican music scene, all themes that reappeared in his music throughout the rest of his career.

Perry left Coxsone and Studio One in 1966 after

> ### At a Glance...
>
> Born Rainford Hugh Perry, March 20, 1936, in Hanover, Jamaica. First marriage to Paulette Perry ended in 1979; married Mireille Ruegg, c. 1989.
>
> **Career:** Worked as an assistant, talent scout, and retail manager for the Kingston, Jamaica label "Studio One" before putting out his first solo records for them in the 1960s; later became a producer of other early reggae acts; affiliated with Amalgamated label, late 1960s; began own label, Upsetter Records, c. 1969; signed with Island Records, 1975; collaborated with a number of other artists over the years, including Bob Marley, Peter Tosh, Adrian Sherwood, and the Mad Professor.
>
> **Addresses:** *Office*—Island Records, Four Columbus Circle, 5th Floor, New York, NY 10019. *Home*—Zurich, Switzerland.

disagreements over songwriting credits and finances. He began working on his own with a young producer named Joe Gibbs and with him put out his first single, the somewhat threatening "I Am the Upsetter"—a reference to Coxsone. The "Upsetter" tag would become one of Perry's aliases. Gibbs had started a label called Amalgamated, and he hired Perry to run it. As the house producer, Perry engineered a number of hits for Jamaican acts on Amalgamated, including a song by the Pioneers called "Long Shot." "Long Shot," according to website author Mick Sleeper's biography on Perry, which he adapted from the book *Reggae, Rasta, Revolution,* edited by Christ Potash, "was the first song to use a new rhythm in Jamaican music." "It didn't have a name at the time," Sleeper explained, "but a year later someone christened the beat 'Reggae.'"

Perry and Bob Marley

Perry's relationship with Gibbs broke down after a few years over questions of rights and royalties, and in 1968 he left Amalgamated and teamed with a backing band called the Hippy Boys. Perry rechristened them the Upsetters, and their first hit, "People Funny Boy," was a lyrical attack on Gibbs. By now a major player in the Jamaican music scene, Perry was able to start his own label, Upsetter Records, and on it issued around a hundred singles with both the Upsetters and other acts in only a few short years. Perry and the band loved to spend afternoons in Kingston movie houses watching spaghetti westerns, and spend all night in the recording studio. His tracks with the Upsetters reflect the on-screen violence in their titles: "Kill Them All," "The Vampire," and "Dig Your Grave," were but a few; another from this era, "Return of Django," became Perry's first top ten hit in England in 1969.

Because of "Return of Django," Perry and the Upsetters became the first reggae act to tour England. Soon, however, Bob Marley lured the Upsetters away from Perry and folded them into the Wailers, his backing band. This ignited a war of words between Marley and Perry, but Perry was mollified when Marley signed a deal for Perry to produce for the band. The resulting work from this period epitomized the reggae sound. "Although it will probably never be known who influenced who, the chemistry between Perry, Marley, the Wailers, and the Upsetters proved to be phenomenal," according to the website biography. It was a short-lived collaboration, however, dissolving in 1971 over issues of songwriting credit and money. Perry and Marley had an alleged deal between themselves to split all profits, but Perry supposedly took off with everything. This resulted in copyright lawsuits and legal problems that persisted well past Marley's death in 1981.

The Black Ark Years

By this time Perry had moved to a nice section of Kingston called Washington Gardens and built a recording studio at his house. Finished in 1974, Perry named it "Black Ark," and it quickly became a tour-de-force in the Jamaican music scene. Breaking away from straight reggae, Perry began to head away toward far more unusual creative avenues. Much of this came from his production techniques. "Perry shot pistols, broke glass, ran tapes backwards, and used samples of crying babies, falling rain, and animal sounds," according to his biography. "Innovation and experimentation became Black Ark trademarks.... He used eccentric methods such as cleaning the tape heads with his t-shirt and blowing ganja smoke onto the master tapes as they rolled, ensuring that the music recorded in the Black Ark would have a dirty, magical quality to it that would never be surpassed."

Most astonishing to music afficionados was that much of the Black Art label recordings were done on a simple four-track mixing board (most studios are 32-track). Perry often ran several tapes at once through each one of the tracks. It resulted in "a dense, multi-layered mixing style that is instantly recognizable," noted the *Guinness Encyclopedia of Popular Music.* Others recognized its unique style, and Perry was signed to Island Records in 1975, a label founded by Chris Blackwell, a white Jamaican of British descent. Perry recorded for them as a solo artist, but also worked as their house producer. From this came a number of hit singles for other acts, such as Max Romeo's "War in a Babylon," Junior Murvin's "Police And Thieves," and "Party Time" from the Heptones. Later, the English ska/punk band the Clash covered "Police and Thieves," and Perry did some studio work with them. He also began recording with King Tubby, considered the primary force behind the birth of dub music.

Infamous Mental Collapse

Perry also continued his own experiments as a recording artist. Many of his songs from this era reflected the turbulent political situation in Jamaica, such as "City Too Hot" and other explicit anti-violence messages. Some tracks were released by Island in 1976 under aliases such as Jah Lion and Super Ape. Yet Perry's personal life took a turn for the worse in 1979, when his wife Paulette left him and took their children with her. In response, Perry set the Black Ark studio afire, completely destroying it. It was a breakdown from which he never seemed to fully recover, and with it came the onset of his famous eccentric personality. He covered the site with graffiti and small crosses, and "journalists arrived at the Black Ark to find Perry worshipping bananas, eating money, and baptizing visitors with a garden hose," his website biography noted.

Escaping Jamaica, Perry moved to Amsterdam and began recording there. He also began performing live, touring North America in 1981 with a white reggae band, the Terrorists, and the following year with another such act, the Majestics. With the latter he recorded his first album in several years, *Mystic Miracle Star,* released on Heartbeat in 1982. Returning to Island, Perry put out *History, Mystery, and Prophecy,* in 1984, but it did not do well.

Perry the Legend

In 1985 Perry once again split with his employer when he put out "Judgment in Babylon," a recording that accused his boss of various evils. "Perry's already shaky deal with the label crumbled when he swore that Island head Chris Blackwell was a vampire and responsible for Bob Marley's death," declared his biography. The accusations only intensified the legend surrounding Perry, and during these years he became a cult figure across Europe. He signed with the Trojan label, and for them released *Battle of Armagideon* in 1986. That same year a compilation of his earliest works was released on Heartbeat, *Some of the Best (1968-1974).* It featured numerous classic reggae tracks and Perry standards that helped connect American rhythm and blues with Jamaican reggae.

In 1987 Perry teamed with English producer Adrian Sherwood to make *Time Boom X De Devil Dead,* recorded with Sherwood's house band, Dub Syndicate. Sherwood had been greatly influenced by early Perry tracks, and the collaboration was a successful one and produced an avant-garde compilation. Perry relocated to Zurich, Switzerland in 1989 with his new wife, a Swiss woman named Mireille Ruegg who also became his manager. He also began building a studio there that he named Blue Ark. That year Heartbeat released another compilation of his early works, *Chicken Scratch.* The record contained tracks done with Rita Marley and the Soulettes as well as with the Wailers. Some of them had not been released in over two decades, while others had never been released at all. One track, "Man to Man," featured Perry with the legends Bob Marley and Peter Tosh singing together.

Perry the Sage

Perry grew increasing eccentric in his middle age. He is known for his unusual pronouncements: he once said that God is black, since the vinyl LP is made of black plastic. "I am the black culture man, super art, super tart, super mind," Perry told Doug Wendt from *Beat* magazine in one interview. "Didn't you hear the words flying like peas?" he said later. Once, he put a microphone in a palm tree to capture what he said was the "living African heartbeat," according to Pareles in the *New York Times.* Perry also renewed his ties with Clement Coxsone Dodd and recorded in New York, but the result, *The Upsetter & The Beat,* was plagued by legal problems.

Perry has continued to make his own records. As a solo artist, "his songs are cagey, cranky rants," wrote the *New York Times's* Pareles. "They're full of advice, messianic pronouncements, come-ons and doggerel, with lucid nuggets surrounded by malarkey." The one exception to this may be his fruitful collaborations with the English producer known as the Mad Professor, which began in the late 1980s. The Mad Professor, a Briton of Guyanan heritage named Neal Fraser and fellow studio genius, runs the Ariwa label. With him Perry has released three records, beginning with *Mystic Warrior* in 1989.

Perry remains a legendary figure in music. The Beastie Boys released a Lee Perry retrospective on their Grand Royal label in 1996, and in the spring of 1997 he signed on with the band's Tibetan Freedom Concert to appear in the New York benefit show. Perry's sold-out shows in San Francisco, held just prior to the Tibetan Freedom Concert, were his first American appearances in over a decade. Afterward, he embarked upon an extensive tour. A three-CD compilation released in 1997 on Island, *Arkology*, featured much of his successful production work for other bands in the 1970s as well as numerous unreleased tracks.

Selected discography

(with the Upsetters)

Super Ape, Mango, 1976.
Roast Fish Collie Weed and Corn Bread, Jamaican Upsetters, 1976.
Cloak and Dagger Dutch Black Art, 1979, Anachron, 1990.
Scratch on the Wire, Island, 1979.
The Return of Pipecock Jackxon, Dutch Black Art, 1980.
The Upsetter Collection, Trojan, 1981.
Scratch and Co.: Chapter One, Jamaican Clocktower, 1982.
Mystic Miracle Star, Heartbeat, 1982.
History, Mystery and Prophecy, Mango, 1984.
Reggae Greats, Mango, 1984.
The Upsetter Box, Trojan, 1985.
Battle of Armagideon, Millionaire Liquidator, Trojan, 1986.
Some of the Best (1968-1974), Heartbeat, 1986.
Time Boom X De Devil Dead, On-U Sound, 1987.
Satan Kicked the Bucket, Bullwackies, 1988, Rohit, 1990.
All the Hits, Rohit, 1989.
Chicken Scratch, Heartbeat, 1989.
Build the Ark, UK Trojan, 1990.
From the Secret Laboratory, Mango, 1990.
Message from Yard, Rohit, 1990.
Lord God Muzick, Heartbeat, 1991.
Revolution Dub, Lagoon, 1993.

(with Mad Professor)

Mystic Warrior, RAS, 1989.
Mystic Warrior Dub, ROIR, 1990.
Black Ark Experryments, Ariwa/Ras, 1995.
Super Ape Inna Jungle, Ariwa, 1995.

(as Jah Lion)

Colombia Colly, Mango, 1976.

Other

"Judgment in Babylon," 12-inch, 1985.
Arkology (3-CD set), Island, 1997.

Sources

Books

Guinness Encyclopedia of Popular Music, edited by Colin Larkin, Guinness Publishing, 1992.

Periodicals

New York Times, November 4, 1997, sec. E, p. 5.
People, September 22, 1997, p. 32.

Online

http://homepage.oanet.com/sleeper/bio.htm
http://www.rollingstone.com
Sleeper, Mick, biography of Lee Perry, http://www.leeperry.com
http://www.trouserpress.com

—Carol Brennan

Ann Petry

1909–1997

Novelist

Ann Petry became the first African American woman to write a best-selling novel. Her 1946 work *The Street,* a tragic story set on a block in Harlem, earned her comparisons to *Native Son* author Richard Wright. In their fiction, both writers demonstrated just how difficult it was for an African American to achieve a dignified, moderately prosperous existence, when racism and violence threatened them from all sides. Petry developed her sympathetic views of black urban life from her own experiences living and working in New York City as a newspaper reporter for prominent black news publications in the 1930s and 1940s. She later fled both the city and her literary fame, retreating back to the small New England town that had been home to several generations of her family.

Ann Lane Petry was born in Old Saybrook, Connecticut, in 1909. She belonged to one of only a handful of African American families in the posh seaside town, where her father had owned a drugstore since the turn of the century. Petry's grandfather was a chemist, and an aunt and uncle were pharmacists like her father. Her mother was first a chiropodist, then began her own linen business. Petry thus grew up in a pleasant, middle-class atmosphere, and planned to enter the family business. A high school teacher, whom Petry later said did not particularly like her, read Petry's assigned piece of fiction aloud to the class and informed her she possessed the talent to become a writer. But when Petry graduated in 1929, she enrolled in the University of Connecticut, and five years later received her doctorate in pharmacy. For the next few years, she worked as pharmacist at family-owned drugstores in Old Saybrook and Lyme, Connecticut, still harboring the dream of writing for a living. During her spare time she penned short stories.

A Wake-Up Call

Ann Lane married George Petry, a writer, in February of 1938, and with her new husband she moved to New York City. Here, far from the quaint towns of the Connecticut shore, she met with her first experiences of just how the majority of African Americans lived during the era. In 1939 she was hired at the *Amsterdam News,* an important African American newspaper, as an advertising salesperson and ad copywriter. Within a few

At a Glance...

Born October 12, 1909, in Old Saybrook, CT; died after a brief illness, April 28, 1997, in Old Saybrook, CT; daughter of Peter C. (a pharmacist and business owner) and Bertha (a barber, chiropodist and business owner; maiden name, James) Lane; married George David Petry, February 22, 1938; children: Elisabeth. *Education:* University of Connecticut, D.Phar., 1934.

Career: Pharmacist at family-owned drugstores in Old Saybrook and Lyme, CT, c. 1934-37; *Amsterdam News*, New York City, began as advertising salesperson and ad copywriter, c. 1939-40; *People's Voice*, New York City, news reporter and editor of women's section, c. 1941; taught at the Young Men's Christian Association; member of American Negro Theatre; founded Negro Women Incorporated (a legislative watchdog group), 1941; first short story under own name published in *The Crisis*, November, 1943; first novel, *The Street*, published by Houghton Mifflin, 1946.

Awards: Houghton Mifflin Literary Fellowship, 1945, for *The Street*.

years she had moved on to another Harlem-focused paper, the *People's Voice*, where she was both a news reporter and editor of its women's section. As a street reporter, she saw firsthand the poverty and terrible circumstances under which many African Americans were forced to live, including unsafe, overpriced housing, police who turned a blind eye to crime, sexual harassment, and chronic unemployment. She spent several years as a reporter before leaving to pursue other career options, including studying painting, founding a legislative watchdog group aimed at African American women, writing and acting in productions with the American Negro Theatre, and teaching business writing courses. She also continued to write fiction.

Petry also became involved in an experimental afterschool program at P.S. 10, a Harlem elementary school on West 116th Street. It was designed to help latchkey children—children whose mothers worked and whose fathers were often absent, or who worked several jobs. Petry pointed out in her first novel, "White folks haven't liked to give black men jobs that paid enough for them to support their families." These children were forced to spend their after-school hours on their own. Much of what she saw during her involvement with the program—especially how such children became easy targets for either abuse and recruitment into criminal activity—became the basis for her first novel.

"I had lived my whole life without paying any attention," Petry said of her affluent upbringing in a 1992 *New York Times* interview with Esther B. Fein. "It wasn't my life. But once I became aware, I couldn't see anything but." The short stories she wrote were now inspired by newspaper clippings, and she met with success when "On Saturday, the Sirens at Noon," appeared in the November 1943 issue of *The Crisis*. An editor at the publishing house Houghton Mifflin read it and contacted her, inquiring as to whether she was working on a novel. George Petry was serving in the Armed Forces at the time, so Petry took a job writing copy for a wig and hairpiece catalog to put together a nest egg, and a year later she gave Houghton Mifflin an outline and five chapters for *The Street*. In turn, they gave her a $2400 fellowship to complete it.

First Novel a Sensation

When it appeared in early 1946, *The Street* quickly became the first best-selling novel ever written by an African American woman. Set in Harlem on the very same stretch of West 116th Street as P.S. 10, it follow the tragic story of a single mother, Lutie Johnson, and her eight-year-old son Bub after Lutie's husband leaves her. She is forced to work long hours, and worries constantly about Bub and the dangers he faces on the streets near their apartment. She harbors a dream of becoming a nightclub singer, earning enough money to escape poverty, and some day sending Bub to a prestigious college. Lutie also finds a role model in Benjamin Franklin, the eighteenth-century American inventor and statesman, who demonstrated how success can come through hard work and honest living. Lutie watches as her neighbor prospers in running a brothel out of her apartment. Bub, like most of his Harlem playmates, eventually wanders down the wrong path. "And they should have been playing in wide stretches of green park and instead they were in the street," Petry wrote. "And the street reached out and sucked them up."

The Street sold 1.5 million copies and was an overnight literary sensation. "*The Street* was a story, not propaganda, wrote Ray Rickman in *American Visions* decades later, "and it was a truer, more intelligent depiction of Harlem than most previous writers were able to accomplish." After two decades of dreaming, Petry found her new celebrity status difficult. "I was a black woman at a point in time when being a writer was not usual," Petry told Fein in *New York Times* interview, "and I was besieged. Everyone wanted a part of me." To escape she fled back to Old Saybrook, purchasing a 200-year-old house in 1947.

Further Explored Themes of Racism

That same year her second novel, *A Country Place,* appeared; its plot revolved around a husband who has returned from the war to learn that his wife has committed adultery. Though it also featured non-stereotypical, sympathetic African American protagonists and still tackled socio-economic prejudices, *A Country Place* achieved nowhere near the success of her debut novel. Arthur P. Davis, writing on Petry in his book *From the Dark Tower: Afro-American Writers 1900 to 1960,* placed it "in the tradition of small-town realistic fiction that goes back to [Sinclair Lewis's] *Main Street*.... *A Country Place* deals with the class lines between aristocrats and nobodies, the antiforeign, anti-Roman Catholic prejudices, and the sexual looseness and the ugliness and viciousness found behind the innocent-appearing life in a small town."

Petry's third and last novel also shows the distance Petry had put between herself and urban life. Published in 1953, *The Narrows* featured an interracial relationship, a distinctly risky literary theme for the time. Its African American protagonist, Link Williams, possesses great gifts, including an Ivy League degree, but still faces prejudice. He becomes romantically involved with a white heiress, and he is later found dead. In an essay on Petry for a 1974 issue of *Critique: Studies in Modern Fiction,* Thelma J. Shinn wrote that Petry's "first concern ... is for acceptance and realization of individual possibilities—black and white, male and female. Her novels protest against the entire society which would contrive to make any individual less than human, or even less than he can be."

The Street Still Timely

Over the next few decades, Petry led a quiet life in Old Saybrook. She wrote children's books, including *Tituba of Salem Village,* and *Harriet Tubman: Conductor on the Underground Railroad,* and saw some of her short stories collected into anthologies such as *Legends of the Saints,* published in 1970. *The Street* was reissued in 1991, and its story still resonated with contemporary single mothers in Harlem: "That's not fiction: That's my life," one such woman told Fein. Though by this time Petry was a relative unknown, her debut novel's place in African American literature was assured. *Essence* writer and novelist Veronica Chambers declared that upon her first reading of *The Street* she was reduced to tears. "And yet I also felt a sense of joy," Chambers wrote. "Petry's writing could do that—encompass a world of characters and emotions with such realism that readers claimed them as their own." The novelist Gloria Naylor, who used to visit her grandparents in Harlem only a few blocks away from West 116th Street, told the *New York Times* she never forgot the book's first scene-setting sentences, and said that Petry "captured the forces that work against the black female." Petry died in a convalescent home in Old Saybrook in April of 1997.

Selected writings

The Street, Houghton Mifflin, 1946, reprinted, 1991.
A Country Place, 1947.
The Narrows, 1953, Beacon, 1988.
Miss Muriel and Other Stories, 1971, Beacon, 1989.
Legends of the Saints (collected short stories), 1970.

Sources

Books

Contemporary Literary Criticism, Gale, Volume 1, 1973, Volume 7, 1977, Volume 18, 1981.
Current Biography, edited by Anna Rothe, H.W. Wilson, 1946.
Davis, Arthur P., *From the Dark Tower: Afro-American Writers 1900 to 1960,*

Periodicals

African American Review, Fall 1992, pp. 495-504.
American Visions, February 1990, p. 56.
Critique: Studies in Modern Fiction, 1974.
Essence, August 1997, p. 148.
New York Times, January 8, 1992; April 30, 1997, p. B9.

—Carol Brennan

Andy Razaf

1895–1973

Lyricist

Popular song lyricist Andy Razaf is best remembered today as the collaborator of pianist and composer Fats Waller. These two men produced numerous hit songs during the 1920s and 1930s, including the classics "Ain't Misbehavin'," "Honeysuckle Rose," and "Black and Blue." Razaf, who lived in obscurity for much of his later life, was much more than just Waller's collaborator. Recent research on Razaf's life has shown that he was an integral part of Harlem's entertainment scene during the late 1920s—a zone of African American creativity that provided crucial underpinnings for the wider American music industry.

As a lyricist, Razaf was something of an anomaly: within the popular-music field, African Americans have been celebrated largely for their musical rather than their poetic contributions. His early life might have given any observer a clue, though, that he was destined for unusual things. Andy Razaf was born Andreamentania Paul Razafkeriefo in Washington, D.C., on December 15, 1895. He had been conceived on Madagascar, an island off the coast of eastern Africa, and was a descendant of Madagascar's Queen Ranavalona.

Descendant of Queen of Madagascar

Razaf's paternal grandfather, John Waller (no relation to Fats Waller), was a Kansas politician and one of several blacks who gained prominence during the Reconstruction Era. As a reward for his work during Benjamin Harrison's presidential campaign in 1888, Waller was appointed U.S. Consul to Madagascar in 1891. He quickly became a close friend of Madagascar's royal family and arranged the marriage of his teenaged daughter to the nephew of Queen Ranavalona. Waller's daughter became pregnant and eventually moved to Washington, where she gave birth to Razaf.

As a teenager, Razaf settled in New York with his mother. While working as an elevator operator in an office building, he was able to sell a song he wrote, "Baltimo", to the James Kendis music-publishing firm. The successful sale of "Baltimo" inspired Razaf to consider a career as a songwriter.

After a brief stint as a semiprofessional baseball player in Cleveland, Razaf returned to New York to become a

At a Glance...

Born Andreamentania Paul Razafkeriefo in Washington, DC, on December 15, 1895; died February 3, 1973, in Los Angeles, CA.

Career: Popular song lyricist, creator or co-creator of over 800 songs; published song, "Baltimo'," at age 17; semiprofessional baseball player in Cleveland; 1920; collaborated with composers Eubie Blake, James P. Johnson, Paul Denniker, and Thomas "Fats" Waller, early 1920s; with Waller created Broadway revue *Keep Shufflin'*, 1928; hired with Waller to furnish music for Connie's Inn, premier Harlem nightclub, 1928; revue *Hot Feet* moved to Broadway as *Hot Chocolates*, 1929; set lyrics to jazz instrumentals, 1930s; paralyzed by a seizure, 1951.

songwriter. He sought out musical collaborators and found several who were interested in working with him. Razaf worked closely with pianists James P. Johnson and Eubie Blake, the white English composer Paul Denniker and Thomas "Fats" Waller, whom he met in 1921 after Waller won a piano contest at Harlem's Roosevelt Theatre. Many of these collaborative relationships flourished for years.

Wrote Blues Songs

Razaf's reputation as a songwriter blossomed throughout the 1920s. He was able to sell several songs each year to established publishing houses and also composed hundreds of blues lyrics, many of which were mildly risque, for tavern floor shows and theatrical presentations. These blues songs, of which the Razaf-Waller title "Ice Cold Papa, Mama's Gonna Melt You Down" is a noteworthy example, were less prestigious for Razaf than more popular mainstream songs. However, they did provide him with a recognizable presence within New York musical circles both in Harlem and on Broadway. Razaf often worried that his blues songs promoted negative stereotypes of African Americans, but they were often performed by legendary blues vocalist Bessie Smith and blues revivalist Alberta Hunter.

In the late 1920s, at the peak of his collaborative relationship with Waller, Razaf reached the high point of his career. The pair's 1928 revue *Keep Shufflin'*, a sequel to the classic Noble Sissle–Eubie Blake stage show *Shuffle Along*, opened on Broadway. Razaf and Waller were also hired to write musical revues for Connie's Inn in Harlem. Connie's Inn was the chief competitor of the famous Cotton Club, which nurtured many black musical careers but employed only white songwriters. Razaf and Waller's revue *Hot Feet* became a smashing success and made an appearance on Broadway. The Broadway show, renamed *Hot Chocolates*, featured the song "Ain't Misbehavin'," which became a huge hit for renowned trumpeter Louis Armstrong. The song, with its relaxed avowal of romantic fidelity, provided a refreshing change from the racy blues lyrics that white audiences had earlier demanded.

Hot Chocolates also included the song "Black and Blue," which was written at the request of gangster Dutch Schultz. Schultz had provided financial backing for the show and wanted a new song added for the show's Broadway premiere. To emphasize the seriousness of his request, Schultz put a gun to Razaf's head. The poignant lyrics of "Black and Blue" were hardly to Schultz's liking. However, when the song became a commercial success, his anger cooled quickly.

Put Lyrics to Instrumental Tunes

Razaf continued to experience success during the early 1930s. He collaborated with Eubie Blake on the *Blackbirds of 1930* revue, which included the pop standard "Memories of You." In 1936, *Variety* magazine reported that Razaf's songs had been played 20,836 times on the radio during the previous year, an impressive showing. As a new form of instrumental music called swing swept the nation, Razaf left his mark by providing lyrics to some well-known band standards, including "Stompin' at the Savoy" and "In the Mood."

As the 1940s dawned, Razaf's career began to steadily decline. His lucrative collaboration with Fats Waller waned after Waller's white managers encouraged him to work with other songwriters. Waller also embarked upon a grueling touring schedule, a schedule that may have contributed to his untimely death in 1943.

Shortly after moving to Los Angeles in 1951, Razaf suffered a syphilitic seizure and was paralyzed. For the next two decades, he was confined to a wheelchair. He continued to write songs and prose and often lamented that he had never been able to realize his full potential. On February 3, 1973, Andy Razaf died of kidney failure. Since his death, revivals of musical revues such as *Ain't Misbehavin'* and *Souvenirs of Hot Chocolates* have rekindled interest in Razaf and his career. Ironically, Razaf's contributions to the world of music have received more attention since his death than when he was alive. Razaf's nearly 800 song lyrics represent a priceless legacy of African American poetic art.

Selected compositions

(as lyricist)

"Ain't Misbehavin'".
"Black and Blue".
"Honeysuckle Rose".
"I'd Give a Dollar for a Dime".
"In the Mood".
"Kitchen Man".
"Stompin' at the Savoy".

Sources

Books

Larkin, Colin, ed., *Guinness Encyclopedia of Popular Music,* Guinness, 1992,
Singer, Barry, *Black and Blue: The Life and Lyrics of Andy Razaf,* Schirmer, 1992.

Periodicals

Billboard, February 6, 1993.
New York Times, February 5, 1973; February 8, 1989, p. C19.
New York Times Book Review, January 3, 1993, p. 8.

—James M. Manheim

J. Paul Reason

1943

Navy admiral

J. Paul Reason, the Navy's first four-star Admiral and Commander of the Atlantic Fleet, was born and raised in Washington D.C. His father Joseph, a former professor of Romance Languages and the holder of a Ph.D., was the director of university libraries at Howard University. His mother Bernice taught science in the Washington D.C. public school system. As a child Reason was drawn to the sea—fishing, crabbing, swimming, or just hanging out on a pier.

In the Navy Reason found a perfect marriage of two of the most prominent influences of his life—education and the ocean. After graduating from high school he did not immediately enlist in the Navy or apply for the Naval Academy, but went to Howard University. He spent three years at Howard before Representative Charles Diggs, a congressman from Michigan, nominated him for the Naval Academy. Reason was accepted and had to start over academically as a freshman. Reason graduated from Annapolis in 1965, but he had previously decided to stay in school and try to enter the Navy's nuclear propulsion program.

In applying for the prestigious program Reason was put to the test by Vice Admiral Hyman G. Rickover, the creator of the nuclear submarine. Reason, who now credits Rickover with helping his career, said that their first meeting was not so comfortable for the young officer in training. Rickover lit into Reason for not being ranked higher in his class with all of his previous education. Rickover told him that he could enter the training program if he promised to improve his class-standing by 20 places. Reason kept his cool and responded that it was impossible to make a promise on that issue because no matter how well he performed, he had no control over the 20 students ahead of him. Rickover became furious at the cool and logical Reason and threw him out of his office. But Reason did not leave the building. One of Rickover's aides told the young midshipman to stay around and hours later a different officer entered the room with a note. Reason told Hans J. Massaquoi of *Ebony* what the deputy told him: "Admiral Rickover says you can have the nuclear power program if will sign this statement that says, 'I swear I will increase my class standing 20 numbers by graduation.'" Reason looked at the statement which guaranteed him entry into the much-coveted program and crossed it out. In its place he wrote: "I will do everything in my power

At a Glance...

Born Joseph Paul Reason in 1943 in Washington, D.C.; son of Joseph (a college professor) and Bernice (a teacher); married in 1965 to Dianne; children: Rebecca and Joseph. *Education:* Attended Howard University for three years before attending the U.S. Naval Academy and graduating in 1965; Masters Degree in Computer Systems Management; Defense policy study at Harvard's Kennedy School.

Career: Served on the USS J.D. Blackwood until 1967; Served on the USS Truxtun, 1968-70; served on the USS Enterprise, 1971-75; again on the USS Truxtun, and became an Assignment Officer at the Bureau of Naval Personnel; Naval Aide to the President of the United States 1976-79; named Executive Officer of the USS Mississippi, 1979-85; Commanding Officer of the USS Coontz and the USS Bainbridge; Commander of Naval Base Seattle, 1986-88; Commander of Cruiser-Destroyer Group One, 1988-94, earned three-star rank and was named Commander, Naval Surface Force, U.S. Atlantic Fleet; Deputy Chief of Naval Operations, 1994-96; Promoted to four-star rank and named Commander in Chief, U.S. Atlantic Fleet, December 1996 to present; First African-American to earn four-star rank in the U.S. Navy.

Awards: First African American to earn four-star rank in the U.S. Navy. Distinguished Service Medal, Legion of Merit, Navy Commendation Medal, the Venezuelan La Medulla Naval Almirante Luis Brion Medal, the Republic of Vietnam Honor Medal, the Navy Unit Commendation, Navy "E", National Defense Service Medal, Armed Forces Expeditionary Medal, the Sea Services Deployment Ribbon, the Republic of Vietnam Meritorious Unit Citation, and the Republic of Vietnam Campaign Medal.

Addresses: *Residence*—Norfolk, VA; *Naval Office*—Commander in Chief, U.S. Atlantic Fleet, 1562 Mitscher Ave., Ste. 250, Norfolk, VA 23551-2487

to improve my class standing by 20 numbers." Rickover's aide tore up the paper and had his secretary type up the first oath again. Reason held his ground knowing that he would be agreeing to something over which he had no control. For the second time in one day he was thrown out of a high-ranking officer's office, but Rickover must have been impressed by something. The next day Reason's name was the third one posted on the list of candidates who had been accepted into the program. Not only did Reason take an enormous step in his Naval career in 1965, but he also got married three days after his graduation from the academy. The new Dianne Reason taught elementary school and was used to military life being the daughter of an Army officer.

On to Active Duty

Reason served as Operations Officer in the destroyer escort USS J.D. Blackwood. After he completed his nuclear training in 1968 he was transferred to the nuclear powered guided missile cruiser the USS Truxtun and immediately sent to Southeast Asia. In 1970 Reason earned a masters degree in computer systems management. He shipped out again in 1971 to Southeast Asia this time on the nuclear powered aircraft carrier, the USS Enterprise. Reason rejoined the crew of the USS Truxtun as the Combat Systems Officer and then went on to the Bureau of Naval Personnel as an Assignment Officer.

Before Christmas in 1976 Reason joined the administration of President Gerald R. Ford as Naval Aide to the White House. When Jimmy Carter took over in 1977 Reason kept his position until going back to the sea in 1979. Reason was named the Executive Officer of the USS Mississippi and then became Commanding Officer of the USS Coontz. From that assignment he assumed command of the USS Bainbridge, a nuclear powered guided missile cruiser. It was at the helm of the USS Bainbridge that Reason met another man who influenced his career—Mike Boorda, the man who would eventually become chief of naval operations. Reason told Rudi Williams of *Sea Services Weekly* about his relationship with the other future admiral: "We got to know West Africa and each other quite well. A bond formed, first a professional bond, then a personal bond. He was the most capable naval officer I ever went to sea with. He knew how to do everything. But at the same time, I was a better engineer because I'd spent most of my time running propulsion plants in cruisers and aircraft carriers ... With his operational expertise and my ability to solve engineering problems, it was a very professionally rewarding cruise to West Africa, the Mediterranean, and the Black Sea."

From 1986 through 1988 Reason was in charge of all naval activities in Washington, Oregon, and Alaska as Commander of Cruiser-Destroyer Group One. At this time he also led Battle Group Romeo through operations in the Pacific and Indian Oceans and the Persian Gulf. As a result of his continued excellence, Reason earned a three-star rank along with the command of the Naval Surface Force of the U.S. Atlantic Fleet. He was then named the Deputy Chief of Naval Operations in August of 1994.

A Four-Star Pioneer

In December of 1996 President Clinton nominated Reason to become the first African American naval officer to achieve the four-star rank. With the elevation in rank Reason was also named Commander in Chief of the Atlantic Fleet—about half of the entire U.S. Navy. Reason overseas a multi-billion dollar budget of a naval armada from the North Pole to the South Pole, the Mediterranean and Caribbean Seas, South America, the African Coast, and the Persian Gulf. He is in charge of the majority of U.S. naval bases along the East and Gulf Coasts in the United States, Puerto Rico, Cuba, and Iceland. In total he is responsible for over 120,000 soldiers, including 26 admirals, 195 warships, 1,357 aircraft on 18 major naval bases.

As the Commander in Chief of the Atlantic Fleet, Reason has several priorities. He wants to make the Navy more efficient by possibly cutting the size of the crews through the use of technology. In addition to making naval warfare cheaper, he wants to make the Navy quicker through new tactics and innovations. The Admiral also maintains an emphasis on creating a fair environment. Reason told Massaquoi of *Ebony:* "I hold every commanding officer responsible for the environment within his command. And every reporting senior, this is every officer in charge of those in command, must evaluate those commanders on their performance of ensuring equal opportunities." Reason had backed up his claim earlier in his tenure by relieving Rear Admiral Robert S. Cole of his command of the Atlantic Fleet's shore facilities after female employees complained about Cole's inappropriate behavior. In a wave of sexual scandals throughout the armed forces in the late nineties, the 32-year Navy veteran became a key part in restoring the credibility of the services and one of the few high-ranking officers to take meaningful action against this type of behavior.

Admiral Reason, who also served on a panel about the future direction of the U.S. Naval Academy, is the father of two. Despite constantly shipping out to different locations around the world during his climb to the top of the Navy, Reason has stayed happily married to his wife Dianne. His daughter Rebecca is an accountant and his son Joseph also joined the Navy. Reason and his son are believed to be the first African American father and son to graduate from the U.S. Naval Academy. He summed up his enormous responsibilities for Williams of *Sea Services Weekly:* "I represent sailors the best way I know how. My test of everything I do, for every decision I make is, is it good for sailors? If I can't prove it's good for sailors, we shouldn't be spending taxpayers' money. And we don't—as long as it's my decision."

Sources

Periodicals

Ebony, April 1998.
The Virginian-Pilot, August 5, 1997.
The Washington Post, August 12, 1997.

Other

Sea Services Weekly Website at http://www.dcmilitary.com/navy/seaservices/feb27/ss_e22798.htm.

Admiral Reason's Homepage at http://www.lantflt.navy.mil/cinbio.htm.

—Michael J. Watkins

Mitch Richmond

1965—

Professional basketball player

In December of 1995, *Sports Illustrated* ran a feature about Mitch Richmond, in which he was described as an expert basketball impressionist. He has the ability, according to the article, to mimic the style and trademark moves of virtually any NBA player. Although he has never been able to attract the media spotlight, one thing is certain: Mitch Richmond is an extremely talented basketball player.

Mitchell James Richmond was born on June 30, 1965 in Ft. Lauderdale, Florida. Growing up in Ft. Lauderdale, his best friend was another native Floridian destined for sports stardom, wide receiver Michael Irvin of the Dallas Cowboys. Irvin, renowned for his talkative nature, was a perfect foil for the more reserved Richmond. "If you wanted to get in a word when you were with Mike, you had to start early," Richmond was quoted as saying in *Sports Illustrated*. Among Richmond's other friends are NFL standouts Benny and Brian Blades and Brett Perriman.

A Rocky Road to Stardom

Richmond's hometown pals called him Smooth, but his road to the NBA was rocky. His attended three different high schools in the Ft. Lauderdale area. After failing an algebra course during his senior year, he almost did not graduate. Realizing that his basketball future was at stake—and at the not-very-subtle urging of his mother, Ernell—Richmond attended summer school and managed to earn his high school diploma. Richmond's next stop was Moberly Area Junior College in central Missouri. Despite intense homesickness, Richmond averaged 13.1 points per game and led the Greyhounds to a two-year record of 69 wins and 9 losses. While he was a student at Moberly, Richmond became close friends with coach Dana Altman, who advised him to beef up both his body and his academic skills. Following Altman's advice, Richmond worked hard in both the weight room and the classroom. On the court, he perfected his outside shooting and rebounding skills. Richmond's grades eventually improved enough for him to secure a transfer to Kansas State University.

At Kansas State, Richmond's game blossomed offensively. As Hank Hersch of *Sports Illustrated* remarked, "Richmond received the ball and orders to create an offense with it." Playing shooting guard instead of the

> **At a Glance...**
>
> Born Mitchell James Richmond June 30, 1965 in Ft. Lauderdale, FL; mother: Ernell O'Neill; married Juli Richmond; children: Phillip and Jerin. *Education:* Kansas State University, B.A.
>
> **Career:** Professional basketball player, Golden State Warriors, 1988-91; Sacramento Kings, 1991-98; Washington Wizards, 1998-.
>
> **Awards:** NBA Rookie of the Year, 1989; member NBA All-Star Team, 1993-97.
>
> **Addresses:** *Office*—Washington Wizards, MCI Center, 601 F St. NW, Washington D.C. 20071.

forward position he had played earlier in his career, Richmond averaged 20.7 points per game. He was at his best at NCAA tournament time, averaging 26.7 points and 9.2 rebounds per game over two seasons. In his senior season, Kansas State advanced to the Final Eight in the NCAA tournament and Richmond broke the school's single-season scoring record. He was also named a Second-Team All-American, and won a bronze medal as a member of the 1988 U.S. Olympic Team. To the delight of his mother, Richmond graduated from Kansas State with a B.A. in social science.

Found Success in the NBA

Richmond was selected by the Golden State Warriors in the first round of the NBA draft and was the fifth pick overall. Warriors coach Don Nelson made Richmond a starter during his rookie season. He responded by scoring 22 points per game and averaging 5.9 rebounds and 4.2 assists per game. Those numbers were good enough to earn Richmond Rookie of the Year honors for the 1988-89 season, and he was the only player unanimously named to the NBA All-Rookie First Team. Richmond's all-around play was praised by coaches, teammates, and opponents alike. "Mitch is doing just about everything I've asked of him," Nelson was quoted as saying in a 1989 *Sports Illustrated* article. "I need him to be dominant, but in the flow of the team, and he's doing that."

The next season, Richmond continued to shine. He scored 22.1 points per game, and his 4.6 rebounds per game average was best among all NBA guards. He was also named Warriors co-captain along with teammate Chris Mullin. Richmond improved his game once again during the 1990-91 season. He averaged 23.9 points per game, and combined with Mullin and Tim Hardaway to form "Run TMC" (for Tim, Mitch, Chris), one of the most explosive offensive trios in the NBA.

Traded to Sacramento

On the night before the 1991 season opener, the Warriors traded Richmond and center Les Jepsen to the Sacramento Kings for Billy Owens. In an instant, Richmond went from being a valued member of a respectable team to being the only respectable member of an awful team. The adjustment was not an easy one for Richmond. The Kings were not only a perennial loser, but they were also a small-market team. This meant that a star player like Richmond would only receive a fraction of the attention—and the accompanying endorsement money—that a player in a major market like New York, Los Angeles, or Chicago received.

Richmond gradually came to terms with his new situation, and continued to thrive as a player. He finished ninth in the league in scoring in 1991-92, and scored 30 or more points per game a dozen times during the season. The following season, Richmond was selected to play in the NBA All-Star Game, becoming the first Sacramento player to be so honored. In a game two days after the announcement, he suffered a broken thumb. The injury forced Richmond to miss both the All-Star Game and the rest of season.

Richmond more than made up for that disappointment during the 1993-94 campaign. He averaged 23.4 points per game during the season, the seventh best average in the league, and was selected to start in the All-Star Game. He performed even better during the 1994-95 season, when he was named Most Valuable Player in the All-Star Game, turning in a 23-point performance in only 22 minutes of play. Despite Richmond's individual success, however, the Kings continued their losing ways. Sacramento won 39 games, which marked the franchise's best season since it moved from Kansas City in 1985. However, the Kings still failed to qualify for the playoffs. The 1995-96 season brought Richmond more success. His 23.1 points per game average was among the NBA's best for guards, and he was named to the All-Star team for the fourth consecutive year. Richmond also earned a gold medal as a member of the U.S. Olympic squad, which was known as the "Dream Team."

Joined the Washington Wizards

After an incredible 1996-97 season, in which he averaged nearly 26 points per game, Richmond desired a change of scenery. At the age of 31, it was clear that he was entering the latter stages of his career. He also tired of playing for a perennial doormat like Sacramento and clamored for a trade to a team that had a realistic chance of making the playoffs. As the NBA's 1998 winter trade deadline approached, a number of deals for Richmond were proposed. Although a few of the deals were nearly completed, they all eventually fell through.

Richmond's wish was finally granted in May of 1998, when he was traded to the Washington Wizards for their talented, but troubled, star forward Chris Webber. Before he had a chance to enjoy the change of scenery, however, a labor squabble resulting in a lockout of players by team owners threw the 1998-99 season into question. Regardless of the outcome of the dispute, Richmond stands to benefit from the greater media exposure that players in major cities like Washington, D.C. inevitably receive.

Sources

New York Times, February 13, 1995, p. C10; February 26, 1997, p. B11; November 10, 1997, p. C7.
Sporting News, May 22, 1989, p. 39; January 18, 1993, p. 33; January 15, 1996, p. 37.
Sports Illustrated, February 6, 1989, p. 20; March 9, 1998, p. 100; May 25, 1998, p. 98.
Time, December 18, 1995, p. 73.
Washington Post, May 15, 1998, p. A1.

—Robert R. Jacobson

Marcus Roberts

1963—

Jazz pianist

Possibly no pianist in jazz today is doing more important work than Marcus Roberts. Generally associated with the neoclassical movement championed by his former mentor, trumpet player Wynton Marsalis, Roberts has emerged as a chief proponent in his own right of the trend toward recapturing the best elements of earlier jazz forms. While he has based the early phase of his career on a mastery of the music of such past giants as Thelonious Monk, Art Tatum, Duke Ellington, and George Gershwin, Roberts stands poised to help synthesize a new blend of music that uses earlier styles as a platform from which to launch jazz in previously unexplored directions.

Roberts was born on August 7, 1963 in Jacksonville, Florida. The younger of two brothers, Roberts went blind from cataracts at the age of four. His mother, a gospel singer at a local church, had gone blind while in her teens. When Roberts was five years old, he began to play on the church organ. His parents noticed this interest in music, and three years later, to encourage their son's involvement, they bought a piano. Roberts began teaching himself to play, spending hours on end at the keyboard. Within a year, he was good enough to give his first public performance, a recital at the church.

Converted to Jazz by Ellington, Tatum

Roberts began taking formal piano lessons at the age of 12 while attending a state school for the blind and deaf in St. Augustine, Florida. After a year of classical piano training, Roberts suddenly was converted to jazz. Scanning radio stations idly one day, he came across a broadcast of music by the great Duke Ellington. "I said to myself then and there, 'That's the kind of music I want to learn how to play,'" Roberts was quoted as saying in a 1989 *Esquire* article. He began collecting all the jazz he could find over the next few years. One of his most important early influences was stride piano wizard Art Tatum. The first time Roberts heard a recording of Tatum, he recounted in *Time,* his response was "Does he have three hands?"

After graduating from high school, Roberts enrolled at Florida State University in Tallahassee, where he began studying piano with Leonidus Lipovetsky. While on a European tour with some high school jazz musicians, Roberts met trumpet player and composer Wynton

At a Glance...

Born Marthaniel Roberts, on August 7, 1963, in Jacksonville, FL; son of a longshoreman and a gospel singer; *Education:* Attended Florida State University.

Career: Toured Europe with high school jazz musicians, c. 1982; toured and recorded with Wynton Marsalis, 1985-91; recorded first album as leader, *The Truth is Spoken Here,* 1989; RCA/Novus recording artist, 1989-94; music dir., Lincoln Center Jazz Orchestra, 1994; Sony/Columbia recording artist, 1994-.

Awards: Great American Piano Competition, Jacksonville, FL, first prize, 1982; Thelonious Monk International Piano Competition, first prize, 1987.

Addresses: *Office*—Sony/Columbia, 51 W. 52nd St., New York, NY 10019.

Marsalis, who was performing at the Montreux Jazz Festival. The following year, Roberts encountered Marsalis's father, pianist Ellis Marsalis, at the 1982 convention of the International Association of Jazz Educators. Through the senior Marsalis, Roberts renewed his acquaintance with Wynton, and the two musicians developed an ongoing dialog about the history and future of jazz.

Meanwhile, Roberts continued to hone his skills at Florida State. He entered and won a handful of piano competitions, including Jacksonville's Great American Competition in 1982. In 1985, during his senior year of college, Roberts was invited to join Marsalis's band for touring and recording, replacing keyboardist Kenny Kirkland. By this time, Roberts had already taken it upon himself to learn the entire Marsalis repertoire, and he eagerly accepted the offer. During his tenure with the Marsalis group, Roberts performed at clubs and festivals throughout the United States, Europe, and Asia. He contributed to several albums, including *J Mood, Marsalis Standard Time, Vol. 1,* and *Live at Blues Alley.* He also found time to undertake an intensive study of the music of Thelonious Monk during this period. The result of this project was a first place finish in the first Thelonious Monk International Jazz Piano Competition in Washington, D.C. in 1987. His renditions of the Monk classics "'Round Midnight" and "Blue Boulevard Blues" earned him a victory over 21 other contestants, and $10,000 in prize money.

Solo Career Boosted by Marsalis

Roberts toured and recorded with Marsalis from 1985 to 1991. It was toward the end of this span that he launched his solo recording career. His first album, *The Truth is Spoken Here,* was released in 1989. His supporting band on the album included both Wynton Marsalis and his brother, trombonist Delfeayo Marsalis. By jazz standards, the album sold extremely well, especially for a first effort. It quickly rose to the top of the *Billboard* jazz chart. Roberts released his next album, *Deep in the Shed,* the following year. Like its predecessor, it was a top seller among jazz recordings. Both albums revealed a developing style that was both cerebral—a bit too cerebral for some critics—and soulful. Comparisons to Monk, whose material was included on both projects, were common. Philip Booth, writing for *Down Beat* in 1990, observed that "if chops, swing, maturity, inspiration, and compositional skills are the qualifications, Roberts has arrived, or at the minimum has established himself as one young jazz pianist with much to offer."

Roberts maintained his streak with a third straight number one jazz album, *Alone With Three Giants,* released in 1991. This album, which made Roberts the first artist ever to see his first three projects top the jazz charts, was a solo piano album featuring the works of three of the most celebrated composers in the history of jazz: Monk, Duke Ellington, and Jelly Roll Morton. Later that year, Roberts put out *Prayer for Peace,* a solo Christmas album. Continuing to record at a feverish pace, he released the album *As Serenity Approaches,* a collection of solos and duets including pieces by Ellington, Morton, Fats Waller, Cole Porter, and others, in 1992. Roberts' next effort was the 1993 release, *If I Could Be With You,* which included several original compositions in addition to works by Ellington, Monk, and other standards. It also featured six challenging stride piano pieces by stride pioneer James P. Johnson. Roberts's performance on this album moved *People* magazine to laud "his ability to make his own brimming compositions sound as if they have always existed, and always will."

The key philosophical approach that Roberts shares with Marsalis, and which his work with Marsalis helped to solidify, is a thorough respect for jazz tradition. "To me, it has to begin with the blues and swing for me to deal with it," Roberts was quoted as saying in a 1993 *Orlando Sentinel* interview. "I think Duke Ellington felt the same way; I think Monk felt the same way, Coltrane—all kinds of other folks. Beethoven felt that way, Haydn, Mozart—you're dealing with the essential component of something sacred." As his recording career continued to gather steam, Roberts's live performances became major events as well. On August 7, 1993—which happened to be his 30th birthday—Roberts premiered his 70-minute commissioned composition "Romance, Swing, and the Blues" as part of the Classical Jazz Series at Lincoln Center in New York. The *New York Post* described the piece as "a rich, life-filled, and quite absorbing extended work." During the winter of 1994, Roberts served as music director for the 19-member Lincoln Center Jazz Orchestra during its nationwide tour of the United States.

Jumped Labels for Gershwin Tribute

After recording his first six albums on the Novus label, Roberts jumped over to Columbia in 1994 to record *Gershwin for Lovers,* a collection of standards, recorded as a trio, by composer George Gershwin. The album reached number one on the jazz charts, selling more than 70,000 copies, spectacular numbers for a jazz recording. His involvement in all things Gershwinian led to a performance with the American Symphony Orchestra of "'I Got Rhythm' Variations," a new interpretation of the Gershwin classic. In 1996 Roberts released two albums simultaneously. *Portraits in Blue,* essentially a follow up to *Gershwin for Lovers,* featured new takes on another batch of Gershwin tunes, in particular a radical transformation of "Rhapsody In Blue." Columbia marketed this recording as a classical album, putting Roberts in a special category of crossover artists exemplified by former associate Wynton Marsalis. Roberts's other 1996 product, *Time and Circumstance,* was an album of original compositions for jazz trio. Critics lauded the maturity of his writing and playing as well as Roberts' grasp of jazz idioms. Wrote Peter Watrous of the *New York Times,* "Marcus Roberts's idiosyncratic, two-handed style sums up the possibilities of jazz in an age of nearly unlimited information."

With the release of *Blues for a New Millennium* in 1997, Roberts cemented his reputation as a leading figure in neoclassical jazz, second in stature only to Marsalis. Even his harshest critics were so pleasantly shocked by *Blues.* While his previous efforts had left no doubt about his technical virtuosity, his mastery of various jazz idioms of the past, or even his own talent as a composer paying tribute to those traditions, questions remained regarding his ability to forge that body of expertise into music that was truly groundbreaking. Writing in *Emerge,* Gene Seymour noted that *Blues* was the album that finally erased his reservations about Roberts' brilliance. "Damned if this wasn't the kind of music that burned on contact," he remarked. "... [H]e seems to have finally taken everything he's learned from his masters and merged it with his own somewhat startling intensity of feeling," Seymour continued. As audiences prepare for a new millennium of listening, they will certainly be expecting further fireworks, rooted in the best of what jazz has to offer, from Marcus Roberts.

Selected discography

The Truth is Spoken Here, Novus, 1989.
Deep in the Shed, Novus, 1990.
Alone With Three Giants, Novus, 1991.
Prayer for Peace, Novus, 1991.
As Serenity Approaches, Novus, 1992.
If I Could Be With You, Novus, 1993.
Gershwin for Lovers, Columbia, 1994.
Time and Circumstance, Columbia, 1996.
Portraits in Blue, Sony Classical, 1996.
Blues for a New Millennium, Columbia, 1997.

(with Wynton Marsalis)

J Mood, Columbia, 1987.
Marsalis Standard Time, Vol. 1, Columbia, 1987.
Live at Blues Alley, Columbia, 1988.
Intimacy Calling, Standard Time, Vol. 2, Columbia.
The Resolution of Romance, Standard Time, Vol. 3, Columbia.
Blue Interlude, Columbia.

Sources

American Visions, April-May 1994, p. 46.
Billboard, May 25, 1996, p. 1.
Christian Science Monitor, March 31, 1992, p. 11.
Down Beat, April 1990, p. 20; July 1996, p. 19. January 1998, p. 52.
Emerge, May 1998, p. 69.
Esquire, September 1989, p. 153.
National Review, September 2, 1996, p. 96.
New York Times, May 14, 1995, p. 28.
Orlando Sentinel, July 13, 1993.
Time, July 17, 1989, p. 85; June 17, 1996, p. 91.

—Robert R. Jacobson

Patrick Robinson

1966—

Fashion designer

Before he turned 30, Patrick Robinson was designing collections for one of the premier names in American sportswear. When the line folded, however, Robinson found himself out of work but with a headful of ideas. The obvious talent that had helped him secure such a plum job in the first place also helped him land a deal with an apparel manufacturer to produce his own line; then the business-savvy designer worked out of his home for several months to produce and show a collection finally under his own name, which was met with positive reviews. "Watch this guy," declared *Harper's Bazaar* writers Jennifer Jackson and Andrea Linett. "He has the potential for first-name designer status."

Robinson was born in Memphis in 1966, but grew up southeast of Los Angeles in the affluent area of Orange County. His father was a doctor, and Robinson, one in a family of five, went to high school in Fullerton and worked at the Nordstrom department store at the Cerritos mall as a teen. It was a fashion-conscious family, he told Rose-Marie Turk of the *Los Angeles Times*—his parents, he said, "subscribed to every magazine in the world and we had a big library." In addition to working at the mall, Robinson also loved to surf, and began his own line of surferwear. He decided to pursue a career as a fashion designer in earnest when he saw a film that featured such homegrown American talent as Calvin Klein and Jeffrey Banks.

Robinson was accepted into the renowned Parsons School of Design in New York City, and also spent time at the American College in Paris. While there, he worked for an up-and-coming young African American designer named Patrick Kelly as his first assistant. After finishing school, Robinson worked for the design houses Albert Nippon and Herman Geist, and was hired by noted Italian designer Giorgio Armani for his bridge line, Le Collezioni. He got the job only when he agreed to start the next day, and had to fly to Italy on extremely short notice. He completed an entire season's worth of clothes just ten days after arriving. "I've done a lot at a young age, but I pushed myself hard, and I gave up a lot of my personal life for my work," Robinson admitted to Julia Chance in *Essence*.

Donna Karan's Footsteps

Being associated with the Armani name, Robinson recognized, was an invaluable experience. "In the '90s,

> ### At a Glance...
>
> Born September 8, 1966, in Memphis, TN. *Education:* Received degree from Parsons School of Design; also attended the American College in Paris.
>
> **Career:** Worked at Nordstrom department store, Cerritos, CA, mid-1980s; affiliated with designer Patrick Kelly, Paris, and with design houses Albert Nippon and Herman Geist, all 1980s; Le Collezioni White Label by Giorgio Armani, Turin, Italy, design director, c. 1990-94; Anne Klein Collection, New York City, designer, 1994-96; launched own collection, 1997.
>
> **Addresses:** *Office*—Patrick Robinson, Inc., 84 Wooster St., Suite 205, New York, NY 10012.

Robinson was responsible for many of the Giorgio Armani power suits that female big shots have relied upon when dealmaking and strong-arming," wrote the *Washington Post*'s Robin Givhan. In late 1994, he was wooed away from Le Collezioni by the Japanese owners of the Anne Klein Collection. The New York-based design house was one of the top purveyors of classic executive gear for American women, but in the 1990s had fallen on hard times. Its image had suffered as its look grew to be considered a bit too staid. The company had hired a Hollywood designer, Richard Tyler, to revitalize it, but the move backfired and the collection was critiqued as too young, too sexy, for the true Anne Klein loyalist. Tyler was unceremoniously fired from the Collection in late 1994 after sales plummeted, and Robinson, still a relative unknown in the industry, was brought on board.

When he arrived back in New York to take over, Robinson found himself the head designer of a major collection at the age of only 28—yet among his predecessors at Anne Klein there had been equal novices: Donna Karan was just 26 when she took the same job in 1973. "This is the only company in America where you can become head designer and really be the designer," Robinson told Chance in *Essence*. The first few weeks were rough, however: he was introduced to baffled staff in the company showroom in a private meeting, and as he recalled in an interview with Kim France in *Harper's Bazaar,* he faced "a bunch of frowning little monsters." One witness to the meeting, Virginia Smith, then head of public relations for the company, told France that the young designer "looked slightly mortified to be in front of this group of people, and I thought, I feel kind of sorry for him."

A Difficult Experience

Just before the debut of his first collection for Anne Klein, Robinson termed himself "28 going on 50" in an interview with Turk in the *Los Angeles Times*. But he loved being back on familiar territory after years abroad. "This is the best country on Earth," he told Turk. "Everything works, I'm the only person, I think, walking around New York grinning." Yet some suspected that Anne Klein, after its Tyler debacle, was a sinking ship. Robinson recalled about this time "that it was almost more important for me to focus on bettering the name," as he told *Harper's Bazaar,* and because of this, he and Smith spent a great deal of time strategizing. A romance eventually blossomed, one that they kept secret for as long as they could.

Meanwhile, Robinson dedicated himself to making Anne Klein Collection a success: with his first collection of clothes, he visited several cities and held seminars with store executives and sales personnel that showed what Turk termed a return to the true Anne Klein look: "safe, sexy, understated, finely tailored day and evening wear in luxurious fabrics." Reviews were mixed: "There are some who think that Patrick Robinson is in way over his head," sniped *Women's Wear Daily* in a late 1995 issue that previewed the Spring 1996 designer lines. But Robinson's third collection for Anne Klein was not even shipped to stores when Japanese executives decided to close the Anne Klein Collection (its lower-priced line, Anne Klein II, was still commercially successful.)

Fortunately for Robinson, his paramour was still gainfully employed—Smith had been offered a job at Calvin Klein shortly before the dark day of the announcement. Out of a job, Robinson traveled through Asia for several weeks as a tonic. Upon his return, he hired a staff and set up a design house in his New York City loft, and began courting backers. A line of clothing finally bearing his own name was launched for the fall/winter season of 1997 after Robinson signed a deal with an Italian manufacturer, Coba. He was rather fortunate in light of the terms of the agreement: Coba, based near Urbino, Italy did not invest in his company and receive a controlling interest, but rather gave him a break on the costs of manufacturing the clothes in return for a promise that the designer would stay with their firm when his business grew successful. "We think Patrick is a very talented designer, even if he didn't have a brilliant experience at Anne Klein," Domenico Toselli, Coba's sole director, told *Women's Wear Daily's* Samantha Conti. "He's young and good, and we want to give him a hand," Toselli continued.

A Successful Launch

Robinson's first trunk show sold $65,000 the first day at Saks Jandel in Washington, D.C. He presented Asian-influenced sportswear carrying price tags ranging from $125 to $1000. Givhan praised the debut collection, and she noted the line was lacking the standard "high-concept theme" that most designers attempt, as she reported in the *Washington Post*. "He simply has created beautiful garments in brushed alpaca, nubuck, python and pony....The clothes have shelf life and relevance," she wrote.

The Asian mood of his first collection fit in perfectly with a late nineties vibe. His catalysts, Robinson told Givhan, would always be global. Theorizing about his "signature look," he said it would always reflect "something about adventure, something with lots of cultures mixed in," he said in the *Washington Post* interview. "I'm looking not only to America for inspiration, but the world....I'm a black man and I love being that. I love being different than other people. That's part of it, too." Early in 1998 Robinson was able to move out of his Soho loft into a separate workspace on Wooster Street. Smith was working for Calvin Klein, and the pair chatted on the phone several times a day. They dine out evenings—often after a very long workday for both—and have no plans to join forces again professionally. "Coming home and seeing her is the highlight of my whole day," Robinson told France in the *Harper's Bazaar* interview. "It's the one thing I cherish. Besides, I couldn't afford her," he added.

Sources

Essence, September 1995, p. 22.
Harper's Bazaar, March 1998; June 1998.
Los Angeles Times, June 29, 1995, p. E1.
Washington Post, August 21, 1997, p. F3.
Women's Wear Daily, December 21, 1994, p. 8; March 1, 1995, p, 8; August 8, 1995, p. G8; November 2, 1995, p. 6; January 7, 1997, p. 2; January 28, 1997, p. 6;

—Carol Brennan

Wendell Oliver Scott

1921–1990

Professional race car driver

Wendell Scott raced stock cars in 506 Winston Cup Grand Nationals from 1961 to 1973 as the first black man to do so at that level and only one of three to race before 1990. His National Association for Stock Car Auto Racing (NASCAR) win occurred in 1963 on the Jacksonville Speedway in Florida. Because of the points he earned during races, he started in the top ten racing positions 147 times.

Scott earned a reputation for speed as a taxi driver and then as a bootlegger in Danville, Virginia, where he lived his entire life. He claimed that all the old race car drivers once were bootleggers like he had been. Bootleggers would race on Sundays after forming a half-mile oval track in the dirt by driving around a cow pasture.

During World War II, before his speeding tickets and moonshine-hauling caught the attention of the Danville police, Scott was trained by the Army to be a mechanic and a paratrooper. His skills as a mechanic would serve him well during his lifetime. In an interview for *Dirt Tracks to Glory,* Scott boasted that his "liquor car would do 95 in second gear, and 118 in high." According to Scott, there were no police cars at the time in Danville that could go over 95 miles per hour. Scott kept his liquor car in topnotch condition.

On one unfortunate liquor run in 1948, Scott skidded on a gravel road to avoid a group of drunks and crashed into a house. After being cited by the police, Scott received three years of probation. When promoter Martin Rogers asked the local police to give him the name of a black man who might be able to drive for him in order to increase the interest at Danville's dirt track, Wendell Scott's name came up. Since stock cars are standard-make automobiles that have been modified for racing, Scott was a natural candidate for Rogers as a skilled mechanic and an accomplished driver.

Determined to Race

In 1949, when Scott began his racing career, motor sports were in their early stages of development. Scott, a NASCAR pioneer, loved racing from day one despite the many problems he encountered. Some tracks would not let him compete. At others, people booed and threw things at him. Drivers slashed his tires or tried to wreck

At a Glance...

Born August 29, 1921, in Danville, VA; died of spinal cancer, December 24, 1990; married Mary; children: Willie Ann, Wendell Jr., Franklin, Deborah, Cheryl, Sybil, and Michael. *Religion:* Baptist.

Career: Taxi cab driver, 1939-43; U.S. Army, 1943-45; city service, 1945-49; driver, 1949-52; NASCAR driver, 1952-73; owner of Scott's Garage, 1949-90.

Member: Honorary lifetime member, Black American Racers Association; Hollywood Screen Actors Guild, 1977-90.

Selected awards: Keys to numerous cities; Virginia State Championship and Southside Speedway Championship, 1959; 127 race wins; Jacksonville Speedway Championship, 1963; State of Florida Citation for Outstanding Achievements, 1965; honorary Lieutenant-Colonel-Aide-de-Camp, Alabama State Militia, 1970; Curtis Turner Memorial Achievement Award, 1971; Special Olympics Service Award, 1974; Schasfer Brewing Company Achievement Award, 1975; subject of the movie and novel, *Greased Lightning*, 1977; Bont Cultural Council Achievement Award, Greenville, SC, 1977; National Black Athletic Hall of Fame, 1977; TobaccoI-and 200 Award for the Finest NASCAR Driver, 1978; Fort Belvair, VA Award for Outstanding Services Rendered, 1979; Black Rose Community Services Award, 1980; Muscular Dystrophy Association Award for Achievements, 1981; Virginia Skyline Girl Scout Council, Inc. Award for outstanding contributions, 1985; Proclamation of Atlanta, GA and Danville, VA, 1986; Wendell Scott Foundation and Scholarship Fund, 1986; Early Dirt Racers Driver of the Year Award, 1990; Wendell Scott Day, Danville, VA, 1990; mourned and honored by the General Assembly of Virginia, January 16, 1991.

his car during races.

Not all discrimination was so blatant. Judges often did not give Scott the scoring points that he deserved. When he went to get paid for his finishing position, no matter where Scott finished, the scorers would have him listed as last. Inspectors would single him out and make him do such things as take a tiny paintbrush and cover chips in his car's paint before allowing him to race. He would win "free dinners" but not be allowed to go into the restaurants to eat them. Despite this racially motivated onslaught, Scott loved to race too much to quit.

Scott knew many drivers like himself who illegally hauled alcohol in half-gallon Mason jars to keep racing. Racing was an expensive sport even for drivers with sponsors and Scott never had a sponsor. He had to use his mechanics skills to build fast cars and was proud that he and his sons had that ability. Because of financial straits, he never got to race in a new car.

Started on the "Dixie Circuit"

Scott got his start in racing on the "Dixie Circuit," the shorter tracks, where he won 127 races. In 1958, Scott competed in a major racing event, the Virginia State Championship and won. In 1961, he moved to the elite form of stock car racing, the Grand Nationals, now known as the Winston Cup. Points were given for each lap completed and for finishing position. The finishing points determined the award money Scott would receive—money needed to feed his large family each week. He finished the races even with broken seats, broken pedals, crushed radiator fins, and crumpled car bodies just to get his points. The competitions consisted of a 100-mile race on a half-mile dirt track. Scott drove his 1962 Chevrolet for many years on those tracks. The superstitious Scott never wore green or allowed green on his cars when he raced, nor did he allow peanuts to be eaten in his pits or his repair garage.

Scott's bittersweet day of glory was December 1, 1963, when his 1962 Chevrolet crossed the finish line first after 202 laps at the Jacksonville Speedway in Florida. Officials flagged Buck Baker as the winner, however. Later, when Scott protested, the officials claimed there had been a scoring error. A recheck showed that Scott's Chevrolet had been two laps ahead of the 22-car field. Scott knew that he had actually been three laps ahead of Baker. By the time the error was pointed out, Baker had taken home the $1,000 purse, the trophy, and the acclaim of racing fans. Scott eventually received his winnings, but never the correct trophy.

Retired After Talladega Wreck

Scott kept driving, eventually earning the accolades he deserved. In 1971, he received the first Curtis Turner Achievement Award for his efforts to promote NASCAR racing. Unfortunately, a disaster struck in 1973 and effectively ended his career. During a race at Talladega, Alabama, Scott sustained severe injuries in a 19-car wreck, including broken pelvis bones, three broken ribs, a leg broken in seven places, and a lacerated arm that required seventy stitches. Despite his injuries, Scott tried to race several more years before retiring from Grand National racing.

Scott received many awards, especially for his contributions to the Danville community. In 1977, he was inducted into the National Black Athletic Hall of Fame. That same year a movie loosely based on Scott's life titled *Greased Lightning* and starring Richard Pryor, was released. Though Scott was a technical consultant and did many of the stunts in *Greased Lightning,* he received little financial compensation. He was also disappointed with the Hollywood stunt drivers. He declared, "They had about three different stunt men who couldn't even drive a car—worst thing I ever seen in my life."

Never Got To Do His Best

After his official retirement from racing in 1973, Scott ran an automobile garage until disease prevented him from working. His reputation as a driver and mechanic brought people with car problems from all over the east coast. He told *Dirt Tracks to Glory,* "It's no fun working on anybody else's cars, especially race cars." Without bitterness, he admitted that racing had not been good to him and regretted that due to lack of funds and equipment, he never got to do his best. In 1986, Les Montgomery of Atlanta, Georgia, with Scott's help, established a Wendell Scott Racing Foundation to begin a scholarship program for young people interested in auto mechanics.

Many acknowledged that Scott had worked harder than any driver they had ever known. In *NASCAR Online,* the president of the Charlotte Motor Speedway, H. A. Wheeler, a man who knew Scott and had watched him race for years, remarked, "He was obviously a much better race driver than the record shows." Though it had been difficult for Scott, he always hoped that his efforts would open doors for other black drivers. Scott, whose children were often his pit crew, managed to put all seven of them through school—quite an accomplishment for a man who earned a total of $188,000 in the 506 NASCAR starts of his career.

In 1983, Scott told *Dirt Tracks to Glory* that he never quit racing. "I just haven't had the time." When Willie T. Ribbs, another black driver, started NASCAR racing in 1986, Scott wished he was 25 years old and just starting out. Scott died of spinal cancer and other problems in 1990, just seven years before his hometown renamed the street he lived on in Danville as "Wendell Scott Drive." He did not get to experience the recognition bestowed upon him December 23, 1997, when an emblem with Scott's number 34 race car and the words, "NASCAR Racing Legend," were put up at intersections near his street.

A month after Scott's death, the Virginia Senate passed a resolution to mourn his death and honor his accomplishments as a "trailblazing sportsman and a man of skill, dedication, and perseverance." Wendell Scott, often called the Jackie Robinson of stock car racing, picked one of the most difficult sports at which a black man might succeed. His efforts in the face of adversity define success.

Sources

Books

Ashe, Arthur R. Jr., *A Hard Road to Glory: A History of the African-American Athlete Since 1946,* Vol. 3, Warner Books, 1988, pp. 231-232.

Golenbock, Peter, *American Zoom: Stock Car Racing—from the Dirt Tracks to Daytona,* Macmillan, 1993.

Porter, David L., editor, *African-American Sports Greats; A Biographical Dictionary,* Greenwood Press, 1995.

Wilkinson, Sylvia, *Dirt Tracks to Glory: The Early Days of Stock Car Racing as Told by the Participants,* Algonquin Books, 1983.

Periodicals

Area Auto Racing News, January 8, 1991.

Atlanta Journal and Constitution, March 15, 1986, pp. 1D, 6D; December 25, 1990, p. E12.

Charlotte Observer, December 27, 1990, pp. 1D, 3D.

Danville Register & Bee, December 24, 1990, pp. 1A-2A; December 17, 1997, pp. 1-2B; December 23, 1997, p. 1A; December 24, 1997, p. 1A.

Jet, August 18, 1986, p. 47; January 26, 1998, p. 54.

New York Times, December 25, 1990.

"Rockets on Wheels: Driver Wendell Scott,"*Racing for Kids,* April 1993.

Southern Motor Sports Journal, December 5, 1963, pp. 1, 3.

USA Today, May 22, 1997, p. 12.

Other

Other information was obtained from a document from

the Virginia Senate Joint Resolution No. 193, January 16, 1991 and from *NASCAR Online,* URL: http://www.nascar.com/news/97news/00656422.html.

—Eileen Daily

Maria W. Miller Stewart

1803–1879

Public speaker, author, teacher

Maria W. Miller Stewart, essayist, teacher, and political activist, is thought to be the first American woman to give public lectures. Stewart is known for four powerful speeches, delivered in Boston in the early 1830s—a time when no woman, black or white, dared to address an audience from a public platform.

Stewart was heavily involved with the abolitionist movement, and most of her lectures deal with this topic. More radically, however, she called for black economic progress and self-determination, as well as women's rights. Other recurring themes included the value of education, the historical inevitability of black liberation, and the need for black unity and collective action. Many of her ideas were so far ahead of their time that they remain relevant more than 150 years later.

Despite the fact that she had little formal education, Stewart continually showed her learning in her lectures, referencing the Bible, the U.S. Constitution, and various literary works. She was deeply influenced by a type of sermon developed by Puritan preachers known as the jeremiad, which applied religious doctrines to secular problems. According to Stewart, the way for African Americans to obtain freedom was to get closer to God; conversely, resistance to oppression was the highest form of obedience to God.

"Maria Stewart was a prototypical black American orator," wrote Halford Ross Ryan in *African-American Orators*. "Her charges against the white racism and hypocrisy that she found in the nineteenth century are still relevant. Her call for black self-help, black education, and black unity still seeks satisfaction."

Maria Miller (later Stewart) was born free in 1803 in Hartford, Connecticut. All that is known about her parents is their surname, Miller; their first names and occupations have been lost to history. At the age of five, Stewart was orphaned and forced to become a servant in the household of a clergyman. She lived with this family for ten years, receiving no formal education but learning as much as she could by reading books from the family's library. After leaving the family at the age of fifteen, she supported herself as a domestic servant while furthering her education at Sabbath schools. Specific details about her employment or where she lived at the time are unknown.

On August 10, 1826, at the age of twenty-three, Maria Miller married James W. Stewart at the African Baptist Church in Boston. At her husband's suggestion, Stewart took not only his last name, but his middle initial as well. James W. Stewart was forty-four years old, and a veteran of the War of 1812; after the war, he earned a substantial living by fitting out whaling and fishing vessels. At the time, African Americans made up just three percent of Boston's population, and the Stewarts were part of an even smaller minority: Boston's black middle class.

> ### At a Glance...
>
> Born Maria Miller, 1803, Hartford, Connnecticut; daughter of Mr. and Mrs. Miller, first names and occupations unknown; married James W. Stewart, a businessman, August 10, 1826; no children. Died December 1879. *Education:* no formal education. *Politics:* Abolitionist. *Religion:* Protestant.
>
> **Career:** Servant, 1808-26, 1829-31; Abolitionist lecturer and writer, Boston, 1831-33; teacher, New York public schools, 1833-52; teacher for paying pupils, Baltimore, 1852-61; teacher in her own school, Washington, D.C., 1861-65; matron, Freedman's Hospital, Washington, D.C., 1870s-1879; Sunday school teacher, 1871-79.
>
> **Selected writings:** Author, "Religion and the Pure Principles of Morality, the Sure Foundation on Which We Must Build" (pamphlet, 1831), "Meditations from the Pen of Mrs. Maria W. Stewart" (pamphlet, 1832), *Productions of Mrs. Maria W. Stewart* (1835), *Meditations from the Pen of Mrs. Maria W. Stewart* (second edition, 1879).

In December of 1829, just three years after the Stewarts were married, James Stewart died; the marriage had produced no children. Although Maria Stewart was left with a substantial inheritance, she was defrauded of it by his white executors after a drawn-out court battle. Once again, she was forced to turn to domestic service to support herself.

Wrote Abolitionist Essays

In 1830, partly due to grief over her husband's death, Stewart underwent a religious conversion. A year later, according to her later writings, she made a "public profession of my faith in Christ," dedicating herself to God's service. For Stewart, her new-found religious fervor went hand-in-hand with political activism: she resolved to become a "strong advocate for the cause of God and for the cause of freedom." In the years to come, when she was criticized for daring to speak in public, Stewart would claim that her authority came from God—that she was simply following God's will.

Meanwhile, the abolitionist movement was beginning to gather strength in Boston. In 1831, William Lloyd Garrison, publisher of the abolitionist newspaper the *Liberator*, called for women of African descent to contribute to the paper. Stewart responded by arriving at his office with a manuscript containing several essays which Garrison agreed to publish.

Stewart's first published work, "Religion and the Pure Principles of Morality, the Sure Foundation on Which We Must Build," appeared as a twelve-page pamphlet, priced at six cents, later that year. An advertisement for the pamphlet, which appeared in the *Liberator*, described it as "a tract addressed to the people of color, by Mrs. Maria W. Steward (sic), a respectable colored lady of this city....The production is most praiseworthy, and confers great credit on the talents and piety of its author."

Delivered Public Lectures

Soon afterward, Stewart began to deliver public lectures. Her first speaking engagement was on April 28, 1832, before the African American Female Intelligence Society of Boston. Aware that she was violating the taboo against women speaking in public, Stewart asserted in her talk that "the frowns of the world shall never discourage me" and that she could bear the "assaults of wicked men." While the main thrust of the speech was to urge African American women to turn to God, she also urged them to stand up for their rights, rather than silently suffer humiliation. "It is useless for us any longer to sit with our hands folded, reproaching the whites; for that will never elevate us," she said.

Six months later, on September 21, 1832, Stewart lectured to an audience of both men and women at Franklin Hall. In that speech, she asserted that free African Americans were hardly better off than those in slavery: "Look at many of the most worthy and most interesting of us doomed to spend our lives in gentlemen's kitchens," she demanded. "Look at our young men, smart, active, and energetic, with souls filled with ambitious fire; if they look forward, alas! What are their prospects? They can be nothing but the humblest laborers, on account of their dark complexions; hence many of them lose their ambition, and become worthless...."

Meanwhile, Stewart continued to submit her writings for publication. In 1832, Garrison published another pamphlet, "Meditations from the Pen of Mrs. Maria W. Stewart." Garrison also printed transcripts of all of Stewart's speeches in the *Liberator*; however, in accordance with the editorial conventions of the day, her contributions were relegated to the paper's "Ladies'

Department."

Was Silenced by Critics

Stewart's third speech, delivered at the African Masonic Hall on February 27, 1833, was titled "African Rights and Liberty." In this speech, she again defended her right to speak publicly, while castigating African-American men. "You are abundantly capable, gentlemen, of making yourselves men of distinction; and this gross neglect, on your part, causes my blood to boil within me," she told her audience. "Had the men amongst us, who have had an opportunity, turned their attention as assiduously to mental and moral improvement as they have to gambling and dancing, I might have remained quietly at home, and they stood contending in my place."

Stewart also condemned the colonization movement, a plan to send free blacks as well as slaves back to Africa. In her conclusion, Stewart recounted how whites first drove the native Americans from their land, then stole blacks from Africa and enslaved them, and now wanted to send them back with nothing. Instead, Stewart argued, blacks should remain in the United States and fight for their freedom.

The response to Stewart's speeches—even from those who supported her cause—was overwhelmingly negative; she was roundly condemned for having the audacity to speak onstage. In the words of African-American historian William C. Nell, writing about Stewart in the 1850s, she "encountered an opposition even from her Boston circle of friends, that would have dampened the ardor of most women."

Stewart delivered her final Boston speech on September 21, 1833, announcing her decision to leave the city. In the speech, she acknowledged that, by lecturing publicly, she had "made myself contemptible in the eyes of many, that I might win some," which she admitted was "like a labor in vain."

Still, Stewart refused to go quietly, asserting that women activists had divine sanction: "What if I am woman; is not the God of ancient times the God of these modern days? Did he not raise up Deborah, to be a mother, and a judge in Israel? Did not Queen Esther save the lives of the Jews? And Mary Magdelene first declare the resurrection of Christ from the dead?"

In 1835, two years after Stewart had left the city, Garrison published a collection of her speeches, *Productions of Mrs. Maria W. Stewart*. Within a year of its appearance, other women, both black and white, began to follow the path Stewart had opened, lecturing in churches and meeting halls across the country.

Became a Teacher and Matron

Contrary to the prejudices of her day, Stewart had long believed that all African Americans—both male and female—deserved the chance to acquire an education. In her speeches, Stewart had often referred to literacy as a sacred quest at a time when it was a crime to teach slaves to read or write. Now that she had given in to public pressure to cease lecturing, she turned her energy to education.

From Boston, Stewart moved to New York, where she taught in public schools in Manhattan and Long Island. She continued her political activities, joining women's organizations—including a black women's literary society—and attending the Women's Anti-slavery Convention of 1837. She also lectured occasionally, but none of these lectures survive. And while she was affiliated with the radical newspaper *The North Star*, later called *Frederick Douglass' Paper*, none of her work appeared there.

In 1852, Stewart moved to Baltimore, earning a small living as a teacher of paying pupils. "I have never been very shrewd in money matters; and being classed as a lady among my race all my life, and never exposed to any hardship, I did not know how to manage," Stewart later wrote about this period. In 1861, she moved to Washington D.C., where again she organized a school.

By the early 1870s, Stewart had been appointed as matron, or head housekeeper, at the Freedman's Hospital and Asylum in Washington. The facility, established by the Freedmen's Bureau, had room for 300 patients, and served not only as a hospital, but also as a refugee camp for former slaves displaced by the Civil War. Stewart continued to teach, even as she lived and worked at the hospital.

In 1878, a law was passed granting pensions to widows of War of 1812 veterans. Stewart used the unexpected money to publish a second edition of *Meditations from the Pen of Mrs. Maria W. Stewart*. The book, which appeared in 1879, was introduced by supporting letters from Garrison and others. It also included new material: the autobiographical essay "Sufferings During the War," and a preface in which she once more called for an end to tyranny and oppression.

Shortly after the book's publication in December of 1879, Stewart died at the Freedman's Hospital at the age of 76. Her obituary in *The People's Advocate,* a Washington-area black newspaper, acknowledged that Stewart had struggled for years with little recognition: "Few, very few know of the remarkable career of this woman whose life has just drawn to a close. For half a century she was engaged in the work of elevating her race by lectures, teaching, and various missionary and benevolent labors." Stewart was buried in Graceland Cemetery in Washington on December 17, 1879—50 years to the day after her husband's death.

> "[I have] made myself contemptible in the eyes of many, that I might win some."

"The emergence of black history and women's studies has reintroduced scholars to the life and work of Maria W. Stewart, but this pioneering black political activist still lacks a critical biographical assessment," wrote Harry A. Reed in *Black Women in America: The Early Years,* which was published in 1983. "Her life and her continuing obscurity illustrate the double pressures of racism and sexism on the lives of black women." Four years later, Indiana University Press published a collected edition of her work, *Maria W. Stewart, America's First Black Woman Political Writer: Essays and Speeches.* While Stewart was criticized and eventually silenced during her lifetime, and her work has been neglected since then, she is finally beginning to be recognized for what she was: a pioneering speaker and essayist.

Sources

African-American Orators, edited by Richard W. Leeman, Greenwood Press, 1996.

Black Women in America: The Early Years, 1619-1899, edited by Darlene Clark Hine, Carlson Publishing, 1993.

The Book of African-American Women, by Tonya Bolden, Adams Media Corporation, 1996.

Maria W. Stewart, America's First Black Woman Political Writer: Essays and Speeches, edited by Marilyn Richardson, Indiana University Press, 1987.

Notable American Women, edited by Edward T. James, Harvard University Press, 1971.

—Carrie Golus

Keith Sweat

1961(?)—

Vocalist

Keith Sweat is one of the earliest practitioners, and some would say the inventor, of "New Jack Swing" music, a style of rhythm and blues that fuses soul singing and hip-hop beats. It should come as no surprise that "New Jack Swing" music became extremely popular, or that Sweat has enjoyed considerable success. Financial success has always been one of the keystones in Sweat's life, from his days working at the New York Stock Exchange to his career in music.

Sweat was born in the early 1960s in Harlem, New York. His father Charles, a factory worker, died in 1973. His mother Juanita, a hairdresser, was forced to raise their five children alone. Sweat would later credit Juanita for his strong sense of values, telling *People Weekly,* "She pushed me hard. I knew I didn't want to be on the street selling drugs—or using them."

An Early Gift for Music

Sweat learned early in life that he had a gift for music, and for affecting women with his voice. "When he was four years old, he'd go outside and sing to the girls," Juanita told *People Weekly.* "I'd say, 'Stop that noise.'" Keith would later remark that he had dreams of performing in concert that often seemed like premonitions. He told *Ebony,* "People might think I'm lying about them, but as a kid I used to go to bed and dream I was onstage giving a concert. I could see myself singing and the people were screaming and the whole thing was so real to me I used to wake up and really believe I had done a show. You couldn't tell me it didn't happen.... I would get up in the morning and start looking in my pockets for all the money I'd made from my shows."

Following his graduation from high school, Sweat enrolled in City College of New York to study communications. He worked as a stock boy at Macy's on weeknights and sang with a band called Jamilah on weekends. After graduating from City College of New York, he went to work on the floor of the New York Stock Exchange, starting in the mailroom at Paine Webber, and working his way up to a lucrative brokerage assistant job in only four years. Although he had advanced quickly in his new career, he still wanted to become a musician.

At a Glance...

Born Keith Sweat circa 1961 in Harlem, New York; son of Charles (a factory worker) and Juanita (a hairdresser) Sweat; three children: Keisha, Keia, and Jordan. *Education:* City College of New York, bachelor's degree in communications.

Career: Paine Webber, mailroom, brokerage assistant; singer for band Jamilah; solo albums, *Make It Last Forever* (1988), *I'll Give All My Love To You* (1990), *Keep It Comin'* (1991), *Get Up On It* (1994), *Keith Sweat* (1996); singles, "I Want Her," "Make You Sweat," "Merry Go Round," "Just One of Them Thangs."

Awards: Double platinum album, *Make It Last Forever*; No. 1 New Male Artist, Black Radio Exclusive, 1988.

Addresses: Singer, c/o Elektra Records, 75 Rockefeller Plaza, New York, New York, 10019.

Near the end of his tenure on Wall Street, Sweat became convinced that he was destined to become a songwriter, not a performer. He spent most of his salary recording demos of his songs, but no one wanted to buy them. "All of the recording companies turned me down flat," he told *Ebony*. "Everybody said the same thing: 'Thanks but no thanks. Your songs just aren't hot enough for our artists to sing,'" he continued.

Received His Big Break

Abandoning his plans to become a major songwriter, Sweat started performing his own material. He finally attracted the attention of Vincent Davis. Davis owned a record label, Vintertainment, and had recently signed a distribution deal with Elektra Records. Sweat soon signed with Vintertainment and recorded his debut album, *Make It Last Forever,* which was a commercial success. It featured the hit single, "I Want Her," and was heavily influenced by a style Sweat called "go-go music," a percussion-based sound which was popular on the East Coast. Much of the material on the album was contributed by the well-known New Jack Swing producer, Teddy Riley. Although the album's credits listed Sweat as a producer, many listeners believed that the album was solely produced by Riley.

Sweat would later tell *Ebony* that the success of the first album could be attributed to his break-up with a long-time girlfriend. "That was a very tough time in my life," he declared. "I was coming out of a relationship where I was hurt and I mean really hurt bad. It was a heart-breaking relationship for me—the kind where you are hurting so much you have to find someone to talk to or go crazy. I didn't really have anyone to talk to so what I did was talk to my album." Sweat also credits Vintertainment with the opportunity to release his debut album. "If I had taken my demo tape directly to Elektra I would have been turned down, I know it," he told the *Los Angeles Times*. "Frankly, a lot of A&R guys can't hear the music. They go home to their big houses in upstate New York and lose touch with what the folks on the street want to hear." Sweat took a leave of absence from his Wall Street job while his debut album climbed the charts. When the album reached No. 1 on the charts, he quit his job on Wall Street. "That's when I knew I could do this for a living," he told *Rolling Stone*.

Continued Success

Sweat's second album, produced without the assistance of Teddy Riley, established more of his individual style. *I'll Give All My Love to You* featured a simpler, more traditional rhythm and blues sound. The album climbed the charts quickly, selling one million copies in less than two months. It produced two more hit singles, including the signature song "Make You Sweat." Although Sweat was pleased that his albums were performing well on the R&B charts, he was disappointed that they were not successful on the pop charts. He told the *Los Angeles Times,* "I want pop fans to know who Keith Sweat is. It's not about ego. It's about selling records—which is what this business is all about. I've hit a stone wall in the black community. There's only so much money there."

Sweat's third album, *Keep It Comin',* offered more of the same style of music expected by his fans. He marked the success of this album by moving to Alpharetta, Georgia, a suburb of Atlanta, and building his dream home. He also concentrated on improving his abilities as a producer by working with other acts, most notably the R&B group Silk. Sweat produced their album, *Lose Control,* which climbed to the top of the R&B charts. That same year, Sweat's music was also featured on the *New Jack City* movie soundtrack.

Sweat returned to the charts in 1994 with his fourth album, *Get Up On It*. This album resembled the musical style of Sweat's other albums and produced another hit single, "How Do You Like It?" In addition to performing, he also pursued other business interests. He began his own record label, Keia Records, and opened a state-of-the-art recording studio called the Sweat Shop. He also produced a hit album for the group Kut Klose. In 1996 Sweat opened a new nightclub, Industry, in Atlanta's Buckhead district. He explained the nightclub's name to *People Weekly,* "This is a spot for people in 'the industry.' There's no other place in Atlanta where celebrities can come and just be themselves. We're people, too."

A few months after opening his nightclub, Sweat released his fifth album entitled *Keith Sweat.* Two songs on the album, "Twisted" and "Nobody," climbed into the top five on the pop charts. The following year, Sweat formed the musical group LSG with Gerald Levert and Johnny Gill. Their debut album produced the hit single "My Body." In 1997 Sweat discovered the group Ol' Skool, which he considered a throwback to the 1960s and 1970s heyday of soul music. He told *Jet* that searching for talent for Keia Records was a full-time occupation, adding that he seeks "people who can sing and people who can put certain things together in terms of performance, stage presence and all of that, overall talent. I'm a hands-on person, so I still pay attention to what's going on. I get demos; I listen to all kinds of music. Atlanta has certainly become a very important place within the music industry, but I search for talent from everywhere."

Sweat believes that simplicity and honesty are the keys to his popularity. He remarked to *People Weekly* in 1997, "If I can't feel it, I don't want to write it. My music is true-to-life relationship music." The consistency of Keith Sweat's success suggests that he will continue to produce and sell hit records for many years to come.

Sources

Billboard, September 30, 1995, p. 22; October 25, 1997, p. 38-39.
Chicago Tribune, January 17, 1991, p. 3, section 5.
Ebony, September 1992, p. 82.
Jet, September 16, 1996, p. 30.
Los Angeles Times, March 20, 1988, p. C70; February 17, 1991, p. C64.
People Weekly, September 26, 1988, p. 115; January 27, 1997, p. 69.
Rolling Stone, November 15, 1990.

—Mike Eggert

Clifton Lemoure Taulbert

1945—

Author, speaker, businessman

In the critically acclaimed book *Once Upon a Time When We Were Colored,* Clifton Taulbert tells the story of his childhood, spent in a small town in rural Mississippi during the Jim Crow years. Although racial injustice is ever present, it is not the focus of Taulbert's bittersweet memoir. Instead, he tries to evoke the sense of community that characterized his hometown—something he believes has been lost in the intervening years.

"In our desire as black Americans to put segregation behind us, we have put ourselves in danger of forgetting the past—the good and the bad," Taulbert wrote in the introduction to *Once Upon a Time.* "I believe that to forget our colored past is to forget ourselves, who we are and what we've come from."

Clifton Lemoure Taulbert was born on February 19, 1945 in Glen Allan, Mississippi, a small town in the western part of the state, near the Arkansas border. His young mother, Mary Morgan Taulbert, had been abandoned by his father, leaving Clifton to be raised by his large extended family. He lived first with his great-grandparents, and then his great-aunt. However, he always maintained close contact with his mother, who became a schoolteacher. The institutionalized racism of the time, which Taulbert would later describe in his books, could have been crushing. Instead, Taulbert remembered the "silent heroes" of the time, such as Louis Fields, a sharecropper. "There was nothing extraordinary about Mr. Fields," Taulbert told the *Chicago Tribune.* "He had very little education....[H]e'd tell me:

'Boy, you can be anything you want to be. Get your education. You can be a doctor, a lawyer, an architect.' He gave me the determination to go to college."

Taulbert began his schooling at a one-room schoolhouse in Glen Allan. Later, he attended the town's new public school for blacks, built under the "separate but equal" rule. Taulbert remembered writing countless essays about four African American role models: Dr. George Washington Carver, Mary McLeod Bethune, Marion Anderson and Jackie Robinson. "I would be out of college before I would fully realize that these four people, although they were great trailblazers, by no means represented the sum total of colored achievements," Taulbert wrote in *Once Upon a Time.*

For all four years of high school, Taulbert had to rise before dawn to catch a bus to a black school in Greenville, 25 miles away—even though there was a white school in Glen Allan just a few blocks from where he lived. By the time the bus had picked up children from far-flung plantations, the trip had stretched to almost fifty miles. Taulbert refused to let this injustice dampen his enthusiasm for schooling, however. His classmates elected him "most studious," and in 1963 he graduated as valedictorian of his class.

Took "Last Train" Up North

Taulbert desperately wanted to go to college, but his

At a Glance...

Born Clifton Lemoure Taulbert, February 19, 1945, Glen Allan, Mississippi; son of Mary Morgan Taulbert; married Barbara Ann Taulbert, December 22, 1973; one son, Marshall Danzy, and one daughter, Anne Kathryn. *Education:* Oral Roberts University, B.A., 1971; graduate degree from Southwest Graduate School of Banking, Southern Methodist University.

Career: Sergeant, US Air Force, 1964-68; administrator, University Village Inc., Tulsa, OK, beginning in 1972; marketing vice president, Bank of Oklahoma, Tulsa, OK; president, Fremount Corporation, Tulsa, OK; president and CEO, Spike USA; professional speaker and leader of community-building workshops; author, *Once Upon a Time When We Were Colored,* 1989; *The Last Train North,* 1992; *Watching Our Crops Come In,* 1997; *Eight Habits of the Heart: The Timeless Qualities That Build Strong Communities—Within Our Homes and Our Lives,* 1997.

Awards: Manager of the Year, Oklahoma Chapter, National Management Association, 1989; National Volunteer, National Arthritis Foundation, 1985.

Addresses: *Home*—Tulsa, OK. *Office*—7802 S. Louisville Ave., Tulsa, OK 74136-8001.

family had little money and there were no scholarships available. Instead, he headed north and settled in St. Louis, where his father was a successful Baptist preacher. In St. Louis, Taulbert had the opportunity to meet his father for the first time. However, the elder Taulbert had since remarried, and his new wife would not allow the two to develop a relationship. "I guess I understood," Taulbert wrote simply in *The Last Train North.*

Upon his arrival in St. Louis, Taulbert received a rude awakening. During his childhood, when northern relatives had come back to visit, Taulbert had built up an elaborate fantasy about what the North was like. Suddenly, he discovered that poverty and discrimination were almost as prevalent in the North as in the South. "Where was the North I had heard about while growing up in Glen Allan?" he wondered over and over again in *The Last Train North.* Taulbert found work as a dishwasher in a restaurant, then as a messenger for Jefferson Bank and Trust. By this time, the civil rights movement had begun and the bank, which refused to promote blacks, was the object of massive civil rights demonstrations. Even as Taulbert started taking night classes at the American Institute of Banking, he realized that he would always be stuck in jobs outside the bank—opening the door for customers, driving the bank president to lunch. "I still marvel that ... the president would place his life in my hands in St. Louis traffic, when he wouldn't trust me with a calculator," Taulbert wrote in *The Last Train North.*

Built Successful Business Career

Taulbert moved to Washington, D.C., where he took classes at the University of Maryland at College Park. Eventually, he earned his bachelor's degree in sociology and history from Oral Roberts University in 1971. He then went on to earn a graduate degree from the Southwest Graduate School of Banking at Southern Methodist University in Dallas, Texas.

Taulbert soon obtained a job at the Bank of Oklahoma, eventually rising to the position of marketing vice president. He later founded a marketing and consulting firm called Freemount Corporation, named after a plantation that had been owned by his ancestors. In the 1980s, he was instrumental in the national marketing of Stairmaster, the exercise machine. In the 1990s, he became chairman and CEO of Spike USA, a manufacturer of isotonic sport drinks.

Despite his business success, Taulbert harbored a different dream. "I had always wanted to be a writer," he told the *Los Angeles Times.* "It was easy for me to write the stories of my family because I had written before. But I was never quite sure when it would happen or if I had the guts to follow my heart."

Wrote Groundbreaking Book

In 1964, Taulbert enlisted in the Air Force and rose to the rank of sergeant. While stationed in Maine, he entertained his fellow soldiers with stories about the people of Glen Allan. With their encouragement, he began to write down some of his reminiscences. "So with pen and paper in hand ..., I started writing about those wonderful 'colored' people, as I called them, who lived in the Mississippi Delta," he recalled in *The Last Train North.* In the 1980s, Taulbert collected these stories into a slim memoir, which he began to send out to publishers. "Then I got rejections from every publisher in New York City," he told the *Chicago Tribune.* In 1987 he met Paulette Millichap, a co-publisher of

Council Oak Books. She told Taulbert that if he reworked the manuscript, she would publish it. *Once Upon a Time When We Were Colored* was published two years later.

The initial press run of *Once Upon a Time* was just 3,000 copies. "The book was easy to underestimate," Paul Galloway wrote in the *Chicago Tribune*. "Although a hardcover, it was closer in size to a paperback and only 153 pages. The author was unknown. It was his first book. It was published to no fanfare by an obscure, financially shaky publishing house in, of all places, Tulsa, a considerable distance from the nation's literary center in New York City." The book was officially launched at a reception in Greenville, Mississippi. To Taulbert's surprise, the reception was attended by the full range of Mississippi society: "In that crowd there were people who were part and parcel of the segregation system. There were 80-year-olds who were plantation owners. There were black doctors, black maids, guys who had just gotten off tractors. A microcosm of all Mississippi was there at one place at one time to share our story," Taulbert told the *Los Angeles Times*.

Taulbert, with his years of marketing experience, worked tirelessly to promote his book. The *Library Journal* was one of the first to review *Once Upon a Time,* calling it "important" and "moving," and recommending it for purchase by major public and academic libraries. Slowly, a few large newspapers decided to run reviews. National Public Radio featured the complete volume on the air. In 1990, Taulbert was one of only 12 authors chosen to address the American Bookseller's Association.

By 1991, the *Once Upon a Time* had turned into a "minor miracle," according to the *Chicago Tribune's* Galloway. Over 20,000 copies had been distributed, it was in its fifth printing, and a paperback edition was planned. (The paperback edition appeared under the title *When We Were Colored.)* Later, the book found its way into the multicultural programs of school systems across the country. "We've only scratched the surface," Michael Hightower, a Council Oak co-publisher, told the *Chicago Tribune* in 1991. "It's not Tom Clancy, but the way it's been building is phenomenal."

While many books about race in the South tended to focus on the civil rights years, *Once Upon a Time...* was set in the forties and fifties. The period had been widely neglected in literature, Galloway wrote in the *Chicago Tribune,* "perhaps because it is so painful for blacks and embarrassing for many whites." In Taulbert's view, however, the pre-civil rights years were a crucial part of American history that should not be allowed to be forgotten. "The era of segregation is like a missing piece of the puzzle," he told the *Chicago Tribune*. "Without it, I don't think we can fully understand the sixties or even today....Segregation was humiliating and cruel, but everyone today should know there was a sense of family and community behind that wall that white society had erected."

Continued Literary Successes

In 1992 Taulbert published the next installment in his memoirs, *The Last Train North,* which was later nominated for a Pulitzer prize. The book begins just after Taulbert's high school graduation, and chronicles his trip north, the period he lived in St. Louis, and his first few years of military service.

Taulbert released the third volume of his memoirs, *Watching the Crops Come In,* in 1996. This volume opens in 1967, while Taulbert was stationed in Washington, D.C., and the civil rights movement was at its height. On leave, he returns to his hometown and finds a South that is slowly being transformed from within. According to a review in *Publishers Weekly,* "his eloquent memoir offers a stirring picture of the birth of the new South." Not all reviews were so positive, however. The *Washington Post* picked up several factual errors in the text, while criticizing Taulbert for writing about a movement that he did not actively participate in: "If there is a story worth telling here, Taulbert has not found it."

In 1996, *Once Upon a Time* was made into a critically acclaimed film starring Phylicia Rashad and Al Freeman, Jr., and directed by Tim Reid. Taulbert co-produced the film, along with Black Entertainment Television and United Image Entertainment. "In a nation torn by racial unhappiness, *Once Upon a Time ... When We Were Colored* is a film we need right now," Roger Ebert wrote in the *Chicago Sun-Times,* calling it "one of the most important films I've seen this year."

Taulbert published his fourth book, *Eight Habits of the Heart: The Timeless Qualities That Build Strong Communities—Within Our Homes and Our Lives,* in 1997. As Taulbert explains in the introduction, the book grew out of a commencement address he delivered at a suburban Chicago high school. Later, he delivered the speech to business groups in the United States, Germany, and Japan and always received an overwhelmingly positive response. Taulbert eventually decided to develop the speech into a book. In the book, he illustrates each of the "eight habits"—a nurturing attitude, dependability, responsibility, friendship, brotherhood, high expectations, courage, and hope—with stories from his childhood.

Taulbert has received numerous awards for his writing, including the 27th annual NAACP Image Award for Literature. He was one of the first African American writers to win the Mississippi Institute of Arts and Letters Award for Nonfiction, and was named one of America's outstanding black entrepreneurs by *Time* magazine. He currently travels around the world lecturing and leading workshops designed to build strong communities.

"Today, I wear a label called 'successful,' but it would not be so if not for them, the leaders of my 'colored' community in Glen Allan, Mississippi, in the 1950s," Taulbert wrote in an article for *USA Weekend*. "Because they cared, shared their lives and trusted each other, they showed me the future. I never want to forget the basic ideals they practiced, he concluded."

Selected writings

Once Upon a Time When We Were Colored, Council Oak Books, 1989.
The Last Train North, Council Oak Books, 1989.
Eight Habits of the Heart, Viking/Dial Books, 1997.

Sources

Boston Globe, *April 4, 1991, p. 65.*
Chicago Tribune, *March 7, 1991, sec. 5, p. 1; November 4, 1997, sec. 5, p. 1.*
Jet, *February 5, 1996, p. 32.*
Los Angeles Times, *September 4, 1990, sec. E, p. 1.*
USA Weekend, *January 19-21, 1996, p. 10.*
Washington Post, *January 26, 1996, sec. F, p. 1.*

—Carrie Golus

Edolphus Towns

1934—

Congressman

Edolphus Towns represents a section of Brooklyn, New York, in the United States House of Representatives. Since 1982, his constituents have re-elected him seven times. Towns's political viability in the Congressional district, which is 57 percent African American and also predominantly Hispanic, depends as much on the intricate, behind-the-scenes maneuvering that characterizes New York City politics as it does upon his service in Washington.

Towns was born in 1934 in Chadbourn, North Carolina, and attended the North Carolina Agricultural and Technical State University. He graduated with a bachelor of science degree in 1956, and then spent two years in the United States Army. By the mid-1960s, he resided in Brooklyn with his wife and children, and had taught in the New York City public school system for several years and at Brooklyn's Medgar Evers College. He became a deputy hospital administrator in 1965, a job that he held for six years, and also returned to school to earn a master's degree in social work from Adelphi University in 1973. In 1976, he ran for and won the deputy president slot for the Borough of Brooklyn. He held this post until 1982, when he was elected to the 98th Congress as a representative from the Eleventh New York District, which encompassed part of Brooklyn. He was re-elected in 1984 and has won six subsequent biennial elections.

During his first years in Congress, Towns became involved in the fight to save family farms—many of which were owned by African Americans. Severe cutbacks in small farm subsidies over a period of decades had left many rural households economically devastated. Towns also chaired the Human Resources and Intergovernmental Affairs committee, and served on the House Commerce committee. Since 1991, he has chaired the Congressional Black Caucus, an influential group of African American lawmakers. When the Los Angeles riots erupted in 1992, Towns spoke on behalf of the Caucus: "America witnessed a terrible travesty of justice," he told the *Los Angeles Times,* and declared that the jury verdict acquitting white police officers of beating motorist Rodney King in 1991 was "a manifestation of prejudice and racism in their most virulent form."

Towns's bid for re-election in the fall of 1992 was more of a challenge than previous campaigns. The boundaries

At a Glance...

Born July 21, 1934, in Chadbourn, NC; married Gwendolyn Forbes, 1960; children: Darryl, Deidra. *Education:* North Carolina Agricultural and Technical State University, B.S., 1956, Adelphi University, M.S.W., 1973. *Politics:* Democrat. *Religion:* Baptist.

Career: Teacher in the New York City public schools, and at Medgar Evers College, Brooklyn, NY, early 1960s; deputy hospital administrator, 1965-71; Borough of Brooklyn, deputy president, 1976-82; elected to the 98th U.S. Congress as a representative from the Eleventh Congressional District (now the Tenth), 1982-; chair of the House Human Resources and Intergovernmental Affairs committee, member of the House Commerce committee, and chair of the Congressional Black Caucus, early 1990s. *Military service:* U.S. Army, 1956-58.

Awards: Honorary degrees from North Carolina Agricultural and Technical State University, and Shaw University.

Member: Congressional Black Caucus; advisory council, Boy Scouts of America.

Addresses: *Office*—2232 Rayburn House Office Bldg., Washington, DC 20515; 16 Court St., 15th Floor, Brooklyn, NY 11241.

of his Eleventh Congressional District had been redrawn to better reflect the changes in Brooklyn's population and demographics. The new boundaries gave Towns a potential constituency that was more Hispanic, but less African American. In addition, the state of New York had lost three of its 34 seats in the House of Representatives. Towns, noted Todd S. Purdum in the *New York Times,* had "fought hard in this year's districting wars to preserve the district's overwhelming concentration of black voters." Voters, both black and Hispanic, responded favorably to Towns and he was re-elected as representative of the renamed Tenth Congressional District.

Towns was re-elected in 1994 and, before facing re-election again in 1996, was a co-sponsor of a provision attached to the important Telecommunications Act of 1996. The provision set up a development fund to provide low-interest loans to help small entrepreneurs launch telecommunications companies. In 1997, Towns became involved in a series of political maneuvers that were symptomatic of the somewhat cutthroat nature of New York City borough politics. He voiced his support of the Reverend Al Sharpton's tentative bid for the New York City Mayor's Office. The endorsement, explained the *Village Voice*'s James Bradley, exposed the divisive alliances within Brooklyn politics. Towns and Sharpton supporters comprised only two of the four factions courting black voters in Brooklyn. Sharpton eventually dropped out of the race and Towns swung his support behind Republican incumbent mayor Rudolph Giuliani.

Towns's support of Giuliani, who was perceived as hostile to the interests of the city's African American community, earned Towns widespread criticism. Giuliani won the race and Sharpton hinted that he might run against Towns for his seat in the 1998 elections. Towns was also at odds with his former mentor and chair of the Brooklyn Democratic Party, Clarence Norman Jr. As Jonathan P. Hicks in the *New York Times* explained, "in the last two years, the two Democrats began sparring, first over competing sets of delegates to the party's convention to select judicial candidates, a race that Mr. Norman won." Hicks went on to note that Towns's endorsement of Giuliani had fanned the flames of the conflict between Norman and Towns. In June of 1998, Norman told the *New York Times* that "we are not supporting Ed Towns" and indicated that the Brooklyn Democratic Party would support Towns's opponent, Harvard-educated lawyer Barry Ford. Towns was unimpressed with the street-level credentials of Ford. "I've never seen him at a town hall meeting, a community board meeting or a tenants association meeting," Towns told the *New York Times.* "So, I don't have any idea of what his record of public service is, and the voters don't either. This is one Ford this Congressional District won't buy."

Towns married Gwendolyn Forbes in 1960 and is the father of two children. His son, Darryl, serves in the New York State Assembly representing the 54th District in Brooklyn. The younger Towns was elected in 1992 and defeated a ten-year incumbent; his State Assembly district overlapped with his father's Congressional one, and Congressman Towns often campaigned with his son. "In a city with a long history of politically active families," noted Jonathan P. Hicks of the *New York Times,* "... it is not surprising that the father-and-son Townses are increasingly viewed as a an emerging political dynasty form the working-class neighborhoods of Williamsburg and Bushwick, where dynasties of any sort are not particularly common." In 1998, Darryl Towns was serving as the Brooklyn district representative at the State House in Albany. "He used to follow me around," Towns told the *New York Times,* "and although I never thought he had an interest in politics when he was young, he developed that interest. He's developed into a good campaigner and a good Assemblyman."

Sources

Entrepreneur, June 1996, p. 134.
Jet, January 27, 1997, p. 46.
Los Angeles Times, May 1, 1992.
New York Daily News, September 30, 1997; March 6, 1998.
New York Times, July 28, 1992, p. B1; September 12, 1994; June 8, 1998, p. B10.
Village Voice, June 10, 1997, p. 26.

—Carol Brennan

Cedric "Ricky" Walker

1953(?)—

UniverSoul Circus founder

(Photo of UniverSoul Circus Performers—Kenyan Black Wizards Acrobatic Troupe)

Bedecked in his bright yellow or cherry red Zoot Suit, matching hat, and tennis shoes, Casual Cal, the ring leader, greets the audience with shouts of "Yo, yo, yo!" The stilt-walking acrobats are costumed in the ritual garments of the stilt-walking shamans of West Africa. The elephants re-enact the saga of Hannibals' army crossing the Alps. The clowns retell the history of blacks in American television. The background music is the theme songs from the television sitcoms *Good Times* and *The Jeffersons*. Is this a comedy show? No, it is the UniverSoul Big Top Circus, the "Cirque du Soul," and the brainchild of Atlanta-based promoter Cedric "Ricky" Walker.

Ricky Walker came to the arts world through an unfortunate but common path, that of troubled adolescence. One of four children born to Frank Walker, an Air Force master sergeant, and his homemaker wife, Alma, Ricky was part of a tough crowd in his Baltimore high school—drinking, drugs, and stealing epitomized his lifestyle. At 18, his father sent him to live with his uncle, William Carr, a nightclub owner in Tuskegee, Alabama. "It was the best thing that ever happened in my life," Walker admitted in an interview with *People Magazine*.

While at his uncle's club and a student at Tuskegee Institute, Walker met the Commodores, who were just beginning their career, and he joined their road crew in 1971. In 1975, he met Cal Dupree, who was also promoting local musical acts. In 1978, they teamed together to promote the Kool Jazz Festivals. They then successfully produced the first national rap tour, the 1984 Fresh Festival, featuring rap artists such as Run-DMC, the Fat Boys, and Whodini. Walker also served as concert promoter for groups, including the O'Jays, the Jackson Five, and Kurtis Blow.

Walker eventually grew disenchanted with the raunchiness of rap music, and his career then moved into theater production. In the early 1990s he produced the gospel plays *A Good Man is Hard to Find* and *Mama Don't*. The plays dealt primarily with problems afflicting African American urban life: drugs, dysfunctional families, and crime. Walker noticed young children leaving these shows late at night, which led him to ponder the options for daytime entertainment for families. It quickly became clear to him that family-oriented entertainment represented a glaring void in the cultural options for African Americans, and he sought to capitalize on this

> **At a Glance...**
>
> Born Cedric "Ricky" Walker in Baltimore; son of Frank Walker (Air Force master sergeant) and Alma Walker (homemaker); married to Cynthia (comptroller and vice president of UniverSoul Circus); children: one son. *Education:* Attended Tuskegee Institute.
>
> **Career:** Founder and chairman, UniverSoul Circus; Music promoter, Commodors, 1971; Kool Jazz Festivals, 1978; Fresh Festival, 1984. Theater producer, *A Good Man is Hard to Find* and *Mama Don't.*
>
> **Addresses:** UniverSoul Big Top Circus, Suite B-5, 2459 Roosevelt Hwy, College Park, GA 30337.

opportunity. As he explained in a July 1995 article by Joyce Jones in *Black Enterprise,* "One of our underlying goals as promoters is to be creative and bring new and different things to the public. We have to look for these types of voids and attempt to fill them."

Family-Based Entertainment

As he considered various options, Walker envisioned a Black variety show, a medley of singing, dancing, and animal acts which would tour the country. When he discussed the idea with longtime friend and partner Cal Dupree, Dupree jokingly responded, "If you're going to have all that, you might as well start a circus." And, after three years of studying circus history, developing the concept for the show, and traveling worldwide to find top Black circus performers, Walker did just that. Walker is now the founder and chairman of the UniverSoul Circus, the first nationally-touring African American circus in more than 100 years.

The UniverSoul Circus is the first Black circus since Ephraim Williams developed Black traveling shows in the late 1880s. Walker intently studied Williams' production, and, in honor of both Williams and the American circus tradition, committed himself to producing a show rich in culture, faith, and history. As a result, his acts pay tribute to such Black figures as the renowned Buffalo Soldier calvarymen and also tell the biblical story of Daniel in the lion's den.

Promoted as "Your Circus of Dreams," the UniverSoul Circus brings together the largest number of African American performers in circus history and showcases everything from aerial and equestrian acts to wild animal and clown skits—all while reshaping the image of the traditional circus. The UniverSoul Circus initially opened in 1994 under a rented tent in the parking lot of Atlanta's Fulton County Stadium. Walker provided the financing from his savings and received some help from Atlanta franchiser La-Van Hawkins. Now, just a few years later, the circus has boasted a 1997 attendance of one million people, it will visit 19 major U.S. cities in 1998, and has 14 acts and 45 performers in the one-ring show—95 percent of whom are African American.

Defined Composition of Circus

Walker's search for Black talent highlights his commitment to his ideal. It was a quest, in fact, which has taken him all over the world. He ultimately signed such famed circus acts as Nayakata, an African-Spanish contortionist, and the Ayak Brothers from South Africa. Monique, who joined the circus in 1998, is the world's first and only African American female lion tamer. He also tapped into the talent of Ringling Brothers and Barnum & Bailey Circus. For instance, all of the clowns in the UniverSoul Circus have graduated from Barnum and Bailey Clown College. The King Charles Troupe of unicyclists, moreover, were the first African American performers hired by Ringling Brothers and are the third generation to perform this act, while Pa-Mela Hernandez was the first Black female aerialist with Ringling.

Initially, one of Walker's biggest challenges was finding his first Black lion tamer. At the time, there were only three in the entire United States, and Walker dreamed of presenting a Black tamer as an inspiration for urban youth. He then thought of a solution: his cousin, Ted McRae, a laborer in Baltimore, MD, owned several poisonous snakes and had made the news when his boa constrictor escaped and terrified the local community. Walker convinced McRae to join the show as a personal favor, and in a period of three weeks, McRae went from driving a forklift to prancing in a pen of lions and elephants. He is now consistently one of the show-stopping acts.

The setting for Walker's circus perfectly complements the show. It is produced outdoors under a striped tent. Far from out-dated, though, the old-world theater-in-the-round with a single ring and 2,100 seats is state-of-the-art, boasting computerized special effects, a rock-style laser show, and high-tech sound. Gospel, jazz, and rhythm and blues accompany the show and further contribute to what Walker terms its "high-energy, hip-hop sound."

Even as his circus has grown both in size and recognition, Walker has not lost sight of his original mission: providing family-based entertainment for African American communities long underserved by the entertainment industry. Thus, the group bypasses suburban areas and heads to the nation's more depressed neighborhoods. Not only does Walker bring his circus into the city, but he also draws the city into his show. The circus hires local people to help with construction, concessions, and security, thereby further contributing to the welfare of these areas. Walker even offers elephant and pony rides before and after the show to give children a taste of circus life. Ticket prices remain affordable thanks to corporate sponsors such as Burger King, General Mills, Ford, and Texaco.

Explored Spiritual Vision of Circus

Walker veritably brims with enthusiasm when discussing his "soulful assault" on the traditional circus. "The enthusiasm is inside of me. I feel like the whole world is in front of me," he told Kevin Chappell in a December 1996 interview for *Ebony*. The passion, moreover, seems in part to stem from his commitment to the vision behind the creation of the circus. Walker not only wants to entertain; he also wants to captivate the children in the audience in a way that allows them to tap into the show's underlying spiritual values.

Thus, not only is the show what *Circus Report* calls a "masterpiece of production, staging, and promotion," but it is also unique in the emphasis it places on the importance of family. The Ringmaster, Casual Cal Dupree himself, actively includes members of the audience to reinforce the message. For example, he implores adults to turn off the television and actively engage their children in other activities. Children in the audience are called upon to take the "ringmaster's pledge" in which they commit to love their families and to reject drugs. He also reminds children to be thankful when people help them and adds, "Whenever faced with adversity, always have faith in your family." At one point in the show, Casual Cal cries, "Our roots come from the church, right? Are you ready to rock this tent like church?" And then he joins the clowns, ushers, and audience in singing, dancing, and stomping through the aisles.

Established Successful Black Role Models

Walker certainly provides his audiences with a plethora of stimuli: visual, oral, and emotional. Most important in Walker's mind, though, is the heightened self-esteem garnered from watching Black performers excel. As Walker commented in *Ebony*, "If you can look in a circus ring and see yourself, that's something you can relate to, and you'll come out to witness it, and you'll tell others about it. But Blacks haven't been given the chance to show they are just like everyone else." As Walker admitted, he himself dreamed of running away with the circus when he was a child. At that time, though, the only role models available for Blacks were janitors. He never aspired to be a lion tamer, he said, because he never saw a black tamer. "When you see someone you can relate to doing it," he told Emory Holmes of the *Los Angeles Times*, "you can aspire to do it. I saw black folks being janitors ... That's how I figured I could be in the circus."

The positive, energy-creating effect of Blacks performing for Blacks is felt on the performers' side of the stage as well. As Walker commented in his discussion with Holmes, "[T]hese guys come from all over the world and have never had the opportunity to stand before their people and do a performance. So their hearts and souls are there." It is this contagious spirit which sets the UniverSoul Circus soaring.

The UniverSoul Circus, then, is a Black circus: about Blacks, by Blacks, and predominantly for Blacks. The show's themes consciously trace black entertainment from slavery until the present time and focus, in Walker's words, on "the expression of a people and a culture." In essence, Walker wants his circus to be different; he wants to make a difference. In his discussion with Holmes, Walker is quick to refute criticism that his show is reminiscent of a twentieth century minstrel show. Rather than a demeaning portrayal of Blacks, Walker sees himself on the opposite end of the spectrum: race conscious but not racist, intent on lovingly and astoundingly conveying positive images of Black life and achievement. As Esther Iverem explained in a *New York Times* review, Walker promotes "race pride, family values and a worldview that does not make Black the Other, but puts it, literally, in the center ring."

Walker is often asked, "What next?" Laughing, he proclaims, "I want to create a Black Disneyland—a Black theme park." Crazy, maybe. But then again, no one believed a rap festival would sell nor did many initially support the idea of a Black circus. Walker's next effort should not really surprise anyone.

Sources

Periodicals

Black Enterprise, July 1995, p. 20.

Cleveland Plain Dealer, June 7, 1998.
Ebony, December 1996, pp. 68-71.
Jersey Journal, May 3, 1997, pp. E1, E4.
Los Angeles Times, October 27, 1996, pp. C6, C93.
New York Times, June 1, 1997.
Parade Magazine, June 7, 1998, pp. 13-14.
People, October 6, 1997, pp. 147-148.
Time for Kids, September 26, 1997.
Village Voice, reference unknown.

Washington Post, July 21, 1997, pp. C1, C4.

Other

Harlem Ontime Features.
Press Releases, UniverSoul Circus.

—Lisa S. Weitzman

Dorothy Porter Wesley

1905–1995

Librarian, writer

Dorothy Porter Wesley was a librarian and curator who, with a passionate single-mindedness, built the Moorland-Spingarn Research Center at Howard University into one of the largest and most comprehensive collections of African American history in the world. Beginning with 3,000 items in 1930, Wesley expanded the Center into an archive of more than 180,000 manuscripts, books, pamphlets, letters, oral history works, and microfilms by the time she retired in 1973. Along the way, Wesley received numerous honors and prizes culminating in the Charles Frankel Award from the National Endowment for the Humanities, which was presented at the White House by President Clinton a year before Wesley died of cancer in December of 1995.

Dorothy Porter Wesley was born Dorothy Burnett on May 25, 1905 in Warrenton, Virginia, the oldest of Dr. Hayes J. Burnett and his wife Bertha Ball Burnett's four children. The Burnetts lived in Montclair, New Jersey, and their children were educated in the public schools. After graduating from high school, Wesley enrolled in Minor Normal School in Washington, D.C. In 1926, she continued her education by transferring to Howard University and began working in the university's Founders Library as a student assistant. Intent on becoming a librarian, Wesley enrolled in the Columbia University School of Library Science where she obtained her bachelor's degree in 1931. She also earned a scholarship to continue her graduate studies at Columbia and became one of the first African American women to receive an M.L.S. from Columbia in 1932.

Asked to Assemble a Collection

In 1928, while pursuing her studies at Columbia, Wesley obtained a position at the Carnegie Library at Howard University as a cataloger. The following year she married James Porter, an artist and chairman of the Howard art department. In 1930, Wesley was asked by her boss, E.C. Williams, to assemble a collection of books by black Americans. She began this process by rooting through dusty, old boxes which contained roughly 3,000 books, pamphlets, and other historical items that had been donated to the university in 1914 by Jesse E. Moorland, a minister and Howard University alumnus and trustee. "Nothing had been done in that collection, nothing had been brought together," Wesley recalled to Phil McCombs of the *Washington Post*. The Moorland collection, along with the 1,600 piece Anti-Slavery collection donated to the university in 1873 by wealthy, New York abolitionist Lewis Tappan, formed the cornerstone of what was called the Moorland Foundation. The Moorland Foundation became the first research library in an American university devoted exclusively to the culture and history of people of African descent.

Although compiling such a collection might seem an incredibly daunting task, it was clear from the outset that Williams had chosen the right person for the job. "First

At a Glance...

Born Dorothy Burnett on May 25, 1905, in Warrenton, Virginia to Dr. Hayes J. Burnett and Bertha Ball Burnett; died December 17, 1995, in Fort Lauderdale, Florida. Married James Porter, 1929; (died 1970); married Charles H. Wesley, 1979; (died 1987). Chilren: Constance. *Education:* Howard Univ., A.B., 1928; Columbia Univ. School of Library Science, B.L.S, 1931; M.L.S., 1932.

Career: Began work as library assistant at Howard University's Founders Library, 1926; appointed curator of Moorland Foundation: A Library of Negro Life, 1930; published *A Selected List of Books by and About the Negro,* 1936; published *North American Negro Poets: A Bibliographical Checklist of Their Writings, 1760-1944,* 1945; advised Howard Univ. to buy the Negro Authors Collection of Arthur Barnett Spingarn, 1946; published *The Negro in American Cities: A Selected and Annotated Bibliography,* 1967; published *Negro Protest Pamphlets: A Compendium,* 1969; published *The Negro in the United States: A Selected Bibliography,* 1970; published *Early Negro Writings, 1760-1837,* 1971; researcher and consultant to the Moorland-Spingarn Research Ctr., 1973; published *Afro-Braziliana: A Working Bibliography,* 1978; named a Ford Foundation visiting fellow at the W.E.B. DuBois Institute for Afro-American Research at Harvard Univ., 1988-89.

Selected awards: Honorary doctorate, Susquehanna Univ., 1971, Radcliffe Coll., 1990; dedication of the Dorothy B. Porter Room in Founders Library, Howard Univ., 1973; Olaudah Equiano Award of Excellence for Pioneering Achievements in African Amer. Culture, Univ.of UT, 1989; Trailblazer Award, Black Caucus of the American Library Assn. (ALA), 1990; Charles Frankel Award, National Endowment for the Humanities, 1994.

I had to teach myself black history," Wesley admitted to McCombs. "Then I went around the [Howard] library and pulled out every relevant book I could find—the history of slavery, black poets—for the collection. Over the years the main thing I had to do was beg—from publishers, authors, families. Sometimes it meant being there just after the funeral director took out the bodies and saying, 'You want all this old junk in the basement?' Then I stretched my searches to Africa, and Latin America, and anywhere in the world that we had what we call the African diaspora."

In addition to her curating duties at the Moorland Foundation, Wesley published many bibliographical works which sought to focus attention on materials for scholars which may have previously gone unnoticed. In 1936 she published the first of these, *A Selected List of Books by and About the Negro,* for the U.S. Government Printing Office, which had an enormous impact on the study of African Americans. Other works published by Wesley included *North American Negro Poets: A Bibliographical Checklist of Their Writings, 1760-1944,* in 1945, *The Negro in American Cities: A Selected and Annotated Bibliography,* on behalf of the National Advisory Commission on Civil Disorders in 1967, and for the Library of Congress, 1970's *The Negro in the United States: A Selected Bibliography.*

Become the Moorland-Spingarn Research Library

In 1946, upon the advice of Wesley, Howard University purchased the nearly 5,000 volume Negro Authors Collection from Arthur Barnett Spingarn and the Moorland Foundation became known as the Moorland-Spingarn Research Library. In addition to African American authors, the Spingarn collection included works by African, African-Brazilian, and Caribbean writers in more than 60 languages. In 1958 the library acquired Spingarn's Negro Music Collection, the largest in the world at the time. Like the authors collection, the music collection featured not just African American composers, but composers from Cuba, Brazil, France, Haiti, and elsewhere.

In order to add to the large collections acquired by Howard University, Wesley relentlessly pursued every avenue. "I would go out and beg for books," she confessed to Linton Weeks of the *Washington Post.* "I would sweep up their basements." Her efforts provided many rewards. Among them, a letter from Benjamin Banneker, a surveyor who helped design the District of Columbia, to then-Secretary of State Thomas Jefferson in 1791 urging Jefferson to consider black people as equals. Another jewel was the brief autobiography of Jarena Lee, the first black woman to seek ordination from the African Methodist Episcopal Church in 1836. The center also includes the papers and manuscripts of actor Paul Robeson, singer Marian Anderson, civil rights activist Mary Church Terrell, sociologist E. Franklin Frazier, and the founder of Union Bethel Church, John

Francis Cook.

A Meeting Place for Scholars

The prominence and breadth of the Moorland-Spingarn collection encouraged many scholars and authors to utilize its 6,000 linear feet of materials for their endeavors. Louis Harlan used the library to research his biography of Booker T. Washington as did Frederick Douglass biographer William McFeeley and writers Taylor Branch and David J. Garrow for their books on Martin Luther King, Jr. Historian John Hope Franklin credits Wesley for the spark that ignited his 40-year project on George Washington Williams, the 19th-century historian and minister. "I was sort of at a loss as to how to get underway," Franklin reminisced to Phil McCombs of the Washington Post. "I had told Dorothy about my problems, and one day she came up to me with a letter from the Moorland-Spingarn collection, the first letter I have in my possession which Williams had written.... It got me going. I don't know where I would have been without that letter. From that point, I took off, and for 35 or 40 years I worked on the book." Franklin published the finished work, George Washington Williams: A Biography, in 1985. The book was a finalist for the Pulitzer Prize and the winner of the Clarence Holte Literary Award for the best book on Afro-American history.

Having created an invaluable collection where scholars and authors interested in African American history could engage in research, Wesley retired from Howard in 1973. To commemorate the occasion and honor Wesley for her years of service, the university dedicated the Dorothy B. Porter Reading Room in the Founders Library. At the ceremony, the historian Benjamin Quarles was quoted by Harriet Jackson Scarupa of New Directions as saying, "Without exaggeration, there hasn't been a major Black history book in the last 30 years in which the author hasn't acknowledged Mrs. Porter's help."

Wesley kept busy during her retirement years. She remained an active researcher and writer and published several books in the 1970s, including Afro-Braziliana: A Working Bibliography in 1978, which is considered to be one of the authoritative volumes on the subject. Wesley also served as a consultant at the Moorland-Spingarn Research Center, which was now the official name of the collection. Nine years after the death of her first husband, she married Charles H. Wesley, a historian and professor at Howard, in 1979. This marriage lasted until his death in 1987. The next year, Wesley was a Ford Foundation visiting fellow at the W.E.B. DuBois Institute for Afro-American Research at Harvard University.

> "The only rewarding thing for me is to bring to light information that no one knows. What's the point of rehashing the same old thing?"

Wesley received many honors and awards for her groundbreaking efforts in documenting and collecting African American history. Chief among these was being named a recipient of the Charles Frankel Award from the National Endowment for the Humanities in 1994. In a ceremony at the White House, Wesley was presented with the award by President Clinton. The following year, ill health forced Wesley to move from Washington, DC, her home of more than 70 years, to Fort Lauderdale, Florida to live with her daughter, Constance. Wesley succumbed to cancer one month later at the age of 91, leaving behind an unprecedented impact on the field of African American history. "The only rewarding thing for me is to bring to light information that no one knows," she revealed to Weeks of the Washington Post one year before her death. "What's the point of rehashing the same old thing?"

Sources

Books

Hildenbrand, Suzanne, ed., Reclaiming the American Past: Writing the Women In, Ablex Publishing Corp., 1996.
Hine, Darlene Clark, et al, eds., Black Women in America, Carlson Publishing, 1993.

Periodicals

Jet, November 7, 1994, p. 32; January 8, 1996, p. 17.
New Directions, January, 1990.
New York Times, December 20, 1995, p. B-15.
Washington Post, December 16, 1989, p. D-1; November 15, 1995, p. C-1; December 19, 1995, p. E-5.

—Brian Escamilla

Cumulative Indexes

Cumulative Nationality Index

Volume numbers appear in **bold.**

American
Aaron, Hank **5**
Abdul-Jabbar, Kareem **8**
Abernathy, Ralph David **1**
Abu-Jamal, Mumia **15**
Adams, Floyd, Jr. **12**
Adams, Oleta **18**
Adams, Yolanda **17**
Adams Early, Charity **13**
Agyeman, Jaramogi Abebe **10**
Ailey, Alvin **8**
Al-Amin, Jamil Abdullah **6**
Alexander, Archie Alphonso **14**
Alexander, Joyce London **18**
Ali, Muhammad **2, 16**
Allen, Byron **3**
Allen, Debbie **13**
Allen, Ethel D. **13**
Amos, John **8**
Amos, Wally **9**
Anderson, Marian **2**
Andrews, Bert **13**
Andrews, Raymond **4**
Angelou, Maya **1, 15**
Ansa, Tina McElroy **14**
Archer, Dennis **7**
Arkadie, Kevin **17**
Armstrong, Louis **2**
Armstrong, Robb **15**
Asante, Molefi Kete **3**
Ashe, Arthur **1, 18**
Avant, Clarence **19**
Ayers, Roy **16**
Bailey, Radcliffe **19**
Bailey, Xenobia **11**
Baker, Dusty **8**
Baker, Ella **5**
Baker, Gwendolyn Calvert **9**
Baker, Houston A., Jr. **6**
Baker, Josephine **3**
Baldwin, James **1**
Bambara, Toni Cade **10**
Banks, Jeffrey **17**
Banks, Tyra **11**
Banks, William **11**
Baraka, Amiri **1**
Barboza, Anthony **10**
Barden, Don H. **9**
Barkley, Charles **5**
Barrett, Andrew C. **12**

Barry, Marion S. **7**
Barthe, Richmond **15**
Basquiat, Jean-Michel **5**
Bassett, Angela **6**
Bates, Daisy **13**
Bates, Peg Leg **14**
Baylor, Don **6**
Beals, Jennifer **12**
Beals, Melba Patillo **15**
Bearden, Romare **2**
Bechet, Sidney **18**
Beckford, Tyson **11**
Belafonte, Harry **4**
Bell, Derrick **6**
Bellamy, Bill **12**
Belle, Albert **10**
Belle, Regina **1**
Belton, Sharon Sayles **9, 16**
Ben-Israel, Ben Ami **11**
Bennett, Lerone, Jr. **5**
Berry, Bertice **8**
Berry, Halle **4, 19**
Berry, Mary Frances **7**
Bethune, Mary McLeod **4**
Bing, Dave **3**
Black, Keith Lanier **18**
Blackwell, Unita **17**
Bluford, Guy **2**
Bluitt, Juliann S. **14**
Bolden, Charles F., Jr. **7**
Bond, Julian **2**
Bonds, Barry **6**
Bontemps, Arna **8**
Borders, James **9**
Bosley, Freeman, Jr. **7**
Bowe, Riddick **6**
Bowser, Yvette Lee **17**
Boyd, T. B. III **6**
Boykin, Keith **14**
Bradley, Ed **2**
Bradley, Thomas **2**
Brandon, Barbara **3**
Brandon, Terrell **16**
Brandy **14**
Braugher, Andre **13**
Braun, Carol Moseley **4**
Braxton, Toni **15**
Brimmer, Andrew F. **2**
Briscoe, Connie **15**
Brock, Lou **18**

Brooke, Edward **8**
Brooks, Avery **9**
Brooks, Gwendolyn **1**
Brown, Donald **19**
Brown, Elaine **8**
Brown, Jesse **6**
Brown, Jim **11**
Brown, Lee P. **1**
Brown, Les **5**
Brown, Marie Dutton **12**
Brown, Ron **5**
Brown, Sterling **10**
Brown, Tony **3**
Brown, Willie L., Jr. **7**
Brown, Zora Kramer **12**
Brunson, Dorothy **1**
Bryant, Kobe **15**
Bryant, Wayne R. **6**
Bullard, Eugene **12**
Bumbry, Grace **5**
Bunche, Ralph J. **5**
Burke, Selma **16**
Burnett, Charles **16**
Burroughs, Margaret Taylor **9**
Burton, LeVar **8**
Busby, Jheryl **3**
Butler, Leroy III **17**
Butler, Octavia **8**
Butler, Paul D. **17**
Butts, Calvin O., III **9**
Byrd, Donald **10**
Byrd, Michelle **19**
Byrd, Robert **11**
Cadoria, Sherian Grace **14**
Caesar, Shirley **19**
Cain, Herman **15**
Calloway, Cab **14**
Camp, Kimberly **19**
Campbell, Bebe Moore **6**
Campbell, Bill **9**
Campbell, E. Simms **13**
Campbell, Tisha **8**
Cannon, Katie **10**
Carroll, Diahann **9**
Carson, Benjamin **1**
Carter, Betty **19**
Carter, Mandy **11**
Carter, Stephen L. **4**
Carver, George Washington **4**

Cary, Lorene 3
CasSelle, Malcolm 11
Catlett, Elizabeth 2
Chamberlain, Wilt 18
Chambers, Julius 3
Chappell, Emma 18
Charles, Ray 16
Chavis, Benjamin 6
Cheadle, Don 19
Chenault, Kenneth I. 4
Chideya, Farai 14
Childress, Alice 15
Chisholm, Shirley 2
Christian, Spencer 15
Christian-Green, Donna M. 17
Chuck D 9
Clark, Celeste 15
Clark, Joe 1
Clark, Kenneth B. 5
Clark, Patrick 14
Clark, Septima 7
Clarke, Hope 14
Clash, Kevin 14
Clay, William Lacy 8
Clayton, Constance 1
Clayton, Xernona 3
Claytor, Helen 14
Cleage, Pearl 17
Cleaver, Eldridge 5
Cleaver, Emanuel 4
Clements, George 2
Cleveland, James 19
Clifton, Lucille 14
Clinton, George 9
Coachman, Alice 18
Cobbs, Price M. 9
Cochran, Johnnie L., Jr. 11
Cohen, Anthony 15
Colbert, Virgis William 17
Cole, Johnnetta B. 5
Cole, Nat King 17
Cole, Natalie Maria 17
Coleman, Bessie 9
Coleman, Leonard S., Jr. 12
Colemon, Johnnie 11
Collins, Albert 12
Collins, Barbara-Rose 7
Collins, Cardiss 10
Collins, Marva 3
Coltrane, John 19
Combs, Sean "Puffy" 17
Comer, James P. 6
Cone, James H. 3
Connerly, Ward 14
Conyers, John, Jr. 4
Cook, Samuel DuBois 14
Cooper, Cynthia 17
Cooper, Edward S. 6
Cooper, J. California 12
Cornelius, Don 4
Cosby, Bill 7
Cosby, Camille 14
Cose, Ellis 5
Cottrell, Comer 11
Crawford, Randy 19
Crew, Rudolph F. 16
Crockett, Jr., George 10
Crothers, Scatman 19

Crouch, Stanley 11
Crowder, Henry 16
Cullen, Countee 8
Curry, Mark 17
Curtis-Hall, Vondie 17
Dandridge, Dorothy 3
Danticat, Edwidge 15
Darden, Christopher 13
Dash, Julie 4
Davidson, Jaye 5
Davis, Allison 12
Davis, Angela 5
Davis, Anthony 11
Davis, Benjamin O., Jr. 2
Davis, Benjamin O., Sr. 4
Davis, Miles 4
Davis, Ossie 5
Davis, Piper 19
Dawes, Dominique 11
Days, Drew S., III 10
Dee, Ruby 8
Delaney, Beauford 19
Delany, Bessie 12
Delany, Sadie 12
Delany, Samuel R., Jr. 9
Dellums, Ronald 2
Devers, Gail 7
Dickens, Helen Octavia 14
Dickerson, Ernest R. 6, 17
Dinkins, David 4
Divine, Father 7
Dixon, Margaret 14
Dixon, Sharon Pratt 1
Dixon, Willie 4
Doby, Sr., Lawrence Eugene 16
Dodson, Howard, Jr. 7
Donegan, Dorothy 19
Dorsey, Thomas 15
Douglas, Aaron 7
Dove, Rita 6
Dove, Ulysses 5
Downing, Will 19
Dr. Dre 10
Draper, Sharon M. 16
Dre, Dr. 14
Drew, Charles Richard 7
Drexler, Clyde 4
Driskell, David C. 7
Driver, David E. 11
Du Bois, W. E. B. 3
Ducksworth, Marilyn 12
Duke, Bill 3
Dumars, Joe 16
Dunbar, Paul Laurence 8
Dungy, Tony 17
Dunham, Katherine 4
Dupri, Jermaine 13
Dutton, Charles S. 4
Dyson, Michael Eric 11
Early, Gerald 15
Edelin, Ramona Hoage 19
Edelman, Marian Wright 5
Edley, Christopher 2
Edmonds, Kenneth "Babyface" 10
Edmonds, Terry 17
Edmonds, Tracey 16
Edwards, Harry 2
Edwards, Teresa 14

Elder, Lee 6
Elders, Joycelyn 6
Ellington, Duke 5
Ellington, E. David 11
Ellison, Ralph 7
Erving, Julius 18
Esposito, Giancarlo 9
Espy, Mike 6
Eubanks, Kevin 15
Europe, James Reese 10
Evers, Medgar 3
Evers, Myrlie 8
Faison, George 16
Farmer, Forest J. 1
Farmer, James 2
Farrakhan, Louis 2, 15
Fattah, Chaka 11
Fauntroy, Walter E. 11
Fauset, Jessie 7
Feelings, Tom 11
Fielder, Cecil 2
Fields, Cleo 13
Fishburne, Larry 4
Fitzgerald, Ella 1, 18
Flack, Roberta 19
Flake, Floyd H. 18
Fletcher, Jr., Alphonse 16
Flipper, Henry O. 3
Flood, Curt 10
Ford, Jr., Harold E. 16
Foreman, George 1, 15
Forman, James 7
Fortune, T. Thomas 6
Fox, Vivica A. 15
Foxx, Jamie 15
Foxx, Redd 2
Franklin, Aretha 11
Franklin, Carl 11
Franklin, Hardy R. 9
Franklin, John Hope 5
Franklin, Kirk 15
Franklin, Robert M. 13
Franks, Gary 2
Frazier, E. Franklin 10
Frazier, Joe 19
Freeman, Al, Jr. 11
Freeman, Charles 19
Freeman, Morgan 2
French, Albert 18
Fudge, Ann 11
Fulani, Lenora 11
Fuller, Charles 8
Fuller, S. B. 13
Fuller, Solomon Carter, Jr. 15
Gaines, Ernest J. 7
Gaither, Alonzo Smith (Jake) 14
Gantt, Harvey 1
Garnett, Kevin 14
Garrison, Zina 2
Gary, Willie E. 12
Gaston, Arthur G. 4
Gates, Henry Louis, Jr. 3
Gates, Sylvester James, Jr. 15
Gaye, Marvin 2
Gayle, Helene D. 3
George, Nelson 12
Gibson, Althea 8
Gibson, Kenneth Allen 6

Cumulative Nationality Index

Gibson, William F. **6**
Giddings, Paula **11**
Gillespie, Dizzy **1**
Gilliam, Sam **16**
Giovanni, Nikki **9**
Gist, Carole **1**
Givens, Robin **4**
Glover, Danny **1**
Glover, Nathaniel, Jr. **12**
Glover, Savion **14**
Goines, Donald **19**
Goldberg, Whoopi **4**
Golden, Marita **19**
Golden, Thelma **10**
Goldsberry, Ronald **18**
Gomes, Peter J. **15**
Gomez-Preston, Cheryl **9**
Goode, Mal **13**
Goode, W. Wilson **4**
Gooding, Jr., Cuba **16**
Gordon, Ed **10**
Gordone, Charles **15**
Gordy, Berry, Jr. **1**
Gossett, Louis, Jr. **7**
Gourdine, Simon **11**
Graham, Lawrence Otis **12**
Graham, Stedman **13**
Gravely, Samuel L., Jr. **5**
Graves, Denyce **19**
Graves, Earl G. **1**
Gray, F. Gary **14**
Gray, William H. III **3**
Green, Al **13**
Green, Dennis **5**
Greene, Joe **10**
Greenfield, Eloise **9**
Gregory, Dick **1**
Gregory, Frederick D. **8**
Grier, Pam **9**
Grier, Roosevelt **13**
Griffey, Ken, Jr. **12**
Griffith, Mark Winston **8**
Grimké, Archibald H. **9**
Guillaume, Robert **3**
Guinier, Lani **7**
Gumbel, Bryant **14**
Gumbel, Greg **8**
Gunn, Moses **10**
Guy, Jasmine **2**
Guy, Rosa **5**
Guy-Sheftall, Beverly **13**
Guyton, Tyree **9**
Gwynn, Tony **18**
Hale, Clara **16**
Hale, Lorraine **8**
Haley, Alex **4**
Hall, Lloyd A. **8**
Hamblin, Ken **10**
Hamer, Fannie Lou **6**
Hamilton, Virginia **10**
Hampton, Fred **18**
Hampton, Henry **6**
Hampton, Lionel **17**
Handy, W. C. **8**
Hannah, Marc **10**
Hansberry, Lorraine **6**
Hansberry, William Leo **11**
Hardaway, Anfernee (Penny) **13**

Hardison, Bethann **12**
Harkless, Necia Desiree **19**
Harper, Frances Ellen Watkins **11**
Harrell, Andre **9**
Harrington, Oliver W. **9**
Harris, Alice **7**
Harris, Barbara **12**
Harris, E. Lynn **12**
Harris, Eddy L. **18**
Harris, Jay T. **19**
Harris, Leslie **6**
Harris, Marcelite Jordon **16**
Harris, Monica **18**
Harris, Patricia Roberts **2**
Harris, Robin **7**
Harsh, Vivian Gordon **14**
Harvard, Beverly **11**
Harvey, Steve **18**
Hastie, William H. **8**
Hastings, Alcee L. **16**
Hathaway, Donny **18**
Hawkins, Coleman **9**
Hawkins, Erskine **14**
Hawkins, La-Van **17**
Hawkins, Steven **14**
Hawkins, Tramaine **16**
Hayden, Palmer **13**
Hayden, Robert **12**
Hayes, James C. **10**
Hayes, Roland **4**
Haynes, George Edmund **8**
Height, Dorothy I. **2**
Hemphill, Essex **10**
Hemsley, Sherman **19**
Henderson, Gordon **5**
Henderson, Wade J. **14**
Hendricks, Barbara **3**
Hendrix, Jimi **10**
Henson, Matthew **2**
Henry, Aaron **19**
Herman, Alexis M. **15**
Hernandez, Aileen Clarke **13**
Hickman, Fred **11**
Higginbotham, A. Leon, Jr. **13**
Hightower, Dennis F. **13**
Hill, Anita **5**
Hill, Calvin **19**
Hill, Grant **13**
Hill, Janet **19**
Hill, Jessie, Jr. **13**
Hilliard, David **7**
Himes, Chester **8**
Hinderas, Natalie **5**
Hines, Gregory **1**
Hinton, William Augustus **8**
Holder, Eric H., Jr. **9**
Holiday, Billie **1**
Holland, Endesha Ida Mae **3**
Holland, Robert, Jr. **11**
Holyfield, Evander **6**
hooks, bell **5**
Hooks, Benjamin L. **2**
Hope, John **8**
Horne, Lena **5**
House, Son **8**
Houston, Charles Hamilton **4**
Houston, Whitney **7**
Howard, Desmond **16**

Howard, Juwan **15**
Howlin' Wolf **9**
Hudlin, Reginald **9**
Hudlin, Warrington **9**
Hudson, Cheryl **15**
Hudson, Wade **15**
Hughes, Albert **7**
Hughes, Allen **7**
Hughes, Langston **4**
Hunt, Richard **6**
Hunter-Gault, Charlayne **6**
Hurston, Zora Neale **3**
Hutson, Jean Blackwell **16**
Hyman, Phyllis **19**
Ice Cube **8**
Ice-T **6**
Iceberg Slim **11**
Ingram, Rex **5**
Innis, Roy **5**
Irving, Larry, Jr. **12**
Jackson, George **19**
Jackson, George **14**
Jackson, Isaiah **3**
Jackson, Janet **6**
Jackson, Jesse **1**
Jackson, Jesse, Jr. **14**
Jackson, Mahalia **5**
Jackson, Mannie **14**
Jackson, Maynard **2**
Jackson, Michael **19**
Jackson, Reggie **15**
Jackson, Samuel L. **8, 19**
Jackson, Sheneska **18**
Jackson, Shirley Ann **12**
Jacob, John E. **2**
Jakes, Thomas "T.D." **17**
James, Daniel Jr. **16**
James, Etta **13**
James, Juanita **13**
James, Rick **17**
Jamison, Judith **7**
Jeffries, Leonard **8**
Jemison, Mae C. **1**
Jenifer, Franklyn G. **2**
Jenkins, Beverly **14**
Jenkins, Ella **15**
Jimmy Jam **13**
Johnson, Beverly **2**
Johnson, Charles **1**
Johnson, Charles S. **12**
Johnson, Earvin "Magic" **3**
Johnson, Eddie Bernice **8**
Johnson, Jack **8**
Johnson, James Weldon **5**
Johnson, John H. **3**
Johnson, Michael **13**
Johnson, Norma L. Holloway **17**
Johnson, Robert **2**
Johnson, Robert L. **3**
Johnson, Robert T. **17**
Johnson, Virginia **9**
Johnson, William Henry **3**
Jones, Bill T. **1**
Jones, Carl **7**
Jones, Cobi N'Gai **18**
Jones, Elaine R. **7**
Jones, Elvin **14**
Jones, Ingrid Saunders **18**

Jones, James Earl 3
Jones, Lois Mailou 13
Jones, Quincy 8
Jones, Star 10
Joplin, Scott 6
Jordan, Barbara 4
Jordan, June 7
Jordan, Michael 6
Jordan, Vernon E. 3
Josey, E. J. 10
Joyner, Matilda Sissieretta 15
Joyner, Tom 19
Joyner-Kersee, Jackie 5
Julian, Percy Lavon 6
Just, Ernest Everett 3
Justice, David 18
Kani, Karl 10
Karenga, Maulana 10
Kearse, Amalya Lyle 12
Keith, Damon J. 16
Kelly, Patrick 3
Kelly, R. 18
Kennedy, Adrienne 11
Kennedy, Florynce 12
Keyes, Alan L. 11
Khan, Chaka 12
Khanga, Yelena 6
Kilpatrick, Carolyn Cheeks 16
Kimbro, Dennis 10
Kincaid, Jamaica 4
King, B. B. 7
King, Bernice 4
King, Coretta Scott 3
King, Dexter 10
King, Don 14
King, Gayle 19
King, Martin Luther, Jr. 1
King, Yolanda 6
Kirby, George 14
Kirk, Ron 11
Kitt, Eartha 16
Knight, Gladys 16
Knight, Suge 11
Komunyakaa, Yusef 9
Kotto, Yaphet 7
Kountz, Samuel L. 10
Kravitz, Lenny 10
Kunjufu, Jawanza 3
L.L. Cool J 16
LaBelle, Patti 13
Lafontant, Jewel Stradford 8
Lampkin, Daisy 19
Lane, Charles 3
Lane, Vincent 5
Langhart, Janet 19
Larsen, Nella 10
La Salle, Eriq 12
Latimer, Lewis H. 4
Lawless, Theodore K. 8
Lawrence, Jacob 4
Lawrence, Martin 6
Lawrence, Jr., Robert H. 16
Lawrence-Lightfoot, Sara 10
Lawson, Jennifer 1
Leary, Kathryn D. 10
Leavell, Dorothy R. 17
Lee, Canada 8
Lee, Joie 1

Lee, Spike 5, 19
Lee-Smith, Hughie 5
Leffall, LaSalle, Jr. 3
Leland, Mickey 2
Leon, Kenny 10
Leonard, Sugar Ray 15
Lester, Julius 9
Lewellyn, J. Bruce 13
Lewis, Byron E. 13
Lewis, Carl 4
Lewis, David Levering 9
Lewis, Delano 7
Lewis, Edmonia 10
Lewis, John 2
Lewis, Reginald F. 6
Lewis, Shirley A. R. 14
Lewis, Terry 13
Lewis, Thomas 19
Lincoln, Abbey 3
Little, Robert L. 2
Little Richard 15
Locke, Alain 10
Lofton, Kenny 12
Logan, Onnie Lee 14
Long, Nia 17
Lorde, Audre 6
Lott, Ronnie 9
Louis, Errol T. 8
Louis, Joe 5
Love, Nat 9
Lover, Ed 10
Lowery, Joseph 2
Lucas, John 7
Lyons, Henry 12
Lyttle, Hulda Margaret 14
Mabley, Moms 15
Madhubuti, Haki R. 7
Madison, Joseph E. 17
Major, Clarence 9
Mallett, Jr., Conrad 16
Malone, Annie 13
Malone, Karl A. 18
Manigault, Earl "The Goat" 15
Manley, Audrey Forbes 16
Marable, Manning 10
Marsalis, Wynton 16
Marshall, Paule 7
Marshall, Thurgood 1
Martin, Louis E. 16
Massey, Walter E. 5
Mayfield, Curtis 2
Maynard, Robert C. 7
Maynor, Dorothy 19
Mays, Benjamin E. 7
Mays, Willie 3
McBride, Bryant 18
McCabe, Jewell Jackson 10
McCall, Nathan 8
McCarty, Oseola 16
McCoy, Elijah 8
McCray, Nikki 18
McDaniel, Hattie 5
McDonald, Erroll 1
McDougall, Gay J. 11
McEwen, Mark 5
McGee, Charles 10
McKay, Claude 6
McKay, Nellie Yvonne 17

McKinney, Cynthia Ann 11
McKinnon, Isaiah 9
McKissick, Floyd B. 3
McKnight, Brian 18
McMillan, Terry 4, 17
McNair, Ronald 3
McNeil, Lori 1
McPhail, Sharon 2
McQueen, Butterfly 6
Mckee, Lonette 12
Meek, Carrie 6
Meredith, James H. 11
Mfume, Kweisi 6
Micheaux, Oscar 7
Miller, Bebe 3
Miller, Cheryl 10
Mingus, Charles 15
Mitchell, Arthur 2
Mitchell, Corinne 8
Monk, Thelonious 1
Moon, Warren 8
Moorer, Michael 19
Morgan, Garrett 1
Morgan, Joe Leonard 9
Morgan, Rose 11
Morrison, Toni 2, 15
Morton, Joe 18
Moses, Edwin 8
Moses, Gilbert 12
Moses, Robert Parris 11
Mosley, Walter 5
Moss, Carlton 17
Moten, Etta 18
Motley, Constance Baker 10
Mourning, Alonzo 17
Moutoussamy-Ashe, Jeanne 7
Mowry, Jess 7
Muhammad, Elijah 4
Muhammad, Khallid Abdul 10
Murphy, Eddie 4
Murray, Cecil 12
Murray, Eddie 12
Murray, Lenda 10
Myers, Walter Dean 8
Naylor, Gloria 10
Ndegéocello, Me'Shell 15
Nelson, Jill 6
Newton, Huey 2
Nichols, Nichelle 11
N'Namdi, George R. 17
Norman, Jessye 5
Norman, Pat 10
Norton, Eleanor Holmes 7
O'Leary, Hazel 6
O'Neal, Shaquille 8
Oglesby, Zena 12
Ogletree, Jr., Charles 12
O'Neil, Buck 19
Owens, Jesse 2
Owens, Major 6
Page, Alan 7
Page, Clarence 4
Paige, Satchel 7
Parker, Pat 19
Parks, Bernard C. 17
Parks, Gordon 1
Parks, Rosa 1
Parsons, James 14

Cumulative Nationality Index

Parsons, Richard Dean **11**
Patrick, Deval **12**
Patterson, Floyd **19**
Patterson, Frederick Douglass **12**
Payne, Allen **13**
Payne, Donald M. **2**
Payton, Walter **11**
Peete, Calvin **11**
Perez, Anna **1**
Perkins, Edward **5**
Person, Waverly **9**
Petry, Ann **19**
Pickett, Bill **11**
Pinchback, P. B. S. **9**
Pinkett, Jada **10**
Pinkney, Jerry **15**
Pippen, Scottie **15**
Pippin, Horace **9**
Pleasant, Mary Ellen **9**
Poitier, Sidney **11**
Porter, James A. **11**
Poussaint, Alvin F. **5**
Powell, Adam Clayton, Jr. **3**
Powell, Colin **1**
Powell, Maxine **8**
Powell, Mike **7**
Pratt, Geronimo **18**
Price, Hugh B. **9**
Price, Leontyne **1**
Primus, Pearl **6**
Prince **18**
Prothrow-Stith, Deborah **10**
Pryor, Richard **3**
Puckett, Kirby **4**
Quarles, Benjamin Arthur **18**
Quarterman, Lloyd Albert **4**
Queen Latifah **1, 16**
Raines, Franklin Delano **14**
Ralph, Sheryl Lee **18**
Rand, A. Barry **6**
Randall, Dudley **8**
Randle, Theresa **16**
Randolph, A. Philip **3**
Rangel, Charles **3**
Rashad, Ahmad **18**
Raspberry, William **2**
Rawls, Lou **17**
Razaf, Andy **19**
Reagon, Bernice Johnson **7**
Reason, J. Paul **19**
Redding, Otis **16**
Reed, Ishmael **8**
Reese, Della **6**
Rhames, Ving **14**
Rhodes, Ray **14**
Rhone, Sylvia **2**
Ribbs, Willy T. **2**
Ribeiro, Alfonso **17**
Rice, Condoleezza **3**
Rice, Jerry **5**
Rice, Linda Johnson **9**
Rice, Norm **8**
Richardson, Nolan **9**
Richie, Leroy C. **18**
Richmond, Mitch **19**
Riggs, Marlon **5**
Riley, Helen Caldwell Day **13**
Ringgold, Faith **4**
Roberts, Marcus **19**
Roberts, Robin **16**
Roberts, Roy S. **14**
Robeson, Eslanda Goode **13**
Robeson, Paul **2**
Robinson, Bill "Bojangles" **11**
Robinson, Eddie G. **10**
Robinson, Frank **9**
Robinson, Jackie **6**
Robinson, Max **3**
Robinson, Patrick **19**
Robinson, Rachel **16**
Robinson, Randall **7**
Robinson, Smokey **3**
Robinson, Sugar Ray **18**
Roche, Joyce M. **17**
Rochon, Lela **16**
Rock, Chris **3**
Rodgers, Johnathan **6**
Rodman, Dennis **12**
Rogers, John W., Jr. **5**
Roker, Al **12**
Rolle, Esther **13**
Rollins, Jr., Howard E. **16**
Ross, Diana **8**
Rowan, Carl T. **1**
Rowell, Victoria **13**
Rudolph, Wilma **4**
Rupaul **17**
Rushen, Patrice **12**
Russell, Bill **8**
Russell, Herman Jerome **17**
Russell-McCloud, Patricia A. **17**
Rustin, Bayard **4**
Saar, Alison **16**
St. Jacques, Raymond **8**
Saint James, Synthia **12**
Samara, Noah **15**
Sampson, Charles **13**
Sanchez, Sonia **17**
Sanders, Joseph R., Jr. **11**
Sapphire **14**
Savage, Augusta **12**
Sayles Belton, Sharon, **9, 16**
Scott, Sr., Wendell Oliver **19**
Sengstacke, John **18**
Shakur, Tupac **14**
Sheffield, Gary **16**
Sherrod, Clayton **17**
Shipp, E. R. **15**
Simmons, Ruth J. **13**
Simone, Nina **15**
Simpson, O. J. **15**
Sinbad, **1, 16**
Singletary, Mike **4**
Sinkford, Jeanne C. **13**
Singleton, John **7**
Sister Souljah **11**
Slater, Rodney E. **15**
Sleet, Moneta, Jr. **5**
Smaltz, Audrey **12**
Smith, Anna Deavere **6**
Smith, Barbara **11**
Smith, Bessie **3**
Smith, Emmitt **7**
Smith, Joshua **10**
Smith, Roger Guenveur **12**
Smith, Tubby **18**
Smith, Will **8, 18**
Smith, Willi **8**
Sneed, Paula A. **18**
Snipes, Wesley **3**
Sowell, Thomas **2**
Spaulding, Charles Clinton **9**
Spikes, Dolores **18**
Stallings, George A., Jr. **6**
Staples, Brent **8**
Staupers, Mabel K. **7**
Steele, Claude Mason **13**
Steele, Shelby **13**
Stephens, Charlotte Andrews **14**
Steward, Emanuel **18**
Stewart, Alison **13**
Stewart, Maria W. Miller **19**
Stewart, Paul Wilbur **12**
Stokes, Carl B. **10**
Stokes, Louis **3**
Stone, Chuck **9**
Stone, Toni **15**
Stringer, C. Vivian **13**
Sudarkasa, Niara **4**
Sullivan, Leon H. **3**
Sullivan, Louis **8**
Sweat, Keith **19**
Swoopes, Sheryl **12**
Tanner, Henry Ossawa **1**
Tate, Larenz **15**
Taulbert, Clifton Lemoure **19**
Taylor, Kristin Clark **8**
Taylor, Meshach **4**
Taylor, Regina **9**
Taylor, Susan L. **10**
Taylor, Susie King **13**
Terrell, Mary Church **9**
Thigpen, Lynne **17**
Thomas, Alma **14**
Thomas, Clarence **2**
Thomas, Frank **12**
Thomas, Franklin A. **5**
Thomas, Isiah **7**
Thomas, Vivien **9**
Thompson, Tazewell **13**
Thurman, Howard **3**
Thurman, Wallace **16**
Till, Emmett **7**
Tolliver, William **9**
Toomer, Jean **6**
Towns, Edolphus **19**
Townsend, Robert **4**
Tribble, Israel, Jr. **8**
Trotter, Monroe **9**
Tubman, Harriet **9**
Tucker, C. DeLores **12**
Tucker, Chris **13**
Tucker, Cynthia **15**
Tucker, Rosina **14**
Turnbull, Walter **13**
Turner, Henry McNeal **5**
Turner, Tina **6**
Tyson, Cicely **7**
Tyson, Neil de Grasse **15**
Underwood, Blair **7**
Upshaw, Gene **18**
VanDerZee, James **6**
Vance, Courtney B. **15**
Vandross, Luther **13**

Van Peebles, Mario 2
Van Peebles, Melvin 7
Vanzant, Iyanla 17
Vaughan, Sarah 13
Vaughn, Mo 16
Vereen, Ben 4
Vincent, Marjorie Judith 2
Von Lipsey, Roderick K. 11
Waddles, Charleszetta (Mother) 10
Walker, A'lelia 14
Walker, Albertina 10
Walker, Alice 1
Walker, Cedric "Ricky" 19
Walker, Herschel 1
Walker, Madame C. J. 7
Walker, Maggie Lena 17
Walker, T. J. 7
Wallace, Michele Faith 13
Wallace, Phyllis A. 9
Wallace, Sippie 1
Warfield, Marsha 2
Warwick, Dionne 18
Washington, Booker T. 4
Washington, Denzel 1
Washington, Fredi 10
Washington, Grover, Jr. 17
Washington, Harold 6
Washington, Laura S. 18
Washington, MaliVai 8
Washington, Patrice Clarke 12
Washington, Val 12
Wasow, Omar 15
Waters, Ethel 7
Waters, Maxine 3
Watkins, Levi, Jr. 9
Watkins, Perry 12
Watkins, Shirley R. 17
Watson, Johnny "Guitar" 18
Wattleton, Faye 9
Watts, J. C., Jr. 14
Watts, Rolonda 9
Wayans, Damon 8
Wayans, Keenen Ivory 18
Weathers, Carl 10
Weaver, Robert C. 8
Webb, Veronica 10
Webb, Wellington 3
Webber, Chris 15
Wells, James Lesesne 10
Wells-Barnett, Ida B. 8
Welsing, Frances Cress 5
Wesley, Dorothy Porter 19
Wesley, Valerie Wilson 18
West, Cornel 5
West, Dorothy 12
West, Togo D., Jr. 16
Wharton, Clifton R., Jr. 7
Wheat, Alan 14
Whitaker, Forest 2
Whitaker, Pernell 10
White, Barry 13
White, Bill 1
White, Michael R. 5
White, Reggie 6
White, Walter F. 4
Whitfield, Lynn 18
Wideman, John Edgar 5
Wilder, L. Douglas 3

Wiley, Ralph 8
Wilkens, Lenny 11
Wilkins, Roger 2
Wilkins, Roy 4
Williams, Bert 18
Williams, Billy Dee 8
Williams, Daniel Hale 2
Williams, Evelyn 10
Williams, George Washington 18
Williams, Gregory 11
Williams, Hosea Lorenzo 15
Williams, Joe 5
Williams, Maggie 7
Williams, Mary Lou 15
Williams, Montel 4
Williams, O. S. 13
Williams, Patricia J. 11
Williams, Paul R. 9
Williams, Robert F. 11
Williams, Vanessa L. 4, 17
Williams, Walter E. 4
Williams, William T. 11
Williams, Willie L. 4
Wilson, August 7
Wilson, Cassandra 16
Wilson, Nancy 10
Wilson, Phill 9
Wilson, Sunnie 7
Winans, BeBe 14
Winans, CeCe 14
Winans, Marvin L. 17
Winfield, Dave 5
Winfield, Paul 2
Winfrey, Oprah 2, 15
Wolfe, George C. 6
Wonder, Stevie 11
Woodard, Alfre 9
Woodruff, Hale 9
Woods, Granville T. 5
Woods, Tiger 14
Woodson, Carter G. 2
Woodson, Robert L. 10
Worrill, Conrad 12
Wright, Bruce McMarion 3
Wright, Louis Tompkins 4
Wright, Richard 5
X, Malcolm 1
Yoba, Malik 11
Young, Andrew 3
Young, Coleman 1
Young, Jean Childs 14
Young, Whitney M., Jr. 4
Youngblood, Johnny Ray 8

Angolan
Bonga, Kuenda 13
Savimbi, Jonas 2

Bahamian
Ingraham, Hubert A. 19

Batswana
Masire, Quett 5

Beninois
Hounsou, Djimon 19
Kerekou, Ahmed (Mathieu) 1
Mogae, Festus Gontebanye 19

Soglo, Nicéphore 15

Bermudian
Gordon, Pamela 17

Brazilian
da Silva, Benedita 5
Nascimento, Milton 2
Pelé 7
Pitta, Celso 17

British
Abbott, Diane 9
Campbell, Naomi 1
Christie, Linford 8
Davidson, Jaye 5
Henry, Lenny 9
Jean-Baptiste, Marianne 17
Julien, Isaac 3
Lindo, Delroy 18
Pitt, David Thomas 10
Seal 14
Taylor, John (David Beckett) 16

Burkinabé
Somé, Malidoma Patrice 10

Burundian
Ndadaye, Melchior 7
Ntaryamira, Cyprien 8

Cameroonian
Kotto, Yaphet 7
Milla, Roger 2

Canadian
Bell, Ralph S. 5
Fuhr, Grant 1
Johnson, Ben 1
McKegney, Tony 3
O'Ree, Willie 5
Reuben, Gloria 15
Richards, Lloyd 2

Cape Verdean
Evora, Cesaria 12

Chadian
Habré, Hissène 6

Costa Rican
McDonald, Erroll 1

Cuban
León, Tania 13
Quirot, Ana 13

Dominican
Charles, Mary Eugenia 10

Dutch
Liberia-Peters, Maria Philomena 12

Ethiopian
Haile Selassie 7
Meles Zenawi 3

French

Baker, Josephine **3**
Baldwin, James **1**
Bonaly, Surya **7**
Noah, Yannick **4**
Tanner, Henry Ossawa **1**

Gabonese
Bongo, Omar **1**

Ghanaian
Annan, Kofi Atta **15**
Jawara, Sir Dawda Kairaba **11**
Nkrumah, Kwame **3**
Rawlings, Jerry **9**
Rawlings, Nana Konadu Agyeman **13**

Guinea-Bissauan
Vieira, Joao **14**

Guinean
Conté, Lansana **7**
Touré, Sekou **6**

Guyanese
Beaton, Norman **14**
Jagan, Cheddi **16**

Haitian
Aristide, Jean-Bertrand **6**
Auguste, Rose-Anne **13**
Charlemagne, Manno **11**
Christophe, Henri **9**
Danticat, Edwidge **15**
Pascal-Trouillot, Ertha **3**
Pierre, Andre **17**

Italian
Esposito, Giancarlo **9**

Ivorian
Houphouët-Boigny, Félix **4**

Jamaican
Ashley, Maurice **15**
Belafonte, Harry **4**
Ewing, Patrick A. **17**
Fagan, Garth **18**
Garvey, Marcus **1**
Johnson, Ben **1**
Marley, Bob **5**
McKay, Claude **6**
Morrison, Keith **13**
Patterson, Orlando **4**
Patterson, P. J. **6**
Perry, Lee "Scratch" **19**
Tosh, Peter **9**

Kenyan
Kenyatta, Jomo **5**
Mazrui, Ali A. **12**

Moi, Daniel **1**

Liberian
Fuller, Solomon Carter, Jr. **15**
Perry, Ruth **15**
Sawyer, Amos **2**

Malawian
Banda, Hastings Kamuzu **6**
Muluzi, Bakili **14**

Malian
Touré, Amadou Toumani **18**

Mozambican
Chissano, Joaquim **7**
Machel, Graca Simbine **16**
Machel, Samora Moises **8**
Mutola, Maria **12**

Namibian
Mbuende, Kaire **12**
Nujoma, Samuel **10**

Nigerian
Abacha, Sani **11**
Achebe, Chinua **6**
Arinze, Francis Cardinal **19**
Azikiwe, Nnamdi **13**
Babangida, Ibrahim **4**
Fela **1**
Obasanjo, Olusegun **5**
Olajuwon, Hakeem **2**
Rotimi, Ola **1**
Sade **15**
Soyinka, Wole **4**

Puerto Rican
Schomburg, Arthur Alfonso **9**

Russian
Khanga, Yelena **6**

Rwandan
Bizimungu, Pasteur **19**
Habyarimana, Juvenal **8**

Senegalese
Diop, Cheikh Anta **4**
Diouf, Abdou **3**
Mboup, Souleymane **10**
N'Dour, Youssou **1**
Sembène, Ousmane **13**
Senghor, Léopold Sédar **12**

Somali
Ali Mahdi Mohamed **5**
Iman **4**

South African
Biko, Steven **4**

Buthelezi, Mangosuthu Gatsha **9**
Hani, Chris **6**
Luthuli, Albert **13**
Mabuza, Lindiwe **18**
Makeba, Miriam **2**
Mandela, Nelson **1, 14**
Mandela, Winnie **2**
Masekela, Barbara **18**
Masekela, Hugh **1**
Mathabane, Mark **5**
Mbeki, Thabo Mvuyelwa **14**
Nzo, Alfred **15**
Ramaphosa, Cyril **3**
Tutu, Desmond **6**

Sudanese
Bol, Manute **1**
Wek, Alek **18**

Tanzanian
Mkapa, Benjamin **16**
Mongella, Gertrude **11**
Mwinyi, Ali Hassan **1**
Nyerere, Julius **5**

Togolese
Eyadéma, Gnassingbé **7**
Soglo, Nicéphore **15**

Trinidadian
Carmichael, Stokely **5**
Guy, Rosa **5**
Primus, Pearl **6**

Ugandan
Museveni, Yoweri **4**

Upper Voltan
Sankara, Thomas **17**

West Indian
Innis, Roy **5**
Kincaid, Jamaica **4**
Staupers, Mabel K. **7**
Pitt, David Thomas **10**
Taylor, Susan L. **10**
Walcott, Derek **5**

Zairean
Mobutu Sese Seko **1**
Mutombo, Dikembe **7**
Ongala, Remmy **9**

Zambian
Kaunda, Kenneth **2**

Zimbabwean
Mugabe, Robert Gabriel **10**
Chideya, Farai **14**
Nkomo, Joshua **4**

Cumulative Occupation Index

Volume numbers appear in **bold.**

Art and design
Andrews, Bert **13**
Armstrong, Robb **15**
Bailey, Radcliffe **19**
Bailey, Xenobia **11**
Barboza, Anthony **10**
Barnes, Ernie **16**
Barthé, Richmond **15**
Basquiat, Jean-Michel **5**
Bearden, Romare **2**
Brandon, Barbara **3**
Brown, Donald **19**
Burke, Selma **16**
Burroughs, Margaret Taylor **9**
Camp, Kimberly **19**
Campbell, E. Simms **13**
Catlett, Elizabeth **2**
Delaney, Beauford **19**
Douglas, Aaron **7**
Driskell, David C. **7**
Ewing, Patrick A. **17**
Feelings, Tom **11**
Gantt, Harvey **1**
Gilliam, Sam **16**
Golden, Thelma **10**
Guyton, Tyree **9**
Harkless, Necia Desiree **19**
Harrington, Oliver W. **9**
Hayden, Palmer **13**
Hope, John **8**
Hunt, Richard **6**
Hudson, Cheryl **15**
Hudson, Wade **15**
Hutson, Jean Blackwell **16**
Johnson, William Henry **3**
Jones, Lois Mailou **13**
Lawrence, Jacob **4**
Lee-Smith, Hughie **5**
Lewis, Edmonia **10**
McGee, Charles **10**
Mitchell, Corinne **8**
Morrison, Keith **13**
Moutoussamy-Ashe, Jeanne **7**
N'Namdi, George R. **17**
Pierre, Andre **17**
Pinkney, Jerry **15**
Pippin, Horace **9**
Porter, James A. **11**
Ringgold, Faith **4**
Saar, Alison **16**
Saint James, Synthia **12**
Sanders, Joseph R., Jr. **11**
Savage, Augusta **12**
Serrano, Andres **3**
Shabazz, Attallah **6**
Simpson, Lorna **4**
Sleet, Moneta, Jr. **5**
Tanner, Henry Ossawa **1**
Thomas, Alma **14**
Tolliver, William **9**
VanDerZee, James **6**
Walker, A'lelia **14**
Walker, Kara **16**
Wells, James Lesesne **10**
Williams, Billy Dee **8**
Williams, O. S. **13**
Williams, Paul R. **9**
Williams, William T. **11**
Woodruff, Hale **9**

Business
Abdul-Jabbar, Kareem **8**
Ailey, Alvin **8**
Al-Amin, Jamil Abdullah **6**
Alexander, Archie Alphonso **14**
Amos, Wally **9**
Avant, Clarence **19**
Baker, Dusty **8**
Baker, Ella **5**
Baker, Gwendolyn Calvert **9**
Banks, Jeffrey **17**
Banks, William **11**
Barden, Don H. **9**
Barrett, Andrew C. **12**
Bennett, Lerone, Jr. **5**
Bing, Dave **3**
Borders, James **9**
Boyd, T. B. III **6**
Brimmer, Andrew F. **2**
Brown, Les **5**
Brown, Marie Dutton **12**
Brunson, Dorothy **1**
Burroughs, Margaret Taylor **9**
Busby, Jheryl **3**
Cain, Herman **15**
CasSelle, Malcolm **11**
Chamberlain, Wilt **18**
Chappell, Emma **18**
Chenault, Kenneth I. **4**
Clark, Celeste **15**
Clark, Patrick **14**
Clay, William Lacy **8**
Clayton, Xernona **3**
Cobbs, Price M. **9**
Colbert, Virgis William **17**
Connerly, Ward **14**
Cornelius, Don **4**
Cosby, Bill **7**
Cottrell, Comer **11**
Delany, Bessie **12**
Delany, Sadie **12**
Divine, Father **7**
Dre, Dr. **14**
Driver, David E. **11**
Ducksworth, Marilyn **12**
Edelin, Ramona Hoage **19**
Edmonds, Tracey **16**
Elder, Lee **6**
Ellington, E. David **11**
Evers, Myrlie **8**
Farmer, Forest J. **1**
Farrakhan, Louis **15**
Fauntroy, Walter E. **11**
Fletcher, Alphonse, Jr. **16**
Franklin, Hardy R. **9**
Fudge, Ann **11**
Fuller, S. B. **13**
Gaston, Arthur G. **4**
Gibson, Kenneth Allen **6**
Goldsberry, Ronald **18**
Gordon, Pamela **17**
Gordy, Berry, Jr. **1**
Graham, Stedman **13**
Graves, Earl G. **1**
Griffith, Mark Winston **8**
Hale, Lorraine **8**
Hamer, Fannie Lou **6**
Handy, W. C. **8**
Hannah, Marc **10**
Hardison, Bethann **12**
Harrell, Andre **9**
Harris, Alice **7**
Harris, E. Lynn **12**
Harris, Monica **18**
Harvey, Steve **18**
Hawkins, La-Van **17**
Henderson, Gordon **5**
Henry, Lenny **9**
Hightower, Dennis F. **13**
Hill, Calvin **19**
Hill, Janet **19**
Hill, Jessie, Jr. **13**
Holland, Robert, Jr. **11**

Houston, Whitney 7
Hudlin, Reginald 9
Hudlin, Warrington 9
Hudson, Cheryl 15
Hudson, Wade 15
Ice Cube 8
Jackson, George 19
Jackson, Mannie 14
Jackson, Michael 19
James, Juanita 13
Johnson, Eddie Bernice 8
Johnson, John H. 3
Johnson, Robert L. 3
Jones, Carl 7
Jones, Ingrid Saunders 18
Jones, Quincy 8
Jordan, Michael 6
Julian, Percy Lavon 6
Kelly, Patrick 3
Kimbro, Dennis 10
King, Dexter 10
King, Don 14
Knight, Suge 11
Lane, Vincent 5
Langhart, Janet 19
Lawless, Theodore K. 8
Lawson, Jennifer 1
Leary, Kathryn D. 10
Leavell, Dorothy R. 17
Leonard, Sugar Ray 15
Lewellyn, J. Bruce 13
Lewis, Byron E. 13
Lewis, Delano 7
Lewis, Reginald F. 6
Lott, Ronnie 9
Louis, Errol T. 8
Lucas, John 7
Madhubuti, Haki R. 7
Malone, Annie 13
Maynard, Robert C. 7
McCabe, Jewell Jackson 10
McCoy, Elijah 8
McDonald, Erroll 1
Micheaux, Oscar 7
Morgan, Garrett 1
Morgan, Joe Leonard 9
Morgan, Rose 11
Nichols, Nichelle 11
Parks, Gordon 1
Parsons, Richard Dean 11
Payton, Walter 11
Perez, Anna 1
Pleasant, Mary Ellen 9
Powell, Maxine 8
Price, Hugh B. 9
Queen Latifah 1, 16
Ralph, Sheryl Lee 18
Rand, A. Barry 6
Rhone, Sylvia 2
Rice, Linda Johnson 9
Rice, Norm 8
Richie, Leroy C. 18
Roberts, Roy S. 14
Robeson, Eslanda Goode 13
Robinson, Jackie 6
Robinson, Rachel 16
Robinson, Randall 7
Roche, Joyce M. 17

Rodgers, Johnathan 6
Rogers, John W., Jr. 5
Ross, Diana 8
Russell, Bill 8
Russell, Herman Jerome 17
Russell-McCloud, Patricia 17
Saint James, Synthia 12
Samara, Noah 15
Sanders, Dori 8
Sengstacke, John 18
Simmons, Russell 1
Sinbad, 1, 16
Smith, Barbara 11
Smith, Joshua 10
Smith, Willi 8
Sneed, Paula A. 18
Spaulding, Charles Clinton 9
Stewart, Paul Wilbur 12
Sullivan, Leon H. 3
Taylor, Kristin Clark 8
Taylor, Susan L. 10
Thomas, Franklin A. 5
Thomas, Isiah 7
Tribble, Israel, Jr. 8
Trotter, Monroe 9
Van Peebles, Melvin 7
VanDerZee, James 6
Walker, A'lelia 14
Walker, Cedric "Ricky" 19
Walker, Madame C. J. 7
Walker, Maggie Lena 17
Walker, T. J. 7
Washington, Val 12
Wasow, Omar 15
Wattleton, Faye 9
Wek, Alek 18
Wells-Barnett, Ida B. 8
Wharton, Clifton R., Jr. 7
White, Walter F. 4
Wiley, Ralph 8
Williams, O. S. 13
Williams, Paul R. 9
Williams, Walter E. 4
Wilson, Phill 9
Wilson, Sunnie 7
Winfrey, Oprah 2, 15
Woodson, Robert L. 10
Yoba, Malik 11

Dance
Ailey, Alvin 8
Allen, Debbie 13
Baker, Josephine 3
Bates, Peg Leg 14
Beals, Jennifer 12
Byrd, Donald 10
Clarke, Hope 14
Davis, Sammy Jr. 18
Dove, Ulysses 5
Dunham, Katherine 4
Fagan, Garth 18
Glover, Savion 14
Guy, Jasmine 2
Hines, Gregory 1
Horne, Lena 5
Jackson, Michael 19
Jamison, Judith 7
Johnson, Virginia 9

Jones, Bill T. 1
McQueen, Butterfly 6
Miller, Bebe 3
Mitchell, Arthur 2
Moten, Etta 18
Nichols, Nichelle 11
Powell, Maxine 8
Primus, Pearl 6
Ribeiro, Alfonso 17
Robinson, Bill "Bojangles" 11
Rolle, Esther 13
Vereen, Ben 4
Walker, Cedric "Ricky" 19
Washington, Fredi 10
Williams, Vanessa L. 4, 17

Education
Achebe, Chinua 6
Archer, Dennis 7
Aristide, Jean-Bertrand 6
Asante, Molefi Kete 3
Baker, Gwendolyn Calvert 9
Baker, Houston A., Jr. 6
Bambara, Toni Cade 10
Baraka, Amiri 1
Barboza, Anthony 10
Bell, Derrick 6
Berry, Bertice 8
Berry, Mary Frances 7
Bethune, Mary McLeod 4
Black, Keith Lanier 18
Bluitt, Juliann S. 14
Bosley, Freeman, Jr. 7
Boyd, T. B. III 6
Brooks, Avery 9
Brown, Sterling 10
Burke, Selma 16
Burroughs, Margaret Taylor 9
Burton, LeVar 8
Butler, Paul D. 17
Callender, Clive O. 3
Campbell, Bebe Moore 6
Cannon, Katie 10
Carver, George Washington 4
Cary, Lorene 3
Catlett, Elizabeth 2
Clark, Joe 1
Clark, Kenneth B. 5
Clark, Septima 7
Clayton, Constance 1
Clements, George 2
Clifton, Lucille 14
Cobbs, Price M. 9
Cohen, Anthony 15
Cole, Johnnetta B. 5
Collins, Marva 3
Comer, James P. 6
Cone, James H. 3
Cook, Samuel DuBois 14
Cooper, Edward S. 6
Cosby, Bill 7
Cottrell, Comer 11
Crew, Rudolph F. 16
Crouch, Stanley 11
Cullen, Countee 8
Davis, Allison 12
Davis, Angela 5
Days, Drew S., III 10

Delany, Sadie 12
Delany, Samuel R., Jr. 9
Dickens, Helen Octavia 14
Diop, Cheikh Anta 4
Dixon, Margaret 14
Dodson, Howard, Jr. 7
Douglas, Aaron 7
Dove, Rita 6
Dove, Ulysses 5
Draper, Sharon M. 16
Driskell, David C. 7
Dyson, Michael Eric 11
Early, Gerald 15
Edelin, Ramona Hoage 19
Edelman, Marian Wright 5
Edley, Christopher 2
Edwards, Harry 2
Elders, Joycelyn 6
Ellison, Ralph 7
Fauset, Jessie 7
Franklin, John Hope 5
Franklin, Robert M. 13
Frazier, E. Franklin 10
Freeman, Al, Jr. 11
Fuller, Solomon Carter, Jr. 15
Gaines, Ernest J. 7
Gates, Henry Louis, Jr. 3
Gates, Sylvester James, Jr. 15
Giddings, Paula 11
Giovanni, Nikki 9
Golden, Marita 19
Gomes, Peter J. 15
Greenfield, Eloise 9
Guinier, Lani 7
Guy-Sheftall, Beverly 13
Hale, Lorraine 8
Handy, W. C. 8
Hansberry, William Leo 11
Harkless, Necia Desiree 19
Harris, Alice 7
Harris, Jay T. 19
Harris, Patricia Roberts 2
Harsh, Vivian Gordon 14
Hayden, Robert 12
Haynes, George Edmund 8
Hill, Anita 5
Hinton, William Augustus 8
Holland, Endesha Ida Mae 3
hooks, bell 5
Hope, John 8
Houston, Charles Hamilton 4
Hunt, Richard 6
Hutson, Jean Blackwell 16
Jeffries, Leonard 8
Jenifer, Franklyn G. 2
Jenkins, Ella 15
Johnson, James Weldon 5
Jones, Ingrid Saunders 18
Jones, Lois Mailou 13
Joplin, Scott 6
Jordan, Barbara 4
Jordan, June 7
Josey, E. J. 10
Just, Ernest Everett 3
Karenga, Maulana 10
Keith, Damon J. 16
Kennedy, Florynce 12
Kilpatrick, Carolyn Cheeks 16

Kimbro, Dennis 10
Komunyakaa, Yusef 9
Kunjufu, Jawanza 3
Lawrence, Jacob 4
Leffall, LaSalle, Jr. 3
Lawrence-Lightfoot, Sara 10
Lester, Julius 9
Lewis, David Levering 9
Lewis, Shirley A. R. 14
Lewis, Thomas 19
Liberia-Peters, Maria Philomena 12
Locke, Alain 10
Lorde, Audre 6
Lyttle, Hulda Margaret 14
Madhubuti, Haki R. 7
Major, Clarence 9
Manley, Audrey Forbes 16
Marable, Manning 10
Marsalis, Wynton 16
Marshall, Paule 7
Masekela, Barbara 18
Massey, Walter E. 5
Maynard, Robert C. 7
Maynor, Dorothy 19
Mays, Benjamin E. 7
McCarty, Oseola 16
McKay, Nellie Yvonne 17
McMillan, Terry 4, 17
Meek, Carrie 6
Meredith, James H. 11
Mitchell, Corinne 8
Mongella, Gertrude 11
Morrison, Keith 13
Morrison, Toni 15
Moses, Robert Parris 11
N'Namdi, George R. 17
Norton, Eleanor Holmes 7
Ogletree, Jr., Charles 12
Owens, Major 6
Page, Alan 7
Patterson, Frederick Douglass 12
Patterson, Orlando 4
Porter, James A. 11
Poussaint, Alvin F. 5
Primus, Pearl 6
Quarles, Benjamin Arthur 18
Reagon, Bernice Johnson 7
Ringgold, Faith 4
Russell-McCloud, Patricia A. 17
Satcher, David 7
Schomburg, Arthur Alfonso 9
Shabazz, Betty 7
Shange, Ntozake 8
Shipp, E. R. 15
Simmons, Ruth J. 13
Sinkford, Jeanne C. 13
Smith, Anna Deavere 6
Smith, Tubby 18
Soyinka, Wole 4
Spikes, Dolores 18
Steele, Claude Mason 13
Steele, Shelby 13
Stephens, Charlotte Andrews 14
Stewart, Maria W. Miller 19
Stone, Chuck 9
Sudarkasa, Niara 4
Sullivan, Louis 8

Taylor, Susie King 13
Terrell, Mary Church 9
Thomas, Alma 14
Thurman, Howard 3
Tribble, Israel, Jr. 8
Tucker, Rosina 14
Turnbull, Walter 13
Tutu, Desmond 6
Tyson, Neil de Grasse 15
Walcott, Derek 5
Wallace, Michele Faith 13
Wallace, Phyllis A. 9
Washington, Booker T. 4
Watkins, Shirley R. 17
Wattleton, Faye 9
Wells, James Lesesne 10
Wells-Barnett, Ida B. 8
Welsing, Frances Cress 5
Wesley, Dorothy Porter 19
West, Cornel 5
Wharton, Clifton R., Jr. 7
Wilkins, Roger 2
Willims, Gregory 11
Williams, Patricia J. 11
Williams, Walter E. 4
Woodruff, Hale 9
Woodson, Carter G. 2
Worrill, Conrad 12
Young, Jean Childs 14

Fashion
Banks, Jeffrey 17
Banks, Tyra 11
Beals, Jennifer 12
Beckford, Tyson 11
Berry, Halle 4, 19
Bailey, Xenobia 11
Barboza, Anthony 10
Campbell, Naomi 1
Davidson, Jaye 5
Henderson, Gordon 5
Iman 4
Johnson, Beverly 2
Jones, Carl 7
Kani, Karl 10
Kelly, Patrick 3
Powell, Maxine 8
Robinson, Patrick 19
Rochon, Lela 16
Rowell, Victoria 13
Smaltz, Audrey 12
Smith, Barbara 11
Smith, Willi 8
Walker, T. J. 7
Webb, Veronica 10
Wek, Alek 18

Film
Amos, John 8
Baker, Josephine 3
Banks, Tyra 11
Bassett, Angela 6
Beals, Jennifer 12
Belafonte, Harry 4
Bellamy, Bill 12
Berry, Halle 4, 19
Braugher, Andre 13
Brown, Jim 11

Brown, Tony 3
Burnett, Charles 16
Byrd, Michelle 19
Byrd, Robert 11
Calloway, Cab 14
Campbell, Naomi 1
Campbell, Tisha 8
Carroll, Diahann 9
Cheadle, Don 19
Clash, Kevin 14
Cosby, Bill 7
Crothers, Scatman 19
Curry, Mark 17
Curtis-Hall, Vondie 17
Dandridge, Dorothy 3
Dash, Julie 4
Davidson, Jaye 5
Davis, Ossie 5
Dee, Ruby 8
Davis, Sammy Jr. 18
Dickerson, Ernest 6, 17
Dr. Dre 10
Driskell, David C. 7
Duke, Bill 3
Dunham, Katherine 4
Dutton, Charles S. 4
Esposito, Giancarlo 9
Fishburne, Larry 4
Fox, Vivica A. 15
Foxx, Redd 2
Foxx, Jamie 15
Franklin, Carl 11
Freeman, Al, Jr. 11
Freeman, Morgan 2
Fuller, Charles 8
George, Nelson 12
Givens, Robin 4
Glover, Danny 1
Glover, Savion 14
Goldberg, Whoopi 4
Gooding, Cuba, Jr. 16
Gordy, Berry, Jr. 1
Gossett, Louis, Jr. 7
Gray, F. Gary 14
Grier, Pam 9
Guillaume, Robert 3
Gunn, Moses 10
Guy, Jasmine 2
Hampton, Henry 6
Harris, Leslie 6
Harris, Robin 7
Hemsley, Sherman 19
Henry, Lenny 9
Hines, Gregory 1
Horne, Lena 5
Hounsou, Djimon 19
Houston, Whitney 7
Hudlin, Reginald 9
Hudlin, Warrington 9
Hughes, Albert 7
Hughes, Allen 7
Ice Cube 8
Iman 4
Ingram, Rex 5
Jackson, George 19
Jackson, Janet 6
Jackson, Samuel L. 8, 19
Jean-Baptiste, Marianne 17

Johnson, Beverly 2
Jones, James Earl 3
Jones, Quincy 8
Julien, Isaac 3
Kirby, George 14
Kitt, Eartha 16
Kotto, Yaphet 7
Kunjufu, Jawanza 3
L L Cool J 3
LaBelle, Patti 13
Lane, Charles 3
La Salle, Eriq 12
Lawrence, Martin 6
Lee, Joie 1
Lee, Spike 5, 19
Lincoln, Abbey 3
Lindo, Delroy 18
Long, Nia 17
Lover, Ed 10
Mabley, Jackie "Moms" 15
McDaniel, Hattie 5
McQueen, Butterfly 6
Mckee, Lonette 12
Micheaux, Oscar 7
Morton, Joe 18
Moses, Gilbert 12
Moss, Carlton 17
Murphy, Eddie 4
Nichols, Nichelle 11
Parks, Gordon 1
Payne, Allen 13
Pinkett, Jada 10
Poitier, Sidney 11
Prince 18
Pryor, Richard 3
Queen Latifah 1, 16
Ralph, Sheryl Lee 18
Randle, Theresa 16
Reese, Della 6
Reuben, Gloria 15
Rhames, Ving 14
Riggs, Marlon 5
Rochon, Lela 16
Rock, Chris 3
Rolle, Esther 13
Rollins, Howard E., Jr. 16
Ross, Diana 8
Rowell, Victoria 13
Rupaul 17
St. Jacques, Raymond 8
Schultz, Michael A. 6
Seal 14
Sembène, Ousmane 13
Shakur, Tupac 14
Simpson, O. J. 15
Sinbad 1, 16
Singleton, John 2
Smith, Anna Deavere 6
Smith, Roger Guenveur 12
Smith, Will 8, 18
Snipes, Wesley 3
Tate, Larenz 15
Taylor, Meshach 4
Taylor, Regina 9
Thigpen, Lynne 17
Thurman, Wallace 16
Townsend, Robert 4
Tucker, Chris 13

Turner, Tina 6
Tyson, Cicely 7
Underwood, Blair 7
Van Peebles, Mario 2
Van Peebles, Melvin 7
Vance, Courtney B. 15
Vereen, Ben 4
Warfield, Marsha 2
Warwick, Dionne 18
Washington, Denzel 1, 16
Washington, Fredi 10
Waters, Ethel 7
Wayans, Damon 8
Wayans, Keenen Ivory 18
Weathers, Carl 10
Webb, Veronica 10
Whitaker, Forest 2
Whitfield, Lynn 18
Williams, Billy Dee 8
Williams, Vanessa L. 4, 17
Winfield, Paul 2
Winfrey, Oprah 2, 15
Woodard, Alfre 9
Yoba, Malik 11

**Government and politics—
international**
Abacha, Sani 11
Abbott, Diane 9
Achebe, Chinua 6
Ali Mahdi Mohamed 5
Annan, Kofi Atta 15
Aristide, Jean-Bertrand 6
Azikiwe, Nnamdi 13
Babangida, Ibrahim 4
Baker, Gwendolyn Calvert 9
Banda, Hastings Kamuzu 6
Berry, Mary Frances 7
Biko, Steven 4
Bizimungu, Pasteur 19
Bongo, Omar 1
Bunche, Ralph J. 5
Buthelezi, Mangosuthu Gatsha 9
Charlemagne, Manno 11
Charles, Mary Eugenia 10
Chissano, Joaquim 7
Christophe, Henri 9
Conté, Lansana 7
da Silva, Benedita 5
Diop, Cheikh Anta 4
Diouf, Abdou 3
Eyadéma, Gnassingbé 7
Fela 1
Gordon, Pamela 17
Habré, Hissène 6
Habyarimana, Juvenal 8
Haile Selassie 7
Hani, Chris 6
Houphouët-Boigny, Félix 4
Ingraham, Hubert A. 19
Jagan, Cheddi 16
Jawara, Sir Dawda Kairaba 11
Kabunda, Kenneth 2
Kenyatta, Jomo 5
Kerekou, Ahmed (Mathieu) 1
Liberia-Peters, Maria Philomena 12
Luthuli, Albert 13

Cumulative Occupation Index

Mabuza, Lindiwe **18**
Machel, Samora Moises **8**
Mandela, Nelson **1, 14**
Mandela, Winnie **2**
Masekela, Barbara **18**
Masire, Quett **5**
Mbeki, Thabo Mvuyelwa **14**
Mbuende, Kaire **12**
Meles Zenawi **3**
Mkapa, Benjamin **16**
Mobutu Sese Seko **1**
Mogae, Festus Gontebanye **19**
Moi, Daniel **1**
Mongella, Gertrude **11**
Mugabe, Robert Gabriel **10**
Muluzi, Bakili **14**
Museveni, Yoweri **4**
Mwinyi, Ali Hassan **1**
Ndadaye, Melchior **7**
Nkomo, Joshua **4**
Nkrumah, Kwame **3**
Ntaryamira, Cyprien **8**
Nujoma, Samuel **10**
Nyerere, Julius **5**
Nzo, Alfred **15**
Obasanjo, Olusegun **5**
Pascal-Trouillot, Ertha **3**
Patterson, P. J. **6**
Perkins, Edward **5**
Perry, Ruth **15**
Pitt, David Thomas **10**
Pitta, Celso **17**
Ramaphosa, Cyril **3**
Rawlings, Jerry **9**
Rawlings, Nana Konadu Agyeman **13**
Rice, Condoleezza **3**
Robinson, Randall **7**
Sampson, Edith S. **4**
Sankara, Thomas **17**
Savimbi, Jonas **2**
Sawyer, Amos **2**
Senghor, Léopold Sédar **12**
Soglo, Nicephore **15**
Soyinka, Wole **4**
Taylor, John (David Beckett) **16**
Toure, Amadou Toumani **18**
Touré, Sekou **6**
Tutu, Desmond **6**
Vieira, Joao **14**
Wharton, Clifton R., Jr. **7**

Government and politics—U.S.
Adams, Floyd, Jr. **12**
Alexander, Archie Alphonso **14**
Ali, Muhammad **2, 16**
Allen, Ethel D. **13**
Archer, Dennis **7**
Avant, Clarence **19**
Barden, Don H. **9**
Barrett, Andrew C. **12**
Barry, Marion S. **7**
Belton, Sharon Sayles **9, 16**
Berry, Mary Frances **7**
Bethune, Mary McLeod **4**
Blackwell, Unita **17**
Bond, Julian **2**
Bosley, Freeman, Jr. **7**

Boykin, Keith **14**
Bradley, Thomas **2**
Braun, Carol Moseley **4**
Brimmer, Andrew F. **2**
Brooke, Edward **8**
Brown, Elaine **8**
Brown, Jesse **6**
Brown, Les **5**
Brown, Ron **5**
Brown, Willie L., Jr. **7**
Bryant, Wayne R. **6**
Bunche, Ralph J. **5**
Caesar, Shirley **19**
Campbell, Bill **9**
Chavis, Benjamin **6**
Chisholm, Shirley **2**
Christian-Green, Donna M. **17**
Clay, William Lacy **8**
Cleaver, Eldridge **5**
Cleaver, Emanuel **4**
Collins, Barbara-Rose **7**
Collins, Cardiss **10**
Connerly, Ward **14**
Conyers, John, Jr. **4**
Cose, Ellis **5**
Crockett, George, Jr. **10**
Davis, Angela **5**
Davis, Benjamin O., Jr. **2**
Davis, Benjamin O., Sr. **4**
Days, Drew S., III **10**
Dellums, Ronald **2**
Dinkins, David **4**
Dixon, Sharon Pratt **1**
Du Bois, W. E. B. **3**
Edmonds, Terry **17**
Elders, Joycelyn **6**
Espy, Mike **6**
Farmer, James **2**
Farrakhan, Louis **2**
Fattah, Chaka **11**
Fauntroy, Walter E. **11**
Fields, Cleo **13**
Flake, Floyd H. **18**
Flipper, Henry O. **3**
Fortune, T. Thomas **6**
Franks, Gary **2**
Fulani, Lenora **11**
Gantt, Harvey **1**
Garvey, Marcus **1**
Gibson, Kenneth Allen **6**
Gibson, William F. **6**
Goode, W. Wilson **4**
Gravely, Samuel L., Jr. **5**
Gray, William H. III **3**
Grimké, Archibald H. **9**
Guinier, Lani **7**
Hamer, Fannie Lou **6**
Harris, Alice **7**
Harris, Patricia Roberts **2**
Harvard, Beverly **11**
Hastie, William H. **8**
Hastings, Alcee L. **16**
Hayes, James C. **10**
Henry, Aaron **19**
Herman, Alexis M. **15**
Hernandez, Aileen Clarke **13**
Holder, Eric H., Jr. **9**
Irving, Larry, Jr. **12**

Jackson, George **14**
Jackson, Jesse **1**
Jackson, Jesse, Jr. **14**
Jackson, Maynard **2**
Jackson, Shirley Ann **12**
Jacob, John E. **2**
Johnson, Eddie Bernice **8**
Johnson, James Weldon **5**
Johnson, Norma L. Holloway **17**
Johnson, Robert T. **17**
Jones, Elaine R. **7**
Jordan, Barbara **4**
Kennard, William Earl **18**
Keyes, Alan L. **11**
Kilpatrick, Carolyn Cheeks **16**
Kirk, Ron **11**
Lafontant, Jewel Stradford **3**
Leland, Mickey **2**
Lewis, Delano **7**
Lewis, John **2**
Mallett, Conrad, Jr. **16**
Marshall, Thurgood **1**
Martin, Louis E. **16**
McKinney, Cynthia Ann **11**
McKissick, Floyd B. **3**
Meek, Carrie **6**
Meredith, James H. **11**
Mfume, Kweisi **6**
Moses, Robert Parris **11**
Norton, Eleanor Holmes **7**
O'Leary, Hazel **6**
Owens, Major **6**
Page, Alan **7**
Patrick, Deval **12**
Payne, Donald M. **2**
Perez, Anna **1**
Perkins, Edward **5**
Pinchback, P. B. S. **9**
Powell, Adam Clayton, Jr. **3**
Powell, Colin **1**
Raines, Franklin Delano **14**
Randolph, A. Philip **3**
Rangel, Charles **3**
Rice, Condoleezza **3**
Rice, Norm **8**
Robinson, Randall **7**
Rustin, Bayard **4**
Sampson, Edith S. **4**
Satcher, David **7**
Schmoke, Kurt **1**
Sears-Collins, Leah J. **5**
Shakur, Assata **6**
Simpson, Carole **6**
Slater, Rodney E. **15**
Staupers, Mabel K. **7**
Stokes, Carl B. **10**
Stokes, Louis **3**
Stone, Chuck **9**
Sullivan, Louis **8**
Thomas, Clarence **2**
Towns, Edolphus **19**
Tribble, Israel, Jr. **8**
Tucker, C. DeLores **12**
Turner, Henry McNeal **5**
Von Lipsey, Roderick K. **11**
Wallace, Phyllis A. **9**
Washington, Harold **6**
Washington, Val **12**

Waters, Maxine 3
Watkins, Shirley R. 17
Watts, J. C., Jr. 14
Weaver, Robert C. 8
Webb, Wellington 3
Wharton, Clifton R., Jr. 7
Wheat, Alan 14
White, Michael R. 5
Wilder, L. Douglas 3
Wilkins, Roger 2
Williams, George Washington 18
Williams, Hosea Lorenzo 15
Williams, Maggie 7
Wilson, Sunnie 7
Young, Andrew 3
Young, Coleman 1

Law
Alexander, Joyce London 18
Archer, Dennis 7
Banks, William 11
Barrett, Andrew C. 12
Bell, Derrick 6
Berry, Mary Frances 7
Bosley, Freeman, Jr. 7
Boykin, Keith 14
Bradley, Thomas 2
Braun, Carol Moseley 4
Brooke, Edward 8
Brown, Lee P. 1
Brown, Ron 5
Brown, Willie L., Jr. 7
Bryant, Wayne R. 6
Butler, Paul D. 17
Campbell, Bill 9
Carter, Stephen L. 4
Chambers, Julius 3
Cochran, Johnnie L., Jr. 11
Conyers, John, Jr. 4
Crockett, George, Jr. 10
Darden, Christopher 13
Days, Drew S., III 10
Dinkins, David 4
Dixon, Sharon Pratt 1
Edelman, Marian Wright 5
Edley, Christopher 2
Ellington, E. David 11
Espy, Mike 6
Fields, Cleo 13
Freeman, Charles 19
Gary, Willie E. 12
Glover, Nathaniel, Jr. 12
Gomez-Preston, Cheryl 9
Graham, Lawrence Otis 12
Grimké, Archibald H. 9
Guinier, Lani 7
Harris, Patricia Roberts 2
Harvard, Beverly 11
Hastie, William H. 8
Hastings, Alcee L. 16
Hawkins, Steven 14
Higginbotham, A. Leon, Jr. 13
Hill, Anita 5
Holder, Eric H., Jr. 9
Hooks, Benjamin L. 2
Houston, Charles Hamilton 4
Jackson, Maynard 2
Johnson, James Weldon 5

Johnson, Norma L. Holloway 17
Jones, Elaine R. 7
Jones, Star 10
Jordan, Vernon E. 3
Kearse, Amalya Lyle 12
Keith, Damon J. 16
Kennard, William Earl 18
Kennedy, Florynce 12
King, Bernice 4
Kirk, Ron 11
Lafontant, Jewel Stradford 3
Lewis, Delano 7
Lewis, Reginald F. 6
Mallett, Conrad, Jr. 16
Mandela, Nelson 1, 14
Marshall, Thurgood 1
McDougall, Gay J. 11
McKinnon, Isaiah 9
McKissick, Floyd B. 3
McPhail, Sharon 2
Motley, Constance Baker 10
Norton, Eleanor Holmes 7
O'Leary, Hazel 6
Ogletree, Jr., Charles 12
Page, Alan 7
Parks, Bernard C. 17
Parsons, James 14
Parsons, Richard Dean 11
Pascal-Trouillot, Ertha 3
Patrick, Deval 12
Richie, Leroy C. 18
Robinson, Randall 7
Russell-McCloud, Patricia A. 14
Sampson, Edith S. 4
Schmoke, Kurt 1
Sears-Collins, Leah J. 5
Stokes, Carl B. 10
Stokes, Louis 3
Taylor, John (David Beckett) 16
Thomas, Clarence 2
Thomas, Franklin A. 5
Vanzant, Iyanla 17
Washington, Harold 6
Wilder, L. Douglas 3
Wilkins, Roger 2
Williams, Evelyn 10
Williams, Gregory 11
Williams, Patricia J. 11
Williams, Willie L. 4
Wright, Bruce McMarion 3

Military
Abacha, Sani 11
Adams Early, Charity 13
Babangida, Ibrahim 4
Bolden, Charles F., Jr. 7
Brown, Jesse 6
Bullard, Eugene 12
Cadoria, Sherian Grace 14
Chissano, Joaquim 7
Christophe, Henri 9
Conté, Lansana 7
Davis, Benjamin O., Jr. 2
Davis, Benjamin O., Sr. 4
Europe, James Reese 10
Eyadéma, Gnassingbé 7
Flipper, Henry O. 3
Gravely, Samuel L., Jr. 5

Gregory, Frederick D. 8
Habré, Hissène 6
Habyarimana, Juvenal 8
Harris, Marcelite Jordan 16
James, Daniel, Jr. 16
Kerekou, Ahmed (Mathieu) 1
Reason, J. Paul 19
Lawrence, Robert H., Jr. 16
Obasanjo, Olusegun 5
Powell, Colin 1
Pratt, Geronimo 18
Rawlings, Jerry 9
Staupers, Mabel K. 7
Stokes, Louis 3
Touré, Amadou Toumani 18
Vieira, Joao 14
Von Lipsey, Roderick K. 11
Watkins, Perry 12
West, Togo, D., Jr. 16

Music
Adams, Oleta 18
Adams, Yolanda 17
Anderson, Marian 2
Armstrong, Louis 2
Avant, Clarence 19
Ayers, Roy 16
Baker, Josephine 3
Bechet, Sidney 18
Belafonte, Harry 4
Belle, Regina 1
Bonga, Kuenda 13
Brandy 14
Braxton, Toni 15
Brooks, Avery 9
Bumbry, Grace 5
Busby, Jheryl 3
Caesar, Shirley 19
Calloway, Cab 1
Campbell, Tisha 8
Carroll, Diahann 9
Carter, Betty 19
Charlemagne, Manno 11
Charles, Ray 16
Cheatham, Doc 17
Chuck D 9
Cleveland, James 19
Clinton, George 9
Cole, Nat King 17
Cole, Natalie Maria 17
Collins, Albert 12
Coltrane, John 19
Combs, Sean "Puffy" 17
Cooke, Sam 17
Crawford, Randy 19
Crothers, Scatman 19
Crouch, Stanley 11
Crowder, Henry 16
Davis, Anthony 11
Davis, Miles 4
Davis, Sammy Jr. 18
Dixon, Willie 4
Donegan, Dorothy 19
Dorsey, Thomas 15
Downing, Will 19
Dr. Dre 10
Dre, Dr. 14
Dupri, Jermaine 13

Edmonds, Kenneth "Babyface" **10**
Edmonds, Tracey **16**
Ellington, Duke **5**
Eubanks, Kevin **15**
Europe, James Reese **10**
Evora, Cesaria **12**
Fela **1**
Fitzgerald, Ella **8, 18**
Flack, Roberta **19**
Foxx, Jamie **15**
Franklin, Aretha **11**
Franklin, Kirk **15**
Gaye, Marvin **2**
Gibson, Althea **8**
Gillespie, Dizzy **1**
Gordy, Berry, Jr. **1**
Graves, Denyce **19**
Gray, F. Gary **14**
Green, Al **13**
Hampton, Lionel **17**
Handy, W. C. **8**
Harrell, Andre **9**
Hathaway, Donny **18**
Hawkins, Coleman **9**
Hawkins, Erskine **14**
Hawkins, Tramaine **16**
Hayes, Roland **4**
Hendricks, Barbara **3**
Hendrix, Jimi **10**
Hinderas, Natalie **5**
Holiday, Billie **1**
Horne, Lena **5**
House, Son **8**
Houston, Whitney **7**
Howlin' Wolf **9**
Hyman, Phyllis **19**
Ice Cube **8**
Ice-T **6**
Jackson, George **19**
Jackson, Isaiah **3**
Jackson, Janet **6**
Jackson, Mahalia **5**
Jackson, Michael **19**
James, Etta **13**
James, Rick **17**
Jean-Baptiste, Marianne **17**
Jenkins, Ella **15**
Jimmy Jam **13**
Johnson, Beverly **2**
Johnson, James Weldon **5**
Johnson, Robert **2**
Jones, Elvin **14**
Jones, Quincy **8**
Joplin, Scott **6**
Joyner, Matilda Sissieretta **15**
Joyner, Tom **19**
Kelly, R. **18**
Khan, Chaka **12**
King, B. B. **7**
King, Coretta Scott **3**
Kitt, Eartha **16**
Knight, Gladys **16**
Knight, Suge **11**
Kravitz, Lenny **10**
L.L. Cool J **16**
LaBelle, Patti **13**
Lewis, Terry **13**
León, Tania **13**

Lester, Julius **9**
Lincoln, Abbey **3**
Little Richard **15**
Lover, Ed **10**
Madhubuti, Haki R. **7**
Makeba, Miriam **2**
Marley, Bob **5**
Marsalis, Wynton **16**
Masekela, Hugh **1**
Mayfield, Curtis **2**
Maynor, Dorothy **19**
McDaniel, Hattie **5**
McKnight, Brian **18**
Mckee, Lonette **12**
Mingus, Charles **15**
Monk, Thelonious **1**
Moses, Gilbert **12**
Moten, Etta **18**
Murphy, Eddie **4**
Nascimento, Milton **2**
N'Dour, Youssou **1**
Ndegéocello, Me'Shell **15**
Norman, Jessye **5**
O'Neal, Shaquille **8**
Ongala, Remmy **9**
Parks, Gordon **1**
Perry, Ruth **19**
Powell, Maxine **8**
Price, Leontyne **1**
Prince **18**
Queen Latifah **1, 16**
Ralph, Sheryl Lee **18**
Razaf, Andy **19**
Reagon, Bernice Johnson **7**
Reese, Della **6**
Rhone, Sylvia **2**
Roberts, Marcus **19**
Robeson, Paul **2**
Robinson, Smokey **3**
Ross, Diana **8**
Rupaul **17**
Rushen, Patrice **12**
Sade **15**
Sangare, Oumou **18**
Seal **14**
Shakur, Tupac **14**
Simmons, Russell **1**
Simone, Nina **3**
Sister Souljah **11**
Smith, Bessie **3**
Smith, Will **8, 18**
Sweat, Keith **19**
Tosh, Peter **9**
Turnbull, Walter **13**
Turner, Tina **6**
Vandross, Luther **13**
Vaughan, Sarah **13**
Vereen, Ben **4**
Walker, Albertina **10**
Walker, Cedric "Ricky" **19**
Wallace, Sippie **1**
Warwick, Dionne **18**
Washington, Grover, Jr. **17**
Waters, Ethel **7**
Watson, Johnny "Guitar" **18**
White, Barry **13**
Williams, Bert **18**
Williams, Joe **5**

Williams, Mary Lou **15**
Williams, Vanessa L. **4, 17**
Wilson, Cassandra **16**
Wilson, Nancy **10**
Wilson, Sunnie **7**
Winans, BeBe **14**
Winans, CeCe **14**
Winans, Marvin L. **17**
Wonder, Stevie **11**
Yoba, Malik **11**

Religion
Abernathy, Ralph David **1**
Adams, Yolanda **17**
Agyeman, Jaramogi Abebe **10**
Al-Amin, Jamil Abdullah **6**
Arinze, Francis Cardinal **19**
Aristide, Jean-Bertrand **6**
Banks, William **11**
Bell, Ralph S. **5**
Ben-Israel, Ben Ami **11**
Boyd, T. B. III **6**
Butts, Calvin O., III **9**
Caesar, Shirley **19**
Cannon, Katie **10**
Chavis, Benjamin **6**
Cleaver, Emanuel **4**
Clements, George **2**
Cleveland, James **19**
Colemon, Johnnie **11**
Cone, James H. **3**
Divine, Father **7**
Dyson, Michael Eric **11**
Farrakhan, Louis **2, 15**
Fauntroy, Walter E. **11**
Flake, Floyd H. **18**
Foreman, George **15**
Franklin, Kirk **15**
Franklin, Robert M. **13**
Gomes, Peter J. **15**
Gray, William H. III **3**
Green, Al **13**
Grier, Roosevelt **13**
Haile Selassie **7**
Harris, Barbara **12**
Hawkins, Tramaine **16**
Hayes, James C. **10**
Hooks, Benjamin L. **2**
Jackson, Jesse **1**
Jakes, Thomas "T.D." **17**
King, Bernice **4**
King, Martin Luther, Jr. **1**
Lester, Julius **9**
Little Richard **15**
Lowery, Joseph **2**
Lyons, Henry **12**
Mays, Benjamin E. **7**
Muhammad, Elijah **4**
Muhammad, Khallid Abdul **10**
Murray, Cecil **12**
Pierre, Andre **17**
Powell, Adam Clayton, Jr. **3**
Reese, Della **6**
Riley, Helen Caldwell Day **13**
Shabazz, Betty **7**
Somé, Malidoma Patrice **10**
Stallings, George A., Jr. **6**
Sullivan, Leon H. **3**

Thurman, Howard **3**
Turner, Henry McNeal **5**
Tutu, Desmond **6**
Vanzant, Iyanla **17**
Waddles, Charleszetta (Mother) **10**
Waters, Ethel **7**
West, Cornel **5**
White, Reggie **6**
Williams, Hosea Lorenzo **15**
Winans, BeBe **14**
Winans, CeCe **14**
Winans, Marvin L. **17**
X, Malcolm **1**
Youngblood, Johnny Ray **8**

Science and technology
Auguste, Rose-Anne **13**
Alexander, Archie Alphonso **14**
Banda, Hastings Kamuzu **6**
Allen, Ethel D. **13**
Black, Keith Lanier **18**
Bluford, Guy **2**
Bluitt, Juliann S. **14**
Bolden, Charles F., Jr. **7**
Bullard, Eugene **12**
Callender, Clive O. **3**
Carson, Benjamin **1**
Carver, George Washington **4**
CasSelle, Malcolm **11**
Christian, Spencer **15**
Cobbs, Price M. **9**
Coleman, Bessie **9**
Comer, James P. **6**
Cooper, Edward S. **6**
Davis, Allison **12**
Delany, Bessie **12**
Dickens, Helen Octavia **14**
Diop, Cheikh Anta **4**
Drew, Charles Richard **7**
Dunham, Katherine **4**
Elders, Joycelyn **6**
Ellington, E. David **11**
Fisher, Rudolph **17**
Flipper, Henry O. **3**
Fulani, Lenora **11**
Fuller, Solomon Carter, Jr. **15**
Gates, Sylvester James, Jr. **15**
Gayle, Helene D. **3**
Gibson, Kenneth Allen **6**
Gibson, William F. **6**
Gregory, Frederick D. **8**
Hall, Lloyd A. **8**
Hannah, Marc **10**
Henson, Matthew **2**
Hinton, William Augustus **8**
Irving, Larry, Jr. **12**
Jackson, Shirley Ann **12**
Jawara, Sir Dawda Kairaba **11**
Jemison, Mae C. **1**
Jenifer, Franklyn G. **2**
Johnson, Eddie Bernice **8**
Julian, Percy Lavon **6**
Just, Ernest Everett **3**
Kountz, Samuel L. **10**
Latimer, Lewis H. **4**
Lawless, Theodore K. **8**
Lawrence, Robert H., Jr. **16**
Leffall, LaSalle, Jr. **3**

Lewis, Delano **7**
Logan, Onnie Lee **14**
Lyttle, Hulda Margaret **14**
Manley, Audrey Forbes **16**
Massey, Walter E. **5**
Mboup, Souleymane **10**
McCoy, Elijah **8**
McNair, Ronald **3**
Morgan, Garrett **1**
O'Leary, Hazel **6**
Person, Waverly **9**
Pitt, David Thomas **10**
Poussaint, Alvin F. **5**
Prothrow-Stith, Deborah **10**
Quarterman, Lloyd Albert **4**
Riley, Helen Caldwell Day **13**
Robeson, Eslanda Goode **13**
Robinson, Rachel **16**
Roker, Al **12**
Samara, Noah **15**
Satcher, David **7**
Shabazz, Betty **7**
Sinkford, Jeanne C. **13**
Staples, Brent **8**
Staupers, Mabel K. **7**
Sullivan, Louis **8**
Thomas, Vivien **9**
Tyson, Neil de Grasse **15**
Washington, Patrice Clarke **12**
Watkins, Levi, Jr. **9**
Welsing, Frances Cress **5**
Williams, Daniel Hale **2**
Williams, O. S. **13**
Woods, Granville T. **5**
Wright, Louis Tompkins **4**

Social issues
Aaron, Hank **5**
Abbott, Diane **9**
Abdul-Jabbar, Kareem **8**
Abernathy, Ralph David **1**
Abu-Jamal, Mumia **15**
Achebe, Chinua **6**
Agyeman, Jaramogi Abebe **10**
Al-Amin, Jamil Abdullah **6**
Ali, Muhammad, **2, 16**
Allen, Ethel D. **13**
Angelou, Maya **1**
Annan, Kofi Atta **15**
Archer, Dennis **7**
Aristide, Jean-Bertrand **6**
Asante, Molefi Kete **3**
Ashe, Arthur **1, 18**
Auguste, Rose-Anne **13**
Azikiwe, Nnamdi **13**
Baker, Ella **5**
Baker, Gwendolyn Calvert **9**
Baker, Houston A., Jr. **6**
Baker, Josephine **3**
Baldwin, James **1**
Baraka, Amiri **1**
Bates, Daisy **13**
Beals, Melba Patillo **15**
Belafonte, Harry **4**
Bell, Derrick **6**
Bell, Ralph S. **5**
Bennett, Lerone, Jr. **5**
Berry, Bertice **8**

Berry, Mary Frances **7**
Bethune, Mary McLeod **4**
Biko, Steven **4**
Blackwell, Unita **17**
Bond, Julian **2**
Bonga, Kuenda **13**
Bosley, Freeman, Jr. **7**
Boyd, T. B. III **6**
Boykin, Keith **14**
Braun, Carol Moseley **4**
Brooke, Edward **8**
Brown, Elaine **8**
Brown, Jesse **6**
Brown, Jim **11**
Brown, Lee P. **1**
Brown, Les **5**
Brown, Tony **3**
Brown, Zora Kramer **12**
Bryant, Wayne R. **6**
Bunche, Ralph J. **5**
Burroughs, Margaret Taylor **9**
Butler, Paul D. **17**
Butts, Calvin O., III **9**
Campbell, Bebe Moore **6**
Carmichael, Stokely **5**
Carter, Mandy **11**
Carter, Stephen L. **4**
Cary, Lorene **3**
Chavis, Benjamin **6**
Chideya, Farai **14**
Childress, Alice **15**
Chissano, Joaquim **7**
Christophe, Henri **9**
Chuck D **9**
Clark, Joe **1**
Clark, Kenneth B. **5**
Clark, Septima **7**
Clay, William Lacy **8**
Cleaver, Eldridge **5**
Claytor, Helen **14**
Clements, George **2**
Cobbs, Price M. **9**
Cole, Johnnetta B. **5**
Collins, Barbara-Rose **7**
Comer, James P. **6**
Cone, James H. **3**
Connerly, Ward **14**
Conté, Lansana **7**
Conyers, John, Jr. **4**
Cooper, Edward S. **6**
Cosby, Bill **7**
Cosby, Camille **14**
Cose, Ellis **5**
Crockett, George, Jr. **10**
Crouch, Stanley **11**
Dash, Julie **4**
da Silva, Benedita **5**
Davis, Angela **5**
Davis, Ossie **5**
Dee, Ruby **8**
Dellums, Ronald **2**
Dickerson, Ernest **6**
Diop, Cheikh Anta **4**
Divine, Father **7**
Dixon, Margaret **14**
Dodson, Howard, Jr. **7**
Dove, Rita **6**
Drew, Charles Richard **7**

Cumulative Occupation Index

Du Bois, W. E. B. **3**
Dunham, Katherine **4**
Early, Gerald **15**
Edelin, Ramona Hoage **19**
Edelman, Marian Wright **5**
Edley, Christopher **2**
Edwards, Harry **2**
Elder, Lee **6**
Elders, Joycelyn **6**
Ellison, Ralph **7**
Esposito, Giancarlo **9**
Espy, Mike **6**
Europe, James Reese **10**
Evers, Medgar **3**
Evers, Myrlie **8**
Farmer, James **2**
Farrakhan, Louis **15**
Fauntroy, Walter E. **11**
Fauset, Jessie **7**
Fela **1**
Foreman, George **15**
Forman, James **7**
Fortune, T. Thomas **6**
Franklin, Hardy R. **9**
Franklin, John Hope **5**
Franklin, Robert M. **13**
Frazier, E. Franklin **10**
Fulani, Lenora **11**
Fuller, Charles **8**
Gaines, Ernest J. **7**
Garvey, Marcus **1**
Gates, Henry Louis, Jr. **3**
Gayle, Helene D. **3**
Gibson, Kenneth Allen **6**
Gibson, William F. **6**
Gist, Carole **1**
Goldberg, Whoopi **4**
Golden, Marita **19**
Gomez-Preston, Cheryl **9**
Gossett, Louis, Jr. **7**
Graham, Lawrence Otis **12**
Gregory, Dick **1**
Grier, Roosevelt **13**
Griffith, Mark Winston **8**
Grimké, Archibald H. **9**
Guinier, Lani **7**
Guy, Rosa **5**
Guy-Sheftall, Beverly **13**
Hale, Lorraine **8**
Haley, Alex **4**
Hamblin, Ken **10**
Hamer, Fannie Lou **6**
Hampton, Fred **18**
Hampton, Henry **6**
Hani, Chris **6**
Hansberry, Lorraine **6**
Hansberry, William Leo **11**
Harper, Frances Ellen Watkins **11**
Harrington, Oliver W. **9**
Harris, Alice **7**
Harris, Leslie **6**
Harris, Marcelite Jordan **16**
Harris, Patricia Roberts **2**
Hastings, Alcee L. **16**
Hawkins, Steven **14**
Haynes, George Edmund **8**
Height, Dorothy I. **2**
Henderson, Wade J. **14**

Henry, Aaron **19**
Henry, Lenny **9**
Hernandez, Aileen Clarke **13**
Hill, Anita **5**
Hill, Jessie, Jr. **13**
Hilliard, David **7**
Holland, Endesha Ida Mae **3**
hooks, bell **5**
Hooks, Benjamin L. **2**
Horne, Lena **5**
Houston, Charles Hamilton **4**
Hughes, Albert **7**
Hughes, Allen **7**
Hughes, Langston **4**
Hunter-Gault, Charlayne **6**
Hutson, Jean Blackwell **16**
Ice-T **6**
Iceberg Slim **11**
Iman **4**
Ingram, Rex **5**
Innis, Roy **5**
Jackson, George **14**
Jackson, Janet **6**
Jackson, Jesse **1**
Jackson, Mahalia **5**
Jacob, John E. **2**
Jagan, Cheddi **16**
James, Daniel, Jr. **16**
Jeffries, Leonard **8**
Johnson, Charles S. **12**
Johnson, Earvin "Magic" **3**
Johnson, James Weldon **5**
Jones, Elaine R. **7**
Jordan, Barbara **4**
Jordan, June **7**
Jordan, Vernon E. **3**
Josey, E. J. **10**
Joyner, Tom **19**
Julian, Percy Lavon **6**
Kaunda, Kenneth **2**
Keith, Damon J. **16**
Kennedy, Florynce **12**
Khanga, Yelena **6**
King, B. B. **7**
King, Bernice **4**
King, Coretta Scott **3**
King, Dexter **10**
King, Martin Luther, Jr. **1**
King, Yolanda **6**
Kitt, Eartha **16**
Lampkin, Daisy **19**
Lane, Charles **3**
Lane, Vincent **5**
Lee, Canada **8**
Lee, Spike **5, 19**
Leland, Mickey **2**
Lester, Julius **9**
Lewis, Delano **7**
Lewis, John **2**
Lewis, Thomas **19**
Little, Robert L. **2**
Lorde, Audre **6**
Louis, Errol T. **8**
Lowery, Joseph **2**
Lucas, John **7**
Madhubuti, Haki R. **7**
Madison, Joseph E. **17**
Makeba, Miriam **2**

Mandela, Nelson **1, 14**
Mandela, Winnie **2**
Manley, Audrey Forbes **16**
Marable, Manning **10**
Marley, Bob **5**
Marshall, Paule **7**
Marshall, Thurgood **1**
Martin, Louis E. **16**
Masekela, Barbara **18**
Masekela, Hugh **1**
Mathabane, Mark **5**
Maynard, Robert C. **7**
Mays, Benjamin E. **7**
McCabe, Jewell Jackson **10**
McCarty, Oseola **16**
McDaniel, Hattie **5**
McDougall, Gay J. **11**
McKay, Claude **6**
McKissick, Floyd B. **3**
McQueen, Butterfly **6**
Meek, Carrie **6**
Meredith, James H. **11**
Mfume, Kweisi **6**
Micheaux, Oscar **7**
Mkapa, Benjamin **16**
Mongella, Gertrude **11**
Morrison, Toni **2**
Moses, Robert Parris **11**
Mosley, Walter **5**
Motley, Constance Baker **10**
Moutoussamy-Ashe, Jeanne **7**
Mowry, Jess **7**
Muhammad, Elijah **4**
Muhammad, Khallid Abdul **10**
Ndadaye, Melchior **7**
Nelson, Jill **6**
Newton, Huey **2**
Nkrumah, Kwame **3**
Norman, Pat **10**
Norton, Eleanor Holmes **7**
Nzo, Alfred **15**
Obasanjo, Olusegun **5**
O'Leary, Hazel **6**
Oglesby, Zena **12**
Owens, Major **6**
Page, Alan **7**
Page, Clarence **4**
Paige, Satchel **7**
Parker, Pat **19**
Parks, Rosa **1**
Patterson, Frederick Douglass **12**
Patterson, Orlando **4**
Patterson, P. J. **6**
Perkins, Edward **5**
Pitt, David Thomas **10**
Pleasant, Mary Ellen **9**
Poussaint, Alvin F. **5**
Powell, Adam Clayton, Jr. **3**
Pratt, Geronimo **18**
Price, Hugh B. **9**
Primus, Pearl **6**
Prothrow-Stith, Deborah **10**
Quarles, Benjamin Arthur **18**
Ramaphosa, Cyril **3**
Rand, A. Barry **6**
Randolph, A. Philip **3**
Rangel, Charles **3**
Rawlings, Nana Konadu Agyeman

13
Reagon, Bernice Johnson 7
Reed, Ishmael 8
Rice, Norm 8
Riggs, Marlon 5
Riley, Helen Caldwell Day 13
Ringgold, Faith 4
Robeson, Eslanda Goode 13
Robeson, Paul 2
Robinson, Jackie 6
Robinson, Rachel 16
Robinson, Randall 7
Rowan, Carl T. 1
Rustin, Bayard 4
Sampson, Edith S. 4
Sapphire 14
Satcher, David 7
Savimbi, Jonas 2
Sawyer, Amos 2
Sayles Belton, Sharon 9, 16
Schomburg, Arthur Alfonso 9
Seale, Bobby 3
Senghor, Léopold Sédar 12
Shabazz, Attallah 6
Shabazz, Betty 7
Shakur, Assata 6
Sifford, Charlie 4
Simone, Nina 15
Simpson, Carole 6
Sister Souljah 11
Sleet, Moneta, Jr. 5
Smith, Anna Deavere 6
Soyinka, Wole 4
Stallings, George A., Jr. 6
Staupers, Mabel K. 7
Steele, Claude Mason 13
Steele, Shelby 13
Stewart, Alison 13
Stewart, Maria W. Miller 19
Stone, Chuck 9
Sullivan, Leon H. 3
Taulbert, Clifton Lemoure 19
Taylor, Susan L. 10
Terrell, Mary Church 9
Thomas, Franklin A. 5
Thomas, Isiah 7
Thurman, Howard 3
Thurman, Wallace 16
Till, Emmett 7
Toomer, Jean 6
Tosh, Peter 9
Tribble, Israel, Jr. 8
Trotter, Monroe 9
Tubman, Harriet 9
Tucker, C. DeLores 12
Tucker, Cynthia 15
Tucker, Rosina 14
Tutu, Desmond 6
Underwood, Blair 7
Van Peebles, Melvin 7
Vanzant, Iyanla 17
Vincent, Marjorie Judith 2
Waddles, Charleszetta (Mother) 10
Walcott, Derek 5
Walker, A'lelia 14
Walker, Alice 1
Walker, Cedric "Ricky" 19

Walker, Madame C. J. 7
Wallace, Michele Faith 13
Wallace, Phyllis A. 9
Washington, Booker T. 4
Washington, Fredi 10
Washington, Harold 6
Waters, Maxine 3
Wattleton, Faye 9
Wells, James Lesesne 10
Wells-Barnett, Ida B. 8
Welsing, Frances Cress 5
West, Cornel 5
White, Michael R. 5
White, Reggie 6
White, Walter F. 4
Wideman, John Edgar 5
Wilkins, Roger 2
Wilkins, Roy 4
Williams, Evelyn 10
Williams, George Washington 18
Williams, Hosea Lorenzo 15
Williams, Maggie 7
Williams, Montel 4
Williams, Patricia J. 11
Williams, Robert F. 11
Williams, Walter E. 4
Williams, Willie L. 4
Wilson, August 7
Wilson, Phill 9
Wilson, Sunnie 7
Winfield, Paul 2
Winfrey, Oprah 2, 15
Wolfe, George C. 6
Woodson, Robert L. 10
Worrill, Conrad 12
Wright, Louis Tompkins 4
Wright, Richard 5
X, Malcolm 1
Yoba, Malik 11
Young, Andrew 3
Young, Jean Childs 14
Young, Whitney M., Jr. 4
Youngblood, Johnny Ray 8

Sports
Ashe, Arthur 1, 18
Aaron, Hank 5
Abdul-Jabbar, Kareem 8
Ali, Muhammad 2, 16
Amos, John 8
Ashe, Arthur 1, 18
Ashley, Maurice 15
Baker, Dusty 8
Barkley, Charles 5
Barnes, Ernie 16
Baylor, Don 6
Belle, Albert 10
Bing, Dave 3
Bol, Manute 1
Bonaly, Surya 7
Bonds, Barry 6
Bowe, Riddick 6
Brandon, Terrell 16
Brock, Lou 18
Brown, Jim 11
Bryant, Kobe 15
Butler, Leroy III 17
Chamberlain, Wilt 18

Christie, Linford 8
Coachman, Alice 18
Coleman, Leonard S., Jr. 12
Cooper, Cynthia 17
Cottrell, Comer 11
Davis, Piper 19
Dawes, Dominique 11
Devers, Gail 7
Doby, Lawrence Eugene, Sr. 16
Drew, Charles Richard 7
Drexler, Clyde 4
Dumars, Joe 16
Dungy, Tony 17
Edwards, Harry 2
Edwards, Teresa 14
Elder, Lee 6
Erving, Julius 18
Ewing, Patrick A. 17
Fielder, Cecil 2
Flood, Curt 10
Foreman, George 1, 15
Frazier, Joe 19
Fuhr, Grant 1
Gaither, Alonzo Smith (Jake) 14
Garnett, Kevin 14
Garrison, Zina 2
Gibson, Althea 8
Gourdine, Simon 11
Green, Dennis 5
Gregg, Eric 16
Grier, Roosevelt 1
Griffey, Ken, Jr. 12
Gumbel, Bryant 14
Gumbel, Greg 8
Greene, Joe 10
Gwynn, Tony 18
Hardaway, Anfernee (Penny) 13
Hickman, Fred 11
Hill, Calvin 19
Hill, Grant 13
Holyfield, Evander 6
Howard, Desmond 16
Howard, Juwan 15
Jackson, Mannie 14
Jackson, Reggie 15
Johnson, Ben 1
Johnson, Earvin "Magic" 3
Johnson, Jack 8
Johnson, Michael 13
Jones, Cobi N'Gai 18
Jordan, Michael 6
Joyner-Kersee, Jackie 5
Justice, David 18
King, Don 14
Lee, Canada 8
Leonard, Sugar Ray 15
Leslie, Lisa 16
Lewis, Carl 4
Lofton, Kenny 12
Lott, Ronnie 9
Louis, Joe 5
Love, Nat 9
Lucas, John 7
Malone, Karl A. 18
Manigault, Earl "The Goat" 15
Mays, Willie 3
McBride, Bryant 18
McCray, Nikki 18

McKegney, Tony **3**
McNeil, Lori **1**
Milla, Roger **2**
Miller, Cheryl **10**
Moon, Warren **8**
Moorer, Michael **19**
Morgan, Joe Leonard **9**
Moses, Edwin **8**
Mourning, Alonzo **17**
Murray, Eddie **12**
Murray, Lenda **10**
Mutola, Maria **12**
Mutombo, Dikembe **7**
Noah, Yannick **4**
O'Neil, Buck **19**
Olajuwon, Hakeem **2**
O'Neal, Shaquille **8**
O'Ree, Willie **5**
Owens, Jesse **2**
Page, Alan **7**
Paige, Satchel **7**
Patterson, Floyd **19**
Payton, Walter **11**
Peete, Calvin **11**
Pelé **7**
Pickett, Bill **11**
Pippen, Scottie **15**
Powell, Mike **7**
Puckett, Kirby **4**
Quirot, Ana **13**
Rashad, Ahmad **18**
Rhodes, Ray **14**
Ribbs, Willy T. **2**
Rice, Jerry **5**
Richardson, Nolan **9**
Richmond, Mitch **19**
Robinson, Eddie G. **10**
Robinson, Frank **9**
Robinson, Jackie **6**
Robinson, Sugar Ray **18**
Rodman, Dennis **12**
Rudolph, Wilma **4**
Russell, Bill **8**
Sampson, Charles **13**
Sanders, Barry **1**
Sanders, Deion **4**
Scott, Sr., Wendell Oliver **19**
Sheffield, Gary **16**
Shell, Art **1**
Sifford, Charlie **4**
Simpson, O. J. **15**
Singletary, Mike **4**
Smith, Emmitt **7**
Smith, Tubby **18**
Steward, Emanuel **18**
Stone, Toni **15**
Stringer, C. Vivian **13**
Swoopes, Sheryl **12**
Thomas, Frank **12**
Thomas, Isiah **7**
Upshaw, Gene **18**
Walker, Herschel **1**
Washington, MaliVai **8**
Watts, J. C., Jr. **14**
Weathers, Carl **10**
Webber, Chris **15**
Whitaker, Pernell **10**
White, Bill **1**

White, Reggie **6**
Wilkens, Lenny **11**
Williams, Venus Ebone **17**
Wilson, Sunnie **7**
Winfield, Dave **5**
Woods, Tiger **14**

Television
Allen, Byron **3**
Allen, Debbie **13**
Amos, John **8**
Arkadie, Kevin **17**
Banks, William **11**
Barden, Don H. **9**
Bassett, Angela **6**
Beaton, Norman **14**
Belafonte, Harry **4**
Bellamy, Bill **12**
Berry, Bertice **8**
Berry, Halle **4, 19**
Bowser, Yvette Lee **17**
Bradley, Ed **2**
Brandy **14**
Braugher, Andre **13**
Brooks, Avery **9**
Brown, Les **5**
Brown, Tony **3**
Burnett, Charles **16**
Burton, LeVar **8**
Byrd, Robert **11**
Campbell, Tisha **8**
Carroll, Diahann **9**
Cheadle, Don **19**
Chideya, Farai **14**
Christian, Spencer **15**
Clash, Kevin **14**
Clayton, Xernona **3**
Cole, Nat King **17**
Cole, Natalie Maria **17**
Cornelius, Don **4**
Cosby, Bill **7**
Crothers, Scatman **19**
Curry, Mark **17**
Curtis-Hall, Vondie **17**
Davis, Ossie **5**
Dee, Ruby **8**
Dickerson, Ernest **6**
Dr. Dre **10**
Duke, Bill **3**
Dutton, Charles S. **4**
Erving, Julius **18**
Esposito, Giancarlo **9**
Eubanks, Kevin **15**
Fishburne, Larry **4**
Foxx, Jamie **15**
Foxx, Redd **2**
Freeman, Al, Jr. **11**
Freeman, Morgan **2**
Gaines, Ernest J. **7**
Givens, Robin **4**
Glover, Savion **14**
Goldberg, Whoopi **4**
Goode, Mal **13**
Gooding, Cuba, Jr. **16**
Gordon, Ed **10**
Gossett, Louis, Jr. **7**
Grier, Pam **9**
Guillaume, Robert **3**

Gumbel, Bryant **14**
Gumbel, Greg **8**
Gunn, Moses **10**
Guy, Jasmine **2**
Haley, Alex **4**
Hampton, Henry **6**
Harrell, Andre **9**
Harris, Robin **7**
Harvey, Steve **18**
Hemsley, Sherman **19**
Henry, Lenny **9**
Hickman, Fred **11**
Hinderas, Natalie **5**
Horne, Lena **5**
Hounsou, Djimon **19**
Hunter-Gault, Charlayne **6**
Iman **4**
Ingram, Rex **5**
Jackson, George **19**
Jackson, Janet **6**
Jackson, Jesse **1**
Johnson, Beverly **2**
Johnson, Robert L. **3**
Jones, James Earl **3**
Jones, Quincy **8**
Jones, Star **10**
King, Gayle **19**
Kirby, George **14**
Kitt, Eartha **16**
Knight, Gladys **16**
Kotto, Yaphet **7**
L.L. Cool J **16**
LaBelle, Patti **13**
La Salle, Eriq **12**
Langhart, Janet **19**
Lawrence, Martin **6**
Lawson, Jennifer **1**
Lewis, Byron E. **13**
Lindo, Delroy **18**
Long, Nia **17**
Lover, Ed **10**
McDaniel, Hattie **5**
McEwen, Mark **5**
McQueen, Butterfly **6**
Mckee, Lonette **12**
Miller, Cheryl **10**
Morgan, Joe Leonard **9**
Morton, Joe **3**
Moses, Gilbert **12**
Moss, Carlton **17**
Murphy, Eddie **4**
Nichols, Nichelle **11**
Payne, Allen **13**
Pinkett, Jada **10**
Price, Hugh B. **9**
Queen Latifah **1, 16**
Ralph, Sheryl Lee **18**
Randle, Theresa **16**
Rashad, Ahmad **18**
Reese, Della **6**
Reuben, Gloria **15**
Ribeiro, Alfonso **17**
Roberts, Robin **16**
Robinson, Max **3**
Rochon, Lela **16**
Rock, Chris **3**
Rodgers, Johnathan **6**
Roker, Al **12**

Rolle, Esther **13**
Rollins, Howard E., Jr. **16**
Ross, Diana **8**
Rowan, Carl T. **1**
Rowell, Victoria **13**
Rupaul **17**
Russell, Bill **8**
St. Jacques, Raymond **8**
Schultz, Michael A. **6**
Shaw, Bernard **2**
Simpson, Carole **6**
Simpson, O. J. **15**
Sinbad **1, 16**
Smith, Barbara **11**
Smith, Roger Guenveur **12**
Smith, Will **8, 18**
Stewart, Alison **13**
Stokes, Carl B. **10**
Stone, Chuck **9**
Tate, Larenz **15**
Taylor, Meshach **4**
Taylor, Regina **9**
Thigpen, Lynne **17**
Tucker, Chris **13**
Tyson, Cicely **7**
Underwood, Blair **7**
Van Peebles, Mario **2**
Van Peebles, Melvin **7**
Vereen, Ben **4**
Warfield, Marsha **2**
Warwick, Dionne **18**
Washington, Denzel **1, 16**
Wattleton, Faye **9**
Watts, Rolonda **9**
Wayans, Damon **8**
Wayans, Keenen Ivory **18**
Weathers, Carl **10**
Whitfield, Lynn **1, 18**
Wilkins, Roger **2**
Williams, Billy Dee **8**
Williams, Montel **4**
Williams, Vanessa L. **4, 17**
Winfield, Paul **2**
Winfrey, Oprah **2, 15**
Yoba, Malik **11**

Theater
Ailey, Alvin **8**
Allen, Debbie **13**
Amos, John **8**
Andrews, Bert **13**
Angelou, Maya **1**
Arkadie, Kevin **17**
Baraka, Amiri **1**
Bassett, Angela **6**
Beaton, Norman **14**
Belafonte, Harry **4**
Borders, James **9**
Brooks, Avery **9**
Calloway, Cab **14**
Campbell, Naomi **1**
Campbell, Tisha **8**
Carroll, Diahann **9**
Cheadle, Don **19**
Childress, Alice **15**
Clarke, Hope **14**
Cleage, Pearl **17**
Curtis-Hall, Vondie **17**

Davis, Ossie **5**
Davis, Sammy Jr. **18**
Dee, Ruby **8**
Duke, Bill **3**
Dunham, Katherine **4**
Dutton, Charles S. **4**
Esposito, Giancarlo **9**
Europe, James Reese **10**
Fishburne, Larry **4**
Freeman, Al, Jr. **11**
Freeman, Morgan **2**
Fuller, Charles **8**
Glover, Danny **1**
Glover, Savion **14**
Goldberg, Whoopi **4**
Gordone, Charles **15**
Gossett, Louis, Jr. **7**
Graves, Denyce **19**
Grier, Pam **9**
Guillaume, Robert **3**
Gunn, Moses **10**
Guy, Jasmine **2**
Hansberry, Lorraine **6**
Harris, Robin **7**
Hemsley, Sherman **19**
Holland, Endesha Ida Mae **3**
Horne, Lena **5**
Hyman, Phyllis **19**
Ingram, Rex **5**
Jackson, Samuel L. **8, 19**
Jamison, Judith **7**
Jean-Baptiste, Marianne **17**
Jones, James Earl **3**
Joyner, Matilda Sissieretta **15**
King, Yolanda **6**
Kitt, Eartha **16**
Kotto, Yaphet **7**
La Salle, Eriq **12**
Lee, Canada **8**
Leon, Kenny **10**
Lincoln, Abbey **3**
Lindo, Delroy **18**
Mabley, Jackie "Moms" **15**
McDaniel, Hattie **5**
McKee, Lonette **12**
McQueen, Butterfly **6**
Moses, Gilbert **12**
Moss, Carlton **17**
Moten, Etta **18**
Payne, Allen **13**
Powell, Maxine **8**
Primus, Pearl **6**
Ralph, Sheryl Lee **18**
Randle, Theresa **16**
Reese, Della **6**
Rhames, Ving **14**
Richards, Lloyd **2**
Robeson, Paul **2**
Rolle, Esther **13**
Rollins, Howard E., Jr.
Rotimi, Ola **1**
St. Jacques, Raymond **8**
Schultz, Michael A. **6**
Shabazz, Attallah **6**
Shange, Ntozake **8**
Smith, Anna Deavere **6**
Smith, Roger Guenveur **12**
Snipes, Wesley **3**

Soyinka, Wole **4**
Taylor, Meshach **4**
Taylor, Regina **9**
Thigpen, Lynne **17**
Thompson, Tazewell **13**
Thurman, Wallace **16**
Townsend, Robert **4**
Tyson, Cicely **7**
Underwood, Blair **7**
Van Peebles, Melvin **7**
Vance, Courtney B. **15**
Vereen, Ben **4**
Walcott, Derek **5**
Washington, Denzel **1, 16**
Washington, Fredi **10**
Waters, Ethel **7**
Whitaker, Forest **2**
Whitfield, Lynn **18**
Williams, Bert **18**
Williams, Billy Dee **8**
Williams, Vanessa L. **4, 17**
Wilson, August **7**
Winfield, Paul **2**
Wolfe, George C. **6**
Woodard, Alfre **9**

Writing
Achebe, Chinua **6**
Abu-Jamal, Mumia **15**
Al-Amin, Jamil Abdullah **6**
Andrews, Raymond **4**
Angelou, Maya **1, 15**
Ansa, Tina McElroy **14**
Aristide, Jean-Bertrand **6**
Arkadie, Kevin **17**
Asante, Molefi Kete **3**
Ashe, Arthur **1, 18**
Azikiwe, Nnamdi **13**
Baker, Houston A., Jr. **6**
Baldwin, James **1**
Bambara, Toni Cade **10**
Baraka, Amiri **1**
Beals, Melba Patillo **15**
Bell, Derrick **6**
Bennett, Lerone, Jr. **5**
Berry, Mary Frances **7**
Bluitt, Juliann S. **14**
Bontemps, Arna **8**
Borders, James **9**
Bradley, Ed **2**
Brimmer, Andrew F. **2**
Briscoe, Connie **15**
Brooks, Gwendolyn **1**
Brown, Elaine **8**
Brown, Les **5**
Brown, Marie Dutton **12**
Brown, Sterling **10**
Brown, Tony **3**
Bunche, Ralph J. **5**
Burroughs, Margaret Taylor **9**
Butler, Octavia **8**
Campbell, Bebe Moore **6**
Carmichael, Stokely **5**
Carter, Stephen L. **4**
Cary, Lorene **3**
Chamberlain, Wilt **18**
Chideya, Farai **14**
Childress, Alice **15**

Clark, Kenneth B. 5
Clark, Septima 7
Cleage, Pearl 17
Cleaver, Eldridge 5
Clifton, Lucille 14
Cobbs, Price M. 9
Cohen, Anthony 15
Cole, Johnnetta B. 5
Comer, James P. 6
Cone, James H. 3
Cooper, J. California 12
Cosby, Bill 7
Cosby, Camille 14
Cose, Ellis 5
Crouch, Stanley 11
Cullen, Countee 8
Curtis-Hall, Vondie 17
Danticat, Edwidge 15
Davis, Allison 12
Davis, Angela 5
Davis, Miles 4
Davis, Ossie 5
Delany, Samuel R., Jr. 9
Diop, Cheikh Anta 4
Dodson, Howard, Jr. 7
Dove, Rita 6
Draper, Sharon M. 16
Driskell, David C. 7
Driver, David E. 11
Du Bois, W. E. B. 3
Dunbar, Paul Laurence 8
Dunham, Katherine 4
Dyson, Michael Eric 11
Early, Gerald 15
Edmonds, Terry 17
Ellison, Ralph 7
Farrakhan, Louis 15
Fauset, Jessie 7
Feelings, Tom 11
Fisher, Rudolph 17
Forman, James 7
Fortune, T. Thomas 6
Franklin, John Hope 5
Franklin, Robert M. 13
Frazier, E. Franklin 10
French, Albert 18
Fuller, Charles 8
Gaines, Ernest J. 7
Gates, Henry Louis, Jr. 3
George, Nelson 12
Gibson, Althea 8
Giddings, Paula 11
Giovanni, Nikki 9
Goines, Donald 19
Golden, Marita 19
Graham, Lawrence Otis 12
Greenfield, Eloise 9
Griffith, Mark Winston 8
Grimké, Archibald H. 9
Guinier, Lani 7
Guy, Rosa 5
Guy-Sheftall, Beverly 13
Haley, Alex 4
Hamblin, Ken 10
Hamilton, Virginia 10
Hansberry, Lorraine 6
Harkless, Necia Desiree 19
Harper, Frances Ellen Watkins 11

Harrington, Oliver W. 9
Harris, Eddy L. 18
Harris, Jay 19
Harris, Leslie 6
Harris, Monica 18
Hayden, Robert 12
Hemphill, Essex 10
Henry, Lenny 9
Henson, Matthew 2
Hilliard, David 7
Holland, Endesha Ida Mae 3
hooks, bell 5
Hudson, Cheryl 15
Hudson, Wade 15
Hughes, Langston 4
Hunter-Gault, Charlayne 6
Hurston, Zora Neale 3
Iceberg Slim 11
Jackson, George 14
Jackson, Sheneska 18
Jenkins, Beverly 14
Johnson, Charles 1
Johnson, Charles S. 12
Johnson, James Weldon 5
Johnson, John H. 3
Jordan, June 7
Josey, E. J. 10
Just, Ernest Everett 3
Karenga, Maulana 10
Kennedy, Adrienne 11
Kennedy, Florynce 12
Khanga, Yelena 6
Kimbro, Dennis 10
Kincaid, Jamaica 4
King, Coretta Scott 3
King, Yolanda 6
Komunyakaa, Yusef 9
Kotto, Yaphet 7
Kunjufu, Jawanza 3
Larsen, Nella 10
Lawrence, Martin 6
Lawrence-Lightfoot, Sara 10
Lester, Julius 9
Lewis, David Levering 9
Locke, Alain 10
Lorde, Audre 6
Louis, Errol T. 8
Madhubuti, Haki R. 7
Major, Clarence 9
Makeba, Miriam 2
Marshall, Paule 7
Mathabane, Mark 5
Maynard, Robert C. 7
Mays, Benjamin E. 7
McCall, Nathan 8
McKay, Claude 6
McMillan, Terry 4, 17
Meredith, James H. 11
Micheaux, Oscar 7
Morrison, Toni 2, 15
Mosley, Walter 5
Moss, Carlton 17
Moutoussamy-Ashe, Jeanne 7
Mowry, Jess 7
Myers, Walter Dean 8
Naylor, Gloria 10
Nelson, Jill 6
Newton, Huey 2

Nkrumah, Kwame 3
Owens, Major 6
Page, Clarence 4
Parker, Pat 19
Patterson, Orlando 4
Petry, Ann 19
Poussaint, Alvin F. 5
Powell, Adam Clayton, Jr. 3
Pryor, Richard 3
Quarles, Benjamin Arthur 18
Randall, Dudley 8
Raspberry, William 2
Reagon, Bernice Johnson 7
Reed, Ishmael 8
Riggs, Marlon 5
Ringgold, Faith 4
Robeson, Eslanda Goode 13
Rodman, Dennis 12
Rotimi, Ola 1
Rowan, Carl T. 1
Saint James, Synthia 12
Sanchez, Sonia 17
Sanders, Dori 8
Sapphire 14
Schomburg, Arthur Alfonso 9
Seale, Bobby 3
Sembène, Ousmane 13
Senghor, Léopold Sédar 12
Sengstacke, John 18
Shabazz, Attallah 6
Shakur, Assata 6
Shange, Ntozake 8
Shaw, Bernard 2
Shipp, E. R. 15
Simone, Nina 15
Simpson, Carole 6
Singleton, John 2
Sister Souljah 11
Smith, Anna Deavere 6
Smith, Barbara 11
Somé, Malidoma Patrice 10
Sowell, Thomas 2
Soyinka, Wole 4
Staples, Brent 8
Stewart, Alison 13
Stone, Chuck 9
Taulbert, Clifton Lemoure 19
Taylor, Kristin Clark 8
Taylor, Susan L. 10
Thurman, Howard 3
Toomer, Jean 6
Townsend, Robert 4
Trotter, Monroe 9
Tucker, Cynthia 15
Turner, Henry McNeal 5
Turner, Tina 6
Tutu, Desmond 6
Tyson, Neil de Grasse 15
Van Peebles, Melvin 7
Walcott, Derek 5
Walker, Alice 1
Wallace, Michele Faith 13
Wallace, Phyllis A. 9
Washington, Booker T. 4
Washington, Laura S. 18
Waters, Ethel 7
Wattleton, Faye 9
Wayans, Damon 8

Webb, Veronica **10**
Wells-Barnett, Ida B. **8**
Wesley, Dorothy Porter **19**
Wesley, Valerie Wilson **18**
West, Cornel **5**
West, Dorothy **12**
Wharton, Clifton R., Jr. **7**
White, Walter F. **4**
Wideman, John Edgar **5**
Wiley, Ralph **8**
Wilkins, Roger **2**
Wilkins, Roy **4**
Williams, George Washington **18**
Williams, Patricia J. **11**
Williams, Robert F. **11**
Wilson, August **7**
Winans, Marvin L. **17**
Wolfe, George C. **6**
Woodson, Carter G. **2**
Worrill, Conrad **12**
Wright, Bruce McMarion **3**
Wright, Richard **5**
Young, Whitney M., Jr. **4**

Cumulative Subject Index

Volume numbers appear in **bold**.

AA
See Alcoholics Anonymous

AAAS
See American Association for the Advancement of Science

AARP
Dixon, Margaret **14**

ABC
See American Broadcasting Company

Academy awards
Freeman, Morgan **2**
Goldberg, Whoopi **4**
Gooding, Cuba, Jr. **16**
Gossett, Louis, Jr. **7**
Jean-Baptiste, Marianne **17**
McDaniel, Hattie **5**
Poitier, Sidney **11**
Prince **18**
Washington, Denzel **1, 16**
Wonder, Stevie **11**

A cappella
Cooke, Sam **17**
Reagon, Bernice Johnson **7**

ACDL
See Association for Constitutional Democracy in Liberia

ACLU
See American Civil Liberties Union

Acquired Immune Deficiency Syndrome (AIDS)
Ashe, Arthur **1, 18**
Gayle, Helene D. **3**
Hale, Lorraine **8**
Johnson, Earvin "Magic" **3**
Mboup, Souleymane **10**
Moutoussamy-Ashe, Jeanne **7**
Norman, Pat **10**
Riggs, Marlon **5**
Satcher, David **7**
Wilson, Phill **9**

Acting
Ailey, Alvin **8**
Allen, Debbie **13**
Amos, John **8**
Angelou, Maya **1, 15**
Baker, Josephine **3**
Banks, Tyra **11**
Bassett, Angela **6**
Beals, Jennifer **12**
Beaton, Norman **14**
Berry, Halle **4, 19**
Borders, James **9**
Braugher, Andre **13**
Brooks, Avery **9**
Brown, Jim **11**
Caesar, Shirley **19**
Calloway, Cab **14**
Campbell, Naomi **1**
Campbell, Tisha **8**
Carroll, Diahann **9**
Cheadle, Don **19**
Childress, Alice **15**
Clarke, Hope **14**
Cole, Nat King **17**
Cole, Natalie Maria **17**
Cosby, Bill **7**
Crothers, Scatman **19**
Curry, Mark **17**
Curtis-Hall, Vondie **17**
Dandridge, Dorothy **3**
Davidson, Jaye **5**
Davis, Ossie **5**
Davis, Sammy Jr. **18**
Dee, Ruby **8**
Duke, Bill **3**
Dutton, Charles S. **4**
Esposito, Giancarlo **9**
Fishburne, Larry **4**
Fox, Vivica A. **15**
Foxx, Jamie **15**
Foxx, Redd **2**
Freeman, Al, Jr. **11**
Freeman, Morgan **2**
Givens, Robin **4**
Glover, Danny **1**
Goldberg, Whoopi **4**
Gooding, Cuba, Jr. **16**
Gossett, Louis, Jr. **7**
Grier, Pam **9**
Guillaume, Robert **3**
Gunn, Moses **10**
Guy, Jasmine **2**
Harris, Robin **7**
Harvey, Steve **18**
Hemsley, Sherman **19**
Henry, Lenny **9**
Hines, Gregory **1**
Horne, Lena **5**
Hounsou, Djimon **19**
Houston, Whitney **7**
Ice Cube **8**
Iman **4**
Ingram, Rex **5**
Jackson, Janet **6**
Jackson, Michael **19**
Jackson, Samuel L. **8, 19**
Jean-Baptiste, Marianne **17**
Jones, James Earl **3**
Kirby, George **14**
Kitt, Eartha **16**
Knight, Gladys **16**
Kotto, Yaphet **7**
L. L. Cool J **16**
Lane, Charles **3**
La Salle, Eriq **12**
Lawrence, Martin **6**
Lee, Canada **8**
Lee, Joie **1**
Lee, Spike **5, 19**
Lincoln, Abbey **3**
Lindo, Delroy **18**
Mabley, Jackie "Moms" **15**
McDaniel, Hattie **5**
Mckee, Lonette **12**
McQueen, Butterfly **6**
Morton, Joe **18**
Moten, Etta **18**
Murphy, Eddie **4**
Nichols, Nichelle **11**
Payne, Allen **13**
Pinkett, Jada **10**
Poitier, Sidney **11**
Prince **18**
Pryor, Richard **3**
Queen Latifah **1, 16**
Randle, Theresa **16**
Reese, Della **6**
Reuben, Gloria **15**
Rhames, Ving **14**
Ribeiro, Alfonso **17**

Richards, Lloyd 2
Robeson, Paul 2
Rock, Chris 3
Rolle, Esther 13
Ross, Diana 8
Rowell, Victoria 13
St. Jacques, Raymond 8
Shakur, Tupac 14
Sinbad 1, 16
Smith, Anna Deavere 6
Smith, Barbara 11
Smith, Roger Guenveur 12
Smith, Will 8, 18
Snipes, Wesley 3
Tate, Larenz 15
Taylor, Meshach 4
Taylor, Regina 9
Thompson, Tazewell 13
Townsend, Robert 4
Turner, Tina 6
Tyson, Cicely 7
Underwood, Blair 7
Van Peebles, Mario 2
Van Peebles, Melvin 7
Vance, Courtney B. 15
Vereen, Ben 4
Warfield, Marsha 2
Washington, Denzel 1, 16
Washington, Fredi 10
Waters, Ethel 7
Wayans, Damon 8
Wayans, Keenen Ivory 18
Weathers, Carl 10
Webb, Veronica 10
Whitaker, Forest 2
Whitfield, Lynn 18
Williams, Bert 18
Williams, Billy Dee 8
Williams, Vanessa L. 4, 17
Winfield, Paul 2
Winfrey, Oprah 2, 15
Woodard, Alfre 9
Yoba, Malik 11

Active Ministers Engaged in Nurturance (AMEN)
King, Bernice 4

Actuarial science
Hill, Jessie, Jr. 13

ACT UP
See AIDS Coalition to Unleash Power

Acustar, Inc.
Farmer, Forest 1

ADC
See Agricultural Development Council

Adoption and foster care
Baker, Josephine 3
Clements, George 2
Gossett, Louis, Jr. 7
Hale, Clara 16
Hale, Lorraine 8

Oglesby, Zena 12

Adventures in Movement (AIM)
Morgan, Joe Leonard 9

Advertising
Barboza, Anthony 10
Campbell, E. Simms 13
Johnson, Beverly 2
Lewis, Byron E. 13
Roche, Joyce M. 17

Advocates Scene
Seale, Bobby 3

AFCEA
See Armed Forces Communications and Electronics Associations

Affirmative action
Berry, Mary Frances 7
Carter, Stephen L. 4
Maynard, Robert C. 7
Norton, Eleanor Holmes 7
Rand, A. Barry 6
Waters, Maxine 3

AFL-CIO
See American Federation of Labor and Congress of Industrial Organizations

African/African-American Summit
Sullivan, Leon H. 3

African American Catholic Congregation
Stallings, George A., Jr. 6

African American folklore
Bailey, Xenobia 11
Brown, Sterling 10
Driskell, David C. 7
Ellison, Ralph 7
Gaines, Ernest J. 7
Hamilton, Virginia 10
Hughes, Langston 4
Hurston, Zora Neale 3
Lester, Julius 9
Morrison, Toni 2
Primus, Pearl 6
Williams, Bert 18

African American folk music
Handy, W. C. 8
House, Son 8
Johnson, James Weldon 5
Lester, Julius 9

African American history
Angelou, Maya 1
Ashe, Arthur 1, 18
Bennett, Lerone, Jr. 5
Berry, Mary Frances 7
Burroughs, Margaret Taylor 9
Camp, Kimberly 19
Cheadle, Don 19

Dodson, Howard, Jr. 7
Douglas, Aaron 7
Du Bois, W. E. B. 3
Dyson, Michael Eric 11
Feelings, Tom 11
Franklin, John Hope 5
Gaines, Ernest J. 7
Gates, Henry Louis, Jr. 3
Haley, Alex 4
Harkless, Necia Desiree 19
Hughes, Langston 4
Johnson, James Weldon 5
Lewis, David Levering 9
Madhubuti, Haki R. 7
Marable, Manning 10
Morrison, Toni 2
Quarles, Benjamin Arthur 18
Reagon, Bernice Johnson 7
Ringgold, Faith 4
Schomburg, Arthur Alfonso 9
Wilson, August 7
Woodson, Carter G. 2

African American Images
Kunjufu, Jawanza 3

African American literature
Andrews, Raymond 4
Angelou, Maya 1, 15
Baker, Houston A., Jr. 6
Baldwin, James 1
Bambara, Toni Cade 1
Baraka, Amiri 1
Bontemps, Arna 8
Briscoe, Connie 15
Brooks, Gwendolyn 1
Burroughs, Margaret Taylor 9
Campbell, Bebe Moore 6
Cary, Lorene 3
Childress, Alice 15
Cleage, Pearl 17
Cullen, Countee 8
Dove, Rita 6
Du Bois, W. E. B. 3
Dunbar, Paul Laurence 8
Ellison, Ralph 7
Fauset, Jessie 7
Feelings, Tom 11
Fisher, Rudolph 17
Fuller, Charles 8
Gaines, Ernest J. 7
Gates, Henry Louis, Jr. 3
Giddings, Paula 11
Giovanni, Nikki 9
Golden, Marita 19
Guy, Rosa 5
Haley, Alex 4
Hansberry, Lorraine 6
Harper, Frances Ellen Watkins 11
Himes, Chester 8
Holland, Endesha Ida Mae 3
Hughes, Langston 4
Hurston, Zora Neale 3
Iceberg Slim 11
Johnson, Charles 1
Johnson, James Weldon 5
Jordan, June 7
Larsen, Nella 10

Lester, Julius **9**
Lorde, Audre **6**
Madhubuti, Haki R. **7**
Major, Clarence **9**
Marshall, Paule **7**
McKay, Claude **6**
McKay, Nellie Yvonne **17**
McMillan, Terry **4, 17**
Morrison, Toni **2, 15**
Mowry, Jess **7**
Naylor, Gloria **10**
Petry, Ann **19**
Pinkney, Jerry **15**
Randall, Dudley **8**
Reed, Ishmael **8**
Ringgold, Faith **4**
Sanchez, Sonia **17**
Schomburg, Arthur Alfonso **9**
Shange, Ntozake **8**
Thurman, Wallace **16**
Toomer, Jean **6**
Van Peebles, Melvin **7**
Walker, Alice **1**
Wesley, Valerie Wilson **18**
Wideman, John Edgar **5**
Wilson, August **7**
Wolfe, George C. **6**
Wright, Richard **5**

African dance
Ailey, Alvin **8**
Fagan, Garth **18**
Primus, Pearl **6**

African folk music
Makeba, Miriam **2**
Nascimento, Milton **2**

African history
Diop, Cheikh Anta **4**
Dodson, Howard, Jr. **7**
Hansberry, William Leo **11**
Harkless, Necia Desiree **19**
Jawara, Sir Dawda Kairaba **11**
Madhubuti, Haki R. **7**
Marshall, Paule **7**

African Methodist Episcopal Church (AME)
Flake, Floyd H. **18**
Murray, Cecil **12**
Turner, Henry McNeal **5**
Youngblood, Johnny Ray **8**

African National Congress (ANC)
Baker, Ella **5**
Hani, Chris **6**
Kaunda, Kenneth **2**
Luthuli, Albert **13**
Mandela, Nelson **1, 14**
Mandela, Winnie **2**
Masekela, Barbara **18**
Mbeki, Thabo Mvuyelwa **14**
Nkomo, Joshua **4**
Nzo, Alfred **15**
Ramaphosa, Cyril **3**
Tutu, Desmond **6**

African Women on Tour conference
Taylor, Susan L. **10**

Afro-American League
Fortune, T. Thomas **6**

Afrocentricity
Asante, Molefi Kete **3**
Diop, Cheikh Anta **4**
Hansberry, Lorraine **6**
Hansberry, William Leo **11**
Sanchez, Sonia **17**
Turner, Henry McNeal **5**

Agency for International Development (AID)
Gayle, Helene D. **3**
Perkins, Edward **5**
Wilkins, Roger **2**

A. G. Gaston Boys and Girls Club
Gaston, Arthur G. **4**

A. G. Gaston Motel
Gaston, Arthur G. **4**

Agricultural Development Council (ADC)
Wharton, Clifton R., Jr. **7**

Agriculture
Carver, George Washington **4**
Espy, Mike **6**
Hall, Lloyd A. **8**
Masire, Quett **5**
Obasanjo, Olusegun **5**
Sanders, Dori **8**

AHA
See American Heart Association

AID
See Agency for International Development

AIDS
See Acquired Immune Deficiency Syndrome

AIDS Coalition to Unleash Power (ACT UP)
Norman, Pat **10**

AIDS Health Care Foundation
Wilson, Phill **9**

AIDS Prevention Team
Wilson, Phill **9**

AIDS research
Mboup, Souleymane **10**

AIM
See Adventures in Movement

ALA
See American Library Association

Alcoholics Anonymous (AA)
Hilliard, David **7**
Lucas, John **7**

All Afrikan People's Revolutionary Party
Carmichael, Stokely **5**
Moses, Robert Parris **11**

Alliance Theatre
Leon, Kenny **10**

Alpha & Omega Ministry
White, Reggie **6**

Alvin Ailey American Dance Theater
Ailey, Alvin **8**
Clarke, Hope **14**
Dove, Ulysses **5**
Faison, George **16**
Jamison, Judith **7**
Primus, Pearl **6**

Alvin Ailey Repertory Ensemble
Ailey, Alvin **8**
Miller, Bebe **3**

AME
See African Methodist Episcopal Church

AMEN
See Active Ministers Engaged in Nurturance

American Association for the Advancement of Science (AAAS)
Massey, Walter E. **5**

American Ballet Theatre
Dove, Ulysses **5**

American Basketball Association (ABA)
Chamberlain, Wilt **18**

American Book Award
Baraka, Amiri **1**
Bates, Daisy **13**
Clark, Septima **7**
Gates, Henry Louis, Jr. **3**
Lorde, Audre **6**
Marshall, Paule **7**
Sanchez, Sonia **17**
Walker, Alice **1**

American Broadcasting Company (ABC)
Christian, Spencer **15**
Goode, Mal **13**
Jackson, Michael **19**
Joyner, Tom **19**
Roberts, Robin **16**
Robinson, Max **3**
Simpson, Carole **6**
Winfrey, Oprah **2, 15**

American Cancer Society
Ashe, Arthur **1, 18**
Leffall, LaSalle, Jr. **3**

American Civil Liberties Union (ACLU)
Norton, Eleanor Holmes **7**

American Community Housing Associates, Inc.
Lane, Vincent **5**

American Enterprise Institute
Woodson, Robert L. **10**

American Express Company
Chenault, Kenneth I. **4**

American Express Consumer Card Group, USA
Chenault, Kenneth I. **4**

American Federation of Labor and Congress of Industrial Organizations (AFL-CIO)
Randolph, A. Philip **3**

American Heart Association (AHA)
Cooper, Edward S. **6**

American Library Association (ALA)
Franklin, Hardy R. **9**
Josey, E. J. **10**

American Negro Academy
Grimké, Archibald H. **9**
Schomburg, Arthur Alfonso **9**

American Nurses' Association (ANA)
Kennedy, Adrienne **11**
Staupers, Mabel K. **7**

American Red Cross blood banks
Drew, Charles Richard **7**

ANA
See American Nurses' Association

ANC
See African National Congress

Anglican church hierarchy
Tutu, Desmond **6**

Anthropology
Asante, Molefi Kete **3**
Bunche, Ralph J. **5**
Cole, Johnnetta B. **5**
Davis, Allison **12**
Diop, Cheikh Anta **4**
Dunham, Katherine **4**
Hansberry, William Leo **11**
Morrison, Toni **2**
Primus, Pearl **6**
Robeson, Eslanda Goode **13**

Antoinette Perry awards
See Tony awards

Apartheid
Ashe, Arthur **1, 18**
Berry, Mary Frances **7**
Biko, Steven **4**
Luthuli, Albert **13**
Makeba, Miriam **2**
Mandela, Nelson **1, 14**
Mandela, Winnie **2**
Masekela, Hugh **1**
Mathabane, Mark **5**
Mbeki, Thabo Mvuyelwa **14**
Mbuende, Kaire **12**
McDougall, Gay J. **11**
Nzo, Alfred **15**
Ramaphosa, Cyril **3**
Robinson, Randall **7**
Sullivan, Leon H. **13**
Tutu, Desmond **6**

Apollo 13
Williams, O. S. **13**

Arab-Israeli conflict
Bunche, Ralph J. **5**

ARCH
See Argonne National Laboratory-University of Chicago Development Corporation

Architecture
Gantt, Harvey **1**
Williams, Paul R. **9**

Argonne National Laboratory
Massey, Walter E. **5**
Quarterman, Lloyd Albert **4**

Argonne National Laboratory-University of Chicago Development Corporation (ARCH)
Massey, Walter E. **5**

Ariel Capital Management
Rogers, John W., Jr. **5**

Arkansas Department of Health
Elders, Joycelyn **6**

Armed Forces Communications and Electronics Associations (AFCEA)
Gravely, Samuel L., Jr. **5**

Arthritis treatment
Julian, Percy Lavon **6**

Artists for a Free South Africa
Woodard, Alfre **9**

ASALH
See Association for the Study of Afro-American Life and History

ASH
See Association for the Sexually Harassed

Association for Constitutional Democracy in Liberia (ACDL)
Sawyer, Amos **2**

Association for the Sexually Harassed (ASH)
Gomez-Preston, Cheryl **9**

Association for the Study of Afro-American Life and History (ASALH)
Dodson, Howard, Jr. **7**
Woodson, Carter G. **2**

Astronauts
Bluford, Guy **2**
Bolden, Charles F., Jr. **7**
Gregory, Frederick D. **8**
Jemison, Mae C. **1**
Lawrence, Robert H., Jr. **16**
McNair, Ronald **3**

Atco-EastWest
Rhone, Sylvia **2**

Atlanta Baptist College
See Morehouse College

Atlanta Board of Education
Mays, Benjamin E. **7**

Atlanta Braves baseball team
Aaron, Hank **5**
Baker, Dusty **8**
Justice, David **18**
Sanders, Deion **4**

Atlanta Chamber of Commerce
Hill, Jessie, Jr. **13**

Atlanta City Council
Campbell, Bill **9**
Williams, Hosea Lorenzo **15**

Atlanta city government
Campbell, Bill **9**
Jackson, Maynard **2**
Williams, Hosea Lorenzo **15**
Young, Andrew **3**

Atlanta Falcons football team
Sanders, Deion **4**

Atlanta Hawks basketball team
Wilkens, Lenny **11**

Atlanta Life Insurance Company
Hill, Jessie, Jr. **13**

Atlanta Negro Voters League
Hill, Jessie, Jr. **13**

Atlanta Police Department
Harvard, Beverly **11**

Cumulative Subject Index

Atlantic Records
Franklin, Aretha **11**
Rhone, Sylvia **2**

Aviation
Bullard, Eugene **12**
Coleman, Bessie **9**

"Little Paris" group
Thomas, Alma **14**

"Back to Africa" movement
Turner, Henry McNeal **5**

Bad Boy Entertainment
Combs, Sean "Puffy" **17**

Ballet
Ailey, Alvin **8**
Allen, Debbie **13**
Dove, Ulysses **5**
Faison, George **16**
Johnson, Virginia **9**
Mitchell, Arthur **2**
Nichols, Nichelle **11**
Parks, Gordon **1**

Baltimore city government
Schmoke, Kurt **1**

Baltimore Colts football team
Barnes, Ernie **16**

Baltimore Orioles baseball team
Baylor, Don **6**
Jackson, Reggie **15**
Robinson, Frank **9**

Banking
Boyd, T. B., III **6**
Brimmer, Andrew F. **2**
Chappell, Emma **18**
Griffith, Mark Winston **8**
Lawless, Theodore K. **8**
Louis, Errol T. **8**
Morgan, Rose **11**
Parsons, Richard Dean **11**
Walker, Maggie Lena **17**

Baptist World Alliance Assembly
Mays, Benjamin E. **7**

Baptist
Gomes, Peter J. **15**

Barnett-Ader Gallery
Thomas, Alma **14**

Baseball
Aaron, Hank **5**
Baker, Dusty **8**
Baylor, Don **6**
Belle, Albert **10**
Bonds, Barry **6**
Brock, Lou **18**
Coleman, Leonard S., Jr. **12**
Cottrell, Comer **11**
Davis, Piper **19**
Doby, Lawrence Eugene **16**
Edwards, Harry **2**
Fielder, Cecil **2**
Flood, Curt **10**
Gregg, Eric **16**
Griffey, Ken, Jr. **12**
Jackson, Reggie **15**
Justice, David **18**
Lofton, Kenny **12**
Mays, Willie **3**
Morgan, Joe Leonard **9**
Murray, Eddie **12**
O'Neil, Buck **19**
Paige, Satchel **7**
Puckett, Kirby **4**
Robinson, Frank **9**
Robinson, Jackie **6**
Sanders, Deion **4**
Sheffield, Gary **16**
Stone, Toni **15**
Thomas, Frank **12**
Vaughn, Mo **16**
White, Bill **1**
Winfield, Dave **5**

Basketball
Abdul-Jabbar, Kareem **8**
Barkley, Charles **5**
Bing, Dave **3**
Bol, Manute **1**
Brandon, Terrell **16**
Bryant, Kobe **15**
Chamberlain, Wilt **18**
Cooper, Cynthia **17**
Drexler, Clyde **4**
Dumars, Joe **16**
Edwards, Harry **2**
Edwards, Teresa **14**
Ewing, Patrick A. **17**
Garnett, Kevin **14**
Gossett, Louis, Jr. **7**
Hardaway, Anfernee (Penny) **13**
Hill, Grant **13**
Howard, Juwan **15**
Johnson, Earvin "Magic" **3**
Jordan, Michael **6**
Justice, David **18**
Kelly, R. **18**
Leslie, Lisa **16**
Lofton, Kenny **12**
Lucas, John **7**
Malone, Karl A. **18**
Manigault, Earl "The Goat" **15**
Miller, Cheryl **10**
Mourning, Alonzo **17**
Mutombo, Dikembe **7**
Olajuwon, Hakeem **2**
O'Neal, Shaquille **8**
Pippen, Scottie **15**
Richardson, Nolan **9**
Richmond, Mitch **19**
Russell, Bill **8**
Smith, Tubby **18**
Stringer, C. Vivian **13**
Swoopes, Sheryl **12**
Thomas, Isiah **7**
Webber, Chris **15**
Wilkens, Lenny **11**

BCALA
See Black Caucus of the American Library Association

BDP
See Botswana Democratic Party

Bear, Stearns & Co.
Fletcher, Alphonso, Jr. **16**

Beatrice International
See TLC Beatrice International Holdings, Inc.

Bebop
Carter, Betty **19**
Coltrane, John **19**
Davis, Miles **4**
Fitzgerald, Ella **8, 18**
Gillespie, Dizzy **1**
Vaughan, Sarah **13**

Bechuanaland Protectorate Legislative Council
Masire, Quett **5**

Bedford-Stuyvesant Restoration Corporation
Thomas, Franklin A. **5**

Ben & Jerry's Homemade Ice Cream, Inc.
Holland, Robert, Jr. **11**

BET
See Black Entertainment Television

Bethann Management, Inc.
Hardison, Bethann **12**

Bethune-Cookman College
Bethune, Mary McLeod **4**

BFF
See Black Filmmaker Foundation

BGLLF
See Black Gay and Lesbian Leadership Forum

Billy Graham Evangelistic Association
Bell, Ralph S. **5**
Waters, Ethel **7**

Bing Steel, Inc.
Bing, Dave **3**

Biology
Just, Ernest Everett **3**

Birth control
Elders, Joycelyn **6**
Williams, Maggie **7**

Bishop College
Cottrell, Comer **11**

BLA
See Black Liberation Army

Black Aesthetic
Baker, Houston A., Jr. 6

Black American West Museum
Stewart, Paul Wilbur 12

Black and White Minstrel Show
Henry, Lenny 9

Black Arts movement
Giovanni, Nikki 9

Black Cabinet
Hastie, William H. 8

Black Caucus of the American Library Association (BCALA)
Josey, E. J. 10

Black Christian Nationalist movement
Agyeman, Jaramogi Abebe 10

Black Consciousness movement
Biko, Steven 4
Muhammad, Elijah 4
Ramaphosa, Cyril 3
Tutu, Desmond 6

Black culturalism
Karenga, Maulana 10

Black Economic Union (BEU)
Brown, Jim 11

Black Enterprise
Brimmer, Andrew F. 2
Graves, Earl G. 1
Wallace, Phyllis A. 9

Black Entertainment Television (BET)
Gordon, Ed 10
Johnson, Robert L. 3

Black Filmmaker Foundation (BFF)
Hudlin, Reginald 9
Hudlin, Warrington 9
Jackson, George 19

Black Gay and Lesbian Leadership Forum (BGLLF)
Wilson, Phill 9

Black Guerrilla Family (BGF)
Jackson, George 14

Black History Month
Woodson, Carter G. 2

Black Horizons on the Hill
Wilson, August 7

Black Liberation Army (BLA)
Shakur, Assata 6

Williams, Evelyn 10

Black literary theory
Gates, Henry Louis, Jr. 3

Black Manifesto
Forman, James 7

Black Muslims
Ali, Muhammad 2, 16
Farrakhan, Louis 2
Muhammad, Elijah 4
X, Malcolm 1

Black nationalism
Abdul-Jabbar, Kareem 8
Baker, Houston A., Jr. 6
Baraka, Amiri 1
Carmichael, Stokely 5
Farrakhan, Louis 2
Forman, James 7
Garvey, Marcus 1
Innis, Roy 5
Muhammad, Elijah 4
Turner, Henry McNeal 5
X, Malcolm 1
Yoba, Malik 11

Black Panther Party (BPP)
Abu-Jamal, Mumia 15
Al-Amin, Jamil Abdullah 6
Brown, Elaine 8
Carmichael, Stokely 5
Cleaver, Eldridge 5
Davis, Angela 5
Forman, James 7
Hampton, Fred 18
Hilliard, David 7
Jackson, George 14
Newton, Huey 2
Pratt, Geronimo 18
Seale, Bobby 3
Shakur, Assata 6

Black Power movement
Al-Amin, Jamil Abdullah 6
Baker, Houston A., Jr. 6
Brown, Elaine 8
Carmichael, Stokely 5
Dodson, Howard, Jr. 7
Giovanni, Nikki 9
McKissick, Floyd B. 3
Stone, Chuck 9

Blackside, Inc.
Hampton, Henry 6

Black theology
Cone, James H. 3

"Blood for Britain"
Drew, Charles Richard 7

Blessed Martin House
Riley, Helen Caldwell Day 13

Blood plasma research/preservation
Drew, Charles Richard 7

Blues
Collins, Albert 12
Dixon, Willie 4
Dorsey, Thomas 15
Evora, Cesaria 12
Handy, W. C. 8
Holiday, Billie 1
House, Son 8
Howlin' Wolf 9
Jean-Baptiste, Marianne 17
King, B. B. 7
Reese, Della 6
Smith, Bessie 3
Wallace, Sippie 1
Waters, Ethel 7
Watson, Johnny "Guitar" 18
Williams, Joe 5
Wilson, August 7

Blues Heaven Foundation
Dixon, Willie 4

Blues vernacular
Baker, Houston A., Jr. 6

Bobsledding
Moses, Edwin 8

Bodybuilding
Murray, Lenda 10

Booker T. Washington Business College
Gaston, Arthur G. 4

Booker T. Washington Insurance Company
Gaston, Arthur G. 4

Boston Bruins hockey team
O'Ree, Willie 5

Boston Celtics basketball team
Russell, Bill 8

Boston Red Sox baseball team
Baylor, Don 6
Vaughn, Mo 16

Botany
Carver, George Washington 4

Botswana Democratic Party (BDP)
Masire, Quett 5
Mogae, Festus Gontebanye 19

Boxing
Ali, Muhammad 2, 16
Bowe, Riddick 6
Foreman, George 1, 15
Frazier, Joe 19
Holyfield, Evander 6
Johnson, Jack 8
King, Don 14

Lee, Canada **8**
Leonard, Sugar Ray **15**
Louis, Joe **5**
Moorer, Michael **19**
Patterson, Floyd **19**
Robinson, Sugar Ray **18**
Steward, Emanuel **18**
Whitaker, Pernell **10**

Boys Choir of Harlem
Turnbull, Walter **13**

BPP
See Black Panther Party

Brazilian Congress
da Silva, Benedita **5**

Breast Cancer Resource Committee
Brown, Zora Kramer **12**

British House of Commons
Abbott, Diane **9**
Pitt, David Thomas **10**

British House of Lords
Pitt, David Thomas **10**

British Parliament
See British House of Commons

Broadcasting
Allen, Byron **3**
Ashley, Maurice **15**
Banks, William **11**
Barden, Don H. **9**
Bradley, Ed **2**
Brown, Les **5**
Brown, Tony **3**
Brunson, Dorothy **1**
Clayton, Xernona **3**
Cornelius, Don **4**
Davis, Ossie **5**
Goode, Mal **13**
Gumbel, Greg **8**
Hamblin, Ken **10**
Hickman, Fred **11**
Hunter-Gault, Charlayne **6**
Johnson, Robert L. **3**
Jones, Star **10**
Joyner, Tom **19**
Langhart, Janet **19**
Lawson, Jennifer **1**
Lewis, Delano **7**
Madison, Joseph E. **17**
McEwen, Mark **5**
Miller, Cheryl **10**
Morgan, Joe Leonard **9**
Roberts, Robin **16**
Robinson, Max **3**
Rodgers, Johnathan **6**
Russell, Bill **8**
Shaw, Bernard **2**
Simpson, Carole **6**
Simpson, O. J. **15**
Stewart, Alison **13**
Stokes, Carl B. **10**

Watts, Rolonda **9**
White, Bill **1**
Williams, Montel **4**
Winfrey, Oprah **2, 15**

Broadside Press
Randall, Dudley **8**

Brooklyn Academy of Music
Miller, Bebe **3**

Brooklyn Dodgers baseball team
Robinson, Jackie **6**

Brotherhood of Sleeping Car Porters
Randolph, A. Philip **3**
Tucker, Rosina **14**

Brown v. Board of Education of Topeka
Bell, Derrick **6**
Clark, Kenneth B. **5**
Franklin, John Hope **5**
Houston, Charles Hamilton **4**
Marshall, Thurgood **1**
Motley, Constance Baker **10**

Buffalo Bills football team
Simpson, O. J. **15**

Bull-riding
Sampson, Charles **13**

Busing (anti-busing legislation)
Bosley, Freeman, Jr. **7**

Cabinet
See U.S. Cabinet

Cable News Network (CNN)
Chideya, Farai **14**
Shaw, Bernard **2**
Hickman, Fred **11**

California Angels baseball team
Baylor, Don **6**
Robinson, Frank **9**
Winfield, Dave **5**

California State Assembly
Brown, Willie L., Jr. **7**
Waters, Maxine **3**

Calypso
Belafonte, Harry **4**

Canadian Football League (CFL)
Moon, Warren **8**
Weathers, Carl **10**

Cancer research
Clark, Celeste **15**
Leffall, LaSalle, Jr. **3**

Capital punishment
Hawkins, Steven **14**

Cardiac research
Watkins, Levi, Jr. **9**

CARE
Gossett, Louis, Jr. **7**
Stone, Chuck **9**

Caribbean dance
Ailey, Alvin **8**
Dunham, Katherine **4**
Fagan, Garth **18**
Nichols, Nichelle **11**
Primus, Pearl **6**

Cartoonists
Armstrong, Robb **15**
Brandon, Barbara **3**
Campbell, E. Simms **13**
Harrington, Oliver W. **9**

Catholicism
See Roman Catholic Church

CBEA
See Council for a Black Economic Agenda

CBC
See Congressional Black Caucus

CBS
See Columbia Broadcasting System

CBS Television Stations Division
Rodgers, Johnathan **6**

CDC
See Centers for Disease Control and Prevention

CDF
See Children's Defense Fund

CEDBA
See Council for the Economic Development of Black Americans

Celebrities for a Drug-Free America
Vereen, Ben **4**

Censorship
Butts, Calvin O., III **9**
Ice-T **6**

Centers for Disease Control and Prevention (CDC)
Gayle, Helene D. **3**
Satcher, David **7**

CFL
See Canadian Football League

CHA
See Chicago Housing Authority

Challenger
McNair, Ronald 3

Chama cha Mapinduzi (Tanzania; Revolutionary Party)
Mkapa, Benjamin 16
Mongella, Gertrude 11
Nyerere, Julius 5

Chamber of Deputies (Brazil)
da Silva, Benedita 5

Chanteuses
Baker, Josephine 3
Dandridge, Dorothy 3
Horne, Lena 5
Reese, Della 6

Che-Lumumba Club
Davis, Angela 5

Chemistry
Hall, Lloyd A. 8
Julian, Percy Lavon 6

Chemurgy
Carver, George Washington 4

Chesapeake and Potomac Telephone Company
Lewis, Delano 7

Chess
Ashley, Maurice 15

Chicago Bears football team
Page, Alan 7
Payton, Walter 11
Singletary, Mike 4

Chicago Bulls basketball team
Jordan, Michael 6
Pippen, Scottie 15
Rodman, Dennis 12

Chicago city government
Washington, Harold 6

Chicago Eight
Seale, Bobby 3

Chicago Housing Authority (CHA)
Lane, Vincent 5

Chicago Negro Chamber of Commerce
Fuller, S. B. 13

Chicago Reporter
Washington, Laura S. 18

Chicago Tribune
Page, Clarence 4

Chicago White Sox baseball team
Doby, Lawrence Eugene, Sr. 16
Thomas, Frank 12

Child abuse prevention
Waters, Maxine 3

Child psychiatry
Comer, James P. 6

Child psychology
Hale, Lorraine 8

Children's Defense Fund (CDF)
Edelman, Marian Wright 5
Williams, Maggie 7

Child Welfare Administration
Little, Robert L. 2

Choreography
Ailey, Alvin 8
Brooks, Avery 9
Byrd, Donald 10
Dove, Ulysses 5
Dunham, Katherine 4
Fagan, Garth 18
Faison, George 16
Glover, Savion 14
Jamison, Judith 7
Johnson, Virginia 9
Jones, Bill T. 1
Miller, Bebe 3
Mitchell, Arthur 2
Primus, Pearl 6

Christian Science Monitor
Khanga, Yelena 6

Chrysler Corporation
Colbert, Virgis William 17
Farmer, Forest 1
Richie, Leroy C. 18

Church for the Fellowship of All Peoples
Thurman, Howard 3

Church of God in Christ
Franklin, Robert M. 13
Hayes, James C. 10

Cincinnati Reds baseball team
Morgan, Joe Leonard 9
Robinson, Frank 9

Cinematography
Dickerson, Ernest 6, 17

Citadel Press
Achebe, Chinua 6

Citizens Federal Savings and Loan Association
Gaston, Arthur G. 4

City government—U.S.
Archer, Dennis 7
Barden, Don H. 9
Barry, Marion S. 7
Bosley, Freeman, Jr. 7
Bradley, Thomas 2
Brown, Lee P. 1
Caesar, Shirley 19
Campbell, Bill 9
Clayton, Constance 1
Cleaver, Emanuel 4
Dinkins, David 4
Dixon, Sharon Pratt 1
Evers, Myrlie 8
Fauntroy, Walter E. 11
Gibson, Kenneth Allen 6
Goode, W. Wilson 4
Hayes, James C. 10
Jackson, Maynard 2
Johnson, Eddie Bernice 8
Kirk, Ron 11
Mallett, Conrad, Jr. 16
McPhail, Sharon 2
Powell, Adam Clayton, Jr. 3
Rice, Norm 8
Sayles Belton, Sharon 9, 16
Schmoke, Kurt 1
Stokes, Carl B. 10
Washington, Harold 6
Webb, Wellington 3
White, Michael R. 5
Young, Andrew 3
Young, Coleman 1

Civil rights
Abernathy, Ralph 1
Abbott, Diane 9
Agyeman, Jaramogi Abebe 10
Al-Amin, Jamil Abdullah 6
Ali, Muhammad 2, 16
Angelou, Maya 1
Aristide, Jean-Bertrand 6
Baker, Ella 5
Baker, Houston A., Jr. 6
Baker, Josephine 3
Bates, Daisy 13
Beals, Melba Patillo 15
Belafonte, Harry 4
Bell, Derrick 6
Bennett, Lerone, Jr. 5
Berry, Mary Frances 7
Biko, Steven 4
Bond, Julian 2
Brown, Elaine 8
Brown, Tony 3
Campbell, Bebe Moore 6
Carmichael, Stokely 5
Carter, Mandy 11
Carter, Stephen L. 4
Chambers, Julius 3
Chavis, Benjamin 6
Clark, Septima 7
Clay, William Lacy 8
Cleaver, Eldridge 5
Cobbs, Price M. 9
Cosby, Bill 7
Crockett, George, Jr. 10
Davis, Angela 5
Days, Drew S., III 10
Dee, Ruby 8
Divine, Father 7
Dodson, Howard, Jr. 7
Du Bois, W. E. B. 3
Edelman, Marian Wright 5

Ellison, Ralph **7**
Evers, Medgar **3**
Evers, Myrlie **8**
Farmer, James **2**
Fauntroy, Walter E. **11**
Forman, James **7**
Fortune, T. Thomas **6**
Franklin, John Hope **5**
Gaines, Ernest J. **7**
Gibson, William F. **6**
Gregory, Dick **1**
Grimké, Archibald H. **9**
Guinier, Lani **7**
Haley, Alex **4**
Hamer, Fannie Lou **6**
Hampton, Fred **18**
Hampton, Henry **6**
Hansberry, Lorraine **6**
Harper, Frances Ellen Watkins **11**
Harris, Patricia Roberts **2**
Hastie, William H. **8**
Hawkins, Steven **14**
Height, Dorothy I. **2**
Henderson, Wade J. **14**
Henry, Aaron **19**
Hill, Jessie, Jr. **13**
Hilliard, David **7**
Holland, Endesha Ida Mae **3**
hooks, bell **5**
Hooks, Benjamin L. **2**
Horne, Lena **5**
Houston, Charles Hamilton **4**
Hughes, Langston **4**
Innis, Roy **5**
Jackson, Jesse **1**
James, Daniel, Jr. **16**
Johnson, Eddie Bernice **8**
Johnson, James Weldon **5**
Johnson, Norma L. Holloway **17**
Jones, Elaine R. **7**
Jordan, Barbara **4**
Jordan, June **7**
Jordan, Vernon E. **3**
Julian, Percy Lavon **6**
Kennedy, Florynce **12**
Kenyatta, Jomo **5**
King, Bernice **4**
King, Coretta Scott **3**
King, Martin Luther, Jr. **1**
King, Yolanda **6**
Lampkin, Daisy **19**
Lee, Spike **5, 19**
Lester, Julius **9**
Lewis, John **2**
Lorde, Audre **6**
Lowery, Joseph **2**
Makeba, Miriam **2**
Mandela, Nelson **1, 14**
Mandela, Winnie **2**
Martin, Louis E. **16**
Mays, Benjamin E. **7**
Mbeki, Thabo Mvuyelwa **14**
McDougall, Gay J. **11**
McKissick, Floyd B. **3**
Meek, Carrie **6**
Meredith, James H. **11**
Morrison, Toni **2**
Moses, Robert Parris **11**

Motley, Constance Baker **10**
Mowry, Jess **7**
Ndadaye, Melchior **7**
Nelson, Jill **6**
Newton, Huey **2**
Nkomo, Joshua **4**
Norman, Pat **10**
Norton, Eleanor Holmes **7**
Nzo, Alfred **15**
Parks, Rosa **1**
Patrick, Deval **12**
Patterson, Orlando **4**
Perkins, Edward **5**
Pinchback, P. B. S. **9**
Pleasant, Mary Ellen **9**
Poitier, Sidney **11**
Powell, Adam Clayton, Jr. **3**
Price, Hugh B. **9**
Ramaphosa, Cyril **3**
Randolph, A. Philip **3**
Reagon, Bernice Johnson **7**
Riggs, Marlon **5**
Robeson, Paul **2**
Robinson, Jackie **6**
Robinson, Rachel **16**
Robinson, Randall **7**
Rowan, Carl T. **1**
Rustin, Bayard **4**
Seale, Bobby **3**
Shabazz, Attallah **6**
Shabazz, Betty **7**
Shakur, Assata **6**
Simone, Nina **15**
Sleet, Moneta, Jr. **5**
Staupers, Mabel K. **7**
Sullivan, Leon H. **3**
Thurman, Howard **3**
Till, Emmett **7**
Trotter, Monroe **9**
Turner, Henry McNeal **5**
Tutu, Desmond **6**
Underwood, Blair **7**
Washington, Booker T. **4**
Washington, Fredi **10**
Weaver, Robert C. **8**
Wells, James Lesesne **10**
Wells-Barnett, Ida B. **8**
West, Cornel **5**
White, Walter F. **4**
Wideman, John Edgar **5**
Wilkins, Roy **4**
Williams, Evelyn **10**
Williams, Hosea Lorenzo **15**
Williams, Robert F. **11**
Williams, Walter E. **4**
Wilson, August **7**
Wilson, Sunnie **7**
Woodson, Robert L. **10**
X, Malcolm **1**
Yoba, Malik **11**
Young, Andrew **3**
Young, Jean Childs **14**
Young, Whitney M., Jr. **4**

Classical singers
Anderson, Marian **2**
Bumbry, Grace **5**
Hayes, Roland **4**

Hendricks, Barbara **3**
Norman, Jessye **5**
Price, Leontyne **1**

Clergy
Caesar, Shirley **19**
Gomes, Peter J. **15**
Jakes, Thomas "T.D." **17**
Winans, Marvin L. **17**

Cleveland Browns football team
Brown, Jim **11**
Hill, Calvin **19**

Cleveland Cavaliers basketball team
Brandon, Terrell **16**
Wilkens, Lenny **11**

Cleveland city government
Stokes, Carl B. **10**
White, Michael R. **5**

Cleveland Indians baseball team
Belle, Albert **10**
Doby, Lawrence Eugene, Sr. **16**
Justice, David **18**
Lofton, Kenny **12**
Murray, Eddie **12**
Paige, Satchel **7**
Robinson, Frank **9**

Clothing design
Henderson, Gordon **5**
Bailey, Xenobia **11**
Jones, Carl **7**
Kani, Karl **10**
Kelly, Patrick **3**
Robinson, Patrick **19**
Smith, Willi **8**
Walker, T. J. **7**

CNN
See Cable News Network

Coaching
Ashley, Maurice **15**
Baylor, Don **6**
Dungy, Tony **17**
Gaither, Alonzo Smith (Jake) **14**
Gibson, Althea **8**
Green, Dennis **5**
Greene, Joe **10**
Miller, Cheryl **10**
O'Neil, Buck **19**
Rhodes, Ray **14**
Richardson, Nolan **9**
Robinson, Eddie G. **10**
Russell, Bill **8**
Shell, Art **1**
Smith, Tubby **18**
Stringer, C. Vivian **13**

Coca-Cola Foundation
Jones, Ingrid Saunders **18**

COHAR
See Committee on Appeal for

Human Rights

Collage
Bearden, Romare **2**
Driskell, David C. **7**

Colorado Rockies baseball team
Baylor, Don **6**

Columbia Broadcasting System (CBS)
Bradley, Ed **2**
McEwen, Mark **5**
Rodgers, Johnathan **6**
Taylor, Meshach **4**

Comedy
Allen, Byron **3**
Amos, John **8**
Beaton, Norman **14**
Bellamy, Bill **12**
Berry, Bertice **8**
Campbell, Tisha **8**
Cosby, Bill **7**
Curry, Mark **17**
Davis, Sammy Jr. **18**
Foxx, Jamie **15**
Foxx, Redd **2**
Goldberg, Whoopi **4**
Gregory, Dick **1**
Harris, Robin **7**
Harvey, Steve **18**
Henry, Lenny **9**
Kirby, George **14**
Lawrence, Martin **6**
Mabley, Jackie "Moms" **15**
McEwen, Mark **5**
Murphy, Eddie **4**
Pryor, Richard **3**
Reese, Della **6**
Rock, Chris **3**
Schultz, Michael A. **6**
Sinbad **1, 16**
Smith, Will **8, 18**
Taylor, Meshach **4**
Townsend, Robert **4**
Tucker, Chris **13**
Warfield, Marsha **2**
Wayans, Damon **8**
Wayans, Keenen Ivory **18**

Comer Method
Comer, James P. **6**

Comic Relief
Goldberg, Whoopi **4**

Commission for Racial Justice
Chavis, Benjamin **6**

Committee on Appeal for Human Rights (COHAR)
Bond, Julian **2**

Communist party
Davis, Angela **5**
Du Bois, W. E. B. **3**
Jagan, Cheddi **16**

Wright, Richard **5**

Computer graphics
Hannah, Marc **10**

Computer science
Hannah, Marc **10**

Conceptual art
Bailey, Xenobia **11**
Simpson, Lorna **4**

Concerned Black Men
Holder, Eric H., Jr. **9**

Conductors
Jackson, Isaiah **3**
Calloway, Cab **14**
León, Tania **13**

Congressional Black Caucus (CBC)
Christian-Green, Donna M. **17**
Clay, William Lacy **8**
Collins, Cardiss **10**
Conyers, John, Jr. **4**
Dellums, Ronald **2**
Fauntroy, Walter E. **11**
Gray, William H. III **3**
Hastings, Alcee L. **16**
Johnson, Eddie Bernice **8**
Mfume, Kweisi **6**
Owens, Major **6**
Rangel, Charles **3**
Stokes, Louis **3**
Towns, Edolphus **19**

Congressional Black Caucus Higher Education Braintrust
Owens, Major **6**

Congress of Racial Equality (CORE)
Dee, Ruby **8**
Farmer, James **2**
Innis, Roy **5**
Jackson, Jesse **1**
McKissick, Floyd B. **3**
Rustin, Bayard **4**

Connerly & Associates, Inc.
Connerly, Ward **14**

Convention People's Party (Ghana; CPP)
Nkrumah, Kwame **3**

Cook County Circuit Court
Sampson, Edith S. **4**

Cooking
Clark, Patrick **14**

CORE
See Congress of Racial Equality

Corporation for Public Broadcasting (CPB)
Brown, Tony **3**

Cosmetology
Cottrell, Comer **11**
Fuller, S. B. **13**
Morgan, Rose **11**
Powell, Maxine **8**
Roche, Joyce M. **17**
Walker, A'lelia **14**
Walker, Madame C. J. **7**

Council for a Black Economic Agenda (CBEA)
Woodson, Robert L. **10**

Council for Social Action of the Congregational Christian Churches
Julian, Percy Lavon **6**

Council for the Economic Development of Black Americans (CEDBA)
Brown, Tony **3**

Council on Legal Education Opportunities (CLEO)
Henderson, Wade J. **14**
Henry, Aaron **19**

Count Basie Orchestra
Williams, Joe **5**

Cow hand
Love, Nat **9**
Pickett, Bill **11**

CPB
See Corporation for Public Broadcasting

CPP
See Convention People's Party

Cress Theory of Color-Confrontation and Racism
Welsing, Frances Cress **5**

Crisis
Du Bois, W. E. B. **3**
Fauset, Jessie **7**
Wilkins, Roy **4**

Cross Colours
Jones, Carl **7**
Kani, Karl **10**
Walker, T. J. **7**

Crucial Films
Henry, Lenny **9**

Crusader
Williams, Robert F. **11**

CTRN
See Transitional Committee for National Recovery (Guinea)

Cubism
Bearden, Romare **2**

Cumulative Subject Index

Culinary arts
Clark, Patrick **14**

Cultural pluralism
Locke, Alain **10**

Cumulative voting
Guinier, Lani **7**

Curator/exhibition designer
Camp, Kimberly **19**
Golden, Thelma **10**
Hutson, Jean Blackwell **16**
Sanders, Joseph R., Jr. **11**
Stewart, Paul Wilbur **12**

Cytogenetics
Satcher, David **7**

Dallas city government
Johnson, Eddie Bernice **8**
Kirk, Ron **11**

Dallas Cowboys football team
Hill, Calvin **19**
Smith, Emmitt **7**

Dance Theatre of Harlem
Johnson, Virginia **9**
Mitchell, Arthur **2**
Tyson, Cicely **7**

DAV
See Disabled American Veterans

David M. Winfield Foundation
Winfield, Dave **5**

Daytona Institute
See Bethune-Cookman College

Dayton Philharmonic Orchestra
Jackson, Isaiah **3**

D.C. Black Repertory Theater
Reagon, Bernice Johnson **7**

Death Row Records
Knight, Suge **11**
Shakur, Tupac **14**

De Beers Botswana
See Debswana

Debswana
Masire, Quett **5**

Defense Communications Agency
Gravely, Samuel L., Jr. **5**

Def Jam Records
L.L. Cool J **16**
Simmons, Russell **1**

Democratic National Committee (DNC)
Brown, Ron **5**
Brown, Willie L., Jr. **7**
Dixon, Sharon Pratt **1**
Fattah, Chaka **11**
Hamer, Fannie Lou **6**
Jordan, Barbara **4**
Mallett, Conrad, Jr. **16**
Martin, Louis E. **16**
Waters, Maxine **3**
Williams, Maggie **7**

Democratic National Convention
Allen, Ethel D. **13**
Brown, Ron **5**
Brown, Willie L., Jr. **7**
Dixon, Sharon Pratt **1**
Hamer, Fannie Lou **6**
Herman, Alexis M. **15**
Jordan, Barbara **4**
Waters, Maxine **3**
Williams, Maggie **7**

Democratic Socialists of America (DSA)
West, Cornel **5**
Marable, Manning **10**

Dentistry
Bluitt, Juliann S. **14**
Delany, Bessie **12**
Sinkford, Jeanne C. **13**

Denver Broncos football team
Barnes, Ernie **16**

Denver city government
Webb, Wellington **3**

Denver Nuggets basketball team
Mutombo, Dikembe **7**

Depression/The Great Depression
Hampton, Henry **6**

Desert Shield
See Operation Desert Shield

Desert Storm
See Operation Desert Storm

Detective fiction
Himes, Chester **8**
Mosley, Walter **5**
Wesley, Valerie Wilson **18**

Detroit City Council
Collins, Barbara-Rose **7**

Detroit city government
Archer, Dennis **7**
Crockett, George, Jr. **10**
Young, Coleman **1**

Detroit entertainment
Wilson, Sunnie **7**

Detroit Golden Gloves
Wilson, Sunnie **7**

Detroit Lions football team
Sanders, Barry **1**

Detroit Pistons basketball team
Bing, Dave **3**
Dumars, Joe **16**
Hill, Grant **13**
Thomas, Isiah **7**

Detroit Police Department
Gomez-Preston, Cheryl **9**
McKinnon, Isaiah **9**

Detroit Tigers baseball team
Fielder, Cecil **2**

Diamond mining
Masire, Quett **5**

Dillard University
Cook, Samuel DuBois **14**

Dime Savings Bank
Parsons, Richard Dean **11**

Diplomatic Corps
See U.S. Diplomatic Corps

Directing
Thompson, Tazewell **13**

Disabled American Veterans (DAV)
Brown, Jesse **6**

DNC
See Democratic National Committee

Documentary film
Byrd, Robert **11**
Dash, Julie **4**
Davis, Ossie **5**
Hampton, Henry **6**
Henry, Lenny **9**
Hudlin, Reginald **9**
Hudlin, Warrington **9**
Julien, Isaac **3**
Riggs, Marlon **5**

Donald Byrd/The Group
Byrd, Donald **10**

Drug abuse prevention
Brown, Les **5**
Clements, George **2**
Hale, Lorraine **8**
Harris, Alice **7**
Lucas, John **7**
Rangel, Charles **3**

Drug synthesis
Julian, Percy Lavon **6**

DSA
See Democratic Socialists of America

Dunham Dance Company
Dunham, Katherine **4**

DuSable Museum of African American History
Burroughs, Margaret Taylor **9**

Earthquake Early Alerting Service
Person, Waverly **9**

Ebenezer Baptist Church
King, Bernice **4**

Ebony
Bennett, Lerone, Jr. **5**
Johnson, John H. **3**
Rice, Linda Johnson **9**
Sleet, Moneta, Jr. **5**

Ebony Museum of African American History
See DuSable Museum of African American History

Economic Community of West African States (ECOWAS)
Sawyer, Amos **2**

Economic Regulatory Administration
O'Leary, Hazel **6**

Economics
Boyd, T. B. III **6**
Brimmer, Andrew F. **2**
Brown, Tony **3**
Divine, Father **7**
Dodson, Howard, Jr. **7**
Gibson, William F. **6**
Hamer, Fannie Lou **6**
Hampton, Henry **6**
Machel, Graca Simbine **16**
Masire, Quett **5**
Raines, Franklin Delano **14**
Robinson, Randall **7**
Sowell, Thomas **2**
Sullivan, Leon H. **3**
Van Peebles, Melvin **7**
Wallace, Phyllis A. **9**
Wharton, Clifton R., Jr. **7**
White, Michael R. **5**
Williams, Walter E. **4**

ECOWAS
See Economic Community of West African States

Edelman Public Relations
Barrett, Andrew C. **12**

Edmonds Entertainment
Edmonds, Kenny "Babyface" **10**
Edmonds, Tracey **16**

Edmonton Oilers hockey team
Fuhr, Grant **1**

Educational Testing Service
Stone, Chuck **9**

EEC
See European Economic Community

EEOC
See Equal Employment Opportunity Commission

Egyptology
Diop, Cheikh Anta **4**

Elder Foundation
Elder, Lee **6**

Emmy awards
Ashe, Arthur **1, 18**
Allen, Debbie **13**
Amos, John **8**
Ashe, Arthur **1**
Belafonte, Harry **4**
Bradley, Ed **2**
Brown, Les **5**
Clayton, Xernona **3**
Cosby, Bill **7**
Curtis-Hall, Vondie **17**
Dee, Ruby **8**
Foxx, Redd **2**
Freeman, Al, Jr. **11**
Goldberg, Whoopi **4**
Gossett, Louis, Jr. **7**
Guillaume, Robert **3**
Gumbel, Greg **8**
Hunter-Gault, Charlayne **6**
Jones, James Earl **3**
La Salle, Eriq **12**
McQueen, Butterfly **6**
Parks, Gordon **1**
Robinson, Max **3**
Rolle, Esther **13**
Stokes, Carl B. **10**
Thigpen, Lynne **17**
Tyson, Cicely **7**
Wayans, Damon **8**
Whitfield, Lynn **18**
Williams, Montel **4**
Winfrey, Oprah **2, 15**
Woodard, Alfre **9**

Endocrinology
Elders, Joycelyn **6**

Energy studies
Cose, Ellis **5**
O'Leary, Hazel **6**

Engineering
Alexander, Archie Alphonso **14**
Gibson, Kenneth Allen **6**
Hannah, Marc **10**
McCoy, Elijah **8**
Williams, O. S. **13**

Environmental issues
Chavis, Benjamin **6**

Epidemiology
Gayle, Helene D. **3**

Episcopal Diocese of Massachusetts
Harris, Barbara **12**

EPRDF
See Ethiopian People's Revolutionary Democratic Front

Equal Employment Opportunity Commission (EEOC)
Hill, Anita **5**
Lewis, Delano **7**
Norton, Eleanor Holmes **7**
Thomas, Clarence **2**
Wallace, Phyllis A. **9**

ESPN
Roberts, Robin **16**

Essence
Parks, Gordon **1**
Taylor, Susan L. **10**
Wesley, Valerie Wilson **18**

Essence Communications
Taylor, Susan L. **10**

Essence, the Television Program
Taylor, Susan L. **10**

Ethiopian People's Revolutionary Democratic Front (EPRDF)
Meles Zenawi **3**

Eugene O'Neill Theater
Richards, Lloyd **2**

European Economic Community (EEC)
Diouf, Abdou **3**

Executive Leadership Council
Jackson, Mannie **14**

Exiled heads of state
Aristide, Jean-Bertrand **6**

Exploration
Henson, Matthew **2**

Eyes on the Prize series
Hampton, Henry **6**

Fairbanks city government
Hayes, James C. **10**

FAIRR
See Foundation for the Advancement of Inmate Rehabilitation and Recreation

Fair Share Agreements
Gibson, William F. **6**

Cumulative Subject Index

Famine relief
See World hunger

Famous Amos Cookie Corporation
Amos, Wally **9**

FAN
See Forces Armées du Nord (Chad)

Fashion
Smaltz, Audrey **12**
Sade **15**

FCC
See Federal Communications Commission

Federal Bureau of Investigaton (FBI)
Harvard, Beverly **11**

Federal Communications Commission (FCC)
Barrett, Andrew C. **12**
Hooks, Benjamin L. **2**
Kennard, William Earl **18**
Russell-McCloud, Patricia A. **14**

Federal Energy Administration
O'Leary, Hazel **6**

Federal Reserve Bank
Brimmer, Andrew F. **2**

Fellowship of Reconciliation (FOR)
Farmer, James **2**
Rustin, Bayard **4**

Fiction
Briscoe, Connie **15**
Danticat, Edwidge **15**
Jenkins, Beverly **14**

Figure skating
Bonaly, Surya **7**

Film direction
Allen, Debbie **13**
Burnett, Charles **16**
Byrd, Robert **11**
Curtis-Hall, Vondie **17**
Dash, Julie **4**
Davis, Ossie **5**
Dickerson, Ernest **6, 17**
Duke, Bill **3**
Franklin, Carl **11**
Freeman, Al, Jr. **11**
Gray, F. Gary **14**
Harris, Leslie **6**
Hudlin, Reginald **9**
Hudlin, Warrington **9**
Hughes, Albert **7**
Hughes, Allen **7**
Jackson, George **19**
Julien, Isaac **3**
Lane, Charles **3**

Lee, Spike **5, 19**
Micheaux, Oscar **7**
Morton, Joe **18**
Moses, Gilbert **12**
Moss, Carlton **17**
Poitier, Sidney **11**
Riggs, Marlon **5**
St. Jacques, Raymond **8**
Schultz, Michael A. **6**
Sembène, Ousmane **13**
Singleton, John **2**
Smith, Roger Guenveur **12**
Townsend, Robert **4**
Underwood, Blair **7**
Van Peebles, Mario **2**
Van Peebles, Melvin **7**
Wayans, Damon **8**
Wayans, Keenen Ivory **18**

Film scores
Jean-Baptiste, Marianne **17**
Jones, Quincy **8**
Prince **18**

Finance
Banks, Jeffrey **17**
Fletcher, Alphonse, Jr. **16**
Griffith, Mark Winston **8**
Lawless, Theodore K. **8**
Louis, Errol T. **8**
Rogers, John W., Jr. **5**

Fisk University
Johnson, Charles S. **12**

Florida A & M University
Gaither, Alonzo Smith (Jake) **14**

Florida Marlins baseball team
Sheffield, Gary **16**

Florida state government
Meek, Carrie **6**
Tribble, Isreal, Jr. **8**

Flouride chemistry
Quarterman, Lloyd Albert **4**

Folk music
Charlemagne, Manno **11**
Jenkins, Ella **15**
Wilson, Cassandra **16**

Football
Amos, John **8**
Brown, Jim **11**
Butler, LeRoy III **17**
Dungy, Tony **17**
Edwards, Harry **2**
Gaither, Alonzo Smith (Jake) **14**
Green, Dennis **5**
Greene, Joe **10**
Grier, Roosevelt **13**
Hill, Calvin **19**
Lott, Ronnie **9**
Moon, Warren **8**
Page, Alan **7**
Payton, Walter **11**

Rashad, Ahmad **18**
Rice, Jerry **5**
Robinson, Eddie G. **10**
Sanders, Barry **1**
Sanders, Deion **4**
Shell, Art **1**
Simpson, O. J. **15**
Singletary, Mike **4**
Smith, Emmitt **7**
Upshaw, Gene **18**
Walker, Herschel **1**
Watts, J. C., Jr. **14**
Weathers, Carl **10**
White, Reggie **6**

FOR
See Fellowship of Reconciliation

Forces Armées du Nord (Chad; FAN)
Habré, Hissène **6**

Ford Foundation
Thomas, Franklin A. **5**
Franklin, Robert M. **13**

Ford Motor Company
Goldsberry, Ronald **18**

Foreign policy
Bunche, Ralph J. **5**
Rice, Condoleezza **3**
Robinson, Randall **7**

Forest Club
Wilson, Sunnie **7**

40 Acres and a Mule Filmworks
Lee, Spike **5, 19**

Foster care
Hale, Clara **16**
Hale, Lorraine **8**

Foundation for the Advancement of Inmate Rehabilitation and Recreation (FAIRR)
King, B. B. **7**

Freedom Farm Cooperative
Hamer, Fannie Lou **6**

Free Southern Theater (FST)
Borders, James **9**

FRELIMO
See Front for the Liberation of Mozambique

French West Africa
Diouf, Abdou **3**

FRODEBU
See Front for Democracy in Burundi

FROLINAT
See Front de la Libération

Nationale du Tchad (Chad)

FRONASA
See Front for National Salvation (Uganda)

Front de la Libération Nationale du Tchad (Chad; FROLINAT)
Habré, Hissène **6**

Front for Democracy in Burundi (FRODEBU)
Ndadaye, Melchior **7**
Ntaryamira, Cyprien **8**

Front for National Salvation (Uganda; FRONASA)
Museveni, Yoweri **4**

Front for the Liberation of Mozambique (FRELIMO)
Chissano, Joaquim **7**
Machel, Graca Simbine **16**
Machel, Samora Moises **8**

FST
See Free Southern Theater

Funk music
Ayers, Roy **16**
Clinton, George **9**
Watson, Johnny "Guitar" **18**

Fusion
Davis, Miles **4**
Jones, Quincy **8**

Gary, Williams, Parenti, Finney, Lewis & McManus
Gary, Willie E. **12**

Gary Enterprises
Gary, Willie E. **12**

Gassaway, Crosson, Turner & Parsons
Parsons, James **14**

Gay Men of Color Consortium
Wilson, Phill **9**

Genealogy
Dash, Julie **4**
Haley, Alex **4**

General Motors Corporation
Roberts, Roy S. **14**

Geometric symbolism
Douglas, Aaron **7**

Geophysics
Person, Waverly **9**

George Foster Peabody Broadcasting Award
Bradley, Ed **2**
Hunter-Gault, Charlayne **6**

Shaw, Bernard **2**

Georgia state government
Bond, Julian **2**
Williams, Hosea Lorenzo **15**

Georgia State Supreme Court
Sears-Collins, Leah J. **5**

Glaucoma treatment
Julian, Percy Lavon **6**

Glidden Company
Julian, Percy Lavon **6**

Golden Globe awards
Allen, Debbie **13**
Carroll, Diahann **9**
Taylor, Regina **9**

Golden State Warriors basketball team
Edwards, Harry **2**
Lucas, John **7**

Golf
Elder, Lee **6**
Gibson, Althea **8**
Peete, Calvin **11**
Richmond, Mitch **19**
Sifford, Charlie **4**
Webber, Chris **15**
Woods, Tiger **14**

Goodwill Games
Swoopes, Sheryl **12**

Gospel music
Adams, Oleta **18**
Adams, Yolanda **17**
Cooke, Sam **17**
Caesar, Shirley **19**
Cleveland, James **19**
Dorsey, Thomas **15**
Franklin, Aretha **11**
Franklin, Kirk **15**
Green, Al **13**
Hawkins, Tramaine **16**
Jackson, Mahalia **5**
Jakes, Thomas "T.D." **17**
Little Richard **15**
Mayfield, Curtis **2**
Reagon, Bernice Johnson **7**
Reese, Della **6**
Walker, Albertina **10**
Winans, BeBe **14**
Winans, CeCe **14**
Winans, Marvin L. **17**

Grammy awards
Adams, Oleta **18**
Belafonte, Harry **4**
Brandy **14**
Caesar, Shirley **19**
Cleveland, James **19**
Cole, Natalie Maria **17**
Cosby, Bill **7**
Davis, Miles **4**

Edmonds, Kenneth "Babyface" **10**
Ellington, Duke **5**
Fitzgerald, Ella **8**
Franklin, Aretha **11**
Gaye, Marvin **2**
Goldberg, Whoopi **4**
Hathaway, Donny **18**
Hawkins, Tramaine **16**
Houston, Whitney **7**
Jackson, Michael **19**
James, Etta **13**
Jimmy Jam **13**
Jones, Quincy **8**
Kelly, R. **18**
Lewis, Terry **13**
Makeba, Miriam **2**
Murphy, Eddie **4**
Norman, Jessye **5**
Price, Leontyne **1**
Prince **18**
Queen Latifah **1, 16**
Reagon, Bernice Johnson **7**
Redding, Otis **16**
Robinson, Smokey **3**
Sade **15**
Smith, Will **8, 18**
Turner, Tina **6**
Warwick, Dionne **18**
White, Barry **13**
Wilson, Nancy **10**
Winans, Marvin L. **17**
Wonder, Stevie **11**

Green Bay Packers football team
Butler, Leroy III **17**
Howard, Desmond **16**
White, Reggie **6**

Groupe de Recherche Chorégraphique de l'Opéra de Paris
Dove, Ulysses **5**

Guardian
Trotter, Monroe **9**

Guitar
Hendrix, Jimi **10**
House, Son **8**
Howlin' Wolf **9**
Johnson, Robert **2**
King, B. B. **7**
Kravitz, Lenny **10**
Marley, Bob **5**
Mayfield, Curtis **2**
Ndegéocello, Me'Shell **15**
Ongala, Remmy **9**
Watson, Johnny "Guitar" **18**
Wilson, Cassandra **16**

Gulf War
Powell, Colin **1**
Shaw, Bernard **2**
Von Lipsey, Roderick K. **11**

Gurdjieff Institute
Toomer, Jean **6**

Cumulative Subject Index

Gymnastics
Dawes, Dominique **11**

Hair care
Cottrell, Comer **11**
Fuller, S. B. **13**
Malone, Annie **13**
Roche, Joyce M. **17**
Walker, Madame C. J. **7**

Haitian refugees
Ashe, Arthur **1, 18**
Dunham, Katherine **4**
Robinson, Randall **7**

Hale House
Hale, Clara **16**
Hale, Lorraine **8**

Harlem Globetrotters
Chamberlain, Wilt **18**
Jackson, Mannie **14**

Harlem Renaissance
Cullen, Countee **8**
Delaney, Beauford **19**
Ellington, Duke **5**
Fauset, Jessie **7**
Fisher, Rudolph **17**
Frazier, E. Franklin **10**
Hughes, Langston **4**
Hurston, Zora Neale **3**
Johnson, James Weldon **5**
Johnson, William Henry **3**
Larsen, Nella **10**
Locke, Alain **10**
McKay, Claude **6**
Thurman, Wallace **16**
Toomer, Jean **6**
VanDerZee, James **6**

Harlem Writers Guild
Guy, Rosa **5**
Wesley, Valerie Wilson **18**

Harlem Youth Opportunities Unlimited (HARYOU)
Clark, Kenneth B. **5**

Harmonica
Howlin' Wolf **9**

Harriet Tubman Home for Aged and Indignet Colored People
Tubman, Harriet **9**

Harvard Law School
Bell, Derrick **6**
Ogletree, Charles, Jr. **12**

HARYOU
See Harlem Youth Opportunities Unlimited

Head Start
Edelman, Marian Wright **5**

Health care reform
Brown, Jesse **6**
Cooper, Edward S. **6**
Davis, Angela **5**
Gibson, Kenneth A. **6**
Norman, Pat **10**
Satcher, David **7**
Williams, Daniel Hale **2**

Heart disease
Cooper, Edward S. **6**

Heidelberg Project
Guyton, Tyree **9**

HEW
See U.S. Department of Health, Education, and Welfare

HHS
See U.S. Department of Health and Human Services

Historians
Berry, Mary Frances **7**
Diop, Cheikh Anta **4**
Dodson, Howard, Jr. **7**
Du Bois, W. E. B. **3**
Franklin, John Hope **5**
Gates, Henry Louis, Jr. **3**
Giddings, Paula **11**
Hansberry, William Leo **11**
Harkless, Necia Desiree **19**
Marable, Manning **10**
Patterson, Orlando **4**
Quarles, Benjamin Arthur **18**
Reagon, Bernice Johnson **7**
Schomburg, Arthur Alfonso **9**
Williams, George Washington **18**
Woodson, Carter G. **2**

Hockey
Fuhr, Grant **1**
McBride, Bryant **18**
McKegney, Tony **3**
O'Ree, Willie **5**

Homosexuality
Carter, Mandy **11**
Delany, Samuel R., Jr. **9**
Gomes, Peter J. **15**
Hemphill, Essex **10**
Julien, Isaac **3**
Lorde, Audre **6**
Norman, Pat **10**
Parker, Pat **19**
Riggs, Marlon **5**
Rupaul **17**
Wilson, Phill **9**

Honeywell Corporation
Jackson, Mannie **14**

House of Representatives
See U.S. House of Representative

Houston Astros baseball team
Morgan, Joe Leonard **9**

Houston Oilers football team
Moon, Warren **8**

Houston Rockets basketball team
Lucas, John **7**
Olajuwon, Hakeem **2**

Howard University
Jenifer, Franklyn G. **2**
Locke, Alain **10**
Mays, Benjamin E. **7**
Porter, James A. **11**
Wells, James Lesesne **10**
Wesley, Dorothy Porter **19**

HRCF
See Human Rights Campaign Fund

Hubbard Hospital
Lyttle, Hulda Margaret **14**

HUD
See U.S. Department of Housing and Urban Development

Hugo awards
Butler, Octavia **8**
Delany, Samuel R., Jr. **9**

Hull-Ottawa Canadiens hockey team
O'Ree, Willie **5**

Human Rights Campaign Fund (HRCF)
Carter, Mandy **11**

Hurdles
Devers, Gail **7**

IBF
See International Boxing Federation

Ice skating
See Figure skating

Igbo people/traditions
Achebe, Chinua **6**

IHRLG
See International Human Rights Law Group

Illinois state government
Braun, Carol Moseley **4**
Washington, Harold **6**

Illustrations
Campbell, E. Simms **13**
Hudson, Cheryl **15**
Pinkney, Jerry **15**
Saint James, Synthia **12**

Imani Temple
Stallings, George A., Jr. 6

IMF
See International Monetary Fund

Indianapolis 500
Ribbs, Willy T. 2

Information technology
Smith, Joshua 10

In Friendship
Baker, Ella 5

Inkatha
Buthelezi, Mangosuthu Gatsha 9

Institute for Black Parenting
Oglesby, Zena 12

Institute for Journalism Education
Harris, Jay T. 19
Maynard, Robert C. 7

Institute for Research in African American Studies
Marable, Manning 10

Institute of Positive Education
Madhubuti, Haki R. 7

Institute of Social and Religious Research
Mays, Benjamin E. 7

Institute of the Black World
Dodson, Howard, Jr. 7

Insurance
Hill, Jessie, Jr. 13
Spaulding, Charles Clinton 9

International Boxing Federation (IBF)
Ali, Muhammad 2, 16
Moorer, Michael 19
Whitaker, Pernell 10

International Free and Accepted Masons and Eastern Star
Banks, William 11

International Human Rights Law Group (IHRLG)
McDougall, Gay J. 11

International Ladies' Auxiliary
Tucker, Rosina 14

International Monetary Fund (IMF)
Babangida, Ibrahim 4
Chissano, Joaquim 7
Conté, Lansana 7
Diouf, Abdou 3
Patterson, P. J. 6

Inventions
Julian, Percy Lavon 6
Latimer, Lewis H. 4
McCoy, Elijah 8
Morgan, Garrett 1
Woods, Granville T. 5

Investment management
Rogers, John W., Jr. 5

Jackie Robinson Foundation
Robinson, Rachel 16

Jamison Project
Jamison, Judith 7

Jazz
Armstrong, Louis 2
Ayers, Roy 16
Bechet, Sidney 18
Belle, Regina 1
Brooks, Avery 9
Calloway, Cab 14
Carter, Betty 19
Charles, Ray 16
Cheatham, Doc 17
Cole, Nat King 17
Coltrane, John 19
Crawford, Randy 19
Crothers, Scatman 19
Crouch, Stanley 11
Crowder, Henry 16
Davis, Anthony 11
Davis, Miles 4
Donegan, Dorothy 19
Downing, Will 19
Ellington, Duke 5
Ellison, Ralph 7
Eubanks, Kevin 15
Fitzgerald, Ella 8, 18
Gillespie, Dizzy 1
Hampton, Lionel 17
Hawkins, Coleman 9
Holiday, Billie 1
Hyman, Phyllis 19
James, Etta 13
Jones, Elvin 14
Jones, Quincy 8
Lincoln, Abbey 3
Madhubuti, Haki R. 7
Marsalis, Wynton 16
Mingus, Charles 15
Monk, Thelonious 1
Nascimento, Milton 2
Reese, Della 6
Roberts, Marcus 19
Ross, Diana 8
Smith, Bessie 3
Vaughan, Sarah 13
Washington, Grover, Jr. 17
Watson, Johnny "Guitar" 18
Williams, Joe 5
Williams, Mary Lou 15
Wilson, Cassandra 16
Wilson, Nancy 10

Jet
Bennett, Lerone, Jr. 5

Johnson, John H. 3
Sleet, Moneta, Jr. 5

John Lucas Enterprises
Lucas, John 7

Johnson Publishing Company, Inc.
Bennett, Lerone, Jr. 5
Johnson, John H. 3
Rice, Linda Johnson 9
Sleet, Moneta, Jr. 5

Joint Chiefs of Staff
See U.S. Joint Chiefs of Staff

Journalism
Ansa, Tina McElroy 14
Abu-Jamal, Mumia 15
Azikiwe, Nnamdi 13
Bennett, Lerone, Jr. 5
Barden, Don H. 9
Borders, James 9
Bradley, Ed 2
Brown, Tony 3
Campbell, Bebe Moore 6
Chideya, Farai 14
Cose, Ellis 5
Crouch, Stanley 11
Cullen, Countee 8
Dunbar, Paul Laurence 8
Edmonds, Terry 17
Forman, James 7
Fortune, T. Thomas 6
Giddings, Paula 11
Goode, Mal 13
Gordon, Ed 10
Grimké, Archibald H. 9
Gumbel, Bryant 14
Gumbel, Greg 8
Hansberry, Lorraine 6
Harrington, Oliver W. 9
Harris, Jay 19
Hickman, Fred 11
Hunter-Gault, Charlayne 6
Johnson, James Weldon 5
Khanga, Yelena 6
Lampkin, Daisy 19
Leavell, Dorothy R. 17
Martin, Louis E. 16
Maynard, Robert C. 7
McCall, Nathan 8
McKay, Claude 6
Mkapa, Benjamin 16
Nelson, Jill 6
Page, Clarence 4
Parks, Gordon 1
Perez, Anna 1
Price, Hugh B. 9
Raspberry, William 2
Reed, Ishmael 8
Roberts, Robin 16
Robinson, Max 3
Rodgers, Johnathan 6
Rowan, Carl T. 1
Shaw, Bernard 2
Shipp, E. R. 15
Simpson, Carole 6
Sowell, Thomas 2

Staples, Brent **8**
Stewart, Alison **13**
Stokes, Carl B. **10**
Stone, Chuck **9**
Taylor, Kristin Clark **8**
Thurman, Wallace **16**
Trotter, Monroe **9**
Tucker, Cynthia **15**
Wallace, Michele Faith **13**
Watts, Rolonda **9**
Webb, Veronica **10**
Wells-Barnett, Ida B. **8**
Wesley, Valerie Wilson **18**
Wiley, Ralph **8**
Wilkins, Roger **2**
Williams, Patricia J. **11**

Journal of Negro History
Woodson, Carter G. **2**

Just Us Books
Hudson, Cheryl **15**
Hudson, Wade **15**

Kansas City Athletics baseball team
Paige, Satchel **7**

Kansas City Chiefs football team
Dungy, Tony **17**

Kansas City government
Cleaver, Emanuel **4**

KANU
See Kenya African National Union

Karl Kani Infinity
Kani, Karl **10**

KAU
See Kenya African Union

KCA
See Kikuyu Central Association

Kenya African National Union (KANU)
Kenyatta, Jomo **5**

Kenya African Union (KAU)
Kenyatta, Jomo **5**

Kikuyu Central Association (KCA)
Kenyatta, Jomo **5**

King Center
See Martin Luther King Jr. Center for Nonviolent Social Change

Kraft General Foods
Fudge, Ann **11**
Sneed, Paula A. **18**

Kwanzaa
Karenga, Maulana **10**

Kwazulu Territorial Authority
Buthelezi, Mangosuthu Gatsha **9**

Ladies Professional Golfers' Association (LPGA)
Gibson, Althea **8**

LAPD
See Los Angeles Police Department

Latin American folk music
Nascimento, Milton **2**

Law enforcement
Alexander, Joyce London **18**
Bradley, Thomas **2**
Brown, Lee P. **1**
Freeman, Charles **19**
Glover, Nathaniel, Jr. **12**
Gomez-Preston, Cheryl **9**
Harvard, Beverly **11**
Johnson, Norma L. Holloway **17**
Johnson, Robert T. **17**
Keith, Damon J. **16**
McKinnon, Isaiah **9**
Parks, Bernard C. **17**
Schmoke, Kurt **1**
Thomas, Franklin A. **5**
Williams, Willie L. **4**

Lawyers' Committee for Civil Rights Under Law
McDougall, Gay J. **11**

LDF
See NAACP Legal Defense Fund

Leadership Conference on Civil Rights (LCCR)
Henderson, Wade J. **14**

League of Nations
Haile Selassie **7**

Leary Group Inc.
Leary, Kathryn D. **10**

"Leave No Child Behind"
Edelman, Marian Wright **5**

Lee Elder Scholarship Fund
Elder, Lee **6**

Legal Defense Fund
See NAACP Legal Defense Fund

Les Brown Unlimited, Inc.
Brown, Les **5**

Lexicography
Major, Clarence **9**

Liberation theology
West, Cornel **5**

Library science
Bontemps, Arna **8**
Franklin, Hardy R. **9**
Harsh, Vivian Gordon **14**
Hutson, Jean Blackwell **16**
Josey, E. J. **10**
Larsen, Nella **10**
Owens, Major **6**
Schomburg, Arthur Alfonso **9**
Wesley, Dorothy Porter **19**

Lincoln University
Randall, Dudley **8**
Sudarkasa, Niara **4**

LISC
See Local Initiative Support Corporation

Literacy Volunteers of America
Amos, Wally **9**

Literary criticism
Baker, Houston A., Jr. **6**
Brown, Sterling **10**
Reed, Ishmael **8**
Wesley, Valerie Wilson **18**
West, Cornel **5**

Lobbying
Brooke, Edward **8**
Brown, Elaine **8**
Brown, Jesse **6**
Brown, Ron **5**
Edelman, Marian Wright **5**
Lee, Canada **8**
Mallett, Conrad, Jr. **16**
Robinson, Randall **7**

Local Initiative Support Corporation (LISC)
Thomas, Franklin A. **5**

Long jump
Lewis, Carl **4**
Powell, Mike **7**

Los Angeles city government
Bradley, Thomas **2**
Evers, Myrlie **8**

Los Angeles Dodgers baseball team
Baker, Dusty **8**
Robinson, Frank **9**

Los Angeles Galaxy soccer team
Jones, Cobi N'Gai **18**

Los Angeles Lakers basketball team
Abdul-Jabbar, Kareem **8**
Bryant, Kobe **15**
Chamberlain, Wilt **18**
Johnson, Earvin "Magic" **3**

Los Angeles Police Department (LAPD)
Parks, Bernard C. **17**
Williams, Willie L. **4**

Los Angeles Raiders football team
Lott, Ronnie 9
Shell, Art 1

Los Angeles Sparks basketball team
Leslie, Lisa 16

Lost-Found Nation of Islam
Ali, Muhammad 2, 16
Farrakhan, Louis 2, 15
Muhammad, Elijah 4
Muhammad, Khallid Abdul 10
X, Malcolm 1

Louisiana state government
Fields, Cleo 13
Pinchback, P. B. S. 9

Louisiana state Senate
Fields, Cleo 13
Pinchback, P. B. S. 9

LPGA
See Ladies Professional Golfers' Association

Lynching (anti-lynching legislation)
Johnson, James Weldon 5
Till, Emmett 7

Lyricist
Dunbar, Paul Laurence 8
Fitzgerald, Ella 8
Johnson, James Weldon 5

MacNeil/Lehrer NewsHour
Hunter-Gault, Charlayne 6

Madame C. J. Walker Manufacturing Company
Walker, A'lelia 14
Walker, Madame C. J. 7

Major League Baseball Properties
Doby, Lawrence Eugene, Sr. 16

Malawi Congress Party (MCP)
Banda, Hastings Kamuzu 6

Manhattan Project
Quarterman, Lloyd Albert 4

MARC Corp.
See Metropolitan Applied Research Center

March on Washington/Freedom March
Baker, Josephine 3
Belafonte, Harry 4
Bunche, Ralph J. 5
Davis, Ossie 5
Fauntroy, Walter E. 11
Forman, James 7
Franklin, John Hope 5
Horne, Lena 5
Jackson, Mahalia 5
King, Coretta Scott 3
King, Martin Luther, Jr. 1
Lewis, John 2
Meredith, James H. 11
Randolph, A. Philip 3
Rustin, Bayard 4
Sleet, Moneta, Jr. 5
Wilkins, Roy 4
Young, Whitney M., Jr. 4

Marie Brown Associates
Brown, Marie Dutton 12

Martin Luther King Jr. Center for Nonviolent Social Change
Dodson, Howard, Jr. 7
King, Bernice 4
King, Coretta Scott 3
King, Dexter 10
King, Martin Luther, Jr. 1
King, Yolanda 6

Marxism
Baraka, Amiri 1
Jagan, Cheddi 16
Machel, Samora Moises 8
Nkrumah, Kwame 3
Sankara, Thomas 17

Massachusetts state government
Brooke, Edward 8

Masters Tournament
Elder, Lee 6

Mathematics
Gates, Sylvester James, Jr. 15

MAXIMA Corporation
Smith, Joshua 10

Maxwell House Coffee Company
Fudge, Ann 11

McCall Pattern Company
Lewis, Reginald F. 6

MCP
See Malawi Congress Party

Medicine
Banda, Hastings Kamuzu 6
Black, Keith Lanier 18
Callender, Clive O. 3
Carson, Benjamin 1
Christian-Green, Donna M. 17
Comer, James P. 6
Cooper, Edward S. 6
Dickens, Helen Octavia 14
Drew, Charles Richard 7
Elders, Joycelyn 6
Fisher, Rudolph 17
Fuller, Solomon Carter, Jr. 15
Gayle, Helene D. 3
Gibson, William F. 6
Hinton, William Augustus 8
Jemison, Mae C. 1
Kountz, Samuel L. 10
Lawless, Theodore K. 8
Leffall, LaSalle, Jr. 3
Logan, Onnie Lee 14
Pitt, David Thomas 10
Poussaint, Alvin F. 5
Satcher, David 7
Sullivan, Louis 8
Thomas, Vivien 9
Watkins, Levi, Jr. 9
Welsing, Frances Cress 5
Williams, Daniel Hale 2
Wright, Louis Tompkins 4

Meharry Medical College
Lyttle, Hulda Margaret 14

Melanin theory of racism
See also Cress Theory of Color Confrontation and Racism
Jeffries, Leonard 8

Men's movement
Somé, Malidoma Patrice 10

Merce Cunningham Dance Company
Dove, Ulysses 5

MESBICs
See Minority Enterprise Small Business Investment Corporations

Metropolitan Applied Research Center (MARC Corp.)
Clark, Kenneth B. 5

MFDP
See Mississippi Freedom Democratic Party

Miami Dolphins football team
Greene, Joe 10

Michael Jordan Foundation
Jordan, Michael 6

Michigan House of Representatives
Collins, Barbara-Rose 7

Michigan State Supreme Court
Archer, Dennis 7
Mallett, Conrad, Jr. 16

Michigan State University
Wharton, Clifton R., Jr. 7

Midwifery
Logan, Onnie Lee 14

Military police
Cadoria, Sherian Grace 14

Miller Brewing Company
Colbert, Virgis William 17

Cumulative Subject Index

Millinery
Bailey, Xenobia **11**

Million Man March
Farrakhan, Louis **15**
Hawkins, La-Van **17**
Worrill, Conrad **12**

Milwaukee Braves baseball team
Aaron, Hank **5**

Milwaukee Brewers baseball team
Aaron, Hank **5**
Baylor, Don **6**
Sheffield, Gary **16**

Milwaukee Bucks basketball team
Abdul-Jabbar, Kareem **8**
Lucas, John **7**

Minneapolis City Council
Sayles Belton, Sharon **9, 16**

Minneapolis city government
Sayles Belton, Sharon **9, 16**

Minnesota State Supreme Court
Page, Alan **7**

Minnesota Timberwolves basketball team
Garnett, Kevin **14**

Minnesota Twins baseball team
Baylor, Don **6**
Puckett, Kirby **4**
Winfield, Dave **5**

Minnesota Vikings football team
Dungy, Tony **17**
Green, Dennis **5**
Moon, Warren **8**
Page, Alan **7**
Rashad, Ahmad **18**
Walker, Herschel **1**

Minority Business Resource Center
Hill, Jessie, Jr. **13**

Minority Enterprise Small Business Investment Corporations (MESBICs)
Lewis, Reginald F. **6**

Minstrel shows
McDaniel, Hattie **5**

Miss America
Vincent, Marjorie Judith **2**
Williams, Vanessa L. **4, 17**

Mississippi Freedom Democratic Party (MFDP)
Baker, Ella **5**
Blackwell, Unita **17**
Hamer, Fannie Lou **6**
Henry, Aaron **19**
Norton, Eleanor Holmes **7**

Mississippi state government
Hamer, Fannie Lou **6**

Miss USA
Gist, Carole **1**

MLA
See Modern Language Association of America

Model Inner City Community Organization (MICCO)
Fauntroy, Walter E. **11**

Modeling
Beckford, Tyson **11**
Berry, Halle **4, 19**
Banks, Tyra **11**
Campbell, Naomi **1**
Hardison, Bethann **12**
Hounsou, Djimon **19**
Houston, Whitney **7**
Iman **4**
Johnson, Beverly **2**
Langhart, Janet **19**
Leslie, Lisa **16**
Powell, Maxine **8**
Rochon, Lela **16**
Smith, Barbara **11**
Tyson, Cicely **7**
Webb, Veronica **10**
Wek, Alek **18**

Modern dance
Ailey, Alvin **8**
Allen, Debbie **13**
Byrd, Donald **10**
Dove, Ulysses **5**
Faison, George **16**
Jamison, Judith **7**
Kitt, Eartha **16**
Miller, Bebe **3**
Primus, Pearl **6**
Vereen, Ben **4**

Modern Language Association of America (MLA)
Baker, Houston A., Jr. **6**

Montgomery bus boycott
Abernathy, Ralph David **1**
Baker, Ella **5**
Jackson, Mahalia **5**
King, Martin Luther, Jr. **1**
Parks, Rosa **1**
Rustin, Bayard **4**

Montreal Expos
Doby, Lawrence Eugene, Sr. **16**

Morehouse College
Hope, John **8**
Mays, Benjamin E. **7**

Morna
Evora, Cesaria **12**

Moscow World News
Khanga, Yelena **6**
Sullivan, Louis **8**

Mother Waddles Perpetual Mission, Inc.
Waddles, Charleszetta (Mother) **10**

Motivational speaking
Brown, Les **5**
Kimbro, Dennis **10**
Russell-McCloud, Patricia **17**

Motown Records
Bizimungu, Pasteur **19**
Busby, Jheryl **3**
Gaye, Marvin **2**
Gordy, Berry, Jr. **1**
Jackson, George **19**
Jackson, Michael **19**
Powell, Maxine **8**
Robinson, Smokey **3**
Ross, Diana **8**
Wonder, Stevie **11**

Mouvement Revolutionnaire National pour la Developpement (Rwanda; MRND)
Habyarimana, Juvenal **8**

MOVE
Goode, W. Wilson **4**
Wideman, John Edgar **5**

MRND
See Mouvement Revolutionnaire National pour la Developpement

"Little Rock Nine"
Bates, Daisy **13**

MTV Jams
Bellamy, Bill **12**

Multimedia art
Bailey, Xenobia **11**
Simpson, Lorna **4**

Muppets, The
Clash, Kevin **14**

Murals
Douglas, Aaron **7**
Lee-Smith, Hughie **5**
Walker, Kara **16**

Music Television (MTV)
Chideya, Farai **14**

Musical composition
Bonga, Kuenda **13**
Braxton, Toni **15**
Caesar, Shirley **19**
Charlemagne, Manno **11**
Charles, Ray **16**

Cole, Natalie Maria **17**
Combs, Sean "Puffy" **17**
Cleveland, James **19**
Davis, Anthony **11**
Davis, Miles **4**
Davis, Sammy Jr. **18**
Edmonds, Kenny "Babyface" **10**
Ellington, Duke **5**
Europe, James Reese **10**
George, Nelson **12**
Gillespie, Dizzy **1**
Gordy, Berry, Jr. **1**
Green, Al **13**
Handy, W. C. **8**
Hathaway, Donny **18**
Jackson, Michael **19**
James, Rick **17**
Jean-Baptiste, Marianne **17**
Jones, Quincy **8**
Joplin, Scott **6**
Kelly, R. **18**
King, B. B. **7**
León, Tania **13**
Lincoln, Abbey **3**
Marsalis, Wynton **16**
Ndegéocello, Me'Shell **15**
Prince **18**
Reagon, Bernice Johnson **7**
Redding, Otis **16**
Rushen, Patrice **12**
Sangare, Oumou **18**
Simone, Nina **15**
Sweat, Keith **19**
Van Peebles, Melvin **7**
Warwick, Dionne **18**
Washington, Grover, Jr. **17**

Music publishing
Cooke, Sam **17**
Edmonds, Tracey **16**
Gordy, Berry, Jr. **1**
Handy, W. C. **8**
Ice Cube **8**
Jackson, George **19**
Jackson, Michael **19**
James, Rick **17**
Knight, Suge **11**
Mayfield, Curtis **2**
Prince **18**
Redding, Otis **16**
Ross, Diana **8**

Muslim Mosque, Inc.
X, Malcolm **1**

Mysteries
Himes, Chester **8**
Mosley, Walter **5**
Wesley, Valerie Wilson **18**

NAACP
See National Association for the Advancement of Colored People

NAACP Legal Defense Fund (LDF)
Bell, Derrick **6**
Chambers, Julius **3**
Edelman, Marian Wright **5**
Guinier, Lani **7**
Jones, Elaine R. **7**
Julian, Percy Lavon **6**
Marshall, Thurgood **1**
Motley, Constance Baker **10**

NABJ
See National Association of Black Journalists

NAC
See Nyasaland African Congress

NACGN
See National Association of Colored Graduate Nurses

NACW
See National Association of Colored Women

NAG
See Nonviolent Action Group

NASA
See National Aeronautics and Space Administration

Nation
Wilkins, Roger **2**

Nation of Islam
See Lost-Found Nation of Islam

National Aeronautics and Space Administration (NASA)
Bluford, Guy **2**
Bolden, Charles F., Jr. **7**
Gregory, Frederick D. **8**
Jemison, Mae C. **1**
McNair, Ronald **3**
Nichols, Nichelle **11**

National Afro-American Council
Fortune, T. Thomas **6**

National Alliance Party (NAP)
Fulani, Lenora **11**

National Association for the Advancement of Colored People (NAACP)
Baker, Ella **5**
Bates, Daisy **13**
Bell, Derrick **6**
Bond, Julian **2**
Bontemps, Arna **8**
Brooks, Gwendolyn **1**
Bunche, Ralph J. **5**
Chambers, Julius **3**
Chavis, Benjamin **6**
Clark, Kenneth B. **5**
Clark, Septima **7**
Days, Drew S., III **10**
Dee, Ruby **8**
Du Bois, W. E. B. **3**
Edelman, Marian Wright **5**
Evers, Medgar **3**
Evers, Myrlie **8**
Farmer, James **2**
Fuller, S. B. **13**
Gibson, William F. **6**
Grimké, Archibald H. **9**
Hampton, Fred **18**
Harrington, Oliver W. **9**
Henderson, Wade **14**
Hooks, Benjamin L. **2**
Horne, Lena **5**
Houston, Charles Hamilton **4**
Johnson, James Weldon **5**
Jordan, Vernon E. **3**
Lampkin, Daisy **19**
Madison, Joseph E. **17**
Marshall, Thurgood **1**
McKissick, Floyd B. **3**
McPhail, Sharon **2**
Meredith, James H. **11**
Moses, Robert Parris **11**
Motley, Constance Baker **10**
Owens, Major **6**
Rustin, Bayard **4**
Terrell, Mary Church **9**
Tucker, C. DeLores **12**
White, Walter F. **4**
Wilkins, Roger **2**
Wilkins, Roy **4**
Williams, Hosea Lorenzo **15**
Williams, Robert F. **11**
Wright, Louis Tompkins **4**

National Association of Black Journalists (NABJ)
Harris, Jay T. **19**
Stone, Chuck **9**
Shipp, E. R. **15**
Washington, Laura S. **18**

National Association of Colored Graduate Nurses (NACGN)
Staupers, Mabel K. **7**

National Association of Colored Women (NACW)
Bethune, Mary McLeod **4**
Harper, Frances Ellen Watkins **11**
Lampkin, Daisy **19**
Terrell, Mary Church **9**

National Baptist Convention USA
Lyons, Henry **12**

National Baptist Publishing Board
Boyd, T. B., III **6**

National Baptist Sunday Church School and Baptist Training Union Congress
Boyd, T. B., III **6**

National Bar Association
Alexander, Joyce London **18**
Archer, Dennis **7**
McPhail, Sharon **2**

National Basketball Association (NBA)
Abdul-Jabbar, Kareem 8
Barkley, Charles 5
Bing, Dave 3
Bol, Manute 1
Brandon, Terrell 16
Bryant, Kobe 15
Chamberlain, Wilt 18
Drexler, Clyde 4
Erving, Julius 18
Ewing, Patrick A. 17
Garnett, Kevin 14
Gourdine, Simon 11
Hardaway, Anfernee (Penny) 13
Hill, Grant 13
Howard, Juwan 15
Johnson, Earvin "Magic" 3
Jordan, Michael 6
Lucas, John 7
Mourning, Alonzo 17
Mutombo, Dikembe 7
Olajuwon, Hakeem 2
O'Neal, Shaquille 8
Pippen, Scottie 15
Rodman, Dennis 12
Russell, Bill 8
Thomas, Isiah 7
Webber, Chris 15
Wilkens, Lenny 11

National Basketball Players Association
Erving, Julius 18
Ewing, Patrick A. 17
Gourdine, Simon 11

National Black Arts Festival (NBAF)
Borders, James 9
Brooks, Avery 9

National Black Gay and Lesbian Conference
Wilson, Phill 9

National Black Gay and Lesbian Leadership Forum (NBGLLF)
Boykin, Keith 14
Carter, Mandy 11

National Book Award
Ellison, Ralph 7
Haley, Alex 4
Johnson, Charles 1
Patterson, Orlando 4

National Broadcasting Company (NBC)
Allen, Byron 3
Cosby, Bill 7
Gumbel, Bryant 14
Hinderas, Natalie 5
Jones, Star 10
Reuben, Gloria 15
Roker, Al 12
Simpson, Carole 6
Stokes, Carl B. 10
Williams, Montel 4

National Center for Neighborhood Enterprise (NCNE)
Woodson, Robert L. 10

National Coalition of 100 Black Women
McCabe, Jewell Jackson 10

National Coalition to Abolish the Death Penalty (NCADP)
Hawkins, Steven 14

National Commission for Democracy (Ghana; NCD)
Rawlings, Jerry 9

National Conference on Black Lawyers (NCBL)
McDougall, Gay J. 11

National Council of Negro Women (NCNW)
Bethune, Mary McLeod 4
Blackwell, Unita 17
Cole, Johnnetta B. 5
Hamer, Fannie Lou 6
Height, Dorothy I. 2
Horne, Lena 5
Lampkin, Daisy 19
Sampson, Edith S. 4
Staupers, Mabel K. 7

National Council of Nigeria and the Cameroons (NCNC)
Azikiwe, Nnamdi 13

National Defence Council (Ghana; NDC)
Rawlings, Jerry 9

National Democratic Party (Rhodesia)
Mugabe, Robert Gabriel 10

National Earthquake Information Center (NEIC)
Person, Waverly 9

National Endowment for the Arts (NEA)
Hemphill, Essex 10
Serrano, Andres 3
Williams, William T. 11

National Equal Rights League (NERL)
Trotter, Monroe 9

National Football League (NFL)
Brown, Jim 11
Butler, Leroy III 17
Green, Dennis 5
Greene, Joe 10
Hill, Calvin 19
Howard, Desmond 16
Lott, Ronnie 9
Moon, Warren 8
Page, Alan 7
Payton, Walter 11
Rhodes, Ray 14
Rice, Jerry 5
Sanders, Barry 1
Sanders, Deion 4
Shell, Art 1
Simpson, O. J. 15
Singletary, Mike 4
Smith, Emmitt 7
Upshaw, Gene 18
Walker, Herschel 1
White, Reggie 6

National Hockey League (NHL)
McBride, Bryant 18
Fuhr, Grant 1
McKegney, Tony 3
O'Ree, Willie 5

National Information Infrastructure (NII)
Lewis, Delano 7

National Institute of Education
Baker, Gwendolyn Calvert 9

National League
Coleman, Leonard S., Jr. 12

National Minority Business Council
Leary, Kathryn D. 10

National Museum of American History
Reagon, Bernice Johnson 7

National Negro Congress
Bunche, Ralph J. 5

National Negro Suffrage League
Trotter, Monroe 9

National Organization for Women (NOW)
Kennedy, Florynce 12
Hernandez, Aileen Clarke 13

National Political Congress of Black Women
Chisholm, Shirley 2
Tucker, C. DeLores 12
Waters, Maxine 3

National Public Radio (NPR)
Early, Gerald 15
Lewis, Delano 7
Abu-Jamal, Mumia 15

National Resistance Army (Uganda; NRA)
Museveni, Yoweri 4

National Resistance Movement
Museveni, Yoweri 4

National Revolutionary Movement for Development
See Mouvement Revolutionnaire National pour la Developpment

National Rifle Association (NRA)
Williams, Robert F. 11

National Science Foundation (NSF)
Massey, Walter E. 5

National Security Council
Powell, Colin 1
Rice, Condoleezza 3

National Union for the Total Independence of Angola (UNITA)
Savimbi, Jonas 2

National Union of Mineworkers (South Africa; NUM)
Ramaphosa, Cyril 3

National Urban Coalition (NUC)
Edelin, Ramona Hoage 19

National Urban League
Brown, Ron 5
Haynes, George Edmund 8
Jacob, John E. 2
Jordan, Vernon E. 3
Price, Hugh B. 9
Young, Whitney M., Jr. 4

National Women's Political Caucus
Hamer, Fannie Lou 6

National Youth Administration (NYA)
Bethune, Mary McLeod 4
Primus, Pearl 6

Nature Boy Enterprises
Yoba, Malik 11

NBA
See National Basketball Association

NBAF
See National Black Arts Festival

NBC
See National Broadcasting Company

NBGLLF
See National Black Gay and Lesbian Leadership Forum

NCBL
See National Conference on Black Lawyers

NCD
See National Commission for Democracy

NCNE
See National Center for Neighborhood Enterprise

NCNW
See National Council of Negro Women

NDC
See National Defence Council

NEA
See National Endowment for the Arts

Nebula awards
Butler, Octavia 8
Delany, Jr., Samuel R. 9

Negro American Labor Council
Randolph, A. Philip 3

Negro American Political League
Trotter, Monroe 9

Negro Digest
Johnson, John H. 3

Negro Ensemble Company
Schultz, Michael A. 6
Taylor, Susan L. 10

Negro History Bulletin
Woodson, Carter G. 2

Negro Leagues
O'Neil, Buck 19
Paige, Satchel 7
Davis, Piper 19
Stone, Toni 15

Negro Theater Ensemble
Rolle, Esther 13

Negro World
Fortune, T. Thomas 6

NEIC
See National Earthquake Information Center

Neo-hoodoo
Reed, Ishmael 8

Nequai Cosmetics
Taylor, Susan L. 10

NERL
See National Equal Rights League

Netherlands Antilles
Liberia-Peters, Maria Philomena 12

NetNoir Inc.
CasSelle, Malcolm 11
Ellington, E. David 11

Neurosurgery
Carson, Benjamin 1

Neurosurgery
Black, Keith Lanier 18

New Concept Development Center
Madhubuti, Haki R. 7

New Dance Group
Primus, Pearl 6

New Jersey Family Development Act
Bryant, Wayne R. 6

New Jersey General Assembly
Bryant, Wayne R. 6

New Jersey Nets
Doby, Lawrence Eugene, Sr. 16

New Negro movement
See Harlem Renaissance

New York Age
Fortune, T. Thomas 6

New York City government
Crew, Rudolph F. 16
Dinkins, David 4

New York Daily News
Cose, Ellis 5

New York Drama Critics Circle Award
Hansberry, Lorraine 6

New York Freeman
Fortune, T. Thomas 6

New York Giants baseball team
Mays, Willie 3

New York Globe
Fortune, T. Thomas 6

New York Institute for Social Therapy and Research
Fulani, Lenora 11

New York Jets football team
Lott, Ronnie 9

New York Knicks basketball team
Ewing, Patrick A. 17

New York Nets basketball team
Erving, Julius 18

New York Public Library
Dodson, Howard, Jr. 7

Schomburg, Arthur Alfonso **9**

New York Shakespeare Festival
Gunn, Moses **10**
Wolfe, George C. **6**

New York State Senate
Motley, Constance Baker **10**
Owens, Major **6**

New York State Supreme Court
Wright, Bruce McMarion **3**

New York Sun
Fortune, T. Thomas **6**

New York Times
Hunter-Gault, Charlayne **6**
Price, Hugh B. **9**
Wilkins, Roger **2**

New York Yankees baseball team
Baylor, Don **6**
Jackson, Reggie **15**
Winfield, Dave **5**

Newark city government
Gibson, Kenneth Allen **6**

Newark Eagles
Doby, Lawrence Eugene, Sr. **16**

Newark Housing Authority
Gibson, Kenneth Allen **6**

NFL
See National Football League

Nguzo Saba
Karenga, Maulana **10**

NHL
See National Hockey League

Niagara movement
Du Bois, W. E. B. **3**
Hope, John **8**
Trotter, Monroe **9**

Nigerian Armed Forces
Abacha, Sani **11**
Babangida, Ibrahim **4**
Obasanjo, Olusegun **5**

Nigerian literature
Achebe, Chinua **6**
Rotimi, Ola **1**
Soyinka, Wole **4**

NII
See National Information Infrastructure

1960 Masks
Soyinka, Wole **4**

Nobel Peace Prize
Bunche, Ralph J. **5**

King, Martin Luther, Jr. **1**
Luthuli, Albert **13**
Tutu, Desmond **6**

Nobel Prize for literature
Soyinka, Wole **4**
Morrison, Toni **15**
Walcott, Derek **5**

Nonviolent Action Group (NAG)
Al-Amin, Jamil Abdullah **6**

North Carolina Mutual Life Insurance
Spaulding, Charles Clinton **9**

North Pole
Henson, Matthew **2**

NOW
See National Organization for Women

NPR
See National Public Radio

NRA
See National Resistance Army (Uganda)

NRA
See National Rifle Association

NSF
See National Science Foundation

Nuclear energy
O'Leary, Hazel **6**
Quarterman, Lloyd Albert **4**

Nuclear Regulatory Commission
Jackson, Shirley Ann **12**

Nucleus
King, Yolanda **6**
Shabazz, Attallah **6**

NUM
See National Union of Mineworkers (South Africa)

Nursing
Auguste, Rose-Anne **13**
Johnson, Eddie Bernice **8**
Larsen, Nella **10**
Lyttle, Hulda Margaret **14**
Riley, Helen Caldwell Day **13**
Robinson, Rachel **16**
Shabazz, Betty **7**
Staupers, Mabel K. **7**
Taylor, Susie King **13**

Nutrition
Clark, Celeste **15**
Gregory, Dick **1**
Watkins, Shirley R. **17**

NYA
See National Youth Administration

Nyasaland African Congress (NAC)
Banda, Hastings Kamuzu **6**

Oakland Athletics baseball team
Baker, Dusty **8**
Baylor, Don **6**
Jackson, Reggie **15**
Morgan, Joe Leonard **9**

Oakland Raiders football team
Howard, Desmond **16**
Upshaw, Gene **18**

Oakland Tribune
Maynard, Robert C. **7**

OAU
See Organization of African Unity

OECS
See Organization of Eastern Caribbean States

Office of Civil Rights
See U.S. Department of Education

Office of Management and Budget
Raines, Franklin Delano **14**

Office of Public Liaison
Herman, Alexis M. **15**

Ohio House of Representatives
Stokes, Carl B. **10**

Ohio state government
Brown, Les **5**
Stokes, Carl B. **10**
Williams, George Washington **18**

Ohio State Senate
White, Michael R. **5**

OIC
See Opportunities Industrialization Centers of America, Inc.

Olympics
Ali, Muhammad **2, 16**
Bonaly, Surya **7**
Bowe, Riddick **6**
Christie, Linford **8**
Coachman, Alice **18**
Dawes, Dominique **11**
Devers, Gail **7**
Edwards, Harry **2**
Edwards, Teresa **14**
Ewing, Patrick A. **17**
Garrison, Zina **2**
Hardaway, Anfernee (Penny) **13**
Hill, Grant **13**
Holyfield, Evander **6**
Johnson, Ben **1**
Johnson, Michael **13**

Joyner-Kersee, Jackie **5**
Leslie, Lisa **16**
Lewis, Carl **4**
Malone, Karl A. **18**
Miller, Cheryl **10**
Moses, Edwin **8**
Mutola, Maria **12**
Owens, Jesse **2**
Pippen, Scottie **15**
Powell, Mike **7**
Quirot, Ana **13**
Rudolph, Wilma **4**
Russell, Bill **8**
Swoopes, Sheryl **12**
Whitaker, Pernell **10**
Wilkens, Lenny **11**

Oncology
Leffall, LaSalle, Jr. **3**

One Church, One Child
Clements, George **2**

OPC
See Ovambo People's Congress

Opera
Anderson, Marian **2**
Brooks, Avery **9**
Bumbry, Grace **5**
Davis, Anthony **11**
Graves, Denyce **19**
Hendricks, Barbara **3**
Joplin, Scott **6**
Joyner, Matilda Sissieretta **15**
Maynor, Dorothy **19**
Norman, Jessye **5**
Price, Leontyne **1**

Operation Desert Shield
Powell, Colin **1**

Operation Desert Storm
Powell, Colin **1**

OPO
See Ovamboland People's Organization

Opportunities Industrialization Centers of America, Inc. (OIC)
Sullivan, Leon H. **3**

Organization of African States
Museveni, Yoweri **4**

Organization of African Unity (OAU)
Diouf, Abdou **3**
Haile Selassie **7**
Kaunda, Kenneth **2**
Kenyatta, Jomo **5**
Nkrumah, Kwame **3**
Nujoma, Samuel **10**
Nyerere, Julius **5**
Touré, Sekou **6**

Organization of Afro-American Unity
X, Malcolm **1**

Organization of Eastern Caribbean States (OECS)
Charles, Mary Eugenia **10**

Orisun Repertory
Soyinka, Wole **4**

Orlando Magic basketball team
Erving, Julius **18**
O'Neal, Shaquille **8**

Osteopathy
Allen, Ethel D. **13**

Ovambo People's Congress (South Africa; OPC)
Nujoma, Samuel **10**

Ovamboland People's Organization (South Africa; OPO)
Nujoma, Samuel **10**

Page Education Foundation
Page, Alan **7**

Paine College
Lewis, Shirley A. R. **14**

Painting
Bailey, Radcliffe **19**
Barthe, Richmond **15**
Basquiat, Jean-Michel **5**
Bearden, Romare **2**
Campbell, E. Simms **13**
Delaney, Beauford **19**
Douglas, Aaron **7**
Driskell, David C. **7**
Ewing, Patrick A. **17**
Flood, Curt **10**
Gilliam, Sam **16**
Guyton, Tyree **9**
Harkless, Necia Desiree **19**
Hayden, Palmer **13**
Johnson, William Henry **3**
Jones, Lois Mailou **13**
Lawrence, Jacob **4**
Lee-Smith, Hughie **5**
Major, Clarence **9**
McGee, Charles **10**
Mitchell, Corinne **8**
Pierre, Andre **17**
Pippin, Horace **9**
Porter, James A. **11**
Ringgold, Faith **4**
Tanner, Henry Ossawa **1**
Thomas, Alma **14**
Tolliver, William **9**
Wells, James Lesesne **10**
Williams, Billy Dee **8**
Williams, William T. **11**
Woodruff, Hale **9**

Pan-Africanism
Carmichael, Stokely **5**
Du Bois, W. E. B. **3**
Garvey, Marcus **1**
Haile Selassie **7**
Kenyatta, Jomo **5**
Madhubuti, Haki R. **7**
Marshall, Paule **7**
Nkrumah, Kwame **3**
Nyerere, Julius **5**
Touré, Sekou **6**
Turner, Henry McNeal **5**

Pan African Orthodox Christian Church
Agyeman, Jaramogi Abebe **10**

Parents of Watts (POW)
Harris, Alice **7**

Parti Démocratique de Guinée (Guinea Democratic Party; PDG)
Touré, Sekou **6**

Parti Démocratique de la Côte d'Ivoire (Democratic Party of the Ivory Coast; PDCI)
Houphouët-Boigny, Félix **4**

Partido Africano da Independencia da Guine e Cabo Verde (PAIGC)
Vieira, Joao **14**

Party for Unity and Progress (Guinea; PUP)
Conté, Lansana **7**

PATC
See Performing Arts Training Center

Pathology
Fuller, Solomon Carter, Jr. **15**

Patriot Party
Fulani, Lenora **11**

PBS
See Public Broadcasting Service

PDCI
See Parti Démocratique de la Côte d'Ivoire (Democratic Party of the Ivory Coast)

PDG
See Parti Démocratique de Guinée (Guinea Democratic Party)

Peace and Freedom Party
Cleaver, Eldridge **5**

Peace Corps
See U.S. Peace Corps

Peace Mission
Divine, Father **7**

Pediatrics
Carson, Benjamin **1**
Elders, Joycelyn **6**

Peg Leg Bates Country Club
Bates, Peg Leg **14**

Pennsylvania state government
Allen, Ethel D. **13**

People Organized and Working for Economic Rebirth (POWER)
Farrakhan, Louis **2**

People United to Serve Humanity (PUSH)
Jackson, Jesse, Jr. **14**

People's Association Human Rights
Williams, Robert F. **11**

People's Liberation Army of Namibia (PLAN)
Nujoma, Samuel **10**

People's National Party (Jamaica; PNP)
Patterson, P. J. **6**

People's Progressive Party (PPP)
Jagan, Cheddi **16**
Jawara, Sir Dawda Kairaba **11**

People United to Serve Humanity (PUSH)
Jackson, Jesse **1**

Performing Arts Training Center (PATC)
Dunham, Katherine **4**

PGA
See Professional Golfers' Association

Phelps Stokes Fund
Patterson, Frederick Douglass **12**

Philadelphia City Council
Allen, Ethel D. **13**

Philadelphia city government
Goode, W. Wilson **4**

Philadelphia Eagles football team
White, Reggie **6**
Rhodes, Ray **14**

Philadelphia Phillies baseball team
Morgan, Joe Leonard **9**

Philadelphia public schools
Clayton, Constance **1**

Philadelphia 76ers basketball team
Barkley, Charles **5**

Bol, Manute **1**
Chamberlain, Wilt **18**
Erving, Julius **18**
Lucas, John **7**

Philadelphia Warriors
Chamberlain, Wilt **18**

Philanthropy
Cosby, Bill **7**
Cosby, Camille **14**
Golden, Marita **19**
Malone, Annie **13**
McCarty, Oseola **16**
Pleasant, Mary Ellen **9**
Thomas, Franklin A. **5**
Waddles, Charleszetta (Mother) **10**
Walker, Madame C. J. **7**
White, Reggie **6**
Wonder, Stevie **11**

Philosophy
Baker, Houston A., Jr. **6**
Davis, Angela **5**
Toomer, Jean **6**
West, Cornel **5**

Phoenix Suns basketball team
Barkley, Charles **5**

Photography
Andrews, Bert **13**
Barboza, Anthony **10**
Lester, Julius **9**
Moutoussamy-Ashe, Jeanne **7**
Parks, Gordon **1**
Robeson, Eslanda Goode **13**
Serrano, Andres **3**
Simpson, Lorna **4**
Sleet, Moneta, Jr. **5**
Tanner, Henry Ossawa **1**
VanDerZee, James **6**

Photojournalism
Moutoussamy-Ashe, Jeanne **7**
Parks, Gordon **1**
Sleet, Moneta, Jr. **5**

Physical therapy
Elders, Joycelyn **6**

Physics
Gates, Sylvester James, Jr. **15**
Jackson, Shirley Ann **12**
Massey, Walter E. **5**
Tyson, Neil de Grasse **15**

Piano
Cole, Nat King **17**
Donegan, Dorothy **19**
Ellington, Duke **5**
Hinderas, Natalie **5**
Joplin, Scott **6**
Monk, Thelonious **1**
Roberts, Marcus **19**
Vaughan, Sarah **13**
Williams, Mary Lou **15**

Pittsburgh Pirates baseball team
Bonds, Barry **6**

Pittsburgh Steelers football team
Dungy, Tony **17**
Greene, Joe **10**

PLAN
See People's Liberation Army of Namibia

Planned Parenthood Federation of America Inc.
Wattleton, Faye **9**

Playwright
Arkadie, Kevin **17**
Childress, Alice **15**
Cleage, Pearl **17**
Gordone, Charles **15**
Jean-Baptistse, Marianne **17**
Kennedy, Adrienne **11**
Moss, Carlton **17**
Sanchez, Sonia **17**
Thurman, Wallace **17**

PNP
See People's National Party (Jamaica)

Playwright
Cheadle, Don **19**

Poet laureate (U.S.)
Dove, Rita **6**

Poetry
Cleage, Pearl **17**
Clifton, Lucille **14**
Angelou, Maya **15**
Dove, Rita **6**
Harkless, Necia Desiree **19**
Harper, Frances Ellen Watkins **11**
Hayden, Robert **12**
Lorde, Audre **6**
Parker, Pat **19**
Randall, Dudley **8**
Sanchez, Sonia **17**
Sapphire **14**
Senghor, Léopold Sédar **12**

Politics
Alexander, Archie Alphonso **14**
Belton, Sharon Sayles **16**
Blackwell, Unita **17**
Chideya, Farai **14**
Christian-Green, Donna M. **17**
Connerly, Ward **14**
Edmonds, Terry **17**
Gordon, Pamela **17**
Henry, Aaron **19**
Ingraham, Hubert A. **19**
Perry, Ruth **15**
Touré, Amadou Toumani **18**
Watts, J. C., Jr. **14**
Wheat, Alan **14**
Williams, George Washington **18**

Pop music
Cole, Nat King 17
Combs, Sean "Puffy" 17
Edmonds, Kenneth "Babyface" 10
Franklin, Aretha 11
Franklin, Kirk 15
Houston, Whitney 7
Jackson, Janet 6
Jackson, Michael 19
James, Rick 17
Jones, Quincy 8
Kelly, R. 18
Khan, Chaka 12
Prince 18
Robinson, Smokey 3
Rupaul 17
Sade 15
Seal 14
Senghor, Léopold Sédar 12
Sweat, Keith 19
Turner, Tina 6
Washington, Grover, Jr. 17
Washington, Val 12
White, Barry 13
Williams, Vanessa L. 4, 17
Wilson, Nancy 10
Wonder, Stevie 11

Portland Trail Blazers basketball team
Drexler, Clyde 4
Wilkens, Lenny 11

POW
See Parents of Watts

POWER
See People Organized and Working for Economic Rebirth

PPP
See People's Progressive Party (Gambia)

Presbyterianism
Cannon, Katie 10

Pride Economic Enterprises
Barry, Marion S. 7

Printmaking
Wells, James Lesesne 10

Prison ministry
Bell, Ralph S. 5

Pro-Line Corp.
Cottrell, Comer 11

Professional Golfers' Association (PGA)
Elder, Lee 6
Sifford, Charlie 4

Proposition 209
Connerly, Ward 14

Psychiatry
Cobbs, Price M. 9
Comer, James P. 6
Fuller, Solomon Carter, Jr. 15
Poussaint, Alvin F. 5
Welsing, Frances Cress 5

Psychology
Fulani, Lenora 11
Staples, Brent 8
Steele, Claude Mason 13

Public Broadcasting Service (PBS)
Brown, Les 5
Davis, Ossie 5
Duke, Bill 3
Hampton, Henry 6
Hunter-Gault, Charlayne 6
Lawson, Jennifer 1
Riggs, Marlon 5
Wilkins, Roger 2

Public housing
Hamer, Fannie Lou 6
Lane, Vincent 5

Public relations
Barden, Don H. 9
Edmonds, Terry 17
Graham, Stedman 13
McCabe, Jewell Jackson 10
Perez, Anna 1
Rowan, Carl T. 1
Taylor, Kristin Clark 8
Williams, Maggie 7

Public television
Brown, Tony 3

Publishing
Achebe, Chinua 6
Barden, Don H. 9
Bates, Daisy 13
Boyd, T. B. III 6
Brown, Marie Dutton 12
Driver, David E. 11
Ducksworth, Marilyn 12
Giddings, Paula 11
Graves, Earl G. 1
Harris, Jay 19
Harris, Monica 18
Hudson, Cheryl 15
Hudson, Wade 15
James, Juanita 13
Johnson, John H. 3
Jones, Quincy 8
Kunjufu, Jawanza 3
Lawson, Jennifer 1
Leavell, Dorothy R. 17
Lorde, Audre 6
Madhubuti, Haki R. 7
Maynard, Robert C. 7
McDonald, Erroll 1
Morgan, Garrett 1
Myers, Walter Dean 8
Parks, Gordon 1
Perez, Anna 1
Randall, Dudley 8
Sengstacke, John 18
Vanzant, Iyanla 17
Walker, Alice 1
Washington, Laura S. 18
Wells-Barnett, Ida B. 8
Williams, Patricia J. 11

Pulitzer prize
Brooks, Gwendolyn 1
Dove, Rita 6
Fuller, Charles 8
Gordone, Charles 15
Haley, Alex 4
Komunyakaa, Yusef 9
Lewis, David Levering 9
Morrison, Toni 2, 15
Page, Clarence 4
Shipp, E. R. 15
Sleet, Moneta, Jr. 5
Walker, Alice 1
Wilkins, Roger 2
Wilson, August 7

PUP
See Party for Unity and Progress (Guinea)

Puppeteer
Clash, Kevin 14

PUSH
See People United to Serve Humanity

Quiltmaking
Ringgold, Faith 4

Race car driving
Ribbs, Willy T. 2
Scott, Sr., Wendell Oliver 19

Race relations
Abbott, Diane 9
Achebe, Chinua 6
Asante, Molefi Kete 3
Baker, Ella 5
Baker, Houston A., Jr. 6
Baldwin, James 1
Beals, Melba Patillo 15
Bell, Derrick 6
Bennett, Lerone, Jr. 5
Bethune, Mary McLeod 4
Bosley, Freeman, Jr. 7
Boyd, T. B. III 6
Brown, Elaine 8
Bunche, Ralph J. 5
Butler, Paul D. 17
Butts, Calvin O., III 9
Carter, Stephen L. 4
Cary, Lorene 3
Chavis, Benjamin 6
Clark, Kenneth B. 5
Clark, Septima 7
Cobbs, Price M. 9
Cochran, Johnnie L., Jr. 11
Cole, Johnnetta B. 5
Comer, James P. 6
Cone, James H. 3

Conyers, John, Jr. **4**
Cosby, Bill **7**
Darden, Christopher **13**
Davis, Angela **5**
Davis, Benjamin O., Jr. **2**
Davis, Benjamin O., Sr. **4**
Dee, Ruby **8**
Dellums, Ronald **2**
Divine, Father **7**
Dunbar, Paul Laurence **8**
Dyson, Michael Eric **11**
Edelman, Marian Wright **5**
Elder, Lee **6**
Ellison, Ralph **7**
Esposito, Giancarlo **9**
Farmer, James **2**
Farrakhan, Louis **2**
Fauset, Jessie **7**
Franklin, John Hope **5**
Fuller, Charles **8**
Gaines, Ernest J. **7**
Gibson, William F. **6**
Goode, W. Wilson **4**
Graham, Lawrence Otis **12**
Gregory, Dick **1**
Grimké, Archibald H. **9**
Guinier, Lani **7**
Guy, Rosa **5**
Haley, Alex **4**
Hampton, Henry **6**
Hansberry, Lorraine **6**
Harris, Alice **7**
Hastie, William H. **8**
Haynes, George Edmund **8**
Henry, Aaron **19**
Henry, Lenny **9**
hooks, bell **5**
Hooks, Benjamin L. **2**
Hope, John **8**
Ingram, Rex **5**
Innis, Roy **5**
Jeffries, Leonard **8**
Johnson, James Weldon **5**
Jones, Elaine R. **7**
Jordan, Vernon E. **3**
Khanga, Yelena **6**
King, Bernice **4**
King, Coretta Scott **3**
King, Martin Luther, Jr. **1**
King, Yolanda **6**
Lane, Charles **3**
Lee, Spike **5, 19**
Lee-Smith, Hughie **5**
Lorde, Audre **6**
Mandela, Nelson **1, 14**
Martin, Louis E. **16**
Mathabane, Mark **5**
Maynard, Robert C. **7**
Mays, Benjamin E. **7**
McDougall, Gay J. **11**
McKay, Claude **6**
Meredith, James H. **11**
Micheaux, Oscar **7**
Mosley, Walter **5**
Muhammad, Khallid Abdul **10**
Norton, Eleanor Holmes **7**
Page, Clarence **4**
Perkins, Edward **5**

Pitt, David Thomas **10**
Poussaint, Alvin F. **5**
Price, Hugh B. **9**
Robeson, Paul **2**
Sampson, Edith S. **4**
Shabazz, Attallah **6**
Sifford, Charlie **4**
Simpson, Carole **6**
Sister Souljah **11**
Smith, Anna Deavere **6**
Sowell, Thomas **2**
Spaulding, Charles Clinton **9**
Staples, Brent **8**
Steele, Claude Mason **13**
Taulbert, Clifton Lemoure **19**
Till, Emmett **7**
Tutu, Desmond **6**
Walcott, Derek **5**
Walker, Maggie **17**
Washington, Booker T. **4**
Washington, Harold **6**
Wells-Barnett, Ida B. **8**
Welsing, Frances Cress **5**
West, Cornel **5**
Wideman, John Edgar **5**
Wiley, Ralph **8**
Wilkins, Roger **2**
Wilkins, Roy **4**
Williams, Gregory **11**
Williams, Hosea Lorenzo **15**
Williams, Patricia J. **11**
Williams, Walter E. **4**
Wilson, Sunnie **7**
Wright, Richard **5**
Young, Whitney M., Jr. **4**

Radio
Abu-Jamal, Mumia **15**
Banks, William **11**
Dee, Ruby **8**
Dr. Dre **10**
Fuller, Charles **8**
Goode, Mal **13**
Gumbel, Greg **8**
Hamblin, Ken **10**
Joyner, Tom **19**
Keyes, Alan L. **11**
Lewis, Delano **7**
Lover, Ed **10**
Madison, Joseph E. **17**
Moss, Carlton **17**
Samara, Noah **15**

Ragtime
Europe, James Reese **10**
Joplin, Scott **6**

Rainbow Coalition
Chappell, Emma **18**
Jackson, Jesse **1**
Jackson, Jesse, Jr. **14**

Rap music
Baker, Houston A., Jr. **6**
Butts, Calvin O., III **9**
Chuck D. **9**
Combs, Sean "Puffy" **17**
Dr. Dre **10**

Dre, Dr. **14**
Dupri, Jermaine **13**
Dyson, Michael Eric **11**
Gray, F. Gary **14**
Harrell, Andre **9**
Ice Cube **8**
Ice-T **6**
Jones, Quincy **8**
Knight, Suge **11**
Lover, Ed **10**
O'Neal, Shaquille **8**
Queen Latifah **1, 16**
Shakur, Tupac **14**
Simmons, Russell **1**
Sister Souljah **11**
Smith, Will **8, 18**
Tucker, C. DeLores **12**

Rassemblement Démocratique Africain (African Democratic Rally; RDA)
Houphouët-Boigny, Félix **4**
Touré, Sekou **6**

Rastafarianism
Haile Selassie **7**
Marley, Bob **5**
Tosh, Peter **9**

RDA
See Rassemblement Démocratique Africain (African Democratic Rally)

Real estate development
Barden, Don H. **9**
Brooke, Edward **8**
Lane, Vincent **5**
Russell, Herman Jerome **17**

Recording executives
Avant, Clarence **19**
Busby, Jheryl **3**
Combs, Sean "Puffy" **17**
Dupri, Jermaine **13**
Edmonds, Kenny "Babyface" **10**
Gordy, Berry, Jr. **1**
Harrell, Andre **9**
Jackson, George **19**
Jimmy Jam **13**
Jones, Quincy **8**
Knight, Suge **11**
Lewis, Terry **13**
Mayfield, Curtis **2**
Queen Latifah **1, 16**
Rhone, Sylvia **2**
Robinson, Smokey **3**
Simmons, Russell **1**

Record producer
Ayers, Roy **16**
Combs, Sean "Puffy" **17**
Dupri, Jermaine **13**
Dre, Dr. **14**
Edmonds, Kenneth "Babyface" **10**
Ice Cube **8**
Jackson, George **19**
Jackson, Michael **19**

Jimmy Jam **13**
Jones, Quincy **8**
Kelly, R. **18**
Lewis, Terry **13**
Prince **18**
Queen Latifah **1, 16**
Sweat, Keith **19**
Vandross, Luther **13**
White, Barry **13**

Reggae
Marley, Bob **5**
Perry, Lee "Scratch" **19**
Perry, Ruth **19**
Tosh, Peter **9**

Republican National Convention
Allen, Ethel D. **13**

Republic of New Africa (RNA)
Williams, Robert F. **11**

Restaurants
Cain, Herman **15**
Hawkins, La-Van **17**
Smith, Barbara **11**

Revolutionary Party of Tanzania
See Chama cha Mapinduzi

Rhythm and blues/soul music
Adams, Oleta **18**
Ayers, Roy **16**
Belle, Regina **1**
Brandy **14**
Braxton, Toni **15**
Busby, Jheryl **3**
Campbell, Tisha **8**
Charles, Ray **16**
Clinton, George **9**
Cole, Natalie Maria **17**
Combs, Sean "Puffy" **17**
Cooke, Sam **17**
Downing, Will **19**
Dre, Dr. **14**
Dupri, Jermaine **13**
Edmonds, Kenneth "Babyface" **10**
Foxx, Jamie **15**
Franklin, Aretha **11**
Gaye, Marvin **2**
Green, Al **13**
Hathaway, Donny **18**
Houston, Whitney **7**
Hyman, Phyllis **19**
Jackson, Janet **6**
Jackson, Michael **19**
James, Etta **13**
James, Rick **17**
Johnson, Robert **2**
Jones, Quincy **8**
Kelly, R. **18**
Knight, Gladys **16**
Little Richard **15**
Mayfield, Curtis **2**
McKnight, Brian **18**
Ndegéocello, Me'Shell **15**
Prince **18**
Redding, Otis **16**

Robinson, Smokey **3**
Ross, Diana **8**
Sade **15**
Sweat, Keith **19**
Turner, Tina **6**
Vandross, Luther **13**
White, Barry **13**
Williams, Vanessa L. **4, 17**
Wilson, Cassandra **16**
Wilson, Nancy **10**
Wonder, Stevie **11**

RNA
See Republic of New Africa

Rock and Roll Hall of Fame
Franklin, Aretha **11**
James, Etta **13**
Wonder, Stevie **11**

Rockefeller Foundation
Price, Hugh B. **9**

Rock music
Clinton, George **9**
Hendrix, Jimi **10**
Ice-T **6**
Kravitz, Lenny **10**
Little Richard **15**
Prince **18**
Turner, Tina **6**

Rockets
Williams, O. S. **13**

Rodeo
Pickett, Bill **11**
Sampson, Charles **13**

Roman Catholic Church
Arinze, Francis Cardinal **19**
Aristide, Jean-Bertrand **6**
Clements, George **2**
Guy, Rosa **5**
Stallings, George A., Jr. **6**

Royal Ballet
Jackson, Isaiah **3**

Royalty
Christophe, Henri **9**

RPT
See Togolese People's Rally

Rush Artists Management Co.
Simmons, Russell **1**

Russell-McCloud and Associates
Russell-McCloud, Patricia A. **17**

SAA
See Syndicat Agricole Africain

SACC
See South African Council of Churches

Sacramento Kings basketball team
Russell, Bill **8**

SADCC
See Southern African Development Coordination Conference

St. Louis Browns baseball team
Paige, Satchel **7**

St. Louis Cardinals baseball team
Baylor, Don **6**
Brock, Lou **18**
Flood, Curt **10**

St. Louis city government
Bosley, Freeman, Jr. **7**

St. Louis Hawks basketball team
See Atlanta Hawks basketball team

San Antonio Spurs basketball team
Lucas, John **7**

San Diego Chargers football team
Barnes, Ernie **16**

San Diego Conquistadors
Chamberlain, Wilt **18**

San Diego Gulls hockey team
O'Ree, Willie **5**

San Diego Hawks hockey team
O'Ree, Willie **5**

San Diego Padres baseball team
Gwynn, Tony **18**
Sheffield, Gary **16**
Winfield, Dave **5**

San Francisco 49ers football team
Edwards, Harry **2**
Green, Dennis **5**
Lott, Ronnie **9**
Rice, Jerry **5**
Simpson, O. J. **15**

San Francisco Giants baseball team
Baker, Dusty **8**
Bonds, Barry **6**
Mays, Willie **3**
Morgan, Joe Leonard **9**
Robinson, Frank **9**

Sankofa Film and Video
Julien, Isaac **3**

Saturday Night Live
Murphy, Eddie **4**
Rock, Chris **3**

Saxophone
Bechet, Sidney **18**
Coltrane, John **19**
Hawkins, Coleman **9**

Washington, Grover, Jr. **17**

Schomburg Center for Research in Black Culture
Andrews, Bert **13**
Dodson, Howard, Jr. **7**
Hutson, Jean Blackwell **16**
Schomburg, Arthur Alfonso **9**

School desegregation
Fortune, T. Thomas **6**
Hamer, Fannie Lou **6**

Science fiction
Bell, Derrick **6**
Butler, Octavia **8**
Delany, Samuel R., Jr. **9**

SCLC
See Southern Christian Leadership Conference

Sculpture
Barthe, Richmond **15**
Bailey, Radcliffe **19**
Brown, Donald **19**
Burke, Selma **16**
Catlett, Elizabeth **2**
Guyton, Tyree **9**
Hunt, Richard **6**
Lewis, Edmonia **10**
McGee, Charles **10**
Ringgold, Faith **4**
Saar, Alison **16**
Savage, Augusta **12**
Shabazz, Attallah **6**

Seattle city government
Rice, Norm **8**

Seattle Mariners baseball team
Griffey, Ken, Jr. **12**

Seattle Supersonics basketball team
Lucas, John **7**
Russell, Bill **8**
Wilkens, Lenny **11**

Second Republic (Nigeria)
Obasanjo, Olusegun **5**

Seismology
Person, Waverly **9**

Senate Confirmation Hearings
Ogletree, Charles, Jr. **12**

Sesame Street
Clash, Kevin **14**
Glover, Savion **14**

Sexual harassment
Gomez-Preston, Cheryl **9**
Hill, Anita **5**
Thomas, Clarence **2**

Shrine of the Black Madonna
Agyeman, Jaramogi Abebe **10**

Sickle cell anemia
Satcher, David **7**

Silicon Graphics Incorporated
Hannah, Marc **10**

Slavery
Asante, Molefi Kete **3**
Bennett, Lerone, Jr. **5**
Douglas, Aaron **7**
Du Bois, W. E. B. **3**
Dunbar, Paul Laurence **8**
Gaines, Ernest J. **7**
Haley, Alex **4**
Harper, Frances Ellen Watkins **11**
Johnson, Charles **1**
Morrison, Toni **2**
Muhammad, Elijah **4**
Patterson, Orlando **4**
Pleasant, Mary Ellen **9**
Stephens, Charlotte Andrews **14**
Stewart, Maria W. Miller **19**
Taylor, Susie King **13**
Tubman, Harriet **9**
X, Malcolm **1**

SNCC
See Student Nonviolent Coordinating Committee

Soccer
Jones, Cobi N'Gai **18**
Milla, Roger **2**
Pelé **7**

Social disorganization theory
Frazier, E. Franklin **10**

Social science
Berry, Mary Frances **7**
Bunche, Ralph J. **5**
Clark, Kenneth B. **5**
Cobbs, Price M. **9**
Frazier, E. Franklin **10**
Harris, Eddy L. **18**
Haynes, George Edmund **8**
Lawrence-Lightfoot, Sara **10**
Marable, Manning **10**
Steele, Claude Mason **13**
Woodson, Robert L. **10**

Social work
Auguste, Rose-Anne **13**
Berry, Bertice **8**
Dunham, Katherine **4**
Hale, Clara **16**
Hale, Lorraine **8**
Harris, Alice **7**
Haynes, George Edmund **8**
Lewis, Thomas **19**
Little, Robert L. **2**
Robinson, Rachel **16**
Waddles, Charleszetta (Mother) **10**
Young, Whitney M., Jr. **4**

Socialist Party of Senegal
Diouf, Abdou **3**

Soledad Brothers
Jackson, George **14**

Soul City, NC
McKissick, Floyd B. **3**

Soul Train
Cornelius, Don **4**

South African Communist Party
Hani, Chris **6**

South African Council of Churches (SACC)
Tutu, Desmond **6**

South African Defence Force (SADF)
Nujoma, Samuel **10**

South African literature
Mathabane, Mark **5**

South African Students' Organization
Biko, Steven **4**

Southern African Development Community (SADC)
Mbuende, Kaire **12**

Southern African Development Coordination Conference (SADCC)
Masire, Quett **5**
Numjoma, Samuel **10**

Southern African Project
McDougall, Gay J. **11**

Southern Christian Leadership Conference (SCLC)
Abernathy, Ralph **1**
Angelou, Maya **1, 15**
Baker, Ella **5**
Chavis, Benjamin **6**
Dee, Ruby **8**
Fauntroy, Walter E. **11**
Hooks, Benjamin L. **2**
Jackson, Jesse **1**
King, Martin Luther, Jr. **1**
Lowery, Joseph **2**
Moses, Robert Parris **11**
Rustin, Bayard **4**
Williams, Hosea Lorenzo **15**
Young, Andrew **3**

South West African People's Organization (SWAPO)
Nujoma, Samuel **10**

Space Shuttle
Bluford, Guy **2**
Bolden, Charles F., Jr. **7**
Gregory, Frederick D. **8**

Jemison, Mae C. **1**
McNair, Ronald **3**

Spectroscopy
Quarterman, Lloyd Albert **4**

Spelman College
Cole, Johnnetta B. **5**

Spingarn medal
Aaron, Hank **5**
Ailey, Alvin **8**
Anderson, Marian **2**
Angelou, Maya **15**
Bethune, Mary McLeod **4**
Bradley, Thomas **2**
Brooke, Edward **8**
Bunche, Ralph J. **5**
Carver, George Washington **4**
Clark, Kenneth B. **5**
Cosby, Bill **7**
Davis, Sammy Jr. **18**
Drew, Charles Richard **7**
Du Bois, W. E. B. **3**
Ellington, Duke **5**
Evers, Medgar **3**
Grimké, Archibald H. **9**
Haley, Alex **4**
Hastie, William H. **8**
Hayes, Roland **4**
Hinton, William Augustus **8**
Hooks, Benjamin L. **2**
Horne, Lena **5**
Houston, Charles Hamilton **4**
Hughes, Langston **4**
Jackson, Jesse **1**
Johnson, James Weldon **5**
Johnson, John H. **3**
Jordan, Barbara **4**
Julian, Percy Lavon **6**
Just, Ernest Everett **3**
King, Martin Luther, Jr. **1**
Lawless, Theodore K. **8**
Lawrence, Jacob **4**
Marshall, Thurgood **1**
Mays, Benjamin E. **7**
Parks, Gordon **1**
Parks, Rosa **1**
Powell, Colin **1**
Price, Leontyne **1**
Randolph, A. Philip **3**
Robeson, Paul **2**
Robinson, Jackie **6**
Staupers, Mabel K. **7**
Sullivan, Leon H. **3**
Weaver, Robert C. **8**
White, Walter F. **4**
Wilder, L. Douglas **3**
Wilkins, Roy **4**
Williams, Paul R. **9**
Woodson, Carter **2**
Wright, Louis Tompkins **4**
Wright, Richard **5**
Young, Andrew **3**
Young, Coleman **1**

Spirituals
Anderson, Marian **2**

Hayes, Roland **4**
Jackson, Mahalia **5**
Joyner, Matilda Sissieretta **15**
Norman, Jessye **5**
Reese, Della **6**
Robeson, Paul **2**

Sports psychology
Edwards, Harry **2**

State University of New York System
Wharton, Clifton R., Jr. **7**

Stonewall 25
Norman, Pat **10**

Structural Readjustment Program
Babangida, Ibrahim **4**

Student Nonviolent Coordinating Committee (SNCC)
Al-Amin, Jamil Abdullah **6**
Baker, Ella **5**
Barry, Marion S. **7**
Blackwell, Unita **17**
Bond, Julian **2**
Carmichael, Stokely **5**
Clark, Septima **7**
Crouch, Stanley **11**
Davis, Angela **5**
Forman, James **7**
Hamer, Fannie Lou **6**
Holland, Endesha Ida Mae **3**
Lester, Julius **9**
Lewis, John **2**
Moses, Robert Parris **11**
Norton, Eleanor Holmes **7**
Poussaint, Alvin F. **5**
Reagon, Bernice Johnson **7**

Sundance Film Festival
Harris, Leslie **6**

Supreme Court
See U.S. Supreme Court

Supreme Court of Haiti
Pascal-Trouillot, Ertha **3**

Surrealism
Ellison, Ralph **7**
Lee-Smith, Hughie **5**

SWAPO
See South West African People's Organization

Sweet Honey in the Rock
Reagon, Bernice Johnson **7**

Syndicat Agricole Africain (SAA)
Houphouët-Boigny, Félix **4**

Synthetic chemistry
Julian, Percy Lavon **6**

Tampa Bay Buccaneers football team
Dungy, Tony **17**

Tanga Consultative Congress (Tanzania)
Nujoma, Samuel **10**

Tanganyikan African National Union (TANU)
Nyerere, Julius **5**

TANU
See Tanganyikan African National Union

Tanzanian African National Union (TANU)
See Tanganyikan African National Union

Tap dancing
Bates, Peg Leg **14**
Glover, Savion **14**
Hines, Gregory **1**

TBS
See Turner Broadcasting System

Teachers Insurance and Annuity Association and the College Retirement Equities Fund (TIAA-CREF)
Wharton, Clifton R., Jr. **7**

Teaching
Early, Gerald **15**
Gates, Sylvester James, Jr. **15**

TEF
See Theological Education Fund

Television scores
Jones, Quincy **8**

Television
Arkadie, Kevin **17**
Bowser, Yvette Lee **17**
Burnett, Charles **16**
Curtis-Hall, Vondie **17**
Cheadle, Don **19**
Eubanks, Kevin **15**
Hemsley, Sherman **19**
Jackson, George **19**
Moss, Carlton **16**
Rollins, Howard E. Jr., **17**
Thigpen, Lynne **17**

Tennis
Ashe, Arthur **1, 18**
Garrison, Zina **2**
Gibson, Althea **8**
Lucas, John **7**
McNeil, Lori **1**
Noah, Yannick **4**
Washington, MaliVai **8**
Williams, Venus **17**

Texas House of Representatives
Johnson, Eddie Bernice **8**

Texas Rangers baseball team
Cottrell, Comer **11**

Texas State Senate
Johnson, Eddie Bernice **8**
Jordan, Barbara **4**

Theological Education Fund (TEF)
Gordon, Pamela **17**
Tutu, Desmond **6**

Theology
Franklin, Robert M. **13**

Third World Press
Madhubuti, Haki R. **7**

Threads 4 Life
Jones, Carl **7**
Kani, Karl **10**
Walker, T. J. **7**

TIAA-CREF
See Teachers Insurance and Annuity Association and the College Retirement Equities Fund

Time-Warner Inc.
Parsons, Richard Dean **11**

TLC Beatrice International Holdings, Inc.
Lewis, Reginald F. **6**

TLC Group L.P.
Lewis, Reginald F. **6**

Today
Gumbel, Bryant **14**

Togolese Army
Eyadéma, Gnassingbé **7**

Togolese People's Rally (RPT)
Eyadéma, Gnassingbé **7**

Tonight Show, The
Eubanks, Kevin **15**

Tony awards
Allen, Debbie **13**
Belafonte, Harry **4**
Carroll, Diahann **9**
Clarke, Hope **14**
Faison, George **16**
Fishburne, Larry **4**
Horne, Lena **5**
Hyman, Phyllis **19**
Jones, James Earl **3**
Richards, Lloyd **2**
Thigpen, Lynne **17**
Vereen, Ben **4**
Wilson, August **7**
Wolfe, George C. **6**

Toronto Blue Jays baseball team
Winfield, Dave **5**

Toronto Raptors basketball team
Thomas, Isiah **7**

Track and field
Christie, Linford **8**
Devers, Gail **7**
Johnson, Michael **13**
Joyner-Kersee, Jackie **5**
Lewis, Carl **4**
Moses, Edwin **8**
Mutola, Maria **12**
Owens, Jesse **2**
Powell, Mike **7**
Quirot, Ana **13**
Rudolph, Wilma **4**

TransAfrica, Inc.
Robinson, Randall **7**

Transition
Soyinka, Wole **4**

Transitional Committee for National Recovery (Guinea; CTRN)
Conté, Lansana **7**

Transplant surgery
Callender, Clive O. **3**
Kountz, Samuel L. **10**

"Trial of the Century"
Cochran, Johnnie L., Jr. **11**
Darden, Christopher **13**
Simpson, O. J. **15**

Trinidad Theatre Workshop
Walcott, Derek **5**

Trumpet
Armstrong, Louis **2**
Davis, Miles **4**
Ellison, Ralph **7**
Gillespie, Dizzy **1**

Turner Broadcasting System (TBS)
Clayton, Xernona **3**

Tuskegee Airmen
James, Daniel, Jr. **16**
Patterson, Frederick Douglass **12**

Tuskegee Experiment Station
Carver, George Washington **4**

U.S. Department of Agriculture
Watkins, Shirley R. **17**
Williams, Hosea Lorenzo **15**

U.S. District Court judge
Keith, Damon J. **16**
Parsons, James **14**

UCC
See United Church of Christ

UFBL
See Universal Foundation for Better Living

UGA
See United Golf Association

Umkhonto we Sizwe
Hani, Chris **6**
Mandela, Nelson **1, 14**

UN
See United Nations

UNCF
See United Negro College Fund

Uncle Noname Cookie Company
Amos, Wally **9**

Underground Railroad
Cohen, Anthony **15**

Unemployment and Poverty Action Committee
Forman, James **7**

UNESCO
See United Nations Educational, Scientific, and Cultural Organization

UNIA
See United Negro Improvement Association

UNICEF
See United Nations Children's Fund

Unions
Clay, William Lacy **8**
Crockett, George, Jr. **10**
Europe, James Reese **10**
Farmer, James **2**
Hilliard, David **7**
Ramaphosa, Cyril **3**
Randolph, A. Philip **3**
Touré, Sekou **6**

UNIP
See United National Independence Party

UNITA
See National Union for the Total Independence of Angola

United Bermuda Party
Gordon, Pamela **17**

United Church of Christ (UCC)
Chavis, Benjamin **6**

United Democratic Front (UDF)
Muluzi, Bakili **14**

United Golf Association (UGA)
Elder, Lee 6
Sifford, Charlie 4

United Methodist Church
Lewis, Shirley A. R. 14

United National Independence Party (UNIP)
Kaunda, Kenneth 2

United Nations (UN)
Annan, Kofi Atta 15
Bunche, Ralph J. 5
Diouf, Abdou 3
Lafontant, Jewel Stradford 3
Mongella, Gertrude 11
Perkins, Edward 5
Sampson, Edith S. 4
Young, Andrew 3

United Nations Children's Fund (UNICEF)
Baker, Gwendolyn Calvert 9
Belafonte, Harry 4
Machel, Graca Simbine 16

United Nations Educational, Scientific, and Cultural Organization (UNESCO)
Diop, Cheikh Anta 4
Frazier, E. Franklin 10
Machel, Graca Simbine 16

United Negro College Fund (UNCF)
Boyd, T. B. III 6
Edley, Christopher 2
Gray, William H. III 3
Jordan, Vernon E. 3
Mays, Benjamin E. 7
Patterson, Frederick Douglass 12

United Negro Improvement Association (UNIA)
Garvey, Marcus 1

United Parcel Service
Washington, Patrice Clarke 12

United Somali Congress (USC)
Ali Mahdi Mohamed 5

United States Football League (USFL)
White, Reggie 6

United Workers Union of South Africa (UWUSA)
Buthelezi, Mangosuthu Gatsha 9

Universal Foundation for Better Living (UFBL)
Colemon, Johnnie 11
Reese, Della 6

University of California administration
Massey, Walter E. 5

University of Colorado administration
Berry, Mary Frances 7

UniverSoul Circus
Walker, Cedric "Ricky" 19

Urban League (regional)
Clayton, Xernona 3
Jacob, John E. 2
Mays, Benjamin E. 7
Young, Whitney M., Jr. 4

Urban renewal
Archer, Dennis 7
Barry, Marion S. 7
Bosley, Freeman, Jr. 7
Collins, Barbara-Rose 7
Harris, Alice 7
Lane, Vincent 5
Waters, Maxine 3

US
Karenga, Maulana 10

U.S. Air Force
Davis, Benjamin O., Jr. 2
Gregory, Frederick D. 8
Harris, Marcelite Jordan 16
James, Daniel, Jr. 16

U.S. Armed Forces Nurse Corps
Staupers, Mabel K. 7

U.S. Army
Cadoria, Sherian Grace 14
Davis, Benjamin O., Sr. 4
Flipper, Henry O. 3
Powell, Colin 1
Watkins, Perry 12
West, Togo D., Jr. 16

U.S. Attorney's Office
Lafontant, Jewel Stradford 3

U.S. Basketball League (USBL)
Lucas, John 7

USBL
See U.S. Basketball League

USC
See United Somali Congress

U.S. Cabinet
Brown, Ron 5
Elders, Joycelyn 6
Espy, Mike 6
Harris, Patricia Roberts 2
Herman, Alexis M. 15
O'Leary, Hazel 6
Slater, Rodney E. 15
Sullivan, Louis 8
Weaver, Robert C. 8

U.S. Circuit Court of Appeals
Hastie, William H. 8
Keith, Damon J. 16

U.S. Commission on Civil Rights
Berry, Mary Frances 7

U.S. Court of Appeals
Higginbotham, A. Leon, Jr. 13
Kearse, Amalya Lyle 12

USDA
See U.S. Department of Agriculture

U.S. Department of Agriculture (USDA)
Espy, Mike 6

U.S. Department of Commerce
Brown, Ron 5
Irving, Larry, Jr. 12
Person, Waverly 9
Wilkins, Roger 2

U.S. Department of Defense
Tribble, Israel, Jr. 8

U.S. Department of Education
Hill, Anita 5
Thomas, Clarence 2
Tribble, Israel, Jr. 8

U.S. Department of Energy
O'Leary, Hazel 6

U.S. Department of Health and Human Services (HHS)
See also U.S. Department of Health, Education, and Welfare
Sullivan, Louis 8

U.S. Department of Health, Education, and Welfare (HEW)
Bell, Derrick 6
Berry, Mary Frances 7
Harris, Patricia Roberts 2
Johnson, Eddie Bernice 8

U.S. Department of Housing and Urban Development (HUD)
Harris, Patricia Roberts 2
Weaver, Robert C. 8

U.S. Department of Justice
Bell, Derrick 6
Campbell, Bill 9
Days, Drew S., III 10
Guinier, Lani 7
Holder, Eric H., Jr. 9
Lafontant, Jewel Stradford 3
Lewis, Delano 7
Patrick, Deval 12
Wilkins, Roger 2

U.S. Department of Labor
Crockett, George, Jr. 10

Herman, Alexis M. **15**

U.S. Department of Social Services
Little, Robert L. **2**

U.S. Department of State
Bethune, Mary McLeod **4**
Bunche, Ralph J. **5**
Keyes, Alan L. **11**
Lafontant, Jewel Stradford **3**
Perkins, Edward **5**
Rice, Condoleezza **3**
Wharton, Clifton R., Jr. **7**

U.S. Department of the Interior
Person, Waverly **9**

U.S. Department of Veterans Affairs
Brown, Jesse **6**

U.S. Diplomatic Corps
Grimké, Archibald H. **9**
Harris, Patricia Roberts **2**
Stokes, Carl B. **10**

USFL
See United States Football League

U.S. Geological Survey
Person, Waverly **9**

U.S. House of Representatives
Chisholm, Shirley **2**
Clay, William Lacy **8**
Collins, Barbara-Rose **7**
Collins, Cardiss **10**
Conyers, John, Jr. **4**
Crockett, George, Jr. **10**
Dellums, Ronald **2**
Espy, Mike **6**
Fauntroy, Walter E. **11**
Fields, Cleo **13**
Flake, Floyd H. **18**
Ford, Harold E., Jr., **16**
Franks, Gary **2**
Gray, William H. III **3**
Hastings, Alcee L. **16**
Jackson, Jesse, Jr. **14**
Jordan, Barbara **4**
Kilpatrick, Carolyn Cheeks **16**
Leland, Mickey **2**
Lewis, John **2**
Meek, Carrie **6**
Mfume, Kweisi **6**
Norton, Eleanor Holmes **7**
Owens, Major **6**
Payne, Donald M. **2**
Pinchback, P. B. S. **9**
Powell, Adam Clayton, Jr. **3**
Rangel, Charles **3**
Stokes, Louis **3**
Towns, Edolphus **19**
Washington, Harold **6**
Waters, Maxine **3**
Wheat, Alan **14**
Young, Andrew **3**

U.S. Joint Chiefs of Staff
Powell, Colin **1**

U.S. Marines
Bolden, Charles F., Jr. **7**
Brown, Jesse **6**
Von Lipsey, Roderick K. **11**

U.S. Navy
Doby, Lawrence Eugene, Sr. **16**
Gravely, Samuel L., Jr. **5**
Reason, J. Paul **19**

U.S. Peace Corps
Days, Drew S., III **10**
Lewis, Delano **7**

U.S. Senate
Braun, Carol Moseley **4**
Brooke, Edward **8**
Dodson, Howard, Jr. **7**
Johnson, Eddie Bernice **8**
Pinchback, P. B. S. **9**

U.S. Supreme Court
Marshall, Thurgood **1**
Thomas, Clarence **2**

U.S. Surgeon General
Elders, Joycelyn **6**

U.S. Virgin Islands government
Hastie, William H. **8**

UWUSA
See United Workers Union of South Africa

Vaudeville
Bates, Peg Leg **14**
Davis, Sammy Jr. **18**
Johnson, Jack **8**
McDaniel, Hattie **5**
Robinson, Bill "Bojangles" **11**
Waters, Ethel **7**

Veterinary science
Jawara, Sir Dawda Kairaba **11**
Patterson, Frederick Douglass **12**
Thomas, Vivien **9**

Vibe
Jones, Quincy **8**

Village Voice
Crouch, Stanley **11**

Virginia state government
Wilder, L. Douglas **3**

Virgina Squires basketball team
Erving, Julius **18**

Voodoo
Dunham, Katherine **4**
Guy, Rosa **5**
Hurston, Zora Neale **3**

Pierre, Andre **17**

Voting rights
Clark, Septima **7**
Forman, James **7**
Guinier, Lani **7**
Hamer, Fannie Lou **6**
Harper, Frances Ellen Watkins **11**
Hill, Jessie, Jr. **13**
Johnson, Eddie Bernice **8**
Lampkin, Daisy **19**
Mandela, Nelson **1, 14**
Moses, Robert Parris **11**
Terrell, Mary Church **9**
Trotter, Monroe **9**
Tubman, Harriet **9**
Wells-Barnett, Ida B. **8**
Williams, Hosea Lorenzo **15**
Woodard, Alfre **9**

Vulcan Realty and Investment Company
Gaston, Arthur G. **4**

WAAC
See Women's Auxiliary Army Corp

WAC
See Women's Army Corp

Walter Payton Inc.
Payton, Walter **11**

War Resister's League (WRL)
Carter, Mandy **11**

Washington Color Field group
Thomas, Alma **14**

Washington Mystics basketball team
McCray, Nikki **18**

Washington, DC City Council
Fauntroy, Walter E. **11**

Washington, DC city government
Barry, Marion S. **7**
Dixon, Sharon Pratt **1**
Fauntroy, Walter E. **11**
Norton, Eleanor Holmes **7**

Washington Post
Maynard, Robert C. **7**
McCall, Nathan **8**
Nelson, Jill **6**
Raspberry, William **2**
Wilkins, Roger **2**

Washington Wizards basketball team
Howard, Juwan **15**
Lucas, John **7**
Webber, Chris **15**

WBA
See World Boxing Association

WBC
See World Boxing Council

WCC
See World Council of Churches

Weather
Christian, Spencer 15
McEwen, Mark 5

Welfare reform
Bryant, Wayne R. 6
Williams, Walter E. 4

West Indian folklore
Walcott, Derek 5

West Indian folk songs
Belafonte, Harry 4

West Indian literature
Guy, Rosa 5
Kincaid, Jamaica 4
Marshall, Paule 7
McKay, Claude 6
Walcott, Derek 5

West Point
Davis, Benjamin O., Jr. 2
Flipper, Henry O. 3

West Side Preparatory School
Collins, Marva 3

White House Conference on Civil Rights
Randolph, A. Philip 3

Whitney Museum of American Art
Golden, Thelma 10

WHO
See Women Helping Offenders

"Why Are You on This Planet?"
Yoba, Malik 11

William Morris Talent Agency
Amos, Wally 9

WillieWear Ltd.
Smith, Willi 8

Wilmington 10
Chavis, Benjamin 6

WOMAD
See World of Music, Arts, and Dance

Women Helping Offenders (WHO)
Holland, Endesha Ida Mae 3

Women's Auxiliary Army Corps
See Women's Army Corp

Women's Army Corps (WAC)
Adams Early, Charity 13

Cadoria, Sherian Grace 14

Women's issues
Allen, Ethel D. 13
Angelou, Maya 1, 15
Baker, Ella 5
Berry, Mary Frances 7
Brown, Elaine 8
Campbell, Bebe Moore 6
Cannon, Katie 10
Charles, Mary Eugenia 10
Christian-Green, Donna M. 17
Clark, Septima 7
Cole, Johnnetta B. 5
Dash, Julie 4
Davis, Angela 5
Edelman, Marian Wright 5
Elders, Joycelyn 6
Fauset, Jessie 7
Giddings, Paula 11
Goldberg, Whoopi 4
Grimké, Archibald H. 9
Guy-Sheftall, Beverly 13
Hale, Clara 16
Hale, Lorraine 8
Hamer, Fannie Lou 6
Harper, Frances Ellen Watkins 11
Harris, Alice 7
Harris, Leslie 6
Harris, Patricia Roberts 2
Height, Dorothy I. 2
Hernandez, Aileen Clarke 13
Hill, Anita 5
Holland, Endesha Ida Mae 3
hooks, bell 5
Jordan, Barbara 4
Jordan, June 7
Lampkin, Daisy 19
Larsen, Nella 10
Lorde, Audre 6
Marshall, Paule 7
McCabe, Jewell Jackson 10
McMillan, Terry 4, 15
Meek, Carrie 6
Mongella, Gertrude 11
Morrison, Toni 2
Naylor, Gloria 10
Nelson, Jill 6
Nichols, Nichelle 11
Norman, Pat 10
Norton, Eleanor Holmes 7
Parker, Pat 19
Rawlings, Nana Konadu Agyeman 13
Ringgold, Faith 4
Shange, Ntozake 8
Simpson, Carole 6
Terrell, Mary Church 9
Tubman, Harriet 9
Vanzant, Iyanla 17
Walker, Alice 1
Walker, Maggie Lena 17
Wallace, Michele Faith 13
Waters, Maxine 3
Wattleton, Faye 9
Winfrey, Oprah 2, 15

Women's National Basketball Association (WNBA)
Cooper, Cynthia 17
Leslie, Lisa 16
McCray, Nikki 18
Swoopes, Sheryl 12

Women's Strike for Peace
King, Coretta Scott 3

Worker's Party (Brazil)
da Silva, Benedita 5

Workplace equity
Hill, Anita 5
Clark, Septima 7
Nelson, Jill 6
Simpson, Carole 6

Works Progress Administration (WPA)
Baker, Ella 5
Douglas, Aaron 7
Dunham, Katherine 4
Lawrence, Jacob 4
Lee-Smith, Hughie 5
Wright, Richard 5

World African Hebrew Israelite Community
Ben-Israel, Ben Ami 11

World beat
Belafonte, Harry 4
Fela 1
N'Dour, Youssou 1
Ongala, Remmy 9
Perry, Lee "Scratch" 19

World Bank
Soglo, Nicéphore 15

World Boxing Association (WBA)
Whitaker, Pernell 10

World Boxing Council (WBF)
Whitaker, Pernell 10

World Council of Churches (WCC)
Mays, Benjamin E. 7
Tutu, Desmond 6

World Cup
Milla, Roger 2
Pelé 7

World hunger
Belafonte, Harry 4
Iman 4
Jones, Quincy 8
Leland, Mickey 2
Masire, Quett 5
Obasanjo, Olusegun 5

World of Music, Arts, and Dance (WOMAD)
Ongala, Remmy 9

WPA
See Works Progress Administration

WRL
See War Resister's League

Xerox Corp.
Rand, A. Barry **6**

Yab Yum Entertainment
Edmonds, Tracey **16**

Yale Child Study Center
Comer, James P. **6**

Yale Repertory Theater
Dutton, Charles S. **4**
Richards, Lloyd **2**
Wilson, August **7**

Yale School of Drama
Dutton, Charles S. **4**
Richards, Lloyd **2**

YMCA
See Young Men's Christian Associations

Yoruban folklore
Soyinka, Wole **4**
Vanzant, Iyanla **17**

Young Men's Christian Association (YMCA)
Butts, Calvin O., III **9**
Goode, Mal **13**
Hope, John **8**
Mays, Benjamin E. **7**

Young Negroes' Cooperative League
Baker, Ella **5**

Young Women's Christian Association (YWCA)
Baker, Ella **5**
Baker, Gwendolyn Calvert **9**
Clark, Septima **7**
Height, Dorothy I. **2**
Jenkins, Ella **15**
Sampson, Edith S. **4**

Youth Pride Inc.
Barry, Marion S. **7**

Youth Services Administration
Little, Robert L. **2**

YWCA
See Young Women's Christian Association

ZANLA
See Zimbabwe African National Liberation Army

ZAPU
See Zimbabwe African People's Union

Zimbabwe African National Liberation Army (ZANLA)
Mugabe, Robert Gabriel **10**

Zimbabwe African People's Union (ZAPU)
Mugabe, Robert Gabriel **10**
Nkomo, Joshua **4**

ZTA
See Zululand Territorial Authority

Zululand Territorial Authority (ZTA)
Buthelezi, Mangosuthu Gatsha **9**

Cumulative Name Index

Volume numbers appear in **bold**.

Aaron, Hank 1934— **5**
Aaron, Henry Louis
　See Aaron, Hank
Abacha, Sani 1943— **11**
Abbott, Diane (Julie) 1953— **9**
Abdul-Jabbar, Kareem 1947— **8**
Abdulmajid, Iman Mohamed
　See Iman
Abernathy, Ralph David 1926-1990 **1**
Abu-Jamal, Mumia 1954— **15**
Achebe, (Albert) Chinua(lumogu) 1930— **6**
Adams, Oleta 19(?)(?)– **18**
Adams Early, Charity (Edna) 1918— **13**
Adams, Floyd, Jr. 1945— **12**
Adams, Yolanda 1961– **17**
Adu, Helen Folasade
　See Sade
Agyeman, Jaramogi Abebe 1911— **10**
Agyeman Rawlings, Nana Konadu 1948— **13**
Aiken, Loretta Mary
　See Mabley, Jackie "Moms" **15**
Ailey, Alvin 1931-1989 **8**
Al-Amin, Jamil Abdullah 1943— **6**
Alcindor, Ferdinand Lewis
　See Abdul-Jabbar, Kareem
Alexander, Archie Alphonso 1888-1958 **14**
Alexander, Joyce London 1949- **18**
Ali Mahdi Mohamed 1940— **5**
Ali, Muhammad 1942— **2, 16**
Allen, Byron 1961— **3**
Allen, Debbie 1950— **13**
Allen, Ethel D. 1929-1981 **13**
Allen, Richard 1760-1831 **14**
Amos, John 1941— **8**
Amos, Wally 1937— **9**
Anderson, Marian 1902— **2**
Andrews, Bert 1929-1993 **13**
Andrews, Raymond 1934-1991 **4**
Angelou, Maya 1928— **1, 15**
Anna Marie
　See Lincoln, Abbey
Annan, Kofi Atta 1938— **15**
Ansa, Tina McElroy 1949— **14**
Archer, Dennis (Wayne) 1942— **7**
Arinze, Francis Cardinal 1932– **19**

Aristide, Jean-Bertrand 1953— **6**
Arkadie, Kevin 1957– **17**
Armstrong, (Daniel) Louis 1900-1971 **2**
Armstrong, Robb 1962— **15**
Asante, Molefi Kete 1942— **3**
Ashe, Arthur Robert, Jr. 1943-1993 **1, 18**
Ashley, Maurice 1966— **15**
Atkins, David
　See Sinbad
Auguste, (Marie Carmele) Rose-Anne 1963— **13**
Avant, Clarence 19(?)(?)– **19**
Ayers, Roy, 1940– **16**
Azikiwe, Nnamdi 1904-1996 **13**
Babangida, Ibrahim (Badamasi) 1941— **4**
Babyface
　See Edmonds, Kenneth "Babyface"
Bailey, Pearl Mae 1918-1990 **14**
Bailey, Radcliffe 1968– **19**
Bailey, Xenobia 1955(?)— **11**
Baker, Constance
　See Motley, Constance Baker
Baker, Dusty 1949– **8**
Baker, Ella 1903-1986 **5**
Baker, George
　See Divine, Father
Baker, Gwendolyn Calvert 1931— **9**
Baker, Houston A(lfred), Jr. 1943— **6**
Baker, Johnnie B., Jr.
　See Baker, Dusty
Baker, Josephine 1906-1975 **3**
Baldwin, James 1924-1987 **1**
Bambara, Toni Cade 1939— **10**
Banda, (Ngwazi) Hastings Kamuzu 1898(?)— **6**
Banks, Jeffrey 1953– **17**
Banks, Tyra 1973— **11**
Banks, William (Venoid) 1903-1985 **11**
Baraka, Amiri 1934— **1**
Barboza, Anthony 1944— **10**
Barden, Don H. 1943– **9**
Barkley, Charles (Wade) 1963— **5**
Barnes, Ernie 1938— **16**
Barrett, Andrew C. 1942(?)— **12**

Barrow, Joseph Louis
　See Louis, Joe
Barry, Marion S(hepilov, Jr.) 1936– **7**
Barthe, Richmond 1901-1989 **15**
Basquiat, Jean-Michel 1960-1988 **5**
Bassett, Angela 1959(?)— **6**
Bates, Clayton
　See Bates, Peg Leg
Bates, Daisy (Lee Gatson) 1914(?)— **13**
Bates, Peg Leg 1907— **14**
Baylor, Don(ald Edward) 1949— **6**
Beals, Jennifer 1963— **12**
Beals, Melba Patillo 1941— **15**
Bearden, Romare (Howard) 1912-1988 **2**
Beasley, Myrlie
　See Evers, Myrlie
Beaton, Norman Lugard 1934-1994 **14**
Bechet, Sidney 1897-1959 **18**
Beck, Robert
　See Iceberg Slim
Beckford, Tyson 1970— **11**
Belafonte, Harold George, Jr.
　See Belafonte, Harry
Belafonte, Harry 1927— **4**
Bell, Derrick (Albert, Jr.) 1930— **6**
Bell, Ralph S. 1934— **5**
Bellamy, Bill 1967— **12**
Belle, Albert (Jojuan) 1966— **10**
Belle, Regina 1963— **1**
Belton, Sharon Sayles 1951–**9, 16**
Ben-Israel, Ben Ami 1940(?)— **11**
Bennett, Lerone, Jr. 1928— **5**
Berry, Bertice 1960— **8**
Berry, Halle 1967(?)— **4, 19**
Berry, Mary Frances 1938— **7**
Bethune, Mary (Jane) McLeod 1875-1955 **4**
Biko, Stephen
　See Biko, Steven (Bantu)
Biko, Steven (Bantu) 1946-1977 **4**
Bing, Dave 1943— **3**
Bishop, Eric
　See Foxx, Jamie
Bizimungu, Pasteur – **19**
Black, Keith Lanier 1955– **18**
Blackwell, Unita 1933–**17**
Blair, Maxine

See Powell, Maxine
Bluford, Guion Stewart, Jr.
  See Bluford, Guy
Bluford, Guy 1942— **2**
Bluitt, Juliann Stephanie 1938— **14**
Bol, Manute 1963— **1**
Bolden, Charles F(rank), Jr. 1946— **7**
Bonaly, Surya 1973— **7**
Bond, (Horace) Julian 1940— **2**
Bonds, Barry (Lamar) 1964— **6**
Bonga, Kuenda 1942— **13**
Bongo, Albert-Bernard
  See Bongo, (El Hadj) Omar
Bongo, (El Hadj) Omar 1935— **1**
Bontemps, Arna(ud Wendell) 1902-1973 **8**
Borders, James (Buchanan, IV) 1949— **9**
Bosley, Freeman (Robertson), Jr. 1954— **7**
Bowe, Riddick (Lamont) 1967— **6**
Bowser, Yvette Lee 1965(?)– **17**
Boyd, T(heophilus) B(artholomew) III 1947— **6**
Boykin, Keith 1965— **14**
Bradley, Ed(ward R.) 1941— **2**
Bradley, Thomas 1917— **2**
Brandon, Barbara 1960(?)— **3**
Brandon, Thomas Terrell 1970– **16**
Brandy 1979— **14**
Braugher, Andre 1962(?)— **13**
Braun, Carol (Elizabeth) Moseley 1947— **4**
Braxton, Toni 1968(?)— **15**
Breedlove, Sarah
  See Walker, Madame C. J.
Brimmer, Andrew F(elton) 1926— **2**
Briscoe, Connie 1952— **15**
Brock, Louis Clark 1939– **18**
Brooke, Edward (William, III) 1919— **8**
Brooks, Avery 1949— **9**
Brooks, Gwendolyn 1917— **1**
Brown, Andre
  See Dr. Dre
Brown, Donald 1963– **19**
Brown, Elaine 1943— **8**
Brown, H. Rap
  See Al-Amin, Jamil Abdullah
Brown, Hubert Gerold
  See Al-Amin, Jamil Abdullah
Brown, James 1933— **15**
Brown, James Nathaniel
  See Brown, Jim
Brown, James Willie, Jr.
  See Komunyakaa, Yusef
Brown, Jesse 1944— **6**
Brown, Jim 1936— **11**
Brown, Lee P(atrick) 1937— **1**
Brown, Les(lie Calvin) 1945— **5**
Brown, Ron(ald Harmon) 1941— **5**
Brown, Sterling (Allen) 1901— **10**
Brown, Tony 1933— **3**
Brown, William Anthony
  See Brown, Tony
Brown, Willie L., Jr. 1934— **7**
Brown, Zora Kramer 1949— **12**
Brown Bomber, The
  See Louis, Joe
Brunson, Dorothy 1938— **1**
Bryant, Kobe 1978— **15**
Bryant, Wayne R(ichard) 1947— **6**
Bullard, Eugene Jacques 1894-1961 **12**
Bullock, Anna Mae
  See Turner, Tina
Bumbry, Grace (Ann) 1937— **5**
Bunche, Ralph J(ohnson) 1904-1971 **5**
Burke, Selma Hortense 1900-1995 **16**
Burley, Mary Lou
  See Williams, Mary Lou
Burnett, Charles 1944– **16**
Burnett, Chester Arthur
  See Howlin' Wolf
Burnett, Dorothy 1905-1995 **19**
Burroughs, Margaret Taylor 1917– **9**
Burton, LeVar(dis Robert Martyn) 1957– **8**
Busby, Jheryl 1949(?)— **3**
Buthelezi, Mangosuthu Gatsha 1928— **9**
Butler, Leroy III 1968– **17**
Butler, Octavia (Estellle) 1947— **8**
Butler, Paul D. 1961–**17**
Butts, Calvin O(tis), III 1950– **9**
Byrd, Donald 1949— **10**
Byrd, Michelle 1965– **19**
Byrd, Robert (Oliver Daniel, III) 1952— **11**
Byron, JoAnne Deborah
  See Shakur, Assata
Cade, Toni
  See Bambara, Toni Cade
Cadoria, Sherian Grace 1940— **14**
Caesar, Shirley 1938– **19**
Cain, Herman 1945— **15**
Callender, Clive O(rville) 1936— **3**
Calloway, Cabell III 1907-1994 **14**
Camp, Kimberly 1956— **19**
Campbell, Bebe Moore 1950— **6**
Campbell, Bill 1954— **9**
Campbell, Charleszetta Lena
  See Waddles, Charleszetta (Mother)
Campbell, E(lmer) Simms 1906-1971 **13**
Campbell, Naomi 1970— **1**
Campbell, Tisha 1969— **8**
Canegata, Leonard Lionel Cornelius
  See Lee, Canada
Cannon, Katie 1950— **10**
Carmichael, Stokely 1941— **5**
Carroll, Diahann 1935— **9**
Carson, Benjamin 1951— **1**
Carson, Josephine
  See Baker, Josephine
Carter, Ben
  See Ben-Israel, Ben Ami
Carter, Betty 1930–1998 **19**
Carter, Mandy 1946— **11**
Carter, Stephen L(isle) 1954— **4**
Carver, George Washington 1861(?)-1943 **4**
Cary, Lorene 1956— **3**
CasSelle, Malcolm 1970— **11**
Catlett, Elizabeth 1919— **2**
Chamberlain, Wilton Norman 1936– **18**
Chambers, Julius (LeVonne) 1936— **3**
Charlemagne, Emmanuel
  See Charlemagne, Manno
Charlemagne, Manno 1948— **11**
Charles, Mary Eugenia 1919— **10**
Charles, Ray 1930– **16**
Chavis, Benjamin (Franklin, Jr.) 1948— **6**
Cheadle, Don 1964– **19**
Cheatham, Doc 1905-1997 **17**
Chenault, Kenneth I. 1952— **4**
Chesimard, JoAnne (Deborah)
  See Shakur, Assata
Chideya, Farai 1969— **14**
Childress, Alice 1920-1994 **15**
Chisholm, Shirley (Anita St. Hill) 1924— **2**
Chissano, Joaquim (Alberto) 1939— **7**
Christian, Spencer 1947— **15**
Christian-Green, Donna M. 1945– **17**
Christie, Linford 1960— **8**
Christophe, Henri 1767-1820 **9**
Chuck D 1960— **9**
Clark, Celeste (Clesteen) Abraham 1953— **15**
Clark, Joe 1939— **1**
Clark, Kenneth B(ancroft) 1914— **5**
Clark, Kristin
  See Taylor, Kristin Clark
Clark, Patrick 1955— **14**
Clark, Septima (Poinsette) 1898-1987 **7**
Clarke, Hope — **14**
Clarke, Patrice Francise
  See Washington, Patrice Clarke
Clash, Kevin 1961(?)— **14**
Clay, Cassius Marcellus, Jr.
  See Ali, Muhammad
Clay, William Lacy 1931— **8**
Clayton, Constance 1937— **1**
Clayton, Xernona 1930— **3**
Claytor, Helen 1907— **14**
Cleage, Albert Buford
  See Agyeman, Jaramogi Abebe
Cleage, Pearl Michelle 1934– **17**
Cleaver, (Leroy) Eldridge 1935— **5**
Cleaver, Emanuel (II) 1944— **4**
Clements, George (Harold) 1932— **2**
Cleveland, James 1932(?)-1991 **19**
Clifton, Lucille 1936— **14**
Clinton, George (Edward) 1941— **9**
Coachman, Alice 1923– **18**
Cobbs, Price M(ashaw) 1928— **9**
Cochran, Johnnie (L., Jr.) 1937— **11**
Cohen, Anthony 1963— **15**

Cumulative Name Index

Colbert, Virgis William 1939– **17**
Cole, Johnnetta B(etsch) 1936– **5**
Cole, Nat King 1919-1965– **17**
Cole, Natalie Maria 1950– **17**
Coleman, Bessie 1892-1926 **9**
Coleman, Leonard S., Jr. 1949– **12**
Colemon, Johnnie 1921(?)– **11**
Collins, Albert 1932-1993 **12**
Collins, Barbara-Rose 1939– **7**
Collins, Cardiss 1931– **10**
Collins, Marva 1936– **3**
Coltrane, John William 1926-1967 **19**
Combs, Sean J. 1969– **17**
Cook, Wesley
  See Abu-Jamal, Mumia
Comer, James P(ierpont) 1934– **6**
Cone, James H. 1938– **3**
Connerly, Ward 1939– **14**
Conté, Lansana 1944(?)– **7**
Conyers, John, Jr. 1929– **4**
Cook, Sam 1931-1964 **17**
Cook, Samuel DuBois 1928– **14**
Cook, Wesley
  See Abu-Jamal, Mumia
Cooks, Patricia 1944-1989 **19**
Cooper, Cynthia 1963– **17**
Cooper, Edward S(awyer) 1926– **6**
Cooper, J. California 19??– **12**
Cornelius, Don 1936– **4**
Cosby, Bill 1937– **7**
Cosby, Camille Olivia Hanks 1944– **14**
Cosby, William Henry, Jr.
  See Cosby, Bill
Cose, Ellis 1951– **5**
Cottrell, Comer 1931– **11**
Crawford, Randy 1952– **19**
Crawford, Veronica
  See Crawford, Randy
Crew, Rudolph F. 1950(?)– **16**
Crockett, George (William), Jr. 1909– **10**
Crothers, Benjamin Sherman
  See Crothers, Scatman
Crothers, Scatman 1910-1986 **19**
Crowder, Henry 1895-1954(?) **16**
Crouch, Stanley 1945– **11**
Cullen, Countee 1903-1946 **8**
Curry, Mark 1964– **17**
Curtis-Hall, Vondie 1956– **17**
Dandridge, Dorothy 1922-1965 **3**
Danticat, Edwidge 1969– **15**
Darden, Christopher 1957– **13**
Dash, Julie 1952– **4**
da Silva, Benedita 1942– **5**
Davenport, Arthur
  See Fattah, Chaka
Davidson, Jaye 1967(?)– **5**
Davis, Allison 1902-1983 **12**
Davis, Angela (Yvonne) 1944– **5**
Davis, Anthony 1951– **11**
Davis, Benjamin O(liver), Jr. 1912– **2**
Davis, Benjamin O(liver), Sr. 1877-1970 **4**

Davis, Lorenzo "Piper" 1917-1997 **19**
Davis, Miles (Dewey III) 1926-1991 **4**
Davis, Ossie 1917– **5**
Davis, Piper
  See Davis, Lorenzo "Piper"
Davis, Sammy Jr. 1925-1990 **18**
Dawes, Dominique (Margaux) 1976– **11**
Days, Drew S(aunders, III) 1941– **10**
de Carvalho, Barcelo
  See Bonga, Kuenda
Dee, Ruby 1924– **8**
Delaney, Beauford 1901-1979 **19**
Delany, Annie Elizabeth 1891-1995 **12**
Delany, Samuel R(ay), Jr. 1942– **9**
Delany, Sarah (Sadie) 1889– **12**
Dellums, Ronald (Vernie) 1935– **2**
Devers, (Yolanda) Gail 1966– **7**
Devine, Major J.
  See Divine, Father
Dickens, Helen Octavia 1909– **14**
Dickerson, Ernest 1952(?)– **6, 17**
Dinkins, David (Norman) 1927– **4**
Diop, Cheikh Anta 1923-1986 **4**
Diouf, Abdou 1935– **3**
Divine, Father 1877(?)-1965 **7**
Dixon, Margaret 192(?)– **14**
Dixon, Sharon Pratt 1944– **1**
Dixon, Willie (James) 1915-1992 **4**
Doby, Lawrence Eugene, Sr. 1924(?)–**16**
Donegan, Dorothy 1922-1998 **19**
Dorsey, Thomas Andrew 1899-1993 **15**
Downing, Will 19(?)(?)– **19**
Dr. Dre **10**
Dodson, Howard, Jr. 1939– **7**
Domini, Rey
  See Lorde, Audre (Geraldine)
do Nascimento, Edson Arantes
  See Pelé
Douglas, Aaron 1899-1979 **7**
Dove, Rita (Frances) 1952– **6**
Dove, Ulysses 1947– **5**
Dr. J
  See Erving, Julius Winfield II
Downing, Will **19**
Draper, Sharon M. 1952– **16**
Dre, Dr. 1965?– **14**
Drew, Charles Richard 1904-1950 **7**
Drexler, Clyde 1962– **4**
Driskell, David C(lyde) 1931– **7**
Driver, David E. 1955– **11**
Du Bois, W(illiam) E(dward) B(urghardt) 1868-1963 **3**
Ducksworth, Marilyn 1957– **12**
Duke, Bill 1943– **3**
Dumars, Joe 1963– **16**
Dunbar, Paul Laurence 1872-1906 **8**
Dungy, Tony 1955– **17**
Dunham, Katherine (Mary) 1910(?)– **4**

Dupri, Jermaine 1972– **13**
Dutton, Charles S. 1951– **4**
Dutton, Marie Elizabeth 1940– **12**
Dyson, Michael Eric 1958– **11**
Early, Deloreese Patricia
  See Reese, Della
Early, Gerald (Lyn) 1952– **15**
Edelin, Ramona Hoage 1945– **19**
Edelman, Marian Wright 1939– **5**
Edley, Christopher (Fairfield, Sr.) 1928– **2**
Edmonds, Kenneth "Babyface" 1958(?)– **10**
Edmonds, Terry 1950(?)– **17**
Edmonds, Tracey 1967(?)– **16**
Edwards, Eli
  See McKay, Claude
Edwards, Harry 1942– **2**
Edwards, Teresa 1964– **14**
Elder, (Robert) Lee 1934– **6**
Elders, Joycelyn (Minnie) 1933– **6**
El-Hajj Malik El-Shabazz
  See X, Malcolm
Ellington, Duke 1899-1974 **5**
Ellington, E. David 1960– **11**
Ellington, Edward Kennedy
  See Ellington, Duke
Ellison, Ralph (Waldo) 1914-1994 **7**
El-Shabazz, El-Hajj Malik
  See X, Malcolm
Erving, Julius Winfield II 1950– **18**
Espy, Alphonso Michael
  See Espy, Mike
Esposito, Giancarlo (Giusseppi Alessandro) 1958– **9**
Espy, Mike 1953– **6**
Eubanks, Kevin 1957– **15**
Europe, (William) James Reese 1880-1919 **10**
Everett, Ronald McKinley
  See Karenga, Maulana
Evers, Medgar (Riley) 1925-1963 **3**
Evers, Myrlie 1933– **8**
Evora, Cesaria 1941– **12**
Ewing, Patrick Aloysius 1962– **17**
Eyadéma, (Étienne) Gnassingbé 1937– **7**
Fagan, Garth 1940– **18**
Faison, George William 1946– **16**
Farmer, Forest J(ackson) 1941– **1**
Farmer, James 1920– **2**
Farrakhan, Louis 1933– **2**
Fattah, Chaka 1956– **11**
Fauntroy, Walter E(dward) 1933– **11**
Fauset, Jessie (Redmon) 1882-1961 **7**
Feelings, T(h)om(a)s 1933– **11**
Fela 1938– **1**
Fielder, Cecil (Grant) 1963– **2**
Fields, Cleo 1962– **13**
Fishburne, Larry 1962– **4**
Fishburne, Laurence III
  See Fishburne, Larry
Fisher, Rudolph John Chauncey 1897-1934 **17**
Fitzgerald, Ella 1918-1996 **8, 18**

Flack, Roberta 1940– **19**
Flake, Floyd H. 1945– **18**
Fletcher, Alphonse, Jr. 1965– **16**
Flipper, Henry O(ssian) 1856-1940 **3**
Flood, Curt(is) 1963– **10**
Folks, Byron
   See Allen, Byron
Forbes, Audrey Manley 1934– **16**
Ford, Harold Eugene, Jr. 1970– **16**
Foreman, George 1948– **1, 15**
Forman, James 1928– **7**
Fortune, T(imothy) Thomas 1856-1928 **6**
Fox, Vivica A. 1964– **15**
Foxx, Jamie 1967– **15**
Foxx, Redd 1922-1991 **2**
Franklin, Aretha 1942– **11**
Franklin, Carl 1949– **11**
Franklin, Hardy R. 1929– **9**
Franklin, John Hope 1915– **5**
Franklin, Kirk 1970– **15**
Franklin, Robert M(ichael) 1954– **13**
Franks, Gary 1954(?)– **2**
Frazier, Edward Franklin 1894-1962 **10**
Frazier, Joe 1944– **19**
Freeman, Al(bert Cornelius), Jr. 1934– **11**
Freeman, Charles Eldridge – **19**
Freeman, Morgan 1937– **2**
French, Albert 1943– **18**
Fresh Prince, The
   See Smith, Will
Fudge, Ann (Marie) 1951(?)– **11**
Fuhr, Grant 1962– **1**
Fulani, Lenora (Branch) 1950– **11**
Fuller, Charles (Henry) 1939– **8**
Fuller, S. B. 1895-1988 **13**
Fuller, Solomon Carter, Jr. 1872-1953 **15**
Gaines, Ernest J(ames) 1933– **7**
Gaither, Jake 1903-1994 **14**
Gantt, Harvey (Bernard) 1943– **1**
Garnett, Kevin 1976– **14**
Garrison, Zina 1963– **2**
Garvey, Marcus 1887-1940 **1**
Gary, Willie Edward 1947– **12**
Gaston, Arthur G(eorge) 1892– **4**
Gates, Henry Louis, Jr. 1950– **3**
Gates, Sylvester James, Jr. 1950– **15**
Gay, Marvin Pentz, Jr.
   See Gaye, Marvin
Gaye, Marvin 1939-1984 **2**
Gayle, Helene D(oris) 1955– **3**
George, Nelson 1957– **12**
Gibson, Althea 1927– **8**
Gibson, Kenneth Allen 1932– **6**
Gibson, William F(rank) 1933– **6**
Giddings, Paula (Jane) 1947– **11**
Gillespie, Dizzy 1917-1993 **1**
Gillespie, John Birks
   See Gillespie, Dizzy
Gilliam, Sam 1933– **16**
Gist, Carole 1970(?)– **1**
Giovanni, Nikki 1943– **9**

Giovanni, Yolande Cornelia, Jr.
   See Giovanni, Nikki
Givens, Robin 1965– **4**
Glover, Danny 1948– **1**
Glover, Nathaniel, Jr. 1943– **12**
Glover, Savion 1974– **14**
Goines, Donald 1937(?)-1974 **19**
Goldberg, Whoopi 1955– **4**
Golden, Marita 1950– **19**
Golden, Thelma 1965– **10**
Goldsberry, Ronald 1942– **18**
Gomes, Peter J(ohn) 1942– **15**
Gomez-Preston, Cheryl 1954– **9**
Goode, Mal(vin Russell) 1908-1995 **13**
Goode, W(oodrow) Wilson 1938– **4**
Gooding, Cuba Jr. 1968– **16**
Gordon, Ed(ward Lansing, III) 1960– **10**
Gordon, Pamela 1955– **17**
Gordone, Charles 1925-1995 **15**
Gordy, Berry, Jr. 1929– **1**
Goreed, Joseph
   See Williams, Joe
Gossett, Louis, Jr. 1936– **7**
Gourdine, Simon (Peter) 1940– **11**
Graham, Lawrence Otis 1962– **12**
Graham, Stedman 1951(?)– **13**
Gravely, Samuel L(ee), Jr. 1922– **5**
Graves, Denyce Antoinette 1964– **19**
Graves, Earl G(ilbert) 1935– **1**
Gray, F. Gary 1969– **14**
Gray, Frizzell
   See Mfume, Kweisi
Gray, William H. III 1941– **3**
Green, Albert 1946– **13**
Green, Dennis 1949– **5**
Greene, Joe 1946– **10**
Greenfield, Eloise 1929– **9**
Gregg, Eric 1951– **16**
Grier, Pam(ala Suzette) 1949– **9**
Grier, Roosevelt (Rosey) 1932– **13**
Griffey, George Kenneth, Jr. 1969– **12**
Griffith, Mark Winston 1963– **8**
Gregory, Dick 1932– **1**
Gregory, Frederick D(rew) 1941– **8**
Grimké, Archibald H(enry) 1849-1930 **9**
Guarionex
   See Schomburg, Arthur Alfonso
Guillaume, Robert 1927– **3**
Guinier, (Carol) Lani 1950– **7**
Gumbel, Bryant Charles 1948– **14**
Gumbel, Greg 1946– **8**
Gunn, Moses 1929-1993 **10**
Guy, Jasmine 1964(?)– **2**
Guy, Rosa 1925(?)– **5**
Guy-Sheftall, Beverly 1946– **13**
Guyton, Tyree 1955– **9**
Gwynn, Anthony Keith 1960– **18**
Habré, Hissène 1942– **6**

Habyarimana, Juvenal 1937-1994 **8**
Haile Selassie 1892-1975 **7**
Hale, Clara 1902-1992 **16**
Hale, Lorraine 1926(?)– **8**
Haley, Alex (Palmer) 1921-1992 **4**
Hall, Lloyd A(ugustus) 1894-1971 **8**
Hamblin, Ken 1940– **10**
Hamer, Fannie Lou (Townsend) 1917-1977 **6**
Hamilton, Virginia 1936– **10**
Hampton, Fred 1948-1969 **18**
Hampton, Henry (Eugene, Jr.) 1940– **6**
Hampton, Lionel 1908(?)– **17**
Handy, W(illiam) C(hristopher) 1873-1937 **8**
Hani, Chris 1942-1993 **6**
Hani, Martin Thembisile
   See Hani, Chris
Hannah, Marc (Regis) 1956– **10**
Hansberry, Lorraine (Vivian) 1930-1965 **6**
Hansberry, William Leo 1894-1965 **11**
Hardaway, Anfernee (Deon)
   See Hardaway, Anfernee (Penny)
Hardaway, Anfernee (Penny) 1971– **13**
Hardaway, Penny
   See Hardaway, Anfernee (Penny)
Hardison, Bethann 19??– **12**
Harkless, Necia Desiree 1920– **19**
Harper, Frances E(llen) W(atkins) 1825-1911 **11**
Harrell, Andre (O'Neal) 1962(?)– **9**
Harrington, Oliver W(endell) 1912– **9**
Harris, Alice 1934– **7**
Harris, Barbara 1930– **12**
Harris, E. Lynn 1957– **12**
Harris, Eddy L. 1956– **18**
Harris, James III
   See Jimmy Jam
Harris, Jay **19**
Harris, Leslie 1961– **6**
Harris, Marcelite Jordon 1943– **16**
Harris, Monica 1968– **18**
Harris, Patricia Roberts 1924-1985 **2**
Harris, Robin 1953-1990 **7**
Harris, "Sweet" Alice
   See Harris, Alice
Harsh, Vivian Gordon 1890-1960 **14**
Harvard, Beverly (Joyce Bailey) 1950– **11**
Harvey, Steve 1957– **18**
Hastie, William H(enry) 1904-1976 **8**
Hastings, Alcee Lamar 1936– **16**
Hathaway, Donny 1945-1979 **18**
Hawkins, Adrienne Lita
   See Kennedy, Adrienne
Hawkins, Coleman 1904-1969 **9**
Hawkins, Erskine Ramsey 1914–

1993 **14**
Hawkins, Jamesetta
    See James, Etta
Hawkins, La-Van 1960(?)- **17**
Hawkins, Steven Wayne 1962— **14**
Hawkins, Tramaine Aunzola 1951– **16**
Hayden, Palmer 1890-1973 **13**
Hayden, Robert Earl 1913-1980 **12**
Hayes, James C. 1946— **10**
Hayes, Roland 1887-1977 **4**
Haynes, George Edmund 1880-1960 **8**
Hedgeman, Peyton Cole
    See Hayden, Palmer
Height, Dorothy I(rene) 1912— **2**
Hemphill, Essex 1957— **10**
Hemsley, Sherman 1938– **19**
Henderson, Gordon 1957— **5**
Henderson, Natalie Leota
    See Hinderas, Natalie
Henderson, Wade **14**
Hendricks, Barbara 1948— **3**
Hendrix, James Marshall
    See Hendrix, Jimi
Hendrix, Jimi 1942-1970 **10**
Hendrix, Johnny Allen
    See Hendrix, Jimi
Henry, Aaron Edd 1922-1997 **19**
Henry, Lenny 1958— **9**
Henson, Matthew (Alexander) 1866-1955 **2**
Herman, Alexis Margaret 1947— **15**
Hernandez, Aileen Clarke 1926— **13**
Hickman, Fred(erick Douglass) 1951— **11**
Higginbotham, A(loyisus) Leon, Jr. 1928— **13**
Hightower, Dennis F(owler) 1941— **13**
Hill, Anita (Faye) 1956— **5**
Hill, Calvin 1947 –**19**
Hill, Grant (Henry) 1972— **13**
Hill, Janet 1947–**19**
Hill, Jesse, Jr. 1927— **13**
Hilliard, David 1942— **7**
Himes, Chester 1909-1984 **8**
Hinderas, Natalie 1927-1987 **5**
Hines, Gregory (Oliver) 1946— **1**
Hinton, William Augustus 1883-1959 **8**
Holder, Eric H., Jr. 1951(?)— **9**
Holiday, Billie 1915-1959 **1**
Holland, Robert, Jr. 1940— **11**
Holland, Endesha Ida Mae 1944— **3**
Holte, Patricia Louise
    See LaBelle, Patti
Holyfield, Evander 1962— **6**
hooks, bell 1952— **5**
Hooks, Benjamin L(awson) 1925— **2**
Hope, John 1868-1936 **8**
Horne, Lena (Mary Calhoun) 1917— **5**

Hounsou, Djimon 1964– **19**
Houphouët, Dia
    See Houphouët-Boigny, Félix
Houphouët-Boigny, Félix 1905— **4**
House, Eddie James, Jr.
    See House, Son
House, Eugene
    See House, Son
House, Son 1902-1988 **8**
Houston, Charles Hamilton 1895-1950 **4**
Houston, Whitney 1963— **7**
Howard, Corinne
    See Mitchell, Corinne
Howard, Desmond Kevin 1970– **16**
Howard, Juwan Antonio 1973— **15**
Howlin' Wolf 1910-1976 **9**
Hudlin, Reginald 1962(?)— **9**
Hudlin, Warrington, Jr. 1953(?)— **9**
Hudson, Cheryl 19(?)(?)— **15**
Hudson, Wade 1946— **15**
Hughes, Albert 1972— **7**
Hughes, Allen 1972— **7**
Hughes, (James Mercer) Langston 1902-1967 **4**
Hunt, Richard (Howard) 1935— **6**
Hunter, Charlayne
    See Hunter-Gault, Charlayne
Hunter-Gault, Charlayne 1942— **6**
Hurston, Zora Neale 1891-1960 **3**
Hutson, Jean Blackwell 1914– **16**
Hyman, Phyllis 1949(?)-1995 **19**
Iceberg Slim 1918-1992 **11**
Ice Cube 1969(?)— **8**
Ice-T 1958(?)— **6**
Iman 1955— **4**
Ingraham, Hubert A. 1947– **19**
Ingram, Rex 1895-1969 **5**
Innis, Roy (Emile Alfredo) 1934— **5**
Irving, Clarence (Larry) 1955— **12**
Jackson, George 1960?— **19**
Jackson, George Lester 1941-1971 **14**
Jackson, Isaiah (Allen) 1945— **3**
Jackson, Janet 1966— **6**
Jackson, Jesse 1941— **1**
Jackson, Jesse Louis, Jr. 1965— **14**
Jackson, Mahalia 1911-1972 **5**
Jackson, Mannie 1939— **14**
Jackson, Maynard (Holbrook, Jr.) 1938— **2**
Jackson, Michael Joseph 1958– **19**
Jackson, O'Shea
    See Ice Cube
Jackson, Reginald Martinez 1946— **15**
Jackson, Samuel L. 1948– **8, 19**
Jackson, Sheneska 1970(?)– **18**
Jackson, Shirley Ann 1946— **12**
Jacob, John E(dward) 1934— **2**
Jagan, Cheddi 1918-1997 **16**
Jakes, Thomas "T.D." 1957– **17**
Jam, Jimmy
    See Jimmy Jam
James, Daniel "Chappie", Jr. 1920-1978 **16**
James, Etta 1938— **13**
James, Juanita (Therese) 1952— **13**

Jamison, Judith 1943— **7**
Jawara, Sir Dawda Kairaba 1924— **11**
Jean-Baptiste, Marianne 1967(?)– **17**
Jeffries, Leonard 1937— **8**
Jemison, Mae C. 1957— **1**
Jenifer, Franklyn G(reen) 1939— **2**
Jenkins, Beverly **14**
Jenkins, Ella (Louise) 1924— **15**
Jimmy Jam 1959— **13**
Johnson, Ben 1961— **1**
Johnson, Beverly 1952— **2**
Johnson, Carol Diann
    See Carroll, Diahann
Johnson, Caryn E.
    See Goldberg, Whoopi
Johnson, Charles 1948— **1**
Johnson, Charles Arthur
    See St. Jacques, Raymond
Johnson, Charles Spurgeon 1893-1956 **12**
Johnson, Earvin "Magic" 1959— **3**
Johnson, Eddie Bernice 1935— **8**
Johnson, Jack 1878-1946 **8**
Johnson, James Weldon 1871-1938 **5**
Johnson, James William
    See Johnson, James Weldon
Johnson, John Arthur
    See Johnson, Jack
Johnson, John H(arold) 1918— **3**
Johnson, Michael (Duane) 1967— **13**
Johnson, Norma L. Holloway 1932- -**17**
Johnson, Robert T. 1948– **17**
Johnson, Virginia (Alma Fairfax) 1950— **9**
Johnson, "Magic"
    See Johnson, Earvin "Magic"
Johnson, Marguerite
    See Angelou, Maya
Johnson, Robert 1911-1938 **2**
Johnson, Robert L. 1946(?)— **3**
Johnson, William Henry 1901-1970 **3**
Jones, Bill T. 1952— **1**
Jones, Carl 1955(?)— **7**
Jones, Cobi N'Gai 1970– **18**
Jones, Elaine R. 1944— **7**
Jones, Elvin 1927— **14**
Jones, Ingrid Saunders 1945– **18**
Jones, James Earl 1931— **3**
Jones, Le Roi
    See Baraka, Amiri
Jones, Lillie Mae
    See Carter, Betty
Jones, Sissieretta
    See Joyner, Matilda Sissieretta
Joplin, Scott 1868-1917 **6**
Jones, Lois Mailou 1905— **13**
Jones, Quincy (Delight) 1933— **8**
Jones, Star(let Marie) 1962(?)— **10**
Jordan, Barbara (Charline) 1936— **4**
Jordan, June 1936— **7**
Jordan, Michael (Jeffrey) 1963— **6**
Jordan, Vernon E(ulion, Jr.) 1935—

3
Josey, E. J. 1924— **10**
Joyner, Jacqueline
   See Joyner-Kersee, Jackie
Joyner, Matilda Sissieretta 1869(?)-1933 **15**
Joyner, Tom 1949(?)– **19**
Joyner-Kersee, Jackie 1962— **5**
Julian, Percy Lavon 1899-1975 **6**
Julien, Isaac 1960— **3**
Just, Ernest Everett 1883-1941 **3**
Justice, David Christopher 1966– **18**
Kamau, Johnstone
   See Kenyatta, Jomo
Kani, Karl 1968(?)— **10**
Karenga, Maulana 1941— **10**
Kaunda, Kenneth (David) 1924— **2**
Kearse, Amalya Lyle 1937— **12**
Keith, Damon Jerome 1922— **16**
Kelly, Patrick 1954(?)-1990 **3**
Kelly, R(obert) 1969(?)– **18**
Kelly, Sharon Pratt
   See Dixon, Sharon Pratt
Kennard, William Earl 1957– **18**
Kennedy, Adrienne 1931— **11**
Kennedy, Florynce Rae 1916— **12**
Kennedy, Lelia McWilliams Robinson 1885-1931 **14**
Kenyatta, Jomo 1891(?)-1978 **5**
Kerekou, Ahmed (Mathieu) 1933— **1**
Keyes, Alan L(ee) 1950— **11**
Khan, Chaka 1953— **12**
Khanga, Yelena 1962— **6**
Kilpatrick, Carolyn Cheeks 1945– **16**
Kimbro, Dennis (Paul) 1950— **10**
Kincaid, Jamaica 1949— **4**
King, B. B. 1925— **7**
King, Bernice (Albertine) 1963– **4**
King, Coretta Scott 1929— **3**
King, Dexter (Scott) 1961— **10**
King, Don 1931— **14**
King, Gayle 1956— **19**
King, Martin Luther, Jr. 1929-1968 **1**
King, Riley B.
   See King, B. B.
King, Yolanda (Denise) 1955— **6**
Kirby, George 1924-1995 **14**
Kirk, Ron 1954— **11**
Kitt, Eartha Mae 1928(?)– **16**
Knight, Gladys Maria 1944–**16**
Knight, Marion, Jr.
   See Knight, Suge
Knight, Suge 1966— **11**
Komunyakaa, Yusef 1941— **9**
Kotto, Yaphet (Fredrick) 1944— **7**
Kountz, Samuel L(ee) 1930-1981 **10**
Kravitz, Lenny 1964— **10**
Kravitz, Leonard
   See Kravitz, Lenny
Kunjufu, Jawanza 1953— **3**
Kuti, Fela Anikulapo
   See Fela
L L Cool J 1968– **16**

LaBelle, Patti 1944— **13**
Lafontant, Jewel Stradford 1922— **3**
Lampkin, Daisy 1883(?)-1965 **19**
Lane, Charles 1953— **3**
Lane, Vincent 1942— **5**
Langhart, Janet 1941– **19**
Larsen, Nella 1891-1964 **10**
La Salle, Eriq 1962— **12**
Latimer, Lewis H(oward) 1848-1928 **4**
Lawless, Theodore K(enneth) 1892-1971 **8**
Lawrence, Jacob (Armstead) 1917— **4**
Lawrence, Martin 1965— **6**
Lawrence, Robert Henry, Jr. 1935-1967 **16**
Lawrence-Lightfoot, Sara 1944— **10**
Lawson, Jennifer (Karen) 1946— **1**
Leary, Kathryn D. 1952— **10**
Leavell, Dorothy R. 1944– **17**
Lee, Canada 1907-1952 **8**
Lee, Don L(uther)
   See Madhubuti, Haki R.
Lee, Gabby
   See Lincoln, Abbey
Lee, Joie 1962(?)— **1**
Lee, Shelton Jackson
   See Lee, Spike
Lee, Spike 1957– **5, 19**
Lee-Smith, Hughie 1915— **5**
Leffall, LaSalle (Doheny), Jr. 1930— **3**
Leland, George Thomas
   See Leland, Mickey
Leland, Mickey 1944-1989 **2**
Leon, Kenny 1957(?)— **10**
Leonard, Sugar Ray 1956— **15**
Lewis, Shirley Ann Redd 1937— **14**
Lewis, Thomas 1939– **19**
León, Tania 1943— **13**
Leslie, Lisa Deshaun 1972– **16**
Lester, Julius 1939— **9**
Lewellyn, J(ames) Bruce 1927— **13**
Lewis, (Frederick) Carl(ton) 1961— **4**
Lewis, (Mary) Edmonia 1845(?)-1911(?) **10**
Lewis, David Levering 1936— **9**
Lewis, Delano (Eugene) 1938— **7**
Lewis, John (Robert) 1940— **2**
Lewis, Reginald F. 1942-1993 **6**
Lewis, Terry 1956— **13**
Lewis, Byron E(ugene) 1931— **13**
Lincoln, Abbey 1930— **3**
Lindo, Delroy 1952– **18**
Little, Malcolm
   See X, Malcolm
Little, Robert L(angdon) 1938— **2**
Little Richard 1932— **15**
Locke, Alain (LeRoy) 1886-1954 **10**
Lofton, Kenneth 1967— **12**
Lofton, Ramona 1950— **14**
Logan, Onnie Lee 1910(?)-1995 **14**

Long, Nia 1970– **17**
Lord Pitt of Hampstead
   See Pitt, David Thomas
Lorde, Audre (Geraldine) 1934-1992 **6**
Lott, Ronnie 1959— **9**
Louis, Errol T. 1962— **8**
Louis, Joe 1914-1981 **5**
Love, Nat 1854-1921 **9**
Lover, Ed **10**
Lowery, Joseph E. 1924— **2**
Lucas, John 1953— **7**
Luthuli, Albert (John Mvumbi) 1898(?)-1967 **13**
Lyle, Marcenia
   See Stone, Toni
Lyons, Henry 1942(?)— **12**
Lyttle, Hulda Margaret 1889-1983 **14**
Mabley, Jackie "Moms" 1897(?)-1975 **15**
Mabuza, Lindiwe 1938– **18**
Machel, Graca Simbine 1945– **16**
Machel, Samora Moises 1933-1986 **8**
Madhubuti, Haki R. 1942— **7**
Madikizela, Nkosikazi Nobandle Nomzamo Winifred
   See Mandela, Winnie
Madison, Joseph E. 1949– **17**
Major, Clarence 1936— **9**
Makeba, (Zensi) Miriam 1932— **2**
Malcolm X
   See X, Malcolm
Mallett, Conrad, Jr. 1953— **16**
Malone, Karl A. 1963– **18**
Malone, Annie (Minerva Turnbo Pope) 1869-1957 **13**
Mandela, Nelson (Rolihlahla) 1918— **1, 14**
Mandela, Winnie 1934— **2**
Manigault, Earl "The Goat" 1943— **15**
Manley, Audrey Forbes 1934– **16**
Marable, Manning 1950— **10**
Marley, Bob 1945-1981 **5**
Marley, Robert Nesta
   See Marley, Bob
Marrow, Tracey
   See Ice-T
Marsalis, Wynton 1961– **16**
Marshall, Gloria
   See Sudarkasa, Niara
Marshall, Paule 1929— **7**
Marshall, Thurgood 1908– **1**
Marshall, Valenza Pauline Burke
   See Marshall, Paule
Martin, Louis Emanuel 1912-1997 **16**
Masekela, Barbara 1941– **18**
Masekela, Hugh (Ramopolo) 1939— **1**
Masire, Quett (Ketumile Joni) 1925– **5**
Massey, Walter E(ugene) 1938– **5**
Mathabane, Johannes
   See Mathabane, Mark
Mathabane, Mark 1960– **5**

Cumulative Name Index

Mauldin, Jermaine Dupri
See Dupri, Jermaine
Mayfield, Curtis (Lee) 1942— **2**
Maynard, Robert C(lyve) 1937-1993 **7**
Maynor, Dorothy 1910-1996 **19**
Mays, Benjamin E(lijah) 1894-1984 **7**
Mays, William Howard, Jr.
See Mays, Willie
Mays, Willie 1931— **3**
Mazrui, Ali Al'Amin 1933— **12**
Mbeki, Thabo Mvuyelwa — **14**
Mboup, Souleymane 1951— **10**
Mbuende, Kaire Munionganda 1953— **12**
McBride, Bryant Scott 1965— **18**
McCabe, Jewell Jackson 1945— **10**
McCall, Nathan 1955— **8**
McCarty, Osseola 1908— **16**
McCoy, Elijah 1844-1929 **8**
McCray, Nikki 1972— **18**
McDaniel, Hattie 1895-1952 **5**
McDonald, Erroll 1954(?)— **1**
McDougall, Gay J. 1947— **11**
McEwen, Mark 1954— **5**
McGee, Charles 1924— **10**
McIntosh, Winston Hubert
See Tosh, Peter
McKay, Claude 1889-1948 **6**
McKay, Festus Claudius
See McKay, Claude
McKay, Nellie Yvonne 194(?)—**17**
McKnight, Brian 1969— **18**
Mckee, Lonette 1952— **12**
McKegney, Tony 1958— **3**
McKinney, Cynthia Ann 1955— **11**
McKinnon, Ike
See McKinnon, Isaiah
McKinnon, Isaiah 1943— **9**
McKissick, Floyd B(ixler) 1922-1981 **3**
McMillan, Terry 1951— **4, 17**
McNair, Ronald (Ervin) 1950-1986 **3**
McNeil, Lori 1964(?)— **1**
McPhail, Sharon 1948— **2**
McQueen, Butterfly 1911— **6**
McQueen, Thelma
See McQueen, Butterfly
Meek, Carrie (Pittman) 1926— **6**
Meles Zenawi 1955(?)— **3**
Meredith, James H(oward) 1933— **11**
Messenger, The
See Divine, Father
Meyer, June
See Jordan, June
Mfume, Kweisi 1948— **6**
Micheaux, Oscar (Devereaux) 1884-1951 **7**
Milla, Roger 1952— **2**
Miller, Bebe 1950— **3**
Miller, Cheryl 1964— **10**
Mingus, Charles Jr. 1922-1979 **15**
Mitchell, Arthur 1934— **2**
Mitchell, Corinne 1914-1993 **8**
Mkapa, Benjamin William 1938– **16**
Mobutu, Joseph-Desire
See Mobutu Sese Seko (Nkuku wa za Banga)
Mobutu Sese Seko (Nkuku wa za Banga) 1930— **1**
Mogae, Festus Gontebanye 1939– **19**
Mohamed, Ali Mahdi
See Ali Mahdi Mohamed
Moi, Daniel (Arap) 1924— **1**
Mongella, Gertrude 1945— **11**
Monk, Thelonious (Sphere, Jr.) 1917-1982 **1**
Moon, (Harold) Warren 1956— **8**
Moore, Bobby
See Rashad, Ahmad
Moorer, Michael 1967– **19**
Morgan, Garrett (Augustus) 1877-1963 **1**
Morgan, Joe Leonard 1943— **9**
Morgan, Rose (Meta) 1912(?)— **11**
Morris, Stevland Judkins
See Wonder, Stevie
Morrison, Keith 1942— **13**
Morrison, Toni 1931— **2, 15**
Morton, Joe 1947– **18**
Moseka, Aminata
See Lincoln, Abbey
Moseley-Braun, Carol
See Braun, Carol (Elizabeth) Moseley
Moses, Edwin 1955— **8**
Moses, Gilbert, III 1942-1995 **12**
Moses, Robert Parris 1935— **11**
Mosley, Walter 1952— **5**
Moss, Carlton 1909-1997 **17**
Moten, Emma Barnett – **18**
Motley, Constance Baker 1921— **10**
Mourning, Alonzo 1970– **17**
Moutoussamy-Ashe, Jeanne 1951— **7**
Mowry, Jess 1960— **7**
Mugabe, Robert Gabriel 1928— **10**
Muhammad, Elijah 1897-1975 **4**
Muhammad, Khallid Abdul 1951(?)— **10**
Muluzi, Elson Bakili 1943— **14**
Murphy, Eddie 1961— **4**
Murphy, Edward Regan
See Murphy, Eddie
Murray, Cecil (Chip) 1929— **12**
Murray, Eddie 1956— **12**
Murray, Lenda 1962— **10**
Museveni, Yoweri (Kaguta) 1944(?)— **4**
Mutola, Maria de Lurdes 1972—**12**
Mutombo, Dikembe 1966— **7**
Mwinyi, Ali Hassan 1925— **1**
Myers, Walter Dean 1937— **8**
Myers, Walter Milton
See Myers, Walter Dean
Nascimento, Milton 1942— **2**
Naylor, Gloria 1950— **10**
Ndadaye, Melchior 1953-1993 **7**
Ndegeocello, Me'Shell 1968— **15**
N'Dour, Youssou 1959— **1**
Nelson, Jill 1952— **6**
Nelson, Prince Rogers
See Prince
Nettles, Marva Deloise
See Collins, Marva
Newton, Huey (Percy) 1942-1989 **2**
Ndungane, Winston Njongonkulu 1941– **16**
Ngengi, Kamau wa
See Kenyatta, Jomo
Nichols, Grace
See Nichols, Nichelle
Nichols, Nichelle 1933(?)— **11**
Njongonkulu, Winston Ndungane 1941– **16**
Nkomo, Joshua (Mqabuko Nyongolo) 1917— **4**
Nkrumah, Kwame 1909-1972 **3**
N'Namdi, George R. 1946– **17**
Noah, Yannick (Simon Camille) 1960– **4**
Norman, Jessye 1945– **5**
Norman, Pat 1939– **10**
Norton, Eleanor Holmes 1937— **7**
Norwood, Brandy
See, Brandy
Nottage, Cynthia DeLores
See Tucker, C. DeLores
Ntaryamira, Cyprien 1955-1994 **8**
Nujoma, Samuel 1929– **10**
Nyerere, Julius (Kambarage) 1922– **5**
Nzo, Alfred (Baphethuxolo) 1 1925– **15**
Obasanjo, Olusegun 1937– **5**
Oglesby, Zena 1947— **12**
Ogletree, Charles, Jr. 1933– **12**
Olajuwon, Akeem
See Olajuwon, Hakeem (Abdul Ajibola)
Olajuwon, Hakeem (Abdul Ajibola) 1963– **2**
O'Leary, Hazel (Rollins) 1937– **6**
O'Neal, Shaquille (Rashaun) 1972– **8**
O'Neil, Buck 1911– **19**
O'Neil, John Jordan
See O'Neil, Buck
Ongala, Ramadhani Mtoro
See Ongala, Remmy
Ongala, Remmy 1947– **9**
O'Ree, William Eldon
See O'Ree, Willie
O'Ree, Willie 1935– **5**
Ousmane, Sembène
See Sembène, Ousmane
Owens, Dana
See Queen Latifah
Owens, James Cleveland
See Owens, Jesse
Owens, J. C.
See Owens, Jesse
Owens, Jesse 1913-1980 **2**
Owens, Major (Robert) 1936– **6**
Page, Alan (Cedric) 1945— **7**
Page, Clarence 1947— **4**

Paige, Leroy Robert
  See Paige, Satchel
Paige, Satchel 1906-1982 **7**
Parker, Pat **1944-19**
Parks, Bernard C. 1943– **17**
Parks, Gordon (Roger Alexander (Buchanan) 1912— **1**
Parks, Rosa 1913— **1**
Parsons, James Benton 1911-1993 **14**
Parsons, Richard Dean 1948— **11**
Pascal-Trouillot, Ertha 1943– **3**
Patillo, Melba Joy 1941— **15**
Patrick, Deval Laurdine 1956— **12**
Patterson, Floyd 1935– **19**
Patterson, Frederick Douglass 1901-1988 **12**
Patterson, Orlando 1940— **4**
Patterson, P(ercival) J(ames) 1936(?)— **6**
Payne, Allen 1962(?)— **13**
Payne, Donald M(ilford) 1934— **2**
Payton, Walter (Jerry) 1954— **11**
Peete, Calvin 1943— **11**
Pelé 1940— **7**
Penniman, Richard Wayne
  See Little Richard
Perez, Anna 1951— **1**
Perkins, Edward (Joseph) 1928— **5**
Perry, Rainford Hugh
  See Perry, Ruth
Perry, Ruth 1936– **19**
Perry, Ruth Sando 1939— **15**
Person, Waverly (J.) 1927— **9**
Peters, Maria Philomena 1941— **12**
Petry, Ann 1909-1997 **19**
Pickett, Bill 1870-1932 **11**
Pierre, Andre 1915– **17**
Pinchback, P(inckney) B(enton) S(tewart) 1837-1921 **9**
Pinkett, Jada 1971— **10**
Pinkney, Jerry 1939— **15**
Pippen, Scottie 1965— **15**
Pippin, Horace 1888-1946 **9**
Pitt, David Thomas 1913-1994 **10**
Pitta, (do Nascimento), Celso (Roberto) 19(?)(?)– **17**
Pleasant, Mary Ellen 1814-1904 **9**
Poitier, Sidney 1927— **11**
Poole, Elijah
  See Muhammad, Elijah
Porter, Countee Leroy
  See Cullin, Countee
Porter, James A(mos) 1905-1970 **11**
Poussaint, Alvin F(rancis) 1934— **5**
Powell, Adam Clayton, Jr. 1908-1972 **3**
Powell, Colin (Luther) 1937— **1**
Powell, Maxine 1924— **8**
Powell, Michael Anthony
  See Powell, Mike
Powell, Mike 1963— **7**
Pratt Dixon, Sharon
  See Dixon, Sharon Pratt
Pratt, Geronimo 1947— **18**
Price, Leontyne 1927— **1**
Price, Hugh B. 1941— **9**
Primus, Pearl 1919— **6**
Prince 1958– **18**
Prothrow, Deborah Boutin
  See Prothrow-Stith, Deborah
Prothrow-Stith, Deborah 1954— **10**
Pryor, Richard (Franklin Lennox (Thomas) 1940— **3**
Puckett, Kirby 1961— **4**
Quarles, Benjamin Arthur 1904-1996 **18**
Quarterman, Lloyd Albert 1918-1982 **4**
Queen Latifah 1970(?)— **1, 16**
Quirot, Ana (Fidelia) 1963— **13**
Raines, Franklin Delano 1949— **14**
Ralph, Sheryl Lee 1956– **18**
Ramaphosa, (Matamela) Cyril 1952— **3**
Rand, A(ddison) Barry 1944— **6**
Randall, Dudley (Felker) 1914— **8**
Randle, Theresa 1967– **16**
Randolph, A(sa) Philip 1889-1979 **3**
Rangel, Charles (Bernard) 1930— **3**
Rashad, Ahmad 1949– **18**
Raspberry, William 1935— **2**
Ras Tafari
  See Haile Selassie
Rawlings, Jerry (John) 1947— **9**
Rawls, Lou 1936– **17**
Razaf, Andy 1895-1973 **19**
Razafkeriefo, Andreamentania Paul
  See Razaf, Andy
Reagon, Bernice Johnson 1942— **7**
Reason, Joseph Paul 1943– **19**
Redding, Otis, Jr. 1941–**16**
Reed, Ishmael 1938— **8**
Reese, Della 1931— **6**
Reuben, Gloria 19(?)(?)— **15**
Rhames, Ving 1961— **14**
Rhodes, Ray 1950— **14**
Rhone, Sylvia 1952— **2**
Ribbs, William Theodore, Jr.
  See Ribbs, Willy T.
Ribbs, Willy T. 1956— **2**
Ribeiro, Alfonso 1971— **17**
Rice, Condoleezza 1954— **3**
Rice, Jerry 1962— **5**
Rice, Linda Johnson 1958— **9**
Rice, Norm(an Blann) 1943— **8**
Richards, Lloyd 1923(?)— **2**
Richardson, Elaine Potter
  See Kincaid, Jamaica
Richardson, Nolan 1941— **9**
Richardson, Pat
  See Norman, Pat
Richie, Leroy C. 1941– **18**
Richmond, Mitchell James 1965– **19**
Ridenhour, Carlton
  See Chuck D.
Riggs, Marlon 1957– **5**
Riley, Helen Caldwell Day 1926— **13**
Ringgold, Faith 1930— **4**
Roberts, James
  See Lover, Ed
Roberts, Marcus 1963– **19**
Roberts, Marthaniel
  See Roberts, Marcus
Roberts, Robin 1960– **16**
Roberts, Roy S. 1939(?)— **14**
Robeson, Eslanda Goode 1896-1965 **13**
Robeson, Paul (Leroy Bustill) 1898-1976 **2**
Robinson, Bill "Bojangles" 1878-1949 **11**
Robinson, Eddie G. 1919– **10**
Robinson, Frank 1935– **9**
Robinson, Jackie 1919-1972 **6**
Robinson, Jack Roosevelt
  See Robinson, Jackie
Robinson, Luther
  See Robinson, Bill "Bojangles"
Robinson, Max 1939-1988 **3**
Robinson, Patrick 1966—**19**
Robinson, Rachel 1922– **16**
Robinson, Randall 1942(?)— **7**
Robinson, Smokey 1940— **3**
Robinson, Sugar Ray 1921– **18**
Robinson, William, Jr.
  See Robinson, Smokey
Roche, Joyce M. 1947– **17**
Rochon, Lela 1965(?)– **16**
Rock, Chris 1967(?)– **3**
Rodgers, Johnathan (Arlin) 1946— **6**
Rodman, Dennis Keith 1961— **12**
Rogers, John W., Jr. 1958— **5**
Roker, Albert Lincoln, Jr. 1954(?)— **12**
Rolle, Esther 1922— **13**
Rollins, Howard Ellsworth 1950-1996 **16**
Ross, Araminta
  See Tubman, Harriet
Ross, Diana 1944— **8**
Rotimi, (Emmanuel Gladstone) Ola(wale) 1938— **1**
Rowan, Carl T(homas) 1925— **1**
Rowell, Victoria 1962(?)— **13**
Rudolph, Wilma (Glodean) 1940— **4**
Rupaul 1960– **17**
Rushen, Patrice 1954— **12**
Russell, Bill 1934— **8**
Russell, Herman Jerome 1931(?)– **17**
Russell, William Felton
  See Russell, Bill
Russell-McCloud, Patricia A. 1946— **17**
Rustin, Bayard 1910-1987 **4**
Saar, Alison 1956– **16**
Sade 1959— **15**
St. Jacques, Raymond 1930-1990 **8**
Saint James, Synthia 1949— **12**
Samara, Noah 1956— **15**
SAMO
  See Basquiat, Jean-Michel
Sampson, Charles 1957— **13**
Sampson, Edith S(purlock) 1901-1979 **4**
Samuel, Sealhenry Olumide 1963— **14**

Sanchez, Sonia 1934– **17**
Sanders, Barry 1968— **1**
Sanders, Deion (Luwynn) 1967— **4**
Sanders, Dori(nda) 1935— **8**
Sanders, Joseph R(ichard, Jr.) 1954— **11**
Sanford, John Elroy
 See Foxx, Redd
Sangare, Oumou 1968– **18**
Sankara, Thomas 1949-1987 **17**
Satcher, David 1941— **7**
Satchmo
 See Armstrong, (Daniel) Louis
Savage, Augusta Christine 1892(?)-1962 **12**
Savimbi, Jonas (Malheiro) 1934— **2**
Sawyer, Amos 1945— **2**
Sayles Belton, Sharon 1952(?)— **9, 16**
Schmoke, Kurt (Lidell) 1949— **1**
Schomburg, Arthur Alfonso 1874-1938 **9**
Schomburg, Arturo Alfonso
 See Schomburg, Arthur Alfonso
Schultz, Michael A. 1938— **6**
Scott, Coretta
 See King, Coretta Scott
Scott, Sr., Wendell Oliver 1921-1990 **19**
Scruggs, Mary Elfrieda
 See Williams, Mary Lou
Seal **14**
Seale, Bobby 1936— **3**
Seale, Robert George
 See Seale, Bobby
Sears-Collins, Leah J(eanette) 1955— **5**
Selassie, Haile
 See Haile Selassie
Sembène, Ousmane 1923— **13**
Senghor, Léopold Sédar 1906— **12**
Sengstacke, John Herman Henry 1912-1997 **18**
Serrano, Andres 1951(?)— **3**
Shabazz, Attallah 1958— **6**
Shabazz, Betty 1936— **7**
Shakur, Assata 1947— **6**
Shakur, Tupac Amaru 1971-1996 **14**
Shange, Ntozake 1948— **8**
Shaw, Bernard 1940— **2**
Sheffey, Asa Bundy
 See Hayden, Robert Earl
Sheffield, Gary Antonian 1968– **16**
Shell, Art(hur, Jr.) 1946— **1**
Sherrod, Clayton 1944– **17**
Shipp, E. R. 1955— **15**
Sifford, Charlie (Luther) 1922— **4**
Simmons, Russell 1957(?)— **1**
Simmons, Ruth J. 1945— **13**
Simone, Nina 1933— **15**
Simpson, Carole 1940— **6**
Simpson, Lorna 1960— **4**
Simpson, O. J. 1947— **15**
Sinbad 1957(?)— **1, 16**
Singletary, Michael
 See Singletary, Mike
Singletary, Mike 1958— **4**

Singleton, John 1968— **2**
Sinkford, Jeanne C. 1933— **13**
Sister Souljah 1964— **11**
Slater, Rodney Earl 1955— **15**
Sleet, Moneta (J.), Jr. 1926— **5**
Smaltz, Audrey 1937(?)— **12**
Smith, Anna Deavere 1950— **6**
Smith, Arthur Lee, Jr.
 See Asante, Molefi Kete
Smith, Barbara 1949(?)— **11**
Smith, Bessie 1894-1937 **3**
Smith, Emmitt (III) 1969— **7**
Smith, Joshua (Isaac) 1941— **10**
Smith, Orlando
 See Smith, Tubby
Smith, Roger Guenveur 1960— **12**
Smith, Tubby 1951– **18**
Smith, Walker Jr.
 See Robinson, Sugar Ray
Smith, Will 1968– **8, 18**
Smith, Willi (Donnell) 1948-1987 **8**
Sneed, Paula A. 1947– **18**
Snipes, Wesley 1962— **3**
Soglo, Nicéphore 1935— **15**
Somé, Malidoma Patrice 1956— **10**
Sowell, Thomas 1930— **2**
Soyinka, (Akinwande Olu)Wole 1934— **4**
Spaulding, Charles Clinton 1874-1952 **9**
Spikes, Dolores Margaret Richard 1936– **18**
Stallings, George A(ugustus), Jr. 1948— **6**
Staples, Brent 1951— **8**
Staupers, Mabel K(eaton) 1890-1989 **7**
Steele, Claude Mason 1946— **13**
Steele, Shelby 1946— **13**
Stephens, Charlotte Andrews 1854-1951 **14**
Stevens, Yvette
 See Khan, Chaka
Steward, Emanuel 1944— **18**
Stewart, Alison 1966(?)— **13**
Stewart, Maria W. Stewart **19**
Stewart, Paul Wilbur 1925— **12**
Stokes, Carl B(urton) 1927— **10**
Stokes, Louis 1925— **3**
Stone, Charles Sumner, Jr.
 See Stone, Chuck
Stone, Chuck 1924— **9**
Stone, Toni 1921-1996 **15**
Stringer, C. Vivian 1948— **13**
Sudarkasa, Niara 1938— **4**
Sullivan, Leon H(oward) 1922— **3**
Sullivan, Louis (Wade) 1933— **8**
Sweat, Keith 1961(?)– **19**
Swoopes, Sheryl Denise 1971— **12**
"The Goat"
 See Manigault, Earl "The Goat"
Tafari Makonnen
 See Haile Selassie
Tanner, Henry Ossawa 1859-1937 **1**
Tate, Larenz 1975— **15**

Taulbert, Clifton Lemoure 1945– **19**
Taylor, John (David Beckett) 1952– **16**
Taylor, Kristin Clark 1959— **8**
Taylor, Meshach 1947(?)— **4**
Taylor, Regina 1959— **9**
Taylor, Susan L. 1946— **10**
Taylor, Susie King 1848-1912 **13**
Terrrell, Mary (Elizabeth) Church 1863-1954 **9**
The Artist
 See Prince
Thigpen, Lynne 19(?)(?)– **17**
Thomas, Alma Woodsey 1891-1978 **14**
Thomas, Clarence 1948— **2**
Thomas, Frank Edward, Jr. 1968— **12**
Thomas, Franklin A(ugustine) 1934— **5**
Thomas, Isiah (Lord III) 1961— **7**
Thomas, Vivien (T.) 1910-1985 **9**
Thompson, Tazewell (Alfred, Jr.) 1954— **13**
Thurman, Howard 1900-1981 **3**
Thurman, Wallace Henry 1902-1934 **16**
Till, Emmett (Louis) 1941-1955 **7**
Tolliver, William (Mack) 1951— **9**
Toomer, Jean 1894-1967 **6**
Toomer, Nathan Pinchback
 See Toomer, Jean
Tosh, Peter 1944-1987 **9**
Touré, Amadou Toumani 1948?– **18**
Touré, Sekou 1922-1984 **6**
Towns, Edolphus 1934– **19**
Townsend, Robert 1957— **4**
Tribble, Isreal, Jr. 1940— **8**
Trotter, (William) Monroe 1872-1934 **9**
Trouillot, Ertha Pascal
 See Pascal-Trouillot, Ertha
Tubman, Harriet 1820(?)-1913 **9**
Tucker, C. DeLores 1927— **12**
Tucker, Chris 1973(?)— **13**
Tucker, Cynthia (Anne) 1955— **15**
Tucker, Rosina Budd Harvey Corrothers 1881-1987 **14**
Ture, Kwame
 See Carmichael, Stokely
Turnbull, Walter 1944— **13**
Turner, Henry McNeal 1834-1915 **5**
Turner, Tina 1939— **6**
Tutu, Desmond (Mpilo) 1931— **6**
Tyson, Cicely 1933— **7**
Tyson, Neil de Grasse 1958— **15**
Underwood, Blair 1964— **7**
Upshaw, Eugene Jr. 1945– **18**
Vance, Courtney B. 1960— **15**
VanDerZee, James (Augustus (Joseph) 1886-1983 **6**
Vandross, Luther 1951— **13**
Vann, Harold Moore
 See Muhammad, Khallid Abdul
Van Peebles, Mario (Cain)

1957(?)— **2**
Van Peebles, Melvin 1932— **7**
Vanzant, Iyanla 1953– **17**
Vaughan, Sarah (Lois) 1924-1990 **13**
Vaughn, Mo 1967– **16**
Vereen, Ben(jamin Augustus) 1946— **4**
Vieira, Joao 1939— **14**
Vincent, Marjorie Judith 1965(?)— **2**
Von Lipsey, Roderick 1959— **11**
Waddles, Charleszetta (Mother) 1912— **10**
Waddles, Mother
  See Waddles, Charleszetta (Mother)
Walcott, Derek (Alton) 1930— **5**
Walcott, Louis Eugene 1933— **2, 15**
  See Farrakhan, Louis
Walker, Albertina 1929— **10**
Walker, Alice (Malsenior) 1944— **1**
Walker, Cedric "Ricky" 1953— **19**
Walker, Herschel (Junior) 1962— **1**
Walker, Kara 1969– **16**
Walker, Madame C. J. 1867-1919 **7**
Walker, Maggie Lena 1867(?)-1934 **17**
Walker, Nellie Marian
  See Larsen, Nella
Walker, Thomas "T. J."
  See Walker, T. J.
Walker, T. J. 1961(?)— **7**
Wallace, Michele Faith 1952— **13**
Wallace, Phyllis A(nn) 1920(?)-1993 **9**
Wallace, Ruby Ann
  See Dee, Ruby
Wallace, Sippie 1898-1986 **1**
Wamutombo, Dikembe Mutombo Mpolondo Mukamba Jean Jacque
  See Mutombo, Dikembe
wa Ngengi, Kamau
  See Kenyatta, Jomo
Warfield, Marsha 1955— **2**
Warwick, Dionne 1940– **18**
Washington, Booker T(aliaferro) 1856-1915 **4**
Washington, Denzel 1954— **1, 16**
Washington, Fred(eri(cka Carolyn) 1903-1994 **10**
Washington, Grover, Jr. 1943– **17**
Washington, Harold 1922-1987 **6**
Washington, Laura S. – **18**
Washington, MaliVai 1969— **8**
Washington, Patrice Clarke 1961— **12**
Washington, Valores James 1903-1995 **12**
Wasow, Omar 1970— **15**
Waters, Ethel 1895-1977 **7**
Waters, Maxine 1938— **3**
Watkins, Frances Ellen
  See Harper, Frances Ellen

Watkins
Watkins, Gloria Jean
  See hooks, bell
Watkins, Levi, Jr. 1945— **9**
Watkins, Perry James Henry 1948-1996 **12**
Watkins, Shirley R. 1938– **17**
Watson, Johnny "Guitar" 1935-1996 **18**
Wattleton, (Alyce) Faye 1943— **9**
Watts, Julius Caesar, Jr. 1957— **14**
Watts, Rolonda 1959— **9**
Wayans, Damon 1961— **8**
Wayans, Keenen Ivory 1958– **18**
Waymon, Eunice Kathleen
  See Simone, Nina
Weathers, Carl 1948— **10**
Weaver, Robert C(lifton) 1907– **8**
Webb, Veronica 1965— **10**
Webb, Wellington, Jr. 1941— **3**
Webber, Chris 1973— **15**
Wek, Alek 1977– **18**
Wells, James Lesesne 1902-1993 **10**
Wells-Barnett, Ida B(ell) 1862-1931 **8**
Welsing, Frances (Luella) Cress 1935— **5**
Wesley, Dorothy Porter **19**
Wesley, Valerie Wilson 194(?)– **18**
West, Cornel (Ronald) 1953— **5**
West, Dorothy 1907— **12**
West, Togo Dennis, Jr. 1942– **16**
Wharton, Clifton R(eginald), Jr. 1926— **7**
Wheat, Alan Dupree 1951— **14**
Whitaker, "Sweet Pea"
  See Whitaker, Pernell
Whitaker, Forest 1961— **2**
Whitaker, Pernell 1964— **10**
White, Barry 1944— **13**
White, Bill 1933(?)— **1**
White, Michael R(eed) 1951— **5**
White, Reggie 1961— **6**
White, Reginald Howard
  See White, Reggie
White, Walter F(rancis) 1893-1955 **4**
White, William DeKova
  See White, Bill
Whitfield, Lynn 1954– **18**
Wideman, John Edgar 1941– **5**
Wilder, L(awrence) Douglas 1931— **3**
Wiley, Ralph 1952— **8**
Wilkens, Lenny 1937— **11**
Wilkens, Leonard Randolph
  See Wilkens, Lenny
Wilkins, Roger (Wood) 1932– **2**
Wilkins, Roy 1901-1981 **4**
Williams, Bert 1874-1922 **18**
Williams, Billy Dee 1937— **8**
Williams, Carl
  See Kani, Karl
Williams, Daniel Hale (III) 1856-1931 **2**
Williams, Evelyn 1922(?)— **10**
Williams, George Washington

1849-1891 **18**
Williams, Gregory (Howard) 1943— **11**
Williams, Hosea Lorenzo 1926— **15**
Williams, Joe 1918— **5**
Williams, Maggie 1954— **7**
Williams, Margaret Ann
  See Williams, Maggie
Williams, Mary Lou 1910-1981 **15**
Williams, Montel (B.) 1956(?)— **4**
Williams, O(swald) S. 1921– **13**
Williams, Patricia J. 1951— **11**
Williams, Paul R(evere) 1894-1980 **9**
Williams, Paulette Linda
  See Shange, Ntozake
Williams, Robert F(ranklin) 1925— **11**
Williams, Robert Peter
  See Guillaume, Robert
Williams, Vanessa L. 1963— **4, 17**
Williams, Venus Ebone Starr 1980– **17**
Williams, Walter E(dward) 1936— **4**
Williams, William December
  Williams, Billy Dee
Williams, William T(homas) 1942— **11**
Williams, Willie L(awrence) 1943— **4**
Williamson, Lisa
  See Sister Souljah
Willis, Cheryl
  See Hudson, Cheryl
Wilson, August 1945— **7**
Wilson, Cassandra 1955– **16**
Wilson, Nancy 1937– **10**
Wilson, Phill 1956— **9**
Wilson, Sunnie 1908— **7**
Wilson, William Nathaniel
  See Wilson, Sunnie
Winans, Benjamin 1962— **14**
Winans, Marvin L. 1958– **17**
Winans, Priscilla 1964— **14**
Winfield, Dave 1951— **5**
Winfield, David Mark
  See Winfield, Dave
Winfield, Paul (Edward) 1941— **2**
Winfrey, Oprah (Gail) 1954— **2, 15**
Wofford, Chloe Anthony
  See Morrison, Toni
Wolfe, George C. 1954— **6**
Wonder, Stevie 1950— **11**
Woodard, Alfre 1953— **9**
Woodruff, Hale (Aspacio) 1900-1980 **9**
Woods, Eldrick
  See Woods, Tiger
Woods, Granville T. 1856-1910 **5**
Woods, Tiger 1975— **14**
Woodson, Carter G(odwin) 1875-1950 **2**
Woodson, Robert L. 1937— **10**
Wooldridge, Anna Marie
  See Lincoln, Abbey

Worrill, Conrad 1941— **12**
Wright, Bruce McMarion 1918— **3**
Wright, Louis Tompkins 1891-1952 **4**
Wright, Richard 1908-1960 **5**

X, Malcolm 1925-1965 **1**
Yoba, (Abdul-)Malik (Kashie) 1967— **11**
Young, Andre Ramelle
   See Dre, Dr.

Young, Andrew (Jackson, Jr.) 1932— **3**
Young, Coleman 1918— **1**
Young, Jean Childs 1933-1994 **14**
Young, Whitney M(oore), Jr. 1921-1971 **4**
Youngblood, Johnny Ray 1948— **8**